What Is Neostructuralism?

Theory and History of Literature
Edited by Wlad Godzich and Jochen Schulte-Sasse

For other books in the series, see p. 483

What Is
Neostructuralism?

Manfred Frank

Translation by Sabine Wilke and Richard Gray

Foreword by Martin Schwab

Theory and History of Literature, Volume 45

University of Minnesota Press, Minneapolis

Copyright © 1989 by the Regents of the University of Minnesota

Originally published as *Was ist Neostrukturalismus?* © 1984 by Suhrkamp, Frankfurt.

Published by the University of Minnesota Press
2037 University Avenue Southeast, Minneapolis, MN 55414.
Printed in the United States of America.

Library of Congress Cataloging-in-Publication Data

Frank, Manfred.
  What is neostructuralism?

  (Theory and history of literature ; v. 45)
  Translation of: Was ist Neostrukturalismus?
  Includes index.
  1. Structuralism. I. Title. II. Series.
  B841.4.F7413   1988   149'.96   87-26689
  ISBN 0-8166-1599-3
  ISBN 0-8166-1602-7 (pbk.)

Permission to quote selected passages from the following is gratefully acknowledged: *The Archaeology of Knowledge* by Michel Foucault, translated by A. M. Sheridan-Smith, 1972. Reprinted by permission of Irvington Publishers, New York. Copyright © Irvington Publishers, Inc., 1972. *Course in General Linguistics* by Ferdinand de Saussure, translated by Wade Baskin. Reprinted by permission of the Philosophical Library. Copyright © 1959. *Dissemination* by Jacques Derrida, translated by Barbara Johnson. Reprinted by permission of The Athlone Press Ltd. and The University of Chicago Press. Copyright © The University of Chicago Press, 1981. *Écrits: A Selection* by Jacques Lacan. Translated by Alan Sheridan from the French. Used by permission of W. W. Norton & Company, Inc. Copyright © 1977 Tavistock Publications Limited. "Introduction to the Origin of Geometry" by Jacques Derrida from Edmund Husserl's *Origin of Geometry*, translated by John P. Leavey, Jr. Reprinted by permission of Nicolas-Hays, York Beach, ME. Copyright © Nicolas-Hays, 1978. "Limited Inc abc. . . ." by Jacques Derrida, from Samuel Weber

Additional copyright information p. 484

The University of Minnesota
is an equal-opportunity
educator and employer.

Contents

II. THREE QUESTIONS FOR NEOSTRUCTURALISM

Foreword
Martin Schwab

I. Frank's Project

This book offers the reader a look at deconstruction from a hermeneutic point of view. Manfred Frank chooses five representative authors from the contemporary French scene—Jacques Lacan, Michel Foucault, Jacques Derrida, Gilles Deleuze, and Jean-François Lyotard—to discuss three of their major issues: *history* (Lectures 6 through 12), *subjectivity* (Lectures 12 through 24), and *semiotics* (sign, meaning, and interpretation; Lecture 25 to the end).[1]

Frank is convinced that "the spiritual situation of the age . . . demand[s] that we give some thought to a new definition of subjectivity and of individuality"(p. 9). Both antirationalists and many rationalists no longer assign an important role to the subject—if they recognize it as a category in its own right at all. Against this, Frank sets his own hermeneutic project by asking: "How can one redeem the fundamental idea of modern humanism which links the dignity of the human being with his use of freedom" *and* "do justice to the fundamental fact that subjects can only form themselves in linguistic, social, cultural, and historical orders?" (pp. 7-8). It is this insistence on "the constitutive role of subjectivity as the primary factor in meaning" and history that makes his contribution a unique voice in the developing debate between rationalism and antirationalism.[2] In *What Is Neostructuralism?* the most recent hermeneutic rationalism challenges present French antirationalism. And this is done not by merely reaffirming the self-transparent and autonomous subject of the tradition, but in the name of a reconceived subjectivity based upon decenteredness and subservience to forces other than its own. The reader will discover that Frank's interest in subjectivity unleashes a particularly lively discussion wherever the subject is at stake. Thus he takes a critical stance toward Foucault's rejection of subjectivity, his contempt for the humanities (*sciences humaines*), and the antihermeneutic ideology of his historiography (Lectures 9 and 10). Similarly, Frank objects to Derrida's elimination of self-consciousness from the essential elements of subjectivity (Lecture 18), and as a unifying force in semiosis (Lectures 26 and 27).

The book challenges antirationalism not merely by criticizing its ideas but also through its method. Frank's approach to French deconstruction is *reconstructive*—another hermeneutic feature. His interpretations translate antirationalist discourse into the discursive language of our intellectual tradition, even systematizing its ideas to some extent. Incidentally, its patient reconstructive effort makes the book a valuable introduction to deconstruction as well. From a theoretical point of view, successful reconstruction demonstrates that the gap between antirationalism and rationalism is not as wide as some antirationalists think it is. Indeed, Frank even thinks that the division between contemporary rationalism and its opponents is not a necessary one. He does not, of course, try to "reconcile" the enemies by explaining away their differences, although he does acknowledge antirationalist positions like the decenteredness of the subject and the impossibility of closure of texts. But Frank does believe that a philosophy yet to be conceived might integrate apparently incompatible propositions now held in either camp into a coherent theory. He supports his belief by the historical observation that the hermeneutic philosophy of Friedrich Schleiermacher was such a successful integration. *What Is Neostructuralism?* aims at preparing the ground for a philosophy that would achieve for the twentieth century what Schleiermacher accomplished for the nineteenth, to "reconstruct a position in the history of modern European philosophy in which what today is broken apart was conceived of as two sides of an integral and dialectical movement" (p. 9).

Instead of summarizing his views this foreword tries to provide background for Frank's specific readings. If *What Is Neostructuralism?* is a statement in the debate between contemporary rationalism and antirationalism, it is important to retrace the history of the intriguing geographical division between French antirationalism and German rationalism (section II). Sketches of general features of antirationalism and of its recent French version (section III) and of the rationalist opposition (section IV) are meant to trace a map on which Frank's contribution can be located. The discussion of hermeneutics (section V) informs us about Frank's position within the hermeneutic movement. The final section (VI) evaluates the rationality of hermeneutics and concludes with a staged debate between hermeneutics and deconstruction on the possibility of constructive interpretation.

II. The History of a Division

How did the sharp division between the rationalist and antirationalist camps emerge? Why is there a French antirationalist group discussed in this book and a German rationalist group to which Frank belongs? The trajectory that has led to the present distribution was set in the nineteenth century. At that time, a process of differentiation and division had generated two feuding intellectual "families." Simultaneously, membership in these families began to be defined in terms of rationality. Previous oppositions, for instance, between Vico and Descartes, Newtonian and Paracelsean science, or between Herder and Kant were spurred by competing conceptions of rationality rather than by the opposition of *the* rational and *the* antirational. As Foucault has emphasized, a certain binarism and the idea of a unitary figure of reason had to emerge before the present constellation became possible.

A bird's-eye view of the last two hundred years of Western intellectual history reveals vigorous growth in the antirationalist family during the nineteenth century. Family ties very often are in or to Germany. Among the earlier antirationalists, the Romantics, Kierkegaard, Schopenhauer, and Nietzsche have the highest visibility today. But other antirational positions also thrived, for instance, on the right and the left wing of the Hegelians, in the historical school, in hermeneutics, or in political and social anarchism. By the end of the century the antirationalist current had broadened and was involved in a number of polemics against rationalist opponents such as Kantians, Hegelians, Marxists, and utilitarians. The antirationalist movement peaked in "philosophy of life" (*Lebensphilosophie*) and in existentialism before and after World War I. At this moment it represented the consciousness of an age (*Epochenbewusstsein*). Again, the German intellectual scene was its main theater, in France, Henri Bergson a major figure. By that time new and strong rationalist adversaries had entered the scene, among them positivism, pragmatism, phenomenology, and the first wave of analytic philosophy. But antirational attitudes were not weakened. They had long since begun to make major inroads into predominantly rationalist territory such as social theory, or psychoanalysis.

At this juncture a decisive event broke the continuity of the antirational evolution. This event is also a main explanatory factor for the present distribution of the rationalist and antirationalist camps. Fascism and Nazism gained political power in Italy and Germany. In both countries antirationalism had, of course, helped to pave their way. The official ideologies of both movements also appropriated elements taken from the antirational intellectual doctrines. As dictatorial powers, the political movements favored antirationalist intellectuals and oppressed rationalist ideas, forcing many of their defenders into retreat or exile. Considering all this, an antirationalist of the time must have come to the conclusion that history was offering him the unique chance to pursue his intellectual efforts from a position of power and to transform his ideas into everyday reality. Many antirationalists joined the ranks of fascism and Nazism. Antirationalism had found its political efficacy, and that was to many of its defendants the criterion of "truth." The twelve-year regime of the Nazis, their crimes, and their downfall have decisively redirected antirationalism. The postwar intellectual scene in France, Germany, and even in America cannot be understood without the unparalleled migration of intellectuals and the accompanying reevaluation of intellectual attitudes during, after, and because of Nazism.

In Germany, antirational thought has never recovered from its involvement with and its instrumentalization by Nazism, at least not to this day. Most of the present generation of thinkers have been exposed to the experience of Nazism, and all of them react to it in their thought. Since Heidegger, who continued to pursue his existentialist project from his forced retreat in the Black Forest, no major antirationalist intellectual has emerged in Germany. Existentialism quickly degenerated into an academic discipline among others, entangled in often sterile Heideggerian philology. The antirational spirit has, at best, been hibernating in Germany since the end of World War II. It has been restricted to historical and philological work on the grand figures of the past or confined to the margins of the intellectual life, borrowing its topics and gestures from French "master thinkers." What is more, antirationalism has also lost most of its influence on other positions. Marxism and the Frankfurt School have revised if not eliminated antirational elements that had found their way into their theories before and during the Second World War. The same revision took place in psychoanalysis where romanticist elements such as the theory of drives have persistently been downgraded or rejected. In a parallel move, Gadamer's hermeneutics subtly transformed Heidegger's predominantly antirational existentialism into a rationalism of sorts. Whenever German thinkers after "the War" have had an option, they have favored the more rationalist alternative. Analytic philosophy, the Frankfurt School, systems theory (Niklas Luhmann), and neoidealism (Dieter Henrich, Michael Theunissen), at present the liveliest movements of ambitious theorizing in Germany, all stress one or the other type of rationality. In this situation, Frank's book also raises antirationalist issues and arguments in an intellectual community that has done its best to ignore or dismiss them.

The antirational drought in Germany has been matched by unprecedented growth in France. French thinkers have moved in directions exactly opposite to those of their German counterparts. In the second half of the twentieth century the country of the Cartesian spirit has become the center of antirationalism. This is a surprising and unexpected development, for, apart from perhaps the period of the *fin de siècle* and Bergson, rationalist currents dominated France until well after the Second World War. Marxists, neo-Hegelians, phenomenologists, and even many existentialists took their inspirations from Hegel, Marx, or Husserl. Is it not remarkable, how much more rationalist Sartre's existentialism is than

Heidegger's? The structuralism of the fifties completes the picture of rationalist dominance in France.

But by the fifties and sixties the trickle of a sporadic and disconnected antirationalist production swells and, for the first time since the beginning of this century, gathers into a self-conscious current again. Three of the authors presented by Frank have strongly contributed to generate this "movement": Jacques Lacan's version of psychoanalysis, Michel Foucault's genealogical historiography and Nietzschean philosophy of history, and Jacques Derrida's deconstruction have been more than isolated variations on antirationalist themes. They have reformulated and reoriented the antirationalist project. Schools and movements were able to crystallize around them. The newly acquired spirit of a movement was also able to draw on the resources of the political "movement" of May 1968, but has never merely been "The Philosophy of '68," as recent opponents would have it. In spite of its strong involvement in politics the movement has been curiously light-handed about the older antirationalist connection with Nazism.

Today a whole array of authors is associated with the antirationalist family. From an older generation, the names of Gaston Bachelard, Henri Lefebvre, Gabriel Marcel, and Georges Bataille should be cited. Authors like Michel Leiris, Emmanuel Lévinas, Jacques Lacan, Michel Foucault, Michel Serres, Gilles Deleuze, Jacques Derrida, Jean Baudrillard, and Jean-François Lyotard document the breadth, variety, and scope of the antirationalist intellectual project. At present, French antirationalism amounts to not more and not less than a theory of our age. As such it is unequaled by any other collective intellectual effort now under way.

III. A Physiognomy of Antirationalism

Antirationalist theorizing denies the possibility or the value of rational knowledge and rational conduct of life (Weber's *rationale Lebensführung*), according to some definition of rationality. This is its negative credo. A general characterization in positive terms is more difficult. Antirationalist projects are too diverse, complex, and, before all, disjointed to be easily summed up. *What Is Neostructuralism?* gives good accounts of some of the concrete theories. It is, however, important to see to what extent more general common traits can be found. The reader must bear in mind that the increasing generality increases injustice to the minute detail of particular theories. In general terms, then, antirationalism is a theory and practice of discourse in general, but also of what its own discourse says, does, and how it achieves its purposes. Thus antirationalists blend the expressive and the cognitive, the perlocutionary and the illocutionary forces of speech acts, generating a new type of discursive speech activity. They also favor a certain ontological model for the things (in the widest possible understanding of thinghood) that are the topics of their theories, for instance, life, texts, history, society, nature, persons. These things basically are presented as processes. Those processes, furthermore, do not fall into preset patterns or follow directions that can be abstracted and separated from the ongoing events themselves. In addition to not being ordered and directed events, those items are also embedded in an equally disorderly environment that exceeds them. The prevalent normative attitude of this "process philosophy," where it is not merely concerned with negative directions, is best summed up by Meister Eckhart's term *Gelassenheit*: an attitude of letting things happen and of putting oneself in the right frame of mind for letting things happen, rather than of bringing them about at will. Both theoretically and practically the process has primacy over the structure, the dynamic over the static. So far my characterization applies to Eastern beliefs, Western mystics, and to "primitive" thought as well as to antirational Western philosophy, from which it differs by its theoretical and discursive frame.

I will now try to present more specific features. They are organized around four themes, typically interwoven in a manner that escapes easy systematization. The four features are order, metaphysics, representation, and history.

Of those four themes, the first, and in my opinion most important, is *order*. The basic "reality" of many antirationalists is chaotic and in constant undirected flux, unordered or alien to order. In this view, order itself either belongs to the register of illusion—mere figment—or is a constraint—imposed upon, consequently suffered by a reality essentially other than and estranged by order. "Basic reality"[3] may be as variously defined as are Lacan's subject, Derrida's textuality, Foucault's history, Deleuze's machinery, or Serres's nature. Orders may likewise vary. They may be systems of categories, or structural or formally definable orders; they may be the mathematical tools used by natural science or metaphysical assumptions like that of a pervasive causal connection among events. Those orders may also be political, institutional, teleological, functional, or of the kind called "Gestalt." Whatever the order and the field of ordered matter may be, the ideal type of antirationalist assumes that no presentation of an order of the relevant kind will ever be an adequate presentation of that field. He will also hold that adequate "knowledge," because it belongs to the field to which it gives access, will exhibit the logic, here the absence of logic, of that field. Discourse participates in the logic of its topic.

Does antirationalism reject *all* order, then? The question is tricky. The rejection of order concerns rational orders of the types just mentioned. From the point of view of some antirational "epistemologies," the existence of orders is as doubtful as is their assertibility. How, indeed, would orders be accounted for in antirational discourse? I can think of two types of order with accompanying discourse that antirationalism might countenance. On the one hand, statistical ideas have been used by antirationalists, from Nietzsche's "eternal recurrence" to Serres's turbulences, because statistical describability is compatible with the assumption that the single event does not arise in a directed manner. On the other hand, participation in an ongoing process may be a means to exhibit its order, without describing it. The idea of a participatory articulation of orders leads to a mimetic notion of order (romanticism, Walter Benjamin, Anton Ehrenzweig). Participation would also solve the problem of conceptual presentation by abolishing the epistemological distance between the thing known and the means used in knowing it. Antirationalism, then, does not need to reject *all* order. It selects certain orders and certain modes of articulation as belonging to rationalism. But it admits odd orders and deviant ways to present them. Antirationalism is not an irrationalism.

A second theme is *metaphysics*, the idea of a second order, a different reality beyond the life-worlds we inhabit. Metaphysicians think that there is a rational way to know a reality beyond the one we face in our everyday lives. Together with many rationalists, contemporary antirationalists *reject* metaphysics. In its most radical form this rejection of metaphysics "flatly" denies all "beyond" or "beneath" of a second level, regardless of whether that level is defined as order or disorder. In this generality the rejection is more a common attitude of our scientific age than a feature specific to antirationalism. Antirationalists do, however, have typical reasons for rejecting metaphysics; for them, metaphysics is not so much a superstition to be overcome by scientific thought, as the core strategy of rationalism. It posits an apparently accessible ontology of order as a means to justify the cognition and production of order. Metaphysics is thus the ideology of order. At first sight the rejection of metaphysics may not look very important. But closer scrutiny shows that this impression is deceptive. For the scope of possible antimetaphysical attitudes is impressive. In each of the following pairs of opposites one of the two terms may be taken to represent a metaphysical "beyond" to the other: world and god, subject and external reality, empirical world and transcendental a priori conditions, language or thought and the world they relate to, an original social contract and a given social situation. To reject one of the terms as metaphysical is ipso facto revising the model according to which the other term has been conceived. Antirationalism is thus engaged in a radical revision of hitherto fundamental notions.

A third group of antirationalist attitudes concerns *language* and *representation*. At the least radical level, antirationalists doubt that conceptual thought (and language) is an adequate means to represent or express the basic truths of our world and our conception of it. A reality that is basically chaotic cannot be rendered conceptually, or it will be violated in the process. The language of concepts is consequently abandoned in favor of expressive, poetical, highly metaphorical, often overtly inconsistent forms of discourse. More radical is the idea that language and thought do not carry representational power at all, that is, do not relate to anything over and above the events of thinking or speaking. This idea applies the antirationalist opposition to order to the field of thought and language, thus integrating the *medium* of our attitude *toward* reality *into* the reality as antirationalism conceives of it. Thought and language are derationalized. By the same token, language and discourse also cease to be *objects* of rational cognition and regulation. There will be no explicit ethics of discourse (there is, of course, a strong implicit normativity in antirational discourse itself), as there will be no reconstruction of ideas, no interpretations of the meanings of works of art. It is simply not possible to take toward the medium the distance necessary for a rational cognition or evaluation of its meanings. The third attitude is obviously directly opposed to hermeneutics.

Finally, antirationalists take typical attitudes toward *history*. Reversing or rejecting historical teleology, antirationalists believe either that we have deviated from a state of anarchic freedom or that history runs in cycles or, most radically, that events are disconnected and random. Therefore, their philosophy of history asserts either that history alienates or deviates us from extrahistorical possibilities or that its form is repetition (Nietzsche's "eternal recurrence") or that it follows no pattern (absence of order at certain levels of events). Many also think that the course of history cannot be influenced by human action, thus adding nonshapability to the features of history. A historiography informed by this refusal of teleology will look for breaks and ruptures instead of continuities, for diversity, plurality, and nonsimultaneity instead of unity and connectedness. It will also look for those elements in the past that are subdued or oppressed by the forces of order. And it will stress that orders are constraints, be they occidental logos or modern rationality.

I have presented four general features that, taken together, would define the ideal type of a modern antirationalist. What is the originality of the present French scene? What does it add to, omit from, how does it vary the general picture? The first trait I would merely like to mention is the particular mixture of intellectual sources. Nietzsche and Heidegger are the two antirationalists, de Saussure is the one rationalist whose doctrines have been most influential in shaping the ideas of the present French "school" of antirationalists in France. The reader will find that *What Is Neostructuralism?* gives careful attention to these affiliations. A second trait is a certain antitraditionalism. Unlike many rational doctrines that have evolved from traditions into which they also insert themselves, many contemporary antirational positions are deviations from or transformations of formerly rationalist disciplines. Lacan's psychoanalysis and Foucault's historiography of discourse are cases in point. Even for Derrida the point of departure has been Husserlian phenomenology, not Heideggerian existentialism or Nietzschean "philosophy of life." Some recent antirationalists seem to break from disciplines with a former strongly rationalist orientation. I refer again to Foucault and Lacan. Their theories can also be viewed as antirational only incidentally, or only as embedded in the concrete enterprise of achieving some goal in their respective disciplines, the writing of history, and the practice and teaching of psychoanalysis. In pursuing those goals they often appropriate tools from the antirationalist arsenal without much concern about their previous usage. The new antirationalism is thus more eclectic and more concrete, more strongly marked by the rup-tures it effectuates *in* a rational field than by its debt and contribution *to* the antira-tionalist tradition itself. This trait is as indicative of foundational difficulties in the disciplines thus transformed, as it is of the weakening force of our intellectual tradition, regardless of its rationalist or antirationalist orientation. A certain ob-liviousness, advocated by Nietzsche about a century ago, is itself a symptom of the crisis of historical tradition.

The second global originality of present French antirationalism is a topical breadth and positivity previous antirationalism did not possess. There is hardly a field in the humanities and social sciences to which it has not made some contri-bution. The vast array of its philosophical topics ranges from Bataille's economics of expense to Lacan's theory of decentered subjectivity, from Foucault's historical reconstructions of forms and constraints of rationality to Baudrillard's sociology of symbolic value and a media-generated simulatory reality, from Serres's in-terpretations of dynamic nature and speculations on cybernetics and systems the-ory to Derrida's all-embracing, uncontrollable textuality that it is constantly "on the move." Frank has to select from a wealth of topics and authors when he chooses history, subjectivity, and semiotics as topics for his presentation in *What Is Neostructuralism?* And contemporary antirationalists, unlike skeptics, do not use up their forces in merely destructing the claims of reason. They offer positive alternative accounts in most of the core fields of rationality. Antirationalism is, as I said earlier, a full-fledged "project," in the sense in which "the project of en-lightenment" has been understood and propagated by Habermas, or the sense in which there have been the projects of ancient philosophy or of romanticism. One may even wonder whether its scope, ambition, and positive articulation have not begun to transform antirationalism into a theory of alternative reason.

Finally, the French movement is specific through its unique philosophical style. (On its own assumptions, the question of style is, of course, simultaneously and undistinguishably a question of substance.) Individual members of the French antirational family have their highly specialized physiognomies. I would even contend that no contemporary current offers a variety and distinctness of personal styles and expressions comparable to that of the vigorously antipersonal family of doctrines gathered under the label of antirationalism. Yet all of its thinkers strike the reader with the highly literary character of their expression. The obvi-ous contrast to the more conceptual tradition has exasperated nonfollowers, par-ticularly philosophers. The change is deep indeed, for contemporary antiration-alists have "poeticized" their expression even when they are compared to Hegel, Kierkegaard, or Nietzsche, all of them "literary" writers and often despised for their literariness. The distinctive new language of present antirational thought is not, as some might think, merely due to an effort to express beautifully or ele-gantly what could also be expressed otherwise. Its style is, on the contrary, the result of the conviction or will that doctrinal substance and expressive presentation must not be separated (antirepresentationalism) and that language, properly spoken, generates "thought" (*Gelassenheit*). Thought and style merge, as meaning and expression were seen to do.

The idea of an indissoluble bond between expression and the expressed is an old one. It has been an integral part of mystic and hermetic traditions and of romanticism. New, however, is the secularized belief that metaphorically "pressed" or "released" language yields a thought all its own, or, more radically even, that only metaphorical procedures are adequate to exhibit the dynamic, indeterminable, and multiple character of all semiosis or, if it is different, of reality at large. Contemporary French antirationalism has aestheticized philosophical discourse. Language has become a "thinking matter," not a datum for or a tool of analysis. This philosophy of language explains why antirationalist writings often read more like surrealist, symbolist, or modern literary texts than like the discursive texts of our tradition, including the oppositional authors of the last century. The same philosophy of language also helps us to understand why many antirationalist texts present themselves in deviant forms. With the exception of romanticism I know of no intellectual movement that has so deliberately experimented with forms of expression in the field of intellectual discourse. Literariness, even poeticity of its theoretical expression and form, is certainly the most conspicuous among the distinctive traits of modern antirationalism.

This concludes my physiognomy of antirationalism. What does present German rationalism look like?

IV. Three Rationalists: Tugendhat, Habermas, and Luhmann

Rationalism asserts what antirationalism rejects. Rationalists think that we are not in principle prevented from conceptual knowledge about reality and argue that we can, indeed ought to, conduct our lives rationally. In choosing the three authors discussed here I have opted for wildly different rationalist approaches united, however, by their ambition toward general inclusive theory. Niklas Luhmann, Jürgen Habermas, and Ernst Tugendhat try to put forward general theories of rationality for and of our era. The positions they reach will, by the same token, define the conflict between the two rival attitudes. It is in the field of rationality staked out by authors such as these that Frank's philosophical position will have to find a place of its own.

Ernst Tugendhat

A theory of rationality proposed by an analytic philosopher will be founded semantically,[4] and rely neither on a metaphysical "beyond" nor on a consensus among reasonable persons. According to Tugendhat, we find out what we accept as reasons for our beliefs and norms by analyzing the ways in which we use words. The analyzability of our language is a methodological premise of his theory of rationality. Fortunately, language also reveals to us the implicit network of our rationality. At its most general level, Tugendhat's rationality is the traditional "justification by reasons," the giving of an account for an attitude we hold (*Ausweisbarkeit*). We are interested in justification because we take positions (*Stellungnahme*) on ourselves and our environment, adopting certain beliefs, rejecting others, and because it makes a difference whether we make the right choices among them. Ultimately, all taking of positions relates back to the fact that we take positions vis-à-vis our own lives. Heideggerian *Dasein* is here rationalized by its insertion into the structure of our language, interpreted in the sense of analytic philosphy.

Tugendhat develops a ramified theory of theoretical reason by examining conditions under which we justify truth claims about the world. In a manner typical for his analytic approach he looks for these conditions, not in the categories of the understanding, but in the semantic structure of assertoric sentences, which we use to make and to argue our truth claims. The fact that we refer to things and say something about them is a basic order of reason, seconded by other orders, notably space and time and the perspectival subjective orders of indexicals ("I," "here," "now"). In a similar manner, Tugendhat approaches the theory of subjectivity. He does not try to elaborate a model of consciousness or self-consciousness, but starts from what he calls "practical self-relatedness" or the taking of a practical attitude toward oneself (*praktisches Sichzusichverhalten*). This relation of self to self obtains, for example, when we deliberate in order to determine what is best to do in a given situation. Finally, Tugendhat proposes an ethics of universalizability in which we accept as morally good only those social norms that can be justified as being equally good for all parties concerned.

Even this very rudimentary outline of Tugendhat's theory of rationality will demonstrate how closely he follows the lines of the philosophical tradition. This proximity, however, should not be allowed to obscure a fundamental difference. Based on semantics rather than on ontology or subjectivity, his analytic rationality aspires to forgo the metaphysical burden incurred by older rationalists. If this model of rationality is successful in its foundational and nonmetaphysical pretensions, then it will not be hurt by the rejection of metaphysics that was seen to be an important part of the antirationalist program. More important still: In agreement with many other analytic philosophers, Tugendhat appeals to order *in* language and to orders that are sustained *by* language, thus directly opposing one of the antirational theorems. Against the idea that orders are fictions or constraints the analytic rationalist sets his contention of a demonstrable and conceptual order of language, and the thesis that those orders are necessary conditions of our worldview.

It has become obvious where the confrontation between antirationalism and analytic rationalism along the line of Tugendhat's thought will take place. On the one hand, it is to be expected that the antirationalist will not accept the analytic claim to be beyond metaphysics. On the other hand, each side disputes the views on language held by the other side. This second topic has indeed been the object of the only major debate between an analytic and a deconstructionist philosopher. It is the polemics that has opposed Jacques Derrida and John Searle over the interpretation of Austin's theory of speech acts. Their debate has not done much to clarify the issues, however.[5]

Jürgen Habermas

If the debate between analytic rationalism and antirationalism remains, in Derrida's word, "unlikely," the confrontation between antirationalism and the "Frankfurt School" is well on its way.[6] "Critical theory of society," originally a critique of capitalist society and culture as well as of orthodox Marxism that had taken its inspirations from the early Marx and Hegel, had absorbed a strong dose of antirationalism before and during the Second World War. The peak of this influence was reached in Max Horkheimer's and Theodor W. Adorno's *Dialectic of Enlightenment*.[7] Its main thesis is antirationalist: reason establishes its rule over alternative beliefs, becomes the ideology of the masters in the struggle between the dominating and the dominated, *and* erects the systems of internal domination and of self-discipline that enable the masters to rule while alienating them from themselves. The conclusion, however, remains rationalist. Adorno and Horkheimer think that enlightenment can be enlightened about its own predicament and might overcome its disastrous consequences.

Confirming the rationalist trend among German philosophers, Habermas has recently "modernized" the "Frankfurt School."[8] He has reduced the weight of the philosophical nineteenth century in critical theory, integrated contemporary sociology and social psychology into its social theory, and renewed the foundations of the theory. His new foundation is here of particular interest because it also introduces a new form of rationalism, the idea of "communicative reason." This idea urges us to accept as rational only those theories, rules, or social institutions whose claims to validity would be found to be acceptable in a general debate itself free of the constraints of a given social situation. Communicative reason is universal consensus without constraint. Habermas historicizes and relativizes his idea of communicative reason so much that the remaining universalism loses most of its dependencies on Enlightenment metaphysics.

Habermas also proposes an analysis of modernity. Social systems, he argues, originally freed individuals from burdens imposed upon them by traditional ways of life. Today, however, the systems have achieved functional autonomy and dominate individuals' life-worlds. As a consequence, autonomous self-realization has become more and more difficult. Frustrated individuals are therefore less and less willing to perform the functions required for the systems. An impoverished life-world ceases to be the resource the systems need to feed from. Social pathologies ensue. Abandoning the idea of an alienation of man from himself or of reason from itself, Habermas diagnoses a historically generated conflict between individual aspirations and the demands of social systems as one of the diseases of modernity.

Communicative reason plays three roles in this critical theory of modernity. Between individuals, it distinguishes permissible self-realization from infringements on others' freedom. Between systems and life-worlds, it mediates between accepted functions of systems and the limitations on the pursuit of individual happiness. Between the systems, finally, a politically institutionalized communicative reason advocates the interests of the whole, a function that includes virtual interests as well as the existing and particular interests of the systems.

Once more, the opposition to antirationalism is palpable. To mention but one central point of dissension: For Habermas the dissolution of the modern pattern of social systems poses a threat to liberty. For antirationalism, the same system is unconditionally a constraint and a form of domination. Habermas's opposition raises two problems for antirationalism. Why should we consider order a *constraint*, something to be overcome? To be sure, concrete orders can become oppressive. But developments are contingent and may be reversible. How does the antirationalist justify his principled rejection of all rational order? Does he not found his assumption that order comes as a constraint on a metaphysics ontologically different from the tradition only by invoking a beyond of freely floating forces? Habermas also recalls to our minds that the project of enlightenment pervades our attitudes, values, and social institutions by reminding us of the genesis of our social institutions. Implicitly, all of us have "always and already" subscribed to some of those values. Should we, then, not also explicitly espouse what we in fact enjoy? Indeed, Habermas thinks that we ought to. In contrast to Tugendhat, however, he offers not a semantic but a communicative argument in support of those values.

His emphasis on an ideal consensus as a criterion for reason uncovers a foundational weakness in the opposition to rationalism. Antirationalism either uses the pathos of freedom (liberation from an oppressive order, leaving the sense of freedom largely undetermined), or it tries to persuade us to adopt certain nonrational attitudes. In both cases it faces the question of why we should adopt its proposals. Antirationalism is thus led into a foundational trilemma which it must resolve. It either bases itself on some metaphysical assumptions (e.g., Nietzsche's will to power) or resorts to some kind of nonmetaphysical basis to give us reasons (e.g., the late Foucault) or is an avowedly arbitrary proposal. Habermas denounces practical consequences of antirationalism and insists on the positive value of autonomy.

Niklas Luhmann

My third example of a contemporary competitor for the position of rationality is Luhmann's systems theory and functionalism.[9] Luhmann's point of departure is the idea that society consists of and is dominated by dynamic systems that emerge, maintain, and transform themselves through activities of their own and in interaction with an environment. He thus asserts the primacy of collective agencies over individuals in society. Self-shaping (and, incidentally, self-preserving) dynamic social systems are the prime agents in modern industrialized societies. Their primacy over other agents (e.g., individuals, groups like parties, unions, etc.) is manifest in the resistance the systems oppose to intentional alteration. Individuals, on the other hand, are formed in systems (e.g., the educational system) to fulfill functions necessary for the systems, and the systems provide what the individuals need to satisfy their wants. But the reverse is not true. Systems are independent of the particular individuals who enact their functions. This practical pessimism would rank Luhmann among the politically conservative antirationalists.

His picture of modernity shows our societies as undergoing a global evolutionary process of social transformation. In its course, the dominant mode of differentiation of Western societies changes from a stratified to a functional mode. Hierarchies such as class, or descending relations running from superior to inferior, lose their importance while relations of mutuality such as exchange or interaction, capacities like mobility or skills that help to adapt to highly variable environments gain in importance. These changes do not occur in a social field separate from the cultural. For all its relative autonomy the semantics of our symbolic systems also changes. And its changes are in accordance with the social transformation under way.

The cognitive rationalism of Luhmann's social theory is obvious enough not to need further emphasis. More interesting, however, is the type of rationality attributed to his primary agents, the systems. They secure their continued existence in time by organizing their behavior into patterns that guide their transactions, both internal and external. These patterns include the symbolic media through which they operate. Social systems thus follow a rationality of self-shaping (*autopoesis*) and adaptation akin to evolutionary biology. The formation of patterns or structures is a rational activity. The systems also try actively to control their "matter," including individuals, and their environment. Here, their aim is to induce their interior and their exterior to function according to the values of the system. There is, therefore, a rationality of systems integration as well as a rationality of systems formation. Finally, Luhmann's social theory contains an implicit ethics addressed to individuals. Its imperative is mimetic: "Do not meddle with the systems; rather, do what is best with regard to the special rationality of the system in which you operate."

The theory may seem to be restricted to the social domain. But the scope of "systems rationality" is really much larger than might appear. It extends to everything that is relevant to the system. Personality, ideologies, personal desires and wants, political and economic attitudes, and semantic values are all subsumed under and evaluated in terms of the social systems. Functionalist rationality posits systems values first, and judges other items according to how they relate to those values. In principle, the criteria of functional rationality are universal. They may be applied to the rationality of hypotheses, of science as an institution, to the question of the good life for a person or the evaluation of art. Functionalism is not just a social theory. It is an ambitious rationalism that gives primacy to the social realm.

I find this theory particularly relevant in a debate between contemporary rationalism and antirationalism. For in Luhmann, antirationalism encounters a contemporary rationalist that draws opposite conclusions from shared observations. Functionalism and antirationalism meet, for instance, in their rejection of enlightenment and of static structuralism. Both insist that we recognize a plurality of freely developing agencies, and that a comprehensive unity or unification is an impediment to the possibly chaotic and desirable development of those agencies. Both emphasize free play, albeit for different types of "players." Both deny teleology in history. And yet Luhmann's interpretations and conclusions tend to contradict antirationalism throughout. Again, I mention only one decisive point of divergence. Where antirationalism states or propagates disorder, Luhmann states and propagates order. To be sure, it is the particular order of the plurality of interacting autopoetic systems. This order is neither preset nor foreseeable nor uniquely determined at any given point in time. Instead, it is a multidimensional order that emerges in the course of events. In short, functionalist order is not "closed." Nevertheless, this functional order of a system and of systems can be analyzed by science. Functionalist rationality thus sees order as an immanent, emerging, and "proper" quality of (social) reality. Antirationalism sees order according to the model of constraint, as nonexistent or "improper," either imposed from the outside or arising from a deviation from a truer unordered reality or self. Here order is a constraint of a chaotic and mobile reality; there a dynamic "autopoetic" reality falls by itself into constantly changing patterns. It would be particularly interesting to confront these two attitudes.

The three members from the rationalist family I have presented all emphasize order, although they favor different types of order in different fields, and on different dimensions. All three look for new foundations of the orders they favor. Language, society, and an ideal community serve as anchoring fields for the principles of rationality. In various ways the three authors try to avoid metaphysical assumptions and traditional philosophies of history. All three, however, raise problems for antirationalism. Can we speak without presupposing that language is a rule-guided conceptual activity embedding a minimal rationality as a prerequisite for all discourse? Do we not have a genuine interest in both individual autonomy and institutions? Does our seemingly chaotic modern life-world not exhibit orders that can be apprehended and recognized?

The present state of the debate between rationalism and antirationalism is confusing. Contemporary French antirationalism has directed most of its arrows against older forms of rationality. Some of the rationalist responses suffer from the same default in refusing to acknowledge the full impact and seriousness of the antirationalist attack. Understandably, there has been a tendency on both sides to perceive the opponent in terms of older positions. Where this happens a strawman, and not the real opponent out there, is set up and torn apart. Unfortunately, a certain belatedness is still the rule in the debate between rationalism and antirationalism. I have tried to point to some of the issues at stake between more recent rationalist attempts and antirationalism. Among the existing samples of the general debate, *What Is Neostructuralism?* is a rare exception, because it both raises the basic issues and does it on the level of their most advanced theorizing.

V. Three Hermeneutic Positions: Gadamer, Ricoeur, and Frank

An account of contemporary hermeneutics, the fourth of my contenders for rationalism, must begin by mentioning Heidegger's not so rationalist analysis of "being there" (*Dasein*) as presented in *Being and Time*, for it is the common paradigm of both Gadamer's and Ricoeur's rationalism. "Being there," as is well known, is concerned with its own being ("Es geht dem Dasein in seinem Sein um dieses Sein," section 4, *Being and Time*). "Dasein" operates and articulates itself in understanding and interpretation. Our condition is therefore hermeneutic throughout, far beyond the utterances we proffer and receive. What is true for the *Entwürfe* of everyday existence is also true for theory: to lay out the existential features of *Dasein* is to engage in interpretation and in hermeneutic theory. Fundamental ontology participates in the hermeneutic character of "being there"; hermeneutics is a universal discipline.[10]

Hans Georg Gadamer

Gadamer transforms Heidegger's global and sketchy hermeneutics by singling out one of its aspects.[11] Instead of pursuing the analysis of *Dasein* or the ontology of *Sein*, he chooses to explore the hermeneutic *experience* and asks how it is grounded in our condition. *Truth and Method* is an ontology of understanding (*Verstehen*).

As a whole, Gadamer's theory oscillates between two points of view, not easily blended into a coherent picture. On the one hand, he adopts a more global, distant, and external perspective that is less rationalist. On the other hand, he also takes a more individualized, proximate, and internal point of view. Here,

Gadamer is much more rationalist. I begin with the more global view in which our sense-making activities are embedded in cultural meanings we neither create nor control. The dynamics of those cultural meanings Gadamer calls *Sinngesche-hen*: a mass and a flux of events that are occurrences of meaning or sense, a slow and continual turnover of cultural meanings, not unlike the matter glaciers transport on their way down from the mountains. All things meaningful fall into this mass. Nothing is beyond that flux or exempt from it. Reason therefore always comes to us in form of a particular section of the moving mass or flux. Gadamer's reason is irredeemably historicized. It does not retain an atemporal and foundational validity prior to and external to *Sinngeschehen*. The movement is not only ungrounded, it is also undirected. There is no measure to state decline, constraint, or progress. Teleology is thus expelled from the history of reason. Furthermore, no unitary or unified being, *Zeitgeist* or *Weltgeist*, realizes itself at any given moment in time. Nothing, therefore, sustains the unity of the many occurrences of meaning at a given time. On the global level, the only classical feature of rationality maintained by Gadamer is continuity clearly favored over discontinuity. Gadamer's faith in continuity may express the pondered "prejudice" of a historian whose culture has taught him that everything is connected. But for him, continuity is a value as well; its loss results in decline. Continuity is, of course, an important and controversial assumption particularly since Foucault has emphasized discontinuities in history; Derrida, the heterogeneity of the text.

This is not yet the end of Gadamer's antirationalist tendencies, for the different occurrences of meaning (*Sinngeschehen*) effect (*bewirken*) each other. History is thus the history of these effects and effectings (*Wirkungsgeschichte*). The flux of events reveals itself to be a web of effectings. By ontologizing these effectings, Gadamer comes close to some of the more recent theories of the text. His occurrences or events of sense are not independent units, which have an existence of their own and enter into relations with each other only contingently. The occurrences *are* the relations of being effected (passive) and of effecting (active). This relational ontology of *Sinngeschehen* overcomes the historicist idea of influence for which occurrences of meaning (*Sinnereignisse*) are connected through bonds of derivation or dependence running from earlier to later meanings (influence). Gadamer advocates the much more radical idea that the effects of those meaningful events contribute to the very identity of those events, and that these effects may lie in the past *and* in the future. Gadamerian "effectuation" has retroactive force, besides effecting the future. The consequences of his ontology are reflected in two of Gadamer's basic concept metaphors: "play" and "dialogue." Both in "play" (*Spiel*) and in "dialogue/conversation" (*Gespräch*), ulterior moves contribute to the meaning of preceding events. Understanding participates in what is to be understood. Specific meanings are constituted in the process of understanding and interpretation.

Thus far, Gadamer's *Sinngeschehen* will not appear to be a rational event. Rationality, if at all, will reside in the ways in which occurrences of meaning are related. Antirationalism would follow if every new event turned out to be entirely unbound by its predecessors and were able to confer on those predecessors whatever meaning it, the later event, happened to choose. Meanings would be erratic and would lack enduring determinacy.

In the global view presented so far, Gadamer's hermeneutics adopts a conservative, pessimistic, and somewhat stoic antirationalism. These traits are particularly visible in his "rehabilitation of prejudice" and in his recommendation that we align with the tradition instead of trying to emancipate from it.

The rationalist countercurrent of this not very strongly unified doctrine appears from a more individual or more internal point of view. Sense-making activities are performed by individual persons, through individual conduct, and result in individual works. The writing or reading of a book, the bringing up of one's children, psychotherapy or reflecting on one's own history, all these activities obviously involve agents and actions. What people do in these instances cannot be reduced to what a switchboard does to the electrical currents that traverse it. Agents come to their sense-making activities with prejudices, interests, and problems. These are internal factors determining understanding. But the current of understanding runs the other way, too: prejudices will be changed by a hermeneutic experience, interests will be redefined, initial problems will be transformed. From a point of view internal to a sense-operating being who, in these transactions, is concerned with his or her own being, the meanings from the cultural environment stand in need of appropriation, adaptation, and application to the situation. In short, they are not externally given data, but meanings individually constituted in the process. The "operation called understanding" has an individual and productive side that remained invisible from the distance of the global view. In the proximity of the sense-making activity itself, two complementary rational traits take profile. The interpreter or understanding agent looks for understanding in order to come to grips with him- or herself, the environment, and the demands of the situation. To be in search of understanding is to be involved in a rational activity. This is why the agent will try to construe his or her meanings as coherently and as comprehensibly as possible.[12] The agent will, for instance, try to understand him- or herself, to make sense of his or her own history or the institutions he or she has to cope with, etc. Sense-making stretches from everyday, piecemeal, and individual problem solving to the collective construction of a mythology or a cosmology. To be sure, no interpretive activity is able to grasp the totality of the cultural or even of the individual meanings attached to the concrete problem to which it is applied. The subject of hermeneutics cannot reach transparency and mastery of his or her own destiny, nor can that subject assemble the totality of the meanings of a work. The subject nevertheless may be able to achieve a limited knowledge and control of his or her life or that work. On the agent's level, Gadamer's rationality goes as far as espousing values borrowed from enlightenment. The agent can be enlightened about the fact that he or she is an "effected meaning." This is the much-discussed *wirkungsgeschichtliches Bewusstsein*, a consciousness arising in history, determined by history, and conscious of arising in history as so determined. Simultaneously, it is also, but only partially, determining history, and likewise conscious of doing so. Historicized "reason" has overcome the prejudices of enlightenment, but it is still capable of being enlightened about itself. And the pathos of Gadamer's plea for a self-consciously hermeneutical attitude suggests that to be or not to be thus enlightened makes a practical difference, for instance, for continuity or forgetfulness.

Understanding turns out to be a bipolar activity. Its two poles are the understanding agents and the "thing" (*die Sache*) to be understood. What is the scope of understanding? Again, it would be too narrow to extend it to the work of art and the text of intellectual discourse alone. The possible subject matter of understanding includes anything that can fill the blank of "x is understood as (meaning) . . ." This allows historical episodes, decisions of courts, and political decisions to be macroobjects; words, sentences, individual actions to be microobjects of understanding.

The "objective" pole of understanding also gives rise to a normative rationality of its own. Here the task is not, as it was for the subject, self-shaping under conditions of limited control. The matter or object requires recognition for what it may be "itself," that is, as something possibly other than what the interpreter thinks it is or wants it to be. Gadamer strongly defends an ethics of otherness at the exact opposite of the interest of appropriation characteristic of the "subjective" pole.

That same otherness is also the source of the cognitive element in hermeneutics. For recognition of otherness includes distance, at times even intentional estrangement, of the understanding agent vis-à-vis the object. Otherness is not given; it needs active construction and recognition. I interpret this as a highly rationalist feature of Gadamer's hermeneutics, as opposed to methodological arbitrariness as to the negation of otherness in some antirationalist theories of the text.

Understanding has to fulfill yet another rational task. Reflection, problem solving, and self-shaping on the subjective side, as well as otherness on the objective side, all call for an interpretation as comprehensive and coherent as possible. Incoherence, scatteredness and disconnectedness are negative values. They are a challenge to an understanding whose task is primarily constructive. Lack of connectedness is not, as it is in deconstruction, propagated, but rather is limited to the smallest amount imposed by the object. The subject has to construe his or her meanings and him- or herself as a thoroughly connected being. Gadamer's ideal is that of the integrated personality, the individual pendant to a closely knit tradition.

To sum up my presentation of Gadamer's hermeneutic rationalism: A radically relativized and historicized reason relegates the subject (and the work) to the limited space of self-shaping. But agents can be enlightened about their limitations as well as their possibilities. Somewhat stoically, the subject continues to construct the most coherent self to be obtained under the circumstances by drawing on the meaning resources of its environment, most notably on its tradition. The collective efforts of the many subjects continue the tradition.

Paul Ricoeur

Ricoeur's impressive oeuvre is the second huge body of contemporary hermeneutic thought.[13] If Gadamer asks "What is understanding and how is it grounded in the human condition?" Ricoeur's questions are "Who are we? What can we know? What are we to do?" In terms of the existentialist framework adopted by Ricoeur the primary interest is in the "Who" of *Dasein*, not in its basic mode of operation. But Ricoeur is convinced that reflection cannot begin by exploring phenomena allegedly presenting themselves, phenomena like *Dasein* (Heidegger) or art (Gadamer). There is no privileged type of experience. Ricoeur therefore opts for working through the dazzling plurality of cultural meanings – religious, aesthetic, or philosophical – in order to detect how we have objectified ourselves into these forms that are simultaneously the forms that shape us. It is important to note that Ricoeur's aim is not a panorama of the objective spirit or of symbolic forms, but hermeneutic reflection on our lived experience. Who are we, beings who not only produce and suffer those symbols but also cast our individual experiences in their terms? From Gadamer's global view we are merely immersed in the mass of our cultural forms. But according to Ricoeur, that "second nature" both obscures, even hides from us, and reveals to us our particular truth at this particular juncture of history. In short, Ricoeur wants to read our existential condition, and a historicized one at that, from the specific symbolic forms of our era.

Such a program changes the theoretical stance itself. Instead of straightforwardly building his own theories Ricoeur constantly discusses other theories pressed to disclose their partial truths about ourselves. I choose *subjectivity*, *interpretation*, and *language* as three topics directly relevant to the frame of Frank's book.

If it is impossible to go straight to the matter of the subject itself, because the truth of the subject is revealed neither by consciousness nor in existential self-disclosedness, then the subject has to gain access to itself as it does to other entities, that is, indirectly. For a symbolic and symbolizing being, self-reflexion is interpretation of the symbolic manifestations of the self. Psychoanalysis, not idealism, is therefore Ricoeur's paradigm for a modern theory of subjectivity. All access to the subject is thus mediate and mediated by cultural meanings. What do these meanings reveal about the subject, notably about his or her predicament to self-fashion freely? How is freedom possible if the conditions of the situation have in advance determined what an agent can choose to bring about? Ricoeur tries to solve the problems to which those questions allude through the *symbol* elevated by him to the rank of an existential concept. The symbol is overdetermined and overdetermining. It is *both*, and simultaneously, determined by factors such as tradition, environment, or archaic heritage *and* produced in a free project constituting a world and a self through the meanings it assumes. The symbol selects its causes and constitutes a project. Freedom and determination coincide and coexist in the symbol. Ricoeur's symbol serves as a medium that provides a feeling, willing, and knowing subject with the distance toward self and environment. This distance is a necessary condition for free self-production. The symbol confers on the subject a space of its own, and simultaneously ties the subject to the larger contexts on which it depends.

The symbol is also what makes the knowledge of self possible. It objectifies a symbolizing activity into works. This symbolizing activity is not in control of its own ground. The work, in turn, does not release its deeper meanings before a special effort is made and special methods are used. This is because the work has been shaped by unconscious and uncontrolled driving forces. And yet they yield to interpretation because they are symbols marked by and exhibiting the impact of those forces that themselves may lie deeply hidden in the material.

Interpretation has the task of uncovering those signifying forces and factors. In addition to its more traditional functions, methodologically controlled interpretation also reflectively reappropriates meanings that are otherwise beyond the realm of conceptual awareness. Interpretation is therefore the proper reflective activity. Is there also a "proper" way to reflect interpretively? Ricoeur puts forward a complex theory of interpretive phases—not, of course, consecutive steps of interpretation—each of which requires a methodological conscience of its own. Interpretation *construes* the immanent meanings of its object, for instance, a narrative. In the constructive phase considerations of application or of consistency do not yet matter. Another, referential, phase is the articulation of the implicit *worldview* of a work. The world to which the work refers is the world implicated by the object, its world "picture," not our "real" world, although the implied world is ultimately related to "our" world. Finally, in the third phase the interpreter interprets him- or herself in the light of the worldview presented by the object. This phase is the *application* of meaning to self. The three phases are moments of a dialectical reflective process.

Another aspect typical of Ricoeur's approach is his discussion of theories that have come as challenges to traditional hermeneutics. Among others, Ricoeur discusses and uses psychoanalysis, linguistic structuralism, and analytic philosophy of language, in sharp contrast to the narrowness, if not parochialness, of Heidegger and Gadamer. Ricoeur's usual strategy is to respond to the challenge of opposing theories by giving up some traditional territory in order to secure the hold of hermeneutics on the rest. He concedes, for instance, that language is rule-governed up to the linguistic level of the well-formed sentence. On this level we deal with a socially and semantically predetermined form that, for that reason, is inappropriate for creative self-projection. Similarly for reference: In referring to a reality that transcends the referring speech or text, and in predicating something of this reality, we have to submit to the semantic and logical bonds of language. But metaphor and symbol are not so determined, nor are the larger and unregulated products of our symbolic activity, among them the text. Texts, moreover, do not depict an outside reality. They *are* the medium in which the freedom of the individual finds expression and design in the invention of selves and worlds.

My concluding observations examine Ricoeur's view of rationality. Compared to Gadamer, Ricoeur's greater emphasis on rationality is palpable. Not only do we not encounter Gadamer's tradition, in advance appropriating each and every individual effort, but everything that has symbolic character is open to reflection and appropriation. Where Gadamer's appropriation of the tradition most often appears as a blind process whose very blindness reflection cannot but acknowledge, Ricoeur insists on the possibility of conceptual elucidation. It is as if he had "appropriated" the idealist project of a reflectively self-producing supersubject, but adapted it to the new conditions of a world and a subjectivity decentered, dispersed, and constituted by symbolic forces beyond reflexive control, but no longer constituted by a self-conscious supersubject. If those constraints bar the idealist project, they do allow us to redefine reflexivity and self-shaping in the symbolic medium. The medium limits the scope of transparency and control, but opens the large intermediate area of interpretive activity. Ricoeur's is a reflexive philosophy based on the symbol (*symbolische Reflexionsphilosophie*). In it, reason has become a mediating and transforming activity. Philosophy has been liberated from the foundational tasks that have overburdened it for so long. Interpretive reason mediates between determinism and freedom, continuity and innovation, poetical and discursive expression, subject and world.

Manfred Frank

My portrait of Frank, who belongs to the generation of hermeneutic philosophers after Gadamer and Ricoeur, concentrates on his two significant contributions to contemporary hermeneutics. He "modernizes" hermeneutics by introducing a structural model of meaning, and he insists on the irreducibility of the individual subject, its uniqueness and the singularity of its sense-making productions.[14]

Structuralism raised two problems for traditional hermeneutics. First, it insisted on the *systematicness* of semiotic units. Signs owe their determinacy to the relations they entertain with other units in a structure or system of relations. This thesis denies that signs have shape or meaning singly entering into relations with each other fully equipped with "Gestalt" and meaning. (We saw that Gadamer's *Bedeutungsereignisse* ["meaning events"] also possessed this feature.) Second, structuralism has proclaimed the primacy of the signifier over the signified (the meaning). According to this second thesis the status of meaning, if indeed it has separate status at all, depends on the relations of or the rules for the signifier. Meanings owe whatever determinacy and identity they have to the stratum of signifiers. In sum, structuralism challenged the autonomy and supremacy of meaning, and with it the primacy of understanding.

Frank's reply to the structuralist challenge is complex but, unlike Ricoeur's, uncompromising. Frank concedes systematicness but resists the idea of a meaningless signifier. He adopts the thesis that signs are indeed constituted in a systematic and historical surrounding and do not have individual existence and determinacy prior to or independently from this environment. But, according to him, far from dispensing with meaning, the systematic and contextual constitution of the sign *requires* meaning. The category of meaning is necessary for the structuralist program and indeed was held by Saussure to be part of his new science of language.

But did structuralism not argue that meaningful activity is *nothing but* the enactment of structures and that "meaning" is *but* the relational network within the structure? If this is true then meaning (the signified) is indistinguishable from the signifier, and is neither an independent category nor the product of a speaker's sense-making activity. This, Frank replies (using Schleiermacher as his mouthpiece), is not true. The structuralist reduction of meaning overlooks that a network of relations among signifiers always occurs as context. The structure of the structuralist, all-embracing and productive as it is to be, is never given otherwise than in the form of some concrete context. Narrative structure, historical *episteme*, systems of kinship, phonological or syntactical structure, are all accessible only by appearing as concrete narratives, myths, tribes, languages, or bodies of knowledge. The phenomenal and contextual element is at least epistemologically primary to the order or structural element it exhibits. Structure and context are not two entities that exist separately and act upon each other. They only exist jointly, and as mutually determining. This ontological feature might be called "interexistence."

What is more, the identity of the order will in part depend on the concrete item allegedly determined by the structure alone because the context always includes the concrete, meaningful element itself. Therefore, signs are constituted by a dynamic interaction between a particular signifier and its context, not by a static and Platonic structural agency intervening in reality. For the same reason, the insertion of a signifier into a structure is the result of a meaningful activity, of a subject or of the particular sign itself.

Let it be assumed that a language shows phonological and syntactical regularities. Were its speakers not to make the distinctions constitutive of the units of that language, there would be nothing to be subsumed under the structural laws. But we can read from the critical attitudes of the speakers themselves that they are observing certain rules, both about units and about combination. If those speakers, as they sometimes do, stop distinguishing units or following rules, then their "meaning-conferring" (Husserl) activity has changed the structure. This, then, is the hermeneutic appropriation of structuralism: structure is constituted by meaning, for it is given as meaning in and through context.[15]

In addition to the structural component, Frank distinguishes yet another dimension of meaning, following Schleiermacher. In the differentiated realm of significances structural meaning calls for but *one* type of interpretive attitude, a generalizing interpretation. We do, however, operate with "sense," too, an individual element in meaning that cannot be reduced to structural meaning. Sense is irreducibly individual. It manifests itself as style, another individualizing concept in Frank's hermeneutics. Sense and style call for an interpretive attitude different from, but dialectically related to, the hermeneutic attitude focusing on structure. Individualizing interpretations grasp what is singular, different, idiosyncratic in a text (or in whatever is the object of interpretation). Over and over again, Frank's paradigm case for sense is Sartre's interpretation of Flaubert.[16] Sartre explores Flaubert, the individual author and his individual "oeuvre," in their most minute detail, but not as separate individual meaning in addition to social, political, structural, or other meaning. Sense is not severable, not even analytically separable, from the structured and structuring environment in which it occurs. And yet sense is also a singular response of a sense-making being in and to that environment. The singularity of that response, lost in interpretations uniquely concerned with the typical and functional aspects of the material, is brought to light only when attention is paid to the particular options, the inconsistencies, the deviations from an established genre or from a paradigm that has become oppressive. Sartre's enterprise is also proof of the feasibility of an individualizing interpretive focus and provides a methodological justification. Frank is one of the few authors to have acknowledged that Sartre's late and much neglected magnum opus is as serious an alternative to structuralism and poststructuralism as it is to Gadamer's integrative hermeneutics and its social and political obliviousness.[17]

Frank, then, counters the structuralist negation of meaning with two theses. Structure, he says, *is* sense and meaning. Or, more precisely, structure is that aspect of meaning that is turned toward order. For there is the other, the individual aspect of meaning; and whatever has meaning also has sense. The uniqueness of sense—this is Frank's second thesis—can be detected in every concrete, meaningful item, from the most ephemeral gesture to the pervading and enduring style of an epoch. Applying his methodology of the individualizing gaze to the authors he discusses in the present volume, Frank discovers interesting individual differences, between, for example, Foucault and Derrida, or Deleuze and Lyotard, thus initiating a differential analysis of contemporary antirationalism.[18]

So far, my presentation of Frank's hermeneutics has deliberately screened out another aspect of his theory: his theory of *subjectivity* and of *individuality*. The "question of the subject" has been a major bone of contention between antirationalism and rationalism. Consequently, Frank accords the largest part of *What Is Neostructuralism?* to the topic of subjectivity and its treatment by Lacan, Derrida, and Deleuze (Lectures 12 through 24). He has also discussed the topic from a different point of view in his latest book.[19] Frank's own theory of subjectivity is still in the process of elaboration.

In its rejection of "the subject," antirationalism affirms two related theses. We are not nor should we try to be unified individuals, reflecting on what we think, do, and are, rationally controlling our actions. In short, the self-conscious and self-controlled individual is neither a fact nor should it be a norm. Consequently, antirationalism abandons the idea of a foundational role of subjectivity, the subject as ultimate ground of knowledge, locus of privileged access and certainty, the subject as a separate ontological realm (mind, spirit) or as the end of a line progressing from less to greater subjectivity. For antirationalists we are nonunified plural beings, ignoring and deluding ourselves as to what we are and do, moved and shaped by forces over which we have no control.

Hermeneutics has consistently opposed this Nietzschean position and has emphasized reflexive self-shaping. We have seen that both Gadamer's and Ricoeur's theories exhibit this attitude. Frank continues along the same lines, but emphasizes subjectivity even more strongly than the two older authors do. His opposition to the Nietzschean position is based on a strong notion of self-knowledge or self-acquaintance (*Selbstvertrautheit*). For Frank, as for his teacher, the neo-idealist Dieter Henrich,[20] self-acquaintance is an original phenomenon evidenced by our lived experience (*Erleben*). Therefore the theory does not need to *argue* for the reality of the phenomenon, although it must give a theoretial account of it. The fact that we are acquainted with ourselves is a certainty.

Self-acquaintance, as conceived by Henrich and Frank, lacks some of the more problematic features of traditional self-consciousness. Being primordial, it does not have access to its sources. It springs, as Henrich puts it, from sources it does not control or master (*aus unverfügbarem Grund*).[21] It is also conceptually impenetrable. Consequently, Frank's self is neither its own author—if an author is someone who knowingly and intentionally brings about a work—nor the locus and agent of order (transcendental agent, bearer of reflexive activity, source and addressee of the law of freedom). Rather, the opposite is true: the self as individual is a constant threat to, an irregularity in, a disturbance and rupture of, orders.

Why does a self-acquaintance that has lost its foundational functions remain important? First, it serves in an account of individuality. Frank distinguishes between the subject, the person, and the individual without, however, offering us more than summary accounts of the distinction. The subject is said to be "general," the person "particular." But the individual is an "unrepresentable, unique being" whose essence cannot be exhausted by concepts.[22] A being possesses this uniqueness because it is related to itself and to itself only in the peculiar mode of self-acquaintance, a familiarity with ourselves that is not cognitive, at least not in the common sense of the term. In an additional thought that one would like to be less abrupt and more elaborate,[23] that same individual is even claimed to be the producer of its meaningful productions. An individual, Frank says, attributes its concept to a totality of which it is an element. The concept is *of* the totality. But it is also *by* an individual element included *in* that totality. The concept thus shares in the uniqueness of its source. In addition, it has the generality of conceptuality through application.

The attribution of the concept to the totality is the work of interpretation. Again, Frank does not tell us why this is accomplished by the individual and not (also?) by the subject or the person, or how the person and the subject manage to be conceptual beings and results of interpretation, and who their conceiver is. Both the subject and the person stand in need of symbolic realization. Do they then have a worldview of their own, or are they merely conceptual projections? Are they conceived by the individual or by the symbolic order? Frank has not yet answered those questions. In addition, he also will need to tell us *how* an individual said to exist "without internal duplicate or double" externalizes and objectifies its inaccessible uniqueness into sense and style that are accessible and amenable to interpretation. Ricoeur's hermeneutics and Merleau-Ponty's phenomenology have more elaborate theories on these issues.

The contours of Frank's design should have become visible. Subjectivity and textuality are the two poles in a hermeneutics equally capable of taking a general and an individual perspective. Frank is working out a theory of subjectivity not based on self-transparency or unification, and therefore not open to the objections raised by antirationalism. Hermeneutics is thus led away from the apparent choice between individualizing and generalizing attitudes. Incidentally, Frank's strategy is also a step toward a hermeneutic model of subjectivity. This is all the more important because hermeneutics focused on understanding, interpretation, and the condition of symbolic man has tended to neglect traditional topics such as society, ethics, and subjectivity. Important fields were thus left to its rationalist and antirationalist rivals. As far as the textual pole is concerned, Frank has incorporated a hermeneutically reinterpreted, structuralist semiotics into contemporary hermeneutics. Hermeneutics overcomes its former dependence on and limitation by antirational Heideggerian existentialism. In addition, Frank creates "elbow room" for a greater variety of hermeneutic attitudes and a better position for hermeneutics in the great doctrinal debates. A semiotically enlightened hermeneutics can accommodate existential, structural, or other interpretive attitudes, among them even deconstructive transactions with texts. Frank's presentations and discussions in *What Is Neostructuralism?* bear witness to the scope of integration his hermeneutics possesses.

VI. Hermeneutic Rationality vs. Antirationalism

In this final section I would like to evaluate hermeneutic rationality more generally, before concluding with a staged debate between hermeneutics and deconstruction on the crucial issue of interpretation.

Hermeneutic rationality is built upon the assumption that we are symbolic, that is, sense-operating, beings. This assumption takes a rationalist turn when the theory asserts — as the three hermeneuticists presented here do — that interpretation has cognitive status, that its claims can be supported or opposed by arguments that relate back to the object to be interpreted for their support. But this is the specialized rationality of interpretive sciences and activities, and yields only a regional or partial rationalism.

Philosophical hermeneutics pursues the more ambitious and larger project of explicating the rationality inherent in our symbolizing or understanding activity itself. Does the fact that we are sense-making beings allow us rationally to conduct our lives? Can our symbolic condition serve as the basis of an epistemology or an ethics? Is the way we model our world through categories and concepts a cognition of that world? Are some interpretations of the world or of ourselves more rational than others? Are there more and less rational ways to deal with our own sense-making capacity? To some of these questions hermeneutics does indeed offer answers, although no systematic account of hermeneutic rationality has been offered by one of the contemporary hermeneutics.

The normative side of the better-known hermeneutical doctrines is perhaps best summed up by the imperative: understand yourself and what is relevant for you; become as differentiated and unified an individual as you can. Most hermeneuticists defend one or the other kind of individuality and of integratedness as values of a rational personality. Rationality, as it emerges from evaluations such as these, applies to self-shaping activities. Its model is the "work" (*ergon*, *Werk*, *oeuvre*) and the making of works, the individual and integrated object or result brought about by the craftsperson or the artist. It is to be noted that *ergon* occupies several places in a rationalism that is, in senses other than Max Weber's, a "work ethics." First and most simply, work is the result of an activity, its objectification into something different from the activity itself. When our activities result in a character, a history, sets of experiences, then we ourselves become works, the joint result of self-shaping and external conditions. As agents, we stand in two relations to our works. We bring them about, or rather, participate in bringing them about. And we encounter them as things to be dealt with. The hermeneutic imperative could therefore also read: become a work (become your work); be a good craftsperson.

In this version, the imperative includes prescriptions as to the ways and means for realizing this ideal. There is thus a "secondary" hermeneutic rationality that applies to the activity through which first-order rationality is acquired or modified. Here, the most important variable is how the individual appropriates the cultural meanings of his or her environment, and how rational that appropriation is. The ideal, again, is a reflexive, selective internalization of those meanings. In the process of internalization the individual works through inherited meanings and gives to them a unique form. To be sure, the individual's potential for innovation is severely limited. Recognition of these limits, itself an interpretive and reflexive task, is therefore an integral part of hermeneutic rationality. In this instance, reflexivity assumes a limiting function, telling an agent what *not* to try to achieve.

In another dimension of graded rationality there are more and there are less genuine ways of pursuing the self-shaping activity. For Gadamer, for instance, the *wirkungsgeschichtliches Bewusstsein*, the reflected self-insertion in one's own tradition, is a positive value, whereas blindness toward, or even willful forgetfulness of, the tradition is negative. For Frank, on the other hand, "emancipation" is a positive value, and emancipation encourages independence from traditional values and the quest for values of one's own.

Still another dimension of rationality concerns the mode of interaction between an agent and his or her tradition. Again, for Gadamer, the appropriation is most successful when it is done in the spirit of a genuine overt dialogue. Ricoeur, on the other hand, favors the model of psychoanalysis as a symbolic integration of forces and meanings from beyond the realm of a self-shaping reason.

The reader of my summary may have felt, as I do, some misgivings about hermeneutic rationality. When elevated to the rank of a universal philosophical theory, hermeneutics begins to sound vague and arbitrary. How, for example, are we going to lead a genuine dialogue? Gadamer tells us that a genuine dialogue transforms all the participants, that the dialogue has unexpected results, etc. Somehow, we recognize such a dialogue when we are engaged in it. But an appeal to nonconceptual knowledge is not what we expect from a theory of reason. Gadamer's dialogue, charitably interpreted, embodies the virtue of wisdom; yet to a less well disposed reader its theoretical propagation may well appear to be a bundle of beautiful but empty phrases.

It may be felt that I am being unjust to Gadamerian hermeneutics. After all, does Gadamer not reject the theoretical claims I have attributed to him? Perhaps he does, thinking that "truth" is properly located not in the theory but in the events (*Wahrheitsgeschehen*). But in this case his hermeneutics moves even closer toward antirationalism, this time toward the anti*theoretical* branch of the antirationalist family. To give another example: Why should we try to be integrated personalities who understand their own history and are well acquainted with their cultural tradition? Why is an individual unique and ineffable? Traditional rationalism derived or justified personal policies for the subject by appealing to its notion of reason. But with the foundational gesture contemporary hermeneutics has given up the justificatory resources of a tradition now more cultivated as a cultural heritage than philosophically defended as a theory. Gadamerian hermeneutics propagates the values of individuality or of an integrated personality without justifying them. At their weaker moments, hermeneutic theories vacillate between a very general and not very interesting metaphilosophy about our condition as sense-making beings, and highly educated, well-intentioned, but ultimately undirected and unorganized, collections of beautiful pieces from our philosophical tradition.

Other problems have been mentioned before. In spite of claims to universality, hermeneutics does not offer elaborate enough theories of its own concerning subjectivity, society, and, most surprisingly, meaning, omissions that are all the more conspicuous given that some of its rival theories address these topics. (Not even Frank's structuralist account of meaning undertakes a systematic account of its topic.) Nor does hermeneutics propose a theory of modernity to be compared to those put forward by Luhmann, Habermas, and Lyotard, unless the theory as a whole is taken as an implicit theory of modernity. In that case, however, it might more adequately be called a symptom. Much of hermeneutics, particularly Gadamer's influential version, presents our era in a pessimistic and highly nonrational way. For the first time in the history of Western thought a period would be characterized by *not* building a theory of its own discursively expressing its self-understanding. It would *not* take upon itself the task of articulating its own worldview in terms it invents for itself, be it in the form of system or of fragments. Instead, for better or for worse, reflexive philosophy would be reduced to the appropriation and modification of the tradition. This would also be the only means for contemporary reason to maintain a reflexive stance toward itself. Theoretical insights are not pursued independently from the fact that they have been thought before, and for their own sake. It is not surprising, then, that hermeneutics emphasizes construction, unity of meaning, coherence, connectedness, and continuity. The theory itself does not realize those values. Instead of offering theories as responses to problems, hermeneutics all too often chooses the flight into metaphilosophy or into a historicizing attitude toward philosophy. Is it not, in this respect, an antirationalism camouflaged as rationalism, much closer to contemporary antirationalism than it likes to admit?[24]

It may seem astounding, then, that the debate between hermeneutics and antirationalism—to which I now turn—has been so lively.[25] At the surface, the main point of contention is clear. The controversy is about language and interpretation. The hermeneuticist advocates construction, cognition, coherence, and unity of meaning; the antirationalist, deconstruction, undecidability, division, and dissemination of meaning. And behind the surface of a debate about interpretation our whole self-definition is at stake. Will we, shall we, define ourselves through one or the other of the two interpretive attitudes?

The observations on interpretation I am going to offer at the end of this foreword are not intended to resolve the case between antirationalist denial and rationalist affirmation of interpretation. The problems I want to raise are different: What kind of a debate are the two parties involved in? How does the controversy proceed? How do the opponents meet? On what grounds, if any, do rationalists and antirationalists oppose each other? To what extent and about what do they have an argument?

Hermeneutics takes constructive interpretation to be possible, and construction to have a cognitive aspect. We can have arguments about the adequacy of an interpretation, because some interpretations fit their object better than others. A strong position against these two theses—construability of meaning and arguability of interpretation—appears to be this: construction of meaning, at least as the hermeuticist understands the term, is impossible. If this position is true, it follows that constructive interpretation is not cognitive but some other kind of activity, more akin perhaps to dreaming than to knowing. Hermeneutics dreams the dream of the unity of meaning. Antirationalism "awakens hermeneutics from its dogmatic slumber," not, of course, "to set hermeneutics on the secure path of science."

On what grounds does antirationalism—here presented in its Derridian or deconstructionist version—reject constructive interpretation?[26] What something "means" is, in the technical language of Derrida, an "undecidable." Let me divide the deconstructionist negation of constructible meaning into two lines of argument. The first, which I will now explore, is based upon the thesis that "meaning" is determined by context, the very thesis Frank used against the structuralist reduction of meaning. Deconstruction pushes the thesis to its radical consequence. No meaning is complete before the last word of the context has been considered. But interpretations are contexts. As long as they continue to "supplement" the text, truth claims about the text cannot be founded on the text. Furthermore, the context is infinite. Therefore no definite meaning can ever be ascertained.

In *What Is Neostructuralism?* Frank replies to the "disseminatory" theory of "meaning." (In its own understanding it is not a "theory of meaning," neither a theory, nor of meaning.) Lecture 25 through the end contains a detailed scrutiny of Derrida's views on interpretation. Frank here challenges the poststructuralist skepticism that denies the assertibility of meaning. He argues that the justifiability of interpretation is always relative. It is relative to an assumed unit to be interpreted, but also to a frame of interpretation, to perspectives, to interests, and so on. Every interpretation constitutes itself as a cellular unit, setting up provisional boundaries against the endlessness of other words, interests, etc., and thus staking out a little territory for itself. If this were impossible there would be nothing determinate enough to be undecidable. Arguments about the adequacy of interpretation function only within the confines of assumptions and presuppositions thus made. Admittedly, neither the boundaries nor the territory are secure and definite. But together they prevent the blankness of the infinite space of possible alternatives, supplements, and disavowals to engulf the emerging interpretation. It is this relative character of interpretation that deconstruction disregards when it passes from the ultimate dependence of all interpretation on the totality of interpretations to the conclusion that *each* and every interpretation is undecidable. Deconstruction conflates the micro- and the macrocosm of interpretation. It may be the case that *ultimately* every interpretation will or may be overcome by some other interpretation refuting the first interpretation. But this is by no means an argument against the feasibility of the particular interpretation in a certain environment, nor against "decidability" (here: arguability) in the confines of such an environment. Is not deconstruction also staking out its own claim in presupposing that a text of departure "deconstructs itself, of its own"? If ever there is an essentialist assumption, this is one. This initial assumption of deconstructive textuality will also determine what counts as an adequate "interpretation" and what can be said in favor of it. Will a nondeconstructive interpretation undo a concrete deconstructive transaction with the text? Will it be acceptable as an adequate transaction with the text of origin?

Frank's reply to the radical skepticism denying the very possibility of controlled interpretation is, then, to grant the premise that all meaning is constituted in (and by) the great chain of meaning, but to reject the conclusion of radical undecidability. Against the radical relativism of deconstruction he affirms the relative controllability of interpretive reconstruction. I think Frank's point is well taken.

Deconstructionist skepticism with regard to constructive interpretation may be based on a more radical thought. This time, the antirationalist argues from the textual fabric of the piece to be interpreted itself. Briefly, the argument asserts that whenever we think we have grasped a meaning of a text, then the same text can also be read as meaning something else, and the two "meanings" are incompatible. A text, or whatever is meaningful, does indeed have meaning effects. But they do not obey any rule, and they fall into no order. The semiotic object will, as it were, license one meaning *and* its opposite (some meaning incompatible with the first). Incoherence is not a particular meaning, dwelling *in* the text side by side with coherent meanings, to be found and spelled out. Neither is incoherence a quality of *some* texts but not of others. Incoherence is the "nature" of textuality or semioticity itself. For a text, it is impossible not to be inconsistent.

This argument raises difficulties of a new kind. As these difficulties are paradigmatic of the more general problems that beset a debate between rationalism and antirationalism, I will try to spell them out here. Indeed, they will turn out to prevent the argument from being an argument, at least in the usual sense of that term.

For how is the hermeneuticist going to deal with a thesis that states that his enterprise is impossible and appeals to the necessary incoherence of textuality for support? His task looks simple enough. The hermeneutic opponent gives a counterexample. He offers a piece of coherent and constructive interpretation that is evidence for the possibility of his favored interpretive attitude. At this point, the antirationalist opponent has to make a decision. If he wants to continue arguing that a "coherentist" interpretation is impossible, he will either have to show that the interpretation of the counterexample is only apparently constructive, but really incoherent, or that it is not an account of the "meaning" of the object at all.[27] Both strategies, however, present self-defeating problems to the antirationalist. Not only does he need to interpret the interpretation and the work in his argument. How else could he say that the apparently "coherent" interpretation is really incoherent or that it fails to do justice to the piece? His own interpretation is also a constructive text in its own right and an interpretation in a minimal sense. The antirationalist runs into this difficulty because, if he wants to argue about the example, he must at least say what he thinks the meaning of a text is *not*. In addition, he must "understand" the interpretation under attack, and he needs to construe its meaning, again at least up to the point where he is able to say that the allegedly constructive interpretation is an inadequate transaction with the original text. Meanings must be assertible and assessable if all this is to take place.

By now it will have become obvious that the debate has been engaged in terms favorable to the hermeneutic position. The antirationalist opponent will consequently try to shift the controversy to a terrain more favorable to his cause. The logical structure of the debate will further highlight the difficulty. "Possibility" and "impossibility" of constructive interpretation are *universal* theses. The hermeneuticist has the advantage of being able to argue for *possibility* from an example of constructive interpretation. But the deconstructionist opponent has the disadvantage that he can be completely successful in his argument against the example, and still does not win his case against the hermeneuticist. There will always be other examples.

Therefore, the antirationalist stands a much better chance if he engages in the debate in general terms. He is also well equipped to do so, for he disposes of a theory of language or of texts saying that the virtual objects of interpretation are incoherent and unconstruable. From this point on, the argument hinges on the plausibility of the theory. I refer the reader to the presentation in *What Is Neostructuralism?*[28] Let it be granted that there is such a theory. Then the debate has indeed changed. It has shifted from the example to the plausibility of the deconstructionist theory. Are texts (in general) "undecidables"? Or are they, for example, pictures of fictionally possible worlds, and thus describable? The roles between the opposing sides are now reversed. At this point, the hermeneutic opponent faces a choice. On the one hand, he can choose to argue against the theory that denounces his favored kind of interpretation. Gadamer, for instance, has invoked a consensual element in understanding as a general presupposition that everyone, including antirationalists, must make.[29] In his reply Derrida has compared Gadamer's will to understand to Kant's "good will," burdening Gadamer with normative assumptions of an ethical kind.[30] Gadamer, of course, did not intend to appeal to a rational will in a Kantian sense, but only to a will that wants to understand. Clearly, wanting to understand what somebody says and wanting to submit to the categorical imperative (or some other ethical standard) are not the same thing. Gadamer is convinced that his will to understand does *not* depend on a particular norm of *any* kind, that there simply is no alternative to willing to understand, short of madness or intentional "misunderstanding" (which seems to be impossible). But Derrida may have wanted to illustrate just this: from the antirationalist point of view, construction of meaning *is* the following of a particular norm, only gradually different from a will that has been subjected to the categorical imperative. For Gadamer, that same will to understand is a transcendental and nonprescriptive condition of communication in general. Clearly, the debate draws arguments from premises or assumptions *not* shared by the adversary. Each side thinks the other does, must, or ought to share those premises, or that arguability begins only after certain rules (or nonrules) have been secured. Yet as a matter of fact, the other party does not think this is the case. The theoretical debate is thus deadlocked. Its participants do not have consensus, either about assumptions or about meanings of fundamental terms. In that situation, an appeal to "understanding" or to grasping each other's meanings is futile because it is part of the position under attack. For each side can maintain its premises only as long as it does *not* make the other's assumptions, or use its own terms as the other does. This is not uncommon in cases of *Grundlagenstreit,* controversies about foundations or fundamentals in which everything, including the basics, is at stake.[31]

Once the hermeneuticist comes to the conclusion just sketched, he may remember that he has another option still. Did the trouble not start when he tried to *refute* the thesis that constructive interpretation is impossible on theoretical grounds? What if instead he asked what *support* the deconstructionist has for his theory? But the same situation will recur. The debate will again and very soon reach premises that cannot be referred to further shared premises or higher-level arguments. The deadlock thus seems complete. The conclusion appears inevitable: the controversy is not an argument. It has not secured the minimal consensus that makes arguments possible. This conclusion is not altogether surprising in a debate between rationalists and antirationalists, at least as long as each side persists in a totalizing attitude. After all, the two camps do not share minimal rationality.

It may seem that we have reached a point where the controversy dissolves into resigned tolerance. Let each party have it its way. This conclusion is, however, premature. The general theories may indeed not be decidable for lack of shared assumptions. But we have stated arguability in our discussion of examples. It is remarkable that deconstructionist and hermeneutic attitudes are genuinely controversial on a level of less ambitious and less general theorizing. Each side, then, chooses examples. In order to reach the less universal and more open type of generality that resides in exemplarity, each side tries to make its case as exemplary as possible. One may wonder, though, what the status of an example can be in the new debate. How should we be able to do through examples what we could not do with the theories themselves? Let the rationalist use his representationalist ideas in choosing and interpreting his examples. The deconstructionist will do the opposite. What is new and different from the previous debate is that now *theories and examples are inextricably entangled.* The theory, "for example," Ricoeur's or Derrida's theory of textuality, is both a presupposition of an interpretation *and* is meant to receive support from that interpretation, provided the theory fares well when applied to the particular text. This also holds for the antirationalist, who uses his disseminatory idea of textuality both as a guiding principle and as something to be shown to be successful. Within its relatively protected area each interpretive attitude may be successful with its own choice of examples. The two attitudes still encounter and oppose each other by claiming exemplarity of their respective interpretations. Within limits difficult to generalize, they can still argue whether one interpretation is more adequate or more successful than the other.

But as I see the situation, rationalism and antirationalism now oppose each other as rational *policies* of interpretation, not as universal theories in the rationalist sense of theory.[32] These policies are "rational" or rationalizable to the extent they aspire to exemplarity of their interpretive results. Beyond the limits of rationalizability, the two attitudes are not in discursive conflict with each other but rather are beliefs and practices that coexist side by side unless they are seized by totalizing desires.

Another thought leads to the same result. Hermeneutics and antirationalism jointly reject the foundational "gesture" of our philosophical tradition. This "gesture" fed the conviction that a theory that had been grounded was therefore entitled to reject other theories, provided they said something different on the same subject matter. The idea of a foundation helped to provide the homogeneous space in which all theories could meet and confront each other. When the idea of an ultimate foundation is abandoned, the many theories may continue to compete for general adoption, but none of them provides the means to refute the other, unless they share a sufficient basis of common assumptions. This is the historical and intellectual situation in which hermeneutics and antirationalism meet. Both try to establish their credentials by relating to the tradition, each in their own way, and by the high-level rhetoric of their appeals and examples. By the same token they cease to be theories that can *criticize* each other. I wonder what will become of the "will to power" that drives their controversies once they recognize that they do not possess the means to give a theoretical explanation of their conflict.

In conclusion, I see Frank's *What Is Neostructuralism?* as a hermeneutic statement in the ongoing debate between contemporary rationalism and antirationalism. In that debate theoretical wills clash and turn their powers of persuasion toward the reader. Frank follows a rationalist strategy of persuading the readers of the well-foundedness of his own attitude by reconstructing the theories and arguments of his adversaries and by attending to those of their weaknesses to which he is most sensitive: the possibility of interpretation, the value of the individual, the connection with our tradition. He thus practices the dialogue hermeneutic theory defends.

Translators' Note

A translation is never anything more — or anything less — than a graphic (or phonic) record of an interpretation. Interpretations, for their part, are always approximations and cannot lay claim to absolute objectivity. Still, as translators, we set ourselves the task of working toward a "faithful" translation of Manfred Frank's text, understanding fully the limitations involved. Derrida has claimed that translation should always be "the transformation of one language by another." In this sense, we hope that Frank's German has transformed our English text in its own characteristic way. His text has, at any rate, constantly challenged ours, and if we have been equal to this challenge in most instances, then we will consider our goal achieved.

There are, aside from the obvious general problems involved in rendering German philosophical discourse in English, some problems specific to this text itself. The most significant of these is Frank's reliance on and employment of numerous subdiscourses of contemporary philosophy. Although schooled in the hermeneutical language of Heidegger and Gadamer, Frank also incorporates the characteristic terminology of psychoanalysis, structuralism, and neostructuralism (as he calls it), phenomenology, romantic idealist philosophy, as well as the language of analytical philosophy. These discourses are not always compatible with one another regarding the signification attributed to certain expressions, and in such cases we have tried to adjust our renderings of the terms according to the given context. The most prominent example of this problem is manifest in the translation of the words *bedeuten/Bedeutung*, *Sinn*, *meinen/Meinung*. Unless otherwise indicated, we have rendered *Sinn* and *Bedeutung*, in the manner relevant to semiology, as "meaning" and "signification," respectively. However, in the context of analytical philosophy, *Sinn* must be translated as "sense," and *Bedeutung* as "meaning" (whereby the rendering of the Fregean distinction between *Sinn* and *Bedeutung* as "sense" and "reference" must be kept in mind). By the same token, in the context of Husserlian phenomenology, *Sinn* and *Bedeutung* are used almost interchangeably, and the third pair of terms, *meinen/Meinung*, comes into play. We have, as a rule, translated these expressions as "to intend" and "intention," in order to emphasize the active sense of the intending of meaning.

The other word complex that presents special problems is that connected with the various meanings of the concept of representation. The latinate verb *repräsentieren* commonly is employed to evoke the notion of re-presencing, and we have translated it thus in such instances. The word *Stellvertreter*, which means representative in the sense of proxy, we have chosen to render as "placeholder." The words *darstellen/Darstellung*, which refer to representation in the aesthetic sense, we have translated as "to portray"/"portrayal."

We are aware that our translation stands in a tradition, and we have sought wherever possible to pay this tradition its due respect. This means that we have followed the established conventions for translating German philosophical concepts. By way of example, *Sein* is always rendered as "Being," *Seiend* as "being." We have consulted and cited the standard translations of the German texts quoted by Frank. In addition, we have relied on the standard English translations of key phrases from the French structuralists and neostructuralists. As a result, of course, the polyphony of voices already inherent in Frank's original has been multiplied by these further voices in our English text.

For the sake of readability, we have tried to keep our interruptions of the text to a minimum. Where we thought it necessary or helpful, we have supplied the German word or phrase in parentheses. Notes added by us are prefixed with the abbreviation TN.

Finally, this translation has been a communal and shared enterprise in the very best sense. It is a product of cooperation, dialogue, mutual respect, and agreement.

Abbreviations

AdS	Michel Foucault, *L'Archéologie du savoir* (Paris: Gallimard, 1969).
AK	Michel Foucault, *The Archaeology of Knowledge*, trans. A. M. Sheridan Smith (New York: Pantheon, 1971).
AO	Gilles Deleuze and Félix Guattari, *Anti-Oedipus*, trans. Helen R. Lane, Robert Hurley, and Mark Seem (New York: Viking Press, 1977).
BN	Jean-Paul Sartre, *Being and Nothingness: An Essay on Phenomenological Ontology*, trans. Hazel E. Barnes (New York: Philosophical Library, 1956).
BT	Martin Heidegger, *Being and Time*, trans. John Macquarie and Edward Robinson (New York: Harper & Row, 1962).
CFS	*Cahiers Ferdinand de Saussure*
CGL	Ferdinand de Saussure, *Course in General Linguistics*, trans. Wade Baskin (New York: McGraw-Hill, 1966).
CM	Edmund Husserl, *Cartesian Meditations: An Introduction to Phenomenology*, trans. Dorion Cairns (The Hague: Nijhoff, 1960).
Coll P	Charles Sanders Peirce, *Collected Papers*, ed. Charles Hartstone and Paul Weiss (Cambridge, Mass.: Harvard University Press, 1953).
Diss	Jacques Derrida, *Dissemination*, trans. Barbara Johnson (Chicago: University of Chicago Press, 1981).
DR	Gilles Deleuze, *Différence et répétition* (Paris: PUF, 1968).

E	Jacques Lacan, *Écrits: A Selection*, trans. Alan Sheridan (New York: Norton, 1977).
E (Fr. ed.)	Jacques Lacan, *Écrits* (Paris: Seuil, 1966).
EC	Ferdinand de Saussure, *Cours de linguistique générale*, Edition critique, ed. Rudolf Engler, 2 vols. (Wiesbaden: Harrassowitz, 1967–74).
EN	Jean-Paul Sartre, *L'Etre et le néant: Essai d'ontologie phénoménologique* (Paris: Gallimard, 1943).
FW	Johann Gottlieb Fichte, *Sämtliche Werke*, ed. I. H. Fichte (Berlin: Veit, 1845–46).
GR	Jacques Derrida, *Of Grammatology*, trans. Gayatri Spivak (Baltimore: Johns Hopkins University Press, 1976).
HuK	Friedrich Schleiermacher, *Hermeneutik und Kritik*, ed. Manfred Frank (Frankfurt: Suhrkamp, 1977).
Ideas	Edmund Husserl, *Ideas: General Introduction to Pure Phenomenology*, trans. W. R. Boyce Gibson (New York: Macmillan, 1931).
IF	Jean-Paul Sartre, *L'Idiot de la famille*, 3 vols. (Paris: Gallimard, 1971–72).
LI	Jacques Derrida, "Limited Inc abc . . .," trans. Samuel Weber, *Glyph 2* (Baltimore: Johns Hopkins University Press, 1977), pp. 162–254.
Logic	Georg Wilhelm Friedrich Hegel, *Science of Logic*, trans. W. H. Johnston and L. G. Struthers, 2 vols. (New York: Macmillan, 1929).
LS	Gilles Deleuze, *Logique du sens* (Paris: Minuit, 1969).
Margins	Jacques Derrida, *Margins of Philosophy*, trans. Alan Bass (Chicago: University of Chicago Press, 1982).
MC	Michel Foucault, *Les Mots et les choses: Une Archéologie des sciences humaines* (Paris: Gallimard, 1966).
MP	Gilles Deleuze and Félix Guattari, *Milles Plateaux* (Paris: Minuit, 1980).
OD	Michel Foucault, *L'Ordre du discours* (Paris: Gallimard, 1971).
OG	Jacques Derrida, "Introduction," *Edmund Husserl's Origin of Geometry*, trans. John P. Leavey, ed. David B. Allison (Stony Brook, N.Y.: Nicolas Hays, 1978).
OT	Michel Foucault, *The Order of Things: An Archaeology of the Human Sciences* (New York: Random House [Vintage Books], 1970).
P	Jacques Derrida, *Positions*, trans. Alan Bass (Chicago: University of Chicago Press, 1981).

PC	Jean-François Lyotard, *The Postmodern Condition: A Report on Knowledge*, trans. Geoff Bennington and Brian Massumi (Minneapolis: University of Minnesota Press, 1984).
PI	Ludwig Wittgenstein, *Philosophical Investigations*, trans. G. E. M. Anscombe (Oxford: Basil Blackwell, 1953).
PL	Edmund Husserl, *The Paris Lectures*, trans. Peter Koestenbaum (The Hague: Nijhoff, 1964).
R	John Searle, "Reiterating the Differences: A Reply to Derrida," *Glyph*, 1 (1977), pp. 189–208.
RC	Louis Althusser and Etienne Balibar, *Reading Capital*, trans. Ben Brewster (New York: Pantheon, 1970).
SA	Claude Lévi-Strauss, *Structural Anthropology*, trans. Claire Jacobson and Brook Grundfest Schoepf (New York: Doubleday, 1967).
SM 1	Claude Lévi-Strauss, *The Raw and the Cooked*, vol. 1 of *Introduction to a Science of Mythology,* trans. John and Doreen Weightman (New York: Harper & Row, 1970).
SM 4	Claude Lévi-Strauss, *The Naked Man*, vol. 4 of *Introduction to a Science of Mythology*, trans. John and Doreen Weightman (New York: Harper & Row, 1981).
SP	Jacques Derrida, *Speech and Phenomena and Other Essays on Husserl's Theory of Signs* (Northwestern University Press, 1973).
SW	Friedrich Wilhelm Joseph Schelling, *Sämtliche Schriften*, ed. K. F. A. Schelling (Stuttgart and Augsburg: Cotta, 1856–61).
Theorie-Werkausgabe	Georg Wilhelm Friedrich Hegel, *Theorie Werkausgabe*, ed. K. M. Michel and E. Moldenhauer (Frankfurt: Suhrkamp, 1968ff.).
TM	Hans-Georg Gadamer, *Truth and Method* (New York: Crossroad, 1975).
Tr	Ludwig Wittgenstein, *Tractatus Logico-Philosophicus*, trans. and ed. C. K. Ogden (London: Routledge & Kegan Paul, 1960).
VP	Jacques Derrida, *La Voix et le phénomène: Introduction au problème du signe dans la phénoménologie de Husserl* (Paris: PUF, 1967).
WD	Jacques Derrida, *Writing and Difference*, trans. Alan Bass (Chicago: University of Chicago Press, 1978).
Werke	Friedrich Nietzsche, *Werke in drei Bänden*, ed. Karl Schlechta (Munich: Hanser, 1966).
Works	Friedrich Nietzsche, *The Complete Works of Friedrich Nietzsche*, ed. Oscar Levy (New York: Macmillan, 1909ff.).

What Is Neostructuralism?

Lecture 1

If some fifteen years ago someone had with some gravity concluded that the so-called German-French friendship was nothing more than the sentimental glorification of an alliance whose sole purpose was economic-political advantage, and that this friendship had few consequences on the profounder level of intercultural dialogue, then this lament would not have made much of an impression in philosophical circles characterized by self-satisfaction. The ship of German philosophy was heading full-sail in the direction of hermeneutics and Critical Theory, both of which were supported at that time by the student revolts. It was believed that the concession to internationalism had been made by means of what in fact was no small integration of Anglo-Saxon positions. What need was there to concern oneself with the French?

To be sure, the situation was not much different in French philosophy. Here there began, almost simultaneously with the Paris May revolts, the joyous ascent of neostructuralism, which promised to be a stable fashion for at least a decade and was not in need of foreign impulses as sources of new energy.

Today this situation is beginning to change markedly. Current historical conditions are not so advantageous to hermeneutic-critical theory as they were ten years ago. The falling star of this theory syndrome, coupled with the incalculable signs that analytical philosophy inspired by Anglo-Saxon models has exhausted its resources, has created conditions under which sections of the younger generation in particular in Germany are beginning to direct their gaze with much more curiosity than previously across the border into France.

A corresponding development appears to be beginning in France today. The interpretive potentials of a philosophy that, as the latest movement, followed first on the heels of existentialism, then on those of classical structuralism, seem to be in a state of decline. Intellectual crises are always favorable catalysts for openness to things foreign, to such things, for example, as the philosophy that has been produced since the Second World War *outre-Rhin* and that has been ignored — *toute compte fait* — in France. The first halting discussions with hermeneutics and with Critical Theory have begun.

These lectures, devoted to the question "What Is Neostructuralism?" are motivated by this situation. They seek to contribute to a reawakening of Central European philosophy, to its engagement for the universal, achieving this, however, not merely in the form of postulates that are received in the native country and formulated in the native language. Furthermore, this engagement should not simply be expressed in the form of a historical reconstruction that explains after the fact what in the time of the philosophers themselves was no transnational subject matter. No, already today we want to make the effort to think within our own age and to write for our contemporaries — for our contemporaries, but not solely for our compatriots, and certainly not on the impaired basis of our own national educational tradition.

Of course, one cannot escape this educational tradition merely by declaring one's goodwill: it must become a part of the dialogue that we wish to initiate with contemporary French philosophy, but only to the extent that a certain point of departure is indispensable and cannot be passed over if one wishes to confront from one's own position something foreign. This position itself, however, is by no means a goal. The goal we set for ourselves here, rather, is expanding the horizons of both partners in this dialogue, that of hermeneutics as well as that of neostructuralism.

Thus my lectures are grounded in a perspective schooled in hermeneutics; however, their gaze is directed at the contemporary philosophy of France. That is why I do not simply want to present an introduction to this foreign subject matter with a German audience in mind; rather, I am seeking a true dialogue with my colleagues in France. Actually being addressed are those French philosophers who would like to discover how what they formulate and think appears from the estranging perspective — and often through the critique — of contemporary hermeneutics. Hermeneutics, for its part, wishes to be informed about those aspects of its formulations that cannot stand up to the criticism of the French.

Those who seek a dialogue with others — especially with interlocutors who speak a different language — are well advised to introduce themselves at the onset. Introducing oneself implies in this instance also presenting the perspective and the position on the basis of which the dialogue is sought. Both of these — perspective and position — are themselves acquisitions that have been shaped in a specific educational context.

From 1964 to 1971 I studied philosophy as well as German and English at the universities of Heidelberg and Berlin. I received my most profound impressions as a student of Hans-Georg Gadamer: his seminars pointed me in the direction of philosophical hermeneutics, i.e., to a set of issues that, as the French (occasionally) know, dominated the philosophical scene in West Germany so completely that someday it will probably be characterized as the specific German contribution to postwar philosophy. Although inspired neither by Heidegger nor by Gadamer with a particularly progressive spirit, hermeneutics nevertheless possessed critical, indeed, even utopian potentials that exerted a powerful influence on the generation of student protesters, to which I also belong, and whose watchword in Germany was *Hinterfragen*, critical questioning. Critical questioning means reminding interpretations, orders, institutions of their traditions and hence of their alterability; reminding them, moreover, of the purely hypothetical nature of their existence; shattering their indigenous and perhaps illegitimate existence by demanding that they justify themselves on the basis of reason, in order that they might pass through this critique purified and renewed. The specific hermeneutical theory that made this intellectual and moral-political attitude into a fundamental political position was the so-called *Kritische Theorie* of the later Frankfurt School. Its main representative, Jürgen Habermas, exerted scarcely less, if yet more moderate influence on the remonstrating university students in West Germany than Sartre did on their French counterparts (in addition, Habermas's ideology-critical approach agrees with that of Sartre on many points).

You must be aware that in Germany around the year 1968 the drive of the young people to come to terms critically with the tradition of their country (i.e., of their parents) was livelier and more urgent than in almost any other nation in Europe. This was quite natural since it appeared to this generation to be absolutely essential for intellectual and moral – and not merely economic – survival that not simply a new morality, but, in fact, any morality whatsoever should be put up against the amorality of the Nazi generation. Yet the most powerful philosophical movement with which we (at the time) younger people could connect, namely, the existential ontology of Martin Heidegger, was, to the extent that it was not compromised by its concessions to the Nazi dictatorship, damaged in our consciousness at the very least by its "incapacity for sorrow." In place of a universal questioning of the history of metaphysics we would above all have been interested to find out how Heidegger would approach philosophically the history of fascism. On this topic, however, he could utter only commonplaces and excuses.

On the other hand, it could not be overlooked that even the Left sympathized with certain aspects of Heideggerian ontology: its emphasis on freedom and simultaneously on the relative dependence of *Dasein* on given conditions; its radical historicism; its critique of metaphysics, etc. Thus there were some lines of connection that led from existential-ontological hermeneutics to the Critical Theory of society; however, these lines could only be drawn to the extent that one was willing to allow Heidegger's philosophical foundations to undergo critical revision. Here one had to carry out what the French neostructuralists call deconstruction: a tearing-down of the philosophical system and its reconstruction on rearranged foundations. Under such prerequisites Germany experienced some lively deconstruction work in the sixties and seventies: Heidegger's ontology was freed from its national restrictions; analytical positions of Anglo-Saxon authors (or of German authors who had emigrated to Anglo-Saxon territory) were brought into play; the thesis of the repression of Being was critically tested on the example of German idealism, of Marx and of Nietzsche; Heidegger's hermeneutics was rewritten both in the spirit of pragmatism (from Peirce to Wittgenstein and Searle) and in the spirit of a critical theory of society.

No one is ever asked under what conditions—in which nation, in which class, at what time—he wants to be brought into the world; no one can escape socialization and culturalization by the currently ruling "order of discourse." In this sense the formation of academic philosophy in the sixties and, in a certain sense, the discourse of existential ontology have been formative for me. But "formative" is not the same as "determining"; and it would be just as false as it would be dangerous to conclude from the precedence of "discourse" over concrete speech, as Heidegger and numerous other linguistic-philosophical determinists of various shades do, that "language itself speaks," and that we are that which is spoken by it. On the contrary, language is no fate; it is spoken by *us* and we are able to critically "question" it at any time. The law of language has the existential status of a mere virtuality: it has an imperative, but no determinative, forcing influence on individual language usage. Precisely this is the fundamental idea of hermeneutics, namely, that symbolic orders, as opposed to natural laws, are founded in interpretations; hence they can lay claim only to a hypothetical existence, they can be transformed and transgressed by new projections of meaning. In the words of the great Geneva linguist: "In relation to the community [the law of language] is absolutely precarious: nothing guarantees its stability; this order is at the mercy of the future. . . . An act of (individual) interpretation, which is active, is (always) necessary."[1]

With this I have touched on the problem that has concerned me considerably (however, not solely) since that time: how can one, on the one hand, do justice to the fundamental fact that meaning, significance, and intention—the semantic foundations of every consciousness—can form themselves only in a language, in a social, cultural, and economic order (in a structure)? How can one, on the other hand, redeem the fundamental idea of modern humanism that links the dignity of human beings with their use of freedom, and which cannot tolerate that one morally applaud the factual threatening of human subjectivity by the totalitarianism of systems of rules and social codes?

I have formulated these two conflicting positions in such a way that you may recognize immediately what I am thinking about. The point of view of the inescapability of structure is represented above all in the France of the sixties and, in somewhat looser form, that of the seventies; in contrast to this, the so-called transcendental hermeneutics of Germany insists on the theory-constitutive role of subjectivity as the primary factor in every formation, interpretation, and alteration of meaning.

The problem was and is that almost no dialogue exists between these two positions—unless one were inclined to attribute to the superficial and narrow-minded polemics on both sides (or for that matter the imitation of French style by some of its German fans who have no standpoint of their own) the honor of such an appellation. My impression was and still is that while hermeneutics has not adequately measured the depth of the structuralist argument against the centrality of the subject, neither has structuralism/neostructuralism questioned down to the roots of a solid theory of the subject. The "decentering of the subject" is grounded just as superficially in France as a theory of the dialectics of structure and attribution of meaning is in Germany.

The more I reflected on this version of a conflict of methods, the more urgent, but also promising, appeared the question of its intellectual-historical genesis. This was my initial reflection: can one reconstruct a position in the history of modern European philosophy in which what today is broken apart was conceived as two sides of an integral and dialectical movement? This reflection was based on two concomitant convictions. The first was that history does not always do us the favor of moving in the direction of progress (sometimes previous standards are lost or forgotten, as, above all, recent German history has taught). The second conviction was that until the consummation of the European Enlightenment in the thought of idealism, the history of philosophy was still represented as a transnational unity and continuity. Only with the historization of thought—with the *linguistic turn* since Herder and Humboldt—could transnational and transhistorical "reason" be reinterpreted as an "image of the world" inscribed in a linguistic order. Reason, relativized into the linguistic world image of a people, was ipso facto nationalized: it disappeared behind the "national spirit" of a culture. Stated in an oversimplified manner, the result of this was a split of reason: on the one hand, the so-called *Weltanschauungsphilosophie*, which historicized all claims to validity by pointing to the cultural, social, or even national genesis of assertions; on the other side, history-blind and positivistic scientism in all its variations. To apply this now to the conflict of methods in the present day: the fatherlands of European civilization are only unified when scientistic claims to knowledge are being discussed, i.e., in all questions concerning technological expediency and natural-scientific truths. On the other hand, the national split in the unity of reason persists in the realm of the human sciences under the influence of classical philosophy (i.e., of philosophy that is not satisfied with being merely *philosophy of science*). This division of reason manifests itself currently in Central Europe in the conflict between structuralist and hermeneutical "knowledge interests," as Habermas has called them.

My hypothesis, once again, is that this conflict can be resolved only if one succeeds in reconstructing the history within which it evolved. This history, however, is the history of the destruction of reason's claim to universality under the blows of "historical consciousness." As a result of this split, among other things, scientistic and hermeneutical, but also structuralist and hermeneutical options could become antagonistic. This antagonism, in my opinion, led to an alarming alienation of German and French philosophy. The remedy that occurred to me is expressed in the incantation from *Parsifal*: "Only the lance that opened the wound can also close it." In other words, one must therapeutically confront this dissolution of the unity of philosophical and human-scientific discourse with its originary conditions, i.e., with the age of romanticism. For example, it is scarcely recognized, but nonetheless true, that the concept of "structure" in its specifically modern and, if you will, specifically French application was written into the terminology of our discipline by a theoretician of early romanticism: the theologian, philosopher, and philologist Friedrich Schleiermacher. Schleiermacher understood under the word "structure" a system of relations among elements, as he expressed it, whereby each element derives its meaning through unequivocal differentiation from all other elements. According to Schleiermacher, this process of differentiation constitutes not only orders such as that of language, but also cultural, social, economic, and juridical orders; in short, all discursive regulations that mediate intersubjective communication. Although my description is rather superficial, you must sense that it was precisely these aspects that were rediscovered and reworked with indubitably more appropriate tools by modern linguistics and discourse analysis in France based on Saussure.

What is surprising and almost unbelievable is that Schleiermacher has survived exclusively as the founder of a "hermeneutics of empathy" (*Einfühlungshermeneutik*), which overtaxes the subjective aspect of interpretation to the disadvantage of structural and historical aspects of that which was to be understood. To his immediate disciples the structural interpretation was still known; for Simmel, Heidegger, Bultmann, Ricoeur, and especially for Gadamer and his school, this was almost totally forgotten. Under the deprecative name "romantic hermeneutics," Schleiermacher's approach became the epitome of an unserious, intuitive, and history-blind model of discourse analysis and textual understanding with whose fictive intention existential hermeneutics shares only an inimicalness to thorough structuring, and the belief in the autonomy of understanding with regard to any form of methodological disciplining.

Unfortunately, Gadamer's opprobation of Schleiermacher and the resulting alternative concept of an "effective-historical hermeneutics" were initially accepted all over, both in philosophy and in the practices of literary criticism. Even the opponents of hermeneutics took over the critique of Schleiermacher. Thus began the aforementioned nationalization and splitting of methods so that structural interpretation—itself originally a romantic enterprise—was only at home in France, and transcendental hermeneutics, with the exception of Sartre and Ricoeur, only in Germany. At Franco-German conferences one experiences yet today, as structuralism has been accepted by a third generation of thinkers, an alarming amount of mutual mistrust, insupportable imputations, and massive unwillingness to understand. Philosophy's claim to universality continues to exist, but it is fractured by the particularistic praxis of the philosophers themselves. On both sides the will for consensus is lacking.

At precisely this point I would like to step outside this critical description and present a positive counterproposal. At the center of this proposal stands the dialectical concept of the "singular universal" (Sartre) or of the "individual universal" (Schleiermacher). How I apply this concept and to what extent I have faith in its ability to overcome the aporia of the contemporary antagonism, that is what I would like to present in an increasingly concrete manner over the course of this lecture series. My lectures will begin with a broadly sketched tour through that which I call neostructuralism, that is, the philosophical-aesthetic position that followed classical structuralism in France. I will begin by introducing this theory in general and highlighting its argumentative strengths. At those points, however, where the premises of this position produce irresolvable aporias, I will attempt a hermeneutical counterapproach that will not only reveal my own position, but will also present objections against hermeneutics as well. In this manner I hope to introduce in a characteristic way a central aspect of my philosophical position. At the same time I wish to lay a foundation for what I want to work out and discuss in the course of these lectures: an archaeology of the individual and a theory of self-consciousness and free praxis of the sort that will stand up to the objections both of structuralism and of analytic philosophy, and which will reconquer for contemporary philosophical discourse one of, if not *the*, central theme of modern metaphysics in deconstructed form.

Indeed, the "spiritual situation of the age" seems to me to demand that we give some thought to a new definition of subjectivity and of individuality (which are not one and the same).[2] Both terms denote concepts that are under attack in contemporary France and are defended perhaps too naively in contemporary Germany. The fact that the time is unfavorably disposed to the subject does not prove anything against its truth (in Hegel's sense). Philosophy—as long as it understands itself morally—must fundamentally guard itself against merely reducing, in the attitude of a "eunuchlike neutrality" (as Droysen called it), the existent to concepts without saying a word about the legitimacy of the process itself. To be sure, the existence of individuality appears threatened, indeed, undetectable in a world that is becoming uniform and totalitarian. It is also true that philosophy must explain and make understandable that process in whose development subjectivity was lost from view. But it is one thing to explain the death of subjectivity as a result of the course of the world, and another thing altogether to greet it with applause, as Foucault does. The factual is not already the true; a "happy positivism" that dissolves this difference mimics, consciously or not, the dominating power. It is true that the individual disappears more and more in the "code" (of the state, of bureaucracy, of the social machine, of all varieties of discourse), which has become autonomous. And it is also correct that a dead subject emits no more cries of pain. However, that interpretation that would like to extract a scientific-historical perspective from the silence of the subject, and which culminates in the gay affirmation of a subjectless and reified machine (à la Deleuze and Guattari), appears to me to be cynical. A neutral description of the crisis of the subject as a factual occurrence is not only nonmoral (in the sense of a standpoint "beyond good and evil," i.e., of an extramoral cognitive position that must be allowed at all times); it is rather *a*moral, for it raises that which is to the measure of that which should be. In this sense, it seems to me, philosophy must always opt for the nonexistent; it must engage itself contrafactually; it must defy reality while recognizing it. The dignity of philosophy always consisted in the fact that it engaged itself for the nonexistent, for it has always been what not (yet) is, with a foresight toward which what is attains its meaning and the ground of its Being (*Seinsgrund*). To use up this reserve of irreality would mean not only strangling the human subject in the mesh of the structural net but also putting an end to philosophy, which would then coincide with positivism and assimilate itself completely to the reified world. In a word, it may be true that the scientific and technical world is not in need of the memory of the dignity of the individual subject in order to survive; indeed, it functions perhaps even better without a philosophy that continually forces upon it a bothersome memory. But the world was always least problematic without human beings; perhaps nature is at present venturing the crucial steps—through the human beings who make themselves its tools—necessary for eliminating the human being forever and eradicating that name from its registry. However, it must be doubted whether, as some contemporaries believe, it is possible to "think" more authentically "in the void of the disappearance of man" than in the fullness of its lost past, at least as long as we are unsuccessful at actually avoiding a theory of consciousness and of praxis that is oriented toward the concept of the subject. Such an alternative theory does not appear to me to be in sight for the present. Therefore I recommend that the diagnostic power of the talk about the death of the subject be taken seriously and made analytically fruitful without meanwhile lapsing into the opposite extreme of applauding the death of the subject on a moral level.

The question about the mode of Being of subjectivity and of individuality is, however, by no means simply a moral one. I am convinced that neither structuralism nor neostructuralism nor, for that matter, any other form of systems theory has truly succeeded in explaining the processes of signification and of the alteration of signification without relying explicitly or implicitly on the category of the individual. Even the reified statement "Language speaks itself," or even the systems-theoretical statement about the "self-reflexivity of systems," has to employ reflexive pronouns that then hypostatize what was earlier considered a characteristic of the speaking subject as a characteristic of language or of the system itself. The subject that is crossed out in the position of the individual recurs in the position of a subject of the universal: this is a classic case of the "return of the repressed." I would like to analyze the logic of this repression, and of the return of the repressed, over the course of this series of lectures in order to explore the place at which the universal and the individual subject are rightfully at home.

Having given this preview, I would like to return from the world of the imaginary—the world of the merely promised and of that for which we hold out prospects—to the real world. In the real world the split between structuralism and hermeneutics plays the role of an indicator or seismograph: it indicates the degree of incredulity connected today with claims to universality in philosophy, and it demonstrates the extent to which the inter-European communication among intellectuals of all nations meanwhile has been disrupted. The pessimistic judgment that the European community is only a community of economic interests, without in addition evoking unlimited intercultural communication, is difficult to deny from this perspective.

Allow me to conclude this general introduction of myself and my project by conjuring up the spirit of one of the great authors of early socialism in France, a man who attempted untiringly to build bridges between French and German philosophy: Pierre Leroux. His grand repost on Schelling's Berlin lectures from 1841 to 1842 culminates in the following exclamation, which completely expresses my own wishes:

> Once again, the time is approaching when there will no longer be one
> or several German philosophies, one or several French philosophies,
> but rather a single philosophy, which will be at the same time a re-
> ligion.[3]

My lectures have as their subject matter a phenomenon that initially can more easily be defined by situating it historically and geographically, rather than by explaining its substance. Before I explain more closely the title, which, I assume, sounds strange to most of you, I would like to try to specify the historical age and the sphere of activity to which you will have to tune in your imaginations whenever I speak of "neostructuralism." I combine under this phrase theoretical tendencies that—for the most part easily datable as belonging to the period just prior to May 1968—shaped intellectual trends in France to such an extent that one could speak abroad (e.g., in West Germany) in abbreviated fashion of its authors as the "new French." Actually, one should speak of the "new Parisians," for just as Paris is the cultural metropolis of France due to the centralism of this country, so too the doctrine of neostructuralism, *if* indeed such a doctrine exists, is concentrated in the centers of the most important Paris universities. From there it has spread to other universities in France, but these are symptoms of infection by contact that simply allow one to locate more clearly the source of the virus in Paris. Everyone who has some knowledge of institutions in France, and especially of French universities, knows of course that my localization of neostructuralist "doctrine" at a few Paris universities and elite colleges (the Collège de France, the Ecole Pratique des Hautes Etudes, the Ecole Normale Supérieure, the former University of Vincennes, to name just a few) is suspect of being a grave distortion. It would have been truer to point to the fact that neostructuralism, as the year of its birth, 1968, indicates, is a movement that developed out of a certain opposition to the ruling doctrine above all in the teaching of philosophy and literature, and which succeeded, despite cultural-political enmity, in effectively conquering a few universities.

A glance at the entirety of French universities (and certainly even a glance at the list of courses offered at Paris universities in numerous years since, let's say, 1965) would probably strengthen the impression that in the instance of neostructuralism it is a matter of a primarily marginal movement that was able to make itself a home at the margins and at the doorstep of dominating instructional practice, and that was able to win over a certain vocal but not dramatic public there. Now one must of course remark that the centers of cultural power—in this instance centers of university power, and within these, those of the human sciences—have always functioned inconspicuously, and that oppositional or even parasitic movements have always found the limits of their development in the absorptive capacity of the ruling doctrinal flood to incorporate them through enclosure. These are observations at which the historian can only arrive in retrospect, for phenomena tend to present themselves differently to contemporaries. They perceive the intensity, the upheaval, and the agitation that deviating positions excite much more clearly than the quiet development of the educational apparatus that is perhaps more representative of the spiritual situation of the age, if only because it is of greater size. This, in fact, may also be true in the case of neostructuralism. I am certain—and I have experienced this before at conferences and lectures in Paris—that the resonant names associated with neostructuralist theory either are considered unimportant or are simply unrecognized by authoritative institutions (by means of their power to ignore, exclude, and render harmless through integration). At a panel discussion held in April 1981 at the Centre culturel allemand (Goethe-Institut) in Paris, at which I served as moderator for, among others, Gadamer and Derrida, there were, aside from my name, as I discovered afterward, two other names that many listeners in Paris—it was really quite a large number—did not recognize: one was Gadamer, the other Derrida.

I am relating this to you not (only) for your amusement but rather to permit the proper caution, which is appropriate for contemporaries when assessing contemporary phenomena, to hold sway. Before maintaining that neostructuralism, whatever it may be, is the trendsetting intellectual movement of the third and fourth decades of the postwar era in France (that is, in Paris), one should not underestimate the power of the nonneostructuralist, i.e., traditional, university discourses. Yet it is still true that in the last fifteen years neostructuralism has received the greatest attention—be it affirmative or negative—that a French intellectual phenomenon can possibly have excited either in France or abroad. Here as always the biblical statement that "the wind bloweth as it will and no one can say whence it comes and whither it goes" remains true. If one interprets "wind" as a metaphor for "intellect" (as, moreover, the passage itself does) and applies this saying to the university situation, then it can be rendered in the following way: intellect—and all intellect is creative and innovative—can be weakened and retarded by institutions and by that which Foucault has called the "dispositive of power," but it will exert its right to exist, it will make its voice audible in the public forum, it will draw attention to itself for a while to such an extent that the official channels will either go along with or eradicate the disruptive voice. I don't believe this description is exaggerated. Simply remind yourselves how small a movement such as German idealism actually was, how little intrainstitutional power supported it, and to how few places of influence it reached. At the time it was heard in Germany, it was the exception and the violation of the norm within the ruling stream of academic philosophy. Yet it appears to subsequent generations, due to a perspectival deception, as though the voice of idealism must have been all-powerful in its day and overwhelmed all that existed next to it. Now please do not be concerned: I do not take neostructuralism to be similarly overwhelming. On the other hand, it is also true that its inconsiderableness in the face of the academic mean does not present us with an image of its intellectual power, something I would like to describe in more detail in this lecture series.

Now that we know when and where one can find neostructuralism, we can take on two other questions: what it deals with and why we should concern ourselves with it. I believe these two questions are intertwined, for as soon as we explain a subject matter we will in every instance immediately also know—i.e., be able to decide—why we should occupy ourselves with this subject matter here and now. An explanation of a subject matter that fails to aid in this decision would treat its object as a "dead dog," as Hegel maintained of Spinoza's philosophy. But neostructuralism seems to me to be in no way a "dead dog."

This is true first of all because neostructuralism is a powerful literary-philosophical movement of the present day, and every contemporary can presume that the circulation and echo this theory evokes in listeners and readers are for the most part attributable to the fact that problems that are our very own have been (and will yet be) spelled out by it. Now we doubtless never have a lack of problems, and you will certainly want to interrupt immediately by asking what the nature of the problems might be with which neostructuralism is especially concerned.

I want to attempt to give an initial orienting answer to this question, as risky as that may be. Neostructuralism, so it appears to me, is the present tip of an approximately 200-year-old tradition of thought that gathers under the remarkably daring collective singular "*the* West" the infinite number of stories and the countless writings, doctrines, actions, and treatises that have arisen or glimpsed the light of day in Europe over the last 2,500 years. That period of human evolution that all of us without hesitation designate as Western has not always been viewed as the unity for which *we* take it. *If* this unity makes itself visible—and Foucault places the birth of this mountaintop overview of the unity of the West in the year 1775—*if* the West proves itself a unit, it does so based only on the awareness of a crisis. The first symptom of this crisis is the uncertainty as to whether we, who perceive the West as a unified and closed whole, even belong to it. You probably are familiar with Hegel's famous comment from the preface to *The Philosophy of Right*, which I cite unabridged and in its context.

> One word more about giving instruction as to what the world ought to be. Philosophy in any case always comes on the scene too late to give it. As the thought of the world, it appears only when actuality is already there cut and dried after its process of formation has been completed. The teaching of the concept, which is also history's inescapable lesson, is that it is only when actuality is mature that the ideal first appears over against the real and that the ideal apprehends this same real world in its substance and builds it up for itself into the shape of an intellectual realm. When philosophy paints its grey in grey, then has a shape of life grown old. By philosophy's grey in grey it cannot be rejuvenated but only understood. The owl of Minerva spreads its wings only with the falling of the dusk.[4]

I shall summarize the kernel of Hegel's reflection: with regard to actuality, thought finds itself in an indissoluble tardiness, for thought is the conceptual substance of the actual itself that is brought into the enclosure of the concept as a harvest is brought into the silo. In order to be conceived, this substance had first of all to *be*; but *if* it is conceived, then it no longer *is*, then it has been, i.e., it has stepped out of its pure Being-there into its essence. Essence (*Wesen*) is that which has been. "Only when knowledge, coming out from the sphere of the immediate Being, *internalizes* itself, does it through this mediation discover Essence," Hegel claims elsewhere. "Language has in the verb *Sein* ("to be") preserved *Wesen* ("Essence") in the past participle *gewesen* ("been"); for Essence is Being which has passed away, but passed away non-temporally."[5]

For Hegel himself this coming to essence (to has-been) of Western Being appeared as a great, indeed as the decisive stage of a history that he also liked to describe as the "history of progress in the consciousness of freedom," and whose conclusion he celebrated in his philosophy of the spirit transparent unto itself. Just as though the history of the West were, to use a metaphor applied with pleasure and frequency in German idealism, a metaphor that for its part cites one of the oldest Western texts, something analogous to the wanderings of Odysseus that, while taking circuitous detours, finally return him to the homeland of Ithaca. Therefore Hegel conceives the history of the European spirit (he is so Eurocentric that one even has to say: he conceives the history of the human spirit) according to the model of *re-flection*. "Reflection" means, literally translated, "turnaround, return to the point of departure, inverted mirroring of the sort that the point of departure appears as the point of destination." Precisely this is – quite literally – the case in the wanderings of Odysseus. It was Hegel's hypothesis that the history of European humanity can also be described as a search for the self and as a failure to find the self. This was expressed by Schelling in 1800.

> Yet the riddle could reveal itself, were we to recognize in it the odyssey of the spirit, which, marvelously deluded, seeks itself, and in seeking flies from itself; for through the world of sense there glimmers, as if through words the meaning, as if through dissolving mists the land of fantasy, of which we are in search.[6]

The history of the West – Schelling applied the same metaphor to the history of nature – would thus be the search for self, initial failure to find, and final finding after all of spirit, which, when the owl of Minerva begins its flight, looking back from the end of its journey comprehends all steps of the return to itself. At the end of its journey spirit comprehends itself as that which it *in itself* already was the entire time, without, however, having had reflective consciousness of it. Its unconscious being becomes – "for it itself" – a conscious possession at the end of its journey: it reflects itself in it *as* that which it is in spirit and in truth. "Tantae molis erat se ipsam cognoscere mentem": Hegel applies this epigraph to his *Lectures on the History of Philosophy*, and in so doing he compares the self-founding of full subjectivity with the toil of Aeneas in founding the Roman nation (*Aeneid*, I, 33). Under this premise Hegel succeeds – and I add: for the last time – in judging the West in its completion *as well as* accommodating himself simultaneously as the last inhabitant in the completed house of the West. When he shuts the door the odyssey of the spirit is complete, the light of transparency is lighted, nothing is hidden any longer, the process *comprehends* its historical identity from within.

Stronger, however, than the light Hegel's philosophy propagated was the effect of the "beginning twilight," about which Hegel also spoke, on the souls of his contemporaries and on posterity. Released from the traditional – and that implies at the same time sheltering – frame of understanding of the West, the European intelligentsia faced a freedom not only cheered but also populated by catastrophic visions. The twilight of the West and of the concept of rationality that had come to power and to self-consciousness over 2,500 years was reflected as a twilight of the gods, as a gradually increasing eclipse of meaning, and as a loss of orientation of the type portrayed in poetic-sensual fashion by Nietzsche's aphorism about the "madman." Before looking at this I want to note that there was profound reason to interpret the conclusion of Western spirit as the conclusion of the rule of God, and therefore as the twilight of the gods. For even in Hegel the absolute spirit is without much ado called God (to be sure, it is a detheologized god because it no longer possesses anything dark and transcendental: it is totally identified with the enlightenment powers of the European spirit). It is therefore not surprising that that "madman," about whom aphorism 125 in the third book of *The Joyful Wisdom* tells, carries out the search for the absent unity of the West as a search for the lost God whose continued rule—as spirit—had lent the West its unity and continuity.

Now this madman lights a lantern on a bright morning and runs across the marketplace crying unceasingly: "I seek God! I seek God!" This cry causes in those who do not believe in God anyway (and this is true of most of them) "a great deal of amusement" that is discharged in ridiculing statements. The madman, however, jumps into the midst of the ridiculers and transfixes them with his glances.

> "Where is God gone?" he called out. "I mean to tell you! *We have killed him,*—you and I! We are all his murderers! But how have we done it? How were we able to drink up the sea? Who gave us the sponge to wipe away the whole horizon? What did we do when we loosened this earth from its sun? Whither does it now move? Whither do we move? Away from all suns? Do we not dash on unceasingly? Backwards, sideways, forwards, in all directions? Is there still an above and below? Do we not stray, as through infinite nothingness? Does not empty space breathe upon us? Has it not become colder? Does not night come on continually darker and darker? Shall we not have to light lanterns in the morning? Do we not hear the noise of the grave-diggers who are burying God? Do we not smell the divine putrefaction?—for even Gods putrefy! God is dead! God remains dead! And we have killed him!"[7]

I break off the quotation here and will summarize the aspects most important for our context. As you see, even the madman notices the fall of darkness, to such an extent that he believes it necessary to light lanterns in the light of day so that one might yet see anything at all. Here, in fact, the completion—and that means simultaneously the conclusion—of Western spirituality is not then perceived as a self-illumination, but rather as a twilight of the gods. You notice, moreover, that it is not the vulgar atheism of those who simply do not believe in God that horrifies the madman; it is not the sublation of that inauthentic relation to the absolute, which is merely devoutly attentive, into absolute knowledge that disquiets him: rather it is the death of *metaphysics* itself, for which the name of God is substituted as a personification.

With this we touch on a concept we will run across often in our lectures and whose specific significance has its origin precisely in Hegel's and Nietzsche's sublation/overcoming of metaphysics. In other words, Hegel, and even more so Nietzsche, are constant discussion partners of neostructuralism, even where they are not mentioned specifically (although they are mentioned almost constantly). But let's save this for later examination. For the moment we are concerned with an initial determination of what "metaphysics" could possibly mean, and we already possess a few criteria for an answer. For if with the death of God the entire system of interpretation, foundation of meaning, and consolation of the Western spirit is supposed to have broken down, then one can surmise what the lowest common denominator has been of all those answers offered to mankind over the last 2,500 years in response to their needs for meaning: namely, the certainty of a *transsensual world*. And "metaphysics" is above all precisely this: the certainty of the transsensual. Its death means for Nietzsche that Western philosophy as Platonism and Christianity is at its end; that the interpretive and meaning-foundational resources have been used up; that that which until now humanity held to be the highest value of its Being-in-the-world has shown itself to be empty. In this sense Nietzsche speaks of the devaluation of all values, which, mind you, is not *his*, as it were, enlightened-critical contribution to the demythologization of the West, but rather what he sees the West itself entering into with romanticism and its pessimism.

After all, it was not the madman who killed God, the paradigmatic panacea of the transsensual: "*We* have killed him!" And: "How have we done it"? By means of enlightenment, by employing our powers for the domination of nature and for self-emancipation from foreign dominance and tutelage. It is not by chance that the madman mentions the Copernican cutting away of the sun from the earth and the early modern discovery of the infinity of the universe in which there is no above and below, i.e., no orientation points for one to get one's bearings in a *Dasein* that has become rootless. Thus the great Western occurrence of the eclipse of meaning began and was completed, the result of which was that by seeking to transform certainties founded merely on faith in certainties grounded in knowledge, it led unintentionally, indeed, against its own will, to the elimination of the category of "value" in itself. (Moreover, it also eliminated the category of meaning, as Nietzsche himself claimed: "The closer one looks, the more our assessment of values disappears—*meaninglessness approaches*.")[8] Enlightenment about the theological prerequisites in our thought led to the destruction of the transsensual world, and this in all its manifestations: as supreme value, as divine creator, as absolute substance, as idea, as absolute spirit, as meaning or communication context, or even only as the producing-conceiving subject of modern technology and natural science. (We will encounter this list of terms in the texts of the neostructuralists again and again.) One could formulate it differently: The rationalist test to determine of what account God and the transsensual prerequisites are in Western thought concluded that they were *of no account*; God and the transcendental values amount to nothing. This is the precise hour at which "the most uncanny of all guests," European nihilism, appears at the door (Nietzsche, *Werke*, III, 881). In the appended fifth book of *The Joyful Wisdom* entitled "We Fearless Ones," Nietzsche wrote in 1886: "The most important of more recent events – that 'God is dead,' that the belief in the Christian God has become unworthy of belief – already begins to cast its first shadows over Europe" (Nietzsche, *Works*, X, 275).

Now you will ask about the specifics of that enlightenment event Nietzsche dealt with under the banner of nihilism. Has it not always been the role of what the Greeks called *episteme* and modernity calls *sci-ence* (*Wissen*[*schaft*]) to sublate the previously believed into the currently known? Of course, but the difference is that previously something believed was left over, whereas now belief itself, the fixed point of orientation for our path through life, has been eroded. With the definitive death of God it is not simply a matter of overcoming an epoch, the Middle Ages and superstitious thought; rather it is a matter of overcoming metaphysics in itself and as such. This means the overcoming of that formation of interpretedness of Being in whose framework all the various answers in the history of the West to the question about the meaning of Being were constituted. The destruction of this framework – i.e., of this world ("world" understood here as a global form of interpretedness of reality, as a meaning context in which we function) – calls forth an orientationlessness of a wholly different type than that which, for example, seized evanescent antiquity when confronted with the dawn of the Christian Middle Ages, or that which seized the natural scientists of the modern period when confronted with the dissolution of the Middle Ages. For in these two epoch-making revolutions the meaning of Being, i.e., the global understanding of the world in which we are anchored, was not destroyed; rather *one* candidate for the meaning of Being was simply replaced by another. Let's just say that "God" was replaced by "reason." But even reason was a fundamentally theological conception, as is made concretely evident in Hegel's remark about a "speculative Good Friday that was otherwise historical."[9] For Hegel the growing feeling that "God Himself is dead" is already expressed in Pascal's comment: "Nature is such that it *marks* everywhere a *lost God*, both in man and outside of man."[10] For Hegel the death of God implies his death as a historic-religious event, an event followed by his resurrection in speculative knowledge into which the God of the West enters in truth and transfiguration, not as if climbing a guillotine. Now, however, in times of nihilism, even supreme knowledge is eroded as a bastion of trust in the world, and "we stray as through infinite nothingness."

With the death of metaphysics, of the certainty of a trans-sensual world, of a supreme (legitimating) value, a situation is created that neostructuralism likes to call "postmodern." I refer with this statement, as I will in later lectures as well, to a popular text by Jean-François Lyotard that has the characteristic title *The Postmodern Condition*,[11] and that wishes to take a position on the "spiritual situation of the age," that is, on the present day. With this we have some initial information, even though it requires further interpretation, about what neostructuralism means, namely, that it is thought under the conditions of the postmodern era. In the next lecture we will consider the sense in which this sentence can be said to be valid.

Lecture 2

In our search for a first and yet preliminary conception of neostructuralist theory, we came across the curious concept of postmodernism. We maintained that neostructuralism conceives itself as a manner of thought founded on the precondition of the closure (*clôture*) of modernity. The word "modern" does not designate only the avant-garde and contemporary; rather it refers to the historical period of the modern age in its totality. Charlie Chaplin's *Modern Times* is not the same as *Les Temps Modernes*. If, for Jean-François Lyotard, a representative of what I am loosely bringing together in the term "neostructuralism," *moderne* means "belonging to the modern age" (in the sense of belonging to the epoch since the Copernican revolution), then *postmoderne* denotes a "condition" posterior to the death of metaphysics. This, as you will recall, was the unintentional effect of the Enlightenment; namely, that by critically questioning unjustified doctrines (e.g., dogmas), it simultaneously collapsed the foundation of its own legitimation. From this point onward philosophy — and bourgeois society as well — has been exposed to the problems arising from this loss of legitimation. There is an absence of unquestionably certain values that could serve to support any claim to justification, regardless of its nature and breadth. Previously such claims had been provided either by religious belief, or by the — itself quasi-religious — faith in the competence of theoretical and practical reason.

At this point, at the very latest, you probably want to interrupt me and interject the following: postmodernism, which Nietzsche had located in the future, must in the meanwhile somehow have made its appearance. The work of Martin Heidegger, on the one hand, and the entrance of European politics into the epoch of fascism, on the other, could be considered symptoms – quite different ones, to be sure – of this eclipse of meaning, as well as symptoms of what an early collaborator and later opponent of Hitler, Hermann Rauschning, called "the revolution of nihilism."[1]

Be that as it may. Earlier I mentioned that neostructuralism, as that particular theoretical movement we want to deal with and examine, forced its way into public consciousness only in the years since 1968. What does this year, which has practically become the year of a revolution, have to do with postmodernity? And why does neostructuralism or poststructuralism carry the reminder of structuralism on its identification tag? Does this have something to do with the "postmodern condition," and thus with "thought in the shadow of nihilism"?

I understand your impatience and I will attempt to pull together the various strands in this web of questions in a coherent fashion. Allow me, therefore, to present a few preliminary theses whose justification can only be brought in the course of this series of lectures. These theses will serve to provide us with an initial rough sketch for the purpose of orientation. The first thesis – it has already been stated – is that neostructuralism, following in the footsteps of Hegel and Nietzsche, is conceived as thought after the end of metaphysics. The second thesis – and the question I imputed to you was aimed in this direction – is that this postmetaphysical thought is simultaneously *thought after structuralism*. This is brought out in differing ways by the terms "poststructuralism" or "neostructuralism," which are both insufficient designations for this phenomenon (a phenomenon that has as yet not run its course, and that thus cannot yet be judged in its entirety). "Poststructuralism" seems to me to be too neutral a designation; after all, even the fall in the value of the dollar and the formation of a peace movement occurred *after* structuralism, without having an inherent connection to it. "Neostructuralism" is also somewhat misleading, for this term implies that the phenomenon we are dealing with is simply a renewal of the older, classical structuralism as we have become acquainted with it through linguistics, literary criticism, sociology, and philosophy as well. Furthermore, this designation is also unfortunate because it does not correspond exactly to such parallel terms as neo-Thomism or neo-Marxism; for these took up *again*, although in altered and revisionistic form, theoretical positions whose development either had been historically interrupted, or – as in the case of neo-Marxism – had been cut off by a dogmatic fixing of the doctrine. This is not the case for neostructuralism: it followed *immediately* upon classical structuralism, represented by such figures as Ferdinand de Saussure (filtered through Bally and Sechehaye), Emile Benveniste, Julien A. Greimas, Claude Lévi-Strauss, Gerard Genette, Tzvetan Todorov, and Roland Barthes, and it retained to this extent an *inherent* connection with structuralism. In other words, neostructuralism is not only, as the term "poststructuralism" suggests, a school of thought that came to light *after* structuralism; it is also critically linked to structuralism and cannot be understood if one ignores this origin.

My third preliminary thesis, finally, is that neostructuralism radicalizes and overthrows the ethnological-linguistic structuralism that precedes it by means of a philosophical perspective. (Structuralism, after all, saw itself more as a methodology of the human sciences than as a philosophical movement.) This perspective is attained through a reconsideration of Nietzsche's overcoming of metaphysics. That is why the names of Heidegger and Freud must be appended to the previously mentioned list of philosophical precursors of neostructuralism. (No doubt we could also add the names of Emmanuel Lévinas and Georges Bataille, who, however, for their part stand profoundly under the influence of the former pair.) Thus our list is composed solely of German philosophers and theoreticians, who, however, have experienced a considerably different interpretation in German-speaking countries, and who confront those German scholars who curiously peer across the border into France in an oddly unfamiliar (yet fascinating) reading. This circuitous detour doubtless has something to do with the discontinuous evolution of recent European history, and especially with the difficulty the Germans had in picking up their own cultural tradition after the catastrophe of the Third Reich. While the postwar era in West Germany is characterized by a gradual movement away from Heidegger and Nietzsche (and toward the theoretical standpoints of Kantian or analytical philosophy, the latter mediated by the immigration of German scholars to Anglo-Saxon countries), the "new French thinkers" appear to want to tell untroubled the uninterrupted story of the German critique of metaphysics from Romanticism all the way to Heidegger. Even Saussure, moreover, is not an exception to this pattern. Recent investigations, which the "Edition critique" by Rudolf Engler made possible,[2] have been able to trace the supposed revolution that Saussure caused in linguistics back to sources in the German idealist philosophy of language (especially to the philosophy of Humboldt, Schleiermacher, and Steinthal, the latter of whom Saussure probably heard lecture in Berlin). This is all noted in passing in order to explain the specific West German interest in neostructuralism. I will return to this issue later.

As already mentioned, the names of Heidegger and Freud must be appended to our honor role of neostructuralism. The former belongs here because he, following Hegel and Nietzsche, seeks to overcome metaphysics in the name of Being — Being that does not wholly abandon its essence to any conceivable theoretical reflection. The latter must be included for a structurally similar reason; namely, because he allows for an unconscious that cannot be completely illuminated, no matter how hard one strains one's power of conceptualization. Illuminate, conceive, explain: these are fundamental desires of that which neostructuralism perceives as the specific European *episteme*, i.e., form of knowledge, which for neostructuralism itself is no longer valid. The postmodern form of knowledge can be neither Platonic idealism nor Christian faith nor even

Hegelian self-consciousness. Nor can it be—and with this I arrive at the justification of my reference to the year 1968—*that epISTEME* manifest in classical structuralism.

Cognizant of the danger of oversimplification, I must nonetheless briefly characterize the *epISTEME* of structuralism in a preliminary manner. The concept "structure," in the specific sense that concerns us here, developed out of a particular reading of Saussure's *Cours de linguistique générale*, although the expression itself cannot be found there. Saussure spoke, rather, of a language system.[3] For Saussure, this expression refers to the ordering principle according to which the lexicon of a language is not only articulated, but articulated, moreover, in such a way that it can be recognized and mastered as the lexicon of one and the same national language. This occurs through acts of differentiation and connection. In the first place, all elements of expression that make a sign hearable or readable must be clearly distinguishable from one another; for the richness, i.e., the differentiation, of my linguistic world is only proportionate to my ability to distinguish among signs. This, according to Saussure, is not immediately possible based on the meaning of signs, but rather only by means of their expression. For meanings in themselves are amorphous, intangible, purely mental, and lacking a distinguishable profile. Therefore, if I wish to distinguish among meanings, I can accomplish this only by distinguishing among sound images or written images—i.e., signifiers. Yet differentiation is merely one aspect of the linguistic system: once linguistic signs have been reduced to their smallest constituents, they must once again be joined to form morphemes, words, phrases, sentences, and finally texts—indeed, ultimately to form a linguistic image of the world. In conclusion, we can now risk a vague definition of "structure": a structure is a system of pairs—meaning/expression, i.e., signified/signifier—such that one and only one signified is assigned to every signifier. This, moreover, occurs according to a firm and lasting rule that allows both the differentiation of signs and their recombination. To take an illustration that structuralism was fond of, call to mind the image of a crystal lattice. Here the individual molecules are both distinct from one another, as well as related (connected) according to strict rules of formation. The formulation of this principle of formation would be the structure (the blueprint) of this crystal.[4]

Here we have touched on a fundamental principle of the structuralism debate. In what follows it will be our objective patiently to work out in detail the mechanism of this principle. My intent here has not been to give a whirlwind introduction to Saussure's linguistics; rather it was a matter of exposing a particular implication of this system-model of language. Let me bring it briefly to light. It is the implication that the individual signs are exact applications of an invariable law to which they are related just as individual instances relate to the concept under which they are subsumed. In a crystal lattice the molecules are not only distinct from one another, they are, at constant low temperature, *fixed to their places*;

i.e., they cannot swarm outward, nor is there any blurring that would make their location and thus their application uncontrollable.

Now it is precisely the concept of uncontrollability that *neo*structuralism interjects into the debate at this point. "Control," thus Derrida, Deleuze, or Lyotard objects, is a move in the language game of rationality, i.e., of metaphysics. Metaphysics not only supplies *Dasein* orientation for human beings, it guarantees and practices this orientation in the form of domination. In the metaphysical cosmos, "order" rules insofar as the laws of the human mind govern the shape of matter – nature, for example. Nature and materiality come into view only as the object or as the realm of application where reason holds sway.

Structuralism itself, as we have just defined it, stands outside metaphysics insofar as it no longer shares a specific basic assumption with it, namely, that the sensual world is a mirror image, a form of expression, or, for that matter, an area of application of the transsensual world. The expression "transsensual world" probably seems overcharged in this context. Yet indeed, the world of "facts and figures" is transsensual, or to put it more simply, nonsensual in the sense of not corresponding to anything in the visible world. The application, for example, of scientific laws to nature is always external to nature itself. It is an exercise of power, of spiritual domination imprinting its formula on nature. Behind the seemingly value-free *theoría* (to be taken in the Greek sense of the word) is a "will to power," a will to overpower. Heidegger convincingly demonstrated this hidden aspect that the traditional idealist metaphysics of the "divine Plato" shares with the drive to dominate nature characteristic of modern technology and the applied sciences. According to Heidegger, the history of metaphysics is the history of a gradually growing self-empowerment of subjectivity that reaches its zenith in modern-day technology's drive to dominate the world. To keep this voluntaristic aspect of theory/technology/science away from the awareness of those who practice it, one devised and perpetuated the strategy of passing reality off as a product, or as a material reflex, of the world of thought. Reality became the sensual re-presentation (i.e., re-presencing) of something in itself nonsensual: the world of ideas, axioms, formulas, terms, and laws that we may thus confidently treat, following Hegel, as a "supersensible world."[5]

As I just said, structuralism as we have encountered it thus far breaks with this working hypothesis still tinged by metaphysics. For structuralism the sensual is not a reflection or expression of something nonsensual in the sensual itself. Let's remain within the more easily comprehensible realm of sign theory: the sound aspect of the sign is conceived of as the represencing of a sign's nonsensual or spiritual aspect, its meaning. Even Aristotle had viewed the word as a simulacrum of psychic and mental processes. This view is inverted by Saussure's thesis that the meaning of a sign is the effect of articulation of its material of expression. By no means is there a prior world of nonsensual psychic or cognitive states or processes that then might be represented by a world of symbols. On the contrary, the nonsensual world of thoughts is itself constituted as a result of differentiation and combination in the realm of the sensual-phonic.

Up to this point, as I mentioned earlier, structuralism is not metaphysical. However, it is metaphysical on the basis of another premise. Insofar as structuralism searches for general ordering principles and universal regularities, the knowledge of which renders the social world capable of technological and scientific mastery, its knowledge interest is dominated by the guiding desire of Western theory, namely, to make nature theoretically accessible. Even without a subject that forms and changes the rules, structuralism remains a traditionally metaphysical endeavor. The talk about an "unconscious spirit," which, according to Lévi-Strauss, is weaving anthropological and grammatical structures, makes this particularly evident. Paul Ricoeur called Lévi-Strauss's structuralism a "Kantism without a transcendental subject."

The French thinkers whom I tentatively bring together under the collective heading of "neostructuralism" try to steer clear of these last encroachments of metaphysical thought. Structuralism for Jean-François Lyotard, for example, is still "modern"; those who want to make allowances for the contemporary provocations of a postmodern condition must break with it (which undoubtedly cannot mean breaking with *all* its premises). The decisive attack the "postmodern" enterprise launches against "modernity" is first of all directed against the (metaphysical) concept of domination and of system. If I am correct, this is the lowest common denominator that connects the writings of otherwise so different theoreticians as Lacan, Derrida, Deleuze, Lyotard, Kristeva, Baudrillard (in the cases of Foucault, Althusser, and Barthes I am as yet undecided). Now you have an idea about why I earlier stressed the revolutionary year of 1968. Around that time the bond that joined classical structuralism (which had remained loyal to the concept of a self-enclosed system) to neostructuralism (which challenged this concept) broke within the consciousness of Parisian intellectuals.[6] There is, so to speak, a touch of revolutionary energy in the anarchism of the neostructuralists. In the duel between the forces of order (preservation of the system) and entropy (dissolution of the system), they side with the latter. However, they establish their position not by rejecting Saussure's conception of a differential articulation of the sign, but rather by challenging the idea that this articulation takes place in a theoretically comprehensive and enclosed system—a "taxonomy," as linguists call it. The "structure" of the neostructuralists no longer knows any specifiable confinement: it is open, subject to infinite transformations, and is not motivated by the ambition formally to master individual "events" (*événements*) in what since then has come to be called "the text in general."[7]

Let me summarize: neostructuralism takes up certain working hypotheses of classical structuralism, i.e., the officially sanctioned version of Saussure's *Cours de linguistique générale*.[8] Among these hypotheses is first of all a brusque rejection of the notion that words are somehow images for prior existing ideas or "παϑήματα τῆς ψνχῆς" (psychic impressions), similar to the way in which syntactical connections reflect logical syntheses that combine thoughts with predicates to form judgments. We will later refer to this hypothesis as the *representational model* of language.

However, in contrast to the working hypotheses of structuralism, neostructuralism rejects the idea of scientific-technological domination of its object. In the idea of a linguistic or a social system, with linguists studying language and socioanthropologists studying the structure of a population, neostructuralists unmask a final encroachment of metaphysical thought, which is thought evolving around concepts of power, of control, mastering, overpowering. The idea of empowerment is bound to that of presence, for only the visibly present, that which shows itself in what it is and how it is (i.e., in its essence), can be dominated conceptually and systematically. Heidegger, however, has taken precisely this to be a basic aspect of the Western interpretation of Being: that it thinks "Being" as "presence" (*ousia, parousia*). To this Western interpretation of Being, neostructuralism juxtaposes the concept of a nonpresence that is never entirely sublatable into presence (a "nonpresent remainder," *LI*, 187),[9] a "structural unconscious" (*LI*, 213), and a principle of "undecidability" (*LI*, 216) of the meaning of signs: "the nonpresent remainder of a differential mark, cut off from its alleged 'production' of origin."[10]

I shall interrupt my introduction at this point. As you realized, I have not been able to go beyond simple assertions. That is the fate of all introductions that are only harbingers of arguments to be presented in what follows. Therefore, the following lectures will try to recapitulate in argumentative fashion what has been asserted here only in the form of theses. I will not proceed by introducing every neostructuralist writer extensively and in "correct" order, for by following such a procedure we would too easily lose track of the unity of our general question about the nature of neostructuralism. I will attempt rather to enter into a *philosophizing* dialogue with neostructuralism, and I will do this in such a way that I segregate the subject matter of neostructuralism from the manner in which it is actually treated in this or that critical text. Let me say in advance that it seems to me that argumentation is the weak side of neostructuralism. And this is not only because argumentative procedure is too easily aligned by the representatives of this movement with traditional Western methodological practices, and therefore considered a *pudendum* — something to be avoided at all cost. It is also the case because, in my opinion, the theoretical insight that forms the origin of neostructuralism can be more forcefully developed than has actually occurred in the critical texts. In other words, one can sometimes uphold the "germinal idea" of neostructuralist theory, while rejecting the blind degeneration it has undergone in texts like those of the later Deleuze or Baudrillard (and thinkers of a comparably rash temperament). I will exploit this procedure as a *constructive hermeneutics* that unfolds a thought as far as, in my opinion, it allows itself to be unfolded. Only after this is done can one begin with critical scrutiny; a thought will be rejected only if it cannot be upheld even in what I consider to be its most complete formulation.

I imagine as a rough organization for my lectures a tripartite division organized around those ideas on the basis of which neostructuralism launches its critique of what it calls the classical *episteme*. First of all there is the attack on thinking in terms of the concepts of *history*; second, there is the attack on the category of the *subject* (or self-consciousness); third, there is the confrontation with a hermeneutics based on the preeminence of *meaning*. In all these fields of contention (which, of course, are connected with the names of different authors), the common denominator is the rejection of metaphysics, which, since it will be universally present, I need not treat separately.

Before I deal with the first field of contention, that concerned with history, I want to uncover more distinctly and patiently neostructuralism's point of departure in classical structuralism (mainly in Saussure's *Cours* and in the writings of Claude Lévi-Strauss). Only then will I turn to Lyotard's, Derrida's, and Foucault's reflections dedicated to that historical occasion out of which sprang the destruction of the very possibility of thinking in terms of structure.

We want to accomplish two things in the second part of this lecture. First, we want to look more closely at the movement with which neostructuralism departs from classical structuralism; in connection to this we want to ascertain in subsequent lectures its motivations for this departure. The second question will already put us on a track that will lead us to the center of the development of neostructuralist theory. This question then reads: what historical configuration shook the paradigm of structural thinking; what point marks the epistemological break that separates modernity from postmodernity?

I wish to remind you of our provisional attempt to make above all else the fundamental concept of *structure* more precise. To be sure, colloquially we designate in appropriate contexts all sorts of forms and ordered constructs as "structures," without, indeed, being able to hope that with this we already possess a key for illuminating structuralist procedure. For this reason we have to proceed more carefully; and I suggest that we begin by once again calling to mind the formula we tentatively agreed upon previously, and that we then later illustrate it through a concrete example.

Not without being influenced by Russian formalism and by the structuralism of the so-called Prague circle, linguists first rendered with the word "structure" what in Saussure was called "the language system." I will ignore for the moment the difficult situation of the manuscripts left after Saussure's death and will not (yet) address the question whether the "structuralist Saussure" was not an ingenious invention of his first editors, Bally and Sechehaye. But even if one affirms this thesis, it still cannot be denied that the text of Saussure's *Cours de linguistique générale* edited by Bally and Sechehaye (from 1915) served as the sole basis of structuralism, just as the Vulgate served as the sole basis of biblical interpretation for the Catholic church.[11] Naturally, *I* hope that there will be a reformation of Saussure scholarship, just as there was one of the church.

Bally and Sechehaye apparently took the thesis about the systematic composition of language to be Saussure's fundamental insight. To be sure, Saussure had distinguished speech (*la parole*), as the manner in which language is present daily in concrete form, from language's system/form, which he called *la langue*. *La langue* is not an ensemble of speech acts by means of which we communicate with one another, but rather the abstract and as such never manifest order that operates, as it were, underneath our speech acts and that stamps its law upon these acts. Saussure also calls this law the "code" of a language (*Cours*, 31). It relates to actual speech acts as a pure possibility (*virtualité*) to its realization (*actualisation*). Only as speech is language *real*; however, that does not mean that it derives its ground of Being from this reality. One can clarify this through a simple consideration: if we had to identify the meaning of a word on the basis of its acoustical form, we would never identify it. For no word, no matter how small it might be, is reproduced in absolutely the same way by all speakers, nor even by the same speaker at different times. Thus if we identify it *as* this particular word at all, then we have to posit a hypothesis; we must draw an ampliative inference that reveals the given chain of voice production (*chaîne phonatoire*) as one instance of a general speech *type*, which as such does not belong to the order of *parole*. This hypothesis, by virtue of which we take a phonetic chain as the stimulus to associate with it a certain meaning, is what first establishes the *Dasein* of a *sign*. What previously—in the realm of concrete speech—was an unrepeatable and unique acoustical figure has now been elevated to the status of a *sign*. You see from this relatively simple reflection that the fact of language mastery demands a theory that strictly differentiates the concrete vocal-graphic event (*événement*) from its never realizable and, to this extent, essentially *ideal* nature as a sign. For the sign by no means connects, as one might at first believe, the vocal-sensual with the nonsensual spiritual aspect of a word; rather it connects, as Saussure expresses it, an acoustical image (*une image acoustique*) with a concept (*concept*). An acoustical *image* does not simply mean a sound. Rather, this expression means that different, never identical phonations (*phonatisations*) are recognized as substrata of one and the same sign only *then*, when one re-cognizes in them articulations of one and the same acoustical image. However, in order to be able to identify essentially different sounds as realizations of *a single* acoustical *image*, one must already have apprehended the acoustical aspect of language from the viewpoint of its possible meaning (*concept, signifié*). And this in turn means that one must have the entire system of *langue* present (one must master it). For only in a *structure* that is neither reliant upon nor subordinate to individual reproduction can signs have a meaning that is both eternally stable and reidentifiable over numerous occurrences (the criterion of *recursivity*). To this extent the system of *langue* is not—as is a realization in concrete speech—itself material; it further is distinguished from speech in that it does not move in time, but rather is strictly timeless (*synchronique*); and finally, it is distinguished from speech in that its status of Being is pure possibility and not actuality. On this basis we can understand that famous statement in the *Cours* that language (*la langue*) is no substance, but rather a form (*CGL*, 113, 122). This statement draws an inference out of two complementary observations we made in the last lecture. I will repeat them here because they are fundamental for all that follows. The first observation claims:

> Psychologically our thought—apart from its expression in words—is only a shapeless and indistinct mass. Philosophers and linguists have always agreed in recognizing that without the help of signs we would be unable to make a clear-cut, consistent distinction between two ideas. Without language, thought is a vague, uncharted nebula. There are no pre-existing ideas, and nothing is distinct before the appearance of language. (*CGL*, 111–12)

Now this is also correspondingly the case for the acoustical aspect of language. The sounds as well are not, as it were, by nature carriers of possible units of meaning, as the naturalist illusion assumes.

> Against the floating realm of thought, would sounds by themselves yield predelimited entities? No more so than ideas. Phonic substance is neither more fixed nor more rigid than thought; it is not a mold into which thought must of necessity fit but a plastic substance divided in turn into distinct parts to furnish the signifiers needed by thought. The linguistic fact can therefore be pictured in its totality—i.e. language—as a series of contiguous subdivisions marked off on both the indefinite plane of jumbled ideas (A) and the equally vague plane of sounds (B). The following diagram gives a rough idea of it:

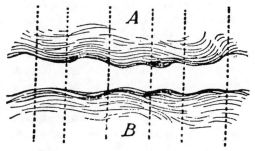

(*CGL*, 112)

If, therefore, there are neither prior existing ideas that might be portrayed by sounds, nor even fixed and firm sounds from which meanings could be wrested, then one must imagine the process of sign synthesis as a stepping-into-the-middle on the part of *langue*, with the result that now at one stroke both a signifier and a signified are born.

> The characteristic role of language with respect to thought is not to create a material phonic means for expressing ideas but to serve as a link between thought and sound, under conditions that of necessity bring about the reciprocal delimitations of units. Thought, chaotic by nature, has to become ordered in the process of its decomposition. Neither are thoughts given material form nor are sounds transformed into mental entities; the somewhat mysterious fact is rather that "thought-sound" implies division, and that language works out its units while taking shape between two shapeless masses. Visualize the air in contact with a sheet of water; if the atmospheric pressure changes, the surface of the water will be broken up into a series of divisions, waves; the waves resemble the union or coupling of thought with phonic substance. (*CGL*, 112).

The illustration used by Saussure is self-explanatory. It dispels the notion that words are names of ideas (or even of things); but it also dispels the notion that ideas might have to accommodate themselves to prior existing acoustical forms. Both streams, that of thought as well as that of sound, are synthesized through the same act; and this act is nothing other than what since the time of Humboldt has been called *articulation* in this specific sense. Articulation means, translated literally, membering (from *articulus*, the member of a body): "Each linguistic term is a member, an *articulus* in which an idea is fixed in a sound and a sound becomes the sign of an idea" (*CGL*, 113).

Both the sound and the thought are distinguished through articulation. However, distinction presupposes differentiation. A thought (and thus a sign as a "unity of thought and sound") is identical with itself only insofar as it is different from all other thoughts of a system. Here we once again come across the idea of determination through contrast (or through negation), which is fundamental to structuralism. To recognize something *as* something means to differentiate it from all other recognizable things. Negation here has the sense of "other than . . ." ("Omnis determinatio est negatio": Spinoza, Hegel). The same is true of the sign: I interpret it as this (and not as that) by differentiating its acoustical image from the acoustical image of all other signs, i.e., by apprehending it from the viewpoint of its possible meaning. The phonic materiality of the sign thus does indeed play a decisive role: only by means of it does identification of meaning occur. However, this should not be taken to mean that one could already read out of the sound as such its meaning (indeed, the sound is amorphous); rather a sound becomes a signifier only when I interpret it as the acoustical image of a *meaning*, and only mastery of the virtual system of *langue* can motivate me to this interpretation. It is in this sense, therefore, that Saussure can say: "Their combination produces a form, not a substance" (*CGL*, 113). Language, viewed as a system of pure differences, has in itself nothing that is substantial: it is not a treasury or storeroom (*trésor*) of *positive* meanings or of *positive signs*; rather it is a web of values (*valeurs*), i.e., of negative references to other values. Saussure expresses it this way in a striking and famous passage.

> Everything that has been said up to this point boils down to this: in language there are only differences. Even more important: a difference generally implies positive terms between which the difference is set up; but in language there are only differences *without positive terms*. Whether we take the signified or the signifier, language has neither ideas nor sounds that existed before the linguistic system, but only conceptual and phonic differences that have issued from the system. The idea or phonic substance that a sign contains is of less importance than the other signs that surround it. Proof of this is that the value of a term may be modified without either its meaning or its sound being affected, solely because a neighboring term has been modified. (*CGL*, 120)

Coming to an end of my summary of Saussure's ideas, I would like to anticipate what is to come by saying that *classical structuralism* developed out of a strong interpretation of this passage (and of the entire fourth chapter of the *Cours* in which it is found). Let's repeat once again the fundamental idea that led to the formula that language, viewed as a system of pure differences, is a form and not something substantial. The basic idea is that the linguistic sign, since there is no "*natural* relationship" between sound (*son*) and idea (*idée*), cannot be conceived on the basis of its "positive" (i.e., material, substantial, innately meaningful) characteristics: there is nothing in the acoustical qualities of the *signifiant* that reminds of the value or the content of that which it signifies. Structuralism rendered a strong interpretation of this state of affairs. An extreme expression of this classical structuralism is found in Hjelmslev, who defines the structure of a language as an "autonomous entity of inner dependencies."[12] This means that structure is nothing but a mere mesh of differences and of relationships among values — lacking any positive (i.e., existing *in itself*) actuality, be it one of meaning or one of expression: it is, therefore, pure form.

> Units and grammatical facts would not be confused if linguistic signs were made up of something besides differences. But language being what it is, we shall find nothing simple in it regardless of our approach; everywhere and always there is the same complex equilibrium of terms that mutually condition each other. Putting it another way, *language is a form and not a substance*. (*CGL*, 122)

As "proof of this," the observation is made in the *Cours* that the value of a linguistic term can be altered without altering the sound or the meaning of this term, and this occurs simply by means of a new differentiation, i.e., through a new articulation of the "unity of sound and thought." Conversely, of course, the structure also remains unchanged when a series of marks (*marques*) is removed from the game and replaced by equivalent terms. Classical structuralism, but not Saussure himself, referred to this possibility as that of *transformation*. Since this is a fundamental concept for the work of Lévi-Strauss, I will insert a few words about the *mechanism of structural transformation* at this point.

When saying that structuralism has to do with systems of transformations, one seeks to express the following: the elements encountered in a structure are *functions* and do not count because of their physical characteristics or because of any characteristics that are determined to be independent of their membership in a structural formation. An element becomes a *function* precisely because it steps out of its material actuality and transforms itself into a systematic value. The same function can be taken over by elements that are materially quite different; conversely, the same material element can fulfill wholly different functions according to the immediate task the system entrusts to it. That sounds complicated, but it is actually quite simple: the knife with which I cut bread is the same physical object as that with whose gleaming blade I reflect rays of light. It simply takes over different functions, the first in the regulated system of housework, the second in the regulated system of an optical experiment. Conversely, the same function can be taken over by different materials; remaining within the current example, the blade of my bread knife can replace a mirror if I have no other instrument at hand, etc.

Of course, transformations of the second type play the greatest role in the framework of structuralism. We saw that structure — as pure form — has to do neither with expressions nor with meanings, but rather with "values." Now the values are equivalent to the functions in our example and can be taken over by any substances whatever: "The opposition between the *simplicity of the structure* and the *multiplicity of elements* is expressed in the fact that several elements compete to occupy the same positions in the structure" (*SA*, 62). This follows from the "arbitrariness" of the sign synthesis (that is, out of the nonnaturalness of the bond between thought and sound). If one then asserts that the values/functions can be represented by random substances (just as the score of the *Eroica* can be performed by random orchestras and random instruments — of the same type, naturally), this, of course, does not mean that the values themselves are random. On the contrary, call to mind the statement of L. Hjelmslev: "Language is an essentially autonomous entity of inner dependencies, and thus a structure."[12] This means that the expandability and the richness of possible transformations are a priori limited and are controlled by the demand of the given system to remain formally identical in all its different substantializations (or realizations). Jean Piaget designated this characteristic of structures with a central concept of his theory as self-regulation (*autoréglage*). The concept means that structures do indeed change, yet always only within the continuum of their self-preservation *as* structures. This presupposes the concept of structural closure: the transformations inherent in a structure may never transgress its limitations; rather it can only produce elements that pertain to its structure and conform to its rules. "These properties of conservation along with stability of boundaries despite the construction of indefinitely many new elements presuppose that structures are self-regulating."[13] This, by the way, is also a basic assumption of so-called systems theory in the social sciences, represented by Parsons and Luhmann, which to this extent is directly traceable to classical structuralism.

We will close here for the moment and investigate the transposition of linguistic structuralism onto the work of anthropology and mythology (in and through the work of Claude Lévi-Strauss) in the next lecture.

Lecture 3

Having glanced at structuralism's magic formula—language is not a substance, but a form—from various sides, and having developed some of its consequences, we would now like to illustrate, as promised earlier, how it works in the nonlinguistic sphere taking the example of Claude Lévi-Strauss. It is general knowledge that Lévi-Strauss, taking Saussure and Troubetzkoy's phonology as his point of departure, tried to discover numerical properties and transformational groups in kinship systems. What is more important for us—and for neostructuralism—is that he traced these structures even within the transition from one classification to another, from one myth to another, and from one collective practice to another, in order ultimately to formulate *the* structure of mankind's supposed "unconscious mind."

Let's first look at the areas where Lévi-Strauss overlaps with Saussure and where *his* version of structuralism goes beyond the linguistic approach. First the areas they have in common. Saussure had already declared linguistics to be a mere (though most important) branch of what he called semiology. Semiology is "a science that studies the life of signs within society; it would be a part of social psychology and consequently of general psychology. . . . Semiology would show us what constitutes signs, what laws govern them" (*CGL*, 16). The rule that the meaning of a social sign is the effect of differential relations to other signs is valid—if, indeed, it is correct—a fortiori not only for linguistic systems in the narrow sense. This is the fundamental assumption on which Claude Lévi-Strauss's structural anthropology is based. All systems of meaning, even nonlinguistic ones, whose laws govern human interaction make use of the universal features that Saussure only coincidentally first discovered within the system of *langue*. To be sure, linguistics, as a science, is enviably far advanced.[1] But there is a close methodological bond between the two disciplines that obliges them to cooperate (see *SA*, 29).

Which procedures of linguistic structuralism could then be adapted by a structural anthropology without any problems? Lévi-Strauss mentions four that he borrows from Nikolai Troubetzkoy.[2]

> N. Troubetzkoy, the illustrious founder of structural linguistics, himself furnished the answer to this question. In one programmatic statement, he reduced the structural method to four basic operations. First, structural linguistics shifts from the study of *conscious* linguistic phenomena to study of their *unconscious* infrastructure; second, it does not treat *terms* as independent entities, taking instead as its basis of analysis the *relations* between terms; third, it introduces the concept of *system* — "Modern phonemics does not merely proclaim that phonemes are always part of a system; it *shows* concrete phonemic systems and elucidates their structure" — ; finally, structural linguistics aims at discovering *general laws*, either by induction "or . . . by logical deduction, which would give them an absolute character." (*SA*, 31)

When, Lévi-Strauss says, an event of such eminent importance takes place in *one* branch of the human sciences, it is not only permissible but even requisite that related disciplines "examine its consequences and its possible application to phenomena of another order" (*SA*, 31). What are these consequences?

> Like phonemes, kinship terms are elements of meaning; like phonemes, they acquire meaning only if they are integrated into systems. "Kinship systems," like "phonemic systems," are built by the mind on the level of unconscious thought. Finally, the recurrence of kinship patterns, marriage rules, similar prescribed attitudes between certain types of relatives, and so forth, in scattered regions of the globe and in fundamentally different societies, leads us to believe that, in the case of kinship as well as linguistics, the observable phenomena result from the action of laws which are general but implicit. The problem can therefore be formulated as follows: Although they belong to *another order of reality*, kinship phenomena are *of the same type* as linguistic phenomena. Can the anthropologist, using a method analogous *in form* (if not in content) to the method used in structural linguistics, achieve the same kind of progress in his own science as that which has taken place in linguistics? (*SA*, 32)

Well it seems to me that the claim is obvious. Let's give further consideration for a moment to what Lévi-Strauss calls the formal analogy between phonology and anthropology. It consists in the "unconscious activity of the mind." This is one of the favorite concepts of this author, and it is nothing but a metaphor for what Saussure called "form" in his *Cours*. Languages share with social structures (and with myths, as we will see in a minute) the characteristic that one cannot conceive their meaning in terms of their content—on the basis of the material properties of their elements—but rather only by conceiving these elements as *values*, i.e., as functions of a system of pure relations. I will cite a characteristic formulation of this analogy.

> In anthropology as in linguistics, therefore, it is not comparison that supports generalization, but the other way around. If, as we believe to be the case, the unconscious activity of the mind consists in imposing forms upon content, and if these forms are fundamentally the same for all minds—ancient and modern, primitive and civilized (as the study of the symbolic function, expressed in language, so strikingly indicates)— it is necessary and sufficient to grasp the unconscious structure underlying each institution and each custom, in order to obtain a principle of interpretation valid for other institutions and other customs, provided of course that the analysis is carried far enough. (*SA*, 21-22)

Let's repeat the central thesis of this passage: the unconscious activity of the mind consists in "imposing forms upon content." If we add "upon previously unarticulated content," then we find ourselves referred immediately back to the beginning of Chapter 4 of Saussure's *Cours* where the principle of the articulation of signs is explained. Mind is in itself just as amorphous as sound; therefore, something has to intervene between the two, namely, the *schematism of articulation* through which a sensually perceptible sound can be related to a nonsensual meaning in the first place.

By supplementing the term "articulation" with the term "schematism," I have recalled in passing a fundamental theorem of idealist language philosophy that Saussure himself, as well as Lévi-Strauss, as you will soon see, made use of. It was Kant who posed the question of how our pure concepts of understanding (which have nothing sensual about them) can be related to the empirical data our experience transmits to us (and which, in turn, have no intellectual quality). His answer was that it is possible by means of a specific operation of our imagination that is capable of relating a pure (or empirical) concept to the objects of experience on the basis of a *scheme*. The scheme is, in Kant's own words, the "representation of a universal procedure of imagination in providing an image for a concept."[3] On the one hand, the scheme is universal like the concept; on the other hand, it is empirical and concrete like the image that I make of a single object. This way it can serve as an intermediary if it is a matter of relating the pure concepts of our mind to particular materials from our world of experience. The same thing is accomplished—and this further conclusion was made by Schelling and Schleiermacher—by the articulation of signs: the sign as well is a synthesis of a concept and a perception (*Anschauung*); it shares the universality of thought with the particularity of its, in each instance, singular reference to an object. A concept alone would be meaningless (i.e., without reference to an object); and, vice versa, perception (*Anschauung*) without conceptual interpretation would be contentless. The scheme serves as intermediary and generates that object, both sensual and intellectual, which we know as the sign.

Precisely this process of schematization or articulation Lévi-Strauss at times calls the unconscious mind, which semiologically (i.e., by means of a structure) relates social reality and the objective; at other times he calls it the "conceptual *scheme*," which mediates between the social praxis of the collective and the practices of the individuals. I shall cite a longer passage from *The Savage Mind* which deals with this.

> If, as I have said, the conceptual scheme governs and defines practices, it is because these, which the ethnologist studies as discrete realities placed in time and space and distinctive in their particular modes of life and forms of civilization, are not to be confused with *praxis* which— and here at least I agree with Sartre (p. 181)—constitutes the fundamental totality for the sciences of man. Marxism, if not Marx himself, has too commonly reasoned as though practices followed directly from *praxis*. Without questioning the undoubted primacy of infrastructures, I believe that there is always a mediator between *praxis* and practices, namely the conceptual scheme by the operation of which matter and form, neither with any independent existence, are realized as structures, that is as entities which are both empirical and intelligible. It is to this theory of superstructures, scarcely touched on by Marx, that I hope to make a contribution.[4]

I believe that after having spent so much time with Saussure's idea of a mediation between sensual sound and intelligible meaning by means of a *form of differential relation*, you will have no difficulty transferring this thought onto the structural anthropology of Lévi-Strauss. The quoted passage essentially asserts nothing more than this: that the undifferentiated activities and actions of a society or a population are not, as it were, inherently connected with the cultural and intellectual processes through which this society articulates its self-understanding, nor are these connected by means of a process of mutual portrayal, but rather by means of *structure*. Human thoughts are related to the actions of the base in the same way as signifier and signified are related in the sign: not by virtue of a *lien naturel*, but rather by means of differential relations between carriers of expression whose interplay founds the unity of thought (of culture) and perception (*Anschauung*) (of the base, of praxis, of the sound) in the first place. Accordingly, there are not two structures, one of social praxis and one of individual (artisan, artistic, and theoretical) practi*ces*; rather, it is one and the same praxis that establishes mind as the mind of *this* base, and base as the base of *this* mind. The structure of society is insofar nothing substantial, but rather a pure form, i.e., a context of assignments or references (in Heidegger's sense) not between objects but between values. Heidegger, by the way, takes up a structuralist thought when he says:

> The context of assignments or references, which, as significance, is constitutive for worldhood, can be taken formally in the sense of a system of Relations.[5]

With this Lévi-Strauss believes he has uncovered the inner relations between a structural theory of society and the procedures of structural linguistics. The fruitfulness of this transferral is generally known, and Lévi-Strauss's works do not need to be praised by me, an amateur in anthropology. We, however, who are for the most part students of philosophy and/or literature, are mostly interested in the application to which Lévi-Strauss put Saussurean linguistics in the field of *mythology*, for myths are narratives that, in contrast to kinship relations or social structures, are located in the immediate realm of the linguistic. There is yet a second reason why we must take a brief look at this new process of the transposition of method: namely, because all of structuralism and neostructuralism, from Foucault through Derrida, has taken up Lévi-Strauss's doctrine at precisely this point. For those of you who would like to know what I mean, I will mention in passing that I am thinking of the establishment of the term "discourse," with whose coining something new is introduced into the human sciences. But let's proceed according to the logical order of the argument.

In his famous essay "The Structure of Myths" (in *Structural Anthropology*) Lévi-Strauss introduced a procedure that he applied with great success to the analysis of myth in his principal work, the *Mythologiques*.[6] We will limit ourselves to a discussion of its methodological maxims on which the analysis follows, and we will compare them to what we know from Saussure.

Lévi-Strauss begins with a fundamental objection addressed at all previous theories of myth. According to these theories, myth is the expression of a hidden reality; for example, of the archetypes of the human mind, of the conditions of a certain society, of a cosmological interpretation of the world, or of the drives and adventures of the human character, etc. Let's first consider the assertion that myth reflects social contents.

> If a given mythology confers prominence on a certain figure, let us say an evil grandmother, it will be claimed that in such a society grandmothers are actually evil and that mythology reflects the social structure and the social relations; but should the actual data be conflicting, it would be as readily claimed that the purpose of mythology is to provide an outlet for repressed feelings. Whatever the situation, a clever dialectic will always find a way to pretend that a meaning has been found. (*SA*, 203)

The essential point of this interpretation of myth is that myth is read as the reflection of a *content*, and precisely not as a structure in the sense that is familiar to us. Lévi-Strauss replies to this that myth *as* myth is completely indifferent to the narrated *contents*, and that it is thus impossible to define the authentic mythic quality of *the* myth on the basis of an investigation of motif and content.

> On the one hand it would seem that in the course of a myth anything is
> likely to happen. There is no logic, no continuity. Any characteristic
> can be attributed to any subject; every conceivable relation can be
> found. With myth, everything becomes possible. But on the other hand,
> this apparent arbitrariness is belied by the astounding similarity between
> myths collected in widely different regions. Therefore the problem: If
> the content of a myth is contingent, how are we going to explain the
> fact that myths throughout the world are so similar? (*SA*, 203–4)

The question must sound rhetorical to us. We will not hesitate to answer: the similarity between myths of different populations cannot be an element of the similarity of the narrated contents, but rather must be a formal feature. Myth, like language, is not a substance, but a form.

Lévi-Strauss, in fact, compares the failure of the motif-oriented approach in the study of myth with the failure of the old theory of the representational character of language.

> For the contradiction which we face is very similar to that which in
> earlier times brought considerable worry to the first philosophers con-
> cerned with linguistic problems; linguistics could only begin to evolve
> as a science after this contradiction had been overcome. Ancient philos-
> ophers reasoned about language the way we do about mythology. On
> the one hand, they did notice that in a given language certain sequences
> of sounds were associated with definite meanings, and they earnestly
> aimed at discovering a reason for the linkage between those *sounds* and
> that *meaning*. Their attempt, however, was thwarted from the very be-
> ginning by the fact that the same sounds were equally present in other
> languages although the meaning they conveyed was entirely different.
> The contradiction was surmounted only by the discovery that it is the
> combination of sounds, not the sounds themselves, which provides the
> significant data. (*SA*, 204)

The *tertium comparationis* of both conceptions is that they do not take into account "the Saussurean principle of the *arbitrary character of linguistic signs*" (*SA*, 204). This principle, which denies a *natural* relation between meaning and sound, forces one to come up with a different explanation of the actual determination and distinction of signs, namely, that of the schematism of articulation, which takes *signifier* and *signified* not for "simple" and "positive" quantities but rather for effects of the differential relations between "values," in short, as effects of linguistic *form* or *structure*. It is the "activity of the unconscious mind" that generates the similarities between myths of peoples, myths that otherwise, as far as their content is concerned, can be extremely different.

At this point in our discussion, where Saussure's working hypothesis — that figures of meaning have to be dealt with not as substances but as forms — seems to have proved itself for a second time in the work of Lévi-Strauss, a decisive problem arises. The thesis is no longer subsumed under Saussure's structuralism; rather it demands its own theoretical legitimation. There is, of course, a decisive difference between the inner form of a language and that of a myth. Myths, although they are linguistic formations (and thus fall under the concept of *langue*), are, on the other hand, events of *parole*: "they arise from discourse" (*SA*, 209; translation modified).

We are now coming across a concept that, as most of you already know, is one of the central marks in the language game of neostructuralism. We have to take a closer look at it. To this end we will gladly allow ourselves to be initially guided by a style as clear and illustrative as that of Lévi-Strauss. The chapter entitled "The Structural Study of Myth" formulates the difference between myth (*qua* discourse) and *langue* as follows:

> In order to preserve its specificity we must be able to show that it is both the same thing as language, and also something different from it. Here, too, the past experience of linguists may help us. For language itself can be analyzed into things which are at the same time similar and yet different. This is precisely what is expressed in Saussure's distinction between *langue* and *parole*, one being the structural side of language, the other the statistical aspect of it, *langue* belonging to a reversible time, *parole* being non-reversible. If those two levels already exist in language, then a third one can conceivably be isolated. (*SA*, 205)

Myth, as a self-enclosed sequence of phrases, i.e., as narrative, is indeed a *linguistic* event, but it is not one of the sort that its individual sequences could be removed without harm from their relative temporal positions. The linearity of the sequence of signs and, what is more, of phrases provides each significant element with a time index; i.e., it is not reversible. The elements of a structure, on the other hand, the values and their relations, are easily reversible. The matrix that generates them as events is strictly atemporal (*atemporelle*). Saussure himself had, as you know, described this difference with the terms "synchrony" and "diachrony." Lévi-Strauss now reminds us that the concept of structure, which so far has been used completely without differentiation, is in itself subdivided in a manifold way: it is a formation within which we can distinguish among different levels of constitution.

I should explain this briefly. It was Émile Benveniste who, in his principal work, *Problèmes de linguistique générale*, introduced the concept of levels of constitution, justifying it in the following way.[7] The point of departure for his idea is that Saussure's insight that linguistic meaning is constituted by phonic differentiation is in need of further discrimination. After all, there are different levels on which this principle, which itself is entirely abstract, can function. There is, for example, the phonetic level, on which one can differentiate the individual sounds of a language; there is further the phonological level, on which the "distinctive features" of an individual language can be sorted out and its possibilities of combination and opposition can be determined; then there is the morphemic level, on which the smallest significant parts of the word are identified; the syntactical level, on which the words are distinguished and combined to syntagms (and phrases); finally, the contextual level, which is concerned with the nuances of meaning of entire expressions within the context of other expressions, etc. Now we can differentiate between those relations that obtain between elements *on* a particular level (for example, phonemes) and those that obtain between elements of *one* level and elements of *another* (for example, words and phrases). Benveniste calls the former "distributional" and the latter "integrative." A structure of a language would thus be the totality of relations, not only between elements of the individually segregated levels, but also between all levels of constitution themselves.

To be sure, Benveniste, as a linguist, ends his analysis on the level of the *sentence*: in the sentence the totality of linguistic rules is exhausted. In contrast to this, myths, as discourses, are structures whose smallest constituent units are not phonemes, morphemes, or syntagms, but rather phrases. But who, Lévi-Strauss continues, would constrain us from climbing up to an even higher level of constitution: a "third level beyond language and parole," namely, the level of "discourse" ("Myth is a *mode of discourse*"; *SA*, 210, translation modified, emphasis added by author). With this we have arrived at a first, still unrefined, definition of a key term for neostructuralism: discourse is a linguistic formation, the smallest constitutive units of which are phrases, or which, as Lévi-Strauss puts it, is constructed out of large (*grosses*), not out of small, units.

Now that we know this, we will, of course, recall the other feature of mythic discourse, namely, its one-dimensionality, which seems to distinguish it from the system of *langue*. After a closer look, however, this distinction does not carry as much weight as its formulation might imply; myths, like *parole*, organize their elements according to a certain order in time; however, it is a temporal order of a peculiar type. Mythical time is always already past, or, to be more precise, it is a timelessly past time. As senseless as it would be to deny the successivity of speech events in myth, it would be just as senseless to assert that the succession of the narrative parts had evolved in an actual historical time. Exactly this, however, is a condition for the succession of phrases in *parole*. A mythic event is, although past, reproducible at any time: it is past, and, at the same time, as long as it is rooted in the collective beliefs of a population, it is timelessly present, just as the message of the birth of the son of God repeats itself every Christmas. This, in turn, myth has in common with *langue*.

> It is that double structure, altogether historical and ahistorical, which explains how myth, while pertaining to the realm of *parole* and calling for an explanation as such, as well as to that of *langue* in which it is expressed, can also be an absolute entity on a third level which, though it remains linguistic by nature, is nevertheless distinct from the other two. (*SA*, 205–6)

We know that this third level of language is the level of discourse, and we want to keep this in mind.

Let's highlight once again as precisely as possible the decisive points. In common with the elements of linguistic systems, the elements of myth do not have a value (or meaning) in themselves, but are meaningful only by virtue of the relations they have with each other; i.e., both are structures. On the other hand, myths, *qua* discourses, are structures composed of large or transphrasal units, and this sets them apart from languages (*langues*). If one nevertheless wishes to analyze them in a structuralist fashion, one needs to draw a conclusion by analogy, and this Lévi-Strauss prepares in two steps.

> (1) Myth, like the rest of language, is made up of constituent units. (2) These constituent units presuppose the constituent units present in language when analyzed on other levels—namely, phonemes, morphemes, and sememes—but they, nevertheless, differ from the latter in the same way as the latter differ among themselves; they belong to a higher and more complex order. For this reason, we shall call them *gross constituent units*. (*SA*, 206–7)

In this passage the idea of what subsequently will be called the linguistics of discourse is born. It was Roland Barthes who formulated most clearly its working hypotheses (although he only repeats, as you see, what Lévi-Strauss had already said).[8] I will give you a small excerpt:

> As is well known, linguistics stops with the *sentence*: it is the ultimate unit that linguistics believes itself to have the right to deal with. . . . And therefore it is evident that *discourse* itself (as made up of sentences) has an organization through which it appears as the message of another *langue*, which is on a higher level than that of the linguists; discourse has its units, its rules, its "grammar": even though it is composed solely of sentences, discourse should naturally be the object of a second linguistics that goes beyond the sentence. . . . if one must establish a working hypothesis for an analysis whose task is immense and whose materials are infinite, *it is most rational to postulate a homologi-*

*cal relationship between sentence and discourse, to the extent that one
sole formal organization probably governs all semiotic systems,* whatever their substances or dimensions: discourse would be a large "sentence" (whose units would not necessarily be made up of sentences),
just as every sentence, within certain limits, is a small "discourse."[9]

Lévi-Strauss, for his part, calls the smallest units of a myth "mythemes." They
share with the "constitutive units" of discourse the property that they are phrases,
yet they are distinct from specifically literary texts in that they do not exhibit any
style.

> Myth is the [mode of discourse] where the formula *traduttore, tradit-*
> *tore* reaches its lowest truth value. . . . Its substance does not lie in
> its style, [its mode of narration], or its syntax, but in the *story* which it
> tells. (*SA*, 206)

This property makes them even more similar to the constitutive units of a merely
formal system of rules, as that of *langue*; for *langue*, too, absolutely ignores the
individual manner of *how* the individual speakers realize their linguistic competence.

In order to remain within the bounds of the analogy (Barthes says: homology)
between mythemes and lower-level linguistic units, myth analysis must observe
the same principles of abstraction as phonology. For the phonologists, the theoreticians of speech sounds and their distinctiveness from other sounds, the phoneme
is not a concrete sound or tone that can be measured and grasped in its acoustic
reality. The phoneme is much rather a certain function at whose definition one
arrives by means of the "commutative method" (i.e., according to the law of substitution or nonsubstitution by another phoneme), and whose value consists in the
fact that it distinguishes itself from (or in opposition to) all other values. Saussure
was sufficiently clear on this point.

> In addition, it is impossible for sound alone, a material element, to be-
> long to language. . . . This is even more true of the linguistic sig-
> nifier, which is not phonic but incorporeal — constituted not by its mate-
> rial substance but by the differences that separate its sound-image from
> all others. (*CGL*, 118–19)[10]

In this sense the phoneme is for Saussure a pure form, no *substance d'expression*,
i.e., a play of contrasting relations without material essence. In precise analogy
to this, a mytheme is not one of the concrete (stylistically, phonetically, or
narrative-technically qualified) phrases of a myth, but rather an "oppositional
value" that can correspond to individual phrases that are realized in very different
ways in the mythic narrative.

According to this selection process, "bundles of such relations" (*SA*, 207) are
generated, that is, columns of phrases that belong together, not because of their

respective individual content, but because they serve the same function. Like the elements of the periodic table, they are vertically aligned in a column according to their valence, and, at the same time, they contrast on all levels with the horizontally facing elements by virtue of shared qualities (valences). In other words, it is not the content of the phrases that determines their membership in a column but rather the fact that they stand in functional contrast to certain other mythemes.

> It is only as bundles that these relations can be put to use and combined so as to produce a meaning. Relations pertaining to the same bundle may appear diachronically at remote intervals, but when we have succeeded in grouping them together we have reorganized our myth according to a time referent of a new nature, corresponding to the prerequisite of the initial hypothesis, namely a two-dimensional time referent which is simultaneously diachronic and synchronic, and which accordingly integrates the characteristics of *langue* on the one hand, and those of *parole* on the other. (*SA*, 207–8)

Let me briefly summarize how Lévi-Strauss illustrates his method using the example of the story of Oedipus. It is characteristic for his approach, for Lévi-Strauss is not a classical philologist; his field of study is the myths of the Indians displaced to the tropics. Well, he arranges four vertical columns in which he distributes according to certain criteria of content – which, to be sure, are entirely independent of their actual narrative succession – all the phrases that make up the myth. In the first column are placed all the phrases (mythemes) that deal with an overrated blood relationship (for example, Oedipus marries his mother, Jocasta; Antigone places blood relation above civil solidarity and buries her brother, Polynices, who is a political aggressor; etc.). In the second column are placed all events that, in contrast to the first, deal with an underrated or ridiculed blood relation (Oedipus kills his father; Eteocles kills his brother, Polynices). To the third column are assigned the monsters that appear in the myth, including the manner in which they are combatted (sphinxes and dragons). In the fourth column, finally, are gathered all proper names occurring in the myth that address a difficulty in walking upright: being lame, awkward, or having a swollen foot, etc. (*Oidi-pûs*, literally translated, means "swollen foot.")

With this the hermeneutical ground, from which further interpretation can proceed, is prepared. As soon as the table is filled in we can engage in a first comparative analysis. Comparison of the four columns brings to light a correlation: between the first and the second there exist correlations insofar as they sometimes overrate, sometimes underrate blood relationships; the third and fourth columns are correlated by a sometimes asserted, sometimes denied autochthonous origin of the human being.[11]

Lévi-Strauss evaluates these correlations in this way:

It follows that column four is to column three as column one is to column two. . . . By a correlation of this type, the overrating of blood relations is to the underrating of blood relations as the attempt to escape autochthony is to the impossibility to succeed in it. (*SA*, 212)

In other words, blood relation, the maternal principle, is victorious over the violent attempt to overcome it (thus father and brother are killed); just as the principle of the earth, the swollen foot, proves itself superior by means of the victory over the sphinx/mother.

The myth thus appears as a kind of logical instrument that groups certain contradictions in order to surmount them in the end.

The inability to connect two kinds of relationships is overcome (or rather replaced) by the assertion that contradictory relationships are identical inasmuch as they are both self-contradictory in a similar way. (*SA*, 212)

This result may seem obscure – like much of that which has recently come to us from across the French border. But that is immaterial. In any case, you will no doubt agree that the chosen method of analysis clearly deserves to be called rational and that it invites imitation, for example, within the framework of other interpretations of myths or fairy tales. That has actually happened frequently and, in some cases, with considerable success; and we can certainly say that some progress was made with regard to the transparency of interpretive procedures that otherwise were subjugated to so-called intuition or to a subjective interpretation in the bad sense of the word.

We can, of course, ask ourselves from a *hermeneutical* standpoint whether Lévi-Strauss's method of discourse *analysis*, which he outlined in "La structure des mythes" and applied with great intelligence, indeed with genius, in his principal work, the *Mythologiques*, is actually tenable as a *scientific* alternative to the classical procedure of *interpretation*, or whether the construction of tables that appear to serve a purely analytic-formalistic end is not itself rather the result of what is basically *semantic interpretation of texts*. This is not the place, however, to pursue this.

In conclusion I would like to direct your attention to a completely different issue, namely, the extent to which the procedure introduced by Claude Lévi-Strauss deserves the name "classical structuralism," for it is as the illustration of this that I briefly presented it to you. You may recall that for a first and rough characterization of this phenomenon I drew on a comparison with the crystal lattice: it was meant to shed light on the similarity between the conception the mineralogist has of his object and that of the taxonomist of language, or, for that matter, of discourse (or myth). And, in fact, Lévi-Strauss admits at the conclusion of his essay that he too was inspired by the model of the crystal lattice.

If this is the case, we should assume that it closely corresponds, in the realm of the spoken word, to a crystal in the realm of physical matter. This analogy may help us to better understand the relationship of myth to both *langue* on the one hand and *parole* on the other. Myth is an intermediary entity between a statistical aggregate of molecules and the molecular structure itself. (*SA*, 226–27)

To be sure, molecular structure adheres even more strictly to regularity than the structure of a crystal seems to. A crystal displays irregularities, distortions, displacements, etc., which accounts for the fact that no matter how similar, two crystals are never completely identical. This also applies to myths, which, indeed, *not only* reproduce an identical scheme, but which at the same time are also charged with new meanings in ever new social and historical circumstances. Let's not forget that myth is *also* a diachronic narrative that extends linearly and is not only realized in the structural correlation of groups of relations. Yet it is precisely this that does not play a decisive role for Lévi-Strauss: in his search for the *invariant structures of the human mind* he emphasizes that the contents, which serve in each case as a means for filling out the scheme, are arbitrary and are of account only as transformations of identical functional values. This is also valid for the supposedly decisive leap the human mind accomplished when crossing the threshold from mythic to scientific thought.

> If our interpretation is correct, we are led toward a completely different view – namely, that the kind of logic in mythical thought is as rigorous as that of modern science, and that the difference lies, not in the quality of the intellectual process, but in the nature of the things to which it is applied. This is well in agreement with the situation known to prevail in the field of technology: What makes a steel ax superior to a stone ax is not that the first one is better made than the second. They are equally well made, but steel is quite different from stone. In the same way we may be able to show that the same logical processes operate in myth as in science, and that man has always been thinking equally well; the improvement lies, not in an alleged progress of man's mind, but in the discovery of new areas to which it may apply its unchanged and unchanging powers. (*SA*, 227)

We don't want to judge here how realistic this claim is and how favorably or unfavorably we are disposed toward its implicit ethics; we only want to highlight that characteristic feature of Lévi-Strauss's work that finds its emblem in the metaphor of the crystal and in the distinction between "hot" and "cold" societies. The structures of discourses are, with the exception of their semantics, invariant. Moreover, the history of mankind is essentially "cold" beneath the surface appearance that gives us the image of constantly "hot" revolutions and changes; i.e., it is a series of transformations of identical functions. The crystal and the steady low temperature that impedes the melting and swarming out of molecules that are bonded in a lattice are *the emblems of taxonomical structuralism*. Taxonomy paints the picture of a history of mankind that is heading toward the absolute freezing point: its aim—the wish-fulfillment dream of the structuralist—is death by hypothermia.

We will see in the next lecture the objections neostructuralism brings against this model and how, without reinstating the former dignity of the old European subject, it brings back into play the experiences of revolution, subversion, and "hot" histories.

Lecture 4

To give you an idea of what, in an abbreviated form, I am calling "classical structuralism" I have referred mainly to two works and two authors: Ferdinand de Saussure and Claude Lévi-Strauss. The former was the first to develop the idea of a structural semiology; the latter was the first to extend it beyond the boundaries of linguistics to include the spectrum of the human sciences in general. To be sure, numerous other persons (and works) could be mentioned: for example, Algirdas Julien Greimas, who first developed the idea of a "structural semantics" and applied structural procedures to literary texts; or Gérard Genette, who on this basis brought literary history, genre theory, and rhetoric into the spectrum of structuralism; or Roland Barthes, who, following Greimas, first made structuralism popular for textual criticism. Nevertheless, it is true that it was above all Saussure and Lévi-Strauss who succeeded in emitting the most decisive impulses and whose names are invoked most frequently in that critical movement that wants to disengage itself from structuralism and that we have provisionally introduced as "neostructuralism." This is true for the work of Lacan as well as for that of Foucault and Derrida.

I indicated earlier that the transition from classical structuralism to neostructuralism was accomplished on the basis of an opening up of the concept of structure. One can observe this turn already in Lévi-Strauss's later works, especially in the "Overture" and in the "Finale" of his *Mythologiques*. Here Lévi-Strauss contradicts the "Cartesian principle" according to which scientific study must uncover in all myths manifestations of one and only one principle.[1] This expectation, says Lévi-Strauss, will be disappointed. Myth analysis is much rather comparable to the work of Penelope.

> There is no real end to mythological analysis, no hidden unity to be grasped once the breaking-down process has been completed. Themes can be split up *ad infinitum*. Just when you think you have disentangled and separated them, you realize that they are knitting together again in response to the operation of unexpected affinities. Consequently the unity of the myth is never more than tendential and projective and cannot reflect a state or a particular moment of the myth. It is a phenomenon of the imagination, resulting from the attempt at interpretation; and its function is to endow the myth with synthetic form and to prevent its disintegration into a confusion of opposites. The science of myths might therefore be termed "anaclastic," if we take this old term in the broader etymological sense which includes the study of both reflected rays and broken rays. But unlike philosophical reflection, which claims to go back to its own source, the reflections we are dealing with here concern rays whose only source is hypothetical. Divergence of sequences and themes is a fundamental characteristic of mythological thought, which manifests itself as an irradiation; by measuring the directions and angles of the rays, we are led to postulate their common origin, as an ideal point on which those deflected by the structure of the myth would have converged had they not started, precisely, from some other point and remained parallel throughout their entire course. (*SM 1*, 5–6)

In this passage, it seems, we come across a considerable reinterpretation of the mode of Being of (mythic) structures. Lévi-Strauss at this point seems to be denying that there is something like an organizing center in which the threads of mythic texture converge or at which the texture is joined. Myths, he rather asserts, never allow the unity of their organization to be seen; this unity has only a tendential or projective character. "If it has any unity, that unity will appear only behind or beyond the text and, in the best hypothesis"—and now follows what could almost be a reception-hermeneutical perspective—"in the best hypothesis, will become a reality in the mind of the reader" (*SM 1*, 6).

Before we draw rash conclusions from this argument (in the direction of a neo-structuralist turn) we have to take a closer look at Lévi-Strauss's formulation. It all depends on whether he denies *myth* or the *structure* of myth an organizing unity, a quasi-transcendental principle that governs its organization. The preceding passage clearly only mentions the missing unity of *myth* and, to be more precise, the "divergence of sequences and themes" of myth. If this is the case, then this text expresses basically what we could already read at the end of "The Structural Study of Myths." There he said:

> And since the purpose of myth is to provide a logical model capable of overcoming a contradiction (an impossible achievement if, as it hap-

pens, the contradiction is real), a theoretically infinite number of slates will be generated, each one slightly different from the others. (*SA*, 226)

This slight difference that separates *one* slate, on which the mythologist identified the structure of the myth, from another slate actually does not affect the "logical model" itself, which remains identical in all myths, different as they might be; rather it affects the changing contents in which this model is realized. And only in this sense is the assertion valid that the unity of myth is only tendential or projective: a narrative that is never wholly complete and that is only completed transitorily in our respective readings.

If this, then, is also applicable to the passage from the "Overture" of the *Mythologiques*, to talk about a decentrality of myth would be only a metaphor for a structural order that is transformational. You remember that we understood a transformation to be the spectrum of content distributions for the same function. At most a transformational structure could be without unity in the sense that the chain of contents or meanings, which in any single instance can occupy the same value, cannot be determined a priori, and in this sense it is infinite and without unity. The structure of values itself, however, would still be thoroughly unified and closed, although it would be constantly subject to the insertion of new contents and new inscriptions. This seems to me to be what Lévi-Strauss actually believes. "What I have tried to give is a syntax of South American mythology" (*SM 1*, 7–8). "Syntax" here means the totality of rules governing the reciprocal connections between signs. Lévi-Strauss even wants us to ignore the semantic side of the signs that are to be connected. Precisely this is the essence of the structural demarche that sets pure form above substance. A structural syntax, therefore, does not need to pay attention to every possible single event, just as a person who is writing a structural grammar of French does not necessarily have to have collected all sentences ever heard or uttered in French. On the contrary, once the fundamentals of a structural syntax are worked out, one can even make a judgment based on them as to whether a single mytheme is actually a case of the underlying (deep) structure that guarantees the reciprocal translatability of all conceivable myths one into the other. I will give you another short passage from the "Overture" that illustrates this.

Mythological patterns have to an extreme degree the character of absolute objects, which would neither lose their old elements nor acquire new ones if they were not affected by external influences. The result is that when the pattern undergoes some kind of transformation, all its aspects are affected at once. And so if one aspect of a particular myth seems unintelligible, it can be legitimately dealt with, in the preliminary stage and on the hypothetical level, as a transformation of the homologous aspect of another myth, which has been linked with the same group for the sake of the argument, and which lends itself more readily to interpretation. This I have done on more than one occasion. (*SM 1*, 13).

A classical case of transformation: if, while one is in the process of structuring a myth, one comes across an element that is difficult or impossible to integrate in it and, at the same time, one is far enough advanced in the formulation of a deep syntax, one may confidently replace this disturbing element with one that has the same valence (in the structural sense of the word), but which fits the content better. Lévi-Strauss, whose brilliant style constantly has to cover up the inexactness of his terminology, proposes the following definitional convention:

> I propose to give the name *armature* to a combination of properties that remain invariant in two or several myths; *code* to the pattern of functions ascribed by each myth to these properties; and *message* to the subject matter of an individual myth. (*SM 1*, 199)

This means that the identity of the code, of the system of functions, allows completely different frameworks, i.e., inscriptions of content. Schelling's *Philosophy of Mythology* supplies us with brilliant illustrations for this procedure: depending on the alternating points of view, Demeter is Persephone's mother, and, at the same time, born later than her; or she is Poseidon's wife, and his parent as well; or she is Zeus's wife, although he, however, is only born after her, etc.[2] Thus the same content can, with regard to the function it fulfills at a given moment, occupy completely different *values* of the mythic syntax, which, for its part, remains always identical — as code.

Yet in the "Finale," the final piece of the *Mythologiques* entitled *The Naked Man* (from 1971), there are formulations that go a step further than those in the "Overture." Let's recall our question: is there a unity of structure, or does one have to conceive the concept of structure as open? In a first attempt to broach this issue we went as far as to say that the openness of the mythic framework does not endanger, or does not have to endanger, the unity of structure. To this extent we were within the realm of transformational structuralism. Lévi-Strauss, however, had, at the same time — and even as early as the "Overture" — excluded Cartesianism and with it also the idea that at the control panel of the organization of structure there sits a subject, regardless of whether we interpret it as an individual, as the subject of the human race, or as "national spirit." Lévi-Strauss accepts it when Paul Ricoeur calls his structuralism a "Kantism without a transcendental subject."[3] That means that there is an order in myths, but this order is not the work of an ordering and self-conscious subjectivity. Neither is there an adequate reflection of myth by the subjects who hand it down, just as no reflective mastery of the phonological apparatus of a language is required for speakers of that language to use it correctly. We already noted earlier that Lévi-Strauss considered this feature, the *unconsciousness* of the rules of the code, to be Saussure's and Troubetzkoy's central discovery. He then arrives at a conclusion that we will have to examine in the light of our question about the unity of structure.

> It is the same with myths as with language: the individual who conscientiously applied phonological and grammatical laws in his speech . . . would nevertheless lose the thread of his ideas almost immediately. In the same way the practice and the use of mythological thought demand that its properties remain hidden. . . . I therefore claim to show, not how men think in myths, but how myths operate in men's minds without their being aware of the fact. (*SM 1*, 11–12)

Here we come across a formulation that seems strange on first sight and for which neostructuralism will supply us with innumerable variations: myth, language, text, they all speak themselves; it is not the subject that, as their author, speaks them. This formulation in part appeals to similar statements by symbolist poets (Mallarmé, for example), in part to Heideggers's "language speaks." Before we ask ourselves whether those who make such formulations understand themselves, let's shed some light on the function of this formulation. Apparently, in this drastic metaphor, the possibility of considering the speaking subject or the subject that hands down myth as the originator of linguistic or mythic structure is supposed to be eliminated. And this indeed contradicts a central aspect of modern metaphysics. For the time being, let's leave this observation as it is without examining its plausibility. At this point we are mainly interested in the fact that the statement "man is structured by structure itself" contradicts a certain idea about the origin of the *unity* of this structure: *if* there is a unity of structure, then it is not—as in the world of Immanuel Kant and German idealism—a precipitate of the ordering activity of a transcendental subject. Nevertheless, it does have a unity, and Lévi-Strauss acknowledges this when he accepts Ricoeur's comparison of structuralism to a "Kantism without a transcendental subject."

Our question must be as follows: can one think of the unity of a structure without at the same time thinking of a unifying center? Some of Lévi-Strauss's formulations (for example, that of the projective unity of myth that finds its completion in our interpretation or reading) seem to imply that he by all means is thinking of such a principle, itself not structural, which, to be sure, is not a subject. Jacques Derrida anticipated this difficulty, or, to be more cautious, this consequence. In his essay "Structure, Sign, and Play in the Discourse of the Human Sciences," which is written in a particularly clear and readable style, he brings together two observations explicitly directed at Lévi-Strauss.[4] The first claims that the ordering of events according to structures (even before the term "structure" was coined) is as old as the history of scientific knowledge itself, i.e., as old as the West. In his second observation, Derrida adds that the coherence of structure is grounded in the fact that all its elements appear to be directed toward a center of meaning: directed at the very object of all scientific endeavors, namely at truth in all those forms the West has successively attributed to it—as God, as Idea, finally as subjectivity. The question remains, staying for the moment with Lévi-Strauss, whether the idea of a grounding center of meaning itself and as such is overcome by excluding subjectivity as the unifying center from this chain of paradigms, or whether it reappears in disguised form. "Even today," Derrida believes, "the notion of a structure lacking any center represents the unthinkable itself" (WD, 297). Let's see first what the later Lévi-Strauss (I mean the author of the "Finale" of the *Mythologiques*) has to say concerning this question. First he takes up, this time in more radical fashion, what he already addressed in his "Overture," i.e., the question of the anonymity of mythic thought that is the work of nobody. The notion of "anonymous thought," he continues,

> also indicated a deeper concern to reduce the subject to what, in an undertaking of this kind, he ought to try to be—if indeed he can ever, in any circumstances, be anything else: the insubstantial place or space where anonymous thought can develop, stand back from itself, find and fulfil its true tendencies and achieve organization, while coming to terms with the constraints inherent in its very nature.[5]

The removal of the subject from a place where it plays no role, i.e., from the anonymous code Lévi-Strauss also calls the activity of the unconscious mind, in no way means that one has to give up one's scientific knowledge interests. On the contrary:

> The subject, while remaining deliberately in the background so as to allow free play to this anonymous deployment of discourse, does not renounce consciousness of it, or rather does not prevent it achieving consciousness of itself through him. Some people pretend to believe that the criticism of consciousness should lead, logically, to the renunciation of conscious thought. But I have never had any other intention than to further knowledge, i.e., *to achieve consciousness*. However, for too long now philosophy has succeeded in locking the social sciences inside a closed circle by not allowing them to envisage any other object of study for the consciousness than consciousness itself. This accounts, on the one hand, for the powerlessness of the social sciences in practice, and on the other for their self-deluding nature, the characteristic of consciousness being that it deceives itself [about itself, as is well-known since Rousseau, Marx, Durkheim, Saussure, and Freud]. (SM 4, 629)

This passage displays a characteristic movement: consciousness, stepping outside of structure, is promised compensation for its dethronement. It is as though one whispered in its ear, give yourself up and you will be regenerated. In other words, the structural human sciences promise the subject, which under the eye of self-reflection (i.e., under the conditions of modern metaphysics) could not achieve any useful knowledge about itself, that it can gain such knowledge if it dissolves itself like a spider in the web of structuralism, the order of which can then be scientifically studied. But precisely this movement only repeats the movement of an essential Hegelian self-reflection: consciousness renounces itself to enter into the nonconscious; thereby it becomes its own object and now knows under what law it exists. This knowledge is nothing other than the return from the state of self-renunciation to the state of absolute self-consciousness.

Formulated in this manner, the thinking of Lévi-Strauss seems to promise very little hope of an overcoming of metaphysics and its central operator, the concept of the subject, which apparently he would like to achieve. In the end he admits that after having studied myth for twenty years he is supported in his conviction that

> the consciousness of the self, the major preoccupation of the whole of Western philosophy, does not withstand persistent application to the same object, which comes to pervade it through and through and to imbue it with an experiential awareness of its own unreality. For the only remnant of reality to which it still dares to lay claim is that of being a "singularity," in the sense in which astronomers use the term. (*SM 4*, 625; translation slightly modified)

Here that sense of the world is already expressed that so pathetically resounds from the last lines of Foucault's *The Order of Things*:

> If those arrangements were to disappear as they appeared, if some event of which we can at the moment do no more than sense the possibility — without knowing either what its form will be or what it promises — were to cause them to crumble, as the ground of Classical thought did, at the end of the eighteenth century, then one can certainly wager that man would be erased, like a face drawn in sand at the edge of the sea.[6]

In both statements, Foucault's as well as Lévi-Strauss's, it is not thinking (let's say, science) that resigns; rather *an episteme* that was in the service of the modern subject gives way to *another one* to which the subject no longer lays claim.

What are the consequences of this for the possible unity of the structure or the *episteme*? Lévi-Strauss has to admit, at least, that there is not only *one*, for if there were only one, then that scientific progress that elevates the structural *episteme* above the modern-day theory of the subject would be uncontrollable. Modern theory of the subject has considered itself the definitive truth of European intellectual history. At least in this point structuralism on the verge of becoming neostructuralism has a historical consciousness that is more acute: it understands itself as a theory of the succession of *epistemes* or structures in analogy to Heidegger's history of interpretations of Being in ever-new images of the world and ever-new philosophies. Only one thing is forbidden to this theory of history (at the price of a relapse into the model of the subject): that is the idea that the structures themselves are generated out of something that is itself nonstructural. The hermeneuticist Friedrich Schleiermacher had already eliminated this possibility of retreat with the phrase: "No newly discovered form is absolutely new."[7] Lévi-Strauss gives voice to a similar conviction.

> Each anterior state of a structure is itself a structure. . . . The process consists of structures which are undergoing transformation to produce other structures, so the *structure itself is a primordial fact*. Less confusion would have occurred in connection with the concept of human nature, that I continue to use, if it had been realized that I do not take it in the sense of a heap of completed and immutable structures, but rather with the meaning of matrices giving rise to structures all belonging to the same set, without necessarily remaining identical throughout any individual existence from birth to adulthood, or, in the case of human groups, at all times and in all places. (*SM 4*, 627)

An ambiguity that is characteristic for Lévi-Strauss permeates this passage. On the one hand, in the first volume of his *Mythologiques* he rigidly distinguished between the code or structure (both of which are unalterable), and the framework of myths (which constantly changes). Now he suddenly asserts the alterability of structures themselves—not in the sense that over the period of historical evolution a structure could ever have been generated out of nothing, as it were, or out of the deed of an understanding subject, but rather in the sense that the constellation of structures is in constant change. If one formulates it this way, one cannot avoid the consequence that *therefore* also the respective *unity* of structure(s) is altered as well. And at this point of our interpretation the text pulls the rug out from under us. For precisely here Lévi-Strauss brings into play the well-known concept of *transformation*, about which we already know that it affects only the content and meaning of a semiological system, not its values. Now both cannot be the case: first, that we are only dealing with transformations, and second, that the transformations alter the structures. Promptly, a subordinated concept surfaces in the text, namely, that of "matrices giving rise to structures all belonging to the same set." In short, the earlier concept of a framework is dissolved into that of structure, and the earlier concept of structure is dissolved into that of a matrix, which remains identical and establishes continuity throughout all transformations. The apparent infinity of the succession of structures turns out to be the old and familiar infinity of contents that one can attribute, one after another, to one and the same semiological value. Even the interpretation of myths belongs in this chain. "It takes its place in sequence after the already known variants of that myth" (*SM 4*, 628); and to clarify what he means, he himself refers to the already cited passage from *Structural Anthropology* (226). With that the return to the model of transformational structuralism is begun.

What are the consequences of this for the unity and/or openness of structure? If the succession of structures is accomplished within the framework of a continuity controlled by matrices, then one cannot possibly avoid the notion of a unity and a center of meaning for structure. One would not even be able scientifically to describe and analyze a structure whose elements, as it were, wander about and swarm out instead of sitting still and remaining where they are. To be sure, something is wandering about and constantly sliding, and Lévi-Strauss knows this well. It is the contents through which humankind—within the framework of an identical structure—comes to terms with the permanently changing demands of its situation and its history. In this way the semantic unity of myths is, as it were, constantly diverted by the peculiarities of the stories in whose guise they present themselves, and by the peculiarities of the sociohistoric constellations reflected in the respective mythic narratives; this diversion, however, remains within the framework of a systematic continuum. A final quote from Lévi-Strauss makes clear the extent to which his theory is held hostage to metaphysics.

> Each version of the myth, then, shows the influence of a twofold determinism: one strand links it to a succession of previous versions or to a set of foreign versions, while the other operates as it were transversally, through the constraints arising from the infrastructure which necessitate the modification of some particular element, with the result that the system undergoes reorganization in order to adapt these differences to necessities of an external kind. (*SM 4*, 628–29)

With this Lévi-Strauss gives an almost classical paraphrase of what Jean Piaget called a system of self-regulation. In order to come to terms with a constantly changing environment, the game marks of structure have to be exchanged constantly for ones that better stand up to the situation or interpret it more precisely. The exchanged marks, however, are always inserted into the same position; i.e., they reveal themselves to be what they essentially always were: variations or transformations of a structure identical according to its *form*. Thus, in the end, the structuralist principle that a semiological system is a pure form and not a substance wins out over the objections of historicity and the openness of contents.

However, what if structure in reality were missing a center? What if transformation emancipated itself from the crystal lattice and actually, not only terminologically, corroded the order of discourse; and what if the power of historicity, which destroys identity, were to intrude into the interior of the structure? Then we would be standing on the ground of a theory that does not speak from within the bounds of classical structuralism, but rather oversteps these bounds. We would stand on the ground of what in this series of lectures is called neostructuralism.

We saw that Lévi-Strauss himself displays a certain ambiguity concerning the question of whether structures indeed possess no organizing center. On the one hand, he displaces the unity of mythic structure into the imaginary, or into the mind of the reader; on the other hand, he characterizes the differences between various versions and/or readings of a myth as transformations of one and the same *set* of matrices that remain formally identical within the changing "frameworks." This ambiguity only vanishes in the *Sémantique structurale* of Greimas, who, without hesitation, speaks of a "total meaning" of structure (*sens total, significa-tion intégrale*).[8] According to him the process of text structuring goes through several levels of constitution, corresponding to what we know from Benveniste: first, the level that combines elementary particles of meaning (semes) in the syn-thesis of a lexeme/sememe; second, the "classematical" level (i.e., the level of lexical units in the meaning context of a phrase); third, the level of what he calls "isotopes" (a level of coherence, whose elements are recurring and semantically *recognized* classemes); and fourth and finally, the level of totality of signification. Let's concentrate completely on the claim put forward when he talks about a total-ity of meaning of the text. It implies nothing less than that textual analysis—to be sure, over several steps—eventually arrives at the discovery of a simple totality of meaning, the understanding of which allows for the text to be masterable *in nuce*. Precisely this would be the center of meaning, the principle, as it were, that permits the structuring of meaning to produce this particular text; just as in an idealist system everything that follows is a necessary consequence of *one* princi-ple, even if, as in Hegel, this principle can be recognized in all its simplicity only in retrospect. In Greimas, classical structuralism reveals particularly clearly its indebtedness to the project of exact science, the latest manifestation of what Heidegger and neostructuralism call metaphysics.

We do not as yet know much about the meaning of the concept of "metaphysics." We are already aware, however, of three pieces of information that we want to recall here: the first states that "metaphysics" means the belief in the subsistence of a transsensual world; the second interprets "metaphysics" as a thinking on the basis of principles; the third seeks to unmask "metaphysics" as a knowledge for mastery. It can easily be seen how these three interpretations connect: those who assert a metabeing over against being hope with this assertion somehow to escape the claim of being—its realm is beyond our world or cannot be entirely absorbed by it. Those who think on the basis of principles hold being under the control of thought: nothing may be taken as correct that has not first passed examination *before* and *on* the principle (for example, the principle of *cogito sum*). The immediate consequence of this is that metaphysics, including the procedures of technology and science, is knowledge for mastery: a special form of what Nietzsche called the "will to power," in the form of the "will to truth," i.e., a form of knowledge that, by controlling being, seeks to master it in the name of the recognizing intellect. Structuralism shares with metaphysics, as we stated earlier, this desire for control and mastery.

Let's recall at this point the question Derrida asked in "Structure, Sign, and

Play": what if the will of metaphysics were grounded in an untenable assumption, namely, that the structures in which being is disclosed to us as a meaningful context are results of constructive actions that, for their part, are grounded in a principle? What if, in other words, structure were decentral? "And even today," Derrida agrees, "the notion of a structure lacking any center represents the unthinkable itself" (WD, 279). For where would we end up if the transcendental place from whence the threads of the structure or of the text are woven to this or that discursive formation were not itself firm and independent of the process of structuring?

Somewhere, I do not recall exactly in which text, Roland Barthes picks up the (biologically somewhat daring) metaphor of a spinning spider that dissolves itself, as it were, into its web. This metaphor could be taken as the radical consequence of Saussure's argument that there are meaning and significance only in the play of distinct sounds. If one develops this thesis further, one would have to conclude that a supposed center of structure, insofar as it is conceived as center of *meaning* (as *signifié transcendantal*), cannot possibly be located within or outside structure. *If* it has a distinct meaning, it can only have this distinct meaning in the differential play of structure itself, i.e., in its difference from other marks of structure. If this is the case, then this distinct meaning cannot be considered central, for it belongs to a structure whose values are all decentral and disseminal as long as this statement is true: all determinateness of meaning is grounded in differences, "omnis determinatio est negatio" ("negation" here understood in the sense of "determined negation," meaning "being different than"). Should meaning, on the other hand, which, like a principle, or (to remain within our metaphor), like a woven pattern, organizes the texture of structure/text indeed be *central*, then it would be impossible to think it, i.e., to distinguish it. It would thus not participate in the distinctions of structure itself: as extrastructural place it would be a nonplace, an *ou tópos*, a utopia.

> Thus it has always been thought that the center, which is by definition unique, constituted that very thing within a structure which while governing the structure, escapes structurality. This is why classical thought concerning structure could say that the center is, paradoxically, *within* the structure and *outside it*. The center is at the center of the totality, and yet, since the center does not belong to the totality (is not part of the totality), the totality *has its center elsewhere*. (WD, 279)

I would like to illustrate with an example this paradox, which is characteristic for many—Derrida would say, for all—great thought systems of Western philosophy. In Fichte's *Science of Knowledge* it is articulated in particularly drastic fashion. On the one hand, Fichte says, subjectivity, which creates world and meaning, is somewhat outside the system, for, as we know, it creates it. To this extent it may be called absolute, a term that, translated literally, means "unconditioned."

On the other hand, Fichte knew quite well that there is determinateness only where there is difference: without imagining something that in itself is *not*-I, I would never be able to grasp the thought of "I" in its determinateness. This insight Fichte also calls "the law of reflection of all our knowledge [*Erkenntnis*]: namely, nothing is recognized as what it is, without thinking at the same time what it is *not*."[9] And he adds: "And precisely this characteristic of our knowledge, to recognize something by means of its opposite, means *to determine* something."[10] Well, "this characteristic of our knowledge," as formulated by the law of reflection, does not exclude the most fundamental of all thoughts, that of the world-creating "I." For when I ask somebody to think *him- or herself*, then I require that person to really concentrate in this moment on *him- or herself* and during that time to keep everything else out of his or her mind. I say, Think yourself, and to this extent do not think anything else, and thus do not think: not-I.[11]

The paradox I would like to direct your attention to consists in the following: on the one hand, the I is supposed to be absolute, a thought that does not need any other thought to be executed (for if it needed another, it would be relative, i.e., referring to something else); on the other hand, "I" cannot be thought as determinate without contrasting it with something else that is not-I. In Derrida's mode of speaking one could say the I must be simultaneously *outside* structure— as its principle or *sens transcendantal*—in order to be able to ground it, and it must be *inside* structure, for otherwise it would have no "value," i.e., no determinateness as opposed to other just as conceivable thoughts.

Derrida believes this paradox to be characteristic of a certain "desire" (*désir*), as he calls it, which lurks in the background of all scientific systems.

> The concept of centered structure is in fact the concept of a play based on a fundamental ground, a play constituted on the basis of a fundamental immobility and a reassuring certitude, which itself is beyond the reach of play. And on the basis of this certitude anxiety can be mastered, for anxiety is invariably the result of a certain mode of being implicated in the game, of being caught by the game, of being as it were at stake in the game from the outset. (*WD*, 279)

One can, I believe, easily grasp what he means. If there were no authority outside structure and outside its play "of pure differences" (as Saussure called it), then, we fear, we would be literally and hopelessly caught in the occurrence of structuring. There would be no meaning and no origin and thus also no purpose *beyond* what the structural context of assignments and references made possible. What the apostle says about the Holy Ghost would apply to structure itself (in an entirely secular sense, of course): in it we live, weave, and are.

To strip this sentence of all theological meaning is at the same time to strip away its metaphysical implications. Derrida, following in Heidegger's footsteps, considers as "metaphysical" every interpretation of being as such and as a whole that wants to ground its *meaning* on a principle that is superior to, indeed, re-moved from that being itself. To be sure, there is nothing in this thought that is stupendous or unintelligible, for it is true of the Platonic idea, as well as of the Christian God, Hegel's spirit, and even of scientific abstraction that they explain what is by relating it to something other, which, in comparison with being in the emphatic sense, is relatively *not* (it is even then *not*, if it declares in a grand inver-sion this relative not-being as the authentic being—τὸ ὄντως ὄν). The principle, the ground of explanation, or even only the rationality of a recognized structure, always implies the notion of a structuring and itself extrastructural center, and it is precisely this thought, which even Lévi-Strauss cannot escape, that according to Derrida is untenable. There is no transcendental center, whether one under-stands it as tutelary meaning, as the *principal* signified of a text, or as major refer-ent (*P*, 45). (I am, by the way, using the expression "transcendental" here and in what follows in an entirely general sense, referring to the condition of some-thing that itself is not, but that by virtue of it comes into being [*ins Dasein tritt*]. Applied to the principle of structure this means that the structuring principle brings about—like the pattern of knitting instructions—the construction of the structure; with relation to the knitting itself, however, it has no absolute exis-tence. Principles allow things to exist, but they do not exist in the same sense as that which they serve as the principle to.)

At this point you perhaps want to interject the following: is it really so impor-tant whether the structure has a center or not? As long as it gives us a framework within which we can orient our endangered lives it serves its purpose, even with-out a principle in the background. It protects us as the "mighty fortress," as relia-ble and stable context of meaning, from the "anxiety" of constant incalculables. It is perhaps this soothing character of structure, which is conceived as enclosed in itself, that has led many intellectuals to turn to structuralism with a certain satis-faction. For behind the abstraction, which in itself would not call forth en-thusiasm, one has always to assume that a passion is evident if it builds up to a movement, for example, the passion for being able to orient one's life in and by means of thought.

Derrida now points out to us the unsettling fact that the unimpedable flow of time, which until now was hardly even mentioned, does in fact imprint its traces onto the mighty fortress of the principle, or even onto the self-enclosed structure. If one looks at the history of culture and philosophy, one finds that the names for the center or principle of the respective structures of *Dasein* have constantly changed. At times it was water, at other times the flickering fire, or at still other times spirit that was said to be the highest principle. Then again there were times when it was the idea of the good, energy, the unifying principle, God, rationality, and finally subjectivity, the will to power, or technology.

From this observation Derrida draws the conclusion—or, to be more cautious, he developed his suspicion—that there is no such thing as the simplicity or timeless presence of such a structuring principle. He further contests that, even if one renounces the idea of a centering principle (as does the later Lévi-Strauss), the power of history exhausts itself in always only triggering transformations of a structure that in its depth remains formally identical. On the contrary, structures can decompose, and this can even affect their form; the changes are more than mere transformations of the always identical.

To back up his suspicion Derrida supplies us with an empirical-historical and a systematic reason. First the empirical one: If there is something like a center of the structure of an *episteme*, why doesn't it remain the same once and for all? Why is it always succeeded and replaced by new candidates for the position of the center?

> Successively, and in a regulated fashion, the center receives different forms or names. The history of metaphysics, like the history of the West, is the history of these metaphors and metonymies. Its matrix—if you will pardon me for demonstrating so little and for being so elliptical in order to come more quickly to my principal theme—is the determination of Being as *presence* in all senses of this word. It could be shown that all the names related to fundamentals, to principles, or to the center have always designated an invariable presence—*eidos, arché, telos, energeia, ousia* (essence, existence, substance, subject) *alétheia*, transcendentality, consciousness, God, man and so forth. (*WD*, 279-80)

Derrida, following Heidegger, emphasizes that the succession of interpretations of Being was always accomplished within the framework of a rule, never blindly or by chance. He emphasizes further that the chain of placeholders of the highest principle (the series of metaphorical and metonymical substitutions for the absence of an authentic and originary meaning of structure) developed within a continuity. They all have in common that they comprehend the meaning of Being as *presence (présence)*; as either a sensual or conceptual being-accessible, being-graspable, or being-attainable of the principle. Yet the main thrust of Derrida's objection seems to me to be in the indicated direction: Derrida confronts metaphysics with the question of how it can concede a nonfinitude of interpretations of Being and, at the same time, hold on to the idea of a structural center. (I am leaving out Hegel's version of metaphysics, which actually holds in reserve a statement as to the historicity of interpretations of Being, at the price, however, of having to take this statement out of historicity itself. The insight into the historicity of all former philosophy is, for its part, no longer historical, but absolute: the center of an absolute structure.)

We are already familiar with the other objection Derrida puts forward against the idea of a principle or a closure (*clôture*) of structure. It is of a systematic nature and maintains that even the signification of a structural principle—in the semantic sense of the word "signification"—cannot escape the law of determination by means of opposition and thus can constitute itself only *within* the referential play of *signifiers* of structure. As a result, one has to give up the idea that the blueprint of structure, its transcendental principle, commandeers structure and keeps it in order from outside of it. One has to concede, on the contrary, that we are, as Derrida says, *entangled* in structures and have no possibility of getting beyond our Being-inside-structures. This objection applies even to Foucault's *Archaeology of Knowledge* and his attempt at multiplying the structural center, while, in the end, merely subduing it by means of discursive regularities. This, at least, is Derrida's view (who otherwise also orients Foucault in the history of metaphysics).

> This is why one perhaps could say that the movement of any archaeology, like that of any eschatology, is an accomplice of this reduction of the structurality of structure and always attempts to conceive of structure on the basis of a full presence which is beyond play. (*WD*, 279)

Now we can hold on to a first result from our occupation with Derrida. By means of a radicalization of the concept of "the structurality of structure," he arrives at a point where he can abandon a fundamental assumption of what we have called classical structuralism, namely, the assumption that there is either a center, or several interdiscursively interwoven centers, or at the very least a formal identity of structure.

Fine, you will say, but what is Derrida's alternative? How would *he* have us think structure? First of all, he introduces a concept of structure, the essence of which is to get along *without* a center. This concept he calls — and with this we come across another major concept of neostructuralism — "decentering," i.e., displacing outside the center. Actually, "decentering" does not mean that formerly there was a center of structure that now, like Louis XVI, is taken to the guillotine in a revolutionary overthrow; rather, the term means that the idea that a structure in its very essence needs a center and a fixed identity is metaphysical (and thus illusionary).

> But a central presence which has never been itself, has always already been exiled from itself into its own substitute. The substitute does not substitute itself for anything which has somehow existed before it. Henceforth, it was necessary to begin thinking that there was no center, that the center could not be thought in the form of a present-being, that the center had no natural site, that it was not a fixed locus but a function, a sort of nonlocus in which an infinite number of sign-substitutions came into play. This was the moment when language invaded the universal problematic, the moment when, in the absence of a center or origin, everything became discourse — provided we can agree on this word — that is to say, a system in which the central signified, the original or transcendental signified, is never absolutely present outside a sys-

tem of differences. The absence of the transcendental signified extends
the domain and the play of signification infinitely. (*WD*, 280)

Let's comment on this passage which is so pregnant with meaning. Its basic theme
is, in short, that if structure in its respective form/order is not secured by an extrastructural principle—and it is not—*then everything is structure and all structurality is an infinite play of differences.* Perhaps the term "play" surprises you;
it comes, however, from Saussure, who not only liked to compare language to
a chess game, but also spoke of a "play of differences." The totality of all differential plays is structure. Thus when Derrida says that "everything is structure," he
does not mean that everything is taxonomy, but rather, every meaning, every signification, and every view of the world is in flux, nothing can escape the play of
differences, there is no interpretation of Being and the world that is valid in and
of itself and for all times. "To interpret"—a hint for hermeneutics—therefore does
not mean that we have to track down something like a self-enclosed and fixed signification beneath the textual surface, but rather, as Roland Barthes says, "to appreciate what *plural* constitutes it."[12] Derrida says the same thing in a similar,
yet more fundamental, fashion. If the movement of totalization of a text proves
itself meaningless,

> it is not because the infiniteness of a field cannot be covered by a finite
> glance or a finite discourse, but because the nature of the field—that is,
> language and a finite language—excludes totalization. This field is in
> effect that of *play*, that is to say, a field of infinite substitutions only be-
> cause it is finite, that is to say, because instead of being an inexhausti-
> ble field, as in the classical hypothesis, instead of being too large, there
> is something missing from it: a center which arrests and grounds the
> play of substitutions. (*WD*, 289)

The idea of a self-enclosed totality of the text, as well as the idea of a binding
or objective interpretation, is not hindered by any "effective-historical" prejudices
or by the factor of subjectivity, which is always irksome to science; rather they
fail for structural reasons. They fail because structures can only be thought of as
decentral, and because texts without a center cannot give rise to a "central interpretation," that is, one that goes to the very heart of the text. Derrida introduces
at this point the concept of supplementarity, which is significant for his thought
in general (*WD*, 289). Supplementarity means the fact of a substitution. If there
is no center of structure or of text, then the respective interpretation must *substitute* for this lack with something, namely, with the interpretation itself. This is
a thought Derrida borrowed from Lévi-Strauss.[13] On the occasion of a discussion
of the status of Being of that undifferentiated substance of the holy, of the *mana*,
Lévi-Strauss says:

Mana is in effect all these things. But is it not precisely because it is none of these things that *mana* is a simple form, or more exactly, a symbol in the pure state, and therefore capable of becoming charged with any sort of symbolic content whatever? In the system of symbols constituted by all cosmologies, *mana* would simply be a zero symbolic value, that is to say, a sign marking the necessity of a symbolic content, *supplementary* to that with which the signified is already loaded, but which can take on any value required, provided only that this value still remains part of the available reserve and is not, as phonologists put it, a group-term. (Quoted by Derrida, *WD*, 290)

In the field of art criticism the early German romanticists already recognized this, and they considered literary criticism a supplement to an irreducible blemish in the work of art itself. Derrida comes very close to this thought. "The movement of signification," he says—and let me add that this applies to the movement of interpretation as well—"adds something, which results in the fact that there is always more, but this addition is a floating one because it comes to perform a vicarious function, to supplement a lack on the part of the signified" (*WD*, 289). Each interpretation, indeed, each use of signs, presents, as it were, a suggestion as to how one can replace the missing central meaning of the text and how one can determine it (provisionally, with reservations). Since the central meaning, however, is missing, interpretation is not so much a matter of *finding* (*Finden*) (finding presupposes the presence of something that can be found) as *inventing* (*Erfinden*), i.e., a supplement, an addition to the text. This addition cannot be lasting, for it has no (objective) correlative in the text, it thus has no permanent place. That is why it is given to it to "float."

Lacan found an especially memorable formulation for this discomforting fact when he said that meaning slides underneath its expression or chain of expressions.

From which we can say that it is in the chain of the signifier that the meaning "insists" but that none of its elements "consists" in the signification of which it is at the moment capable. . . . We are forced, then, to accept the notion of an incessant sliding of the signified under the signifier . . . with an image resembling the wavy lines of the upper and lower Waters in miniatures from manuscripts of *Genesis*.[14]

I believe that with this conclusion both the structural model of the *Cours* and the transformational model of Lévi-Strauss are overcome. We are standing on the ground of neostructuralism.

Lecture 5

Our reading of Derrida's essay "Structure, Sign, and Play in the Discourse of the Human Sciences" gave us a first impression of how neostructuralism steps beyond the structural model of classical structuralism. We saw that, above all, he rejects the explicit or implicit assumption that there is something like a principle, a blueprint, or a central meaning that contains, as though in a nutshell, the essence of a structure, be it that of a text or of a *langue*. Now you will rightly say that neither the Saussure of the *Cours* nor Lévi-Strauss explicitly makes use of this idea. Nevertheless, it turns out to be an implication of the taxonomical model of structure whose analogy to the crystal lattice remained a leitmotif throughout our discussion. Even without a central meaning holding together the threads of structure, structure is self-enclosed; for it is *structure* in the first place only insofar as it is a finite context of assignments and references among a finite number of oppositive values. What can be *changed* in a structure are, at the most, the contentual and significational attributions, not the order of values itself (we called this the working hypothesis of "transformational structuralism"). Now Derrida, and also Lacan, launches an attack on the thought of structural closure; the constellation of values is no longer under attack in the name of transformation, but rather in the name of its "structurality" itself.

I promised to explain this attack as a historical event through Lyotard and especially through Foucault. Before one can accomplish something of the sort, however, one has to understand precisely which event is actually in question, and, what is more, how it justifies itself. You will hardly take what I have told you so far for a plausible justification, and you are quite right. Therefore, we should begin by taking a closer look at this attack on the structural model. I will do this on the basis of the interview "Sémiologie et grammatologie," which Derrida granted to Julia Kristeva shortly after his book *De la grammatologie* appeared.[1] In this interview, Derrida not only reiterates in abbreviated form several central theses of his *Grammatology*—and that with a precision and brevity other texts by this author so often are lacking; he also tries to explain his approach by contrasting it with a certain Saussurean tradition that culminates in structuralism. What is interesting here is that he by no means understands himself as an opponent of Saussure, but rather as someone who rescued Saussure's concept of the sign from its last metaphysical connections, and to this extent merely radicalized it.[2] I cannot present this important text in all its details; thus I shall limit my discussion to what seems to me to be most pressing for a first argumentative examination of the phenomenon of neostructuralism.

Derrida first admits that Saussure, with his theory of articulation and differentiality of the sign (which was mainly developed in the fourth chapter of his *Cours*), came very close to what Derrida himself calls the infinite play of signs or "le texte (en) générale." It is mainly two achievements Derrida definitely wants to hold on to: first of all, Saussure's insight into the inseparability of signified and signifier; second, his emphasis on the differential and formal character of the sign-constituting schematism, i.e., on "the *differential* and *formal* character of semiological functioning" (*P*, 18), which deny any relation whatsoever between the material character of the phonic material and *langue*. Derrida then continues: for reasons which I don't (yet) want to discuss, Saussure made certain concessions in his theory. He first of all acceded to the classical-dualistic concept of the sign and thus to its unconscious metaphysical heritage, despite his insight into the fact that this designation can only be a preliminary solution ("As regards *sign*, if I am satisfied with it, this is simply because I do not know of any word to replace it, the ordinary language suggesting no other"; *CGL*, 67).

At this point I have to insert a remark: Derrida was not aware that Saussure, as is recorded in his posthumously published *Notes item*, actually considered replacing his binary concept of the sign with the simple concept of the "seme." The seme no longer subsists as a synthesis of the (seemingly independent) elements *vocal image* and *concept*, but rather only as an immediate effect of differential relations which it has to other semes that subsist alongside it. Saussure calls the differential neighbor-semes "parasemes." Derrida replaces the term "sign" with "mark" for exactly the same reason.

> What should also suffice is the suspicion concerning the *sign* and even concerning the opposition signifier/signified: this suspicion, legible in every line, bears on the entire system that supports this opposition, and consequently, among others, on that of an intention hidden behind the

"visible sign" (the signifier). Hence, the substitution of "mark" for "sign," of intentional effect for intention, etc. (*LI*, 205)

This entanglement in the metaphysical dialectics of signified (*signifié*) on the one hand and signifier (*signifiant*) on the other made it possible for Saussure—and this is Derrida's second observation—to grant the signifying part of the sign a certain preeminence, i.e., to "leave open the possibility of thinking a *concept signified in and of itself*, a concept simply present for thought, independent of a relationship to language, that is of a relationship to a system of signifiers" (*P*, 19). This reproach is correct insofar as Saussure, in his *General Linguistics*, defends the view that the significance of an object remains unaltered even when the linguistic values are displaced.

> A few examples will show clearly that this is true. Modern French *mouton* can have the same signification as English *sheep* but not the same value, and this for several reasons, particularly because in speaking of a piece of meat ready to be served on the table, English uses *mutton* and not *sheep*. The difference in value between *sheep* and *mutton* is due to the fact that *sheep* has beside it a second term while the French word does not. (*CGL*, 115–16)

Here we are touching on a problematic aspect of reading Saussure that has something to do with the problem of translatability from one language to the other. Derrida grants the necessity of respecting this possibility; he suggests, however, the following terminological change:

> In the limits to which it is possible, or at least *appears* possible, translation practices the difference between signified and signifier. But if this difference is never pure, no more so is translation, and for the notion of translation we would have to substitute a notion of *transformation*: a regulated transformation of one language by another, of one text by another. (*P*, 20)

This objection essentially boils down to the recommendation that we give up the distinction between meaning (signified/signification)—which, after all, is only one side of the sign—and value (*valeur*), the differential determination of the sign. Derrida argues that one should not exclude the determination of meaning from the play of the parasemes, as Saussure's sheep/mutton and *mouton* example suggests. In an interview with Henri Ronse, "Implications," from 1967, Derrida supported this recommendation with an interesting additional argument.

> The movement of *différance*, as that which produces different things, that which differentiates, is the common root of all the oppositional concepts that mark our language, such as, to take only a few examples, sensible/intelligible, intuition/signification, nature/culture, etc. (*P*, 9)

That means that it would be senseless to work with a two-sided concept of the sign, if, at the same time, one accepts that the two sides of a sign, signifier and signified, are not originary, but rather themselves derive their difference on the basis of differentiation/articulation of values.

In a third objection, Derrida states that Saussure privileged the phonic aspect of the sign, although he himself asserted that the phonic is foreign to the essence of language (*CGL*, 7, 118). In other passages, however, he speaks of a "natural link" (*CGL*, 25) between voice and thought (*P*, 21).

This, in turn, results, fourth, in an unexpected reliance on the part of Saussure on the old Western idea that has found its most beautiful formulations in Hegel; namely, that "*phoné*, in effect, is the signifying substance *given to consciousness* as that which is most intimately tied to the thought of the signified concept. From this point of view, the voice is consciousness itself" (*P*, 22). This objection seems unimportant — if not unintelligible — on first sight. Derrida, however, in his publications that concern themselves with Husserl and, above all, in his *Grammatology*, has demonstrated quite convincingly and supported with profuse examples that, according to a metaphor deeply etched in European grammar, the voice, in contrast to writing, for example, was considered more spiritual, more closely related to breath, which, itself, is considered to be spiritual. In light of *this* interpretation one can hardly reject Derrida's fifth objection, in which he complains about a psychologization of semiology (*P*, 22–23). Whereas sounds are *heard*, the voice is *perceived*. That is a fundamental difference: *perception is not hearing, but rather implies understanding*. If voice (*la phonè*) itself is already spiritual in its essence, then in perceiving the speaking voice one intellect, as it were, speaks to another: "The exteriority of the signifier seems reduced" (*P*, 22). (At this point I want to interject something into Derrida's criticism of Saussure: Derrida seems to me to pay little attention to the fact that the voice has the advantage of being one-dimensional and that it is *this* circumstance that assures it its privileged status from Hegel through Saussure, and not its metaphorical nonsensuality.[3] Only in the flow of speech can semes be parasemically distinguished from each other, i.e., transformed into distinct values.)

I do not want to decide to what extent this last reproach actually touches the historical Saussure and not merely his editors and successors, who took many freedoms. Derrida himself relies mainly on Saussure's structuralist successors, particularly on Roman Jacobson who, indeed, plays a key role in the history of European structuralism. Be that as it may, in the thus interpreted Saussure Derrida takes exception, sixth and finally, to the fact that he oriented himself on an untenable model of communication that itself, in turn, was burdened by the underlying concept of the sign.

> This equivocality, which weighs upon the model of the sign, marks the "semiological" project itself and the organic totality of its concepts, in

particular that of *communication*, which in effect implies a *transmission charged with making pass, from one subject to another, the identity* of a *signified* object, of a *meaning* or of a *concept* rightfully separable from the process of passage and from the signifying operation. Communication presupposes subjects (whose identity and presence are constituted before the signifying operation) and objects (signified concepts, a thought meaning that the passage of communication will have neither to constitute, nor, by all rights, to transform). *A communicates B to C. Through the sign the emitter communicates to a receptor, etc. (P, 23–24)*

From this we get an idea about the point Derrida wants to put his finger on: it is the question of whether structure can guarantee the semantic identity of the sign either during the exchange or during two different usages of it. From now on when I say "semantic identity," I mean the presupposition that the meaning of a sign, insofar as it is an element in the crystal lattice of *langue* or of *discours*, is not altered in the course of communication. All of classical structuralism rests on this assumption, and even large parts of Anglo-Saxon language philosophy presuppose the semantic identity of the linguistic sign, for example Searle, when he says that "any conventional act involves the notion of repetition of the same."[4] This assumption rests, according to Derrida, on an ambiguity in the concept of "structure."[5] Everything depends upon the use to which it is put. We already know one: it is the application in communication theory, which assumes that for the sake of its transmittability a sign must be able to be attributed by the listener or reader to the same completed system of *langue* out of which it was generated by the speaker or author. Thus the signifier would be a mere medium that transplants the signified from one brain to another, it would simply be an indispensable instrument of transportation. This view, however, is incompatible with Saussure's idea of articulation, which, in a radical form, says no more and no less than that there is no meaning where there is no expression. Yet expression, for its part, is not indigenously at hand; rather it is the effect of oppositive differentiations from other expressions. But who could possibly know in advance how many other expressions I distinguish my expression from? Saussure's law of the differential determination of value simply states that the value of a term is what distinguishes it from other terms. The chain of negations ("a is not b and not c and not d, etc.") presumably runs *ad infinitum*: in the end, it is up to the individual's interpretive and linguistic competence, indeed, even imagination, to decide which term it distinguishes from which other terms in what manner, and with which terms it associates it (metaphorically, metonymically). *Thus nothing requires that one connect the structurality of sign articulation with the idea of enclosed structure.* If this is the case, classical structuralism has become untenable and with it that type of communication theory that wagers that a content encoded according to rules must be decoded by a speaker of the same competence in the exact same way.

For this to occur, one would have to assume that in the head of every competent speaker the exact same quantity of established oppositions has to be associated with each term—an assumption that gives us a vivid picture of the passionate denial of reality that can be found in the project of scientific idealization and mastery of reality. *Actual* communication, in contrast to the wishful thinking of structural science, is semantically uncontrollable and completely incompatible with that deterministic machine that underlies the model of input-output. We can note this as the second conclusion of our reading of Derrida: the differentiality of the formation of signs in no way implies the systematicity of structure. On the contrary,

> This principle [of difference] compels us not only not to privilege one substance—here the phonic, so called temporal, substance—while excluding another—for example, the graphic, so called spatial, substance—but even to consider every process of signification as a formal play of differences. That is, of traces.
>
> Why traces? And by what right do we introduce grammatics at the moment when we seem to have neutralized every substance, be it phonic, graphic, or otherwise? Of course it is not a question of resorting to the same concept of writing and of simply inverting the dissymmetry that now has become problematical. It is a question, rather, of producing a new concept of writing. This concept can be called *gram* or *différance*. The play of differences supposes, in effect, syntheses and referrals which forbid at any moment, or in any sense, that a simple element be *present* in and of itself, referring only to itself. Whether in the order of spoken or written discourse, no element can function as a sign without referring to another element which itself is not simply present. This interweaving results in each "element"—phoneme or grapheme—being constituted on the basis of the trace within it of the other elements of the chain or system. This interweaving, this textile, is the *text* produced only in the transformation of another text. Nothing, neither among the elements nor within the system, is anywhere ever simply present or absent. There are only, everywhere, differences and traces of traces. (*P*, 26)

Actually, this passage tells us nothing new, yet one feels slightly at a loss with Derrida's statement, presumably because he employs in an exemplary fashion a technique he calls "deconstruction." It consists in adapting the classical terminology of semiology, but then wearing it out through use, and thus distorting and deforming it in such a way that the Western-metaphysical (Derrida likes to say "logocentric") implications are avoided wherever possible. Let's take a closer look at this process. There is first the concept of the trace, which also, to be sure, has its Western, for example, Humboldtian tradition, but which appears rather as a troublemaker in a Saussurean context. "Trace" denotes the being-related-to-one-another of distinct elements. So far, so good. But why does he designate this condition of being-related with a new, artificial term, *différance*? Obviously, Derrida is not satisfied with Saussure's term *différence*. For traditional thinking can deal with difference. Let me remind you of Hegel, who makes short work of difference, sublating it in the reconstructed "simple unity" of the spirit which is present to itself. Derrida does not have in mind such a preliminary difference, which, in the end, can be subordinated to system or to structure. For the differentiality of the trace is *not* supposed to come to a standstill in a closed system of signs, i.e., not in a taxonomically understood "text." "Texts," Derrida says, are always transformations of other texts; signs transformations of other signs. Lévi-Strauss said this, as you might recall, in the "Finale" of his *Mythologiques* in almost the same words. But the difference between his and Derrida's formulation is that in his model the transformation leaves structure intact, whereas it influences it in Derrida's conception. And why? Because for Derrida the thought of difference simultaneously implies that no sign, as he says, is immediately present to itself.

This is not an easily graspable formulation. Let's make an effort to understand it: Its comprehension (*Verständnis*) will essentially decide whether we can join sides with neostructuralism and its critique of systems, or whether we want rather to remain with metaphysics. "No sign is ever present to itself" means that if a sign acquires its determined meaning only through distinction from all other signs, then it obviously does not refer first to *itself*. Rather, it takes the detour, so to speak, over all other signs of the system, and only thereafter does it come back to itself identifiably. Thus one could actually say that it is separated from *itself* by nothing less than the universe of all other signs and texts, if one wants to establish the argument on the level of the text. This means that difference is more primordial than (*ursprünglicher als*) identity: a statement that has scarcely fathomable consequences if we decide to go along with it. If one does this, one already stands outside metaphysics, which, after all, always grants to *one* element of the system (or outside the system), i.e., to the center or the principle, the feature of being immediately familiar with itself.

Today we cannot possibly overlook the consequences of Derrida's thesis. The course of this lecture series will, we hope, bring us to a point where we will be more familiar with some of them. For today I want to avoid leaving the context in which Derrida's interview moves. This context is Saussure's theory of the sign and the system. Let's then ask ourselves what consequences Derrida's *différance* might have for the reinterpretation of Saussure's *Cours*.

The most striking consequence would be the destruction of Saussure's concept of opposition. Saussure places a limit on the "play of differences": once the values of a linguistic system are established by means of the differentiating activity, he believes, one must no longer speak of differences, but rather of oppositions. Oppositions are fixed differences between terms, and as such they have a clear identity with themselves, which Saussure regards as positive.

> Although both the signified and the signifier are purely differential and negative when considered separately, their combination is a positive fact. (*CGL*, 120)

To be sure, the origin of the opposing elements is negation or differentiality, but their purpose, the condition they enter by virtue of being oppositions, is the positivity of a fixed self-reference, of a unity or an identity. If the signs were not identical with themselves, *langue* would not be a *system*; i.e., there would be innumerable differential references, and the ultimate identification of the meaning of the signs would have to fail. In fact, however, Saussure speaks of the "system of language," and "system" means, literally, coexistence of many under *one* central concern. If this central concern is absent from the free "play of differences" in its pure negativity, this does not mean, Saussure explains, that it is also absent from the linguistic system, viewed no longer as a limited context of assignments and references among values, but rather as one among fixed *terms* ("When we compare signs—positive terms—with each other, we can no longer speak of difference. . . . Between them there is only *opposition*"; *CGL*, 121). In other words, as soon as differentiation as articulation of the sound and image material is complete, we are dealing with positivities (with terms and oppositions), and no longer with pure negativities, about which Saussure had said earlier that "in language there are only differences *without positive terms*" (*CGL*, 120).

In an insightful essay, Samuel Weber has identified this transition from the anarchical power of differentiation to a transparent order of oppositions as a contradiction in Saussure's approach.[6] And he also added that this contradiction is linked to Saussure's (or rather Bally and Sechehaye's) *systematical* interest. For if both were simultaneously true (first, that in language there are no positivities, but only negative relations; and second, that language is a finite arsenal of signs), a transition from the free play of differences to the fixed referentiality of oppositions would necessarily have to be found. The only question is, What authority determines the free play of relations? Saussure gives a cautious answer to this question. He says that the unity of concern that allows the free play of differences to become a fixed context of assignments and references of oppositions is supplied by the unity of a collective consciousness ("by the collective mind"; *CGL*, 100).

How, one might ask, can we imagine this unifying of the linguistic material by means of a collective consciousness, if, at the same time, it is supposed to be true that thought in itself is amorphous and articulated only through the free play of differences? Saussure, indeed, seems to correct his fundamental insight into the inseparability of sound and thought when he says that "maintaining the parallelism between the two classes of differences is the distinctive function of the linguistic institution" (*CGL*, 121).

But if, inversely, the so-called collective consciousness of the participants in language is a result of articulation, it cannot appear at the same time as determining authority in the service of a system. This, in turn, seems to imply that the boundary between oppositions and differences can never be fixed. Saussure had, for his part, expressed this opinion already at an earlier point of his *Cours* when he stated:

> The synchronic law is general but not imperative. Doubtless it is imposed on individuals by the weight of collective usage (see p. 73), but here I do not have in mind an obligation on the part of speakers. I mean that *in language* no force guarantees the maintenance of a regularity when established on some point. (*CGL*, 92)

Derrida is of the exact same opinion, namely, that the text is infinite and that the signs can*not* be identified (with themselves) with absolute certainty, either beforehand or afterward. For in differential systems, he says, there is no (final) authority whatsoever that defines its limits. Each speech act is a continuing test of whether the other speakers articulate their ideas in a similar fashion. There is no policing of language, as he says in "Limited Inc": "Everything becomes possible against the language-police; for example, 'literatures' or 'revolutions' that as yet have no model" (243; see also 250); and that is because the radicalized thought of differentiality of structure suspends the idea — or at least renders it untenable — that there is an extrastructural principle (and be it even the identity of a collective consciousness) that watches over its unity.

In discussions of Derrida's criticism of Saussure one often comes across the objection that his criticism of the system of language and of the unity of meaning goes too far, indeed, that it is senseless when it posits as absolute the "structurality of structure." Deviations and transformations that can no longer be recognized as deviations *from* something (which to this extent has to remain identical with itself) are no longer deviations. Even the notion of an "unlimited play of differences" must, for that reason, insist on a minimum of uniformity among the signs. Without giving a final answer to this question, I would like to add at this point by way of explanation that Derrida explicitly admits this, most clearly in section o of his "Limited Inc." There he says that there is a certain constancy of the sign. Yet this constancy ought not be misunderstood as "permanence," i.e., in the sense of a timeless self-presence of a meaning; rather it should be interpreted as a kind of non-self-present "remainder" (*LI*, 187). *Restance* is a neologism born of the caution that the idea of the conservation of a sign's signification over the course of its innumerable uses could include a metaphysical assumption. Namely, if it is true that each new usage of a sign *can* contest the meaning of the first use, then we are dealing not with a mere eventuality but rather with a structural possibility (*LI*, 184). Structural possibilities are not refuted by de facto arguments, and thus not by the objection that *this* use of signs did in fact *not* alter the meaning of the sign. A sufficiently fundamental theory of language has to account for this contestant and irrefutable possibility. Yet if the signification of a sign *can* be altered, then a timeless-synchronous self-presence (*présence à soi*) of meaning can in any case be excluded: "The structure of the remainder, implying alteration, renders all absolute permanence impossible" (*LI*, 191). To grant this is not, inversely, to assert that there is no expectancy whatsoever about the attribution of meaning for signs. For precisely this reason Derrida speaks of a nonpresent remainder: something remains, but what is remaining is not the self-presence of a meaning, not even the permanence of the phonic or graphic material by means of which meaning is expressed; it is rather something like the schematic unity of a sign, about which Schleiermacher said that it is a unity with movable edges that can even wipe out or newly determine the presumed kernel of meaning. Let's see how Derrida himself (to be sure, only in a preliminary fashion) responds to our doubts.

> Iterability supposes a minimal remainder (as well as a minimum of
> idealization) in order that the identity of the *selfsame* be repeatable and
> identifiable *in*, *through*, and even *in view of* its alteration. For the struc-
> ture of iteration—and this is another of its decisive traits—implies *both*
> identity *and* difference. Iteration in its "purest" form—and it is always
> impure—contains *in itself* the discrepancy of a difference that constitutes
> it as iteration. The iterability of an element divides its own identity *a
> priori*, even without taking into account the fact that this identity can
> only *determine* or delimit itself through differential relations to other
> elements and that it hence bears the mark of this difference. It is be-
> cause this iterability is differential, within each individual "element" as
> well as between the "elements," because it splits each element while
> constituting it, because it marks it with an articulatory break, that the
> remainder, although indispensable, is never that of a full or fulfilling
> presence: it is a differential structure escaping the logic of presence or
> the (simple or dialectical) opposition of presence and absence, upon
> which opposition the idea of permanence depends. This is why the
> mark qua "non-present remainder" is not the contrary of the mark as
> effacement. Like the trace it is, the mark is neither present nor absent.
> This is what is *remarkable*. . . . It is iterability itself, that which is
> remarkable in the mark, passing between the *re-* of the repeated and the
> *re-* of the repeating, traversing and transforming repetition. (*LI*, 190)

The main argument (but, at the same time, the main difficulty) of this passage seems to me to lie in the statement that differentiation not only divides one sign from others (*qua* oppositum) but that it already divides the unity of this sign itself by virtue of its irrefutable possibility of repetition. So that you can more easily familiarize yourself with this difficult, but in no way unintelligible, thought, I want to present to you Derrida's own explanation of the concept of "différance." First of all, he says, the occurrence of *différance* can no longer be explained on the basis of the opposition of signifier and signified, nor on that of absence and presence.

> *Différance* is the systematic play of differences, of the traces of differences, of the *spacing* by means of which elements are related to each other. This spacing is the simultaneously active and passive (the *a* of *différance* indicates this indecision as concerns activity and passivity, that which cannot be governed by or distributed between the terms of this opposition) production of the intervals without which the "full" terms would not signify, would not function. (*P*, 27)

In French the verb *différer* has two meanings: to establish a distance between two conditions of a thing (thus, "to delay," also in the sense of "to defer") and, "to be different." In *différance* both meanings are present. The interval that separates meaning from meaning and thus determines it, is, at the same time, the deferral of presence on the basis of which meaning is not simple and immediately present to itself: full, saturated, atemporal, identical with itself. *La différance* has the oscillation of the term between active and passive in common with Humboldt's *energeia* (as opposed to the product as *ergon*). We have to imagine both as vital and historical processes: deferral presupposes temporality. It is *time* that separates one meaning from another and thus thwarts its self-presence. For time, according to a famous definition taken from Hegel's *Encyplopaedia*, is "Being which, because it *is*, is not, and *is* because it is *not*":[7] i.e., the contradiction of *Dasein* or the nonpresence of *Dasein*.

The *espacement*, the spatial separation of signs, has therefore its raison d'être in temporization. Only temporality allows the rupture with all options for synchrony or presence.

> This is why the *a* of *différance* also recalls that spacing is temporization, the detour and postponement by means of which intuition, perception, consummation—in a word, the relationship to the present, the reference to a present reality, to a *being*—are always *deferred*. Deferred by virtue of the very principle of difference which holds that an element functions and signifies, takes on or conveys meaning, only by referring to another past or future element in an economy of traces. (*P*, 28–29)

Indeed, two sign values can be distinguished from each other only if both do not abide in the present, but rather pass on so that one can make room for the other. This is the only way the ideality of a sign *meaning*, released from its material baggage (sunken into the past), can come to light. If time, however, is the condition of possibility of articulation and of differentiality, then it would be very strange to believe that it could be frozen into an idealized concept, like that of the system of language. No, not even as values in a supposedly "synchronic" system do the signs have (timeless) presence: they are divided not only from their other signs (as their *opposita*), but also from themselves, simply because their *self* exists in time, i.e., it is a being that, because it *is*, is *not*, and *is*, only because it is *not*. To close this part of today's lecture I am going to cite a passage from Derrida's interview in which the classical structuralist concept of structure, understood as a system of simultaneous oppositions, is both taken up as well as critically overcome. It is exactly by reason of this movement that we speak of "neostructuralism."

> The activity or productivity connoted by the *a* of *différance* refers to the generative movement in the play of differences. The latter are neither fallen from the sky nor inscribed once and for all in a closed system, a static structure that a synchronic and taxonomic operation could exhaust. Differences are the effects of transformations, and from this vantage the theme of *différance* is incompatible with the static, synchronic, taxonomic, ahistoric motifs in the concept of *structure*. But it goes without saying that this motif is not the only one that defines structure, and that the production of differences, *différance*, is not astructural: it produces systematic and regulated transformations which are able, at a certain point, to leave room for a structural science. The concept of *différance* even develops the most legitimate principled exigencies of "structuralism." (*P*, 27–28)

We now have at our disposal—after the reading of two texts by Derrida—not only a definition of what is meant by "neostructuralism" but also a first illustration of its content and methods. Neostructuralism radicalizes Saussure's basic idea according to which the meaning of the speech acts, by means of which we communicate with each other, is grounded for its part in something that itself is not meaningful, namely, in the differential play of what the later Saussure calls "semes" and Derrida "marks" or "nonpresent marks." The fundamental structuralist idea is radicalized insofar as it now challenges even the *concept of taxonomy*, of a self-enclosed structure of signs governed by a *set* of rules. The closed text is confronted by the open text, interpretation (as search for the central meaning of a text) by plural reading that does not look for a unified meaning but rather is interested in semantic "dissemination."

So far, so good. You will say, however, that one example does not make a rule, and Derrida's texts do not constitute a large enough basis to justify our use of the term "neostructuralism." Before I come back to Derrida, I therefore want to broaden the terrain on which we are working by introducing other names and voices; at the same time, I want to study neostructuralism under *a historical perspective*. The second part of my program for today one could also characterize as follows: primarily on the basis of *The Order of Things*, I want to clarify the actual historical presuppositions on the basis of which the thought of an open structure and of a nonrepresentational concept of the sign could emerge. The historical question will turn into a *question about the essence of history* over the course of our investigation.

Not very long ago people looked at the number of individual histories in which mankind is entangled under the collective concept of history (in the singular). In Germany, it was mainly the works of the historian Reinhart Koselleck that pointed to that so-called turning point (*Sattelzeit*)—around 1750—in which the event of the unification of the many histories under one (universal) history took place. Foucault, mainly in *The Order of Things*, made the same observation, and placed this turn, on the basis of data from French culture, at almost the same point in time, the year 1775. We will learn more about this when we engage in the discussion of Foucault's major works. For now a single observation should suffice: the overcoming of histories is an ambiguous process. On the one hand, it emancipates the power of time that is at work in the historical process—it destroys the idea of a universal reason that is valid for all time and that in an exemplary fashion manifests itself in all individual histories. On the other hand, it also furthers the expansion of the concept of reason insofar as from now on not only what exists in space but also what exists in time will be subordinate to reason. In this sense one was able to celebrate Hegel's philosophy of spirit and history as the greatest triumph of Western rationality, succeeding for the first time in understanding even the facts of history as manifestations of reason. To apply the concept of unity to history already points to this kind of appropriation, for one could scarcely speak of *one* history (as opposed to *many* histories) if one had not already conceived the totality of history under the perspective of its possible unity of meaning, i.e., as a meaningfully unfolding process. If one calls, with Foucault, the age that concludes with the discovery of history the age of representation or the age of structure, one would have to characterize the period after 1750 or 1775 as the age that broke with the model of representation in the name of history. And indeed, this is what Michel Foucault does. On the other hand—and this would be more or less the opinion of Derrida or of Jean-François Lyotard (to mention only them at this point)—universal history itself displays a structural similarity with the thinking of representation or of structure insofar as it orients the decentering power of time around the concept of a unity that history always and unforgettably imagines as its final aim. Philosophy calls this teleology: the direction of a process toward a *telos* (τέλος). This idea would allow us to grasp history as completed or as capable of completion, as Hegel does, for example.

Hegel—as we said in one of our first lectures—still, as it were, finds a place in the closed construction of Western history: he is still "at home" in the West, to employ a metaphor he liked to use. He experiences its completion from within, for the idea that a history of the West is completed with consciousness of itself still belongs to metaphysics (i.e., to Western thought).

This is no longer true for neostructuralism's interpretation of modern times. For Jean-François Lyotard, whose book *The Postmodern Condition* we have already mentioned, thinking of the future is postmodern; i.e., it looks at the closed (or supposedly closed) house of metaphysics as if from the outside, without itself still being a resident. This looking in from the outside is a standard metaphor of neostructuralism. I am sure that some of you know the statement that we should "observe our civilization with the eyes of an anthropologist." That means that one cannot be a member of society and identify with its customs; rather one has to observe it as a theoretician, with the alienating gaze of someone who does not belong to it. It is precisely this perspective that Lyotard chooses with regard to modern times. Its agony and final decline represent themselves to him in the gradual perishing of its legitimation. From a West German perspective this point of view is both strange and exciting at the same time. Our philosophy has for quite some time been struggling with the question of a "legitimation of modern times," as it was formulated (and answered positively) by Hans Blumenberg in his book of the same title; it has likewise been excited by the question that, above all, Jürgen Habermas brought to our attention, namely, the question of how one can overcome the loss of legitimation of the modern state. The first deals with a defense of modern rationality against either theological, political, or ecological doubts about its humanistic substance; in other words, it treats the simple but consequential question of whether reason that has become autonomous redeems humankind from the constraints of nature, or whether it enslaves humankind by means of new, even worse constraints, indeed, whether it threatens humankind with extermination. (That is the question raised by Adorno and Horkheimer's *Dialectic of Enlightenment*.) The second question concerns itself with what since romanticism and Marx is called the alienation of state and society. The formulation means, as you know, that in societies that function on a capitalist basis the system of means (economy, administration, social labor, etc.) no longer serves the ends of politics, i.e., no longer reflects the value decisions that can be obtained through consensus of the citizens. However, since, according to the idea of democracy, politics derives its legitimacy from the agreement of rationally generalizable decisions by the citizens, the state, as the administrator of the general will, loses its legitimacy under the described conditions. Niklas Luhmann, the main representative of the so-called systems theory of society, contests in the face of this the view that the need for legitimacy can be reduced to that of legality: factual legality is substituted in this view for the "old European" concept of a "counterfactual" legitimation on the basis of reason. As the title of one of his books, *Legitimation durch Verfahren* (Legitimation by means of procedure), drastically shows, he believes that nostalgic longings for legitimation can be soothed by means of procedure—by the state's handling of its monopoly of power in such a way that the question of a possible (normative) legality of its decrees becomes a question of the examination of its actual agreement with the constitution.[8] The problem is that this factual criterion can be claimed by any state, even

Chile; there is, after all, an ultraconservative tradition, as Luhmann knows, for example, in the prefascism of Carl Schmitt.

I am mentioning the names of Habermas and Luhmann because Lyotard himself does so. He is one of the few thinkers of neostructuralism who commands some knowledge of contemporary German (and Anglo-Saxon) philosophy. This makes the dialogue with his work an exciting event for a German reader. However, I have to limit my discussion to what is significant for our present context.

When Lyotard defines "postmodernity" as the inapplicability of modernism's traditional means to legitimate society, we are mainly interested in this idea from the point of view of whether it contains something analogous to the opening of the system (or of structure). And this is indeed the case. For Lyotard is working with a three-step scheme. According to this scheme, scientific knowledge has overcome a form of social self-legitimation that stood at the beginning of this development. In the beginning—in premodernity—the European cultures and civilizations justified themselves by means of narratives, *récits*, (for example, mythic narratives). This option was succeeded by the universal, no longer narrative-mythical, but rather rational legitimation requirement of scientific discourse. The claim for universality of the scientific discourse of legitimation, however, has shown itself to be flawed today, because it brings into play an assumption that, for itself, cannot be justified; namely this: there is a philosophical metadiscourse that is superior to all other language games and unifies them. Structuralism, too, with its characteristic claims to universality that we encountered in Saussure and especially in Lévi-Strauss, takes part in this assumption (and has this in common with Luhmann's "systems theory" as well as Habermas's "universal pragmatics"). In reality, there is no universal grammar that encompasses the individual language games, and thus the difference or dissemination of linguistically codified "forms of life" or "language games" is pragmatically insurmountable. The closed, but universally conceived, system is confronted by the open system, or the plurality of systems, which are never unified in a metadiscourse. Let me give you a longer passage from the introduction to Lyotard's book.

> Science has always been in conflict with narratives. Judged by the yardstick of science, the majority of them prove to be fables. But to the extent that science does not restrict itself to stating useful regularities and seeks the truth, it is obliged to legitimate the rules of its own game. It then produces a discourse of legitimation with respect to its own status, a discourse called philosophy. I will use the term *modern* to designate any science that legitimates itself with reference to a metadiscourse of this kind making an explicit appeal to some grand narrative, such as the dialectics of Spirit, the hermeneutics of meaning, the emancipation of the rational or working subject, or the creation of wealth. For example, the rule of consensus between the sender and addressee of a statement with truth-value is deemed acceptable if it is cast in terms of a possible

unanimity between rational minds: this is the Enlightenment narrative, in which the hero of knowledge works toward a good ethico-political end—universal peace. As can be seen from this example, if a metanarrative implying a philosophy of history is used to legitimate knowledge, questions are raised concerning the validity of the institutions governing the social bond: these must be legitimated as well. Thus justice is consigned to the grand narrative in the same way as truth.

Simplifying to the extreme, I define *postmodern* as incredulity toward metanarratives. This incredulity is undoubtedly a product of progress in the sciences: but that progress in turn presupposes it. To the obsolescence of the metanarrative apparatus of legitimation corresponds, most notably, the crisis of metaphysical philosophy and of the university institution which in the past relied on it. The narrative function is losing its functors, its great hero, its great dangers, its great voyages, its great goal. It is being dispersed in clouds of narrative language elements—narrative, but also denotative, prescriptive, descriptive, and so on. Conveyed within each cloud are pragmatic valencies specific to its kind. Each of us lives at the intersection of many of these. However, we do not necessarily establish stable language combinations, and the properties of the ones we do establish are not necessarily communicable.

Thus the society of the future falls less within the province of a Newtonian anthropology (such as structuralism or systems theory) than a pragmatics of language particles. There are many different language games—a heterogeneity of elements. They only give rise to institutions in patches—local determinism.

The decision makers, however, attempt to manage these clouds of sociality according to input/output matrices, following a logic which implies that their elements are commensurable and that the whole is determinable. They allocate our lives for the growth of power. In matters of social justice and of scientific truth alike, the legitimation of that power is based on its optimizing the system's performance—efficiency. The application of this criterion to all of our games necessarily entails a certain level of terror, whether soft or hard: be operational (that is, commensurable) or disappear.

The logic of maximum performance is no doubt inconsistent in many ways, particularly with respect to contradiction in the socioeconomic field: it demands both less work (to lower production costs) and more (to lessen the social burden of the idle population). But our incredulity is now such that we no longer expect salvation to rise from these inconsistencies, as did Marx.

Still, the postmodern condition is as much a stranger to disenchantment as it is to the blind positivity of delegitimation. Where, after the metanarratives, can legitimacy reside? The operativity criterion is technological; it has no relevance for judging what is true or just. Is

legitimacy to be found in consensus obtained through discussion, as Jürgen Habermas thinks? Such consensus does violence to the heterogeneity of language games. And invention is always born of dissension. Postmodern knowledge is not simply a tool of the authorities; it
refines our sensitivity to differences and reinforces our ability to tolerate
the incommensurable. Its principle is not the expert's homology, but the
inventor's paralogy. (*PC*, xxiii-xxv)

I decided to cite almost unabridged the introduction to Lyotard's book so that you
can familiarize yourself not only with his central themes and theses but also with
the discernible feeling for life that makes itself apparent between the lines. Let's
summarize briefly his essential statements: while premodern societies legitimated
themselves by means of (mythic or religious) narratives, modernism invented the
new paradigm of social legitimation by means of universalization of the requirement for legitimation that first appeared in the exact sciences, namely, legitimation on the basis of a discourse of rationality. Lyotard also calls it metadiscourse,
for it—suspended above all individual discourses and transcending their particularity—formulates the pure form of legitimate speech as such in which all individual discourses take part insofar as they themselves step forward with the
claim of speaking legitimately: enlightened reason; the absolute spirit of the
idealists; the subject of the working class in Marx's theory; the system of the
structuralists and systems theoreticians; the universal discourse, which is free of
domination, of the pragmatic consensus theory à la Peirce, Habermas, and Apel.
Lyotard seeks to prove that although these theoreticians are opposed to each other
on ideological grounds, they nevertheless share a common assumption: the claim
to universality and with it the ambition to set *one* homogeneous medium of rationality *above* all individual discourses (i.e., above all language games). To this extent, according to Lyotard, the most important contemporary opponents, systems
theory of society and the Critical Theory of the more recent Frankfurt School,
are in agreement. The former is working with a code model that both guarantees
the identicality of input and output and that places mechanical operability above
the question of the possible meaning of an operation. The latter links the question
of meaning to a social consensus, which, at the same time, has to be conceived
as universal for the sake of its rationality, and which thus violates the heterogeneity of the individual language games in whose irreducible variety we articulate our private and social life.[9] In this context Lyotard expresses a wish we do
not want to take foremost as an argument, but rather as the expression of an image
of the world, namely, the wish for innovation, for the change of each encrusted
code. Lyotard also adds that the dissent of innovative changes in meaning offers
more advantageous conditions than the universal "consensus obtained through
discussion."

I presume that, in spite of the differences in style and theme, you can get an idea of the similarities of the intellectual climate in which Derrida's and Lyotard's discourses unfold. Both break with all varieties of totalitarian thinking (which here denotes thinking that aims at the interpretation of the world as totality); for both the idea of a closed system is unbearable; both stand on the side of innovation, of systematically uncontrollable change in meaning; both emphasize difference, indeed, irreducible variety rather than uniform unity and singularity of language games. In the work of both, the term "dissemination" plays an important role, and both believe, as we will see later, that even the fundamental idea of modern-day philosophy — the idea of the subject which is identical with itself and which constitutes world — must fall victim to it. And both borrow in this context in a certain sense from Nietzschean vitalism, which suspected rational consensus and the morality founded on it of being a conspiracy of the many and the weak against the less numerous strong and nonmoral individuals who, however, justifiably act in accord with the will to power. It is not the supposed truth, but the powerfulness (understood completely in a vital, life-conserving and life-intensifying sense), the *force* of an argument that determines its possible truth; the pretended will to truth unmasks itself, viewed discourse strategically, as a particularly sly variant of the will to power. Speech-act theory, which goes back to Wittgenstein's pragmatism, had, as Derrida emphasized in his argument with Austin and Searle, revalidated the notion that arguments are actions that have a certain power that initially is articulated not in terms of truth or falsehood but rather in terms of strength or weakness. Indeed, we rarely call arguments (even logical ones) "true" or "false," but rather "weak" or "strong" or "compelling" etc. Here is what Lyotard concludes from this.

> This last observation brings us to the first principle underlying our method as a whole: to speak is to fight, in the sense of playing, and speech acts fall within the domain of a general agonistics. This does not necessarily mean that one plays in order to win. A move can be made for the sheer pleasure of its invention: what else is involved in that labor of language harassment undertaken by popular speech and by literature? Great joy is had in the endless invention of turns of phrase, of words and meanings, the process behind the evolution of language on the level of *parole*. But undoubtedly even this pleasure depends on a feeling of success won at the expense of an adversary — at least one adversary, and a formidable one: the accepted language, or connotation.
>
> This idea of an agonistics of language should not make us lose sight of the second principle, which stands as a complement to it and governs our analysis: that the observable social bond is composed of language "moves." An elucidation of this proposition will take us to the heart of the matter at hand. (*PC*, 10–11)

Lyotard believes that this fundamental reality of the adversary character of all speech is neglected in all sociological concepts that work with the model of a self-regulating mechanism. According to him, all social technologies of the type of Luhmann's systems theory belong in this category. In contrast to them, Marx's theory of class struggle has obvious advantages. However, it is weakened and deradicalized by its utopian perspective—a thought that is hardly intelligible in a contemporary German context. Class struggle is for Marx, and even more so for the Frankfurt School, only a transitional condition, which, like Hegel's difference, is sublated for the sake of a new, no longer agonal, totality. The idea of such a totality, however, is part of modernism's heritage: for a thinking under the condition of the closure of modernity, it no longer has validity.

This certainly sounds strange to a generation educated in the spirit of German idealism and its successor theories (and Marxism as well as Critical Theory are born of the spirit of idealism). Yet, before we arrive at a premature judgment and accuse Lyotard's conception of an "agonal discourse" of wanting to palm off on us the Social Darwinism of an early capitalist society of competition as postmodern thinking, we want especially to emphasize one point: Lyotard says that a structure conceived to be uniform (be it as system, as universal consensus, or as classless society) would have to renounce completely the idea of innovation. As soon as the balanced state of forces was achieved, nothing could ever change again. Above all, it would be difficult to explain what a saturated structure should change in itself in the first place, and how it would go about it if all its elements are merely parts of a whole. Parts of a whole always execute only the movements prescribed by the laws of the whole. Only a part of the sort that, for itself, had a certain autonomy, i.e., could not be reached from the concept of the whole by an ordered sequence of deductive steps, could rise up against the whole. These conditions, according to Lyotard, are only guaranteed in his idea of a "paralogy" of the individual language games liberated from the systematic reference to the whole—language games that in the realm of the philosophy of language sought to imitate a form of organization known to us, for example, in classical anarchism or anarcho-syndicalism. Lyotard's imagined enemy is "the system" and "totality" in all their manifestations, above all in the form of bureaucraticized institutions that paralyze the will to innovation, indeed, to "displacement" and "disorientation," whether in the form of bureaucratic capitalism or of actually existing socialism. Even consensus that is free from domination, as long as it is not kept alive by the freedom to infinite discussion, does not escape his suspicion that it, in reality, is a bureaucratic instrument for avoiding discussion or bringing it to a standstill; only *that* revolution would truly be nontotalitarian that would be permanent. (From here, I believe, one can in part explain the attraction that not only Nietzscheanism, but also Maoism—a strange constellation—had for the neostructuralist intellectuals.)

In all texts of neostructuralism, by the way, we encounter a certain skepticism toward the feasibility of absolute consensus. This occurs most powerfully in the work of Jacques Lacan, who suspects discursive agreement of being a *narcis-*

sisme à deux. Every consensus — and we have to understand the term in the broad sense in which it also designates customs, traditional forms of life, phrases held to be true or binding — establishes agreement on a system of exclusions on the part of those who concur in it: the binding force of the binding, or the truth of the correct, excludes the unallowable and the incorrect, just as in scientific discourse the language game of the pertinent statement excludes all other language games (for example, the narrative, the religious, the prescriptive, the promissory language game, etc., *PC*, 25ff.). Lyotard recognizes the university of Humboldt and Schleiermacher as an attempt to transfer the concept of universality onto the interdisciplinary dialogue among departments, which itself is philosophy (*PC*, 31ff.). This conception of a university was viewed as nonexclusionary (as opposed to the exact sciences in the narrower sense), for it sought to ground the individual disciplines and discursive forms either by means of the idea of philosophical speculation, or through the idea of the universal, principally unlimited hermeneutical dialogue. If this last attempt dialectically to unify scientifically and narratively mediated legitimation failed, there were at least two reasons for this failure. The first was brought to light by Nietzsche: the loss of meaning of scientific thinking developed as a consequence of the application of the scientific claim to truth to this claim itself ("he shows that 'European nihilism' resulted from the truth requirement of science being turned back against itself"; *PC*, 39). As soon as the scientific attitude turns the imperative of scientific legitimation, with the same rigor as against everything nonscientific, against its own principles, science collapses into the ungrounded. "The speculative hierarchy of learning gives way to an immanent and, as it were, 'flat' network of areas of inquiry, the respective frontiers of which are in constant flux. The old 'faculties' splinter into institutes and foundations of all kinds, and the universities lose their function of speculative legitimation" (*PC*, 39). A second reason for the delegitimation of the scientific attitude is the impossibility of a universal metadiscourse. Doubts about its existence connect romantic hermeneutics with the work of Wittgenstein, Gadamer, and the neostructuralists. This is not the place to ground this doubt philosophically: Schleiermacher, Wittgenstein, and Derrida all do it in quite different ways. I limit our discussion to the consequences Lyotard derives from it. Science, he says, has ceased to be capable of legitimating, as the last metalanguage, all other forms of knowledge and action (as speculative discourse had believed it could do). Prescriptive discourse, for example, or the discourse of desire escape it. Instead of *one* language of science, there appear many irreducible language games.

> The social subject itself seems to dissolve in this dissemination of language games. The social bond is linguistic, but is not woven with a single thread. It is a fabric formed by the intersection of at least two (and in reality an indeterminate number of) language games obeying different rules. . . .

We may form a pessimistic impression of this splintering: nobody speaks all of those languages, they have no universal metalanguage, the project of the system-subject is a failure, the goal of emancipation has nothing to do with science, we are all stuck in the positivism of this or that discipline of learning, the learned scholars have turned into scientists, the diminished tasks of research have become compartmentalized and no one can master them all. Speculative or humanistic philosophy is forced to relinquish its legitimation duties, which explains why philosophy is facing a crisis wherever it persists in arrogating such functions and is reduced to the study of systems of logic or the history of ideas where it has been realistic enough to surrender them. (*PC*, 66, 113)

This pessimism, however, is not the only possible reaction to the "crisis of meaning" that occurred with the delegitimation of the claim for universality. Lyotard finds positive aspects in it. According to him, the loss of universality emancipates the variety of the knowable and sayable. This, of course, presupposes that the meaning of the word "knowledge" changes (*PC*, 60). From now on, it should no longer serve to designate a system of exclusions that can anticipatingly control its results on the basis of secure premises, as classical structuralism still imagined possible. This newly understood "knowledge" "is producing not the known, but the unknown. And it suggests a model of legitimation that has nothing to do with maximized performance, but has as its basis difference understood as paralogy" (*PC*, 60). In short, in the face of the absence of a universally valid metalanguage, be that Luhmann's system or Habermas's consensus, one has to get acquainted with a "model of an 'open system' " (*PC*, 64) whose principal instability gives dissent much greater chances than consensus. Dissent, moreover, is innovative; consensus leans toward conservatism, for it brings antagonistic arguments to a standstill and reduces difference to identity. In its extreme it is even terroristic, "as is the behavior of the system described by Luhmann. By terror I mean the efficiency gained by eliminating, or threatening to eliminate, a player from the language game one shares with him. . . . It [terror] says: 'Adapt your aspirations to our ends – or else' " (*PC*, 63–64). In another sense even the consensus theory of Habermas's *Diskurs* is "terroristic": first, because it determines in advance the universal-pragmatic rules on the basis of which one opens a conversation (they cannot be debated); and second, because it prescribes consensus as the aim of our entering into a conversation; consensus, however, can only be a state of our discussion, never its purpose and its end. If it were its purpose, each society would be required to limit its conversations with a view toward its requirement for consensus, which thus would assume terroristic traits, as confirmed by Sartre's pessimistic analysis of the transition from "fusing societies" to those held together only by terror.

To be sure, the positive and alternative things Lyotard proposes are far from being clear; and one can hardly make more sense of his visions of the future than from the monthly changing manifestos of the political "alternatives," in whose intellectual climate *The Postmodern Condition* belongs. The lack of concreteness in terms of a feasible alternative does not, however, diminish, to my mind, the right of an author to articulate his discontent with the axioms of the dominating state of society. And in this articulation we find—to be sure, in essay form—striking similarities with what we already know from Derrida: a fundamental suspicion of consensus formations of whatever kind (and their identification with the concept of metaphysics); a preference for differentiation and for change of the system (instead of the stabilization of systems as in structuralism or systems theory);[10] a language-theoretically founded doubt in the claim for universality of the (speculative) intellect, even when it appears in the much more moderate form of a universal hermeneutics; a certain return to the vitalism of desire in resistance to the demands of the superego, which is allied with the system. Both have further in common the inability to formulate truly feasible alternatives, but we do not want to criticize even that too rashly, for ignorance about how our future is to be formed after the decline of traditional practices is our common condition, even if, with good reason, one refrains from retrogressing to Nietzsche, hastily characterizing our status quo as "postmodern." It could indeed be that the essence of modern times (of the *Temps Modernes*) is not correctly thought out in the programs of neostructuralism and that we have to submit "deconstruction" to a revision.

Lecture 6

Jean-François Lyotard's *The Postmodern Condition* not only serves as additional evidence for our working hypothesis, according to which neostructuralism is thinking that jettisons metaphysic's demand for system and domination. This book also develops a thesis about the historical coming-into-Being of the "postmodern situation." As we recall, Lyotard explains the necessity of thinking in "open systems" without internal unity on the basis of the disintegration of the possibility of maintaining a universal metalanguage. This possibility presupposes that the individual language games through which we perspectively live our Being-in-the-world can be gone beyond by some sort of speech that itself is not relative. Such nonrelative speech, for its part, presupposes an authority that modern metaphysics conceives as "the Absolute." If it can be demonstrated — and Derrida has shown this more clearly than Lyotard — that the thought of the Absolute itself cannot escape the "structurality of structure," then one can no longer lay claim to a transhistorical frame of orientation beyond linguistic differentiality. Systems without internal unity and without absolute center become the inescapable condition of our *Dasein* and our orientation in the world.

  This, in essence, is the fundamental insight of all post-Hegelian philosophy from Schelling, Kierkegaard, and Marx, through Nietzsche to Heidegger, Sartre, and Gadamer. One could speak of it as a philosophy of finitude. The *minimal accord* of all these approaches, which shape and have shaped the face of our present, is the standpoint that it is not possible to interpret our world from an Archimedean point, from an "infinite consciousness," as Gadamer says. Modern consciousness, after all, is not therefore finite because it is unfree and limited in its possibilities, but rather in the exact sense that it is not the ground of itself, i.e., of its own subsistence.

Heidegger called this not-Being-the-basis-for-itself "thrownness," and he made clear that the inescapable dependence of *Dasein* presents no limit to its freedom. "As being, Dasein is something that has been thrown; it has been brought into its 'there,' but *not* of its own accord" (*BT*, 329). That simply means that "as existent, it never comes back behind its thrownness"; however, it does not mean that it is not the basis for the possibilities through which it relates to its thrownness and to its future:

> The Self, which as such has to lay the basis for itself, can *never* get
> that basis into its power; and yet, as existing, it must take over Being-a-
> basis. To be its own thrown basis is that potentiality-for-Being which is
> the issue for care. (*BT*, 330)

In other words, if the subject of *Dasein* is not the author of its factual subsistence, then this not-Being-a-basis "does not signify anything like not-Being-present-at-hand or not-subsisting; what one has in view here is rather a 'not' which is constitutive for this *Being* of Dasein—its thrownness. The character of this 'not' as a 'not' may be defined existentially" (*BT*, 330): namely, as a having a potentiality for Being. This having a potentiality for Being "belongs to *Dasein*'s Being-free for its existential possibilities" (*BT*, 331). Because it is not the basis for its own Being, it is—by virtue of its essential nullity—nonetheless precisely the basis of its not-Being, i.e., of the modifications it allows to occur to Being. (Sartre's point of departure in *Being and Nothingness* is founded in precisely this reflection.)

This not Being the basis for itself can be interpreted differently: in Marx's terms as dependence of consciousness on its (social) Being; in Darwin's and Nietzsche's terms as descendance of our consciousness from the phenomenon of the will to life; in terms of the historicists as the insurmountability of history; in Freud's terms as consciousness's not being master in its own home (i.e., as its incapability of ever completely making present the unconscious portion); or in Heidegger's and Gadamer's terms as an overhang of Being over every possible interpretation we make of it. "To exist historically," Gadamer says very concretely, "means that knowledge of oneself can never be complete."[1] That implies that consciousness that understands meaning can never dissociate itself completely from "what is historically pre-given" (*TM*, 269) and can never enlighten itself about its Being. "In the last analysis," Gadamer adds, "*all* understanding is self-understanding, but not in the sense of a preliminary self-possession or of one finally and definitely achieved. . . . The self that we are does not possess itself; one could say that it 'happens.' "[2]

I do not (yet) want to investigate the epistemological problematics of such formulations here; rather, I want to call your attention to a presupposition neostructuralism shares with post-Hegelian philosophy in its entirety, and this is something which, for the most part, it shares consciously, as the frequent references to Marx, Nietzsche, Freud, and Heidegger demonstrate. This prerequisite can be summarized most briefly as follows: that consciousness – or, and this is the same thing, that understanding – through which we observe the world is not, once again, a work of our consciousness or understanding, but rather something that happens or occurs to us. There *is* consciousness, but consciousness is no originary phenomenon, it is no principle (as it still was for Kant and Fichte, and, in a certain sense, for Husserl and Sartre). If our view of the world were a product of our consciousness, then we would be able to explain our condition completely by means of our consciousness. Nothing would be obscure, everything would be masterable, the world would lie before our eyes as an open book we ourselves had written. "In fact," says Gadamer, "history does not belong to us, but we belong to it" (*TM*, 245); and further: "Understanding is not to be thought of so much as an action of one's subjectivity, but as the placing of oneself within a process of tradition, in which past and present are constantly fused" (258). As those thrown into history, we always "arrive, as it were, too late if we want to know what we ought to believe" (446); if we, that is, want to bring before us the significance of our speech that is independent of our historicity (i.e., "objective") by means of a reflection that itself is historical-linguistic. The historical tradition of our system of communication is our inescapable condition; our understanding is always already an implanted understanding; the reflection through which we strive to gain absolute clarity about our situation always protrudes with one of its poles into the unprescribable, into that which is never totally dissolvable in knowledge.

I have intentionally heaped this long list of metaphors, all of which pursue one intention, in order to illustrate the derivativeness of reflection vis-à-vis Being or, for that matter, tradition. These metaphors turn up in the history of philosophy as soon as German idealism – as the last great climax of metaphysical interpretation of Being as Being-at-one's-disposal, i.e., as graspable presence – enters into the phase of self-critique. Here are two examples of this: the first is Fichte's reinterpretation of absolute self-consciousness as a "power into which an eye is implanted."[3] In this formulation the eye of reflection, to which the originality of self-knowledge portrays itself, is given a secondary position, the primary one belonging to force. Indeed, Fichte spoke of a "*feeling* of dependence and conditionality";[4] this formula does not question the originality of consciousness and of freedom, but it does admit that both of these, precisely because of their originality, cannot be brought back once again to a ground, and in this sense they indeed are groundless and ungroundable. The second example I want to present to you picks up directly at this point: Friedrich Schleiermacher introduced the expression "feeling of absolute dependence" into the debate about the originality of consciousness; with this he sought to express that the supreme consciousness of which the human being is capable cannot provide once more for itself, but rather remains inaccessible in its very Being. Schleiermacher distinguishes these two forms of causation—in the discourse of philosophical terminology—as real ground and knowledge ground (*ratio essendi/ratio cognoscendi*). The real ground founds the *Dasein* of a state of affairs; the knowledge ground founds its knowability. Applied to absolute consciousness this means that the self is the basis of its own self-*knowledge*, but not the basis of its own *Being* (and not even of the Being of its self-knowledge). Schleiermacher also distinguishes between both of these grounds when he claims that the innerliness of self-consciousness "simply takes place *in* the subject," but is not "effected *by* the subject."[5] From its first appearance in section 3 of Schleiermacher's *Christian Faith* onward, the concept of "feeling" carries the additional meaning of "determinateness." What is so distinguishing about feeling (in which knowledge has its origin) is "that we are conscious of our selves as absolutely dependent."[6] One can also express it in this way: the principle and last securing ground of all recent philosophy, the evidence of our immediate self-experience, is itself "somehow *determined*, but it is irrelevant exactly how." "This transcendent determinateness of self-consciousness is the religious aspect of the same, or the *religious feeling*, and in this the transcendental ground or the highest being is itself represented."[7]

I have presented the example from Schleiermacher in more detail because it allows an interpretation that is interesting for us. Namely, it allows us to translate the inaccessible determinateness of self-consciousness as *être signifié*. That would mean—and you certainly remember what we described as the paradox of Fichte's *Science of Knowledge* a few lectures ago—that self-consciousness itself carries the trace of a "transcendent determinateness" (in the sense of "signification d'origine transcendante"), by virtue of which it is marked in its Being in the first place, as well as distinguished from other beings. Derrida called this act of differentiation or articulation, as we know, *différance*. And we also know he is of the opinion that self-consciousness does not escape, to the extent that it is determined, the law of the "structurality of structure." In other words, insofar as self-consciousness grasps itself *as* that which it is, it is already marked by the trace of a tardiness vis-à-vis that by which it feels itself shaped, i.e., upon which it is dependent—on the basis of its absolute determinateness. As soon as it opens its eyes it is robbed of its presence.

Thus here the experience of the groundlessness or secondariness of self-consciousness—from which follow both the historicity of *Dasein* and the inescapability of structure—found its first significant expression.[8] We only need to show that even neostructuralism refers back to this experience. I want to give you a few especially characteristic examples of this from the work of Michel Foucault and of Louis Althusser. They all basically vary Fichte's formula of the implanted gaze or the implanted eye, a formula, thus, that wants to express figuratively that the gaze through which we make our world accessible was not created by us, but rather implanted into us; we were—to play with the metaphor—in-oculated. As soon as we see something *as* something, we are already in a (Heideggerian) clearing of Being that unfolds itself *in* us but not *through* us, and with a view to which we experience ourselves as dependent.

For Foucault it is a certain order of discourse that implants into us the gaze for our world.

> The field of relations that characterizes a discursive formation is the locus in which symbolizations and effects may be perceived, situated, and determined.[9]

Everything that in classical philosophy was taken to be an activity of the subject—its ability to perceive objects, to ascertain their relation to each other and thereby to determine them—is seen by Foucault as a secondary effect of what he calls the discursive formation of an age. Before I explain this expression I want to give a few more quotations that have the same thrust.

> This group of elements, formed in a regular manner by a discursive practice, and which are indispensable to the constitution of a science, although they are not necessarily destined to give rise to one, can be called *knowledge*. Knowledge is that of which one can speak in a discursive practice, and which is specified by that fact: the domain constituted by the different objects that will or will not acquire a scientific status (the knowledge of psychiatry in the nineteenth century is not the sum of what was thought to be true, but the whole set of practices, singularities, and deviations of which one could speak in psychiatric discourse); knowledge is also the space in which the subject may take up a position and speak of the objects with which he deals in his discourse; . . . archaeology finds the point of balance of its analysis in *savoir*—that is, in a domain in which the subject is necessarily situated and dependent, and can never figure as titular (either as a transcendental activity, or as empirical consciousness). (*AK*, 182–83)

I will add two quotations from the introduction to Louis Althusser and Étienne Balibar's *Reading Capital*, in order to expand our list of examples.

> Any object or problem situated on the terrain and within the horizon, i.e., in the definite structured field of the theoretical problematic of a given theoretical discipline, is visible. We must take these words literally. The sighting is thus no longer the act of an individual subject, endowed with the faculty of "vision" which he exercises either attentively or distractedly; the sighting is the act of its structural conditions, it is the relation of immanent reflection between the field of the problematic and *its* objects and *its* problems. Vision then loses the religious privileges of divine reading: it is no more than a reflection of the immanent necessity that ties an object or problem to its conditions of existence, which lie in the conditions of its production. It is literally no

longer the eye (the mind's eye) of a subject which *sees* what exists in
the field defined by a theoretical problematic: it is this field itself which
sees itself in the objects or problems it defines—sighting being merely
the necessary reflection of the field on its objects. (This no doubt explains a "substitution" in the classical philosophies of vision, which are
very embarrassed by *having* to say *both* that the light of vision comes
from the eye, *and* that it comes from the object.)[16]

If the structural conditions that implant the eye into the theory change, then even
such a "change of terrain" cannot be explained as the effect of an innovative action
on the part of the subject (or subjects).

Here I take this transformation for a fact, without any claim to analyse
the mechanism that unleashed it and completed it. The fact that this
"change of terrain" which produces as its effect this metamorphosis in
the gaze, was itself only produced in very specific, complex and often
dramatic conditions; that it is absolutely irreducible to the idealist myth
of a mental decision to change "view-points"; that it brings into play a
whole process that the subject's sighting, far from producing, merely
reflects in its own place; that in this process of real transformation of
the means of production of knowledge, the claims of a "constitutive
subject" are as vain as are the claims of the subject of vision in the
production of the visible; that the whole process takes place in the dialectical crisis of the mutation of a theoretical structure in which the
"subject" plays, not the part it believes it is playing, but the part which
is assigned to it by the mechanism of the process—all these are questions that cannot be studied here. (*RC*, 27)

Let's summarize the decisive common points of these four passages. The first
states that the field of relations that constructs a "discursive formation" is what
initially allows the subject introduced into this field to interact symbolically, to
perceive objects, to relate them to other objects, to differentiate them from other
objects: in short, to determine and differentiate its world. The second quotation
applies this fundamental thesis to a particular case of knowledge (*savoir*) in which
it underscores that neither subjective certainty nor possible truth elevates a statement to the status of a knowledge (in Foucault's sense), but rather that "to know"
means to be inscribed in a field of symbolic practices (*pratiques*) whose rules reproduce the knowledge. The subject that supposedly performs these practices
sovereignly and critically projects their meaning, proves itself to be "necessarily
situated and dependent," without ever being able to appear as proprietor or primary authority of the discursive field. If the subject has consciousness of itself,
it will mainly be the consciousness of its own utter dependence.

In both passages from Althusser and Balibar we come across variations of the
metaphor of the implanted eye that we first found in Fichte. The first passage addresses the being-implanted of the gaze—thus of the theoretical attitude to the

world; the second addresses the being-implanted of praxis as well, which exchanges one structural formation for another.

In the first passage it is stated that the gaze through which a state of the world presents itself to us as a meaningful context of involvements is forestructured. "Forestructured" is to be understood quite literally: the significations and concepts we invest in a particular theoretical worldview are not expressions of our intentions, i.e., not the externalization of our prearticulated (*vorausdrücklich*) interior, as Husserl calls it; rather the signs, through whose application we theoretically survey (articulate) reality, are put at our disposal by structure. As soon as we use them, our assertion that *we* are the ones who established them comes too late. The gaze that is permitted to us by a certain context of signs pregiven by the discursive entirety of an age is always a gaze implanted into us—it is inoculated into us "literally."[11] *How* exactly does one explain the phenomenon of consciousness and self-consciousness, for which, undoubtedly, an immediate access to itself is indispensable, if one, in addition, simultaneously maintains that consciousness is an effect that appears in and through the differential play of the marks of a structure? Before formulating objections one must first, in fact, know precisely the thesis at which they are directed and understand well its motivations. As you see, I am concentrating on presenting to you the main features of neostructuralism; and this presupposes that I attempt first of all to *understand* as well as possible the causes that have led to its formulation. And in my opinion what Foucault and Althusser give us to consider can certainly be understood.

We saw that the fundamental insight of structuralism (which is perhaps identical with the fundamental insight of postclassical philosophy in its entirety, insofar as it participates in the *linguistic turn*) is that in the world there are no thoughts in themselves, and that thoughts require for their distinction the structuring of the material of expression. Most of you were certainly convinced by this thesis and by the way Saussure justified it. Now we do not want to abandon it too quickly just because of a few oddities that arise when one considers its consequences. For the consciousness that I have of my psychic and mental acts or states is yet doubtless in every case a *thought*. If that is the case, it must distinguish itself from other thoughts in order to determine itself; i.e., it must articulate itself. But to articulate itself means to inscribe itself in a structural texture through whose "play of difference" it can first become that thought as which we—apparently immediately—grasp it. Now Foucault and Althusser say precisely this about the genesis of our self-consciousness.

On the other hand, we have been warned in advance: Derrida and Lyotard have given reasons that cause us to doubt that structures are ever "whole," i.e., closed in themselves. If the play of differences has to be conceived as infinitely open, the thought of our self must also be alterable and without final identity. We might like to spontaneously protest against the imputation that lies in this consequence. In philosophy, however, protestations must be fundamentally better grounded than the position against which they are directed. And as long as we are not capable of rejecting or limiting the notion that there is no thought where there is no sign (and thus no structure), we should not repress our doubts, but rather think them through thoroughly. One thing can be ascertained: even if structures are conceived as open, this does not disqualify the structuralist principle that meaning and significance (and therefore thoughts) are only formed interstructurally, and that, since even I-ness (*Ichheit*) is a thought, this is likewise valid for the self.

Althusser, by the way, whose revolutionary Marxism would otherwise remain unfounded, explicitly takes into account the fact of the alteration of structure. We find it in the last of the quotations I cited: the transformation of structures is the result of very complex conditions; we would like to know something more definite about this, but at any rate, it seems to be a fact that subjectivity that is practical and projects meaning plays no role in the alteration of structure. And this is exactly what we wanted to know. Althusser says in strangely hypnotizing formulations that there is no such thing as a "constitutive subject," not even in the practical field; but even the *practices* of subjects are not the causes but rather the effect of structural processes that must be conceived as changes in relations of production (relations of production are, however, as the phrase itself implies, structured). Thus Althusser arrives at the conclusion that structure both implants the gaze into the subject, and also prescribes its practices.

But precisely how, one might ask, does this occur? Especially the Saussure of the *Edition critique* had always admitted that articulation of the material of expression is only one side of the process of meaning formation, the other side of which consists in interpretation. In other words, Saussure thought that articulation is indeed a necessary condition for the distinction of thoughts, but not a sufficient condition, just as a cause *without* which something else does not occur is far from having to be that cause *through* which the effect is positively triggered. For example, no one will doubt that the suspension or reduction of philosophy classes at some Paris universities and high schools necessarily presupposes a world-economical crisis, without already wanting to imply that the recession is positively responsible for the measures of Giscardist educational policy in Paris. The same could be true of the relationship of articulation and interpretation: it could be true—and here we have to agree completely with structuralism—that there is no meaning where no play of differences governs; and it could further be true that the play of differences, when left to itself, does not positively found meaning. The examination of this will be a main task of coming lectures, especially those that address details of the neostructuralist theory of the subject and of meaning. At this point I only want to mention, with Foucault and Althusser in mind, that Saussure himself, in fact, believed that the (speaker's) consciousness creates the units in the flow of the spoken mass (*masse parlée*): "Thought is what defines the units: there is always a relationship with thought."[12] Another passage reads:

> The *langue* can be considered as something that, from one moment to the next, *interprets* the generation that it receives; *langue* is an instrument that one tries to understand. The present collectivity does not at all interpret it like the preceding generations, for the conditions have changed, and the means for understanding it are no longer the same. *Thus there has to be the first act of interpretation, which is active. . . . This interpretation will be revealed by distinguishing the units* (which is what all *langue* activity leads to).[13]

Therefore, while there is no distinctness without differentiation of the "spoken mass," this differentiation occurs for its part, however, in light of an interpretation of which Saussure claims no less than that *it* is what posits the distinctions of the units (i.e., determines them and, on the basis of a new interpretation, dissolves them again).

This is not the place to investigate *how* this interpreting activity appears from close up. Foucault and Althusser are, at any rate, not aware of it and are driven for this reason to a characteristic formulation: it is not the eye of a subject (or of the idealistic spirit) that makes visible the context of involvements of a symbolic order; rather the eye of the subject is seen, for its part, by the structural field. In other words, the consciousness that begins in and with each use of signs is not the effect of a projection of meaning, but rather a process of self-reflection of this field. (With this Althusser finds himself in argumentative proximity to Marx, who also criticized idealistic philosophy for calling the subject, in an unusual *quid pro quo*, what "in reality" is only a predicate [namely, the self-consciousness of subjects], while it views the authentic subject of the historical process [the social reality in flesh and blood] as a mere predicate of the absolute spirit.) In this way not only the *theory* of a society is a reflex generated by structures, but even the *praxis* of subjects is nothing more than a reflection of the subjects on the latitude of their actions assigned to them by the structure. Here you must recall the terminology of Marx and Engels, who liked to translate *reflection* as *mirroring* (*Widerspiegelung*) (of pregiven infrastructures).

Before we examine the dethroning of the self-consciously acting subject in the theory of Foucault and Althusser for its practical consequences, and, in addition, for its concrete execution, I want to make four remarks about the argument itself. The fact that these remarks to a certain extent have a critical accent does not mean that I take the argument with Foucault and Althusser (and other authors of neostructuralism) to be complete and capable of a final judgment. On the contrary, I would like to mention a few motifs that also recur in other texts of neostructuralism, and for which we want to be prepared. First of all, I find in the formulation

"*We* are not the ones who see the discursive field, but much rather the field that sees us," a circle characteristic of all similar formulations. It appears in more intensive form when it is maintained that "the sighting . . . is the relation of immanent reflection between the field of the problematic and *its* objects and *its* problems" (*RC*, 25). This immanent reflection of the field onto itself (and its elements) is not only equivalent to what Hegel calls "intro-Reflection" (and thus to a figure from classical philosophy of the subject); it also misses its critical intention in another way. This intention, after all, was to allow the supposedly autarchic subject to step down as the author of structure. However, what was achieved by the formulation just given was that what, up to this point, was considered the achievement of the "constitutive subject," now has to be attributed to structure itself, namely, the capacity for self-reflection and practical change. Both capacities are now given over to structure (or to the field, or to the discursive formation), without, at the same time, having brought a fundamental objection against the theorem of praxis and of self-reflection. Thus Althusser's objection to idealism, that, *quid pro quo*, the constitutive subject takes over the position of structure, turns against Althusser himself. Subjectivity, which was repressed in the position of the individual, returns as subjectivity of the reflecting and actively transforming structure—return of the repressed.

Second, I discover certain parallels to neutral monism's theory of consciousness in the explanation of the phenomenon of "consciousness" as we were introduced to it in rudimentary form through the passages from Foucault and Althusser. Neutral monism is a position represented by William James, Ernst Mach, and, for some time, Bertrand Russell. As the name suggests, it remains neutral concerning the alternative of an idealist or a materialist explanation of the phenomenon of consciousness. To put it briefly, this position maintains that consciousness is a feature of relations between elements, not, however, between an I and an object. We will come across this position again when we criticize in more detail the neostructuralist theory of the subject. At this point, we will only mention that the idea of an "implanted gaze" is, to a large extent, similar to that of neutral monism, for the gaze is indeed no longer constituted by a meaning-projecting practical subject, but rather appears as a secondary effect of relations within the structural (or discursive) field.

Among the thinkers of neostructuralism, Lacan has found the strongest formulations for this. He speaks of the subject as an effect of language, or, to be more precise, as an "effect of the signifier."[14] According to Lacan, even the passive grammatical form through which we express the significance of a sign—*signifié*, signified—is an indication of this. The supposedly prior self-possession of meaning must hand over its authority to the action of the signifier that prescribes the effects, "in which the signifiable appears as submitting to its mark, by becoming through that passion the signified" (*E*, 284).

Of course, this is an abbreviated expression: *one* signifier can for itself alone effect nothing at all. This makes clear Lacan's definition of the signifier, which at first glance seems obscure.

> My definition of a signifier (there is no other) is as follows: a signifier is that which represents the subject for another signifier. This signifier will therefore be the signifier for which all the other signifiers represent the subject: that is to say, in the absence of this signifier, all the other signifiers represent nothing, since nothing is represented only *for* something else. (*E*, 316)

I would summarize the quintessence of this "definition" as follows: the subject (or the meaning in which it resides) is what occurs in the play of references between at least two signifiers, just as for Saussure the value of a sign occurs in the play of at least two "verbal images." I conclude that this interpretation correctly represents Lacan's opinion because the only parallel formulation that I found in his *Écrits* corroborates it: "The subject . . . is produced by the appeal made in the Other [this is Lacan's standard phrase for Freud's unconscious] to the second signifier" (*E* [Fr. ed.], 835). I understand him to say that subjectivity is explained here as a (negative) effect of differential relations between elements of the structure: negative, because this effect only occurs if the subject renounces its positivity and thereby is subsumed thoroughly by the negative "play of differences." (This explains its relative "nullity," its mode of Being a "nothingness of Being," which was already recognized by idealism.)

My third remark addresses certain parallels between formulations by Foucault or Althusser, on the one hand, and similar ones by Gadamer, on the other hand, concerning the passivity of the subject. I do not want to look at them individually, rather I will only indicate what kind of language usage I am thinking of: Gadamer likes to say that it is less true that the subject speaks language, than that it is what is spoken by language (*TM*, 421). Likewise we "fall into" a conversation, rather than "conduct" it (*TM*, 345). The coming-into-language of the truth of a discourse shows itself as "something that the thing itself does, and which thought 'suffers.' This activity of the thing itself is the real speculative moment that takes hold of the speaker" (*TM*, 431). "Thus here it really is true to say that this event is not our action upon the thing, but the act of the thing itself" (*TM*, 421). This chain of metaphorical expressions always has the same intention: to deny the idea that the subject chooses its interpretation of the world sovereignly and by virtue of its own autarchy; on the contrary, it in fact arrives at its self-understanding conversely by virtue of standing in a tradition—and this view connects Gadamer's hermeneutics with Foucault's archaeology. It makes no difference in this context whether I say "tradition" (like Gadamer), "discourse" (like Foucault), or "structural field" (like Althusser): it is enough to understand that even traditions, insofar as processes of communication are stored in them, as is also the case for what

Foucault calls "archive," obey *rules*, for every symbolic interaction is guided by rules.

Fourth and finally, I want to recall a common source of hermeneutic and of neostructuralist expression in the metaphor of the implanted gaze—a source that is cited neither by Foucault nor by Althusser (although it is by Derrida and Lacan): I am referring to Heidegger's metaphor about the clearing of Being. This metaphor seeks to express that the frame of interpretation within which we live our relations to the world and to other subjects is not the work of our sovereignty, but rather is something sent by Being that shows itself (or lets us see it) precisely under this particular interpretation. Heidegger also speaks of "disclosure." The "world" in which we exist and through which we understand ourselves precedes our self-understanding and our self-consciousness: only with the aid of signs, which an already constituted context of references puts at our disposal, can we attain a consciousness of our world, of our situation, and of our self (*BT*, sections 17 and 18). You see that even Heidegger had already denied the subject a prior subsisting self-consciousness: for him the subject is tendered (*veräussert*) to its world completely ek-statically, and it gains knowledge of itself only out of the reflection that "relucently" falls back on it from the objects of the world. Understanding, Heidegger says, is *Dasein's* (this is his name for the subject) most authentic possibility of transgressing Being in the direction of its meaning, in order to let be announced "relucently" to itself from *Dasein* what it itself is (*BT*, 42).[15] The model of consciousness that underlies this formulation by Heidegger is similar to that of neostructuralism in a decisive point: both assume that consciousness has no prior access to itself, but rather that it learns what is the case with itself from the "order of things," from that which Heidegger calls its "world."

> The kind of Being which belongs to Dasein is rather such that, in understanding its own Being, it has a tendency to do so in terms of that entity towards which it comports itself proximally and in a way which is essentially constant—in terms of the "world." In Dasein itself, and therefore in its own understanding of Being, the way the world is understood is, as we shall show, reflected back ontologically upon the way in which Dasein itself gets interpreted. (36–37)

Now we could assume that what Heidegger calls "world" is semiologically scarcely articulated. The structuralists take issue with the possibility of a self-reflection prior to the "world" with the argument that there is no meaning where expression fails. But Heidegger, without, however, referring to Saussure, comes very close to this conclusion. In the chapters of *Being and Time* dedicated to the "idea of the worldhood of the world," there are sections entitled "Reference and Signs" (section 17) and "Involvement and Significance: The Worldhood of the World" (section 18). Here Heidegger demonstrates very exactly that the understandability of the "world" is an effect of its disclosure by means of "signs"; or, said differently, of its articulating taking into possession through a being that approaches it practically. Its referentiality to other signs is essential to the sign: the quantity of signs becomes a world — the frame of a structure that orients me — only if all are connected to one another. The totality of such a context of references Heidegger also likes to call a "totality of involvements" (*un tout finalisé*, as the French translators write). In such a "totality of involvements" (116), the totality is always prior to the individual parts: it is, as Heidegger expresses it, the condition of possibility for the fact that a single being is familiar to me under the point of view of its applicability. For I know the "world" in which this "equipment" is involved, i.e., in which this object of use or this sign functions.

> But what does it mean to say that that for which entities within-the-world are proximally freed must have been previously disclosed? To Dasein's Being, an *understanding* [emphasis added] of Being belongs. Any understanding [*Verständnis*] has its Being in an act of understanding [*Verstehen*]. If Being-in-the-world is a kind of Being which is essentially befitting to Dasein, then to understand Being-in-the-world belongs to the essential content of its understanding of Being. The previous disclosure of that for which what we encounter within-the-world is subsequently freed, amounts to nothing else than understanding the world — that world towards which Dasein as an entity always comports itself. . . .
>
> In the *act of understanding* [*Verstehen*], which we shall analyse more thoroughly later (compare Section 31), the relations indicated above must have been previously disclosed; the act of understanding holds them in this disclosedness. It holds itself in them with familiarity; and in so doing, it holds them *before* itself, for it is in these that its assignment operates. The understanding lets itself make assignments both in these relationships themselves and of them. The relational character which these relationships of assigning possess, we take as one of *signifying*. . . . *Dasein, in its familiarity with significance, is the ontical condition for the possibility of discovering entities which are encountered in a world with involvement (readiness-to-hand) as their kind of Being, and which can thus make themselves known as they are in themselves* [*in seinem Ansich*]. . . .
>
> But in significance itself, with which Dasein is always familiar, there lurks the ontological condition which makes it possible for Dasein, as something which understands and interprets, to disclose such things as "signification"; upon these, in turn, is founded the Being of words and of language. (*BT*, 118, 120–21)

We will see that Foucault strictly distinguishes his procedure from what Heidegger calls "understanding" and Gadamer calls "hermeneutics." The essential reason for this is that in French *herméneutique* and *compréhension* have different connotations from those of their German equivalents. *One* difference, however, does not occur between Foucault and Heidegger, namely, that one made semiologic order of discourse the basis of his analyses, while the other sought to interpret a semiologically unarticulated "world." Heidegger, as I have said, owes a French-educated reader much with regard to the determination of the status of Being of the sign and of the symbolic order; but he does not owe the reader this: that, for example, he did not understand the "context of involvements" as a *structured* totality. Earlier (Lecture 3) I cited the quotation that supports this assertion, but I now repeat it in its context, preserved from a structuralist and formalizing appropriation.

> The context of assignments or references, which, as significance, is constitutive for worldhood, can be taken formally in the sense of a system of Relations. But one must note that in such formalizations the phenomena get levelled off so much that their real phenomenal content may be lost, especially in the case of such "simple" relationships as those which lurk in significance. The phenomenal content of these "Relations" and "Relata"—the "in-order-to," the "for-the-sake-of," and the "with-which" of an involvement—is such that they resist any sort of mathematical functionalization; nor are they merely something thought, first posited in an "act of thinking." They are rather relationships in which concernful circumspection as such already dwells. This "system of Relations," as something constitutive for worldhood, is so far from volatilizing the Being of the ready-to-hand within-the-world, that the worldhood of the world provides the basis on which such entities can for the first time be discovered as they are "substantially" "in themselves." And only if entities within-the-world can be encountered at all, it is possible, in the field of such entities, to make accessible what is just present-at-hand and no more. By reason of their Being-just-present-at-hand-and-no-more, these latter entities can have their "properties" defined mathematically in "functional concepts." Ontologically, such concepts are possible only in relation to entities whose Being has the character of pure substantiality. Functional concepts are never possible except as formalized substantial concepts. (121–22)

One will see this diatribe against the procedures of formalization as unsophisticated. They apparently are directed against Cassirer's *Substance and Function in Einstein's Theory of Relativity*, which appeared in 1910, and whose thematics philosophers already discussed quite early on in connection with the statement from the *Cours* that language is not a substance but a form, and which probably influenced the terminology of the early Wittgenstein. Be that as it may, Heidegger admits that "disclosure" *can* be conceived as a context of signs, and this, in turn, can be conceived as a structure of the type of a system of relations. The expression "system of relations" that Heidegger uses here (I assume, as already stated, that he borrows it from Cassirer) is in no way terminologically neutral. Indeed, it is generally assumed that with precisely this phrase one describes in a conceptually correct manner what the structuralist conception of language understands under a structure in general, and a linguistic structure in particular—and which, in addition, Rudolf Carnap, for example, conceives of in a similar way in his *The Logical Structure of the World*, which appeared in 1928. The term "relational structure" can be developed most succinctly out of a differential comparison with the concept of "algebraic structure." An algebraic structure is a triple function (E, R, O), whereby E refers to the elements or set of individuals, R to a set of relations, and O to a set of operations. "If a structure contains only operations and no relations, we are dealing with an *algebra*; if a structure contains only relations, i.e., if the set O is empty, then one speaks of a *relational structure* or of a *relational system*, just as is the case with the system of a *language*."[16]

When Heidegger admits this, on the one hand, for his concept of the context of signs or references, and limits it, on the other hand, his caution seems to me to have a simple reason. What he calls "mathematical formalization" could in the worst case portray the inert reproduction of a prior interpretation (or disclosure/clearing) of the meaning of Being; and it is to this extent not "autonomous" or "purely formal," as presupposed by Hjelmslev's famous definition of linguistic structure as an "autonomous entity of inner dependencies." Against this type of formalization Heidegger insists on what he, perhaps clumsily, calls the "substantial": namely, the ontic priority of a clearing of Being (i.e., of a world disclosed to our praxis) before its ontological and, in an extended sense, scientific theoretization and reduction to presence at hand.

We will see in what follows the extent to which this objection also pertains to Foucault's analysis of discourse.

Lecture 7

In our previous lecture we described several figures of thought that recur in Foucault's procedure of historiography called "archaeology." What first seemed striking to us was the metaphor of the "implanted eye" (or "gaze") in which we recognized a figure of idealism's self-criticism at the turn to what the later Schelling first called "existential philosophy." Then we mentioned some of the difficulties that arise when one abandons the concept of a subject that sovereignly projects its meaning, without renouncing the claim to an always possible self-reflection (no longer of the subject, to be sure, but of structure). Finally, we recalled the theoretical impulse that Foucault's thought received from Heidegger's idea of a history of Being in the form of images of the world that indomitably prefigure (*vorgeben*) all our thinking and understanding (I consider this impulse more significant than that which Foucault received from Bachelard's and Canguilhem's epistemology, although he refers more frequently to these predecessors than to Heidegger). In this context we also mentioned that Heidegger himself described the "world," from which subjects "relucently" allow their self-understanding to be mediated to them, as a context of signs and even designated it with the specifically structuralist term "system of relations." To be sure, we have not yet gathered all the constitutive elements out of which Foucault constructs what he calls the "order of discourse," but we already have the essential parts in our hands.

We want to examine these questions by means of a cursory reading of *The Order of Things*. This book, one of the most debated works by this author, is subtitled *Une Archéologie des sciences humaines* and appeared in 1966. For us it is interesting not only for methodological reasons but also because of the content it presents in its four hundred or so pages: namely, the history of two epochal ruptures—that which occurred at the transition from the Renaissance to the Enlightenment (Foucault says: to the "classical age"); and that which took place during romanticism (as the dislodging of "classical learning") and which still shapes our present time. This history seeks, among other things, to explain how the "paradigm of representation" was overcome and how the human subject could have assumed such a central place in the so-called historical sciences, as we know them from the nineteenth century. This break with the representational model of cognition has something to do with the question that above all others motivates us, namely, the question of whether we have to see the concept of the sign system as open or as closed. In this regard we may expect quite a bit from a reading of this text by Foucault, for this reading is the first that lets us see, and not only systematically think through, the decay of taxonomical thinking as something that actually took place, as a *historical* process.

But first we are curious to know what kind of historiography we are dealing with here. In the preface to the German translation of *The Order of Things*, Foucault expressly refused the honor of being called a "structuralist."[1] And indeed, I think we should heed his request. (I myself cautiously insert Foucault's works into the frame of neostructuralism without overlooking that the authors I gather here would also reject this title.) Foucault objected just as strenuously to being viewed as a thinker in whose work the concepts of history (as a meaningful and teleological movement) and of the transcendental subject play a role. And indeed, his concept of *discourse*, which we want to approach step-by-step (since Foucault himself nowhere introduces it in a plausible way), shares with the concept of synchrony as it was developed by Saussure's editors the refusal to explain the meaning of elements of a symbolical order in any other manner than from within the totality of this order itself, i.e., specifically, not diachronically. The question, of course, is how one can still pass as a historian after such a comprehensive preliminary decision of a theoretical order. Sartre was one of the first who asked Foucault this question. He expressed his opinion about *The Order of Things* in an interview that appeared under the title "Jean-Paul Sartre répond."

> What Foucault presents us with, as Kanters saw very well, is a geology: the series of successive layers that make up our "ground." Each one of these layers defines the conditions of possibility of a certain type of thought which prevailed during a certain period. But Foucault tells us neither what would be most interesting, namely how each thought is constructed on the basis of these conditions, nor how men move from one thought to another. In order to do this he would have to bring in praxis, and therefore history, and this is precisely what he refuses to do. Of course his perspective remains historical. He distinguishes between epochs, a before and an after. But he replaces cinema with a magic lantern, and movement with a succession of immobilities.[2]

Despite their critical intention, Sartre's remarks are absolutely appropriate as a description of Foucault's procedure (I am leaving the polemics of the interview aside: it answers a prior polemic on the part of Foucault against Sartre that is also of little interest to us). What he does not mention, however, is that Foucault is by no means the inventor of this type of historiography, but that—apart from the French epistemologists—Heidegger too, whom many consider the one in whom the thinking of historicity culminated, completely severed the history of Being from the opinions and actions of subjects. For the essential thought that gave the ultimate impulse to the strange talk about a history of Being was, after all, that subjects always only arrive at their self-understanding in an already "cleared" world, i.e., in a world that is already furnished with meaning; and to this extent they cannot—except at the price of a circle—be considered the hermeneutical or practical authors or coauthors who establish such a symbolical order. By holding on to this idea—which Bachelard also presupposes, without supporting it ontolog- ically or epistemologically—Foucault is in a sense more consistent than Sartre. Therefore we do not want to reject immediately and polemically the fundamental insight of Foucault's archaeology—the Schleiermacherian "germinal idea." Rather we want to concede that it has a certain consistency.

At the beginning of his book, Foucault claims in a biographical note that it was through a text by Jorge Luis Borges the he was first struck with the idea of writing *The Order of Things*. Borges quotes a certain Chinese encyclopedia that suggests the following classification of animals.

> (a) belonging to the Emperor, (b) embalmed, (c) tame, (d) sucking pigs, (e) sirens, (f) fabulous, (g) stray dogs, (h) included in the present classification, (i) frenzied, (j) innumerable, (k) drawn with a very fine camelhair brush, (l) *et cetera*, (m) having just broken the water pitcher, (n) that from a long way off look like flies.

Foucault comments:

> In the wonderment of this taxonomy, the thing we apprehend in one great leap, the thing that, by means of the fable, is demonstrated as the exotic charm of another system of thought, is the limitation of our own, the stark impossibility of thinking *that*. (*OT*, xv)

The amused wonderment about the fact that a foreign culture collects what is so obviously disconnected under the heading of "classification of animals" makes ap- parent, through contrast, the nonnecessity (i.e., the historical relativity) of our own schemes of thought. We then turn to them "with the estranging eye of the anthropologist" or the "archaeologist" for whom familiarity with a culture—with *his* culture—could only be an obstacle preventing him from studying attentively and without prejudice the foreignness of the foreign. For indeed, what could be a greater obstacle to the study of the thought processes according to which the

Chinese classification was accomplished than the Eurocentric refusal "of thinking *that*"? One thing, of course, is necessary to make sure that the wonderment about the foreignness of the foreign reflects back on the archaeologist as a wonderment about the foreignness and non-self-evidence of the familiar: one has to make certain that the foreign (and the familiar as well) are effects of what Foucault calls a "thinking." Apparently all thinking moves within the context of a symbolic order by virtue of which "Being" is disclosed – in a way that is linguistically and culturally determined – to the members of a specific linguistic and cultural context. To admit this is not to maintain that it always is, or must be, one and the same order within which the members of this order communicate. If we call *discourse*, in a still-vague approximation, a cultural order that allows all subjects socialized under its reign to talk with each other and to interact, then we will presume that there is *always* an *order* of discourse, but not necessarily always *one* order of *all* discourses. Such a superorder, such a universal metadiscourse, was the dream of the European *episteme* as manifest in differing ways in the Enlightenment, in idealism, and in the utopia of technical-scientific world domination. If one only and without exception calls "thinking" a movement within the boundaries of rational discursive formation, then it is very difficult – and Foucault jokingly demonstrates these difficulties – to accept the Chinese classification for animals as the product of *thinking*. At least this is how Foucault seems to use the term "thinking," for he calls this classification unthinkable since it holds no smallest common denominator and no intelligible reasons for its divisions, unless the rules of the language in which it is composed can be considered to be such: "Yet, though language can spread them before us, it can only do so in an unthinkable space" (xvii). No "*u*topia," but rather an "*a*topia": i.e., the loss of a "common space" (tópos) among the listed objects and thus of *one* (image of the) world that unites them (xviii).

I am not certain whether it is very apt to call what is foreign unthinkable. Whoever speaks in this fashion presupposes that only the familiar can be understood (or thought), whereas, as we know, no order of thinking was, is, or will ever be stable; and yet we nevertheless can communicate with each other more or less successfully about our world and our intentions. The ability to "divine" and disclose foreign meaning, even without completely mastering the underlying "code," is generally greatly underestimated in structuralism.

Be that as it may, the actual deprivation – or what was experienced as such – of a familiar scheme of order can suddenly make us aware that our presumably so freely moving thoughts always hold on to an instituted contextual order whose reliability alone allows us to think something *as* something (and not as something else), and to arrive at a consensus with other thinking beings about it. To this extent an exclusion of the unthinkable lies at the origin of all order: a keeping-at-a-distance of everything that will be rejected by the rules of the discourse as something that does not make sense, or that will be prohibited as hostile to the system.

Foucault amply demonstrated this in his previous books on the history of madness and on the birth of the clinic (and of the medical gaze). In his preface he remarks:

> What historical *a priori* provided the starting-point from which it was possible to define the great checkerboard of distinct identities established against the confused, undefined, faceless, and, as it were, indifferent background of differences? The history of madness would be the history of the Other—of that which, for a given culture, is at once interior and foreign, therefore to be excluded (so as to exorcize the interior danger) but by being shut away (in order to reduce its otherness); whereas the history of the order imposed on things would be the history of the Same—of that which, for a given culture, is both dispersed and related, therefore to be distinguished by kinds and to be collected together into identities. (*OT*, xxiv)

According to this observation, discursive (or, as Lacan likes to say: symbolic) orders function in the first instance by excluding or including/confining (in order to keep under control) whatever opposes their principle of construction; second, they function by gathering under the unity of the same whatever is consistent with this principle. This is exactly how we defined a closed system (a closed structure): all distinctions produced by articulation disclose themselves as effects of one and the same act of structuring (for *struere* means to construct what was formerly divided and disconnected according to an order). This is likewise true for the great systems of philosophy or of classical physics: they distinguish and divide their elements, but according to rigid principles that let the different be recognized as instances of one and the same (the ground of differentiation and the ground of relation only occur together). An image of the world knows many words and expressions, and yet it remains the same in all of them. Likewise, Hegel's spirit remains the same in all its manifestations. On this point Foucault comments:

> In fact, there is no similitude and no distinction, even for the wholly untrained perception, that is not the result of a precise operation and of the application of a preliminary criterion. A "system of elements"—a definition of the segments by which the resemblances and differences can be shown, the types of variation by which those segments can be affected, and, lastly, the threshold above which there is a difference and below which there is a similitude—is indispensable for the establishment of even the simplest form of order. Order is, at one and the same time, that which is given in things as their inner law, the hidden network that determines the way they confront one another, and also that which has no existence except in the grid created by a glance, an examination, a language; and it is only in the blank spaces of this grid that order manifests itself in depth as though already there, waiting in silence for the moment of expression. (xx)

A completely conventional characterization of what we called structure or system; at the conclusion of the passage, however, we again find the characteristic attempt to exclude from "order" any contribution of a constitutive subject. (One could make a fitting observation already at this point, one that will be developed later: what is excluded from Foucault's thinking is the subject; it is put under the thought prohibition he so penetratingly examined in the "dispositives of power" and in the exclusionary mechanisms of penalty and confinement.) This is given away by the phrase that is so characteristic of Foucault and other neostructuralists: in the domain of order things look at each other. That means that it is not a subject observing or reflecting on them; rather order itself, as their autonomous self-reflection, is what metaphysics called the subject. The old subject disappears — as the confined Other of the order — in the white squares of the graph paper, only to rise again as the potential of a possible statement. (I have deliberately chosen my words, although I have only paraphrased Foucault: for structuralism/neostructuralism does not completely succeed in the banishment of the subject; it survives as a kind of potential, as an empty position pregnant with meaning. We will yet have occasion to ask ourselves whether the idealists, or Husserl, or Sartre actually conceived the subject much differently than this.)

Foucault, by the way, does not simply leave the given definition of order as it is. Similar to Lévi-Strauss, who defined myth as something in between the reversible order of *langue* and the irreversible order of *parole*, he wants to see *the* discourses, whose investigation *The Order of Things* pursues, understood as second-degree orders. Unfortunately, it is not especially clear what Foucault means with this definition of his key term. If I am correct, this second-degree order or "middle region" (xxi) means something like this: no culture presents the simple and unequivocal mirror image of what we know as its "fundamental codes," for example, "those governing its language, its schemas of perception, its exchanges, its techniques, its values, the hierarchy of its practices" (xx). Nor is culture identical with the scientific or philosophical theories that either justify this order on the basis of a principle, or examine it in its systematic composition, i.e., that take a reflective and systematic position with regard to the order of the life-world. The "empirical" and "philosophical-theoretical" view of order tends rather toward extremes between which a third can be inserted — the one we are looking for — about which Foucault maintains that it is not less fundamental (*pas moins fondamental*), although its blueprint is less strict and thus more difficult to analyze.

It is here that a culture, imperceptibly deviating from the empirical orders prescribed for it by its primary codes, instituting an initial separation from them, causes them to lose their original transparency, relinquishes its immediate and invisible powers, frees itself sufficiently to discover that these orders are perhaps not the only possible ones or the best ones; this culture then finds itself faced with the stark fact that there exists, below the level of its spontaneous orders, things that are in themselves capable of being ordered, that belong to a certain unspoken order; the fact, in short, that order *exists*. As though emancipating itself to some extent from its linguistic, perceptual, and practical grids, the culture superimposed on them another kind of grid which neutralized them, which by this superimposition both revealed and excluded them at the same time, so that the culture, by this very process, came face to face with order in its primary state. It is on the basis of this newly perceived order that the codes of language, perception, and practice are criticized and rendered partially invalid. It is on the basis of this order, taken as a firm foundation, that general theories as to the ordering of things, and the interpretation that such an ordering involves, will be constructed. Thus, between the already "encoded" eye and reflexive knowledge there is a middle region which liberates order itself. (xx-xxi)

I assume that Foucault understands by this intermediate order all those culture-specific and epoch-specific interpretations that, on the one hand, are "less orderly" (*plus confus, plus obscur*) than what he calls the level of *econnaissances*; i.e., scientifically supported knowledge; on the other hand, they are richer and more concrete than the "primary codes" that uniformly determine our language, our manners, our perception, and our social conventions. We could be dealing with something that has affinities in part with Husserl's "life-world," and in part with traditional "worldviews" or "ideologies." Foucault says that they can "se donner comme [l'ordre] la plus fondamentale": more familiar, more everyday, more deeply rooted, more reliable even than words, perceptions, and gestures through which they are expressed; more solid, original, archaic and, so to speak, "truer" than the theories that seek to sublate them in a comprehensive and explicit explanation; something which, it seems to me, is thoroughly comparable to Heidegger's "world" — understood as an articulated context of assignments and involvements — since it likewise "preontologically" precedes the knowledge of signs and life forms, as well as scientific reflection and formalization. In any case — it is, of course, unsatisfying not to know exactly what the object of a scientific study is — Foucault's book concerns itself with these second-degree grids of order. They are designated as "historical a prioris" that indicate, prior to any scientific examination, the empirical and "positive" conditions of possibility on the basis of which a certain civilization organizes its speech acts, accomplishes its acts of exchange, lives its social life, and looks at its world. Again, Ricoeur's formula (of a "Kantism without a transcendental subject") fits quite well as a description of Foucault's approach. Foucault departs from the epistemological and knowledge-sociological endeavors of Bachelard or the "Annales" group, for example, in that he does not treat traditional disciplines and "objective" knowledge; rather he researches the discursive conditions under which, among other things, they too (but also all prescientific orders) were able to arise (which only in part are reflected and completed in *epistemes*, in veritable modes of knowledge). Foucault is more interested in the conditions of creation than in the structures of what is created. But one should not understand the term "constitution" in the sense of a historistic or transcendental-philosophical "deduction": for Foucault, the ground on which an order is constituted can never be a subject; rather it is, once again, an order – that of discourse in its last stage with its *regard déjà codé*. For the same reason the succession of "positivities" cannot – in a Hegelian manner – be conceived as a teleological process.

> I am not concerned, therefore, to describe the progress of knowledge towards an objectivity in which today's science can finally be recognized; what I am attempting to bring to light is the epistemological field, the *episteme* in which knowledge, envisaged apart from all criteria having reference to its rational value or to its objective forms, grounds its positivity and thereby manifests a history which is not that of its growing perfection, but rather that of its conditions of possibility; in this account, what should appear are those configurations within the *space* of knowledge which have given rise to the diverse forms of empirical science. Such an enterprise is not so much a history, in the traditional meaning of that word, as an "archaeology." (*OT*, xxii)

It would be useful if we could find out more about the methodological details of the conception of archaeology. Unfortunately, Foucault only satisfies our wish for more information in a later book, his *Discours de la méthode,* as it were: namely, his *Archaeology of Knowledge* to which he refers at this point. We will concern ourselves with it in lecture 11.

In *The Order of Things* we have to infer the breadth of the concept of "archaeology" from the manner of its concrete and historical application; for here Foucault is interested not so much in a methodological as in a contentual problem. One can express it with the following question: how did this strange phenomenon of the human sciences (*sciences humaines*) historically evolve? What are its discursive "conditions of possibility"? (*The Order of Things*, after all, has the subtitle: *An Archaeology of the Human Sciences.*)

This question is of special interest to us, for the human sciences – the scientific analysis of the human being as something that in its mode of Being is radically different from all other beings in nature – constitute a paradigm of scientific questioning whose right to exist is emphatically put into question by discourse analysis. One should not rashly confuse "human sciences" with what in Germany is called *Geisteswissenschaften* or with what in the Anglo-Saxon world is termed "moral sciences" (since Mill), that is, with what we call hermeneutics, for example. Instead, Foucault includes disciplines like linguistics, philology, biology, anthropology, and economics in this category; we could also add sociology or psychology, including psychoanalysis, which Foucault mentions at times (*OT*, 373ff.). All these are "sciences" (*Wissenschaften*), in the literal sense of the word, which would not uncritically accept Gadamer's division of "truth and method" – of hermeneutical-historical approaches and procedures that are oriented on the ideal of objectivity characteristic of the exact sciences – as valid for their disciplines. Nevertheless, we must and may at least also hear echoes of the (German) concept of *Geisteswissenschaften* in the concept of the human sciences. Foucault, to be sure, does not speak very penetratingly about the discussion of hermeneutics in the nineteenth and twentieth centuries (his book is rather Franco-centric with regard to its sources, despite its claim to all-European validity). Some of his theses about the human sciences and the image of the world inscribed in them, however, seem to me to make sense only if one also relates them to hermeneutics (in the German sense of the word). Foucault states very clearly that neither biology nor linguistics is, as it were, a human science per se: they become such only on the basis of a certain *interpretation* of their subject matter. According to this interpretation, underlying all cognitive processes there exists a subjective being (*Wesen*) without whose "representations" nothing of that which occurs in society, life, and language would acquire meaning. Using the example of linguistics (which, as we said, is not a human science per se) Foucault says:

> The object of the human sciences is not language (though it is spoken
> by men alone); it is that being which, from the interior of the language
> by which he is surrounded, represents to himself, by speaking, the
> sense of the words or propositions he utters, and finally provides him-
> self with a representation of language itself. (353)

This recourse, which, according to Foucault, is inherent to all human sciences, to an all-representing subject which itself, however, cannot be represented in all its depth (since it constitutes all representability) has obvious hermeneutical ambitions that we should not ignore (for explicit references to historical hermeneutics, see 372–73). Foucault's "archaeology," therefore, was soon understood, especially in Germany, as an alternative to the hermeneutically founded social sciences, and, I believe, rightly so. Thus it is all the more strange that hermeneutics with characteristic magnanimity thus far has ignored Foucault's challenge. Why?

Foucault's procedure is not teleological, i.e., not directed toward a goal. He does not assert (as do, for example, Schelling, Heidegger, and Derrida) that in the West (or, to speak more moderately, in modern times) an interpretation of Being exists and is reinforced that is nothing but the fantasy of a self-empowerment of subjectivity, and this means at the same time, an obscuration of Being, whose twilight we experienced in the human sciences.[3] By contrast, the process, whose "historical a priori foundations" Foucault as archaeologist discovers, is nonnecessary and contingent. Nevertheless, he is of the opinion that each form of knowledge can be described as a transformation of the previous form of knowledge, and thus, as a succession of *epistemes* – to be sure, not a meaningful transformation (carried out in the service of an intentional projection). To the extent that this is the case, Sartre was completely correct in speaking of a *geology* of the human sciences, and in adding that Foucault leaves us completely in the dark about how the transition from one form of knowledge to another takes place. Without the possibility of *understanding* this process, there is no way of distinguishing archaeology from something like a natural history in which a species *Homo sapiens sapiens* appears and perishes – a brief bright flame before the planet burns itself out. Foucault, in fact, actually sees it this way, and he even derives a certain comfort and profound peace of mind from this natural-historical gaze that thinks in millennia rather than in centuries. For my part, I am not certain to what extent this can cheer up the reader and lull her/his soul into a state of peace. Judge for yourselves.

> Strangely enough, man – the study of whom is supposed by the naive to be the oldest investigation since Socrates – is probably no more that a kind of rift in the order of things, or, in any case, a configuration whose outlines are determined by the new position he has so recently taken up in the field of knowledge. Whence all the chimeras of the new humanisms, all the facile solutions of an "anthropology" understood as a universal reflection on man, half-empirical, half-philosophical. It is comforting, however, and a source of profound relief to think that man is only a recent invention, a figure not yet two centuries old, a new wrinkle in our knowledge, and that he will disappear again as soon as that knowledge has discovered a new form. (xxiii)

Basically, genealogy (in the sense of Darwin and Nietzsche) and historicism are allied in this concept. It is historistic – I know that this label estranges on first sight – that Foucault describes the history of the images of the world as one that is subject to no teleology. Each history has the same right as every other one, none brings to light the definitive truth of humanity; all are, according to Ranke's famous phrase, "equally immediate to God." But Foucault's archaeology only shares with historicism the moral and epistemological indifference, not the claim to *understanding* (see *OT*, 372–73). It shares this renunciation of *understanding*, on the other hand, with genealogy. "Genealogical" does not mean "genetic," but rather almost the opposite. When Darwin overthrew Lamarck's model for the evolution of species (which assumed that the transformation of species was the result of meaningful and inherited acts of adaptation), he destroyed, to make a long story short, the paradigm of teleology in the human sciences. The human being did not evolve from the animal kingdom by virtue of some secret "decision of nature for freedom" (as in Hegel or Herder), but rather on the basis of genetic mutations and mechanisms of selection that offered the best chances of survival to the best-adapted organism. Whoever describes history in terms of genealogy never seeks to *understand* the transition from one formation to another as something subjective or intended by God's guiding will; he rather describes in a completely value-free manner the different configurations that, without intelligible reason, offered a greater chance of survival to one type of knowledge rather than to the previous one.[4] The genealogical procedure (Foucault occasionally calls it this himself, referring to Nietzsche, of course) describes transformations of paradigms, *epistemes*, or "discursive orders" as events without intelligible reason. If he were to mention a reason for the change from one *episteme* to another, then his procedure would be comparable to that of teleology, which would bring into play a praxis that meaningfully projects itself onto its future. This renunciation of explanation of meaning and of motivated derivation of *epistemes* forces Foucault's "archaeology" into a characteristic narrative gesture: in retrospect, everything is described as if it *had* to occur as a necessary derivation from a "historical a priori."[5] This historical a priori, however, is, in reality, only a ground of legitimation projected into the transcendental (or, as Foucault says, into the "empirical transcendental") for the factual subsistence of this already existing discursive order.[6] The ineffectuality of taking up the standpoint of a counterreality (a "counterfactuality") over against the positively existing, and then to criticize it from that standpoint, seems to me to give Foucault's "archaeology" a conservative bent, which – based on his approach, not on the subjective morality of the author – drives it even deeper into positivism (i.e., into the factual collaboration with the factual) than what was probably meant by Foucault's audacious self-characterization of himself as a happy positivist (*AK*, 125).

I say "was probably meant," for I am in no way overlooking the fact that the temperament Foucault's attacks on the human sciences display on all fronts also has a critical motive, just as his analyses of clinical, psychiatric, and penal confinement derive from a critical impulse. What I mean, simply, is that the radicalized historicism of the archaeological procedure presents no possibility for justifying the inherent implicit ethics of the procedure as such, for an ethics reduced to a historical a priori loses its normative power and becomes one impotent "positivity" (to use Foucault's favorite term) among others. A positivity is *given* (*gegeben*), but a task that needs to be done is *set* (*aufgegeben*). A positivity *is*; the liberation of subjects from governmental repression *should be* (and thus is *not*). In my opinion, Foucault can only deceive himself about the nature of the ethics that secretly guides him (and thus, his teleology) by taking his *interpretations* of the discursive formations that he analyzed as objective characteristics of the things themselves, and thus as results of deductive conclusions from *epistemes* whose historical a priori was supposedly only just brought to light. In reality, however, "positivity" – even that of the human sciences – is only the precipitate, projected into the objective, of a teleological process of exegesis and interpretation.

Be that as it may, Foucault's "archaeology of the human sciences" deserves to have its fundamental characteristics presented, if only for the sake of its concrete assertions. The book is concerned with two paradigm changes: one between late medieval/early modern thinking and the thinking of the Enlightenment (Foucault calls this enlightened thinking, with an eye for the situation in France, the "thinking of the classical age"); and another such rupture between the thinking of the Enlightenment and that of the nineteenth and twentieth centuries, that is, of the epoch which is characterized by the discovery of man and the human sciences.

To preclassical thinking, Foucault says, the world was interpretable on the basis of the universal analogy of all realms of Being: due to correlations based on similarity, everything is reminiscent of everything else, and the totality of all living beings, for its part, appears in the form of analogy to the superior Being (*summum ens*). What interests Foucault most is that even the relation between the signifying form (*form signante*) and the form of the signified (*form du signe*) is conceived as a correlation based on similarity of the sort that the sign as thing is connected with what it signifies by virtue of a relation of participation.

> Let us call the totality of the learning and skills that enable one to make the signs speak and to discover their meaning, hermeneutics; let us call the totality of the learning and skills that enable one to distinguish the location of the signs, to define what constitutes them as signs, and to know how and by what laws they are linked, semiology: the sixteenth century superimposed hermeneutics and semiology in the form of similitude. To search for a meaning is to bring to light a resemblance. To search for the law governing signs is to discover the things that are alike. The grammar of beings is an exegesis of these things. And what the language they speak has to tell us is quite simply what the syntax is that binds them together. The nature of things, their coexistence, the way in which they are linked together and communicate is nothing other than their resemblance. And that resemblance is visible only in the network of signs that crosses the world from one end to the other. (*OT*, 29)

This conception of the sign (and also of writing) as a thing that, although it does not preserve a fully transparent view through to the *summum ens*, does, however, preserve an (indirect, mediated by similarity) participation in it (35–36), is shaken in the transition to the classical *episteme*, i.e., at the beginning of the eighteenth century. We note in passing how traditional Foucault's treatment of the conceptions of epoch is in the final analysis, and to what extent he falls into the trap of employing such collective singulars of classical intellectual historiography – in spite of his persuasive methodological objections to the use of stratified concepts such as, for example, the "spirit of the age" (*Zeitgeist*) or the "objective spirit." Up to this point—at least, since Stoicism—in the Western world the system of signs was founded on a tripartite relation: /signans—*signatum*— τύγχανον (*conjoncture*) (*OT*, 42). Signifier (*signifiant*) and signified (*signifié*) were interconnected by means of something that stood between them and that bridged their irreconcilability (for example, similarity). This bond of a natural proximity of words and things breaks down with the entrance into the epoch of Enlightenment. From this point on the sign relation is only binary: assignment of one signifier to one signified. However, since the connecting element—τὸ τύγχανον (*la conjoncture*)—is missing, this assignment has to be grounded differently, and, according to Foucault, this is accomplished by means of representation (42ff.). A text that exhibits this "epistemological break" exceptionally well is, according to Foucault, *Don Quixote*, whose protagonist, constantly searching for similarities, instead everywhere comes across the chimeras and reflexes of his eccentric reading of chivalric romances. The reader's laughter unmasks the fact that this world of similarities no longer functions.

> Resemblances and signs have dissolved their former alliance; similitudes have become deceptive and verge upon the visionary or madness; things still remain stubbornly within their ironic identity: they are no longer anything but what they are; words wander off on their own, without content, without resemblance to fill their emptiness; they are no longer the marks of things; they lie sleeping between the pages of books and covered in dust. (47–48)

In the Enlightenment world the relation between the world of words and the world of things is no longer given: it must first be established (arbitrarily) by means of intervention of procedures of ordering and coordination. The classical *episteme*, defined as the totality of historical a prioris (or conditions of possibility) that determine the thinking of the epoch, is therefore based on a general science of order within whose framework analysis (the hollowing out or dekernelization of identities and the segregation of differences) becomes the universal principle of cognition. Reason becomes "analytical," it takes apart the complex syntheses of feudalism, of synthetic reason, and of correlations of similarity. The loss of a *natural* synthesis between things and signs forces reason, as it were, to develop—in a countermove—artificial orders, taxonomies, grammars, etc., in which the pertinence of the signs is based on positing, on arbitrary assignment. And this arbitrary principle of assignment Foucault calls *représentation*. Knowledge no longer reproduces the natural orderedness of the world; rather it brings the world in order, so to speak, for the first time: "since it [the order of the world] was now accomplished according to the order laid down by thought, progressing naturally from the simple to the complex" (54). The naturalness of a world based on relations of similarity is torn down and reconstructed according to the blueprint of analytical rationality in which the deceptive semblance of the sensual world is cognitively penetrated ("enlightened"), and in which from now on everything is assigned to the place that is appropriate to it "in reality" and "by right." The old hierarchies are abraded and stratified by dismantling—"analysis" means literally "to dismantle, to take apart." Similarity cannot stand up to the procedure of differentiating comparison; the supposedly synthetic unity of the world gives way to the endeavor of compiling as complete as possible a list of its details; the intellectual activity of the mind consists no longer in the connection of circumstances and things, but rather in their separation. And finally—for knowledge is differentiation—history and science are strictly segregated: historical traditions are deceptive, and thus one has to examine them from the judgment bench of reason; traditions are not pertinent merely because they were thus far believed and because they have remained a part of a living tradition, but rather because, and to the extent that, they survive critical examination (55–56). (It is well known that Kant was negatively disposed to historical education as the concern of transcendental philosophy: the educated person thinks in terms of traditions, and thus *believes* in this or that, instead of authentically examining it here and now and making a decision through use of transhistorical rationality.)

Foucault, of course, is mostly interested in the sign theory of the Enlightenment.[7] "What is a sign in the classical age?" (*OT*, 58). And what he tells us about it was justifiably called one of the most informative, stimulating, but also most confusing passages of his book. The fundamental thought is the idea that in the absence of a "natural bond" between signified and signifier (as was still present in the Renaissance in the thought of similarity), "representation" had to step into the middle ("a bond of representation"; 65) in order to establish the referential character of signs. Representation, therefore, does not belong to the natural order, but has its origins in convention: the sign becomes, in short, an instrument of the analytically controlled use of reason, of knowledge (60ff.). Whether something is a sign or not, and if it is, to what it refers, is decided by the conclusions of a transhistorical reason, and these conclusions *re-present* themselves in the use of signs, for example, as "universal language," or as *characteristica universalis*. The conventionality of the sign presupposes

> that the relation of the sign to its content is not guaranteed by the order of things in themselves. The relation of the sign to the signified now resides in a space in which there is no longer any intermediary figure to connect them: what connects them is a bond established, inside knowledge, between the *idea of one thing* and the *idea of another*. (63)

This missing mediation between sign and signified is difficult to conceive. In fact, Foucault claims, it is the only possibility the sign has for being a direct representation of thought or knowledge: no intermediary element intrudes into the synthesis of the sign and obscures its transparency.

This is because there is no intermediary element, no opacity intervening between the sign and its content. Signs, therefore, have no other laws than those that may govern their contents: any analysis of signs is at the same time, and without need for further inquiry, the decipherment of what they are trying to say. Inversely, the discovery of what is signified is nothing more than a reflection upon the signs that indicate it. (66)

This transparency derives from the fact that the things that take on the function of a sign (and thus represent another thing) do this in such a way that they represent their act of representing in themselves a second time: "The signifying idea becomes double, since superimposed upon the idea that is replacing another there is also the idea of its representative power" (64). "From the Classical age, the sign is the *representativity* of the representation in so far as it is *representable*" (65). From this one can infer, according to Foucault: first, the coexistence of representing (of using a sign) and thinking (every thinking is an image, a representation *of* something, but in a way that it, for its part, penetrates and recognizes its representativity); and second, that there is no need for a special theory of the sign (for one cannot theorize about the sign as though about a particular object of thinking, because all thinking is self-conscious and reasonable representing).

You probably noticed that Foucault uses the concept of representation in a slightly different manner than we would expect after our still superficial knowledge of Saussure's and Derrida's critique of the representational model of language. Saussure proved that the naive conception, according to which there are ideas in themselves (or thoughts, or elementary perceptions) that are then assigned a name according to convention, is untenable. But when Foucault asserts about the thinking of the Enlightenment that in it words "have been allotted the task and the power of 'representing thought' " (78), he does not want to say that previously existing representational contents are retroactively translated into signs.

> But representing in this case does not mean translating, giving a visible version of, fabricating a material double that will be able, on the external surface of the body, to reproduce thought in its exactitude. Representing must be understood in the strict sense: language represents thought as thought represents itself. (*OT*, 78)

However, if this is supposed to be the opinion of the Enlightenment, then to what extent, you will ask, does this classical model essentially differ from the general semiology of Saussure? Not fundamentally, is Foucault's brief and surprising answer.

> If the sign is the pure and simple connection between what signifies and what is signified . . . then the relation can be established only within the general element of representation: the signifying element and the

signified element are linked only in so far as they are (or have been or can be) represented, and in so far as the one actually represents the other. It was therefore necessary that the Classical theory of the sign should provide itself with an "ideology" to serve as its foundation and philosophical justification, that is, a general analysis of all forms of representation, from elementary sensation to the abstract and complex idea. It was also necessary that Saussure, rediscovering the project of a general semiology, should have given the sign a definition that could seem "psychologistic" (the linking of a concept and an image): this is because he was in fact rediscovering the Classical condition for conceiving of the binary nature of the sign. (67)

With this Saussure would become the rediscoverer and reutilizer of a classical formation of knowledge that was temporarily buried or disturbed by three figures (from Schleiermacher to Nietzsche and Freud) and by three theories that challenge the sign's self-representativity in different ways (*OT*, 74–75). With Saussure there occurred what at the end of *The Order of Things* is called the return of language (*le retour du langage*) (384).

The task of the next lecture will be to attempt to explain this rehabilitation of "representation," which is astonishing within the context of a discussion of neo-structuralism, in order to pave the way for what Foucault calls the overthrow of the paradigm of "representation" by the paradigm of "historical consciousness."

Lecture 8

Following up on the history of two epochal ruptures presented by Foucault in *The Order of Things*, we find ourselves at a point where a world interpreted by means of similarities is replaced by a relationship between signs and states of affairs founded on the principle of representation. Foucault views representation as the central feature of discourse in the Enlightenment, that is, in seventeenth- and eighteenth-century Europe (and mainly France).

Over the course of this series of lectures we have already come across the concept of representation—of "re-presencing" something previously already present—as one of the main targets of neostructuralism's critique. A model of signs based on representation assumes that signs portray either elementary perceptions of the senses, or elementary (inherent) ideas of the human mind, i.e., that they give in retrospect (and for the purpose of communication) a sensual form to entities that are immediately present to the mind's eye even without designation. Needless to say, neither mind nor language consists solely of simple elements; there are also synthetic combinations. However, the classical model of representation assumes that the syntheses by means of which speech combines words of different classes (and thus representations of different types of intellectual and/or sensual activities or apperceptions) to form sentences are linguistic representations of the preceding syntheses by means of which the mind joins word images of elementary impressions or of thoughts with predicates to make judgments. The syntax of a language, thus, would be the mirroring of the logical forms of judgment as they are characteristic of the mind. Given this precondition, there exists a preestablished harmony between the eternal conclusions of (theo-

118

logically or rationally conceived) reason and the linguistic forms in which rational judgments are articulated in sentences and as sentences. To understand a sentence would hence mean to understand what is reasonable in it (the unreasonable, for example, the *res imperceptibilis* of the Evangelists who believed in miracles, cannot be understood); and reasonable is (in a strangely circular conclusion) "whatever kind of thoughts words, according to reason and the laws of the soul, can awaken in us."[1]

Such reasonable thoughts composed according to the invariant "laws of the soul" always depict things as they in themselves *are*, independent of individual interpretation. Therefore, sentences that are based on axioms of reason, and that as such can immediately lay claim to truth (necessity of thought, pertinence, and generality), do not, strictly speaking, need to be mediated by acts of understanding. Indeed, one could say that they are understandable "on their own" by virtue of equal participation of the communicating partners in one common reason. At any rate, history is not the measure of their truth; rather the historical context in which they appear is suspected of disguising their reasonableness, of obscuring it or holding it hostage in a web of myths and other superstitious patterns of interpretation such as those that are characteristic of primitive populations. The task of interpretation consists, then, in liberating the possible truth of a given text (or a perceived speech)—and this in general means at the same time: liberating the truth of the thing or idea that is signified by that text or speech—by means of procedures of critical segregation, or by historically explaining the unreasonable estrangements they have undergone. The famous perspectival limitation of the interpreter, as it is expressed in Chladen's theory of the *viewpoint* (*Sehe-Punckt*), only appears to relativize this standpoint; in reality, he claims no more and no less than that a thing can be observed from numerous sides, without the different judgments made about it (for example, "the rose is pale red" and "the rose smells strong") being logically incompatible.[2] In broad simplification one could say that until the middle of the eighteenth century interpretation did not play a role as a specific problem in the language-grounded forms of knowledge because linguistic form, in its truth, mirrors a logical form, and because the logical form of the synthetic judgments refers immediately to facts, so that reasonable speech coincides with speech pertinent to the facts; the problem of an agreement about the specific use of a statement or about the manner of the linguistic construction of the world does not even arise. If, however, the laws of reason are universal, the same must be true for the laws of grammar in which reason is represented. Enlightenment's system of relations is conceived as universal grammar, i.e., as a system of signifieds that is arbitrarily represented by different signifiers in different languages, without fundamental problems of translation between these languages occurring, at least insofar as these languages are manifestations of the same universal reason.

Now as we recall, Saussure (and Derrida who even outdid him) took exception to this model of linguistic representation of reasonable thoughts and reasonable judgments, asserting that mind, without mediation by signs, remains amorphous and thus cannot be thought as something that, portraying itself, is merely repeated in the order of signs. What Foucault presents with the word *représenter* as the feature of the classical *episteme* deviates in a strange fashion from such a description of the function of representation. For Foucault believes that Saussurean structuralism does not introduce an epistemological revolution in the twentieth century, but rather that it accomplishes a mere reconstruction of the classical concept of representation. The so-called historical grammar—from Bopp through Meillet—is nothing other than a "philological episode" that interrupted the continuity between the grammar of Port Royal and Saussurean semiology.

> And after all, between the last "philosophical," "general," or "reasoned" grammars and Saussure's *Cours*, less than a century passed; in both, there is the same reference, whether explicit or not, to a theory of signs of which the analysis of language would only be a particular and singularly complex case; in both, the same attempt to define the conditions of functioning common to all languages; in both, the same privilege accorded the present organization of language and the same reference to explain a grammatical fact through evolution or historical remanence: the same will to analyze grammar not as a set of more or less coherent precepts, but as a system inside of which a reason would have to be found for all the facts, and for the very ones which appear to be the most deviant.[3]

If this is the case, then either structuralism ("modern linguistics") is in reality a premodern discourse formation, or, inversely, the discourse of the Enlightenment was already structural. Foucault agrees that "it is not easy to give a precise meaning to these coincidences" (iv). We are dealing, of course, with "two different epistemological configurations," which, nevertheless, maintain a number of obvious similarities. Foucault even speaks of a "partial isomorphism of two figures that are in principle foreign to one another" (iv). Chomsky's idea of a "Cartesian linguistics" points in this direction (v). (The work of Karl Marx undergoes in Foucault a similarly ambiguous demotion; it deviates from the work of the bourgeois economist Ricardo only "on the level of opinion": "At the deepest level of Western knowledge, Marxism introduced no real discontinuity"; *OT*, 261.) Comparing Grimm's and Bopp's historical grammar with Saussure's semiology, Foucault actually concludes:

> And it was for this very reason that Saussure had to by-pass this moment in the history of the spoken word, which was a major event for the whole of nineteenth-century philology, in order to restore, beyond its historical forms, the dimension of language in general, and to reopen, after such neglect, the old problem of the sign, which had con-

tinued to animate the whole of thought from Port-Royal to the last of the "Idéologues." . . .

It is well known that Saussure was able to escape from this diachronic vocation of philology only by restoring the relation of language to representation, at the expense of reconstituting a "semiology" which, like general grammar, defined the sign as the connection between two ideas. (*OT*, 286, 294)

One can hardly imagine a greater antithesis, both to Derrida's and to the hermeneutical interpretation of Saussure. And although we do not want to overlook the fact that Foucault, in contrast to Derrida, does not simply describe linguistic representation as the sensual expression of something in itself nonsensual, it is nevertheless clear that he takes over the definition of Port Royal that states: "The sign encloses two ideas, one of the thing representing, the other of the thing represented; and its nature consists in exciting the first by means of the second."[4] Such a binary concept of the sign, however, falls prey to all those objections that Derrida already brought against Saussure's division of signification and value, for as long as the side of expression is distinguishable from the side of meaning, one cannot reduce the "meaning" of a sign entirely to the "principle of difference"; i.e., one cannot dissolve it entirely in the occurrence of articulation. Like a jack-in-the-box it rises again and again as articulation's authentic and distinguishable purpose from the chain of voice production (*chaîne phonatoire*).

Be that as it may, the fact that Foucault treats (although not necessarily trenchantly) Saussure's semiology under the chapter heading "The Return of Language" (*OT*, 303ff.), and that he welcomes it as an event that sounds the funeral bell for the human sciences, allows two conclusions. First, the Foucault of *The Order of Things* is by no means that consistent representative of an anti-Enlightenment attitude for which Jean Améry's polemics attacked him; at least in regard to his clinging to a representational model of language he himself is rather a premodern thinker, at heart archivistic (and rational). Second, we can see that Foucault takes on a special, or marginal, position within the totality of neostructuralism since he is the only one who does not let go of the (although modified) representational model of the sign.

It was François Wahl who, in the second part of his essay "La Philosophie entre l'avant et l'après du structuralisme," most penetratingly pointed out this second consequence.[5] There he states that in Foucault we can observe the strange phenomenon of a critic of the Western *episteme* who believes that he can approach the structures that underlie all thought processes with, of all things, the prestructuralist representational model of designation or of knowledge as it was developed in the Enlightenment. Not only Derrida's classification of Foucaultian archaeology under logocentrism supports this observation; in addition, we can cite numerous confessions by Foucault himself. We already mentioned the most important one: Foucault speaks of a complete transparency of the signifier to the signified.

> In fact, the signifying element has no content, no function, and no determination other than what it represents: it is entirely ordered upon and transparent to it. But this content is indicated only in a representation that posits itself as such, and that which is signified resides, without residuum and without opacity, within the representation of the sign. (*OT*, 64)

This complete transparency of the sign to itself is in many ways similar to the language-theoretical model of reflection of several idealist philosophers. Novalis, for example, says:

> The first signifier [he means the schematizing activity of sign foundation] will have unnoticeably painted its own picture in front of the mirror of reflection, and it will also not be forgotten that the picture is painted in the position in which it paints itself.[6]

Foucault says fundamentally the same thing when he asserts:

> An idea can be the sign of another, not only because a bond of representation can be established between them, but also because this representation can always be represented within the idea that is representing. Or again, because representation in its peculiar essence is always perpendicular to itself: it is at the same time *indication* and *appearance*; a relation to an object and a manifestation of itself. (*OT*, 65)

Those who are familiar with neostructuralism's critique of the concept of the self-representation of self-consciousness are certainly more than a little surprised to see that Foucault takes over this concept, applied to the sign, without much ado. *The Order of Things*, by the way, begins with a now-famous description of *Las meniñas* by Velásquez, a painting in which exactly what Foucault and Novalis describe takes place, namely, a painting-himself of the painter in the position *in which* he paints himself; or, a representation of representation that even brings into the picture the viewer of the painting, who finds himself in the position of the one who is viewed, and which also represents the model by means of a reflection in a mirror (see also *OT*, 307–8).

Before one examines the possibility of such an implicit self-representation in each reference to *something*, one has to ask oneself, of course, whether Foucault justifiably cites this characteristic as a feature of the Enlightenment—his book makes, after all, a historicizing claim. In fact, Foucault worked out this historical relation more clearly in his preface to the *Grammaire général et raisonnée* of Arnauld and Lancelot than in *The Order of Things*. There he asks himself why the logic, but not the grammar, of Port Royal contains an explicit theory of the sign.

His answer is that the generality of grammar cannot be derived from the individual usages of the speakers, not even from the average usage, and certainly not from the side of the word: "General grammar traces particular usages back to universally valid principles" ("Préface," ix-x).

The question is, "What instance guarantees this passage and how can one be sure that, starting from a singular fact, one has indeed attained to an absolutely general form?" (x). The answer is that the generality of correct speech (and thus of grammar) is guaranteed by the unity of reason, which represents itself uniformly, if in changing signifiers, in all languages.

> For the "reason" that traverses the singularity of the languages is not of the order of the historical fact or the accident; it is of the order of what men in general can want to say or mean (*vouloir dire*). (x)

The rules of correct thinking, however, are determined by logic; thus the theory of signs is grounded in logic as well.

There is another thing to consider: while one can use the term "grammar" to designate both the immanent order of speech and the *theory* of this order, there is no such duplication in logic. Logic is nothing but a reflection onto the unconsciously obeyed rules of correct thinking.

> In other words, logic, in relation to the natural art of thinking, is a light that allows us to know ourselves and to be sure that we possess the truth. . . . Its task is purely reflexive; it undertakes to explain only when there is a matter of nontruth. Logic is the art of thinking enlightening itself of itself and formulating itself into words. (xiv-xv)

If we take our first observation (namely, that the generality of grammar is grounded in the general validity of logical thought) with the second (namely, that the art of thinking is reflected in itself), we arrive exactly at Foucault's assertion that every speech act has to once more represent its representing-something in itself. For when I speak, I follow rules; if I want to know why I have to follow precisely these rules in order to speak correctly, then I have to uncover the principles that found them. These founding principles, however, are formulated by *logic*, and they are reflected in themselves.

Foucault also traces this in Enlightenment's concept of the sign (xviff.). The sign (whose rules of usage are formulated by grammar) is, according to the grammar of Port Royal, the representation of a thing for our mind. Foucault paraphrases this definition as follows:

> To give a sign to an idea is to give oneself an idea whose object will be the representative of what constituted the object of the first idea; the object of the sign will be substitutable for and equivalent to the idea of the signified object. (xvii)

This formula is not easily understood. It means this: to designate the idea (or *representation*) that I have of a thing, I have to choose a second representation (or idea), namely, the sign. This second idea—the sign—must have the same object as the first in order to actually serve as the placeholder for the first (original) one. In other words, its object (the object of the sign) must be the representative of that object to which the idea of the mind refers. In this way the completely unfolded sign is a four-part system that can be illustrated as follows:

$$\text{Representation} \rightarrow \text{thing}$$

$$\downarrow$$

$$\text{Representation} \rightarrow \text{thing}$$

or again:

$$\text{Idea} \rightarrow (\text{object} = \text{idea} \rightarrow) \text{object (xviii)}$$

In this schematization one can see more easily than in *The Order of Things* what, according to Foucault, is the nature of this strange self-duplication of representation: "The relation of the idea to its sign is thus a specification or rather a doubling of the idea to its object" (xviii). This reflexivity is nothing other than the inscription of logic within grammar, i.e., the being-dominated of sign usage by the reflexivity of thought that only externally represents itself in the sign usage, which in itself, however, is immediately familiar with itself—by means of its reflexivity: "word and meaning appear to be linked at a level that arises not from grammar but from the speculativeness of thought translucent for itself" (xix).

What Foucault tells us here closely follows the grammar or logic of Port Royal (from the middle of the seventeenth century) and may be considered historically valid, even if it brings to light only a partial aspect of the (early) "classical age." It is also true that the concept of *repraesentatio* (German: *Vorstellung*, French and English: *idée*/"idea") "is promoted to the status of organizing principle of the theory of consciousness and of language, above all by Leibnitz and Wolff."[7] Birus also confirms the correctness of Foucault's assertion that this term gained "more and more a subjective-psychological signification" until the meaning of this placeholding representation (*Stellvertretung*) (by a sign) finally disappeared behind the meaning of the self-reflexivity of a (mental) representation (*Vorstellung*). "This historical development of the term culminated in Kant's treatment of *Vorstellung* in itself (*repraesentatio*) as the most general generic concept of theoretical philosophy"[8] and in K. L. Reinhold's elevation of representation to the status of the general principle of deduction of all philosophy: here the link between "classical knowledge" and philosophical idealism is touched upon. But already Leibnitz had conceived representation as self-reflexive, as the phrase *sibi repraesentare* proves.[9]

Although Foucault can present historical data to support his thesis that the representational model of language implies not only a dependence of speech on thought but also a reflexivity of the representational procedures, one still has to ask oneself whether a representation that is reflected in itself is indeed *possible*. The question is all the more appropriate since Foucault does not clearly reject the representational model in his melding of classical and structuralist thought. (On the contrary, he considers historical criticism of it to be a "mere episode" in the history of philology, which at present is in the process of being replaced by a "return of language.")

Now if a representation that is reflected in itself is possible, one could escape the structurality of structure and we could, without further ado, return to the early idealist model of consciousness in which—as in the early Fichte—the I not only posits itself, but posits itself *as* self-positing.[10] In this case what is represented would always already be disclosed in light of a previous consciousness that jumps outside the play of designation. Foucault, in fact, says that language represents thought in exactly the same way as thought presents itself ("Representing must be understood in the strict sense: language represents thought as thought represents itself"; *OT*, 78). In other words, a sign that simultaneously also designates its being-a-sign dissolves the necessity for *re*presentation in favor of the immediate self-presence of something present.

> And language exists in the gap that representation creates for itself. Words do not, then, form a thin film that duplicates thought on the outside; they recall thought, they indicate it, but inwards first of all, among all those representations that represent other representations. The language of the Classical age is much closer to the thought it is charged with expressing than is generally supposed; but it is not parallel to it; it is caught in the grid of thought, woven into the very fabric it is unrolling. It is not an exterior effect of thought, but thought itself. (*OT*, 78)[11]

We can observe a strange turn in this paragraph that is characteristic of Foucault's image of classicism: the first part of the passage emphasizes that language—the material aspect of language—does not hide thought, so to speak, behind the facade of the signifier; rather it grants it self-reflection as a form of self-presencing precisely by means of the moving away from the represented thing that is inscribed in all representation. The second part of the passage describes this self-reflection that suffuses the materiality and autonomy of the sign completely in terms of Saussurean "articulation": as a being-interwoven of "thought" and "sound" in the differential unity of the sign, and not as a mere "parallelism" of signifier and signified. Nevertheless, the sign is only supposed to be the immediate manifestation of a thought that knows itself even without the sign. This explains why Foucault can understand Saussure's semiology as a return of the representational model of the classical age.

We saw earlier that Fichte uncovered the circular logic in the conception of an immediate being-familiar-with-itself of thought. Since 1800 the formula of to-posit-itself-as-self-positing has been replaced by the formula of the "force with an implanted eye." This formula seeks to take account of the fact that self-consciousness cannot be held responsible a second time for this task of representation *if* it possesses an immediate representation of its self; only when the task of representation occurs is there self-consciousness. In other words, the consciousness of representation cannot simultaneously posit (or know) itself as the ground of the task of representation to which it owes its self-consciousness. And from this we infer that designation is prior to self-consciousness, a conclusion in whose effective history we also located Foucault's "archaeology" — at least until we saw how it itself is caught up in the model of representation. From this François Wahl concludes that Foucault's "archaeology" in no way excludes the recourse to a "transcendental subject," although it renders impossible any compatibility with the principles of neostructuralism. [12]

At this point we do not want to make a final conclusion about the justifiability of this strict judgment (which, we note, was made by a representative of neostructuralism, not by one of its adversaries). Even if Foucault again and again — most obviously in his support of Saussure *as* a thinker who reestablished the Enlightenment formation of thought — expressed his sympathy with a modified form of the model of representation, he still never asserted that the evolution of modern *epistemes* was completed within this model. On the contrary, he dedicated half of his book to the dawn of a new discursive formation, which he discussed not under the heading of *Représenter*, but rather under "The Age of History" (*OT*, 217ff.). The paradigm of representation, which can fairly easily be dated between 1775 and 1825, is transformed by a paradigm that in Germany was called "historical consciousness" (*OT*, 221). Foucault believes that the blossoming of the human sciences follows from it and is built on the foundation of its "historical a priori."

This "epistemological break" has shaken classical thought (which Foucault at this time still broadly calls "discourse") to a greater extent than the thought of the Renaissance was shaken by the classical age. Foucault probably did not exaggerate when he called the break with the model of representation and the dissolution of the paradigm of *order* into that of *history* a fundamental event:

And it took a fundamental event — certainly one of the most radical that ever occurred in Western culture — to bring about the dissolution of the positivity of Classical knowledge, and to constitute another positivity from which, even now, we have doubtless not entirely emerged. . . .
From this springs an almost infinite series of consequences. (220, 243)

Foucault carried out his analysis of the epistemological break under the viewpoints of life (biology), production of value (economy), and production of meaning (philology, linguistics). All these disciplines, he believes, depart from the taxonomical element in classical thought: from the classification of living things, from the analysis of wealth, and from the universal regularities of general grammar and hermeneutics; and they move toward a thinking that dynamizes these ordering disciplines. In biology the concept of organization and evolution appears; analysis of wealth gives way to the reconstruction of its material production (from Adam Smith through to Marx); and the grammatical and rhetorical systems expose a transcendental subject in their depth that originarily produces meaning and uses it in different constellations differently according to its own interpretation. The knowledge of philosophy appears under the auspices of the loss of an origin that it seeks to retrieve in the future.

This rearranging of the historical a priori of (classical) "discourse" necessarily and primarily destroys the concept of representation as well. It is relatively easy to see why. The classical *episteme* is grounded in the assumption that a complete dissolution of the signifier in the signified can be obtained; no property of the sign opposes the thought that represents itself by means of the sign, especially not if the order of thoughts is conceived as atemporal *in its truth*. For something is true, according to classical thought, not because it can be felt, believed, or viewed as true by me here and now, but rather because it simply cannot be felt, believed, or viewed in any other way; what is true is a fortiori always true. This premise is invalidated when time (or History: *l'Histoire*) intervenes or makes its nest in the synthesis of representation. To be temporal means (among other things) not to be simply present. A temporally mediated synthesis of signifier and signified thus cannot simply be described as a relationship of representation. For to represent means to make a prior presence present again in the sign. If, however, the object that the sign "represents" becomes a fact of a historical world, then the sign assumes an index of temporality; i.e., the annotation that the semiological synthesis accomplished by it could be undertaken differently and will be undertaken differently by future generations. Words and things come into flux.

> Obviously, History in this sense is not to be understood as the compilation of factual successions or sequences as they may have occurred; it is the fundamental mode of being of empiricities, upon the basis of which they are affirmed, posited, arranged, and distributed in the space of knowledge for the use of such disciplines or sciences as may arise. . . . History, as we know, is certainly the most erudite, the most aware, the most conscious, and possibly the most cluttered area of our memory. (*OT*, 219)

If one calls thinking in taxonomical orders "metaphysical," then, Foucault maintains, one could go as far as to say that "historical consciousness" overcomes old metaphysics in the same manner as Kant's criticism of metaphysics and Hegel's logical sublation of metaphysics (*OT*, 219, 242–43). (I emphasize this statement by Foucault because it again brings his "archaeology" into noticeable contrast with Derrida's "deconstruction," which, judging from Foucault's perspective, is merely a later event in the course of the evolution of historical-hermeneutical consciousness, whereas Derrida declares even historicism and hermeneutics to be metaphysical, to the extent that they cling to some form of self-relation, and that simply of a temporal-historical sort.)

Be that as it may, historical consciousness introduces — with the nonidentity of the temporal — something obscure into the transparency of the relation of representation: "an element that cannot be reduced to that representation" (*OT*, 237). Within the analysis of wealth it is productive labor (*le travail*) that leaves the dark stain. Within the domain of *histoire naturelle* it is *organization*; in the sphere of language it is the inflectional system (*le système flexionnel*).

> From this event onward, what gives value to the objects of desire is not solely the other objects that desire can represent to itself, but an element that cannot be reduced to that representation: *labour*; what makes it possible to characterize a natural being is no longer the elements that we can analyse in the representations we make for ourselves of it and other beings, it is a certain relation within this being, which we call its *organic structure*; what makes it possible to define a language is not the way in which it represents representations, but a certain internal architecture, a certain manner of modifying the words themselves in accordance with the grammatical position they take up in relation to one another: in other words, its *inflectional system*. In all these cases, the relation of representation to itself, and the relations of order it becomes possible to determine apart from all quantitative forms of measurement, now pass through conditions exterior to the actuality of the representation itself. (237)

What exactly is the nature of these external conditions that obscure the transparency of representation? They can probably best be understood through a comparison: In the Enlightenment (*savoir classique*) the individual signs and the sign chains were considered marks of elementary ideas or of connections of ideas, and they derived their evidence from this recourse to reason. The world of words and the world of things or ideas were one and the same; their referentiality was preestablished. This is no longer the case when reason is viewed as a historical institution that, while following rules, by no means follows rules that are valid for all time.

What does that mean, "to follow rules that are not valid for all time?" Apparently, it means that the elements of the order of reason are not equipped from the beginning with a signification that guarantees their reference to the world.[13] Precisely this was presupposed by classical thought, and precisely this explained the transparency of the signs to the ideas *whose* signs they were. However, if the relation of ideas to their objects is *not* previously defined (and "preestablished" means nothing other than this), then the medium that puts ideas and things in a relation acquires a certain autonomy; and this medium is language, taken as a system of relations or as a schematism. A schema is a rule that indicates how reason has to proceed in order to furnish its categories and concepts with signification and thus with a reference to an object. For in contrast to what the Enlightenment thought about language, ideas are not naturally represented by signs; this occurs only when a schematism—i.e., a language—becomes a mediator. Once a language—and thus a certain intersubjectively accepted manner of interpreting the world—is constituted, then there are indeed also rules of reason; however, these rules can no longer be segregated from the concept of a linguistic interpretation and schematization of the world. One could phrase this in Herder's terminology as follows: neither the world (as the sum of objective facts) nor reason (as the system of ideas) is an originary entity; prior to both is the process of synthesis that can be carried out very differently at different times in the evolution of humankind. Reason and the language that represents it are thus—literally—institutions of a synthetic activity, such as imagination, as expressed in particularly drastic fashion by Herder.

> Our reason is formed only *through fictions*. We incessantly seek and create for ourselves a *One in the Manifold* and give it a form; out of this arise *concepts, ideas, ideals*.[14]

This formulation opens up a series of insights into the theory of language of the nineteenth century, at the end of which stands Nietzsche's essay "On Truth and Falsity in Their Ultramoral Sense."[15] If truth, according to Nietzsche, understood as the correspondence of thought and reality, is itself only an institution of (something instituted by) language and thus by imagination, then one cannot control speech by means of a truth criterion that is independent of language. On the contrary, the concepts of a language and its syntax are nothing other than

> a mobile army of metaphors, metonymies, anthropomorphisms: in short a sum of human relations which became poetically and rhetorically intensified, metamorphosed, adorned, and after long usage seem to a nation fixed, canonic and binding; truths are illusions of which one has forgotten that they *are* illusions; worn-out metaphors which have become powerless to affect the senses; coins which have their obverse effaced and now are no longer of account as coins but merely as metal.[16]

I hope that you can see the point of this interpretation of language, which—despite the many contemporary approaches in linguistics that rely on classical thought, be it "Cartesian linguistics" or taxonomical linguistics—is basically still our own.

It states that the rules of reason, on whose timeless validity the Enlightenment uncritically relied, are the precipitates of synthetic activities behind which, in the final analysis, there is a "transcendental," vital, or laboring subject that founds value and meaning and that simply institutes the circulating signs or life functions or commodities into their respective order and to this extent is not part of this order itself. The founding subject is always one that falls through the mesh of structure: in relation to being it is something that is relatively non-being:

> The very being of that which is represented is now going to fall outside representation itself.
> It is the activity that has produced them [objects, other symbolic orders] and has silently lodged itself within them. (*OT*, 240, 238)

These, then, are the two characteristics of the founding activity: it *founds* the order of representations, and it *escapes* this order. Whatever sees to it that something else enters into a certain order is not a member of this order itself. One of the significations of "transcendental" means exactly this: the condition of possibility for the mode of Being of something other, but not itself falling under the mode of Being of what is founded. Hermeneutics will become the central discipline that tracks down the constituting activity of an organizing subjectivity in the background of (nineteenth-century) orders; this subjectivity presents itself, according to the domain from which it at any given time draws its object, as the force of life ("will to life," "will to power"), as the force of production ("value-producing labor"), or as linguistic *enérgeia*, i.e., as the capacity of creating signs and altering meaning. In each case and in each of these domains it is the ground for the unity and unitedness of the field, and thus for its systematic nature (if we define "system" as a coexistence of many in the unity of one central concern).

> The condition of these links resides henceforth outside representation, beyond its immediate visibility, in a sort of behind-the-scenes world even deeper and more dense than representation itself. (*OT*, 239)

You may have noted that Foucault characterizes the value- and meaning-producing activity as "synthetic," whereas he calls the classical *episteme* "analytic" (*OT*, 243ff.), for example, in the preceding quotation, where he (indirectly) calls it the "condition of these links" that allows the representations to become members of one unified order. Insofar as this is the case, one can also describe the transition from the Enlightenment to postromantic modernism as a transition from the paradigm of analytic reason to that of synthetic reason.[17] Historical consciousness indeed asserts that analysis would literally have nothing to analyze (i.e., dismantle and differentiate), if previously something had not been put together by a synthetic act. For Kant the pure concepts of understanding (*Verstandesbegriffe*) (whose application, for their part, lends unity to all concepts of experience [*Erfahrungsbegriffe*]) are grounded in an overriding synthetic act that he calls the transcendental synthesis of self-consciousness (or of apperception). In the same way, all moral (*sittliche*) actions are grounded in a pure desire that vouches for their unity. And even aesthetic or teleological judgments derive their unity on the basis of an anticipation of a pure purpose of reason that founds them.

> From this, there springs an almost infinite series of consequences—of unlimited consequences, at least, since our thought today still belongs to the same dynasty. In the first rank, we must undoubtedly place the simultaneous emergence of a transcendental theme and new empirical fields—or, if not new, at least distributed and founded in a new way. (243)

This schism between what in a narrow sense is the transcendental-philosophical realm and the empirical domain seems to be connected to the schism between the analytic and the synthetic. In the next lecture we want to investigate what the consequences are of this schism and to what extent it shapes the image of the human sciences.

Lecture 9

If in the previous lecture we informed ourselves particularly thoroughly about what Foucault contributes to the theory of representation in the Enlightenment, this was because we saw that he expressed certain sympathies with this model. From the standpoint of this model he develops — contrastively in *The Order of Things* — the genesis of the human sciences, which he calls a mere "episode" in the course of modern thought. Well, an "episode" is an incident, something that suddenly occurs and then disappears. If one designates the dawn of historical consciousness, which breaks with the model of representation, a mere episode within the flow of Western thought, then one pays all the more attention to the immediately prior, namely, the classical form of knowledge. A simple return to classical discourse is out of the question, of course.[1] Even to consider this possibility would be naive, Foucault admits. He adds, however, that this return would be "all the more tempting, it must be said, because we are so ill-equipped to conceive of the shining but crude being of language, whereas the old theory of representation is there, already constituted, offering us a place in which that being can be lodged and allowed to dissolve into pure function" (*OT*, 338–39). Thus it is probably more than mere sympathy that causes Foucault to dream of Saussure's semiology, of Nietzsche's thought, of Mallarmé's absolute literature, and of other phenomena as the return of language (383–84). The model of representation seems to serve Foucault as the orientational framework for his critique of modernism's image of the world — under the conditions of the insufficiency of a postmodern or "still unknown thought." One could almost maintain that the tenor of his critique of modernism does not so much bear the mark of neostructuralism as it bears that of the Enlightenment (as he sees it).

All the more reason why we are interested in discovering how Foucault explains historical consciousness, and at which points he considers it incompatible with the model of representation. The previous lecture has already provided us with some pieces of information in this regard. The most important was that the model of representation presupposes a preestablished relation between thought and the sign that represents it, and, on top of this, it must be conscious of the representativity of this relation. To designate ideas always simultaneously means knowing that the signs are mere signs. It is precisely this transparency of the relation "thought"/"sign" that is clouded if one conceives it as something that was implanted, as something that has to be established either by a transcendental or by a historical force which produces the relation between the sign and the signified from the outset and which can no longer be controlled by a timeless-universal reason. It is not as if there would no longer be rules for speech; it is not even questioned that these rules are at the same time rules of reason. What is new is that the rules of reason, or of language, are grounded in synthetic acts that precede analysis and remain exterior to it. Analysis would have nothing to sink its teeth into if synthesis had not previously produced something. The dependence of analysis on synthesis, however, clouds the transparency of the relation of depiction that is articulated in analysis; it obscures the bond between language and representation.

Foucault believes that an almost infinite number of consequences arise from this transformation of the classical *episteme* (*OT*, 243). The most important of these is the simultaneous surfacing of the transcendental theme and of new empirical fields. This splitting off of what, in a narrower sense, is transcendental-philosophical from the issue of empiricism seems to be connected with the schism between the synthetic and the analytic. Formerly, Foucault says, there was only *one* general science of order ("*mathesis* as a general science of order"; 243); its field of application embraced not only a priori knowledge (for example, mathematical knowledge) but also empirical knowledge. These two domains of knowledge now fall apart. On the one side there is transcendental philosophy, which founds the conditions of possibility of knowledge (*Erkenntnis*) and explains them on the basis of the performance of a subject that itself is nonempirical (243). On the other side there is a type of thinking that "questions the conditions of a relation between representations from the point of view of the being itself that is represented: what is indicated, on the horizon of all actual representations, as the foundation of their unity" (244). Although even the principles that found the unity of the being that is represented by knowledge are never objectifiable as such (otherwise they would not be principles), they are, in contrast to the subject of transcendental philosophy, nonetheless objective principles, as it were, since they found the concrete context for the world of experience. Foucault calls them "transcendentals" (*transcendantaux*), and as illustrations he mentions "the force of labour, the energy of life, the power of speech" (244).

> In their being, they are outside knowledge, but by that very fact they are conditions of knowledge; they correspond to Kant's discovery of a transcendental field and yet they differ from it in two essential points: they are situated with the object, and, in a way, beyond it. (244)

They thus stand *on the side of the objects*, for they found the context for the concrete realm of experience; they accomplish this foundation of coherence, however, on the basis of a principle that itself is not objective: a regulating idea of the realm of experience, as Kant calls it in his transcendental dialectics. This idea of Kant concerns not the a priori truths but rather the a posteriori (and thus empirical) truths (or syntheses). In this schism between empirical and purely a priori syntheses Foucault recognizes the germ for that schism of intellectual disciplines so characteristic for the nineteenth century: the schism between disciplines oriented toward the methodological ideal of mathematics, and disciplines that, like the *Geisteswissenschaften*, bring an impenetrable synthetic activity into play that is not subject to this ideal of exactitude. One side of this schism, the disciplines of the *transcendantaux*, splits itself further, according to Foucault, into metaphysics and positivism. The metaphysical systems (for example, those of German idealism) seem in a certain sense precritical, for they again dare to present a great systematic explanation of the world (even of the concrete-empirical world) on the basis of *one* idea; positivism, on the other hand, refrains from any recourse to a founding ground that explains the rationality of the realm of experience.

> Thus, on the basis of criticism—or rather on the basis of this displacement of being in relation to representation, of which Kantian doctrine is the first philosophical statement—a fundamental correlation is established: on the one hand there are metaphysics of the object, or, more exactly, metaphysics of that never objectifiable depth from which objects rise up towards our superficial knowledge; and, on the other hand, there are philosophies that set themselves no other task than the observation of precisely that which is given to positive knowledge. (245)

But despite their manifest inimicality to each other, Foucault believes that the disciplines of the "transcendentals"—i.e., of objective syntheses—are epistemologically connected in their common incompatibility with the demand of the analytical sciences (of the purely a priori, the formal-deductive sciences, namely, logic and mathematics).

> The analytic disciplines are found to be epistemologically distinct from those that are bound to make use of synthesis. . . . In this double affirmation—alternating or simultaneous—of being able and not being

able to formalize the empirical, perhaps we should recognize the
ground-plan of that profound event which, towards the end of the eighteenth century, detached the possibility of synthesis from the space of
representations. It is this event that places formalization, or mathematicization, at the very heart of any modern scientific project; it is this
event, too, that explains why all hasty mathematicization or naive formalization of the empirical seems like "pre-critical" dogmatism and a
return to the platitudes of Ideology. (246)

Here we recall an observation expressed in particularly impressive fashion in
Lyotard's *The Postmodern Condition*: the decay of the classical *episteme* is the
decay of the axiom of universality or of a general metalanguage. The general
metalanguage was supposed to guarantee the unity of the individual language
games into which our social and cultural context, as well as our life-world, is
divided. This metadiscourse, which overrides and unifies all individual discourses, would be universal in the original sense of the word: it would be a *unum
versum*, a One that has been turned into a manifold, the consistent unity of a Manifold, i.e., a totality (unity in the manifold is universality). With the decline of
what in France was called "ideology," on the one hand, and of German idealism,
on the other, this postulate of universality became theoretically and practically
untenable as something that is founded a priori.

This is also Foucault's opinion, but, in contrast to Lyotard, he regrets this rupture, and he is inclined to belittle it as a mere "episode" and fight it polemically.

At the beginning of the nineteenth century, the unity of the mathesis
was fractured. Doubly fractured: first, along the line dividing the pure
forms of analysis from the laws of synthesis, second, along the line that
separates, when it is a matter of establishing syntheses, transcendental
subjectivity and the mode of being of objects. (*OT*, 247)

At the time of Descartes and Leibnitz "the reciprocal transparency of knowledge
and philosophy was absolute" (247). With Kant these two forms of knowledge are
divided: from now on they are no longer held together by the same unifying principle. What now became problematical—since it could not be arbitrated through
the unity of a common principle—was the rivalry between formal and transcendental claims for knowledge on the one hand, and that between the domain of empiricities and their transcendental foundation on the other. Foucault concludes his
observations about the break of the nineteenth century with the Enlightenment
model of representation with the following summary:

The most distant consequences—and the most difficult ones for us to
evade—of the fundamental event that occurred in the Western *episteme*
towards the end of the eighteenth century may be summed up as follows: negatively, the domain of the pure forms of knowledge becomes
isolated, attaining both autonomy and sovereignty in relation to all em-

pirical knowledge, causing the endless birth and rebirth of a project to formalize the concrete and to constitute, in spite of everything, pure sciences; positively, the empirical domains become linked with reflections on subjectivity, the human being, and finitude, assuming the value and function of philosophy, as well as of the reduction of philosophy or counterphilosophy. (248–49)

At this point we, for the first time, come across the clearly expressed second worry of Foucault. When representation becomes opaque there evolves a completely new interest in the human subject: the human being, according to Foucault, is, strictly speaking, an invention of romanticism (at the turn of the eighteenth to the nineteenth century), an invention completely foreign to (classical) discourse and that one day will again disappear, like a facial impression in the sand on the seashore.

Before I present the evidence that Foucault cites for his thesis, I want to interrupt my report by expressing a doubt. We saw that Foucault conceives the figure of self-reflection to be inscribed in classical thought. He demonstrated with clever and instructive interpretations that the figure of representation—*stat aliquid pro aliquo*—implies an immanent duplication of referentiality: the idea stands for an object, but not directly, rather it stands for it by letting itself be represented by another idea (the sign), whose object becomes the placeholder of that which constituted the object of the first idea (see the "Préface" to the *Grammaire générale et raisonnée* of Arnauld and Lancelot, xvii). In this way each sign reference is once again embedded or contained in itself: it is always simultaneously conscious of itself *as* something mediated through signs. Furthermore, we saw that this reflexivity that is inscribed in the sign reference brought with it in the course of the Enlightenment an ever-stronger subjectification/psychologization of the term "representation." Initially conceived as linguistic representation (in the sense of "to present, represent, or express something"), *représentation* in the end becomes *représentation* in the sense of the Kantian term *Vorstellung*: the significative representation (*Vertretung*) disappears behind the "self-reflexive relation onto the subject of representing (*Vorstellung*)."[2] This subject of representing (*Vorstellen*), in the philosophy of Johann Gottlieb Fichte at the very latest, stakes its claims as the principle of representing (*Vorstellen*): other than in Kant and Reinhold, "the 'theory of the capacity for representation' is now transposed into a theory of subjectivity."[3] Hendrik Birus draws from this the following conclusion:

> Foucault [gives] no convincing proof for his (more Hegelian than "Classical") thesis of a force specific to *representation* for representing *itself*, this "folding of representation back upon itself" having materialized into something like "the human being" as the theme of anthropology only at the end of the eighteenth century (cf. Foucault, *MC*, esp. 78ff., 85, 92, 319ff.). In contrast to this, Foucault's (at this point, however, sup-

pressed) main authority, Heidegger, emphasizes justifiably the immediate interrelationship between the rise of *representatio* as "Vor-stellung" since Descartes, and the representing human being as the "setting, in which the existent must from now on represent itself, that is, be a view or picture."[4]

In short, the development of classical German (and European) philosophy of the subject took place *gradually*, and not, as Foucault would have it, in the form of a (discontinuous) rupture out of classical philosophy of representation and its idea about the self-reflexivity of representation.[5] Without such a deep continuity of the sort Heidegger and Derrida always emphasized, even Foucault's harmonizing conception of a "destiny of Western philosophy" (*OT*, 248) would remain unintelligible; for what could destiny possibly be if not the unity of an inescapable fate that was gradually executed throughout history: namely, an all-Western interpretation of Being in the sense of presence or disposability—an interpretation that is only fatalistic insofar as it is not based on a wanton act as whose authors the subjects would see themselves?

At this point I discover a decisive weakness in the theoretical foundation that has to support *The Order of Things*. On the one hand, Foucault has to insist on the unfathomable discontinuity of epochs, since the alternative would be continuity, i.e., the stability of a One that would basically remain the same through all transformations. In the final analysis, such a One could only be thought of as a subject. To conceive a subject of history, however, would mean to betray the concept of "archaeology," i.e., its initial fundamental insight. Foucault thus ends up in the conflict of, on the one hand, having bluntly to reject the modern, i.e., postclassical *episteme* and, on the other hand, having to do this by means of the model of representation that—however unconsciously or unintentionally—carries in itself the model of a self-reflecting subject of representations (*représentations*) as an immanent consequence, and which openly brings it to light by the end of the eighteenth century. The herewith admitted continuity between the phase of the Enlightenment and that of postromanticism, however, would make it difficult to talk about an epistemological break between the eighteenth and the nineteenth centuries, and would indicate that it is more a matter of a mere change in emphasis. In regard to Foucault's point of departure—namely, that a subject is out of the question as the source of the historical process since it achieves self-consciousness only in an already encoded world (remember the concept of the "implanted gaze" [*regard déjà codé*])—precisely this thesis has an unwilling similarity to knowledge in the nineteenth century. First of all, because it was the nineteenth century that questioned the self-authorization of the subject (it was Fichte who introduced the concept of the "implanted gaze"); second, because the nineteenth century, as Foucault himself convincingly demonstrated, works with deep structures as an explanatory model, i.e., with structures that, although unconscious themselves, determine our thinking, acting, and feeling from a deeper level. With this, knowledge's own foundation is obscured: history loses its unity and continuity. Surprisingly, Foucault regrets precisely this feature, "that from the nineteenth century the field of knowledge can no longer provide the ground for a reflection that will be homogeneous and uniform at all points" (*OT*, 279). To express it paradoxically and strikingly: Foucault's model of archaeological orders in whose net a knowledge is formed that for the first time mediates between subject and object ("knowledge itself as an anterior and indivisible mode of being between the knowing subject and the object of knowledge"; 252) so resembles the models that he calls "transcendentals" and that he takes to be the characteristic forms of organization of knowledge in the much hated nineteenth and twentieth centuries, that it could be mistaken for one of them. It is a question of synthetic principles, as we saw, which operate from a deeper level like the forces of a magnet that arranges iron chips on a piece of paper into a structured order. Thus also the structured orders of which the eighteenth century was conscious become secondary effects of an energy that is untransparently operating beneath the surface and whose depth cannot be fathomed by any reflection: something that in the literal sense of the word is irrepresentable (*OT*, 251), which ipso facto will be historical because it will produce an infinite number of finite forms none of which will be an adequate expression of the principle, so that the chain of productions will continue on indefinitely.

In the realm of economic facts the acts of exchange that are noticeable on the surface disappear (but not those that initiate the circulation of wealth); they are now explained as practical-inert reflexes of a force that can never be brought to the surface and that since Adam Smith and Ricardo is referred to as the productive force (*Produktivkraft*) of labor. Marx will add that it is a question of the discovery of a commodity "whose use value possesses the peculiar property of being a source of value, whose actual compensation, therefore, is itself an embodiment of labour, and, consequently, a creation of value."[6] This general condition of possibility of wealth in fact corresponds, in the realm of the empirical, to what Kant called "transcendental" in the realm of pure acts of consciousness; thus Marx occasionally speaks of the "seemingly transcendental power" of objectified labor.[7]

Similarly, the hitherto mechanically-analytically explained facts of natural history (*histoire naturelle*) do not disappear from the scientific consciousness of the nineteenth century: now they are deduced, however, from a deep force; namely, from life (*vie*) as a teleological and synthesizing principle on the basis of which the objectified manifestations can ultimately be grasped, while the deep force itself escapes knowledge. The animated world is, as the title of Schopenhauer's principal work indicates, only seemingly "representation"; in reality, however, it is primordial *will* that is prior to all representing and that founds it.[8] The actual moving force is, as Foucault demonstrates nicely with the example of the comparative anatomy of Cuvier, the "internal organic structure of living beings" (*OT*,

252): the principle of production that is common to all species. At the center of the life sciences stands the concept of the *organ*, defined since Kant as the point of intersection of two types of causality: a mechanical cause, which also rules in the domain of inorganic beings, and a finalistic one. Under a final cause Kant understands a purpose that lies in the future, toward which the entire chain of organic production is directed in such a way that the purpose has to be regarded as the cause of the mechanical relation of cause and effect. Even without this speculative cloaking, this idea governs biology in the nineteenth century, for example, in the distinction between structure and function of an organ. With Cuvier the functionalist perspective (which replaces Kant's finalist viewpoint) gains the upper hand and forces the structural-descriptive standpoint more and more into the background. The analytically identifiable blueprints no longer form a feature for classification; rather, living beings are sorted according to the principle of identity, analogy, or inner dependency of their life functions.

> Life is no longer that which can be distinguished in a more or less certain fashion from the mechanical; it is that in which all the possible distinctions between living beings have their basis. It is this transition from the taxonomic to the synthetic notion of life which is indicated, in the chronology of ideas and sciences, by the recrudescence, in the early nineteenth century, of vitalist themes. From the archaeological point of view, what is being established at this particular moment is the conditions of possibility of a *biology*. (269)

Finally—the third "transcendental" is language—the taxonomy of language does not disappear from the consciousness of linguistics in the transition from the eighteenth to the nineteenth century; it is now, however, explained—as in economics and biology—as a secondary effect of a dynamic force of language: as *enérgeia*, not as *ergon* (if we let Humboldt's classical distinction jump in as a placeholder). Foucault follows this process from Friedrich Schlegel's "Essay on the Language and Philosophy of the Indians" (1808), through Jacob Grimm's *Deutsche Grammatik* (1818), to Bopp's *Analytical Comparison of the Sanskrit, Greek, Latin and Teutonic Languages, Shewing the Original Identity of Their Grammatical Structure* (1816). One discovers the "inner form" of the national languages, the respectively different articulation of "world" in the linguistic image of a culture, and grammar as an organic system;[9] but even the relationship among languages is discovered, this time no longer to the extent that they are arbitrary representations of one reason that is common to all humankind, but rather to the extent that they have a common historical origin: the primordial Indo-European language, for example. This is demonstrated by etymological laws of derivation and laws of linguistic transformation (laws of modification of vowels, series of graded vowels, etc.) that enable one to describe every existing national language as a regulated variation of one primordial language. However, the reference to the common primordial language no longer redeems the national languages, as it still did in the Enlightenment, from their irreducible individuality; the comparison remains "lateral because the comparison does not reach back to the elements shared by all languages or to the representative stock upon which they draw; it is therefore not possible to relate a language to the form or the principles that render all other languages possible" (*OT*, 291).

> It is apparent, then, that historicity was introduced into the domain of languages in the same way as into that of living beings. For an evolution—other than one that is solely the traversal of ontological continuities—to be conceived, the smooth unbroken plan of natural history had to be broken, the discontinuity of the sub-kingdoms had to reveal the plans of organic structure in all their diversity and without any intermediary, organisms had to be ordered in accordance with the functional arrangements they were to perform, and thus establish the relations of the living being with what enables it to exist. In the same way, for the history of languages to be conceived, they had to be detached from the broad chronological continuity that had linked them without interruption as far back as their origin; they also had to be freed from the common expanse of representations in which they were caught; by means of this double break, the heterogeneity of the various grammatical systems emerged with its peculiar patternings, the laws prescribing change within each one, and the paths fixing possible lines of development. (292–93)

The scrutiny of the "transcendentals"—"life, labor, language"—leaves us with a division that is virtually impossible to remove. On the one hand, we know that Foucault strictly rejects as an idealistic premise a subject that adequately represents/reflects itself in its activities; the gaze of the archaeologist is the *regard déjà codé*. On the other hand, Foucault blames the historical disciplines of the nineteenth century for distorting the adequate representation of meaning in expression by historicizing the synthesis of the sign; in this context he dreams of a "return of language" and welcomes the first rays of light of a returning age of representation in Saussure, Nietzsche, and Mallarmé.

This immanent contradiction in Foucault's conception is so stunning that I have to support it with additional evidence. In fact, he reproaches historical grammar with frustrating absolute self-recognition and transparency of the recognizing spirit, in contrast to general grammar, which guaranteed precisely this possibility.

> The preeminence that enabled *general grammar* to be *logic* while at the same time intersecting with it has now been lost. To know language is no longer to come as close as possible to knowledge itself; it is merely to apply the methods of understanding in general to a particular domain of objectivity. (*OT*, 296)

According to Foucault, this development was effected by the dissociation of the Enlightenment ideal of a universal science (*mathesis universalis*); from now on languages no longer represent a priori forms; formalization and interpretation fall apart ("Interpretation and formalization have become the two great forms of analysis of our time"; 299). This means that "discourse" no longer, as before, is immediately capable of truth on the basis of its participation in the logic inscribed within it: truth and method now fall apart. On the one side there are linguistic images of the world; they are systematically composed and form the a priori of what can be said and thought ("The grammatical arrangements of a language are the a priori of what can be expressed in it. The truth of discourse is caught in the trap of philology"; 297). On the other side there is the trend toward formalization and toward analysis that culminates in logistics, Russellian and language-analytic philosophy, or in logical empiricism; this trend aims at the control of speech by means of rules that themselves are not produced from linguistic traditions and which to that extent are "objective."

The former trend — the hermeneutical — Foucault identifies with several names: Schleiermacher, Marx, Nietzsche, Freud (78, 298). According to him, they all are looking for a hidden depth of meaning or of actions beneath the surface of a text with the knowledge of which the constellation of the surface could only first be understood, although this depth — like Freud's unconscious — does not even appear on it. The trend toward formalization Foucault supports only with the (misspelled) name "Russel" (corrected in *OT*, 299). What is original is that he considers both trends to be sad results of one and the same epistemological shock, namely, the breaking apart of the model of representation. While from now on hermeneutics yearns for rules and justifications for a successful formalization, logical atomism is desperately looking for an empirical field to which its rules can be assigned. Pure thought and world are estranged from one another. Therefore, Foucault concludes, it is not surprising that both — interpretation and formalization — frequently seek to connect with one another, for example, in different fashions in structuralism and in phenomenology (299). Both trends, however, the search for *sens* as well as for *signifiant*, are two sides of the same coin.

It is true that the division between interpretation and formalization presses upon us and dominates us today. But it is not rigorous enough: the fork it forms has not been driven far enough down into our culture, its two branches are too contemporaneous for us to be able to say even that it is prescribing a simple option or that it is inviting us to choose between the past, which believed in meaning, and the present (the future), which has discovered the significant. In fact, it is a matter of two correlative techniques whose common ground of possibility is formed by the being of language, as it was constituted on the threshold of the modern age. The critical elevation of language, which was a compensation for its subsidence within the object, implied that it had been brought nearer both to an act of knowing, pure of all words, and to the unconscious element in our discourse. It had to be either made transparent to the forms of knowledge, or thrust down into the contents of the unconscious. This certainly explains the nineteenth century's double advance, on the one hand towards formalism in thought and on the other towards the discovery of the unconscious—towards Russell and Freud. It also explains the tendency of one to move towards the other, and of these two directions to cross: the attempt, for example, to discover the pure forms that are imposed upon our unconscious before all content; or again, the endeavour to raise the ground of experience, the sense of being, the lived horizon of all our knowledge to the level of our discourse. It is here that structuralism and phenomenology find, together with the arrangements proper to them, the general space that defines their *common ground*. (299)

There is, Foucault adds, a third possibility of self-presentation of the new paradigm of language: this is romantic-symbolist poetry (300). Only since its existence is there "*la* littérature": it embodies the harshest break with classical knowledge because it points to itself instead of pointing to things, because it becomes radically intransitive and self-reflexive. While it is apparently the opponent of philology, in reality its obstinate silence is only philology's obverse side (*figure jumelle*): the autonomous expression of the refusal to represent world or ideas, i.e., to communicate.

At the moment when language, as spoken and scattered words, becomes an object of knowledge, we see it reappearing in a strictly opposite modality: a silent, cautious deposition of the word upon the whiteness of a piece of paper, where it can possess neither sound nor interlocutor, where it has nothing to say but itself, nothing to do but shine in the brightness of its being. (300)

A strange constellation: analytical philosophy, hermeneutics, structuralism, phenomenology, psychoanalysis, and absolute literature. They all, according to Foucault, spring up on the same archaeological ground: namely, the nineteenth-century conception of language, reworked and revolutionized by historical consciousness. A stronger contrast to Derrida, who finds a completely new discourse initiated with Mallarmé, Nietzsche, and Freud, can hardly be conceived. For Foucault these figures are typical exponents of the nineteenth century, and the "return of language" can occur only after the paradigm embodied in them has exhausted itself. Even a key concept, which Derrida holds up against the harmonizing gesture of the nineteenth-century conception of language, namely, *la dissémination*, the systematic uncontrollability of effects of meaning, the dissemination of meaning, is converted by Foucault into a feature of precisely this nineteenth-century conception of language.

Once detached from representation, language has existed, right up to
our own day, only in a dispersed way: for philologists, words are like
so many objects formed and deposited by history; for those who wish
to achieve a formalization, language must strip itself of its concrete
content and leave nothing visible but those forms of discourse that are
universally valid; if one's intent is to interpret, then words become a
text to be broken down, so as to allow that other meaning hidden in
them to emerge and become clearly visible; lastly, language may sometimes arise for its own sake in an act of writing that designates nothing
other than itself. This dispersion imposes upon language, if not a privileged position, at least a destiny that seems singular when compared
with that of labour or of life. When the table of natural history was dis-
sociated, the living beings within it were not dispersed, but, on the contrary, regrouped around the central enigma of life; when the analysis of
wealth had disappeared, all economic processes were regrouped around
the central fact of production and all that rendered it possible; on the
other hand, when the unity of general grammar—discourse—was broken
up, language appeared in a multiplicity of modes of being, whose unity
was probably irrecoverable. It is for this reason, perhaps, that philosophical reflection for so long held itself aloof from language. (304)

I cite this passage so extensively because even this aspect of Foucault's analysis
is astonishing. In the texts of Derrida or Deleuze there begins with Mallarmé and
Nietzsche a counter movement against the ruling stream of the idea of a sign's
mode of Being that is oriented on the paradigm of reflection and interpretation.
For Foucault, however, the connection of philosophy to the so-called linguistic
turn is simply the executing of an imperative inscribed in the human sciences: to
render the Being of language independent of the demand of a world that exists
unto itself. For Foucault, Nietzsche and Mallarmé are not the surpassers but
rather the culmination of hermeneutics, if only because he dismisses them in one
big sweep with all the human sciences. In this he is consistent: the fragmentation
of language, its liberation from the referent, its irreducibility to a truth value, its
historicization, its self-empowerment, etc., are all simply consequences of the
break with the model of representation of the classical age.

These questions were made possible by the fact that, at the beginning of
the nineteenth century, the law of discourse having been detached from
representation, the being of language itself became, as it were, fragmented; but they became inevitable when, with Nietzsche, and Mallarmé, thought was brought back, and violently so, towards language itself, towards its unique and difficult being. The whole curiosity of our
thought now resides in the question: What is language, how can we find
a way round it in order to make it appear in itself, in all its plenitude?
(306)

On the one hand, Foucault continues, the "transcendental" *language* shares this alleged special position with the "transcendentals" life and labor. On the other hand, the dawn of a new kind of thought pattern seems to be indicated in the becoming-theme of language, and the thinking of the archaeologist belongs to this new age: a thinking from beyond the grammer on the basis of which the West until now has formed its discourse.

> Is it a sign of the approaching birth, or, even less than that, of the very first glow, low in the sky, of a day scarcely even heralded as yet, but in which we can already divine that thought—the thought that has been speaking for thousands of years without knowing what speaking is or even that it is speaking—is about to re-apprehend itself in its entirety, and to illumine itself once more in the lightning flash of being? (306)

Note again the strange division in Foucault's argument: in order to be able to speak at all of all-Western thought, one has to conceive its grammar as a continual and goal-directed unity, completely in the sense of the nineteenth century. At this point the dramatization of epochal ruptures that explode the relations of continuity between epochs becomes superfluous. But even if that were possible, if the West could demonstrate to the gaze of the archaeologist that its discourse is a unity, then archaeology, which guarantees this unity, would not be an undertaking in any way distinguishable from Hegel's self-consciousness of history. At the conclusion of Western spirituality, this spirit would understand itself in retrospect as what it always was: through recognition it would liberate itself from the thus far unconsciously forcing laws of its thought and would make room for a new phase of thought. A new clearing of Being would dawn, a new flash, in which meaning is disclosed, would inundate us in its light.

Be that as it may, Foucault attributes both the dawn of a pattern of thought that is announced in Nietzsche's overcoming of Western grammar, as well as the thought of Grimm, Humboldt, and Bopp, to *one* common event that by now we know sufficiently well.

> In attempting to reconstitute the lost unity of language, is one carrying to its conclusion a thought which is that of the nineteenth century, or is one pursuing forms that are already incompatible with it? The dispersion of language is linked, in fact, in a fundamental way, with the archaeological event we may designate as the disappearance of Discourse. To discover the vast play of language contained once more within a single space might be just as decisive a leap towards a wholly new form of thought as to draw to a close a mode of knowing constituted during the previous century. (307)

In short, if the completely new thought that begins with Foucault's archaeology and the thought of the historic-hermeneutic nineteenth century are based on the same conditions of constitution, then they obviously are *figures jumelles*, just as philology on the one side and absolute poetry on the other. The division in Foucault's thought thus would be the irreconciled schism in the thought of the nineteenth century itself, and not the archaeological overcoming of this schism. Foucault admits this himself.

It is true that I do not know what to reply to such questions, or, given these alternatives, what term I should choose. I cannot even guess whether I shall ever be able to answer them, or whether the day will come when I shall have reasons enough to make any such choice. Nevertheless, I now know why I am able, like everyone else, to ask them—and I am unable not to ask them today. (307)

Nevertheless, Foucault believes that he still has something to say in regard to the "human sciences," for example, that there was no such form of science in the classical age.

Faced with so many instances of ignorance, so many questions remaining in suspense, no doubt some decision must be made. One must say: there is where discourse ends, and perhaps labour begins again. Yet there are still a few more words to be said—words whose status it is probably difficult to justify, since it is a matter of introducing at the last moment, rather like some *deus ex machina*, a character who has not yet appeared in the great Classical interplay of representations. (307)

He is speaking of the human being. In the previously mentioned painting by Velásquez, *Las meniñas*, Foucault believes that the human being was totally missing as subject-center of representation. This painting shows a painter in the position in which he is painting his model, the king. The king himself remains outside the painting in a position that is in the vicinity of the position of the actual viewer. While the king, however, participates in the play of representations (one can detect his mirror image in the background to the right), the real subject of the viewer remains outside this play of representations: the personage for whom the image is an image is not present. Foucault draws from this the following conclusion:

In Classical thought, the personage for whom the representation exists, and who represents himself within it, recognizing himself therein as an image or reflection, he who ties together all the interlacing threads of the "representation in the form of a picture or table"—he is never to be found in that table himself. Before the end of the eighteenth century, *man* did not exist—any more than the potency of life, the fecundity of labour, or the historical density of language. He is a quite recent creature, which the demiurge of knowledge fabricated with its own hands less than two hundred years ago: but he has grown old so quickly that it has been only too easy to imagine that he had been waiting for thou-

sands of years in the darkness for that moment of illumination in which
he would finally be known. (308)

Here we come across one of the most famous theses in Foucault's archaeology,
and it is not particularly shocking to us, for we already encountered it in the preface to *The Order of Things*. Of course it is not Foucault's opinion that the human
being was not already a theme of knowledge in the classical age or even in earlier
ages; but it was not a theme in the sense of being an irreducible and transcendental
knowledge subject, without the presupposition of which the entire world of objectivities and positivities would collapse into nothingness, as it is expressed in
Schopenhauer's concise statement: "No subject, no object." In other words, the
human being was not a particular epistemological problem as such; it was not that
which above all was knowledgeable and which had to be known (*OT*, 309), that
which in part reshaped the sciences into human sciences or *Geisteswissenschaften*.

We formulated our doubts already at an earlier point: it is extremely hard to
make plausible that the self-reflecting human subject is not supposed to be a direct
and continual consequence of the classical view, according to which every
representation (*représentation*) is self-reflexive. How could anyone who conceives the capacity for representation as endowed with the capability to represent
itself possibly see a new paradigm in Kant's and Fichte's philosophy of consciousness, especially since the old claims to universality of the Enlightenment are
preserved in the act of absolute self-consciousness?

We also saw, however, that Foucault's antipathy is not so much directed at this
theorem of self-reflexive representation. To state it outright: his objection is in no
way aimed at absolute self-consciousness (and this distinguishes him, obviously,
from other thinkers of neostructuralism). He expressly refers to Descartes who,
after all, is considered the founder of modern philosophy of self-consciousness.

The transition from the "I think" to the "I am" was accomplished in the
light of evidence, within a discourse whose whole domain and functioning consisted in articulating one upon the other what one represents to
oneself and what is. (311–12)

Such a representational relation between Being and thinking of the human subject, according to Foucault, does not place excessive demands on the limits of
classical discourse; on the contrary, it is its consummate expression. Human
nature is a folding of representation back upon itself (309): it is self-conscious
representing *of* something. Foucault even speaks of a being-represented of things
in the mind's eye.

In the Classical age, discourse is that translucent necessity representation and beings must pass—as beings are represented to the mind's eye
and as representation renders beings visible in their truth. (311)

If it is not this absolute self-transparency that Foucault rebukes as specific to post-classical, human-scientific knowledge, then what is it?

The answer seems astonishing, even if we are by now prepared for such surprises in Foucault: it is the romantic reinterpretation of the subject as self-relation without fathomable ground. What Foucault has to say about this is extremely stimulating. Let's concentrate for now on the kernel of his idea. If representation, according to Foucault, in the process of folding back upon itself meets at the same time something other that cannot be completely dissolved into the gaze of consciousness, then self-relation, which representation exists as, literally feels itself to be overextended. Self-consciousness senses itself as having risen from a ground to which it is not itself ground, and which it can also no longer dissolve into absolute self-consciousness. This basic figure of thought—which we first come across in such a pointed manifestation in Novalis and Hölderlin, then in the later Fichte, in Schelling, Solger, Schleiermacher, Kierkegaard, and Feuerbach as well—can appear in various guises: first of all, as the finality of the human being that does not hold in its hand the conditions of its existing; or as consciousness without access to the infinite, and thus without the possibility of continuing to think within the boundaries of metaphysics; second, as a "doublet empirico-transcendantal." On the one hand, each knowledge and action can only be grounded in a transcendental reflection; on the other hand, this reflection does not escape empirical reality, finality, and historicality: discourse becomes empirico-transcendental and empirico-critical at the same time. And third, the figure of the unfathomable ground appears in the imagery of "*cogito* and the unthought" (*OT*, 322ff.): the unthought and unthinkable is the shadow, as it were, that falls upon self-consciousness and obscures it, insofar as it has an apodictic, but in no way adequate, knowledge of itself (as the classical age had assumed). Self-consciousness is thus no longer absolutely present to itself.

> In the modern *cogito*, on the other hand, we are concerned to grant the highest value, the greatest dimension, to the distance that both separates and links thought-conscious-of-itself and whatever, within thought, is rooted in non-thought. The modern *cogito* . . . must traverse, duplicate, and reactivate in an explicit form the articulation of thought on everything within it, around it, and beneath it which is not thought, yet which is nevertheless not foreign to thought, in the sense of an irreducible, an insuperable exteriority. (*OT*, 324)

The best-known expression of this would be the (romantic, Schopenhauerian, or Freudian) unconscious (327), but the "ineffaceable and fundamental relation to the unthought" can also be, as in Husserl's and Heidegger's phenomenology, "the implicit, the inactual, the sedimented, the non-effected" (327) or an "ontology of the unthought that automatically short-circuits the primacy of the 'I think' " (326). "The unthought," Foucault adds, "is, in relation to man, the Other" (326), from which we can conclude in passing that he certainly would consider Lacan's psychoanalysis to be a human-scientific form of knowledge. But we still have to look at the fourth form in which the figure of the indisposable ground of knowledge is cloaked, namely, temporality as search for the lost ground (*OT*, 328ff.). To exist without ground means not only to exist without justification but also to achieve self-consciousness on a basis that always already is cast off and overcome. This kind of nonpresence is the temporality or noncontemporaneousness of the human being in the face of that under whose presupposition it exists ("thought reveals that man is not contemporaneous with what makes him be"; 334).

> Time—the time that he himself is—cuts him off not only from the dawn from which he sprang but also from that other dawn promised him as still to come. It is clear how this fundamental time—this time on the basis of which time can be given to experience—is different from that which was active in the philosophy of representation: then, time dispersed representation, since it imposed the form of a linear sequence upon it; but representation was able to reconstitute itself for itself in imagination, and thus to duplicate itself perfectly and to subjugate time. . . . In the modern experience, on the contrary, the retreat of the origin is more fundamental than all experience, since it is in it that experience shines and manifests its positivity; it is because man is not contemporaneous with his being that things are presented to him with a time that is proper to them. And here we meet once again the initial theme of finitude. (335)

This basic premise of modern knowledge also, of course, touches on the discourse in which and through which modern knowledge articulates itself. Classical discourse—and we saw that Foucault considers it to be discourse as such—could unfold itself on a permanent table of stable differences and limited identities (339). This is entirely different from the "discourse of the analytic of finitude": it operates within an irreversible time order and on the assumption that the origin has been lost. But the mere Being-related to the thought of a lost origin makes it into thought of the Same (*une pensée du Même*) in the form of thought in continuities. Continuity presupposes both difference and identity; for everything that is continuous bridges different aggregates or states of Being, and thus different times. But the same is true for identity, for we call continuous only that time span in which One remains dynamically identical with itself over the course of changing states. Foucault justifiably finds in this disposition of modern thought the archaeological origin for the formation of dialectics. In contrast to classical thought, to which the Manifold of differences and limited identities was harmless, since it did not impinge upon the concept of a homogeneous, but analytical and time-indifferent reason, modern thought has to integrate dialectically its dissemination: it is both loss of a grounding unity and search for the lost ground. (A note in passing: We can tell to what extent Foucault's definition of modernism is inspired by the self-understanding of romanticism.) Foucault speaks of thought of the Same that is always to be conquered anew by means of contradiction ("a thought of the Same, still to be conquered in its contradiction: which implies . . . a dialectic"; 339–40);

> a dialectical interplay and an ontology without metaphysics: for modern thought is one that moves no longer towards the never-completed formation of Difference, but towards the ever-to-be-accomplished unveiling of the Same. Now, such an unveiling is not accomplished without the simultaneous appearance of the Double, and that hiatus, minuscule and yet invincible, which resides in the "and" of retreat *and* return, of thought *and* the unthought, of the empirical *and* the transcendental, of what belongs to the order of positivity *and* what belongs to the order of foundations. Identity separated from itself by a distance which, in one sense, is interior to it, but, in another, constitutes it, and repetition which posits identity as a datum, but in the form of distance, are without doubt at the heart of that modern thought to which the discovery of time has so hastily been attributed. (340)

Hastily (*hâtivement*) because, according to Foucault, the model of a "distance creating a vacuum within the Same" (ibid.) can more easily be questioned by means of metaphors of *spatial* division, whereas classical taxonomical thought operates with the model of a continuous sequence of *time* that is ever-to-be-returning to its ubiquitous origin. According to this, the *espacement*, of which Mallarmé and Derrida dream as the prerequisite for a "disseminal discourse," is a specific "historical a priori" of *modernism*, and not of a coming "postmodern condition": a new kind of thought first outlined in Nietzsche in which it will be possible to think "in the void left by the disappearance of the human being" ("It is no longer possible to think in our day other than in the void left by man's disappearance"; *OT*, 342).

We cannot at this moment decide what this thought beyond the "human being" who stands in the center might look like. I will report what Foucault has to say about it in my next lecture.

Lecture 10

These lectures, concerned with the question "What is neostructuralism?," roughly follow this outline: after making some preliminary observations regarding the systematical and historical limits of the phenomenon, we wanted to investigate neostructuralism in terms of three questions. First, what does it say about the phenomenon of history? Second, how does it explain the phenomenon of subjectivity? And third, what theory of sign formation and of meaning effects does it have at its disposal?

So far we only began to answer the first question and have in no way exhausted it. It was obvious that we should direct this question at Michel Foucault and Louis Althusser, for both thinkers search for a structural explanation of the phenomenon of "history" on comparable theoretical foundations. First of all, we decided to start with an exploration of Foucault's most readable book — I hesitate to call it his major work, since neostructuralism knows no "major works." We did this not just in order blindly to begin somewhere, but rather because this work supplies us with illustrative material — not only with its methodological abstraction, but with the example of a concrete piece of knowledge-sociological historiography — of what Foucault understands under "archaeology." Moreover, we began with this work because it promises to give us an idea of what we call *Geisteswissenschaften* or "human sciences" in a manner that itself is not human-scientific.

We saw that Foucault rejects for his own historiography the concept of a human being that sovereignly projects its history. He considers the human subject to be a recent, i.e., romantic invention that will perish much as it began. Supported by Heidegger's "history of Being," he wants to explain the change of what he calls *epistemes* (orders of knowledge), not on the basis of the acts of subjects, but by means of sendings (*Schickungen*) whose origin we cannot understand, but whose "historical a prioris" can be analytically reconstructed. The theory that exposes the historical a priori of a momentarily dominant discourse would be "archaeology."

This apparently purely methodological observation implies a massive thesis on the essence of subjectivity that is a persistent element in all of neostructuralism. This procedure assumes that subjectivity always finds itself in the position of something that has been implanted, or to be more exact, in the position of something that is instituted by a symbolic order. The gaze with which we disclose our world and ourselves is implanted into us, or, taken literally, "in-oculated" into us by the inescapable a priori of the epistemic structure. *As soon as* a symbolic order has intervened in us, it is too late to declare ourselves to be the instituters of this gaze.

One can understand this standpoint entirely independently of the question of whether it correctly explains subjectivity. It even seems that certain subject-centric overaccentuations of traditional historiography are favorably corrected. What was confusing to us, however, was a certain ambiguity in Foucault's attitude toward the model of representation of knowledge. Applied to the theory of the subject, this means that the subject at any given time is able to account for the actions through which it discloses the world because it also represents *itself* in all representations *of* something. This theory of knowledge appeared toward the end of the eighteenth century — in Kant, Reinhold, and the early Fichte — and we saw that it developed continuously out of what Foucault called the representationism of the classical age. One would expect Foucault bluntly to reject this theory, for it is incompatible with the view that the subject springs up on a ground that not only escapes its consciousness, but even determines this consciousness. But it is precisely this step that Foucault does not take; he does not attack Cartesianism — the principle of the transparency of knowledge unto itself; rather he attacks its obscuration by the romantic discovery of the unconscious or the unthought that is prior to consciousness and not at its disposal, be it "absolutely transcendental Being" (Schelling), or "unconscious" (Schopenhauer). In every case, however, it is that ungraspable identity that escapes all representation that allows the relation of self-consciousness to arrive at the certainty of being the relation of One to *itself* (and not to something else): "a thought of the Same, still to be conquered in its contradiction" (*OT*, 339). Our question, which remains open, was whether Foucault does not also tear down the foundations of his own archaeology with his critique of such a widely introduced formation of modern thought, especially since he leaves no doubt that he is willing to exclude neither Nietzsche's nor Marx's nor Freud's nor Mallarmé's thought from the game-rules of modern discourse (or at least, as in Nietzsche's case, only with characteristic reservations). It is these authors, however, to whom neostructuralism commonly refers as the forerunners of a still unknown future thought "in the void left by the disappearance of the human being."

To answer our question we have to take a closer look at what Foucault describes as characteristic of the "human sciences." This *episteme* that is characteristic for the nineteenth and twentieth centuries rises, according to Foucault, out of the decline of the Enlightenment axiom of universality: universal formalization and research of the fundamental principles of empirical events from now on do not go hand in hand. Thus formal logic, the deductive and exact natural sciences, and analytical philosophy on the one hand, as well as the hermeneutically founded disciplines, are simultaneously formed. The dispute in which they are engaged is preprogrammed and cannot be decided on the basis of a dominating paradigm.

> Hence that double and inevitable contestation: that which lies at the root of the perpetual controversy between the sciences of man and the sciences proper—the first laying an invincible claim to be the foundation of the second, which are ceaselessly obliged in turn to seek their own foundation, the justification of their method, and the purification of their history, in the teeth of "psychologism," "sociologism," and "historicism"; and that which lies at the root of the endless controversy between philosophy, which objects to the naïveté with which the human sciences try to provide their own foundation, and those same human sciences which claim as their rightful object what would formerly have constituted the domain of philosophy. (*OT*, 345–46)

This schism, as I said, is preprogrammed in the division of the empirical and the transcendental. Since Kant and German idealism, however, there have been constant attempts to overcome this division, i.e., attempts to find constitutive (and not only regulative) principles—to this extent one may call these attempts "transcendental"—which at the same time cover the field of the empiricities (to this extent these attempts are "positive"). After the decline of idealism, *anthropology* inherits this claim to reconciliation: a completely new discipline that claims to be both transcendental and empirical and that lends the entire epoch the pattern of its *episteme*. Marxism and historicism, hermeneutics and psychoanalysis, even the social sciences—all take part in it. Anthropology is transcendental: the world is explained from the standpoint of the human being and of the specifically human production or attribution of meaning. At the same time, anthropology is empirical, for it takes human activity, as Marx calls it, as an "objectified activity," and no longer as a purely spiritual or transcendental spontaneity that can only intervene in the realm of the existing world by means of several mediations. Reference to the "historico-transcendental" or the "empirico-transcendental" can indeed be found in the texts important for the formation of theory in the human sciences, from romanticism (Friedrich Schlegel) to Jürgen Habermas. Foucault speaks of an infringement of the transcendental upon the empirical, or also of a fold.

> In this Fold, the transcendental function is doubled over so that it covers with its dominating network the inert, grey space of empiricity; inversely, empirical contents are given life, gradually pull themselves upright, and are immediately subsumed in a discourse which carries their transcendental presumption into the distance. And so we find philosophy falling asleep once more in the hollow of this Fold: this time not the sleep of Dogmatism, but that of Anthropology. (341)

Here Foucault alludes to the well-known statement by Kant that David Hume awoke him from his "dogmatic slumber" (*Prolegomena*, A 13). What is needed, therefore, is a new Kant who would again prohibit the inadmissible mixture of the transcendental with the empirical for which the epistemological phantom of a constitutive human subject (which simultaneously is never completely transparent to itself) is responsible. Nietzsche, who dreams of the overcoming of the human being by Superman, could be such a Kant of postmodern thought, if not for the fact that his vitalism and historicism share important presuppositions with the historical a priori of the anthropological slumber (341–42). The "will to power" shows all too obviously the traces of early capitalist society of competition, the study of which even led the economist Malthus to the idea that only the best-adapted individuals, i.e., those who are most competitive, could possibly survive, so that one would have to prevent the population explosion of "the poorest and most numerous class." From his reading of Malthus, Darwin, in turn, on his voyage to the New World, developed his working hypothesis that it is the "struggle for existence" that reduces the natural overproduction by means of natural selection to the number of individuals who are best adapted to their biotope. On the basis of this historical a priori Nietzsche ultimately comes to the conclusion that the will that dominates in the West's orientation to truth is "in truth" a will to seize power: a will not only to the preservation of existence, but also to intensification of existence. Thus there arises in him the vision of the "breeding" (*Züchtung*) (conceived completely in terms of genetics) "of a new type of human being" of the *Homo natura* or of the Superman who recognizes the will to truth as a lie of life, and who in joyful acquiescence to fate (*amor fati*), says "Yea and Amen" to the "beautiful cruel life" and who stands above the species *Homo sapiens sapiens* just as the latter stands above the primates (*Works*, XI, 6-9).

To be sure, in comparison with metaphysics this is a "new kind of thinking," and it is also true that it is a thinking *dans le vide de l'homme disparu*. But it is just as true, and Foucault recognizes this, that Nietzsche's thought believes it has uncovered once again in the "will to power" a principle that is simultaneously transcendental and empirical, and whose functioning epistemologically is totally in keeping with Humboldt's language energy and Marx's productive force of labor, and to this extent it reveals itself to be a typical product of anthropological knowledge. This is also valid for the being-obscure-to-itself of the "will to power," as it is lyrically expressed in Zarathustra's *Dancing-Song*: "Of late did I gaze into thine eye, O Life! And into the unfathomable did I there seemed to sink" (*Works*, XI, 127). Even more telling is the metaphor with which the essay "On Truth and Falsity in their Ultramoral Sense" describes human consciousness: it is "hanging in dreams on the back of a tiger" (*Works*, II, 176). This life (*vie*) is simultaneously unfathomable (*unergründlich*) as well as grounding (*gründend*). Thus it is transcendental, but it is at the same time the *ens realissimum*, the realest and most familiar, and thus an empirical and by no means intelligible power. Even teleology is not missing in Nietzsche's dream of the overcoming of the current human being: "The Superman is the meaning of the earth. Let your will say: The Superman *shall be* the meaning of the earth!" (*Works*, XI, 7).

If one suppresses these traces of the nineteenth century in Nietzsche's works, one could predict *ex negativo* the direction in which postanthropological thought would have to unfold according to Foucault's wish.

> If the discovery of the Return is indeed the end of philosophy, then the end of man, for its part, is the return of the beginning of philosophy. It is no longer possible to think in our day other than in the void left by man's disappearance. For this void does not create a deficiency; it does not constitute a lacuna that must be filled. It is nothing more, and nothing less, than the unfolding of a space in which it is once more possible to think. (*OT*, 342)

Under the "obstacle standing obstinately in the way of an imminent new form of thought" (342), Foucault numbers above all the obstacle that exists in the assertion that one cannot think without immediately also thinking that it is the human being that is thinking, and he continues:

> To all these warped and twisted forms of reflection we can answer only with a philosophical laugh—which means, to a certain extent, a silent one. (343)

We did not really want to know so clearly, you will say, in which direction that "imminent new form of thought" moves. Since we now know it, however, we have to take a stand on it.

First of all, we can state that the ambiguity of Foucault's approach does not decrease, but rather increases in the case of his position on the human sciences. Under the conditions of a strictly archaeological approach, a positive or negative judgment on the epistemic formations should not be possible. Furthermore, it seems just as illegitimate to say that a certain epistemic form no longer allows thought, whereas the most recent one still allowed it. For with this, "thought" would be defined in a transarchaeological manner and would no longer arise from the simultaneously positive and relative ground of a symbolic order: "thought" would become, in other words, a *signifié transcendantal*. At this point in Foucault's argument we observe a clear, no longer archaeologically demonstrable opting for the model of representation: in it "thought" was obviously still possible. Even a political—and certainly more Nietzschean than ethical—option is implied in Foucault's theoretical antihumanism, namely, opting against "a leftist thought" in which the human origin of all institutions, all *epistemes*, and all practices is constantly emphasized. This antidemocratic option, too, strictly contradicts the premises of archaeology, which may reconstruct the positive ground of a knowledge, but may not evaluate this knowledge on a moral or argumentative basis. To be sure, such an evaluation seems inevitable *to me*, but I believe that it effaces the basic lines of Foucault's theoretical approach. Once the field of ethics and of argumentation is reopened, we find ourselves in the middle of the epistemic field of the nineteenth century in which left and right positions fight each other, in which better arguments are weighed against worse ones, in which claims to validity are examined transcendentally as well as empirically, etc. Even Foucault's implicit (and not reflected) ethics (which perhaps manifests, despite some poignant statements that received more applause from the political Right, for example, from the *Nouvelle Droite*, than from the Left, not a truly "Right," but rather an anarchistic thinking) does not circumvent the game-rules of the human sciences simply because it ignores them or does not expressly reflect on them. The opinion, moreover, that in premodern knowledge "thought" was still possible on the basis of the model of representation of knowledge and designation turns out to be archaeological in a sense that Foucault himself cannot possibly have intended, and that makes his endeavor—through a trick of reason—outdated and antiquarian. It does not open up a new thinking; rather it opens the backdoor to what we already know and do not necessarily wish the return of.

The final chapter of *The Order of Things* is dedicated to the human sciences as such, but it hardly lends new insights to what we already know. Foucault places what he calls the human sciences into a scarcely intelligible relation with a triad of existing and exact sciences ("The three faces of knowledge"; *OT*, 344ff.). Its three faces are: first, the purely deductive sciences, above all mathematics and physics; second, the empirical sciences (linguistics, biology, economy); and third, philosophical reflection. The human sciences do not belong to any of these three forms of knowledge and consequently are not sciences at all. They do, however, maintain relationships with the three types of knowledge he lists. What Foucault has to say about this is not particularly illuminating. What is more important is how he grasps the difference between the human sciences and the real sciences: according to him, the human sciences do not have different methods or even a different object than the sciences in the strict sense; rather they interpret their object differently. The human being appears in them "as the foundation of all positivities . . . man became that upon the basis of which all knowledge could be constituted as immediate and non-problematized evidence; he became, *a fortiori*, that which justified the calling into question of all knowledge of man" (345). Thus the "essential instability" of the human sciences (348). For a representation that is based on subjective constitution (cf. 352–53) ipso facto becomes a revisable representation whose inconstancy continuously falls back on the human subject in the background of all regularities and occurrences. The human sciences pose as metasciences or hypersciences vis-à-vis the real sciences (whose validity Foucault here, as often, underlines; cf. 354–55) in that they duplicate them in a subject-theoretical manner.

> Here, the human sciences, when they duplicate the sciences of language, labour, and life, when at their finest point they duplicate themselves, are directed not at the establishment of formalized discourse: on the contrary, they thrust man, whom they take as their object in the area of finitude, relativity, and perspective, down into the area of the endless erosion of time. (355)

However, how is the transposition of scientific methods onto human-scientific methods accomplished? Foucault mentions three "models" (taken from biology, from economy, and from linguistics), which he also calls human-scientific "categories" (357): these are the pairs *function and norm, conflict and rule, signification (signification)* or *meaning (sens) and system* (357). With the first term of each of these pairs, the constituting and, so to speak, active or genetic element of the relationship is given; with the second, the deep-structural order that, although itself not falling under consciousness, guarantees the course, the interpretability, and the masterability of the first. In the course of the nineteenth century, Foucault believes, the deep-structural element attracted more and more the interest of the human sciences. Whereas formerly function sought its norm, conflicts remained unregulated if possible, and significations did not fit into a system, now functions, conflicts, and significations are vouched for by norm, rule, and linguistic system. "Everything may be thought within the order of the system, the rule, and the norm" (360). Freud's name represents the zenith of this movement.

> [Freud] prefigures the transition from an analysis in terms of functions, conflicts, and significations to an analysis in terms of norms, rules, and systems: thus all this knowledge, within which Western culture had given itself in one century a certain image of man, pivots on the work of Freud, though without, for all that, leaving its fundamental arrangement. But even so, it is not here—as we shall see later on—that the most decisive importance of psychoanalysis lies. (361)

We already said more than once that it is not easy to render in a clear way the difference that Foucault apparently ordains between the process of unveiling in psychoanalytic hermeneutics, for example, which functions human-scientifically, and the process of unveiling in his own archaeology. When he says about history (which he places in the vicinity of the human sciences), for example, that "to each of the sciences of man it offers a background, which establishes it and provides it with a fixed ground and, as it were, a homeland; it determines the cultural area . . . in which that branch of knowledge can be recognized as having validity" (371), then we may justifiably ask ourselves whether archaeology does not want the same thing or something indistinguishably similar: namely, to survey the symbolical, discursive, or epistemic ground that determines as historical a priori the thought and actions of an epoch. A second analogy comes up in this context: in order to escape the trap of the theory of self-consciousness of the human subject, archaeology assumes that the historical ground on which an epistemic formation rests is unconscious and not representable; but even this it shares with what it says about the theoretical premises of the human sciences. We will see in a concluding discussion of *Les Mots et les choses* how this precarious and, at the very least, ambiguous relation is explained.

The question we are asking ourselves is, to what extent does the archaeological reduction of an epochal self-understanding to an unconscious historical ground depart from the human-scientific one? This question obviously is tied to the question about the role that "representation" plays in the human sciences on the one hand, and in Foucault's archaeology on the other. Freud, the theoretician of the unconscious (as system), spoke of the "regard for representability," or of "drive representations"—in conformity with an old romantic model that, once again, is most clearly brought to light in Schopenhauer's major work: on the one hand, being is unconscious wanting, and, on the other, indirectly the object of our representations. Without denying that the will has primacy in self-consciousness,[1] this conception nevertheless concedes that there are representations of the will without which the unconscious could not be scientifically thematized. Foucault emphasizes this as a constant trait of the ambiguous position the human sciences have toward the model of representation: to be able to be represented does not fundamentally mean to appear to an explicit consciousness (*OT*, 361–62); it only means *to be able* to appear to a consciousness.

> In fact, representation is not consciousness, and there is nothing to prove that this bringing to light of elements or structures that are never presented to consciousness as such enables the human sciences to escape the law of representation. (361)

Applied to language theory of the nineteenth century this means that the role of the concept of signification, so says Foucault, implies the representability of speech for consciousness, even if this speech is neither explicitly nor consciously penetrated with it; in contrast to this, the concept of the linguistic system (in the sense of Humboldt and Schleiermacher) is principally unconscious: "in relation to the consciousness of a signification, the system is indeed always unconscious since it was there before the signification" (362). But this unconsciousness of the system is not principally given; it arises because "the system is always promised to a future consciousness which will perhaps never add it up" (362). That is, the unconsciousness is not based on a principle but rather is structural. Due to the irreducible cooperation of the speaking subjects in the process of meaning formation, that the system controls only as a mere virtuality, one never commands a view of the entire system: its unconsciousness is the here and now not yet realized potentials of meaning formation whose absolute and conscious presencing is thwarted by the openness of human history.

Foucault thus believes that the significance of unconsciousness that the human sciences confer on the system, the rule, and the norm, does not, as it were, endanger the primacy of representation ("It must not be forgotten, therefore, that the increasingly marked importance of the unconscious in no way compromises the primacy of representation"; 363). For without the possibility of making their unconscious present, the human sciences would have to renounce any claim to being forms of *knowledge* of something. Insofar as they insist on the claim of mediating a specific knowledge of the human being, they approach classical thought (for all thought, Foucault obviously believes, is representation; 363–64). On the other hand, the human sciences take up a critical position vis-à-vis the means that elevate them to the status of sciences, and thus vis-à-vis representation: they ask—transcendentally oriented—about the conditions of possibility of such knowledge, and this condition of possibility itself is supposed to be representable.

> They never cease to exercise a critical examination of themselves. They proceed from that which is given to representation to that which renders representation possible, but which is still representation. . . . This quasi-transcendental process is always given in the form of an unveiling. It is always by an unveiling that they are able, as a consequence, to become sufficiently generalized or refined to conceive of individual phenomena. On the horizon of any human science, there is the project of bringing man's consciousness back to its real conditions, of restoring it to the contents and forms that brought it into being, and elude us within it; this is why the problem of the unconscious . . . is not simply a problem within the human sciences which they can be thought of as encountering by chance in their steps; it is a problem that is ultimately coextensive with their very existence. A transcendental raising of level that is, on the other side, an unveiling of the non-conscious is constitutive of all the sciences of man. (364)

Fine, one will say; as a description of the human-scientific method and its knowledge interests what Foucault says is not inappropriate. But at which location can he set the lever of archaeology in order to lift the methodology of the human sciences off the hinges on which they have pivoted (*pivoté*) for a hundred years, i.e., since Freud?

As far as I can see, *The Order of Things* provides no clear answer to this important question. We can, however, sketch the site where it could have been given. Foucault reproaches the human sciences for using circular argumentation: they allow for an unconscious in the background of the subject (of labor, of life, of speech), and to this extent they depart from the paradigm of the universal self-representation of knowledge; on the other hand, they need representation, which is always representation-for-a-consciousness, in order to establish themselves as sciences. These claims, however, are incompatible with one another.

If I have correctly reproduced Foucault's view of what he calls "this peculiar property of the human sciences" (364), then one could, in contrast to this, depict the concept of such an unconscious that cannot be converted into representation. To be sure, even archaeology seeks to lay bare the historical substratum of a form of knowledge in a manner that can be described as "quasi-transcendental." Yet it does not do this, as do the human sciences, in such a way that it lays bare a foundation of this knowledge that is representable to knowledge, which, in the final analysis, would have to be interpreted as a subject untransparent unto itself. The substratum of knowledge, even of that of the human sciences, is not the human being but rather the *episteme*, the symbolic configuration of the "positivity" ruling at any given time.

> In any case, we can see that what manifests this peculiar property of the human sciences is not that privileged and singularly blurred object which is man. For the good reason that it is not man who constitutes them and provides them with a specific domain; it is the general arrangement of the *episteme* that provides them with a site, summons them, and establishes them—thus enabling them to constitute man as their object. (364)

Even if I cannot make out precisely where the argument lies here, one can easily see the point of defense against, and of contrast to, the human sciences: the transcendental self-reflection of the human sciences remains narcissistic; in the structural unconscious—in norm, rule, or system—it always finds only what it already brought into play as its premise, namely, the grounding power of the human being. Precisely for this reason it misses its *real* ground; namely, the positivity of the *epistemes*.

How is one supposed to think about this positivity without falling back into the aporias of the human sciences? As eloquent and garrulous as Foucault otherwise is, what he says about this point at the end of *The Order of Things* is laconic. The book concludes with a view of two forms of knowledge, psychoanalysis and ethnology (373ff.). In them the transition from the modern to the postmodern *episteme* is accomplished; or to be more correct, these two disciplines inspire

Foucault's thinking to gather courage for his belief that "something new is about to begin, something we glimpse only as a thin line of light low on the horizon" (384). What is just barely touched upon here is the finitude of the human being. But how does that come about? Through a return of language, Foucault answers. Re-turn: the semantics of this expression implies a recurrent movement. Only what has already existed can return. That is also Foucault's opinion. In the work of Freud, Lévi-Strauss, and Saussure the structure (of language, of life, of economy) becomes once again autonomous, it uncouples itself from speech, and thus from effects of meaning. Herewith we see what the human sciences always tried anew to reduce to the performance of a subjectivity: the reduction of the unconscious in its absolute irreducibility to the consequence of occurrences that are generated by it and from it (376-77). The human being dissolves; it vanishes in the universality of unconscious structures.

> Ethnology, like psychoanalysis, questions not man himself, as he appears in the human sciences, but the region that makes possible knowledge about man in general; like psychoanalysis, it spans the whole field of that knowledge in a movement that tends to reach its boundaries. But psychoanalysis makes use of the particular relation of the transference in order to reveal, on the outer confines of representation, Desire, Law, and Death, which outline, at the extremity of analytic language and practice, the concrete figures of finitude; ethnology, on the other hand, is situated within the particular relation that the Western *ratio* establishes with all other cultures; and from that starting-point it avoids the representations that men in any civilization may give themselves of themselves, of their life, of their needs, of the significations laid down in their language; and it sees emerging behind those representations the norms by which men perform the functions of life, although they reject their immediate pressure, the rules through which they experience and maintain their needs, the systems against the background of which all signification is given to them. The privilege of ethnology and psychoanalysis, the reason for their profound kinship and symmetry, must not be sought, therefore, in some common concern to pierce the profound enigma, the most secret part of human nature; in fact, what illuminates the space of their discourse is much more the historical *a priori* of all the sciences of man—those great caesuras, furrows, and dividing-lines which traced man's outline in the Western *episteme* and made him a possible area of knowledge. It was quite inevitable, then, that they should both be sciences of the unconscious: not because they reach down to what is below consciousness in man, but because they are directed towards that which, outside man, makes it possible to know, with a positive knowledge, that which is given to or eludes his consciousness. (378)

This long passage obviously distinguishes the archaeological from the human-scientific unveiling of the epistemic basis of the historical self-understanding of an epoch by asserting that only the former explains the structural presuppositions that can never be made conscious by the human being, whereas the latter reflectively repeats its historical self-understanding: the image it has of itself and in regard to which it deceives itself. Let's recall the earlier requirement of observing our own culture with the eyes of the anthropologist. As soon as the human sciences are studied under this attitude, the consciousness they acquire about themselves (with the aid of hermeneutical, Marxist, or vitalist categories) disappears, much in the same sense as the editors of the *Cours* had asserted: "Language is not a function of the speaker; it is a product that is passively assimilated by the individual" (*CGL*, 14).

Foucault reminds one of Saussure when he speaks about the return of language. Modern linguistics—as the third discipline, the one that finally brings to completion the intentions of psychoanalysis and ethnology—is the actual model for archaeology.

> Whereupon there is formed the theme of a pure theory of language which would provide the ethnology and the psychoanalysis thus conceived with their formal model. . . . In linguistics, one would have a science perfectly founded in the order of positivities exterior to man (since it is a question of pure language), . . . Thus we see the destiny of man being spun before our very eyes, but being spun backwards; it is being led back, by those strange bobbins, to the forms of its birth, to the homeland that made it possible. And is that not one way of bringing about its end? For linguistics no more speak of man himself than do psychoanalysis and ethnology. (*OT*, 381)

Do you remember that the metaphor of the homeland, to which the self-consciousness of the human being is led back, already had to function as the characteristic trait of the innermost intention of the human sciences? Again it is extremely difficult to detect the actual and radical difference between archaeology and the human sciences beyond the absolutely intelligible assertions of which Foucault gives us plenty. For, first of all, even the human sciences bring the human being to the consciousness of the epistemic ground in which its self-consciousness is rooted (Marxism and psychoanalysis, after all, *are* human sciences); second, it would be entirely absurd to maintain that the human sciences reduce the unconscious to that knowledge which the human subject gains about the unconscious through its "unveiling," whereas archaeology brings to light *no* knowledge about the epistemic positivity. What could this "archaeology of the human sciences," which Foucault presents to us in four hundred pages, be other than a conversion of unconsciously knowledge-producing structures into explicit knowledge *of* these structures. There is even less justification for claiming it is precisely the human sciences that make use of the representation of the unconscious in a circular way, since Foucault explicitly speaks of a *re*turn of language and not of its invention. Is, according to this, the new thought that has become possible with the death of the human being in a certain sense a new edition of classical thought of representation and universality? It indeed seems so.

The question as to what language is in its being is once more of the greatest urgency.

At this point, where the question of language arises again with such heavy over-determination, and where it seems to lay siege on every side to the figure of man (that figure which had once taken the place of Classical Discourse), contemporary culture is struggling to create an important part of its present, and perhaps of its future. On the one hand . . . questions arise which before had seemed very distant from them: these questions concern a general formalization of thought and knowledge; and at a time when they were still thought to be dedicated solely to the relation between logic and mathematics, they suddenly open up the possibility, and the task, of purifying the old empirical reason by constituting formal languages, and of applying a second critique of pure reason on the basis of new forms of the mathematical *a priori*. . . .

For the entire modern *episteme* — that which was formed towards the end of the eighteenth century and still serves as the positive ground of our knowledge, that which constituted man's particular mode of being and the possibility of knowing him empirically — that entire *episteme* was bound up with the disappearance of Discourse and its featureless reign, with the shift of language towards objectivity, and with its reappearance in multiple form. If this same language is now emerging with greater and greater insistence in a unity that we ought to think but cannot as yet do so, is this not the sign that the whole of this configuration is now about to topple, and that man is in the process of perishing as the being of language continues to shine ever brighter upon our horizon? Since man was constituted at a time when language was doomed to dispersion, will he not be dispersed when language regains its unity? . . . Ought we not to admit that, since language is here once more, man will return to that serene non-existence in which he was formerly maintained by the imperious unity of Discourse? Man had been a figure occurring between two modes of language; or, rather, he was constituted only when language, having been situated within representation and, as it were, dissolved in it, freed itself from that situation at the cost of its own fragmentation: man composed his own figure in the interstices of that fragmented language. Of course, these are not affirmations; they are at most questions to which it is not possible to reply; they must be left in suspense, where they pose themselves, only with the knowledge that the possibility of posing them may well open the way to a future thought. (382–83, 385–86)

No matter how many question marks Foucault appends to his thesis about the advent of a new thought and the end of the human being, they cannot bridge the basic schism in his theory. Whatever an *episteme* might be, it is first of all unconscious, and as "historical a priori" it constitutes, second, the totality of the relations that in a given epoch lend *unity* to the discursive practices and forms of knowledge ("By *episteme*, we mean, in fact, the total set of relations that unite, at a given period, the discursive practices that give rise to epistemological figures, sciences, and possibly formalized systems"; *AK*, 191). To what extent could such an over abstract definition of the "historical a priori" be different from what romanticism called the "Historic-Transcendental"?[2] Historic-transcendental refers to the condition of possibility of knowledge, speech, and actions. But in contrast to Kant's categories of the timelessly valid pure reason, here it is a matter of conditions of possibility that, according to Herder and Hamann, no longer originate in pure reason, but are abstracted from a discursive praxis and discursive form that itself is historical. Foucault spoke of "transcendentals" (*transcendantaux*), and we want to ask to what extent what (since *The Archaeology of Knowledge*) he calls "archive"—the system of discursive regularities that characterizes a certain epoch—can be distinguished from a human-scientific "transcendental." Both are unconscious, both shape a discursive formation, and both, we should not forget, can be scientifically re-presented.

The attitude toward the concept of representation is among the most untransparent notions in *The Order of Things*. On the one hand, Foucault condemns the clouding of the model of representation by the historicization of the sign synthesis, just as romanticism had done; on the other hand, he still reproaches psychoanalysis for gradually converting the unconscious into representations. Thus it never becomes clear whether Foucault rejects or appropriates the model of representation. That he appropriates it in modified form is supported by the talk of a "return of language": only something that already existed can "return," "resurface," or "reassume its former power." This is also supported by the fact that he welcomes Saussure and modern linguistics both as return of eighteenth-century semiotics, and as the overthrow of subject-centric thought. Above all, I believe it is most strangely supported by the fact that Foucault, as far as I can see, equates the meaning of the term "to think" with that of "to represent," for example, when he says that only with the death of the human being will thought again be possible (which implies that only with the decline of a paradigm of knowledge that is *not* founded on the model of representation of the sign will one again be able "to think"). I assume that Foucault wishes the same transparency for the "new thought" that he praises in the universal-grammatical thought of the classical age. For one could scarcely strive for an even greater transparency than that which is found in the formalized grammars of modern linguistics, and thus Foucault repeatedly applauds it. To be sure, we do not want to overlook that the regularities of the discursive field are fundamentally distinct from those of logic or mathematics in that they are the rules of actual speech and not those of a preexisting and, in its performances, incessantly identical code. We will come back to this issue in our reading of *The Archaeology of Knowledge*. We may, however, critically remark that both the rules of formal logic as well as those of a historical "archive" radically disregard the concrete fashion in which individuals deal with them in thought and in speech, in order, where possible, to achieve something entirely different from what the rules of the code prescribe. And disregard for this links Foucault's variant of structuralism with the universal-grammatical concepts of the classical age in which thought also represents (*représente*) itself—and thus its unconquerable regularity—in the use of signs. This representation is successful only if one ignores the irreducible capacity of the thinking and speaking individuals to relate themselves to a general concept in a singular manner in each instance. And it is not successful if one takes into account the meaning-creating energies of individual sign use. Foucault seems to know this very well, for the cooperation of the individual element in sign synthesis is exactly that which at the inception of romanticism clouded the transparency of the Enlightenment model of the sign, and that now, with the suicide of the human being for the benefit of anonymous systems, again steps into the background of the archive. I want to bring out this point, which is of great importance, in yet a different manner. A system like *langue* or logic can only be transparent (and thus be reduced to an order that is wholly unrelated to application) if, and as long as, the acts of concrete application (the discourses, the propositions) are completely taken up with the execution of the imperatives of the system: each occurrence of a sign or of a statement would be the *token* of an invariant *type*. If, however, the application of elements of *langue* were subject to individual interpretation, then the pure relation of representation would be clouded: the effects of meaning could never be anticipated with absolute certainty on the level of the system, they could not be mastered systematically. This is the standpoint of hermeneutics, that Foucault is fighting, and for whose expiration he is hoping.

This hope seems to me to be irreconcilable with the premises of Foucaultian archaeology. First, because it brings into play a teleology of the overcoming of the subject that is legitimated by nothing except perhaps the individual preference of the author; second, because the model of a system that remains identical in its application—as above all Heidegger and Derrida have demonstrated—is completely unsuited to breaking with the predominance of the subject, insofar as in this model the dream of the subject to remain transparent in the acts of its "representing world mastery" climbs its highest Western peak (to this extent Foucault himself is justifiably suspected of scientism); third, because a discourse that is reduced to *langue* cannot function as the basis of an "archaeology" that presupposes that the gaze with which human knowledge grasps itself is implanted into it beyond its control: this uncontrollability would be restricted to the rank of something provisional—which is the same criticism Foucault directed at the human sciences—if one were to describe that on which knowledge is supposed to depend as a codified system whose order could be converted into the pure transparency of one and the same knowledge. Thus the dependence of knowledge on discourse would only be the relative and provisional dependence of immediate consciousness that Hegel deals with, and of which he demonstrated that it can enlighten itself about its presuppositions and thus elevate itself to the status of a no longer relative and, to this extent, absolute knowledge. Foucault's critique of the human sciences is written to such a large extent from the point of view of "thought that is made possible again" that his concept of "thought" does not unequivocally escape a secret ahistoricism or Hegelianism. Fourth, however, Foucault's archaeology becomes a theory of *history* only because it theoretically explains the noneternity of certain discourse-formations, the possibility and the reality of epistemological breaks. The most effective and, at the same time, most trivial characteristic of an "epistemological break," consists in destroying the orders of a discourse, disorganizing it, and putting it back together in a new form that is not reducible to the old one. If the new discourse is really not reducible to the game-rules of the old one, then the theory of representation has to be dismissed in a most radical fashion. To summarize in the form of a thesis, I mean that the break with the idea that discursive systems are stable and unchangeable in fact brings Foucault close to what we here are calling "neostructuralism"; what differentiates him from Derrida and Lacan, for example, is, however, the theoretical impotence vis-à-vis the mode of Being of this rupture: it actually appears as if Foucault imagines the succession of epochs (whose "*unity*" he emphasizes in quite traditional terms, much as if it were a "spirit of the age") in such a way as if, as in a theatrical piece, the historical curtain went down between two acts of representation to rise again in order to make space for a new discursive formation in which thought is again articulated transparently in signs for itself and for the scientist. The model of representation is not revised as such, as in Derrida, by the fact of the instability of all codes: it is just periodically suspended in order that it might celebrate happy primordial states (*Urstände*) in a new clearing of Being or in a "new thought."

Perhaps it was an awareness of these difficulties that caused Foucault to rethink his concept of an archaeology of knowledge in 1969 in a methodological study entitled *The Archaeology of Knowledge.*

Lecture 11

With *The Archaeology of Knowledge* Foucault wants to finish up what he announced and already presented in concrete analysis in *The Order of Things* but had not yet theoretically legitimated, namely, he wants to supply some information about the methodological status of an "archaeology" that differs from the procedures of "history" (*histoire*), understood in the traditional sense of the word (*OT*, xxii).

The Archaeology of Knowledge works out the foundations for the formation and transformation of discourses.[1] "Discourse" no longer means, as in *The Order of Things*, the form of knowledge of the classical age (*âge classique*) and the model of representation that is characteristic for it; rather it means every system of statements (*système d'énoncés*) that occurs in history that holds together the set of statements mastered by it by means of a finite number of rules and that protects them from dissolution into another system of statements. I know that this definition is once again rather vague and almost unusable according to the rigid standards of analytical philosophy; nonetheless (or even: for that very reason), the fashionable use of the term "discourse" has its origin in this broad definition.

The Archaeology of Knowledge is a difficult book. This is true not only because it is intellectually especially strenuous but also because it – deviating from the tradition of all comparable "*Discours de la méthode*" (from Descartes to Sartre) – defines its concepts either not at all, or badly (although it constantly mentions the word "definition"; see above all *AK*, 79ff.).

This is primarily the case, as we will see, for its concept of *énoncé* (with appropriate self-irony Foucault speaks of the "indiscriminate use that I have made of the terms statement, event, and discourse"; *AK*, 31). "Statement" (*énoncé*) does not mean, as an expert in analytical or especially in pragmatic language philosophy would immediately associate, the descriptive *proposition*, and also not the pragmatically interpreted *utterance*. In this way the assertions of Foucault's study remain overabstract, in Hegel's sense of the word: they allow one to detect without difficulty neither the field of their application nor the general concept to which they appeal. The only salvation in this case seems to me the supply of concrete questions that we, as readers, can direct at Foucault's book.

One of several difficulties we came across in our reading of *The Order of Things* was the uncertainty about the standpoint from which Foucault actually speaks as an archaeologist. Since he unfolds a concrete and well-documented history of the transformations of the classical and the modern *epistemes*, it remains undecided in most instances whether he is reporting the thematized position of representation in indirect speech, that of history, or his own. *The Archaeology of Knowledge* places itself above this dispute and explicates its own procedure without constant reference to the Enlightenment and to postromanticism. This liberates it from a number of ambiguities, for example, from the uncertainty of whether "archaeology" organically grows out of the historical reflections of, say, Marxism, or out of the psychoanalytical founding of the unconscious through a kind of overintensification, or whether it actually introduces an entirely new form of knowledge. Since 1969 we can positively determine that Foucault means the latter; however, he still must answer the question of whether archaeology seeks to be a "true" theory of the succession of discourses, as it were, or whether it only puts a new, itself relative discourse in the place of the discourse that was recently dismissed (namely, the "modern" one). This question, of course, applies analogously to hermeneutics and historicism (taken as forms of knowledge) and throws us once again into the uncertainty of whether the schism between archaeology and presumably traditional and historical questioning is really methodologically and theoretically so radical and total. Should archaeology itself turn out to be one discourse among others, one would not be able to determine whence it derives the right *theoretically* to criticize forms of thought such as hermeneutics, speculative dialectics, or historicism; if it situates itself, however, as a theory beyond those Western discourses that de facto have occurred, then it would inherit the ancient Western claim to being a definite *theoria*, a unified total view of objects and speeches in their *truth* that itself is not affected by historical change; i.e., it would resemble the explanatory claim of Hegel's philosophy, for example, even though not the explanatory means that Hegel's philosophy employs. *The Archaeology of Knowledge* unfortunately does not provide us with an answer to this first question. In its concluding chapter, well worth reading, it defends its standpoint against a representative of classical subject-related philosophy of history in a fashion similar to the way that a representative of subject philosophy would critically and argumentatively set his position apart from positivism. This implies a theoretical *parti pris* whose epistemological self-understanding remains unclear to me. But let's first look at something in Foucault's *Archaeology of Knowledge* that provides us with a positive and less problematical response to our other questions mentioned earlier.

First of all there is the theme of discontinuity. You recall that in *The Order of Things* Foucault declared thinking in discontinuities to be an invention of the postclassical age, and that he rejected it in an obscure way. He does this because he himself simultaneously introduces the concept of discontinuity at this central point in order to contradict a supposedly subject-centric and dialectical model of history that conceives of history as a continual movement of reappropriation of a lost origin (for example, Hegel). This model is the (perhaps imaginary) adversary of Foucault, with whom he converses in a fictitious dialogue at the end of his *Archaeology of Knowledge* (191ff.). Regardless of whether he is fictitious, we have to get to know this other thinker in order to be able better to understand Foucault's methodological standpoint. Since in earlier publications he did not play such a comparatively large role as in *The Archaeology of Knowledge*, one may presume the influence of another thinker who is also mentioned at the beginning of *The Archaeology of Knowledge* (5), namely, Louis Althusser. In order to be able positively to throw into relief Marx's *Capital* over against idealist dialectics of history and to make it possible to read it as a structuralist analysis of society *avant la lettre*, Althusser strictly differentiates the "theoretical praxis" of Marx's approach from the subject-centric and anthropological praxis of Feuerbach, but also from thinking in continuities (in Hegel).

The latter pattern of thought he calls ideological, his own (with reference to Marx) scientific. The former is ideological because it formulates its problems in the light of an already given and fixed solution (and thus does not ask any real question). Hegel, for example, thinks of the absolute as the way that leads to it; this movement is obviously a circular one: it supplies that as its genesis that necessarily had to lead to the aim envisioned from the very beginning, therewith theoretically transfiguring the existing.

I say that this posing of the "problem" of knowledge is *ideological* insofar as this problem has been formulated on the basis of its "answer," as the exact *reflection* of that answer, i.e., not as a real problem but as the problem that had to be posed if the desired *ideological* solution was to be the solution to this problem. I cannot deal here with this point which defines the essentials of ideology, in its ideological form, and which in principle reduces ideological knowledge . . . to a phenomenon of *recognition*. In the theoretical mode of production of ideology (which is utterly different from the theoretical mode of production of science in this respect), the formulation of a *problem* is merely the theoretical expression of the conditions which allow a *solution* already produced outside the process of knowledge because imposed by extra-theoretical instances and exigencies (by religious, ethical, political or other "interests") *to recognize itself* in an artificial problem manufactured to serve it both as a theoretical mirror and as a practical justification. (*RC*, 52)

The entire Western theory of knowledge (*Erkenntnistheorie*), culminating in Hegel, is in this sense ideological, namely, justifying in the mirror image of theory a praxis that leads up to it. The space of the problem of knowledge thus turns out to be a closed space: "a closed space, i.e., a vicious circle (the vicious circle of the mirror relation of ideological recognition), . . . from the famous 'Cartesian circle' to the circle of the Hegelian or Husserlian teleology of Reason" (*RC*, 53).

That his model of history is conceived as a circular movement Hegel himself emphasized often and gladly.[2] He speaks of "the anticipation that the Absolute is subject."[3] Hegel, as we know, also liked to speak of the Absolute Spirit as of a coming-to-itself of something that formerly appeared to be lost in externality. Already Schelling reproached him for employing the vicious circle, and Marx was the first to add to this the characteristic of the ideological (circle).[4] To escape this consequence, Althusser, for his part referring to Foucault's earlier works, describes "a revolution in the traditional concept of the history of the sciences" (*RC*, 44).

We are beginning to suspect, and even to be able to prove in a number of already studied examples, that the history of reason is neither a linear history of continuous development, nor, in its continuity, a history of the progressive manifestation or emergence into consciousness of a Reason which is completely present in germ in its origins and which its history merely reveals to the light of day. We know that this type of history and rationality is merely the effect of the retrospective illusion of a given historical result which writes its history in the "future anterior," and which therefore thinks its origin as the anticipation of its end. The rationality of the Philosophy of the Enlightenment to which Hegel gave the systematic form of the development of the concept is merely an ideological conception both of reason and of its history. The real history of the development of knowledge appears to us today to be subject to laws quite different from this teleological hope for the religious triumph of reason. We are beginning to conceive this history as a history punctuated by radical discontinuities (e.g., when a new science detaches itself from the background of earlier ideological formations), profound re-organizations which, if they respect the continuity of the existence of regions of knowledge (and even this is not always the case), nevertheless inaugurate with their rupture the reign of a new logic, which, far from being a mere development, the "truth" or "inversion" of the old one, *literally takes its place*. (44)

In Althusser's relatively clear argumentation one can immediately recognize the crucial point: one has to describe history as a series of ruptures between which no teleological Reason establishes continuity, and which are also not held together by a higher necessity. To be sure, it is amusing to imagine that "today" anybody would assert such a teleology; Althusser, however, does Hegel the honor of fighting him as our contemporary, and in occasional lapses Sartre has to stand in as Hegel's most recent incarnation.

With this we at least have also identified the point of departure of Foucault's *Archaeology of Knowledge*: the history that archaeology studies is not one of continuities in the service of a grounding subject mind; it is rather a series of contingently connected levels of discourse. But the historical epochs are not only discontinuous in terms of their succession; they are also, according to Foucault, discontinuous in themselves. Indeed, precisely in the so-called humanities it was for a long time customary to speak of the "spirit of the Age of Goethe," for example, as if this time span were a homogeneous block:[5] the manifold and differentiated "expression" (this is a favorite concept of the humanities since Dilthey) of a life feeling or of a spirit. In contrast to this, Foucault justifiably called for caution and demonstrated just how many unsimultaneities constitute the supposed homogeneity of epochs, what immense differences crisscross and dismember the unity of the so-called spirit of the age (*Zeitgeist*) or "national spirit" (*Volksgeist*). (One will only come to understand that, for example, in the Third Reich "something archaic" asserts itself when one abandons the totalitarian concept of the hermeneutical unity of this age and uncovers the differences of the codes that here have their gloomy rendezvous.) Thus history appears as an interweaving of disparate structures that are not reducible to each other, as the succession of discontinuous "specificities" that in no way are completely absorbed in a terminal concept of "spirit."

> The notion of discontinuity assumes a major role in the historical disciplines. For history in its classical form, the discontinuous was both the given and the unthinkable: the raw material of history, which presented itself in the form of dispersed events—decisions, accidents, initiatives, discoveries; the material, which, through analysis, had to be rearranged, reduced, effaced in order to reveal the continuity of events. Discontinuity was the stigma of temporal dislocation that it was the historian's task to remove from history. It has now become one of the basic elements of historical analysis. (*AK*, 8)

I just spoke of "specificities" into which the former unity of the historical process or of the spirit of the age dissolves. Foucault used this expression in his inaugural lecture at the Collège de France in 1970 (*L'Ordre du discours*).[6] Specificity is here introduced as a methodological necessity, indeed, as a "principle." To study historical events in their specificity means not to look at them as cases that fall under a general concept but rather to consider them in their irreducible singularity and individuality. The individual, to be sure, is the most stubborn adversary of the general (for example, of Hegel's spirit) since it, in contrast to the particular, is not an element of the system: everything individual or singular is not capable of being subordinated to, and deducible from principles, because it modifies the principles in a way that is unforeseeable from the standpoint of these principles themselves. That is an interesting piece of information for our reading of Foucault, and in terms of *The Order of Things* it seems to be new, or at least to have a new emphasis. You remember that there Foucault spoke in a rather deductive manner of *the* classical and *the* modern knowledge: a manner that, in the final analysis, was hardly distinguishable from global concepts like the spirit of the age or "total history" (*AK*, 9), or *de la longue durée* (*OD*, 57). If the singular event (*l'événement singulier*) evades generalization in a concept like "epoch," "spirit of the age," or "total history" because of its irreducible distance from the particular that is always subordinated to its general law or its rule, then it is obviously particularly appropriate as an element of an archaeology of knowledge, insofar as the latter wants precisely to interrupt the smooth flow of continuities and universalities. Foucault actually sees it this way. About archaeology he says:

> It has led to the individualization of different series, which are juxtaposed to one another, follow one another, overlap and intersect, without one being able to reduce them to a linear schema. Thus, in place of the continuous chronology of reason, which was invariably traced back to some inaccessible origin, there have appeared scales that are sometimes very brief, distinct from one another, irreducible to a single law, scales that bear a type of history peculiar to each one, and which cannot be reduced to the general model of a consciousness that acquires, progresses, and remembers. (*AK*, 8)

The principle of the individuality of events is supported by the principle of exteriority (*extériorité*) (229f.). We are so accustomed to thinking of individuality as a special case of subjectivity (and/or inwardness) that the associability of individuality and exteriority is confusing on first sight. Actually, Foucault refers to only one aspect that was already implied in the idea of the singular individual, namely, its irreducibility to a discursive principle or to a core of meaning of discourse. The law of exteriority thus states: "we are not to burrow to the hidden core of discourse, to the heart of the thought or meaning manifested in it" (229). The procedure of archaeology is thus exterior because it wants to leave the "series" of singular events that are not reducible to one another (according to a teleological principle) "outside" of any totalizing general concept. The theory of history that Foucault calls Western operates in a manner directly opposite to this, it itself being based on unpenetrated historical assumptions that are brought to light only by archaeology, e.g., the historical maxim that all individual events are to be totalized in "a system of homogeneous relations," in a

> network of causality that makes it possible to derive each of them, relations of analogy that show how they symbolize one another, or how they all express one and the same central core; it is also supposed that one and the same form of historicity operates upon economic structures, social institutions and customs, the inertia of mental attitudes, technological practice, political behaviour, and subjects them all to the same type of transformation; lastly, it is supposed that history itself may be articulated into great units—stages or phases—which contain within themselves their own principle of cohesion. (9–10)

Foucault here vividly objects both to the principle of the one-dimensional explanation of all historical events on the basis of *one* type of occurrence, as well as to the principle of deduction of the events from one structural principle. In this sense Foucault's archaeology is indeed clearly distinguishable from taxonomical structuralism in, let's say, Lévi-Strauss.

> The fundamental notions now imposed upon us are no longer those of consciousness and continuity (with their correlative problems of liberty and causality), nor are they those of sign and structure. They are notions, rather, of events and of series. . . . And now, let those who are weak on vocabulary, let those with little comprehension of theory call all this—if its appeal is stronger than its meaning for them— structuralism. (*AK*, 230, 234)

Jean Piaget spoke of a "structuralism without structures" in regard to Foucault, and Foucault himself points in this direction when he comments in retrospect on his procedure.

> For me, the problem was certainly not how to structuralize it, by applying to the development of knowledge or to the genesis of the sciences categories that had proved themselves in the domain of language (*langue*). My aim was to analyse this history, in the discontinuity that no teleology would reduce in advance; to map it in a dispersion that no pre-established horizon would embrace; to allow it to be deployed in an anonymity on which no transcendental constitution would impose the form of the subject; to open it up to a temporality that would not promise the return of any dawn. My aim was to cleanse it of all transcendental narcissism; it had to be freed from that circle of the lost origin, and rediscovered where it was imprisoned. (203)

Even if we want to concede that Foucault attempts to distinguish himself from classical structuralism with such bold assertions, we still have to take a closer look at whether he is really successful at this. Over the course of this lecture we will have many occasions to recognize that the appeal to an irreducible individuality is indeed an appropriate tool for putting into question rigid structuralism. For if the smallest discursive units, the discursive atoms, so to speak, are individuals, then there is no law that prescribes how one gets from one to another. To be more precise: If one takes the individual – in a strictly inductive fashion – as the point of departure, then one will never arrive at the definitive formulation of a rule. If that induction, however, remains incomplete, then that in no way means that this does not occur, indeed must occur, in light of the projection of a *unity*. For without the dialectically conceived oppositional concept of the system or of the general one could not even speak of individuals. If one concedes that each measurement of the terrain on which the individualities are found is made with foresight to a totality, as whose particulars these individualities can be identified, then one is still far from asserting that the projected unity is the firm core of the system from which the individuals can be derived as elements. The unity is rather a merely projected one, and it is projected by each individual in a singularly different manner. To this extent one can absolutely agree with the thesis about the discontinuity and dissemination (*dispersion, dissémination*) of history, without at the same time falling into the other extreme of denying it any unity (as teleological concept) whatsoever.

And this is not at all what Foucault has in mind. Although his concept of the historical epoch is no longer as monolithic as it was in *The Order of Things*, he is still working with unified concepts – though in a scarcely intelligible manner. In the introduction to *The Archaeology of Knowledge* he still declares that he does not want just to dismember the unity of history with an anarchist gesture.

> This is not because it is trying to obtain a plurality of histories juxtaposed and independent of one another: that of the economy beside that of institutions, and beside these two those of science, religion, or literature; nor is it because it is merely trying to discover between these different histories coincidences of dates, or analogies of form and meaning. The problem that now presents itself – and which defines the task of a general history – is to determine what form of relation may be legitimately described between these different series; what vertical system they are capable of forming; what interplay of correlation and dominance exists between them; what may be the effect of shifts, different temporalities, and various rehandlings; in what distinct totalities certain elements may figure simultaneously, in short, not only what series, but also what "series of series" – or, in other words, what "tables" it is possible to draw up. A total description draws all phenomena around a single centre – a principle, a meaning, a spirit, a world-view, an overall shape; a general history, on the contrary, would deploy the space of a dispersion. (10)

Even without the definition of the "rule of formation" of discourses, or of the archive, for that matter, as the space of the dissemination of the "statements," we are beginning to understand one thing: archaeology cannot get by without the assumption of a minimal unity and regularity (the latter being a concept that *The Order of Discourse* numbers as one of the basic concepts of discourse analysis; see *AK*, 299). Otherwise it would not even be a theory, but simply a conceptless and thoughtless list of singularities that are not the singularities *of* something (for example, of a discourse). That discourse is conceived as order is betrayed by the notion of a *vertical system* that holds together the different series of the histories occurring at a certain time. It is obviously—in the logic of the metaphor—perpendicular to the individual histories and penetrates them like a lance. But even if there were *no* such supersystem, there still would remain the game-rules of the individual histories as such. When Foucault first used the term "individuality," he simply meant to attack the thesis that all historical events are deducible from *one* global meaning (spirit, origin, subject, system). An epoch much rather consists of singular events that are not reducible to one another ("irreducible to a single law"; *AK*, 8). If these individualities are not reducible to *one* single and overriding law, that does not mean that they are not reducible to any law at all, for example, that of the series to which they belong. In other words, *a multiplication of the codes from which events are deducible is no principal dismissal of the code model of classical structuralism*; with this there are only *many* subcodes at work instead of *one* global code—as is analogically the case in Roland Barthes's analysis of Balzac's story *Sarrasine*.[7] The démarche of multiplying the codes would, of course, be methodologically unsatisfying. Analysis, after all, (Foucault underlines this himself) has to make the interconnection among the individual series intelligible: a table, he says, is a series of series, and thus itself a series that fundamentally must be able to be described just as exactly as a subseries or an individual series that is simply contained in the table.

To this extent we can begin to see that Foucault's discourse analysis (as we assumed from the beginning) finds itself in close proximity to structuralist text analysis: its smallest units are not phonemes or morphemes, but phrases. In Foucault the term "phrases" is replaced by "statements" (*énoncés*). We now want to examine how Foucault explains to us the mode of Being of a table—as a series that contains other series in itself. The title of his inaugural lecture, at any rate, sounds very similar to the concept of order of textual structuralism.

We just developed certain consequences that arise from Foucault's opting for discontinuous historiography and came across the concept of the "singular event" that does not submit to a single general concept. Now we want to address another question to Foucault's archaeology: how can it still identify itself as a methodically masterable procedure if it operates under the assumption that the smallest parts of its system of statements are individuals? (Since Schleiermacher, it has been hermeneutics that refers to the individual, the adversary of discourse analysis, to the extent that the latter understands itself as a deductive procedure.)

Our question can also be rephrased in this manner: how is one to imagine what Foucault calls the system of statements of an epoch—as a table, as a series of series—if it is no structurally describable structure in the emphatic sense?

If we remember at this point what we observed earlier on the occasion of a discussion of the concept of structure, we will, above all, recall the feature of the one-dimensional dependence of the event (*événement*) on structure: an event is generatively produced out of the competence a speaker has by virtue of the "code," as the editors of Saussure's *Cours* express it. What is obvious is that the code theory of language can never conceive an event in any other way than as a simple case of application whose reality can be nothing other than the actualization of the laws that exist merely virtually in the "language system." This deductive dependence of the individual speech act on the law of its formation makes a science of *parole* superfluous, for, according to the epistemological premises of the model, nothing can occur in *parole* the knowledge of which was not already assured on the level of *langue*.

Foucault wants to free his archaeology from this model. Archaeology's basic concept—discourse—is located somewhere between structure and event; it is not subsumable under the "structure/development opposition" (*AK*, 11). Why not? We can already imagine the reason: because archaeology deals with discourses whose elements are not types but rather individuals. If discourses are generalities in comparison with their elements, then they are at least individualized generalities: systems of a different sort than, say, logic.

What, then, exactly are discourses? Foucault concedes that he uses this central term in at least three significations.

> Lastly, instead of gradually reducing the rather fluctuating meaning of the word "discourse," I believe that I have in fact added to its meaning: treating it sometimes as the general domain of all statements, sometimes as an individualizable group of statements, and sometimes as a regulated practice that accounts for a certain number of statements. (*AK*, 80)

In all three cases, discourses are something like frames, and what they frame are statements. We would know more about them if we knew what a statement was. For a system of a higher order grasps itself according to whatever is contained in it as the set of elements.

Foucault gives a number of negative answers to this question. Statements, he says, are neither propositions nor phrases nor speech acts (81ff.), although under certain circumstances they can take on the function of these forms of speech. But propositions, phrases, and illocutionary acts are elements of closed systems: of grammar, of logic, of conventionalized speech acts. In regard to these systems they are, so to speak, "atoms of discourse" (80): the last, undecomposable (*indécomposables*) elements "isolated and introduced into a set of relations with other similar elements" (80). Just these conditions are not true for statements as elements of discourses, because they are individualized, in contrast to the elements in a taxonomical system.

> When one wishes to individualize statements, one cannot therefore accept unreservedly any of the models borrowed from grammar, logic, or "analysis." (*AK*, 84)

"Individualized," in this context, means not foreseeable from the perspective of structure, contingent with regard to its Being-such. Foucault says this expressly when he distinguishes an *énoncé* (as element of discourse) from an *événement de la parole* (as element of *langue*). Language (*langue*) exists, as we know, only as a virtual system of the formation of *possible* statements; discourse analysis, however, has to do with individual and actual statements whose formative origins are not reducible to those of *langue* (although they presuppose *langue* as a necessary condition) (85–86). *The statement thus takes account of the never-to-be-closed distance that exists between that which could be said according to the rules of language (langue), conventions, and correct thinking, and that which is actually said.* The statement maintains this distance on all orders that can be described as systems in the strict sense of the word (with which we mean rule apparatuses through whose mastery the singular events can be deductively derived without changes having occurred). All systems have to ignore—that is their nature—the individuality and the content specificity of the statement; they cannot—even if they wanted to—account for historical singularity and the traditional ballast of a historically situated speech act.

This brings us to another feature of the statement. We can again introduce it by means of contrast with the event of a system. For an event of a system it is essential to be able to be repeated without significant loss of meaning; elements of systems are, after all, not individuals, but rather types (or schemes) that can be reproduced as that which they are in any context whatever (even contexts are, when they are dominated by means of rules, types). In contrast to this, the following holds for the statement:

> A statement exists outside any possibility of reappearing; and the relations that it possesses with what it states is not identical with a group of rules of use. It is a very special relation: and if in these conditions an identical formulation reappears, with the same words, substantially the same names—in fact, exactly the same sentence—it is not necessarily the same statement. (*AK*, 89)

This is a thought that brings Foucault in very close proximity to romantic hermeneutics. Schleiermacher asserted in the same sense the impossibility that the statement can be mastered by the (language) system. His basic idea was that from the standpoint of the system one can only reach the types that have been grasped and formulated by the system, the particular cases that are encoded according to the imperative of the system and that are decoded by the interpreter according to the inverse of the same rule. What one does *not* comprehend (for logical reasons) is that which the speaking individual made out of them or, to be more precise, added to them by means of his manner of using the linguistic possibilities that is unforeseeable by the system. This unbridgeable distance between the universal system and the individual statement is the imperishable "individual component" that manifests itself in style and that one has to guess at, or, for that matter, pass over by means of an effort of imagination.

You can probably imagine that Foucault would immediately put on the brakes if he were to hear what conclusions I am drawing here from his thesis. In the absence of the author the text already does this by differentiating the previously cited observation about the unrepeatability of the statement. It now introduces a distinction between statement (*énoncé*) and enunciation (*énonciation*). Only the latter, Foucault says, is individual in the strictest sense, it is, in fact (because of the irreversibility of the flow of time) an unrepeatable enunciative *act* (*acte d'énonciation*). Before we listen to how Foucault specifically justifies this, we can already imagine why he *has* to introduce this distinction. For even if he distinguished discourse from system in a satisfactorily strict manner, there still exists an unavoidable analogy between the relation of a system to a type, and the relation that obtains between discourse and a statement. Since discourse analysis defines itself in strict contrast to human-scientific hermeneutics of the individual, it must avoid absolute opposition to the code model. It ultimately must only mollify it, even if I do not see how this can be accomplished (Dali's painting of the soft clocks, which are, after all, a surrealist fantasy and to which nothing real can correspond, occurs to me in this context). If archaeology wants to show itself to be a science (in the strict sense) of discourse, then it must describe discourses as *orders*; to be sure, as orders of a special sort. But one can modify the concept of order as long as one wishes: the hermeneutical idea of the unforeseeability of the effects of meaning (*effets de sens*), which is also subscribed to by Derrida and Lacan, is not reconcilable with the idea of an order. But precisely this, it seems to me, is what Foucault is trying to accomplish.

After having softened the clocks of the code all too much—by means of his all too harsh contrast between discourse and system—he now is concerned with making them stiff again. He proposes to define the statement according to its *function* in discourses at any given time.

> One should not be surprised, then, if one has failed to find structural criteria of unity for the statement; this is because it is not in itself a unit, but a function that cuts across a domain of structures and possible unities, and which reveals them, with concrete contents, in time and space. (*AK*, 87)

Note the metaphor of the vertical unification of statements in one and to one discourse (a metaphor with which we are already familiar):

> as a function that operates vertically in relation to these various units [logical, grammatical, or locutionary], and which enables one to say of a series of signs whether or not they are present in it. (86)

I do not want to go into detail and individually discuss the four functional types. According to Foucault, a statement can be, first, a function of the sort similar to how a domain of objects or a meaning dimension is disclosed (88ff., esp. 91), that is, a condition of the possibility of reference and/or significance; second, a function of the positions that in each instance it grants the subjects of the statement (92ff.); third, a function of the real or verbal context (98), understood as "an associated domain" or as "related to a whole adjacent field"/"collateral space" (96, 97), in which it surfaces and which does not overlap with the context rules of syntagmatics or pragmatics (97–98); and fourth, the enunciative function has to satisfy the condition of having a material existence (100ff.) which provides it with a minimal identity.

One can speak of functions only in regard to a—I am expressing this gropingly—frame similar to a system that defines its conditions. By way of example, the failure to greet somebody I know functions as an insult only within an institutional frame of forms of interaction and rules of courtesy. Without such a frame no action could be recognized as such a function, and thus associated with another action (or another state of affairs).

What can we conclude from this about the individuality of the statement? You recall that Foucault denied its exact iterability. He thus drew a radical conclusion from his distinction between discourses and semiological systems. Now he has to temper this conclusion, for as function the statement must indeed be identifiable in some sense. (If it were not, then there would be no analysis of discourses.)

This is the point at which Foucault thinks it is apt to distinguish between statement and (the act of) enunciation. "The enunciation is an unrepeatable event: it has a situated and dated uniqueness that is irreducible" (101). This nonrepeatability has to do with the irreversibility of the time during which a speech act (*acte de parole*) occurs; this nonrepeatability, therefore, does not imply that the enunciation does not show "a certain number of constants": grammatical, semantic, logical, pragmatic types that I can repeat as often as I wish *as* types (but not at one and the same time). With the statement it is different.

> But the statement itself cannot be reduced to this pure event of enunciation, for, despite its materiality, it cannot be repeated. . . . And yet the statement cannot be reduced to a grammatical or logical form because, to a greater degree than that form, and in a different way, it is susceptible to differences of material, substance, time, and place. (102)

The statement therefore stands between the exclusive singularity of the enunciation and the identical and uniform repeatability of a linguistic, logical, or any other system-related scheme. In various different enunciations one and the same statement can be expressed; inversely, in different phrases that are repeated with the same meaning and formed in a grammatically correct manner, a different statement can have been expressed in each instance.

To guarantee this repeatability one has to have recourse to an *order* that encodes the statement as a *scheme*: to be sure, an infinitely more sensitive, susceptible, and alterable one, but a scheme nevertheless. And Foucault indeed draws this conclusion: first of all, he speaks of an "order of the institution" in which the statements are inscribed and to which they are subordinated as elements identical with themselves (103); and, second, he speaks of a *"field of use*, in which it [the statement] is placed" (104).

> The schemata of use, the rules of application, the constellations in
> which they can play a part, their strategic potentialities constitute for
> statements a *field of stabilization* that makes it possible, despite all the
> differences of enunciation, to repeat them in their identity; but this same
> field may also, beneath the most manifest semantic, grammatical, or
> formal identities, define a threshold beyond which there can be no fur-
> ther equivalence, and the appearance of a new statement must be recog-
> nized. (103)

Institutions and fields of uses are, to be sure, more subtle and more loosely knit orders than formalized grammars, logics, and taxonomically prepared speech-act conventions; they are—and that is the point here—nevertheless orders. If Foucault grants them a "status that is never definitive, but modifiable, relative, and always susceptible of being questioned" (102), then he could account for this only within the framework of a hermeneutics of divination that divines systematically unforeseeable innovations of meaning; within the epistemological framework of discourse analysis, innovation necessarily rigidifies in the steel casing of institutional dogma that does not put up with any individuals.

We now understand the sense in which Foucault can speak of the *unity* of an "archive" (defined as the sum of all discursive regularities that characterize a certain epoch). Even the concepts "discursive formation" and "rules of formation" (53) are comprehensible from this perspective, especially if one takes into account the following definition:

> The rules of formation are conditions of existence (but also of coexis-
> tence, maintenance, modification, and disappearance) in a given discur-
> sive division. (38)

Foucault, of course, asks himself again and again: "can one really speak of unities?" (71), "in what way can we speak of unities and systems?" (72). These questions and doubts, however, at the end of a series of qualifying restrictions, are affirmed, or rather appeased, with beautiful regularity. And at decisive points the metaphor of the vertical unit that unifies discourses that are self-enclosed and different from one another recurs like a leitmotif or like a unifying thread.

> In this way, there exists a vertical system of dependences: not all the positions of the subject, all the types of coexistence between statements, all the discursive strategies, are equally possible, but only those authorized by anterior levels. (72–73)

And another significant passage:

> By system of formation, then, I mean a complex group of relations that function as a rule: it lays down what must be related, in a particular discursive practice, for such and such an enunciation to be made, for such and such a concept to be used, for such and such a strategy to be organized. To define a system of formation in its specific individuality is therefore to characterize a discourse or a group of statements by the regularity of a practice. (74)

Especially the emphasis on the "singular individuality" of such a system brings to mind the theory of style in the hermeneutics of the individual. Style, too, is indeed a unity – even the unity of a "discursive practice." Moreover, true for style is also what Foucault says about the unity of discursive practice, namely, that "a discursive formation, then, does not play the role of a figure that arrests time and freezes it for decades or centuries; it determines a regularity proper to temporal processes" (74). Style, too, cannot be anticipated on the basis of the grammatical system, but for exactly the same reason it is also not formalizable; i.e., it cannot be inscribed into a generic or institutional order, or even into an order of use. This small but decisive gulf separates Foucault's appropriation of a "singular individuality" from all hermeneutical applications of this phrase from Schleiermacher through to Sartre.

Of course, I am not reproaching Foucault for not being a hermeneutical thinker (perhaps he would not have so very much to criticize in Schleiermacher); at this point we are not yet in a position to draw such a comparison. Rather, I reproach him for the fact that his emancipation of discontinuity, of the epistemological rupture and of individuality, in the final analysis subordinates itself to the well-known code model in its somewhat more moderate form as the dogma of institutions. We therefore can pass the judgment that Foucault is a thinker at the border between classical structuralism and neostructuralism. With structuralism he shares thinking in orders and in relations of parts and whole (statement/discourse, for example); with neostructuralism he shares the interest in a transformation of orders of the sort that no longer serves the preservation of units of meaning, but rather their multiplication.

In the years of research since *The Archaeology of Knowledge*, Foucault was constantly searching for a theoretical foundation for his archaeology. Above all, he wanted to know—and this question was left open in his book—whether the authority that lends discourses and archives their order could not be concretized and named. His inaugural lecture at the Collège de France formulated precisely this question and opened up the field of studies in which Foucault was subsequently involved. They are subsumed under the phrase "theory of power."

I can only give a hint about this direction. *The Order of Discourse* evolves consequences from the (not unfamiliar) hypothesis that society controls the production of discourses by means of a certain number of mechanisms of exclusion: through prohibitions and restrictions, for example, which can extend to the object, to the context, as well as to the speaker of the discourse; or alternatively, it controls them through the banishment of madness from the system of (medical and spiritual) normality or reason (*raison*); finally, it controls them through the "opposition between the true and the false" that puts sanctions on wrong thinking, whereby the criterion of "within the true" (223–24) is based on an "institutional support" (218). To this is connected a criticism of rationality on a Nietzschean basis. In all forms of rationality—regardless of whether as "will to truth," as "will to knowledge," or as "goodwill" of morality—one can discern a will that itself is by no means rational and whose essence Nietzsche characterized as the *will to power*. To be sure, the thought of the driving desire that operates below the surface of "value-free" rationality is put under sanctions itself (it belongs to the game-rules of rationality that it should assert its autonomy); the archaeologist who steps down into this subterranean level of value-free thinking, meanwhile, rediscovers there Nietzsche's will to overpowering—the will to conserve and intensify life—supported mainly by a reading of the *Genealogy of Morals*, the Bible of neostructuralist theory of power.[8] We will come across it again when we examine Deleuze and Guattari's contribution to the topic of our lecture series. For today I am satisfied with demonstrating that with the (re)discovery of the will to power (which, in the internalized form of a will to order and to truth/reason, cuts back all discourses), the principle is simultaneously found that lends discourses that mysterious unity that Foucault again and again identifies.

With this hypothesis Foucault can simultaneously provide an answer to our question that he would have had to leave unanswered during his work on *The Archaeology of Knowledge*, namely, whether the subordination of discourse to a unity and order (let's say, its taxonomization) does not stand in contradiction to his opting for the semantic-pragmatic unconquerability of discourse. Foucault will now give us the following answer to this (and therewith he prepares the breakthrough into the theoretical domain of neostructuralism): this is indeed the case, but this is not a natural characteristic of discourses as such, but rather the effect of their mutilation by the systems of exclusion that the will to power—beneath the mask of rationalization—introduces into them.

This conclusion can easily be understood, and I do not want to challenge the fruitfulness it demonstrated in Foucault's more recent works, especially in his *Surveiller et punir*. It undoubtedly also has a political dimension in that it throws the mechanisms of exclusion, by means of which instituted power in all its manifestations gets rid of its enemies, into a brighter light, thus making them visible and combatable. Foucault's political engagement leaves no doubt about the applicability and significance of his theory for practical action. Nevertheless, we will have to ask some questions about this most sophisticated form that his thought has attained.

Lecture 12

In the previous lecture we were able to provide only a brief look at the theoretical work of Michel Foucault in the seventies. What we were able to determine was that at this time he sought to explain the phenomenon of the "order" in which discourses subsist by turning to Friedrich Nietzsche's theory of power. It is not a natural feature of discourses that joins the set of statements (*énoncés*) contained by them into the unity of an order. It is rather the mechanisms of exclusion, of prohibition, and of internal disciplining by means of which the will to power trims back their natural wildness. We saw that this hypothesis provides both an illuminating explanation of the unification of the discursive field, and can also serve as the basis for a political engagement against the "dispositives of power."

Nevertheless, some questions seem to remain unanswered and we want to formulate them now, before going on to another topic. The first question concerns the criterion that allowed Foucault to draw from his theory of power precisely *those* consequences that he in general drew, and whose moral engagement we appreciate (although Foucault himself would certainly never speak of "moral," or of "engagement"). In other words, in whose name—through an appeal to whom or what—can he announce a call to arms against the power that manifests itself in exclusion? One cannot overthrow existing conditions or orders without referring to a value—in opposition to these realities—in whose name the existing falls prey to criticism. This "contrafactual" value, moreover, would have to be in the service of an alternative order, but an order nevertheless, for it is impossible (and scarcely stimulating, even as a pure fantasy) to engage oneself against an order in the name of pure, abstract nonorder. For a nonorder would be a completely characterless formation, similar to the mythical Tohuwabohu, or chaos, in which nothing could be distinguished and in which, among other things, one could identify neither happiness, desire, freedom, nor justice. (The thought of an unstructured chaos contradicts, by the way, the rules of the game of semiological differentiation, and thus the theoretical foundation of both structuralism and neostructuralism; remember Saussure's characterization of unstructured thought as a "shapeless and indistinct mass"; *CGL*, 111.)

In fact, Foucault's critique of order is directed not against some particular order (such as late-capitalist order) but against order *as* order, i.e., as a system of exclusions as such. When the attack on order *as* order becomes universal, it is no longer directed at any order in particular; i.e., the targets of the attack become indifferent and interchangeable.[1] This fight against order is very similar to the "gratuitous act" of some of the surrealists, e.g., blind flailing (without principles) or running amok. That my assessment is not overstated is supported by the fact that the guardians of the state can look upon this new sort of enemies of order with relative calm; since they are against everything (and not against this or that in particular), they are in the final analysis preservers of the state (in the case of Sartre it was different). This is a danger that, in my opinion, becomes exponentially greater in the texts of some of Foucault's students—especially in the more recent works of Deleuze—and which I will respond to as soon as I examine these texts. The other danger is that Foucault fails to take into account that political fights were never directed against order as idea, but always against a certain *state* of order that enslaves, deprivileges, and violates the subject; every political engagement stands in the service of an alternative order and an alternative organization of our social interchange, but never in the service of disorder or nonorder: a concept that even with the utmost effort of our imagination cannot be filled with content, because it is and remains "amorphous" when one reflects on it. Chaos was never the wish-fulfillment dream of the political revolutionary, and I do not believe that will ever be the case.

Connected with this is that Foucault speaks ambiguously and misleadingly about the order of discourse as a net of mechanisms of repression. On the one hand, one cannot even describe discursive formations and regularities unless the will to power in some way arranged (i.e., structured) them in the form of a system; on the other hand, describability, on the presupposition of which Foucault's work is based, is nothing other than the precipitate of violent acts on the part of the will to power. Is then archaeology itself—similar to what it calls the order of reason—in alliance with the will to power? The fact that it rejects an extradiscursive center of orders—something like a transcendental condition of possibility for the "orderliness" of orders—as a human-scientific notion speaks in favor of this. But what could the will to power be, if not a ground for the possibility of discourses that itself is not discursive, a ground that forces the manifoldness of human activities and thoughts into the unity of a structure or of an institution (in a structurally homologous manner to Kant's self-consciousness that imprints the unity of its categories on the manifoldness of empirical reality)?

An isolated reflection in *The Archaeology of Knowledge*, which allows some room for such questions, points in this direction.

> Behind the visible façade of the system, one posits the rich uncertainty of disorder; and beneath the thin surface of discourse, the whole mass of a largely silent development (*devenir*): a "presystematic" that is not of the order of the system; a "prediscursive" that belongs to an essential silence. Discourse and system produce each other—and conjointly—only at the crest of this immense reserve. (*AK*, 76)

To this conjecture Foucault responds that when the archaeology of knowledge speaks of the conditions of possibility for discursive orders, these conditions of possibility are always of the nature of discourse itself. Discourses are therefore inescapable.

> Behind the completed system, what is discovered by the analysis of formations is not the bubbling source of life itself, life in an as yet uncaptured state; it is an immense density of systematicities, a tight group of multiple relations. Moreover, these relations cannot be the very web of the text—they are not by nature foreign to discourse. They can certainly be qualified as "prediscursive," but only if one admits that this prediscursive is still discursive, that is, that they do not specify a thought, or a consciousness, or a group of representations which, *a posteriori*, and in a way that is never quite necessary, are transcribed into a discourse, but that they characterize certain levels of discourse, that they define rules that are embodied as a particular practice by discourse. One is not seeking, therefore, to pass from the text to thought, from talk to silence, from the exterior to the interior, from spatial dispersion to the pure recollection of the moment, from superficial multiplicity to profound unity. One remains within the dimension of discourse. (76)

If discourses are inescapable, then the anarchical option, in the polemics against those mechanisms that force the supposedly wild acts of speech into the Procrustean bed of a discourse, becomes unintelligible: discourses are alterable, and they constantly alter themselves as "singular practices," but the goal of these transformations will never be extradiscursive or a condition of disorder.

Since *The Order of Discourse* makes the will to power responsible for the task of unification that creates discourses and, on the other hand, cannot hold up anything extradiscursive against the order and violence manifested in discourses, the theory becomes contradictory in itself: the will to power—in the guise of rationality—is an instrument of torture (*la Raison, c'est la torture*), its work is the institutions, the disciplines, the prohibitions, and commandments that constrain wild acts of speech in orders; on the other hand, on the basis of the language-theoretical premises of Foucault's work it would be absurd to believe that one could transgress discourse and arrive at a state that would not itself be discourse. Thus we see that Foucault has nothing to hold up against the omnipresence of power that he unmasks: his theory becomes willy-nilly fatalistic, just as Nietzsche's theory, which celebrates the will to power with a "tremendous and unlimited saying of Yea and Amen" and turns to *amor fati* as a final consequence, is fatalistic.[2]

This consequence, however, could have been avoided—but on other theoretical foundations than those with which Foucault operates. I can only sketch the alternative here: it becomes more visible in that which we already saw, and will yet see, on the occasion of an examination of Derrida's theory of discourses and signs. Foucault distinguishes other ("internal," *internes*) "systems for the control and delimitation of discourse" (220) from the external (*externes*) mechanisms of repression that constitute discourses. They are called "internal" "where discourse exercises its own control" (220). Foucault numbers among them, above all, the task of textual commentary that, as it were, in the form of secondary texts, repeats, consolidates, and seeks to restrict the meaning of primary texts to the reproduction of their authentic original meaning (220ff.). A second internal control procedure consists in the institution of authorship (221ff.), which seeks to bind the discourse to the writing or speaking subjectivity of an author as its "unifying principle in a particular group of writings of statements, lying at the origins of their significance, at the seat of their coherence" (221).

> Commentary limited the hazards of discourse through the action of an *identity* taking the form of *repetition* and *sameness*. The author principle limits this same chance element through the action of an *identity* whose form is that of *individuality* and the *I*. (222)

The third internal principle of arrangement is the becoming-"discipline" of the discourses: on the one hand, their subordination to institutions (academic, educational, political, medical, military, etc.) (224ff.); on the other hand, their disciplining by means of socioepistemic organizational conditions and "theoretical fields" (223: "certain type[s] of theoretical field[s]") in which a branch of scholarship (*Wissenschaft*) can unfold at a given time. Thus the paradigm of evolutionary biology, for example, deprives certain taxonomical discourses, which deal with the mode of Being of life, of their basis for existence; certain epistemological horizons define at the outset the space for possible truths and untruths: "In short, a proposition must fulfil some onerous and complex conditions before it can be admitted within a discipline; before it can be pronounced true or false it must be, as Monsieur Canguilhem might say, 'within the true' " (224).

I do not want to follow up on the often inspiring observations Foucault makes about these "internal" principles of limitation: the brilliant simplicity with which *The Order of Discourse* presents them requires no commentary. I want rather to put my finger on the point I had in mind when I said that the fatalistic consequence of Foucault's idea of the inescapability of order is not necessary. Foucault speaks of the internal rules that dominate the constitution of discourses (among which he, surprisingly enough, does not even count the grammatical rules that make speech possible and that, indeed, also exercise internal restrictions, even on the wildest manner of speech), and behind which stands the will to power, as a *discursive policy* ("if one obyed the rules of some discursive 'policy' "; 224). The discipline, the paradigm, the epistemological framework are such policing authorities of control in the production of discourses: "[Discipline] . . . fixes its limits through the action of an identity taking the form of a permanent reactivation of the rules" (224; translation modified).

Behind this thesis—which in its context is entirely intelligible—there seems to me to stand a false model of (discursive) grammar or of order that again brings me back to the idea that Foucault's thinking stops short of the threshold of neostructuralism. To be sure, his newly introduced theory of power provided a plausible explanation for the possible unity and orderedness of discourses. Moreover, it gives an inkling of an anarchical space of unregulated speech—beyond discourses—that archaeology, however, cannot have access to because it cannot conceive of extradiscursive speech and action (and thus it remains faithful to the *linguistic turn*). It thus remains subjugated to the repressive effect of the will to knowledge itself—as theory, which it is.

This is a paradox that Foucault cannot escape. It has to do with the fact that he can only think of the effects of a symbolical order as determination of the events by its underlying structure. Only this conception makes the comparison of the discursive discipline with the police state possible. In reality, the talk of the "prison house of language" (which goes back to Nietzsche) is theoretically untenable. Discursive orders, rather, are unstable and uncontrollable—we saw this in our initial glance at Derrida's work—*for internal reasons*: first of all, because the relationship between linguistic law and speech act is not one of simple derivation, but rather presupposes the application of a hypothesis and thus a free interpretation; second, because the view that discourses consist of stable and identical elements can only be justified with reference to an extrastructural principle of organization, but at this point, however, it would escape the basic law of linguistic differentiation; third, because a structure *without* such a principle of unity has to be conceived as decentral and thus could not govern and limit the free play of the formation of differences by means of a law. To be sure, I do not wish to overlook that Foucault depicts such a law in an unfavorable light. It is nevertheless true that he cannot imagine discourses *without* such disciplining and determination. The talk about "an identity taking the form of a permanent reactivation of the rules" (224) borrows extensively from the code model of understanding, with the rejection of which neostructuralism as a theoretical movement actually commences.

For Derrida, as we saw, this rejection is self-evident. For him there is no external and no internal law that could determine the course of a "discursive praxis" at the outset, not even the police code.[3] The police always stay behind the scenes of speech because each adherence to a rule of discourse can amount to its uncontrollable transformation.

If the police [are] always waiting in the wings, it is because conventions are by essence violable and precarious *in themselves*. (*LI*, 250)

Another passage—also taken from his answer to Searle—seems to reply ironically to Foucault's police metaphor.

Once iterability has established the possibility of parasitism, of a certain fictionality altering at once—*Sec* too [*aussi sec*]— the system of (il- or perlocutionary) intentions and the systems of ("vertical") rules or of ("horizontal") conventions, inasmuch as they are included within the scope of iterability; once this parasitism or fictionality can always add *another* parasitic or fictional structure to whatever has preceded it— what I elsewhere designate as a "supplementary code" [*supplément de code*]—everything becomes possible against the language-police; for example "literatures" or "revolutions" that as yet have no model. Everything is possible except for an exhaustive typology that would claim to limit the powers of graft or of fiction by and within an analytical logic of distinction, opposition, and classification. (243)

The "order of discourse" is thus no phantom, but its status of Being is pure possibility, whereas its reality is the permanent (not fetterable or thwartable by any will to power) transformation and new creation of constituted meaning.

With this look at Foucault's power-theoretical foundation of his "archaeology," we have closed one chapter of our lectures on neostructuralism and opened a new one. The completed chapter was devoted to the *theory of history*; the new chapter will treat the *theory of the subject*.

You will certainly object that my report was very incomplete. I concentrated almost entirely on Michel Foucault and only occasionally presented comparable positions from Louis Althusser. Yet poststructuralism has taken up other positions (I am thinking of what Maurice Godelier, for example, has written about the phenomenon of history, and of Louis Althusser's suggestion that the "structural causality" be conceived as a relationship between discontinuous structures of which *one* dominates "as the final authority").

I gladly admit to all this and defend my approach with a reminder about the agreement we made at the outset of our lectures, namely, to limit ourselves to an explanation of the phenomenon of *neo*structuralism (and thus to use classical structuralist approaches only as a foil).[4] Furthermore, we agreed not to have "positions of poststructuralism" stand for review in a rhapsodic series, but rather to enter into a *philosophizing* examination of what neostructuralism actually and essentially is. In doing this we only wanted to concern ourselves with authors and individual works insofar as they are indispensable (and, moreover, practical) for the explanation of intellectual attitudes. It was not my intention to report on the intellectual biography of Michel Foucault, and even a glance at his investigations about the birth of the clinic, the history of madness, and the penal code, as well as the archaeology of sexuality, all of which are abundant in material, was beyond the boundaries within which these lectures are intentionally defined. On the example of Foucault and Althusser I wanted to give you an idea of what neostructuralism's philosophy of history accomplishes and what it objects to in the philosophy of history of the human sciences. For even neostructuralism submits (as far as I can tell) to an accepted game-rule of philosophical discourse that says that the explanation of a phenomenon, as it was transmitted by an earlier manner of thought, may be rejected only if simultaneously a different and better explanation of the same phenomenon is offered. I believe that this demand does justice to Foucault's self-understanding, for his archaeology, indeed, seeks to send a tremor through a century-old discursive practice, but also to replace it completely with a new thinking.

This is also true for the explanation of the phenomenon of *subjectivity*. You noticed, even before I had the chance to broach this subject as such, what an extraordinary weight the texts discussed so far have lent it. You know or imagine at the same time that this interest is critical, or even negative. "The subject," whatever this might be, is out of the question as the point of departure for the "new thinking": it appears to be the last retreat of a thinking that is outdated and backward, and which it now has to remove from the center of philosophizing (i.e., decentralize) in order for that which Foucault all too simply called "thought" and (somewhat more intricately) a "felicitous positivism" to be possible again ("let us say that, if the critical style is one of studied casualness, then the genealogical mood is one of felicitous positivism" (*AK*, 234).

The challenge of the concept of the subject thus grows organically out of neostructuralism's philosophy of history: "the subject" designates the point of departure of premodern (for example, Cartesian), and particularly of modern (for example, Kantian, Fichtean, Sartrean) thought. If the archaeology of modern knowledge comes down to the subject's euthanasia — to thought in the void left by the disappearance of the subject — then it obviously enters the space in which thought will be "possible again," namely, an entirely anonymous thinking (like that of mythology): a thinking that no longer is the predicate of a subject, as in the work of Kant, and which only makes sense in connection with the first-person singular pronoun (as that "I am thinking that has to be able to accompany all my ideas": I-ness and thought are coextensive concepts in this formula).

Before I document this universal challenge of the concept of the subject with names of individual neostructuralist authors and with texts and examine it in detail, I want to draw a rough sketch of the position of these attacks and also discuss it in an intellectual-historical fashion. Despite the fact that neostructuralism likes to designate itself in aporetical metaphors as a new thought—as thought after the decline of the West—it still fails to escape a tradition that anteceded it by decades, indeed by centuries. The decline of the West is a thought that accompanies modern times like a thoroughbass, and that has become a main subject of philosophy at the very latest since the critical turn (Kant, Fichte). "The West" becomes a collective singular in romanticism; Hegel's philosophy conceives itself as the completion and conclusion of Western thought; Nietzsche and Heidegger prepare the advent of a thought on this side or beyond the "grammar" that had determined Western discourses.

Simultaneously, what the neostructuralists will call the "decentering of the subject" is prepared. Heidegger had reproached Western and particularly modern thought for a step-by-step repression of the thought of Being in favor of the fantasy of a "self-empowerment of the subject." (We cannot, of course, strictly speak of a "reproach": it is rather a matter of a diagnosis of the Western direction of thought founded in the "history of Being," a diagnosis that, however, does not always escape the speech act of the moral judgment, as we could document on the example of Foucault.) The history that Heidegger narrates to us from *Being and Time* through to his last dark and laconic texts tells us the following: the human being—or (to burst the human-scientific/humanistic fetter of the expression "human being") *Dasein*—is that kind of being that in its Being is concerned with its Being. This inquiring circular movement allows *Dasein* a self-relation whose mode of Being Heidegger calls hermeneutic. "Hermeneutic" means "related to interpretation" (*Deutung, Interpretation, Auslegung*). Relating itself to itself-in-its-Being, *Dasein* attempts an interpretation of its Being and of Being in general. We know how this interpretation (as Heidegger reconstructs it) turned out: in the Western tradition from Parmenides to Sartre's phenomenology (the last contemporary with whom, aside from the mere mentioning of names, Heidegger took issue), *Dasein* persistently posed the question of Being in the form "*What* is Being?" To inquire about *what* a thing is means to inquire about its essence ("Being-what-it-is" and "essence" [Latin, *quidditas*] are, as the idealists already pointed out, words of a similar origin in German). "Essence" in Greek means οὐσία, but in such a way that it at the same time means "Being":[5] Essence-Being in absolute possibility of being identical. That Heidegger, furthermore, is of the opinion that the "meaning of Being" (that is, the signification as which the term "Being" is disclosed at any given time in the history of European thought) unveils itself within the horizon of time (as having-been, presence, and becoming-Being), one can state more precisely by saying that οὐσία interprets Being from the vantage point of being-present, i.e., of presence, of perceptibility, and of graspability (παρουσία). Thus, over the course of centuries Being-as-Being (τὸ ὄν ᾗ ὄν) got out of sight and came to coincide with essence: Being-what-it-is and presence. Being was interpreted as "being-ness"; and as totality of being it became *object*: something that stands over against representing and acting in order to be manipulated by it.

Under the conditions of this positioning of the epistemic switch, the place of the subject is conceived from the very beginning, as it were, as a vacant position. "Subject" designates that which executes the activity of re-presenting and of action and which is something like the owner of the same. This owner also has a relation of objectivity and presence to itself: it *represents* itself in its Being as that which it is: as sovereign self-consciousness that "presences" itself and all other beings (as Heidegger says). Heidegger conceived this process, which leads from the repression of Being-as-Being to the idea of re-presenting, as the history of the gradual self-empowerment of subjectivity. In *his* "archaeology" the central evidence is, first, Parmenides' identification of *Sein* ("to be," "Being") (as anonymous infinitive: τὸ εἶναι) and *Seiendes* (being) (the present participle of *Sein*: τὸ ὄν) as the correlative of thought (νοεῖν) – whereby, by the way, νοεῖν, similar to εἰδέναι (to know) and θεωρεῖν (to observe intellectually), was originally an expression taken from the semantic sphere of sensual perception and took on the signification of a nonsensual perceiving, as in "thought," only by means of this Western reinterpretation. Thus Being, narrowed down to being, became the object of a necessary thought – a switching point that is completely codified in the Platonic idealization of being as εἶδος. The second major evidence Heidegger cites for his thesis of the successive empowerment of subjectivity is the becoming-subject of idea (at the latest) in Descartes, and finally – the third state of the repression of Being – the absolutization of the subject as "subject-object" (i.e., as unity of object and thought) in German idealism, above all in Johann Gottlieb Fichte. Here the thesis of Parmenides that "Being and thought, however, are the same" arrives at its goal; the West completes itself by sublating its origin through thought. (This occurs in the chapter entitled "The Doctrine of Being" in Hegel's *Logic*, which explicitly refers to Parmenides: what appeared to be "Being," turns out to be "essence," thought through in the mind and in truth; and essence turns out to be a necessary moment in the dialectical self-relation of what Hegel calls "idea.")

The brilliance of this "archaeology" of European knowledge is undisputed, and nobody will deny that the evidence Heidegger presents has great explanatory force. Yet we still have to ask ourselves whether the history Heidegger tells us is correct *in the way* he tells it. The kernel idea of Heidegger's "history of Being" is the thesis that Western thought comes down to a gradual "subjectivization" of Being. And in fact, one can and may characterize philosophy, at least modern philosophy (and within it above all German philosophy), as thought deriving from the unity of the subject. *If* there was one theme that gave profile and coherence to thought in modern times, it was the role this one and central thought of the *sub-*

ject played in it. To this extent one cannot maintain that Heidegger and the neostructuralists were focusing on a marginal theoretical outpost.

Heidegger's reconstruction of the path of Western thought — neostructuralism's theory of the subject relies primarily on it — seems, nevertheless, incorrect, or at least one-sided. I will summarize the points at which I wish to give notice of my contradiction. As soon as I turn to a more extensive examination of Lacan, Derrida, and Deleuze, I will provide the necessary differentiations.

1. Heidegger thinks of subjectivity, as it were, as the owner of the representations that reduce Being to the sum of being, i.e., of occurring objects. In its extreme manifestation — in Fichte — the subject then appears as power over beings, as that which "posits" itself and world. Subjectivity thus fuses with sovereignty, it inherits the capacity formerly attributed to God to be ground of itself. A being that owes its Being only to itself and not to the relation to something Other may justifiably be called absolute (*omnibus relationibus absolutum*).

Now it can be demonstrated that the modern idea of the absoluteness of subjectivity is ambiguous. Looked at more closely, it is far from being one-sidedly directed toward mere self-empowerment which would be continued in taking power over the world. Even in Descartes the *cogito* can be explained only on the basis of the relationships it has with itself; however, it is not yet capable of grounding its own Being through this self-relation (and he refers to the divine guarantee). In other words, "The self-relation of conservation (*conservatio sui*) together with its reflection, is what it is not through itself, and thus it evokes the question about its ground."[6] This ground can no longer be an external ground under the conditions of the epistemic framework of the philosophy of self-Being; it must be a matter of an unfathomableness, the experience of which the subject makes in the attempt of identifying itself with itself, and thus in its own internal sphere. "Thus the experience that self-Being, by virtue of an inner principle, is related to itself and only to itself, has as its complement not only the certainty of being nevertheless from an unfathomable ground, but also the knowledge that this ground remains inaccessible to it. The more the thought of self-relation and self-determination of the human being was developed in modern philosophy, the more the other side of the same consciousness had to become its theme."[7] This experience that the subject of modern philosophy experiences itself as not-being-ground-of-its-own-subsistence[8] has never been more clearly articulated in modern times than in the thought of early romanticism, in the philosophy of Schelling (with his coinage of the term "unprereflective Being"), and of Fichte (with his idea of the "absolute dependence" of the subject). According to Heidegger, this is the age of the greatest obscuration of Being and of the greatest subjectivization. Indeed, Fichte reinterpreted the absolute subject, at the very latest around 1800, as a being that can account for its essence and for its deeds (in short, for its *mode* of Being), but not for the fact *that* it is. To the romantic philosophers and Schelling, self-consciousness presented itself from the very beginning as a relation that comes about only on the precondition of a grounding identity that escapes the play of relations as such. What Lacan will call the *assujettisation du sujet* is, therefore, not a new thought, but the renewed taking up of a specifically modern idea that extends from Descartes and Spinoza in a continuous line through Rousseau, Fichte, Schelling, Feuerbach, Kierkegaard, and Schopenhauer to Darwin, Nietzsche, Marx, and Freud, all of whom, although with different accentuation, allow for the grounding of the self-conscious subject in something that itself is not conscious and on which it depends absolutely (and which is its *internal*, not its *external*, ground).

2. The second objection relates to Heidegger's thesis that in modern times the owner of the "capacity for representation" was specified as the "subject." This thesis states — I am only repeating it in a new light — that the subject fuses with the capacity for representation in such a way that in the end (since Kant and Reinhold; actually, since Leibniz) we can say that there is no representation that is not the representation of a subject *who* has it (and *whose* representation it is). All acts of representation (I am using this expression in the Kantian sense, meaning all mental and volitional acts, and all acts of perception) are acts of I-ness, of the "transcendental synthesis of apperception." Kant's monstrous expression, which can be translated simply with self-consciousness, is nevertheless illuminating. It refers back to the doctrine of perception that now is also being applied to the knowledge the I has of itself. The knowledge the I has of itself is an analogue of the "representation" (perception/apperception) one can have of external objects. In other words, the I is immediately objectifiable to itself.

Looked at through the spectacles of Heidegger's "fundamental ontology," to "re-present" means "to put something in front of oneself," to "make an object out of something" in order to dominate it through the power of consciousness. Thus, in every act of representing two poles can be distinguished. If, then, the I is also thought of according to the model of representation — and that was already true for Descartes's *cogito sum* — then the phenomenon of self-consciousness is conceived as bipolar: as the relation of one thing to itself. Such a relation, insofar as it is accompanied by consciousness, is called reflection. Self-consciousness is conceived as reflection (as an explicit placing itself in front of itself) in the epistemic framework of "representation." The tense of reflection is the present. As that which has itself constantly before its own eyes, self-consciousness is simultaneously both "something objective" and "something present," just as that which representation perceives (the things in the world) is always something present.[9] Self-consciousness thus is not only reflection, but it is also self-presence: "Being-alongside-itself."

Is that really correct? You will see that Foucault, and particularly Derrida, but also Lacan, always describe and criticize the phenomenon of self-consciousness as self-presence. If self-consciousness, however, was not conceived as self-

presence by the influential thinkers of modernism, then this criticism becomes ob-
solete, or, to be more precise, it is deprived of its historical object.

It is true that Leibniz, Kant, Hegel, and after them many others (for example,
Husserl) actually described self-consciousness as reflection: as a representing-
itself whose effect was the knowledge the I had about itself. It is also true that
they thought of self-consciousness as a Being-present-to-itself. That is particularly true for Husserl, to whom Derrida devoted his first works.

It is not true, however, for early romanticism and not, for example, for Fichte,
Franz Brentano, Hans Schmalenbach, or Sartre. These thinkers explicitly rejected the model of reflection of knowledge as insufficient when it is a matter of
describing the experience that consciousness has of itself. And they did this without exception along the lines of the following argument. If the experience of self-
consciousness were a result of self-reflection, then the following process would
have to take place: the I, still without knowledge of itself, turns to itself during
the process of representation and becomes aware of: itself. But how is it supposed
to register this insight if it has not already previously had a concept of itself?[10]
For the observation of something (even if it is of *me*) will never provide me with
information about that particular characteristic of my object that makes evident
that it is *I* whom I am observing. I must rather have already had this insight, and
I now bring it into play. (Only if I already know myself can the mirror tell me
that it is *I* who is looking at him/herself. And reflection is precisely such a mirror.) *If* I gain this insight, and this with apodictic evidence, then it cannot have
been the result of a reflection, for (as Novalis says) "what reflection *finds*, *seems*
to have been there already."[11] In other words, that it is *I* whom I make present
in the act of reflection — of self-mirroring — cannot be the product of cognition; it
must rather be the result of *re*cognition, the reidentification of something already
known: in this instance, of myself. If this is the case — and it *is* the case — then self-
consciousness has to be explained differently than on the basis of reflection,
namely, as a Being-familiar-with-itself prior to all reflection which since Novalis
is characterized as a nonpositing self-consciousness.[12] Hölderlin's friend Isaac
von Sinclair spoke of the "athetical,"[13] Schleiermacher of the "immediate" self-
consciousness: the "immediate" self-consciousness must not be confused with the
"*reflected self-consciousness* where one has become an object to oneself."[14] If
self-consciousness, according to this, is not and *cannot* be grounded on presencing, then what becomes of the view that with the philosophy of self-consciousness
(and thus, in short, with Fichte) the will to self-empowerment of subjectivity
reached its Western zenith? The question is a rhetorical one: this thesis by
Heidegger is deprived of its object and at very best has to be reworked or revised.

3. Our third objection is closely related to the second. It asserts two things:
(a) self-consciousness was not conceived as *I-ness* by all significant philosophers
of modern times, for example, not by Novalis, not by Schleiermacher, and not
by Sartre. Where Novalis is concerned, I refer to my book on *Das Problem "Zeit"*

in der deutschen Romantik;[15] Schleiermacher expressly emphasized in the passage cited earlier that under the term "immediate self-consciousness" he understands only the familiarity of *consciousness* with itself, not the knowledge of an *I*—as the owner of consciousness—about itself.[16] Consciousness is thus apersonal, it is not the consciousness of an I. The I, according to Schleiermacher, is generated as a by-product, or in the background of a *reflection* (it is not an inhabitant of the nonpositing self-consciousness). "We have no representation of the I without reflection"; "self-consciousness and I relate to one another as the immediate to the mediate."[17] Or another passage: the *"immediate self-consciousness* = feeling . . . is 1) different from reflected self-consciousness = I, which expresses the identity of the subject only in the difference of moments, and thus is based on the summary of the moments that is always mediated; 2) different from sensation *(Empfindung)*, which is the subjective and personal element in a given moment, and thus posited by means of affect."[18] In his famous essay *La Transcendance de l'Ego*, Sartre says almost the same thing: prereflective self-consciousness is both I-less and apersonal.[19] The only philosopher from the spectrum of neostructuralism who took cognizance of this feature in the tradition of the theory of self-consciousness seems to be Gilles Deleuze. In *Logique du sens* he writes, referring to Sartre:[20]

> I am trying to determine an impersonal and preindividual transcendental
> field that does not resemble the corresponding empirical fields and yet
> is not identical with an undifferentiated depth. This field cannot be de-
> termined as that of a consciousness: in spite of Sartre's attempt to do
> so, one cannot retain consciousness as a *milieu* and at the same time
> take exception to the form of the person and the point of view of in-
> dividuation. A consciousness is nothing without a unifying synthesis,
> but there is no unifying synthesis of consciousness without a form of
> the I and a point of view of the Ego. (*LS*, 124)

I will return to Deleuze later, who in this context was important only as evidence for a neostructuralist approach that wishes to uphold a modified transcendental-philosophical standpoint. He, to be sure, thinks that one has to renounce the category of consciousness (because consciousness supposedly always has to be thought of as personal as well as unified structure).

(b) We yet have to cover the second aspect of our third question addressed at Heidegger's archaeology of self-consciousness. It asserts that self-consciousness was not only (frequently) conceived as I-less; already for the early romantics and, for example, for Schelling there was no necessity of attributing to it the present tense—as self-presence. In *Das Problem "Zeit" in der deutschen Romantik* I demonstrated that with the liberation from the model of reflection the bond to the present was simultaneously overcome. Husserl had the problem of imagining a consciousness beyond the present. He believed that our consciousness was indeed a flow, but one that "retains" (*retinieren*) immediately past phases of consciousness and "protains" (*protinieren*) immediately following experiences of consciousness, and it does this always from the position of presence. Thus Sartre's polemical metaphor of the common houseflies that press their noses hard against the windowpane of presence, but that never step into the past or into the future, was justified.[21] The *cogito* that is banned to the circle of self-reflection remains instantaneous and cannot get away from itself: it is its own re-presentation and is condemned to exist always in the present of its own gaze. This is not true for prereflective self-consciousness: it is always consciousness *of* something, and this, moreover, is something other than itself. Compared to the being *of* which it is consciousness, it *is* not being itself; it is not an object at all, not even its own object. It is, on the contrary, the absolute nonobject, something that is relatively nonbeing compared to the world of objects. By virtue of its own relative non-Being it is always already outside itself: in the future with its projections, in the past with its factual Being. It is thus thrown into time, even before it is with itself—as reflection; the meaning of Being, therefore, unveils itself as being-past, and on the ground of this being-past self-consciousness projects its future as that which it now is not, but which it at some time will be (and at that time, to be sure, in the manner of being-past). Thus it is emphatically not true of prereflective self-consciousness that it is a present identical with itself; it has, rather, the structure of "absent-presence" (*BN*, 103).

As far as this part of our correction of Heidegger's equation of self-consciousness with self-presence is concerned, we will see that Derrida is in part not affected by it. His little known first publication, the long introduction to Edmund Husserl's *L'origine de la géométrie*,[22] emphasized on the basis of Husserl's analysis of temporality that in his last notes even Husserl found a way out of the entanglement of the self in the sphere of the "living present" (*du présent vivant*).

4. The final objection I want to formulate with regard to the theoretical basis concerning the subject shared by Heidegger and neostructuralism is directed at the assumption that the fact of self-consciousness, which nobody denies, not even Heidegger and Derrida, can be derived from something itself not conscious, such as a structure.

To be sure, this objection does not retract what we conceded in point (1), namely, that self-consciousness experiences itself as something dependent, as nonground of its subsistence. Our present objection has nothing to do with the absolute dependence of the subject on its ground; it deals rather with the thesis that self-consciousness can be derived from a structure that itself does not imply consciousness. I want to speak very briefly to this point since neostructuralist attempts to derive self-consciousness from a play of signifiers are much more differentiated, though also bolder, than Heidegger's attempt to deduce subjectivity from the care structure of *Dasein*.

Heidegger understands care as the mode of Being of Having-to-be. *Dasein* has "to be" its Being in the same sense as Christ had to take up his cross. *Dasein* is thus a negative reference to itself: it is concerned with itself, it constantly refers back to its facticity from the future of its projections; in short, it subsists as self-reference.

To subsist as self-reference: Self-caring *Dasein* obviously shares this characteristic with self-consciousness. Since Heidegger no longer wants to recognize self-consciousness as a point of departure of ontology, he arrives at the idea of deriving it as secondary effect from a much more fundamental structure, namely, of care, or of self-understanding. The objection we made earlier to the model of reflection of the subject is also valid in this instance: one can never gain consciousness from something that is not already conscious. Sartre emphasized this clearly in a famous objection to Heidegger.

> Heidegger, wishing to avoid that descriptive phenomenalism which leads to the Megarian, antidialectic isolation of essences, begins with the existential analytic without going through the *cogito*. But since the *Dasein* has from the start been deprived of the dimension of consciousness, it can never regain this dimension. Heidegger endows human reality with a self-understanding which he defines as an "ekstatic pro-ject" of its own possibilities. It is certainly not my intention to deny the existence of this project. But how could there be an understanding which would not in itself be the consciousness (of) being understanding? This ekstatic character of human reality will lapse into a thing-like, blind in-itself unless it arises from the consciousness of ekstasis. In truth the *cogito* must be our point of departure, but we can say of it, parodying a famous saying, that it leads us only on condition that we get out of it. (*BN*, 73–74)

In other words, consciousness is always and only what it is (for itself): "*en acte*," as Sartre liked to say; there is no possible or latent consciousness, but only consciousness of virtualities and latencies.[23] If Heidegger wants to have a prereflective "having a mood," "experiencing," or "self-understanding" precede consciousness (cf. *BT*, 175–76), then this makes sense only on the basis of the terminological agreement to take consciousness as synonymous with cognition, and self-consciousness as synonymous with self-cognition, i.e., with reflection. In this sense one can indeed say, as Heidegger does, "that only because the 'there' has already been disclosed in a state-of-mind can immanent reflection come across 'Experiences' at all" (*BT*, 175). This "unreflecting devotion to the 'world' with which it is concerned and on which it expends itself" (*BT*, 175–76) could, of course, only then include "understanding" if it also were conscious (which does not mean: if it also reflects), for an understanding without consciousness of understanding would simply be no understanding (although one can easily think of comprehension without reflection that is given over to the world). If Heidegger seriously denies the possibility of understanding consciousness, then this is based on a confusion of consciousness and self-cognition. If one erases the traces of this confusion, then there is nothing miraculous about the thesis that explicit and objectifying consciousness (as the scientist applies it and as it was thematized by Descartes in his *cogito*) is something that over against prereflective consciousness, as it is manifested in understanding, caring, and having a mood, is "derived" (*abkünftig*).

This thesis says nothing more than that the scientific "looking-at . . ." (and thus explicit and objectified observation and knowledge) always presupposes consciousness and, more precisely, self-consciousness. Heidegger, indeed, states this frequently.

> This understanding [he means the "prereflective" self-understanding], like any understanding, is not an acquaintance derived from knowledge about them, but a primordially existential kind of Being, which, more than anything else, makes such knowledge and acquaintance possible. . . .
> By showing how all sight is grounded primarily in understanding (the circumspection of concern is understanding as *common sense* [*Verständigkeit*]), we have deprived pure intuition [*Anschauen*] of its priority, which corresponds noetically to the priority of the present-at-hand in traditional ontology. "Intuition" and "thinking" are both derivatives of understanding, and already rather remote ones. Even the phenomenological "intuition of essences" [*Wesensschau*] is grounded in existential understanding. . . .
> [The scientific ideal of knowledge] is itself only a subspecies of understanding. (*BT*, 161, 187, 194)

This claim by Heidegger to have *derived* the idealist or phenomenological "consciousness" from something itself not conscious — an existential structure — collapses as soon as one introduces the terminological differentiation of nonpositing and positing consciousness. Neither the neostructuralists nor Heidegger know this differentiation. They constantly speak of self-consciousness, where they should speak of self-reflection; it is fairly easy, however, to demonstrate (as Fichte has already done) that self-reflection is grounded in something that itself is not reflected. But this nondifferentiation is not simply a terminological lapse: neostructuralism does not seem to be aware of the theory of the prereflective *cogito*, so that the phenomenon of subjectivity shrinks to the entirely different phenomenon of self-cognition. The neostructuralist attempt to derive self-reflection from the differential play of signifiers is, of course, more daring than Heidegger's (easily correctable) thesis that knowledge is a derived form of understanding.

Over the course of the next lectures we will see in what way the neostructuralists develop and found their view of the subject. Prior to this, however, we want to track down another tradition.

Lecture 13

In the previous lecture I looked at Heidegger's view of essence and the "history of Being" of subjectivity. We found that Heidegger describes the history of European thought as the history of a successive repression of Being in the direction of essence, i.e., in the direction of the objectified characteristics of being that manifest themselves in re-presentation and that are sublated in thought. At the culmination of this movement, according to Heidegger, appears the owner of those representations, namely, the subject. Following Nietzsche, he characterizes it as generated by a will to domination of the world, whose Being shrinks to mere presence at hand: to an object for scientific and technical manipulation.

This view of the essence of the subject fundamentally influenced the theory of neostructuralism, above all Derrida. Because Heidegger's influence is also evident at the weaker points, which Derrida's theory of the subject does not evade, I formulated at the outset four objections against Heidegger in order to be able to refer to them in what follows. I want to repeat Heidegger's theses and my criticism in abbreviated fashion.

1. Heidegger conceives subjectivity as being in the service of the will to self-empowerment and world domination. In contrast to this, modernity, however, and particularly German idealism, thought of subjectivity as absolute Being-dependent on an (as Schelling says) "unprereflective Being."[1]

2. Heidegger believes—according to his thesis that the West interprets Being as presence—that the subject is alongside itself as presence, or as something that represents itself, i.e., as reflection. This model, however, was overcome at the

very latest by Fichte and the early romantics, who no longer think of self-consciousness as relation of reflections.

3. The thus conceived familiarity of consciousness with itself is to be thought of neither as I-ness nor as instantaneousness except from time or bound to the present. In contrast to what Heidegger maintains, neither the romantic philosophers nor Sartre did this; rather without exception they described self-consciousness as I-less and temporal.

4. Heidegger wants to understand self-consciousness as a "derived mode" of the structure either of understanding or of care. This attempt fails because the relations that *Dasein*, in understanding and caring, has with itself must already have the character of consciousness if one is supposed to be able to distinguish them from relations in inorganic nature, and then put them up against a reductionistic materialism.

Heidegger's theory of the subject is apparent in all of neostructuralism, and this is unfortunately also true for the errors inscribed in his model. Heidegger was, of course, not the only, maybe not even the decisive authority for neostructuralism's theory of the subject. Nietzsche's and Freud's discovery of the unconscious as an autonomous aspect of spiritual life also had its effect. Nietzsche never systematically presented his theory of the subject, and it is difficult to try to report in a coherent way on what he uttered on the theme of the subject and of consciousness in various phases of his life. Neostructuralism's reading of Nietzsche, however, itself has an eclectic character, and this provides us with the justification for highlighting some basic ideas that found resonance in neostructuralism.

Nietzsche, first of all, declares the "subject" to be a mere "fiction": "the *ego* of which every one speaks when he blames egoism, does not exist at all" (*Works*, XIV, 294). The subject is much rather an epiphenomenon of the will to power or of life. This formulation, however, is misleading. *On the one hand*, it permits conclusions like the following: The human being "as a rule can perceive nothing of himself but his outworks. The actual fortress is inaccessible, and even invisible, to him" (*Works*, VI, 357). In this sense the subject is an organ of misunderstanding that, far from conducting the will to power, is rather itself in the service of it (*Works*, XV, 40), and it developed evolutionarily-biologically for the purpose of the sustaining of the herd nature of the human being (*Works*, X, 298–99).[2] Communicability presupposes identical schematization of experiences within a communicative community; in order to assure such an identity of schemes, reality, which is constantly in flux, has to be subjected to rules: it is a matter of "a particular species of animal which can prosper only by means of a certain *exactness*, or, better still, *regularity* in recording its perceptions" (*Works*, XV, 11). This subjecting to rules is, of course, entirely external to reality; it is a mere fiction without which a certain species of animal called human being would not be able to cope with life. The will to knowledge, or the will to truth, both centered in the subject, are therefore secondary operations of the will to power for the sake of preserving a bearable social condition. To this extent the subject is a "projection" of identities and regularities into nature that in itself is chaotic (cf. *Works*, XV, 116). And "all our so-called consciousness is a more or less fantastic commentary of an unknown text, one which is perhaps unknowable but yet felt" (*Works*, IX, 127), that of the unconscious will. This is also true for the tasks of morality that, just like words and the rules for their combination, are bound to iterability as their law of Being: actions, the neglect of which is penalized by sanctions, and which therefore can be expected from others and presupposed with some reliability, support sociability; they stabilize the "herds" in which the human being prospers as "factory product of nature" (Schopenhauer). In the human being "nature" has succeeded in "the breeding of an animal that *can promise*," i.e., that assumes the responsibility for the predictability of its actions (*Works*, XIII, 61). For this the introduction of conscience was necessary. Nietzsche compares it to a "*system of mnemonics*" that burns "memory" into the human being (*Works*, XIII, 66). This process, as a result of which the human being in the natural incalculability and arbitrariness of its amoral striving for power becomes "to a certain extent, necessitated, uniform, like among his like, regular, and consequently calculable" (*Works*, XIII, 63), Nietzsche likes to describe as a process of inscription in the sense of branding.[3] This is an idea that, above all, is picked up again and again by Foucault and Deleuze when they talk about the subject as the effect of mutilation, entirely in the spirit of Nietzsche, who in *The Genealogy of Morals* says:

> When man thinks it necessary to make for himself a memory, he never accomplishes it without blood, tortures, and sacrifice; the most dreadful sacrifices and forfeitures (among them the sacrifice of the firstborn), the most loathsome mutilation (for instance, castration), the most cruel rituals of all the religious cults (for all religions are really at bottom systems of cruelty) – all these things originate from that instinct which found in pain its most potent mnemonic. In a certain sense the whole of asceticism is to be ascribed to this: certain ideas have got to be made inextinguishable, omnipresent, "fixed," with the object of hypnotising the whole nervous and intellectual system through these "fixed ideas." . . . The worse memory man had, the ghastlier the signs presented by his customs; the severity of the penal laws affords in particular a gauge of the extent of man's difficulty in conquering forgetfulness, and in keeping a few primal postulates of social intercourse ever present to the minds of those who were the slaves of every momentary emotion and every momentary desire. (*Works*, XIII, 66–67)

The most internalized form of social memory is rationality or the will to truth.

> The will to truth is a process of *establishing things*; it is a process of *making* things true and lasting, a total elimination of that *false* character, a transvaluation of it into *being*. . . . Life is based on the

hypothesis of a belief in stable and regularly recurring things; the mightier it is, the more vast must be the world of knowledge and the world called being. Logicising, rationalising, and systematising are of assistance as means of existence. (*Works*, XV, 60–61)

The ascetic ideal of truth and rationality, however, is not in the service of the strong and cruel life of the individual, of the powerful human being who serves as a bridge to the Superman; rather it is in the service of the herd, which pays attention to the transferability of experiences, to the equivalence of claims, and the comparability of legal means: in short, to the rationality of the forms of intercourse whose most internalized form is reason. Viewed from this perspective, reason is "Life turned against Life" (*Works*, XIII, 153). For this reason the will to truth—as the internalization of the claims of the will to survival of the "all-too many"—is itself in need of a critique for the sake of the breeding of the Superman. "The Will for Truth needed a critique . . . the value of truth is tentatively *to be called into question*" (*Works*, XIII, 198). Instead of a critique of reason that uncovers a subject subservient to morality and truth as the condition of all yea-saying (be that as affirmation or as a positing of values), there rather is need of a "self-critique of reason" (*Works*, XIII, 201). It unmasks the morally autonomous and truthful subject as an instrument of the will to life, insofar as this will to life is already weakened ("degenerated") and sickened by the respect for "the general."

So far we have illuminated, as I said earlier, only one side of Nietzsche's theory of the subject. The subject, according to this view, is simply an organ of misapprehension in that it considers itself to be the ruler of the dark life, whereas it is actually ruled by it. Nietzsche's attack on the "superstitions of logicians" is well known: according to this view "the subject 'I' is the condition of the predicate 'think' "; whereas in reality, "*One* thinks; but that this 'one' is precisely the famous old 'ego,' is, to put it mildly, only a supposition, an assertion, and assuredly not an 'immediate certainty' " (*Works*, XII, 24). This already points ahead to Lacan's formula: "I think where I am not, therefore I am where I do not think" (*E*, 166).

If one pays close attention, both in Nietzsche's and in Lacan's formulation subjectivity is not simply denied, rather it is differentiated or duplicated. Obviously, one can distinguish the subject of modern philosophy—as the place of misapprehension—from a true subject, from that which is real and not mere "*fraud*" and invented, and about which Lacan speaks as the "true subject." Between the two a correspondence takes place: the fiction Nietzsche describes the I (or the subject, consciousness, or thought) to be is always the product of a useful mistake, that is, of a life-preserving misapprehension of Being and the will to power. In this respect Nietzsche remains a Kantian: he considers the outer and the inner world to be an undifferentiated chaos that is in need of synthetic acts in order to be articulated for us. He calls these syntheses, from which he derives morality and reasonableness, fictions. They do not describe actual being, but rather forms by which life adapts to external conditions. Truth, as we saw, is a fiction that makes it easier for the masses to live together by binding its manifestations to the rule of verification and reiteration, and thus to commensurability for everyone.

> Thus, "truth" is not something which is present and which has to be found and discovered; it is something *which has to be created* and which *gives* its name *to a process*, or, better still, to the Will to overpower, which in itself has no purpose: to introduce truth is a *processus in infinitum*, an *active determining* — it is not a process of becoming conscious of something, which in itself is fixed and determined. . . . Man projects his instinct of truth, his "aim" to a certain extent beyond himself, in the form of a metaphysical world of Being, a "thing-in-itself," a world already to hand. His requirements as a creator make him *invent* the world in which he works in advance; he anticipates it: this anticipation (this faith in truth) is his mainstay. . . .
>
> The *assumed world* of subject, substance, "reason," etc., is necessary: an adjusting, simplifying, falsifying, artificially-separating power resides in us. "Truth" is the will to be master over the manifold sensations that reach consciousness; it is the will to *classify* phenomena according to definite categories. (*Works*, XV, 60-61, 33)

Even if with this Kant's subject — the representation of a representation that lends unity and profile to the manifoldness of empirical reality — is declared to be something that is derived, the will to power simply inherits the task that in Kant was assigned to the subject, namely, to bring order into sensual chaos.[4] To the degree that the subject of modern philosophy is rejected as a mere "thing of fantasy" (*Works*, XV, 59), the subject of the will to power inherits the function that the transcendental subject vacated.

Nietzsche actually draws this conclusion. If the world of phenomena — "adjusted" and "made logical" for the sake of communicability and recognizability — is not the true world, but rather a pure fiction, then one can still ask "whether this creating, rationalising, adjusting, and falsifying be not the best-guaranteed *reality* itself: in short, whether that which 'fixes the meaning of things' is not the only reality: and whether the 'effect of environment upon us' be not merely the result of such will-exercising subjects . . . *The subject alone is demonstrable*; the *hypothesis* might be advanced *that subjects are all that exist*, — that the object [is] only . . . a *modus of the subject*" (*Works*, XV, 73-74). Nietzsche thus acknowledges a certain subjectivism — for which Heidegger will reproach him — even though it is not an idealistic, but rather a voluntaristic subjectivism of the sort that the will to power that produces representations and values is the *true subject*. This true subject does not, of course — like Kant's — represent itself in its truth; it has no truth whatsoever. All of its representations — as I, as substance, causality, or autonomy — is deception: a perspectival "*interpretation*" (cf. *Works*, XIV, 213, and XV, 16) of the in itself "unknowable" and "amorphous and unadjustable world consisting of the chaos of sensations" (*Works*, XV, 73). The genesis of the word "I" consists in the gradually accepted "absurd habit" of assuming a "sort of perspective in seeing which makes sight a *cause of seeing in itself*: this was the feat in the invention of the 'subject' and the 'ego' " (*Works*, XV, 54). In the institution of this double sight not the I (as intellect-subject) but the will to power is operating, the power-subject. This will to power represents itself before its own eyes as truth; i.e., it imagines the spectacle of a world that is brought in order, subjected to the *principium contradictionis*, morally reliable, and, with regard to its significations, repeatable.[5] This world of truth—which "in truth" is fictitious and in which the concept of a self-identical and active subject plays its role—is not, however, the aim of the will to power, but only something like a means of its desire for intensification: "not a 'substance,' but rather something which in itself strives after greater strength; and which wishes to 'preserve' itself only indirectly (it wishes to *surpass* itself)" (*Works*, XV, 17). The phenomenon of subjectivity thus seems to be derived from a unified principle in two steps: in the first step the will-subject invents the subject of the fictitious world in order to provide itself with a basis for self-preservation. What we call "truth" is, therefore, only a projection of "*our* conditions of existence as the *attributes of being* in general. Owing to the fact that, in order to prosper, we must be stable in our belief, we developed the idea that the real world was neither a changing nor an evolving one, but a world of *being*" (*Works*, XV, 26). However, once this basis for self-preservation is provided (on which the "herd" would like to retire once and for all), it is instantly transgressed by the true subject of the will. For the will to power is concerned not only with preservation but also with growth and intensification—this being the second step. Any mere preservation would be decline. The assurance of living space (*Lebensraum*) is always only a means, never the aim of the will. The purpose is surpassing, overpowering of the self, the will-to-become-stronger and as such "of more value than truth" (*Works*, XV, 292).

From this follows the conclusion that the true subject—like the true world—is indeterminable in its essence: "The sphere of a subject *increasing* or *diminishing* unremittingly, the centre of the system continually *displacing* itself" (*Works*, XV, 17). Each fixation of this fluctuation of the subject, enforced upon it by the law of intensification of the self, is the work of an "interpretation" (understood as the most general "means in itself to become master of something" [*Works*, XV, 125], as "a form of the Will to Power" [*Works*, XV, 65]). The world is frozen into a "logical form" by means of interpretation, but its iterability, formulizability, calculability, and necessity are "not an established fact, but an interpretation" (*Works*, XV, 59): "from the fact that something happens regularly, and that its occurrence may be reckoned upon, it does not follow that it happens *necessarily*" (*Works*, XV, 58). The subject of the will to power is the actual *movens* of the evolving world, which is always only transitorily forced to obey the law of deception (i.e., the law of identical iterability and of logicalness), whose character, however, is "in truth" "non-formulizable," "false," and "self-contradictory." "*Knowledge* and the process of *evolution* exclude each other. *Consequently*, knowledge must be something else: it must be preceded by a will to make things knowable, a kind of Becoming in itself must create the *illusion of Being*" (*Works*, XV, 33–34).

Innumerable other passages could be cited that would support this ambiguous theory of consciousness and subjectivity. It is not Nietzsche, however, who is the subject of our investigation, but rather neostructuralism's theory of the subject, to which Nietzsche transmitted important impulses. Let's summarize the most important observations. Like Heidegger (even if with different means), Nietzsche thinks of the subject as something "derivative"; like Heidegger, he conceives it as an explicit self-relation of the sort of representation that an I directs toward itself (whereby the I is, of course, itself the result of an "error": the projection of an "agent," which "lay at the root of all things"; *Works*, XVI, 37). From behind this derived subject—the unifying agent of the fictitious world—the true subject, which is necessarily misapprehended by the conscious subject (and this accounts for the "unconquerable distrust of the *possibility* of self-knowledge"; *Works*, XII, 252), steps forward. It can also not be known because it is in constant flux and because the determinations, into which the fictitious subject forces it, only serve as stepping-stones to new interpretations behind which the will to self-intensification operates. For semantics this leads to the consequence that the process of interpretation (of the permanent self-explanations in which the will to power aesthetically mirrors itself) is infinite: "all existence is . . . essentially an *explaining* existence" (*Works*, X, 340). "The world . . . has once more become 'infinite' to us: in so far as we cannot dismiss the possibility that it *contains infinite interpretations*" (*Works*, X, 340–41). Lacan will reformulate this insight in language-theoretical terms as follows:

> From which we can say that it is in the chain of the signifier that the meaning "insists" but that none of its elements "consists" in the signification of which it is at the moment capable.
> We are forced, then, to accept the notion of an incessant sliding of the signified under the signifier. (*E*, 153–54)

Like Nietzsche, Lacan thinks of this unconquerability of the effects of meaning as the linguistic manifestation of a "true subject" that can never be reduced to Being and that is always becoming. That portion of the deeds of the true subject that arrives at consciousness is never the subject in its entirety (both of these, consciousness and the true subject, do not have the same center, they are eccentrically opposed to each other in such a way that the unconscious subject surrounds the subject of consciousness [*E*, 165–66 and 163]).

Lacan, too—like Nietzsche—thinks of the conscious subject as a fictitious (or

as he prefers to say, "imaginary") self-reflection. He imagines this quite pictori-
ally: consciousness (and thus meaning) evolves when the productivity of the unconscious subject is reflected back on itself by means of a kind of arresting of its
gliding. Lacan calls the point at which this reflection occurs the "anchoring point"
(*E*, 154).

> The diachronic function of this anchoring point is to be found in the
> sentence, even if the sentence completes its signification only with its
> last term, each term being anticipated in the construction of the others,
> and, inversely, sealing their meaning by its retroactive effect. . . .
>   This is a retroversion effect by which the subject becomes at each
> stage what he was before and announces himself—he will have been—
> only in the future perfect tense.
>   At this point the ambiguity of a failure to recognize that is essential
> to knowing myself (*un méconnaître essentiel au me connaître*) is in-
> troduced. For, in this "rear view" (*rétrovisée*), all that the subject can
> be certain of is the anticipated image coming to meet him that he
> catches of himself in his mirror. (303, 306)

The pun "*méconnaître*"/"*me connaître*"already indicates what Lacan thinks is important: the function of self-consciousness, he believes, is a function of missap-
prehension that he—like Nietzsche—designates as "imaginary."

> The only homogeneous function of consciousness is in the imaginary
> capture of the ego through its specular reflection and in the function of
> the failure to recognize which remains attached to it. (E[Fr. ed.], 832)

I will come back to this later. For the moment, I only wanted to supply evidence
for the fact that Nietzsche's differentiation of a true and a fictitious subject recurs
in Lacan and has a recognizably similar function.

But Nietzsche's theory of the subject brings into play something else besides
the idea of necessary misapprehension: first, the idea that the subject cannot be
subjected to a concept, not even a scientific concept, because of its ungraspability
(as semantic variable it shares the indeterminateness of all semantic phenomena
and permits "infinite interpretations"); second, it brings into play the language-
philosophical foundation of the theory of subject that is so characteristic for neostructuralism. According to this theory, self-consciousness is not simply dependent on the "true subject," on the unconscious; it rather proves to be an effect of
language, or, as Lacan says, of the signifier.

> My own presence to myself has been preceded by a language. Older
> than consciousness, older than the spectator, prior to any attendance, a
> sentence awaits "you": looks at you, observes you, watches over you,
> and regards you from every side. . . .
>   The text occupies the place before "me"; . . . announces me to my-

self, keeps watch over the complicity I entertain with my most secret present.[6]

We have to take a closer look at the presuppositions of this linguistic reinterpretation of the dependence of self-consciousness.

At an earlier point in our series of lectures we came across the name of Nietzsche in the context of a *language-philosophical reinterpretation of the transcendental subject*. In his essay "On Truth and Falsity in Their Ultramoral Sense," he popularized certain ideas of Hamann, Herder, and Humboldt. They can be summarized as follows: first, the idea that the thought of a synthesizing and constituting subject must somehow be "determined" for the sake of its distinguishability from other thoughts (and all determination presupposes distinction, i.e., formation of signs); and second, the idea that the transcendental subject is no longer the author of meaning-effects, but rather itself is an effect of the linguistic schematism. Reason, as Herder put it, is only constituted in fictions; it is the abstract form that is stripped of the concrete schematization of the world in signs, the reflection of the syntheses by means of which representations are connected with sound-images in the regulated unity of a life praxis, and differentiated as signs from other signs. The concepts thus do not determine the words but are invested, as it were, in the words. They are the relations between perceptions that have become rigid and binding for a thought community, and as such they are "illusions of which one has forgotten that they *are* illusions; worn-out metaphors which have become powerless to affect the senses; coins which have their obverse effaced and now are no longer of account as coins but merely as metal" (*Works*, II, 180). Just as the coins are the abstract expression of functional value, words are the abstract expression of the syntheses of imagination or of our capacity to perceive: transpositions of nerve stimuli that have to be schematized and made "canonical" for the sake of their intersubjective validity.

In reference to this turn against classical philosophy of consciousness (according to which the word represents a prior thought), Heidegger spoke of a simple "overturning."[7] Nietzsche inverts the directional meaning of the relation between perception and concept by making the concept dependent on full perception. Formerly the metaphor used to be one of a deviation controlled by the law of similarity ("analogy"), which perception could allow itself in order to sensualize a thought that in itself was nonsensual. In Nietzsche, however, it is the original mode of Being of everything linguistic, and the concept appears as the product of a subsequent abstraction (as *"the residuum of a metaphor,"* [*Works*, II, 181]).[8] Nietzsche thus does not escape the thought of re-presentation, only he no longer takes the word as representation of thought, but rather takes thought as representation of the word. In this "overturning" is grounded his claim to "grammar." What he contributes to this is, from a language-philosophical standpoint, diffuse and immature, but it has, however, had its effect. He can now derive all achievements of a culture, that formerly had to be attributed to a transcendental consciousness, from grammatical functions by means of that which he calls "the common philosophy of grammar" (*Works*, XII, 29). All thinking is caught up in "the spell of certain grammatical functions" (*Works*, XII, 29). (At this point I am neglecting the disturbing fact that Nietzsche attributes this spell, for its part – "in the last analysis" – to the "spell of *physiological* valuations and racial conditions," and therewith not only allows for the Gobineau syndrome, but also rehabilitates a rather clumsy representationism: thus the "grammar" of the late nineteenth century and of prenazism is prefigured in Nietzsche's thought.)

Be that as it may, the fact that thought is placed in the service of grammar (in which, according to Nietzsche, is always engraved a sort of "popular metaphysics" [*Works*, X, 300]) ipso facto subjects thought (the subject, consciousness) to the demands of grammar. Here Nietzsche includes, above all, schematization and regularity: identity of the rules of usage and iterability of the signs without loss of signification. Those are demands without which language would not be able to function intersubjectively, i.e., without which a consciousness could never become *linguistic*. Language is by nature intersubjective, it does not exist privately. Nietzsche is already thinking of the "philosophy of grammar" when he says of "*consciousness*" that it "*generally has only been developed under the pressure of the necessity for communication*" (*Works*, X, 297). This necessity Nietzsche interprets – in analogy to the paradigm of Darwinism – genealogically: it articulates the will to life and the will to power from the side of a certain weakness (insofar as the human being needs the "herd" – thus the social bond – in order to survive; "the recluse and wild-beast species of men would not have needed it" [*Works*, X, 297]).

> It is essential that one should not mistake the part that "consciousness" plays: it is our *relation to the outer world*; *it was the outer* world that developed it. (*Works*, XV, 39)

This means that our consciousness is not "the general sensorium and highest ruling centre," thus "*not* the conducting force, but an *organ of the latter*" (*Works*, XV, 40). It is formed under the pressure of "a sort of directing committee, in which the various *leading desires* make their votes and their power felt" (*Works*, XV, 39). The function it has to fulfill in the service of surviving within the herd is already familiar to us; "it is only a *means of communication*: it was developed by intercourse, and with a view to the interests of intercourse" (*Works*, XV, 40). In *The Joyful Wisdom* Nietzsche is most elaborate about this point.

> The very fact that our actions, thoughts, feelings and motions come within the range of our consciousness – at least a part of them – is the

result of a terrible, prolonged "must" ruling man's destiny: as the most
endangered animal he *needed* help and protection; he needed his fel-
lows, he was obliged to express his distress, he had to know how to
make himself understood—and for all this he needed "consciousness"
first of all: he had to "know" himself what he lacked, to "know" how he
felt, and to "know" what he thought. For, to repeat it once more, man,
like every living creature, thinks unceasingly, but does not know it; the
thinking which is becoming *conscious of itself* is only the smallest part
thereof, we may say, the most superficial part, the worst part:—for this
conscious thinking alone *is done in words, that is to say, in the symbols
for communication*, by means of which the origin of consciousness is
revealed. In short, the development of speech and the development of
consciousness (not of reason, but of reason becoming self-conscious) go
hand in hand. Let it be further accepted that it is not only speech that
serves as a bridge between man and man, but also the looks, the pressure and the gestures; our becoming conscious of our sense impressions, our power of being able to fix them, and as it were to locate
them outside of ourselves, has increased in proportion as the necessity
has increased for communicating them to *others* by means of signs. The
sign-inventing man is at the same time the man who is always more
acutely self-conscious; it is only as a social animal that man has learned
to become conscious of himself,—he is doing so still, and doing so
more and more.—As is obvious, my idea is that consciousness does not
properly belong to the individual existence of man, but rather to the social and gregarious nature in him; that, as follows therefrom, it is only
in relation to communal and gregarious utility that it is finely developed; and that consequently each of us, in spite of the best intention of
understanding himself as individually as possible, and of "knowing himself," will always just call into consciousness the non-individual in him,
namely, his "averageness";—that our thought itself is continuously as it
were *outvoted* by the character of consciousness—by the imperious
"genius of the species" therein—and is translated back into the perspective of the herd. Fundamentally our actions are in an incomparable
manner altogether personal, unique and absolutely individual—there is
no doubt about it; but as soon as we translate them into consciousness,
they *do not appear so any longer*. (*Works*, X, 297–99)

Although Nietzsche by no means takes the side of language or consciousness—on
the contrary, he despises them as "characteristic of the herd"; their achievements
are "a great, radical perversion, falsification, superficialisation, and generalisation" (*Works*, X, 299)—he nevertheless points to something that in his later
philosophizing will be treated as the impossibility of a private language. For
Nietzsche this attack on the inwardness of the individual has the form of "an invisible spell" (*Works*, XII, 28) to which the individual succumbs as a result of the

pressure to adapt to the equalizing "herd" that substitutes the universal sign for individual impression. If one were to talk of the individual—and Nietzsche expressly does not do so—as the true subject, then one could characterize the step into the linguistic as a "subversion of the subject by the *ordre symbolique*." We will see in a moment that Nietzsche himself is thinking within "the spell of grammar" at this point. His distinction between the individual and the universal—where the individual is the object of perception, the universal the object of a concept—follows the language game of Kant's critique of knowledge by inverting its preference for the communicable and the universal.

But let's remain for a moment with what he calls the philosophy of grammar. Here Nietzsche is obviously not thinking of something like a philosophy that has the grammar of a language as its object, but rather of a worldview inserted into an existing language, or, as he sarcastically expresses it, a "popular metaphysics" (*Works*, X, 300). The philosophy of philosophers is only its translation or its thinning out into something abstract. Behind this assertion there lurks the hermeneutical thesis that the philosophy of an age remains dependent on the terms and categories that are supplied by the linguistically articulated worldview, and that it is greatly deceived if it believes that it can free itself from the "toils of grammar" by means of thought (*Works*, X, 300). The distinction between subject and object is Nietzsche's favorite example for a compulsion of thought engraved into European grammar, at the bottom of which lies absolutely no higher necessity.[9] One believed in " 'the soul' as one believed in grammar and the grammatical subject: one said, 'I' is the condition, 'think' is the predicate and is conditioned" (*Works*, XII, 72). Such philosophical propositions prove to be nothing more, however, than a "deception on the part of grammar" (*Works*, XII, 2). "The wonderful family resemblance of all Indian, Greek, and German philosophising," for example, is explained by them (*Works*, XII, 29). Philosophical thought is thus "far less a discovery than a re-recognising, a remembering, a return and a home-coming" to the "common-household" of the underlying linguistic construction of the world (*Works*, XII, 29).

> In fact, where there is affinity of language, owing to the common philosophy of grammar—I mean owing to the unconscious domination and guidance of similar grammatical functions—it cannot but be that everything is prepared at the outset for a similar development and succession of philosophical systems; just as the way seems barred against certain other possibilities of world-interpretation. (*Works*, XII, 29)

With this conclusion, which comes close to a veritable linguistic determinism—think of the famous statement in *The Twilight of the Idols*: " 'Reason' in language!—oh what a deceptive old witch it has been! I fear we shall never be rid of God, so long as we still believe in grammar" (*Works*, XVI, 22)—he denies in a certain way the openness and infiniteness of interpretation and the grammatical nonfixability of the subject that only becomes real in becoming; namely, the will-subject. This is one of many contradictions in Nietzsche's thought that accounts for the fact that linguistic determinists as well as hermeneuticists and neostruc-turalists could appeal to him.

But let's return to the argument that language essentially excludes the expression of the individual or the private (Nietzsche does not distinguish between the two). This argument (or maybe we should speak of a thesis) stands in harsh contrast to the romantic and to the Humboldtian view of language, which was dialectic and which conceived the process of linguistic tradition as a reciprocal action of the universal ("the law of language") and the individual ("language usage"). According to this, the universal has a motivating, but no determining power over individual speech: the sign syntheses are hypotheses that themselves are grounded in interpretations and that are open to new interpretations, so that the system of language is incalculably transformed over the course of its individual uses.

Not so in Nietzsche: Individual perception is destroyed as soon as the linguistic community accepts it into its repertoire; as word-coin, the meaning of an individual experience shows the same face to everybody, and becomes "thereby shallow, meagre, relatively stupid, – a generalisation, a symbol, a characteristic of the herd" (*Works*, X, 299).

This theorem of the incompatibility of the private and the linguistic was taken up, in a distinguishable, yet nevertheless related manner, by Anglo-Saxon analytical philosophy, as well as by neostructuralism. Best known is Wittgenstein's version of a critique of the idea of a "private language." In his conception it has the function of the decisive evasion in the face of the reproach of solipsism, whose phantom haunted him for a long time. Under solipsism one understands an extreme form of idealism, namely, the extension of the doubt in the existence of a world independent of consciousness onto the existence of other thinking beings. (*If* they exist, then only mediated by my consciousness and as relative, not as absolute beings.) For this radical doubt – which accepts the givenness only of one's own consciousness – Wittgenstein (like some idealists before him) saw only one remedy, namely, the reconsideration of our Being-in-language. This reconsideration was not only supposed to make the extreme of epistemological solipsism impotent, but was also supposed language-philosophically to overthrow idealist subject philosophy in its entirety from Berkeley though Kant, Fichte, Schopenhauer, Natorp, and Husserl to Sartre; and in this sense it was also decisive for the neostructuralist critique of subject-thought. One spoke of it as the *linguistic turn*; it belongs to the few epistemological presuppositions that neostructuralism shares with hermeneutics (since Schleiermacher) and with analytical philosophy, i.e., to be thought of along the lines of language. For this reason alone we have to take a closer look at the language-philosophical subversion of the idealist subject of knowledge before we turn to the work of Derrida and Lacan. Otherwise we will understand poorly – even after all we know about Heidegger's and Nietzsche's roles as predecessors—why neostructuralist theory of the subject unfolded on the basis of philosophy of language.

The oldest version of Wittgenstein's thesis, according to which the subject has no privileged knowledge of its experiences of consciousness, can be found in Schleiermacher: it is the germinal cell of the *linguistic turn* of all of modern philosophy. In extreme simplification it states that the idea of a thought, a perception, or a representation independent of language (and thus not articulated) arises from a pure abstraction. Differences in the medium of the ideal can present themselves only on the basis of a material and temporal (for example, phonic) difference. Otherwise thought would remain an amorphous and foggy mass (*HuK*, 367) that for the sake of its distinctness has to be led through what Lacan calls the *défilé du signifiant*. But precisely this argument thrives on the attack on the model of representation of the seventeenth and the eighteenth centuries, according to which speech designatively re-presents, as it were, almost as a nomenclature, the simple ideas (or primordial impressions) of the soul and the connections that reason established between them. Once it is demonstrated that distinctions in thought are bound to differences between the carriers of expression—to "the determined distinguishing of significant units" (*HuK*, 365) and their recombination in words and sentences[10]—then the supposed difference between thought and speech is reduced to the difference between internal and spoken speech:

> This leads us to the unity of speech and thought; language is the mode of thought in which it is real. For there is no thought without speech. The pronunciation of words merely refers to the presence of something else and is therefore arbitrary. But nobody can think without words. Without words thought is not yet completed and clear. (*HUK*, 77)

We have already seen that Saussure takes up this idea. In Wittgenstein it appears in another variant that has so frequently been presented in detail or even attacked that I will draw only a very brief sketch. Wittgenstein saw himself confronted with a philosophical tradition that assumed that experiences were given to consciousness in the form of "internal perceptions" in a manner that was evident only to it. Wittgenstein, by contrast, seeks to show that the predicates by means of which we designate our experiences of consciousness have a signification that remains identical from the first-person and the third-person perspective. My pain and my sensations are not more familiar to *me* than they are to *you* or *him*. The limits of knowing something are coextensive with the limits of being able to speak about something (Wittgenstein obviously shares this assumption with Nietzsche). Wittgenstein justifies it in the following way: to have a certain sensation means to distinguish it from other, comparable sensations, and thus to be able to identify it over the course of time.[11] Only within the system of a language can one distinguish and identify something; a language system, in its nature, however, is intersubjective and transindividual. The epistemological problem of how I am able to know my own or somebody else's inner states thus is transformed into a semantic problem: how can I master a language and be certain that I have mastered it? If I master the language, then the question about the subsistence of a private component of signification is superfluous. For this concept contradicts the game-rules of a meaningful use of linguistic expressions. Linguistic expressions do not identify their signified by themselves, and also not by pointing to it (ostension), but rather only by virtue of a rule that supplies an intersubjective criterion for the correctness of the association of signifier and signified. To master a rule means to be able to repeat identically the once established association (for instance, on the example of an individual state of sensation that must lie in the past) in any number of cases of application. As soon as I identify something by speaking, I am acting in conformity with a rule; i.e., I am following a convention I learned, and the mastery of which enables me to distinguish between correct and incorrect uses of an expression in any number of speech situations. If, however, it were within my power to designate private sensations with a name, then even *I* could not definitively come to know my sensations; for I either proceed according to a rule that distinguishes correct and incorrect applications of the word, which my neighbor can also then learn; or I do not proceed according to a rule, and in this instance even I do not recognize and designate my own states of consciousness. Wittgenstein concludes from this that the accessibility of the *signification* of my inner conditions is just as unproblematic from the "I" perspective as it is from the "he" perspective.[12]

You will say that only I can know whether I am in pain or whether I am in love; somebody else could only presume it (*PI*, section 246). To this extent I have epistemologically privileged access to my experiences of consciousness. Wittgenstein takes exception to this with a somewhat sophistic argument. He says that a word can have a significance only if it has a function, a function that only the word can fulfill. That is not true for the use of the verb "to know," in the expression "I know that I am in pain." For this expression means exactly the same as: "I am in pain" (*PI*, sections 533f.).[13] If one is in pain, then one is simply in pain. The term "to know" is not appropriate as a designation for this, for in the case of knowledge it must be logically possible to doubt what one previously knew. That, however, is not and will never be the case for the expression of sensations; therefore, the use of the predicate has no function in this case, it is meaningless. This, of course, does not mean that when I *am* in love, the other person too has to be in love; it does mean, however, that when I have *knowledge* of my being in love, this knowledge has to be expressed on the level of signification, the regulated use of which I share with the other language participants in the framework of our common membership in a "form of life." *I* do not know this better than anyone else.

Thus the reproach of solipsism is dissolved: one can mean something — such as an internal condition of consciousness — *as* something only within a language.

If, however, I already need the language I share with my neighbor to identify my self and its states, then it is obviously too late to doubt their existence and to consider the certainty I have concerning my experiences to be exclusive or private.

We will see in our next lecture how Derrida (and Lacan) take up the *linguistic turn* of the philosophy of the subject and how they transform it.

Lecture 14

In our search for antecedents to neostructuralism's theory of the subject, we eventually came across analytical philosophy. At first glance its proximity to neostructuralism seems rather doubtful. This is especially the case because analytical philosophy takes seriously the dimension of the "meaning" (*Sinn*) and "signification" (*Bedeutung*) of linguistic expressions, whereas neostructuralism "critically questions" meaning in order ultimately to arrive at something not meaningful in itself. The method of analytical philosophy, as presented, for example, by Ernst Tugendhat in his introductory lectures on analytical philosophy, consists in the clarification of concepts by means of an exposition of the rules for the use of the words to which they correspond.[1] As a fundamental discipline of philosophy, language analysis is "formal semantics"; i.e., it is concerned with clarification of the signification of concepts. It is a form of universal pragmatics whenever it makes clarification of the signification of words contingent on contexts of practical action, at least to the extent to which this action is sufficiently general that it can be characterized formally.

To be sure, by proceeding in this way analytical philosophy attains (it would be more correct to say that it presupposes) a rigid concept of rule and regularity. Even its preference for the formal and the universal ("formal semantics," "universal pragmatics," etc.) expresses this. The demand that one work only with defined concepts and clarify the signification of concepts by uncovering the rules for their use testifies to a staunch belief in the dogma of unequivocality, of semantic identity, and of "capacity for presence" (*Gegenwärtigen-Können*). It is precisely this that connects analytical philosophy with the deepest tradition of European

215

metaphysics. Tugendhat expressly affirms this view when he says that "the traditional idea" of a philosophical "fundamental discipline as ontology . . . comes into its own only in the idea of formal semantics."[2] This is a Hegelian formulation: a tradition grasps its own truth only in that final philosophizing that provides the "concept" for, or "brings into its concept," as Hegel says, the activity of metaphysics that prior to that point had been relatively unconscious. Formal semantics believes, in much the same way, that it has grasped the essence, discovered the "concept" of Western ontology, and to this extent it belongs to this tradition itself.

On the other hand, analytical philosophy resembles the "knowledge interest" of neostructuralism in that it criticizes metaphysical thought. We are all familiar with the accusation that metaphysics operates with "pseudoconcepts" (*Scheinbegriffe*). These are concepts to which no signification (in the sense of a retrospective coupling to a legitimate word *usage*) can be assigned and which, therefore, are used "falsely." Examples of this are concepts like "the I," "the for- itself," or "the nothing," i.e., nominalizations of pronouns, adverbs, etc., whose grammaticality is thereby abused. The best known example for such a critique of metaphysics is Rudolf Carnap's polemic against Heidegger's "the nothing nots" (*das Nichts nichtet*). But the universal incrimination of senselessness, on the basis of which language analysis denounces metaphysical thinking, simultaneously "brings into its concept" the most profound passion of Western thought: the passion for unequivocality, enlightenment, and exactitude.

This does not prevent us from bringing out certain parallels between language analysis and neostructuralism: first, the renunciation of metaphysics; second, recourse to language and language use; and third, repudiation of the model of linguistic representation.

Where the renunciation of metaphysics is concerned, we already saw that analytical and neostructuralist philosophy each understands it quite differently. The incrimination of senselessness, with which language analysis for a long time — and in a truly foolish fashion — assailed idealist philosophy and all possible forms of ethics and dialectics, finally indenturing itself to thoroughly conservative (rule-affirming and rule-preserving) manners of thinking, remains in our memory today only as a piece of cast-off history. Heidegger himself reacted by pointing out the metaphysical heritage of this incrimination of senselessness: analytical philosophy in its rigorously positivistic and scientistic extremes, according to Heidegger, is the conceptual form of the technological and scientific age, and as such it is the culmination of an interpretation of Being along the lines of the "presencing the present" (knowledge for mastery).

The procedure that Derrida calls "deconstruction" is fundamentally distinct from this form of an (alleged) critique of metaphysics. In the instance of this term we are dealing with a neologism modeled on Heidegger's "The Task of Destroying the History of Ontology" (section 6 of *BT*, pp. 41ff.). What Heidegger means by this is the endeavor of destroying that "metaphysics" that is operative in the Western interpretation of "Being" "until we arrive at those primordial experiences in which we achieved our first ways of determining the nature of Being" (*BT*, 44). He explains this procedure as follows:

> In thus demonstrating the origin of our basic ontological concepts by an investigation in which their "birth certificate" is displayed, we have nothing to do with a vicious relativizing of ontological standpoints. But this destruction is just as far from having the *negative* sense of shaking off the ontological tradition. We must, on the contrary, stake out the positive possibilities of that tradition, and this always means keeping it within its *limits*; these in turn are given factically in the way the question is formulated at the time, and in the way the possible field for investigation is thus bounded off. On its negative side, this destruction does not relate itself towards the past; its criticism is aimed at "today" and at the prevalent way of treating the history of ontology, whether it is headed towards doxography, towards intellectual history, or towards a history of problems. But to bury the past in nullity [*Nichtigkeit*] is not the purpose of this destruction; its aim is *positive*; its negative function remains unexpressed and indirect. (*BT*, 44)

Derrida speaks of "deconstruction" in order to emphasize this positive — or, to be more precise — constructive aspect of the destruction of the Western interpretation of Being. "Deconstruction" means the tearing down of the walls of Western metaphysics, not with the purpose of destroying it, but rather in order to reconstruct it (*reconstruire*) anew and differently. To be more precise, "deconstruction" means initiating within that discourse as which the West presents itself a discussion with what Heidegger calls Being, and Lacan and Lévinas like to call "the Other" (*l'Autre*). Deconstruction to this extent resembles psychoanalysis, which also questions each utterance in regard to what is actually "thought" in it beyond its "manifest content." In this sense we can say that Derrida, even in his criticism of the concept of the subject, always takes cognizance of that voice that acknowledges the subject even if only in the form of its repression.

So much for the critique of metaphysics. Another point of agreement between analytical and neostructuralist philosophy is discernible in the fact that both movements presuppose the so-called *linguistic turn*. In a moment I will become more specific about this point, supporting my arguments on the basis of Derrida's texts. But we already know from our previous reading of Saussure, and from what we learned about Schleiermacher and Wittgenstein, that the *linguistic turn* consists in the transferral of the philosophical paradigm of consciousness onto that of the sign. It is no longer consciousness that is the transcendental place of the "condition of possibility" for meaning, significance, and reference, rather it is the sign. Transcendental philosophy is transformed or dissolved into semiology, i.e., into the theory of signs. This transpires because, in order to be able to set itself off in its own identity from other thoughts, a thought (even the thought of myself as subject) needs to be articulated; i.e., it must go through the "parade of the signifier." Analytical philosophy concurs with this, just as does the hermeneutics of the younger Frankfurt School (Karl-Otto Apel, Jürgen Habermas, Alfred Lorenzer, and others).

The third and last point of agreement that we could detect between neostructuralism and analytical philosophy concerns their common critique of the representational model of language. This model supposes that to speak means to mimetically represent (*abbilden*) thoughts or ideas by means of words. Wittgenstein demonstrates in radical fashion the untenability of this view, which he himself had held at an earlier stage of his philosophizing. The frequently varied premise of his later philosophy states, after all, that the significance of a word does not consist in its correspondence with a thought or a perception, but rather that this significance makes itself manifest in the "rule for its usage." This is also the case for the concept of self-consciousness. In fact, for a long time self-consciousness had been interpreted according to the model of the relationship of a subject to an object, whereby in the case of self-consciousness the object would simply be the subject itself (the classical instance of reflection). Apart from the fact that the reflectional model is contradictory in itself, it is also untenable for language-philosophical reasons because it attempts to reduce consciousness to acts of (sensual or mental) *perception (Anschauung)*. In the case of self-consciousness we are merely dealing with a kind of "inner viewing" or "inner perception." The fallaciousness of this can be demonstrated by a reflection on our use of language. Tugendhat devoted particular attention to it in the lectures mentioned earlier. There is, according to him, no objectivity, not even of a subject, that is independent of language, and this is so because we cannot determine what is meant by objectivity or "state of affairs" (*Sachverhalt*) without referring back to propositions and their meanings (*Bedeutungen*). Only within a language can something have meaning (*Bedeutung*), for meaning is nothing other than a nonautonomous component of the use of signs.[3] Tugendhat reproaches Husserl's analysis of intentionality for having neglected this fact in particularly drastic fashion,[4] and it is interesting to note in this respect the parallel to Derrida. In order to make this more apparent, I have specifically selected Tugendhat as a representative of analytical philosophy, since both he and Derrida derive their positions from a critique of the model of language-independent consciousness à la Husserl. This phenomenological model assumes that the "positing" (*das meinende*) (intentional) consciousness is immediately "directed" toward the "states of affairs" or "facts" of the real or imagined world. Let's first look at what Tugendhat objects to in this position, so that we can then compare his critique of consciousness from the perspective of the philosophy of language with Derrida's critique of Husserl.

Tugendhat asserts that propositions in which intentional "acts" or "experiences" are articulated are not two-part, but rather three-part: they express the relation of an intention not with regard to an object, but rather with regard to a "state of affairs." A "state of affairs," however, is nothing to which one could refer by means of nominal expressions; it is itself something synthetic that is made up of at least two elements: the object of a "singular term," and its characterization by means of an act of predication. In other words, a "state of affairs" is not a *thing* (*Sache*); rather it is a judgment about a thing by means of predication: "It is the case for A that it is b."

In reality I never see things, as the model of intentionality suggests, but always only states of affairs, i.e., complex things or things that are immediately furnished with properties. (I do not, for example, as Husserl wants us to believe, first see the castle in Heidelberg and only subsequently synthesize this perception with the perception that it is also red; on the contrary, the proposition by means of which the states of affairs are expressed is both the cognitive and the semantic minimum of all intending and speaking about objects of consciousness.)[5] If this is the case, then I will have to make corrections with regard to the notion of "seeing something": I do not see something (whereby "something" stands for an object that can be expressed by a "sigular term"); rather I see *that* something is the case (expressible by means of a propositional expression). What analytical philosophers call the *propositional attitude* is the basic form of all intentional consciousness, including even self-consciousness. Thus for me as well it is the case that when I reflect on my internal states, I do it in the following way: "I know (feel, sense, or understand, etc.) *that* I p"; I do not "look at my feeling, my thinking, or my perceiving." On this Tugendhat remarks:

> The evidence that all intentional consciousness is propositional lends the analytical program of a theory of the proposition an additional historical value: just as the ontological question about being as being dissolves into the question about understanding the proposition, the question of consciousness dissolves into the question of propositional understanding."[6]

Tugendhat returned to this topic in his lectures on self-consciousness and self-determination. In the introductory lecture he once again (critically) refers to Husserl, who described self-consciousnes in analogy to the consciousness we direct toward objects ("intentional experiences" like perceiving, knowing, loving, desiring, intending, i.e., those experiences our language constructs by means of a direct object). To be sure, Husserl rejected with regard to intentionality the crude representational model: consciousness does not furnish us with something like a representative in the sense of a placeholder (*Stellvertreter*) for the object; rather it "constitutes" it (and even this it accomplishes with the restriction that it does not find out anything about its existence, but only about its essence). In a stricter sense, however, Husserl does not really get away from the representational model: he considers the "directedness of consciousness towards . . ." to be the relation of a conscious subject to an object. The metaphor of sight, a metaphor that itself has an old Western tradition (νοεῖν, ϑεωρεῖν, εἰδέναι, ἰδέα, etc., are expressions that originally designated sensory perception), serves him as a model for thought. Husserl knows that the object of consciousness is a state of affairs and thus something complex. However, he believes that he can take account of this fact by declaring that the object of consciousness is composed of synthetic acts, composed, for example, of syntheses of acts that constitute the object itself, and acts that constitute its conditionedness (*Zuständlichkeit*). The same is true for self-consciousness: Husserl takes it to be the synthesis of an invariant ego pole and a varying set of consciousness experiences that are coordinated with it. Behind all this, as we know, is the model of direct *representing* (*Vorstellen*) or *seeing*. Yet this model, according to Tugendhat, stands in contradiction to the way in which self-consciousness is given to us as language.

> If we look at relations of consciousness such as wishing, meaning, knowing, intending, fearing, then we realize that their grammatical object is never an expression that designates a common object, a spatiotemporal object; rather we see that their grammatical object is always a nominalized proposition. One cannot wish, know, etc., spatiotemporal objects; if one expresses a wish, one always wishes that something is or would be the case; the expression "I know" cannot be supplemented by expressions such as "the chair," "Mr. X," etc.; I know rather "that it is raining today," or "that this chair is brown," or even "that there is a chair standing there."[7]

The "something" at which the expressions of intentional consciousness are directed, then, is not an object, but a contracted (a nominalized) *proposition*: "that p (is the case)," for example, "that it is raining today," "that I'm feeling well," "that I'm looking at you," etc. Objects of this sort (contracted propositions) Husserl called *Sachverhalte*, the Anglo-Saxon tradition speaks of "propositions," "and in British philosophy those intentional experiences whose objects are propositions, i.e., attitudes toward 'propositions' or 'states of affairs,' are therefore called *propositional attitudes*."[8]

This is also true, according to Tugendhat, for those intentional acts that thematize (reflect) themselves. The "something" in the structure of "consciousness of something" is in this instance also a contracted or abridged proposition: "it has or implies the structure *consciousness that p*."[9] If self-consciousness, as Tugenhat further assumes, is a form of knowledge, then it is also true that it exhibits the structure *knowledge that p*. One cannot, accordingly, know an experience (*Erlebnis*); rather one can only know *that* someone (e.g., I myself) takes part in it. This then implies that there can be no knowledge of an isolated self (of an "I"), but only of a cognitive, emotional, or volitional state of affairs, whose mode of Being analysis of language discloses to be that of a linguistic entity—that of a proposition. In this sense it is quite clear that analytical philosophy passionately takes exception to the idea that there is something like a nonpropositional (and thus translinguistic) intentional consciousness, self-consciousness included. (Here I am passing over the fact that Tugendhat is faithful to Husserl insofar as he still takes self-consciousness—falsely—to be a special case of the positing consciousness, i.e., to be an act of reflection, a principally *identifiable* object of *knowledge*.)

With these references to Wittgenstein and Tugendhat I want to conclude the section of my lectures dedicated to the epistemological prehistory of neostructuralism's theory of the subject. My intention was to make evident that there never was a radical break or a new beginning; rather we discover here one of the numerous transformations by means of which a new form of thinking connects with an existing formation of knowledge, partly preserving it and partly transfiguring it. The idea of a radical beginning is in itself contradictory, for any "beginning" must evolve on the basis of language (a historical-epistemic a priori) whose signs it can twist and transmute, but never create (anew) in their entirety.

Derrida does not have much to say about Wittgenstein, or about Ernst Tugendhat, for that matter. He has, however, concerned himself considerably with a certain movement in Anglo-Saxon pragmatics that is based on Wittgenstein, namely, with Austin's and Searle's speech-act theory. In his retort to Searle's criticism of the lecture he delivered in Montreal in August 1971,[10] he says about the theory:

> Among the many reasons that make me unqualified to represent a "prominent philosophical tradition," there is this one: I consider myself to be in many respects quite close to Austin, both interested in and indebted to his problematic. This is said in *Sec*, very clearly. . . .
> Above all, however, when I do raise questions or objections, it is always at points where I recognize in Austin's theory presuppositions which are the most tenacious and the most central presuppositions of the *continental* metaphysical tradition. . . . *Signature Event Context* analyses the metaphysical premises of the Anglo-Saxon—and fundamentally moralistic—theory of the performative, of speech acts or discursive events. In France, it seems to me that these premises underlie the hermeneutics of Ricoeur and the archaeology of Foucault. (*LI*, 172, 173)

Here Derrida concedes that he stands in very close proximity to analytical pragmatics; indeed, that he is indebted to it. Yet he claims at the same time not to be part of the metaphysical tradition evident in it. This certainly does not mean that one might simply be able to escape this tradition. On the contrary, Derrida emphasized again and again that discussions of Western grammar cannot simply put its game rules out of action: speech that does not make use of traditional grammar would be forced to express itself in "monstrous" ways. Derrida does, however, claim to diagnose the metaphysical tradition as that which it actually is. Thereby he links up with a tradition that has already prepared his "discourse," namely, that tradition for which the names of Nietzsche and Heidegger are exemplary.

Let's examine by means of a concrete example just how Derrida employs his deconstructive hermeneutics. The metaphysical tradition of the *langage herité* cannot be eliminated, and Derrida's remarks about Husserl are just as valid for Derrida himself.

> The unity of ordinary language (or the language of traditional metaphysics) and the language of phenomenology is never broken in spite of the precautions, the "brackets," the renovations or innovations. Transforming a traditional concept into an indicative or metaphorical concept does not eliminate its heritage; it imposes questions, rather, to which Husserl never ventured a response.[11]

Derrida also depends heavily on the metaphysical tradition, and he discusses its classical themes: sign, self-reference, the relation of transcendental and empirical world, etc. However, he does it in such a way that he estranges his subject matter by means of an interpretive procedure that goes against the grain, a procedure that from the standpoint of phenomenology appears to be a distortion, but which from the perspective of diagnostics, however, seems to divulge profitable new recognitions.

Unfortunately, Derrida has not yet published a text whose sole thematic emphasis is that which concerns us most at the moment: the problematics of (modern) subjectivity. Therefore we will have to rely on texts that consider this question – if with special attentiveness – as one among others. I am intentionally taking as my point of entry (mainly, although not solely) Derrida's earliest publications, namely his introduction to Edmund Husserl's *Origin of Geometry*,[12] and his work on Husserl's theory of signs (*Speech and Phenomena*). The basic ideas of both works are summarized (or supported through the examples of other texts by Husserl) in his interview with Julia Kristeva ("Semiology and Grammatology"), which we discussed earlier, as well as in the two essays " 'Genesis and Structure' and Phenomenology" (*WD*, 154–68) and "Form and Meaning" (*Margins*, 155–73).

It makes sense for us to orient our investigation around these texts, not only because we can thereby become aware of the genesis of Derrida's thought, but also because Derrida's treatment of the concept of the subject is developed precisely on the example of Husserl, just as Ernst Tugendhat explicitly developed his analytical countermove as a reaction against Husserl's idealist explanation of the constitution of "states of affairs." In this way the line, which is by no means easy to draw, between the analytical and the neostructuralist "critique of meaning" (*Sinnkritik*) becomes visible.

Those works by Derrida devoted to Husserl exhibit, judged within the context of neostructuralist texts in general, an exceptional clarity. One can scarcely reproach them with the claim that they thrust upon their subject matter consequences that are completely foreign to it. On the contrary, in his readings of Husserl Derrida is amplifying a voice resonant in Husserl's texts themselves, but one which can assert itself against the epistemic framework of his philosophizing only with great effort. It is this less apparent aspect of—and in—Husserl's works that interests Derrida the most.

Derrida's ideas are discriminating and he develops them in small argumentative steps. Therefore it seems useful first to provide a global survey of his position and particularly of the themes that he treats most thoroughly. In a second step we can then supplement this rough framework with the necessary refinements.

First of all, one has to know that Derrida—much like Tugendhat—approaches the phenomenon of "self-consciousness" or "subjectivity" from the angle of the so-called experiences of consciousness or *states* of consciousness. Derrida tries to demonstrate that Husserl believed it was possible to distinguish a "preexpressive" stratum from an expressive stratum in these "states of consciousness." The consciousness experience, according to this, would thus be cognizant of its meaning or its signification even before it is consigned to the expressive substance (*Ausdruckskörper*).

> 2. This layer of pure meaning, or a pure signified, refers, explicitly in Husserl and at least implicitly in semiotic practice, to a layer of prelinguistic or presemiotic (preexpressive, Husserl calls it) meaning whose presence would be conceivable outside and before the work of *différance*, outside and before the process or system of signification. (*P*, 31)

As in Tugendhat's critique of Husserl, it is the idea of a presemiotic internal perception against which Derrida lashes out. In his opinion, meaning can be formed only in a language, and language generates its significations by means of the differentiations of expressions.

We are already acquainted with this sort of critique of the paradigm of a language-independent transcendental consciousness from the works of Herder, Schleiermacher, Humboldt, and, of course, Saussure. In contrast to Tugendhat, Derrida acknowledges this tradition at least in part. Already in his earliest longer text, in his introduction to *Edmund Husserl's Origin of Geometry*, he pointed in a longer footnote to Herder's role as predecessor.

> Did not Herder, in his *Verstand und Erfahrung: Eine Metakritik zur Kritik der reinen Vernunft* . . . already reproach Kant for not taking into consideration the intrinsic necessity of language and its immanence in the most apriori act of thought? (*OG*, 70)

Herder's criticism of Kant thus appears as an argumentative parallel to Derrida's critique of Husserl. The only difference is that Derrida does not simply criticize Husserl; rather he merely demonstrates that, and to what extent, this nonreducibility of language becomes a problem for Husserl himself. On the other hand, Husserl leaves no doubt that, to his mind, "it would be absurd for sense not to precede – de jure (and here de jure is difficult to make clear [*une évidence difficile*]) – the act of language whose own value will always be that of expression" (*OG*, 69). On the other hand, it by no means escapes Husserl when he discusses language that "[language] offers the most dangerous resistance to the phenomenological reduction, and transcendental discourse will remain irreducibly obliterated by a certain ambiguous worldliness" (*OG*, 68–69). In a certain sense, language is the condition of possibility for the phenomenological reduction, and if this is true, then transcendental consciousness is not the appropriate authority to turn to when one abstracts from language.

> It is rather significant that every critical enterprise, juridicial or transcendental, is made vulnerable by the irreducible factuality and the natural naiveté of its language. We become conscious of this vulnerability or of this vocation to silence in a *second* reflection on the possibility of the juridico-transcendental regression itself. . . . Attentiveness to the "fact" of language in which a juridical thought lets itself be transcribed, in which juridicalness would like to be completely transparent, is a return to factuality as the de jure character of the de jure itself. It is a reduction of the reduction and opens the way to an infinite discursiveness. (69–70)

We will have to take a closer look at the thoughts that lead to this conclusion. But that belongs to those refinements that we still have to append to our initial orientational framework. First of all, however, we want to look at how Husserl actually develops his thesis of the preexpressivity of meaning, and only then will we examine how Derrida uncovers its contradictoriness.

Husserl discusses the relationship between intentional and expressive acts in the clearest and most compact fashion in sections 124 to 127 of his *Ideas: General Introduction to Pure Phenomenology*.[13] In this text he writes of "pre-expressive intentions," i.e., acts of consciousness that are directed at ideal objectivities and that possess knowledge about themselves, yet which are not linguistically articulated. Such a preexpressive intention, Derrida remarks, would be "a presence to itself of the subject in a silent and intuitive consciousness" (*Margins*, 16). Husserl assumes, as we stated earlier, that there actually is something like this, but, by the same token, he insists that he wants to explain not only the preexpressivity of intentional acts but also their relation to linguistic expressions. He is both amazed that preexpressive meaning and expression can "coincide," and amazed about the manner in which this occurs, and he concludes that "we clearly have title-headings here indicated for phenomenological problems that are not unimportant" (*Ideas*, 319). In order to eliminate these problems at the outset, Husserl takes flight into the metaphor of *interwovenness* (*Verwebung*): meaning and expression, he says, are interwoven (318).

Husserl does not feel entirely comfortable with the choice of this metaphor, whose "unavoidable ambiguity" rather disturbs him (318). "Ambiguity is dangerous," he continues, however, "only so long as it is not known to be such, or the parallel structures have not been kept apart" (319). By parallel structures he means 1) the "expressing stratum," as the "logical act-stratum" or pure "intentional meaning," and 2) the stratum that "suffers expression," i.e., the linguistic stratum (318 and 322). We can already tell from this formulation how Husserl hopes to be able to uphold the notion that the intending and the expressing theses are in fact unitary: only the stratum of expression, he asserts, is active and productive. "The stratum of expression—and this constitutes its peculiarity—apart from the fact that it lends expression to all other intentionalities, is not productive" (321). Thus the act of meaning production seems to move unidirectionally from the "non-sensory 'mental' aspect" to the "sensory, the so to speak bodily aspect of expression" (319). Husserl also differentiates between the two aspects by calling them the "lower stratum" and the "upper stratum." On the other hand, he concedes that

> the attempt to clarify here the relevant structures meets with considerable difficulties. Already the recognition that after abstracting from the stratum of sensory verbal sound, there lies before us in reality still another layer which we here presuppose, thus in every case—even in that of a thinking that is ever so vague, empty, and merely verbal—a stratum of meaning that expresses, and a substratum of expressed meaning—is not one that is easy to make, nor again is the understanding of the essential connexions of these stratifications easy. For we should not hold too hard by the metaphor of stratification; expression is not of the nature of an overlaid varnish or covering garment; it is a mental (*geistige*) formation, which exercises new intentional influences (*Funktionen*) on the intentional substratum and experiences from the latter correlative intentional influences. (322)

Although Husserl does not escape the representational model of language, neither does he welcome it. What is so remarkable about the foregoing passage, to be sure, is that it abjures the thesis of the relative passivity of the expressing stratum contained in the spirit of the metaphor of interweaving: not only does the intentional substratum stamp itself in the expressive upper stratum, but this sensory upper stratum also exercises a certain retroactive effect on the "intentional function." This is confirmed when Husserl writes of a "remarkable blending together" of both strata. "From the noetic standpoint the rubric 'expressing' should indicate a special act-stratum to which all other acts must adjust themselves in their own way, and with which they must blend remarkably in such wise that every noematic act-meaning, and consequently the relation to objectivity which lies in it, stamps itself 'conceptually' in the noematic phase of the expressing" (320). Only substances of the same order can be blended together, not something productive with something unproductive. Blending or interweaving of meaning and expression: that would be something quite different from a mere "mirroring" of one in the other ("reflecting back as from a mirror"; 320). In the case of mirroring, one element is the mere copy of the other and, therefore, not autonomous in itself. In the case of interweaving, however, there are two equally autonomous components: woof and warp, which literally are woven (Latin, *texere*) to form a cloth, a textile.

It is precisely at this point that Derrida inserts his critique, and he does so by spelling out the implications of the metaphor of *interweaving* (*texere*). The "bodily stratum," he says, can be "blended together" with the preexpressive act (the meaning) of the "animating intention" (thus with the "non-sensory, 'mental' aspect" of the sign) *only according to a textual order*: for example, according to a language (understood not as a system of expressions but rather as a system of signs, i.e., of syntheses of meaning and expression).

> The interweaving (*Verwebung*) of language, the interweaving of that which is purely language in language with the other threads of experience constitutes a cloth. The word *Verwebung* refers to this metaphorical zone. The "strata" are "woven," their intercomplication is such that the warp cannot be distinguished from the woof. If the stratum of the logos were simply *founded*, one could extract it and bring to light its underlying stratum of nonexpressive acts and contents. But since this superstructure acts back upon the *Unterschicht* in an essential and decisive manner, one is indeed obliged, from the very outset of the description, to associate a properly *textual* metaphor with the geological metaphor: for cloth means *text*. *Verweben* here means *textere*. The discursive is related to the nondiscursive, the linguistic "stratum" is intermixed with the prelinguistic "stratum" according to the regulated system of a kind of *text*. (*Margins*, 160)

Derrida then shows that Husserl can avoid this consequence only with difficulty—and only at the price of certain contradictions—when he asserts that the "expressing stratum . . . is completely one in essence with that which finds expression, and in the covering process absorbs its essence" (*Ideas*, 321–22). In order to explain this unity, Husserl extends the meaning of the word *Sinn* ("Sense or Meaning *simpliciter*"; *Ideas*, 319) to make it include the entire noematic aspect (i.e., the signified aspect, understood in a limited sense) of all experiences (independent of whether they are actually expressed or only silently intended [*gemeint*]), and he declares the expressive "meaning something" (*Bedeuten*) to be an actual *re*production of the preexpressive "meaning" (*Sinn*).[14] "Thus, sense already would be a kind of blank and mute writing redoubling itself in meaning" (*Margins*, 165). The one-sidedness of this explanation in fact only shifts the problem of how a sign is formed from the "bodily" aspect of expression to the aspect of "nonsensory" meaning, without escaping the semiotic conclusion that even meaning, if it is conceived as a distinct quantity, has to inscribe itself into a differential texture that has the constitution of a text. At this moment, however, the difference between inside and outside collapses: meaning is that which is expressible according to its essence, "and when the two cover each other we find not two theses to be kept separate, but *one thesis only*" (*Ideas*, 322).[15]

At this point Husserl himself runs up against the conclusion that he so painstakingly tried to avoid, namely, that there can be no preexpressive meaning (*Meinen*) because, first of all, all meaning (*Meinen*) is a function of the use of significations (*Bedeutungen*), and, second, because significations, for their part, are interwoven with expressions. The smallest and most elementary unit of all thought is the sign; only prelinguistic self-perception has to be excluded.

This is the first result of Derrida's reading of Husserl that we want to take note of: meaning attains to consciousness of itself not through some mysterious internal perception (*Anschauung*) but rather, on the contrary, by means of a total exteriorization onto the stratum of expression: exteriority of expression is always prior to the internalness of its signifying (*Bedeuten*). Husserl succumbs all the more to this conclusion— against his own will—since in principle he always held on to the representational model of consciousness: his differentiation between noesis and noema turns out to be a mere transformation of the classical distinction between subject and object. If one assumes on top of this, as Husserl does, that noesis always finds out what it is only from a subsequent reflection onto itself or based on the way its noema is constituted, then one arrives at the conclusion that there can be no immediate (i.e., prereflective) self-consciousness of intentional acts. Moreover, if it is true that the distinction among noemata themselves is possible only on the basis of distinctions among expressions, then not only is there no immediate self-consciousness of intentional acts, there is also no prelinguistic self-consciousness of intentional acts. Thus the fact that Husserl holds on to the model of self-consciousness as reflection leads him first to the insight into the interwovenness of meaning and expression, and from there to the unintended conclusion that all consciousness, including consciousness that is conscious of itself, is dependent on language.

In highlighting this point, Derrida is not only more consistent than Husserl himself; he can justifiably claim that his reading of Husserl develops the internal consequences of phenomenology only by going beyond the metaphysical obstacles put in place by Husserl's idealism, and that in so doing he does it justice. The fact that he respects Husserl's premises, however, has its price for Derrida's thought: by developing the consequences of the model of self-consciousness as reflection he—*mutatis mutandis*—still upholds this model in itself undisturbed. This model assumes that consciousness finds out only in retrospect what it is, as the result of an explicit self-thematization. This is an epistemological premise that Hegel's dialectics and Husserl's phenomenology have in common. Derrida's thought shares this premise in a modified form, for he too assumes that consciousness learns its meaning (*Bedeutung*) from the reflection of signs, and that it does not invest at a stage preliminary to this in the deciphering of its signs. Based on this we can understand how he can concede with regard to Hegel that there are "relations of profound affinity that *différance* thus written maintains with Hegelian discourse" (*Margins*, 14; translation modified). We will see to what extent this minimal consensus between Hegel, Husserl, and Derrida also involuntarily furnishes Derrida's thought with a historical index and limits its validity.

With this projected task, however, we are going considerably beyond that which we have been able to demonstrate thus far, namely, that the idea of a language-independent consciousness is an illusion. Our intention, however, reaches much further than merely to this not particularly exciting insight. We are not so much concerned with consciousness, as we are with self-consciousness. Therefore we have to return to Husserl's text and read him—along with Derrida—more thoroughly than before.

Lecture 15

In the last lecture we found that our assertion of a profound connection between the *linguistic turn* of analytical philosophy and that of neostructuralism could be confirmed. And the fact that individual representatives from the analytical and neostructuralist camps—for example, Ernst Tugendhat and Jacques Derrida— established their positions by means of a critique of Husserl underlined the affinity between the two movements. Both Tugendhat and Derrida take exception to the idea that consciousness is a kind of perception (*Anschauung*) and that, correspondingly, self-consciousness is a kind of internal perception. The subject-object scheme accounts neither for the fact that the elementary data of consciousness are states of affairs rather than things (i.e., entities that are articulated in propositions), nor for the fact that intentional acts can acquire significance only within a language. The meaning of an intention is the minimum of what could be conscious to a consciousness, and this meaning only occurs "interwoven" with an expression, i.e., in the form of a sign that is differentially distinguished from other signs.

However, we are not so much concerned with the theory of consciousness (and the consequence that it is only possible as a theory of language) as with the question of a neostructuralist theory of *self*-consciousness. This question can also be addressed by following the thread of Derrida's reading of Husserl, and, in fact, the answer emerges as a consequence of Husserl's theory of consciousness. This has to do with the fact that Husserl considers self-consciousness to be a special case of consciousness, that is, as its self-reflection. Derrida follows him in this respect, although with a deconstructive intent.

229

We observed earlier that the meaning of the expression "self-consciousness" does not coincide with the meaning of the expression "I," or at least does not *have to* coincide with it. Subjectivity (in the sense of I-ness [*Ichheit*]) is not the same as consciousness, even though it presupposes consciousness as the dimension in which it can evolve. At any rate, it is clear that one does not necessarily have to deconstruct the concept of the *subject* in order to demonstrate that consciousness experiences acquire their meaning only within a language.

As a matter of fact, self-consciousness in the sense of I-ness was never a central problem in Husserl's philosophy, in contrast to Fichte's idealism or Sartre's phenomenology, for example. Perhaps it was only his encounter with neo-Kantianism (which still viewed the transcendental ego as the only explanation for the unification of the material of experience) that led Husserl eventually to integrate (particularly in the confrontation with Paul Natorp) the notion of a "transcendental ego" or a "pure ego pole" into his reflections. And to this extent Derrida is quite correct in observing that

> Husserl in the end never asked *what it* [consciousness of oneself or consciousness in general] *was*, in spite of the admirable, interminable, and in so many respects revolutionary, meditation he devoted to it. (*SP*, 15)

If "self-consciousness" itself never became a cardinal problem in Husserl's thought, that still does not mean that this theorem does not serve a decisive *function* in his phenomenology. In order to give a preliminary characterization of this function, we can say that it allows intentional acts, with which Husserl is concerned, to have a pure self-referentiality. We want to define a "pure self-reference" as the potential of the consciousness experience to refer back to itself without having to come into contact with the empirical, the material, and, above all, the linguistic world. The phenomenological attitude—to be sure, only as a methodological procedure—systematically disregards external reality, linguisticality, transcendence, and the materiality of the body. Husserl calls this process of setting aside ἐποχή or also "reduction," i.e., the disconnection of existence and concentration on "pure intuition," on that which is "given" to consciousness acts in themselves, wholly independent of the question of any reality that extends beyond this (which Husserl calls "transcendence"). This disconnection, of course, has to be founded philosophically; it implies Husserl's opting for a kind of idealism that rigorously limits "the validity" of its statements to that which reveals itself as valid to the "internal life of consciousness."[1] One can speak of an internal life, of course, only when it is juxtaposed with an external life; Husserl calls this external life (of consciousness) "the psychical." It is the result of a "self-Objectivation" (*CM*, 26, 131), or, to be more precise, a "*mundanizing self-apperception*": "by virtue of this mundanization everything included in the ownness belonging to me transcendentally (as this ultimate ego) enters, as something *psychic*, into 'my psyche' " (99–100). This implies that the psycho-physical (and the personal) ego is something derivative over against the transcendental ego. Husserl calls it a "component pertaining to my world-apperception," and, therefore, it is "something *transcendentally secondary*" (100), an "être au milieu du monde," as Sartre would say. In other words, it is a being of the sort of inner-worldly existing objects *of* which the pure transcendental ego is conscious, which themselves, however, by no means have consciousness of their own mode of Being. Because the transcendental ego can refer back to itself without having to come into contact with the domain of the psychic ego or with mundane reality, it founds itself as an absolute principle, i.e., as something internal that is antecedent to any exteriority. To be more precise, it founds itself as something internal that does not owe its knowledge of itself to the mediation of something external. Husserl repeatedly characterizes this *im*mediate (i.e., nonmediated) self-knowledge, acquired neither through signs nor through objects, by means of metaphors of presence: as Being present to itself [*sich-gegenwärtig-sein*], as living present, as self-appresentation, etc. This figurative language, according to Derrida, is not simply an unsuspected residue of traditional philosophical terminology; rather it implies a "metaphysical presupposition," indeed "a dogmatic or speculative commitment," that inherently constitutes phenomenology

> from within, in its project of criticism and in the instructive value of its own premises . . . precisely in what soon comes to be recognized as the source and guarantee of all value, the "principle of principles": i.e., the original self-giving evidence, the *present* or *presence* of sense to a full and primordial intuition. (*SP*, 5)

I mentioned earlier that the potential of consciousness to make itself present to itself without contact with the world serves less a thematic than a theory-constitutive function for phenomenology. We can now indicate more precisely what function it is a matter of: pure self-consciousness guarantees the idea of a purely ideal world (*idéalité*), i.e., "what may be indefinitely *repeated* in the *identity* of its *presence*, because of the very fact that it *does not exist*, is *not real* or is *irreal*" (*SP*, 6), and this is to be taken not in the sense of a mere fiction but rather in the sense of a transreality that goes infinitely beyond all aspects of mundane being. According to Derrida, this idea exhibits the most profound desire of that sort of thinking that is articulated in the project of metaphysics, namely, the desire for a mysterious bodyless self-appresentation, which is evident in Aristotle's definition of the divine spirit as a νόησις νοήσεως, all the way to Hegel's "self-consciousness of the absolute spirit"; this metaphysical desire has left its imprint on phenomenology as well.[2] The bodily, the external, the worldly always appear as the reprehensible side of a distinction that is virtualized with great effort. Of course there is the body, the world, the external, the nonpresent, the Other, and temporality. But if one presupposes that absolute self-consciousness exteriorizes *itself* in all these entities, then this sphere of exteriority appears either as something posited, derived, and secondary, or as something that is merely virtual. However, an opposition that has the unity of self-consciousness as its prerequisite can no more endanger this unity itself than can a merely virtual opposition; i.e., an opposition that attains no autonomy over against the transcendental ego, but that is rather inscribed in it. In the latter case the "psychic life" would not be another life that stands opposed to the "inner life of the transcendental self"; rather it would be *the Other of itself.* The point of this formulation is that the difference between the ideal and the real, the internal and the external, the mental and the physical, etc., which is inscribed in the self, can never bring into play something that is independent of the self; for the Other is already taken into account from the outset as the other side of the self, i.e., as the Same. The division between the transcendental and the psychic ego ultimately is incorporated into the sphere of "transcendental life" itself.

> One finds out quickly enough that the sole nucleus of the concept of *psyché* is as self-relationship, whether or not it takes place in the form of consciousness. "Living" is thus the name of that which precedes the reduction and finally escapes all the divisions which the latter gives rise to. But this is precisely because it is its own division and its own opposition to its other. (*SP*, 14–15)

Without getting bogged down in the details of Husserl's theory of consciousness, we want to emphasize its theory-constitutive function. It consists precisely in the fact that it allows "bodily nature" (*Körperlichkeit*) — for example, that of language that expresses the consciousness experiences — to be sublated and reinterpreted as "flesh" (*Leiblichkeit*), or, to be more precise, as "spiritual flesh," which in the midst of its exteriority rescues pure self-reference and thereby escapes worldliness.

> The phenomenological voice would be this spiritual flesh that continues to speak and be present to itself — *to hear itself* — in the absence of the world. (16)

Derrida, of course, is mainly interested in the bodily aspect of language, its materiality that can never be entirely dissolved into spirituality. If it were the case that its bodily aspect — much as the remainder of the physical world — could be disconnected by means of the transcendental reduction, then a whole domain of "preexpressive" meaning would be secured, a world of pure signifieds not borne by signifiers. At the same time, the preeminence of difference for the production of meaning would be challenged, for if there is meaning of consciousness experiences in pure "self-presence," then for this sphere of meaning, at least, what holds for all other significations does not seem to be the case, namely, that they can be produced only on the basis of unequivocal distinctions among their physical substrates, i.e., on the basis of differences among their signifiers.

Indeed, transcendental life knows no differentiation and is nevertheless immediately conscious of itself. But does this description truly hit the mark? Is self-consciousness really a nondifferential entity? Husserl, at any rate, does not admit any other conception of self-consciousness than that of reflection. Reflection, as we saw, is something mediate: the reference of a consciousness to itself. If one pays attention to the language by means of which this mediation is articulated, then one cannot help but notice that Husserl is talking about two poles between which reflection mediates: between the pole of the subject of reflection, and the pole of the object of reflection; between that which reflects, and that which is reflected. This duality is already implied in the semantics of the pronouns "self" and "itself" (*selbst/sich*): something refers to itself, but mediately, by taking a detour. Husserl constantly described transcendental consciousness-life as something mediate in this sense, as a relation of reflection, as the "place of reflexive articulation, i.e., the *mediation* of a Logos retaking possession of *itself* through this consciousness" (*OG*, 146). A consciousness that has to bridge a difference in order to become consciousness of *itself* can hardly be defined as predifferential.

Yet Husserl would not dispute this internal differentiality of self-consciousness (contrary to his teacher Franz Brentano, Husserl describes self-consciousness as self-*relation*). He would, however, emphasize that in the case of this differentiality of self-consciousness, it is actually only a matter of a *virtual* difference, i.e., of a difference that evolves only on the basis of a prior unity, and that remains bound up with this unity. If the Other exists only as the Other of itself, then it is inscribed in the sphere of the self and thus could not possibly assert any independence of it. (Difference stands in relation to a unity, and the latter is the decisive factor.)

If Husserl's characterization were correct, then self-consciousness in its totality would have to be something merely virtual, for reality presupposes determination, and differentiation is a necessary part of determination. In order for differentiation to be able to become effective, it for its part would have to be real. A real opposition, however, would necessarily explode the shackle in which unity encloses difference in self-consciousness. Thus the elimination of the physical from the sphere of pure ideality takes its revenge by making self-consciousness into an unreal element, depriving it of its Being. Even if it were the case that in self-consciousness unity describes a circle around the difference of the two connected components (in order to guarantee the sameness of their meaning), this unity itself would still first of all have to *be*. A consciousness that *is* not real would *not* be; i.e., it would be no *consciousness*. The idea of a merely virtual consciousness annuls itself; there is a consciousness of virtualities, but no virtual consciousness. *If* a consciousness experience is given, then it is *given*; i.e., it no longer exists as potentiality, but rather as act(uality). In order to provide this actuality for self-consciousness, one would have to introduce into it an existing difference; this, however, would destroy both its claim to being the "principle of principles," and the assertion of its absolute "primordiality."

> At the heart of what ties together these two decisive moments of description we recognize an irreducible nonpresence as having a constituting value, and with it a nonlife, a nonpresence of nonself-belonging of the living present, an ineradicable nonprimordiality. (*SP*, 6–7)

Derrida considers this to be an immediate consequence of the model of a reflective consciousness. To be sure, reflection means mirroring (*Widerspiegelung*). This model seeks to guarantee the unity of the divided consciousness by transforming the Other into the Other of itself. To accomplish this, however, reflection has to (temporarily) surrender itself to the reality of the opposition, to the division, and to the nonsimultaneity of the two moments of consciousness (*Bewusstseins-Relate*). Once delivered over to the medium of reality, of temporal sequentiality, and of contrast, reflection can no longer return to the sphere of pure ideality and instantaneousness, at least as long as this sphere is understood as pure nonbodily and transtemporal autoaffection:

> A pure difference comes to divide self-presence. In this pure difference is rooted the possibility of everything we think we can exclude from auto-affection: space, the outside, the world, the body, etc. As soon as it is admitted that auto-affection is the condition for self-presence, no pure transcendental reduction is possible. But it was necessary to pass through the transcendental reduction in order to grasp this difference in what is closest to it—which cannot mean grasping it in its identity, its purity, or its origin, for it has none. We come closest to it in the movement of differance.
>
> This movement of differance is not something that happens to a transcendental subject; it produces a subject. Auto-affection is not a modality of experience that characterizes a being that would already be itself (*autos*). It produces sameness as self-relation within self-difference; it produces sameness as the nonidentical. (*SP*, 82)

Here we once again come across that concept of *différance* with which we are already acquainted. The context has changed, however: here *différance* not only serves to explain the nonidentity of significations within the framework of a system of signs (and, a fortiori, explaining the nonclosure of this system); rather it now also appears as the condition of possibility for self-consciousness. Derrida arrives at this conclusion by means of what at first sight seems to be a minimal reinterpretation of the (Husserlian) model of reflection, which, as we saw earlier, presupposes (and by no means denies) the distance between the two moments of consciousness. Yet in contrast to the interpretation that Husserl himself provides (that which reflects, affirms, and demonstrates its *identity* with what is reflected),

Derrida is of the opinion that the detour reflection takes in order to identify the
self with itself suffices to put its identity in question once and for all.

> The present can only present itself as such by relating back to itself; it
> can only aver itself by severing itself, only reach itself if it breaches it-
> self, (com)plying with itself in the angle, along a break [*brisure*]
> (*brisure*: "crack" and "joint," created by a hinge, in the work of a lock-
> smith. *Littré*): in the release of the latch or the trigger. Presence is
> never present. The possibility—or the potency—of the present is but its
> own limit, its inner fold, its impossibility—or its impotence. . . .
> What holds for the present here also holds for "history," "form," the
> form of history, etc., along with all the significations that, in the lan-
> guage of metaphysics, are indissociable from the signification: "pres-
> ent." (*Diss*, 302–3)

Indeed, once we are moving within the epistemological framework of the model
of reflection, we can no longer escape its logic. In other words, if the self originally does not know itself, but rather needs the mirror of reflection to acquire
knowledge of itself, then one can distinguish at least three temporal moments:
first, the moment of a still-unconscious innerliness; second, the moment of going
outside of itself and mirroring itself; and finally, a third moment of reinternalizing
the mirror image within the self. One cannot speak in strict terms of an instantaneity in the case of this event. Incidentally, we are now touching a ticklish point
in Husserl's philosophy, which argued for an internal temporality of self-
consciousness, but distinguished it strictly from the external time sequence of the
psychic ego. If it is true, however, that the self can by no means obtain consciousness of itself unless it *really* reflects itself, then this attempted distinction breaks
down. Either there is self-consciousness, in which case several stages have to be
traversed in this coming to consciousness; or consciousness remains in its pure
presence, in which case it has—as pure instantaneity—no consciousness of itself.
As we now see, even the idea of an *inscription* of difference into a superposed
unity is untenable within the framework of the model of reflection (that is, the
idea of a difference that exists only as difference of unity itself, as unity's *own*
difference). This means that self-consciousness can no longer answer for its
"unity." This unity becomes an *indécidable* (*Diss*, 219ff.). The model of reflection
presupposes, of course, that the beam consciousness aims at itself will actually
hit its target. This is not the case in Derrida's model. We recall that in the last
passage cited, he spoke of a folding of presence back upon itself, rather than of
a reflection ("[com]plying with itself in the angle"; 302). "But the fold is not a
form of reflexivity" (271). The fold bends back upon itself, without, however,
reaching itself entirely. The model of reflection, on the other hand, assumes "that
the mirror does unite the self with its image . . . deliberately and unilaterally
closes the fold, interprets it as a coincidence with self, makes opening into the

precondition of self-*adequation*, and reduces every way in which the fold also marks dehiscence, dissemination, spacing, temporization, etc." (271).

At another point Derrida speaks of a barricaded street of reflection.

> Following a pattern we have already experienced in the "*entre*," the quasi-"meaning" of dissemination is the impossible return to the rejoined, readjusted unity of meaning, the impeded march of any such *reflection*. (268)

The metaphor implies that a criterion is missing that would guarantee the identification of the gaze directed at the mirror with the image that comes back from the mirror to the eye. After all, nothing about the mirror itself betrays that it is in fact a mirror. Similarly, I can only testify to the identity of the mirror image with myself if I have access to a prereflective knowledge of myself, but that idea does not come up at all in Derrida's reading of Husserl, although Husserl himself considered it, especially in his later work.[3]

Derrida liked to illustrate his conclusion by means of unsettling metaphors, letting his own metaphors take their inspiration from the original metaphor of the mirror as manifest in the model of reflection. What if the mirror of reflection had no tain, he asks; what if it were to reflect back to me an uncontrollable alterity?

> The truth that lifts the veil-screen . . . is already regulated according to a mirror, and in particular a tainless mirror, or at any rate a mirror whose tain lets "images" and "persons" through, endowing them with a certain index of transformation and permutation. . . . But this is an effect of the specular nature of philosophical reflection, philosophy being incapable of inscribing (comprehending) what is outside it otherwise than through the appropriating assimilation of a negative image of it, and dissemination is written on the back—the *tain*—of that mirror. . . . the structure of a very strange mirror. A mirror which, despite the aforementioned impossibility, does indeed come to stand as a source, like an echo that would somehow precede the origin it seems to answer—the "real," the "originary," the "true," the "present," being constituted only on the rebound from the duplication in which alone they can arise. (314, 33, 323)

Each of these passages culminates in the same aporia: consciousness identifies itself by means of its mirror image; yet the mirror image has no criterion at hand that permits such a reidentification. The mirror image could very well be the Other of consciousness, without which, on the one hand, *consciousness* as such would not exist, and, on the other hand, through whose mediation the identity of *consciousness* is threatened and made into something that is "undecidable."

We will encounter this distortion of the model of reflection once again when we discuss Derrida's theory of the sign in more detail. For the moment we are left with the task of recognizing the *operating of language* in that irreducible difference that is no longer the Other of *itself*. Based on what we already know about Derrida, it is not hard to imagine that he will even etch the trace of meaning-constituting difference into the alleged innerliness of self-consciousness.

Before continuing we want to describe as precisely as possible the place from which our questions derive. We saw that Derrida's deconstructive critique of Husserl is argued in two steps. In a first advance he unmasks the contradictions that make Husserl's concept of a preexpressive "meaning" (intending) problematic (this area of criticism thus concerned Husserl's conception of a consciousness of *something*); Derrida advances to the second step of his critique when he takes aim at the other type of consciousness that Husserl conceives, namely, at that consciousness that is not necessarily conscious of something else, but rather of itself (self-consciousness).

The idea of a preexpressive intending is disputed by Derrida with one argument that we already are familiar with from Saussure and (in a slightly modified form) from Wittgenstein: in order to be able to identify something *as* something, one has to distinguish it from other objects. This distinction presupposes a universe of expressions that oppose one another, i.e., a language. It is only in a language that I can mean something (an object) with something (a word, a thought).

Husserl, however, wants to evade this conclusion. The only possibility he has for doing so consists in the thesis that consciousness that is directed at objects in the world can be directed at itself in a like manner, and that it achieves this by means of a prelinguistic self-perception (*Selbstanschauung*). Since consciousness is the condition of possibility for the givenness of objects (of any kind whatsoever), the totality of objects in the world would in this case depend on a preexpressive knowledge, namely, on the knowledge that consciousness possesses, as self-reflection, prior to all knowledge of *something*. According to Derrida, this is the strategic motivation for Husserl's recourse to the thesis of an immediate and preexpressive consciousness that is present to itself. One could also characterize this strategy in the following way: in order to be able to ascertain positively that consciousness does not intermix with the sphere of exteriority at which it is directed, one only has to be able to demonstrate that it is, first, the condition of possibility for the knowledge of exteriority, and that it, second, does not incorporate in itself anything exterior. Proof for the second point is supposed to be brought by pointing to the possibility that consciousness has for thematizing itself prior to all knowledge about the world—a possibility it possesses precisely as consciousness of itself or as reflection. In reflection the innerliness of consciousness is directed solely at itself; no trace of exteriority blurs the pure self-transparency of this relationship.

We also saw that the first part of Husserl's program has to be viewed as a failure: facts or states of affairs acquire significance and meaning only in a language. And even self-consciousness is not exempt from this truth, at least as long as one thinks of it, as Husserl does, in terms of reflection. Reflection is the cognizant reference of One to itself; yet precisely in this formulation it becomes obvious that even reflection is articulated as a *duality* of moments, or, let us say, as a division of One within itself. To be sure, the additional qualification that we are actually dealing with a *cognizant* reference is supposed subsequently to return this division to a predifferential unity of both moments. Yet if it is true—and Husserl does not have any theoretical instruments at his disposal with which he could dispute it—that the preservation of unity has this passing through a division as its prerequisite, then unity is obviously founded in a difference, indeed, in a difference that is prior to the consciousness of unity both as real ground *and* as knowledge ground. Especially the notion of the presence of One alongside itself destroys the strategic meaning of the expression "presence," inasmuch, at least, as one is not thinking only of the simultaneity of two moments that are different from each other, but rather of a *cognizant identification* that as such goes beyond the presentness of mere Being-related-to-each-other.

Husserl deprives himself of the possibility of accomplishing a sublation of the two moments of reflection into the *knowledge* of their unity because he considers reflection to be a special case of consciousness, i.e., consciousness of *something* (Other). In this case the alterity of the Other of consciousness is insurmountable; the alleged innerliness of self-reference is fractured in order to give way to the exteriority of an irreducible Other. And it is precisely this on which Derrida puts his finger.

One thing should be noted here: *I* do not believe that self-consciousness is adequately defined as a special case of intentional consciousness; rather I believe that it is constituted as nonrelational, and thus as nonreflective, and therefore cannot be conceived as the result of an identification. In such an instance the unity characteristic of it could not be rescued. At the moment, however, we only have to underline that Husserl is not aware of this alternative, and that he thus is not able to name a *criterion* for the identity of the two moments related to each other in the process of reflection. As long as this criterion is lacking, then one cannot clearly distinguish self-reference from reference to something other (*Fremdbezug*), and we can join Derrida in his suspicion that the metaphor of mirroring and of the mirror image inscribed in the model of reflection resembles rather a gaze into a mirror that has no tain, and which therefore returns to us images and representations we—wanting a criterion for comparison—can neither identify with nor positively distinguish from ourselves. The unity of self-consciousness with itself thus becomes an *indécidable*; self-consciousness appears as a special case of a disseminal, a unityless, a decentered structure without instantaneity, i.e., without lasting presence. We are living in a world without identical significations; and likewise our self-consciousness, of which it was our task to demonstrate that it can grasp itself only by means of a system of significations, i.e., by means of a language, is a fortiori affected by this fact. In this sense Derrida's statement is correct.

> My own presence to myself has been preceded by a language. Older than consciousness, older than the spectator, prior to any attendance, a sentence awaits "you": looks at you, observes you, watches over you, and regards you from every side. (*Diss*, 340)

This statement, by the way, could easily have been uttered by Wittgenstein. But the observations we have made thus far already permit us to draw a clear line that separates Derrida's thesis of the dependence of self-consciousness on language from that proposed by Wittgenstein (and Tugendhat). Whereas the latter two believe that the dependence of the cognizant self-reference on the system of language usage simultaneously secures the unity and identifiability of the self (secured, at least, within the limits of the range of a practical language game), Derrida, on the other hand, believes that the linguistically dependent self-consciousness a fortiori also participates in the equivocality of linguistic signs whose significations, according to his view, are produced in open diacritical references to other signs, that is, in open systems. The alterity of the reference to the Other is insurmountable: it not only destroys temporarily, as in Hegel's dialectics; rather it permanently (because principally) destroys any possibility of return to a point of departure. This becomes imaginary and undeterminable precisely because there is no *criterion* for it.

This is exactly the point at which for Husserl the undemonstrated factual unity of the *transcendental ego* is transformed into an "idea in the Kantian sense," i.e., into a regulative idea that I have to keep in mind if I want to be able to think of the ego as one identical with itself, yet as one that remains "merely an idea" and which thus cannot "constitute" the unity of this ego as a fact. Now a discipline that needs to fall back on such regulative principles has to give up the claim of being "exact" and must be satisfied with being called "rigorous." This is an ever-recurring contrastive pair in Husserl's later writings, and it is simultaneously the symptom of a crisis Derrida never tires of interpreting.

The crisis in Husserl's phenomenology is, to be sure, also a symptom of the honesty of its author, who uncovers the limits of metaphysics, as it were, to the detriment of his own philosophical project. It is this that constitutes the "rigor" of phenomenology. Husserl develops this contrast primarily in his confrontation with Dilthey's "philosophy of worldview" (*Weltanschauungsphilosophie*). This hermeneutical historicism can be characterized as a kind of genetic structuralism. It reconstructs the forces and interpretations at work in the construction of a picture of the world and shows in what manner they are woven into a "ratioid" structure. I am using a favorite expression of Robert Musil's, "ratioid," and not "rational," because it is a theoretical implication of radical historicism that it is not capable of founding a rationality criterion that is independent of the factual order of a worldview. Factual data thus acquire the status of inescapable truths: they are similar to rational truths, "ratioid," but precisely only similar to them, and thus only similar to truth (*ratiosimila* or *verisimila*), since every order of a world image bears the index of its historicality and temporariness on its forehead. Thus historicism is transformed into a radical skepticism, since it cannot distinguish between truths of reason and truths of fact, reducing the former to the latter.

> In Husserl's eyes the structuralism of the *Weltanschauungsphilosophie* is a historicism. And despite Dilthey's vehement protests, Husserl will persist in thinking that, like all historicism, and despite its originality, the *Weltanschauungsphilosophie* avoids neither relativism nor skepticism. For it reduces the norm to a historical factuality, and it ends by confusing, to speak the language of Leibniz and of the *Logische Untersuchungen* (vol. I, p. 188), the *truths of fact* and the *truths of reason*. Pure truth or the pretension to pure truth is missed in its *meaning* as soon as one attempts, as Dilthey does, to account for it from within a determined historical totality, that is, from within a factual totality, a finite totality. (*WD*, 160)

In other words, the scientific masterability of an object or a domain of objects presupposes its closure as a totality of *facts*. This closure of an object would be assured if it could be merged with structures as they are thematized both by the natural sciences (e.g., biology) and by the structural-hermeneutical human sciences. Phenomenology, however, cannot merge as a "rigorous science" with such disciplines, for it is concerned with the transstructural and, so to speak, transfinite conditions of possibility for such structures, i.e., with the *validity* of the propositions made about such structures and thus with their possible truth.

> Now the Idea or the project which animates and unifies every *determined* historical structure, every *Weltanschauung*, is *finite*: on the basis of the structural description of a *vision of the world* one can account for everything except the infinite opening to truth, that is, philosophy. Moreover, it is always something like an *opening* which will frustrate the structuralist project. What I can never understand, in a structure, is that by means of which it is not closed. (*WD*, 160)

There will always be an irreconcilable difference between the comprehensibility of the factual or the positive, and its explanation on the basis of foundations ("This irreducible difference is due to an interminable *delaying* [*différance*] of the theoretical foundation"; *WD*, 161). Derrida spells *différance* with an "a," since we are dealing not with a difference between the parts of a system or a structure but rather with the difference that distinguishes the totality of differences in a closed structure from the openness of the thought of this structure: "it is a question of *closure* or of *opening*" (162). Even an advance into the unity of the field that constitutes the essences of pure consciousness can never reach the exactitude of mathematics.

> An eidetic descriptive science, such as phenomenology, may be rigorous, but it is necessarily inexact—I would rather say "anexact"—due to no failure on its part. Exactitude is always a product derived from an operation of "idealization" and of "transition to the limit" which can only concern an abstract moment, an *abstract* eidetic element (spatiality, for example) of a thing materially determined as an objective body, setting aside, precisely, the other eidetic elements of a body in general. This is why geometry is a "material" and "abstract" science. It follows that a "geometry of experience," a "mathematics of phenomena" is impossible: this is an "attempt doomed to miscarry." This means in particular, for what concerns us here, that the essences of consciousness, and therefore the essences of "phenomena" in general, cannot belong to a structure or "multiplicity" of the mathematical type. Now what is it that characterizes such a multiplicity for Husserl, and at this time? In a word, the possibility of *closure*. . . . What Husserl seeks to underline by means of this comparison between an exact and a morphological science, and what we must retain here, is the principled, essential, and structural impossibility of closing a structural phenomenology. It is the infinite opening of what is experienced, which is designated at several moments of Husserlian analysis by reference to an *Idea in the Kantian sense*, that is, the irruption of the infinite into consciousness, which permits the unification of the temporal flux of consciousness just as it unifies the object and the world by anticipation, and despite an irreducible incompleteness. It is the strange *presence* of this Idea which also permits every transition to the limit and the production of all exactitude. (162)

This idea, however, which preserves the unity of self-consciousness *despite* the flow of inner time and *beyond* the irreducible exteriority of reflection, has the character of a pure postulate. It rests, therefore, on the concession that "*within* consciousness in general there is an agency which *does not really* belong to it" (163). This "failure" inscribed within self-consciousness—conceived as ego-logical reflection—can take on various forms. It can be a matter of the irreducible materiality (*hylē*) with which the consciousness-independent *reality* of the givenness of "noemata" announces itself. It could further be a matter of the nonsimultaneity of consciousness with and to itself that can never be eliminated. This was something Husserl came across when he first studied the temporality of the "stream of consciousness," which internally undermines consciousness, and he was barely able to escape the conclusion that an exteriority and nonpresence that found all the operations of constitution would have to be given priority over the innerliness and presence of consciousness. The irreducible alterity of the Other ultimately remains entirely external to the ego-logical structure of reflection.

It is that the constitution of the other and of time refers phenomenology to a zone in which its "principle of principles" (as we see it, its *metaphysical* principle: the *original self-evidence* and *presence* of the thing itself in person) is radically put into question. (164)

Husserl, as we saw, believes that he is able to assure the "principle of principles" in the intuitive self-presence of an ego, and to derive all other knowledge from this evidence.

I exist for myself and am continually given to myself, by experiential evidence, as "*I myself.*" This is true of the transcendental ego and, correspondingly, of the psychological pure ego; it is true, moreover, with respect to any sense of the word ego. Since the monadically concrete ego includes also the whole of actual and potential conscious life, it is clear that the problem of *explicating this monadic ego phenomenologically* (the problem of his constitution for himself) must include *all constitutional problems without exception.* Consequently the phenomenology of this *self-constitution* coincides with *phenomenology as a whole.* (*CM,* 68)

If, however, the unity of this transcendental ego, which founds the *validity* of all other consciousness experiences as *cognizant* unity, becomes a mere postulate, an idea in the Kantian sense, then the scientific unity of phenomenology as such is threatened. The unity of the self and of the knowledge founded by the self *opens itself* in order to make room for the historical and temporal infinity of interpretations.

Logos is *nothing* outside history and Being, since it is discourse, infinite discursiveness and not an actual infinity, and since it is meaning. . . .
Since *Telos* is totally open, is opening itself, to say that it is the most powerful structural a priori of historicity is not to designate it as a static and determined value which would inform and enclose the genesis of Being and meaning. It is the concrete possibility, the very birth of history and the meaning of becoming in general. Therefore it is structurally genesis itself, as origin and as becoming. (*WD,* 166, 167)

This means that philosophy, inasmuch as it, as a rigorous science of facticity, wants to escape merely historical truths and seeks to ascend to truths of reason, must testify to the unbridgeable gap separating the factual from the counterfactual. This gap also traverses—in the form of nonidentity, of time flux—the unity of self-consciousness, from whose evidence and undeniable validity the certainty and validity of all other knowledge were supposed to be derived. Now the ego, as Husserl concedes in the *Cartesian Meditations,* is apodictically but by no means adequately given (*CM,* 22–23). The consciousness of its "living present" is not coextensive with the totality of the time phases in which it extends. Self-consciousness, for that matter, is essentially more and quite different than "living present": it is a projection of its future motivated by its own past. The structural totality of *Dasein* (to use a Heideggerian expression) is in the "thrown projection," the ekstatic reaching out of past Being to its future essence. But in the living self-present of the tripartiteness of this structure, only the "core" of the present is "adequately" given. Here are Husserl's own words:

> In such experience the ego is accessible to himself originaliter. But at any particular time this experience offers only a core that is experienced "with strict adequacy," namely the ego's living present (which the grammatical sense of the sentence, *ego cogito*, expresses); while, beyond that, only an indeterminately general presumptive horizon extends, comprising what is strictly non-experienced but necessarily also-meant. To it belongs not only the ego's past, most of which is completely obscure, but also his transcendental abilities and his habitual peculiarities at the time. External perception too (though not apodictic) is an experiencing of something itself, the physical thing itself: "it itself is there." But, in being there itself, the physical thing has for the experiencer an open, infinite, indeterminately general horizon, comprising what is itself not strictly perceived — a horizon (this is implicit as a presumption) that can be opened up by possible experiences. Something similar is true about the apodictic certainty characterizing transcendental experience of my transcendental I-am, with the indeterminate generality of the latter as having an open horizon. Accordingly the actual being of the intrinsically first field of knowledge is indeed assured absolutely, though not as yet what determines its being more particularly and is still not itself given, but only presumed, during the living evidence of the I-am. (*CM*, 22–23)

From this it follows that the transhistorical self-present of the ego, which transgresses the difference of the time phases, exists only in the form of a motivated postulate, i.e., as a regulative idea; in other words, it does not *really* exist. Postulates *demand* the existence of what is postulated, but they do not *affirm* this existence. In the case of the stream of consciousness, the unreachability of the idea is also compelling, for time is essentially unclosed and extends into the infinite. As long as self-consciousness exists in time, its unity is only presumptive (as Husserl says). This is a fortiori also true for all regional truths derived from the apodictic evidence of the *ego cogito*, like, for example, the truths of all structural sciences, be they a priori (as in geometry), empirical (as in biology), or historical (as in the genetic structuralism of the philosophy of *Weltanschauung*).

> Were we to respect and to repeat these numerous mediations once again, we would thus be led back once more toward primordial temporality. The "again and again" which hands over exactitude inscribes the advent of mathematics within the ethico-teleological prescription of

the infinite task. And the latter is grounded, then, in the movement of primordial phenomenological temporalization, in which the Living Present of consciousness holds itself as the primordial Absolute only in an indefinite protention, animated and unified by the Idea (*in the Kantian sense*) of the total flux of lived experience. (*OG*, 136)

If this is the case—and the impressively aporetic reflections of *The Phenomenology of Internal Time-Consciousness* have shown it to be the case—then one has to go one step further than Husserl does in the quoted formulation from the *Cartesian Meditations*. Not only past and future, not only the habits and capacities of consciousness lie in the darkness of a horizon that can*not* now be experienced; even the *present*, the now of the "living self-present," slips into the darkness of the nongiven. For only in casting itself off from its immediate past (Husserl calls it "retention") can self-consciousness identify its presence. A present undistinguishable from its immediate past simply *would have* no past, and this would simultaneously mean that it would not have at its disposal a criterion for the *knowledge* of its own present. If, however, the differential relation to something nonpresent precedes the consciousness of its own presence, then one can go so far as to say that even the self-presence of the *ego cogito* is no absolute. For one can only call such a being absolute that completely constitutes its Being in itself, not having to obtain it from the reference to some other being. However, it is exactly this reference that establishes for the first time the alleged absoluteness of the living present of self-consciousness. That means that even the self is *primordially* differentiated, that its cleavage (*Spaltung*) comes prior to its possible unity. We will take a closer look at this idea in the next lecture.

Lecture 16

In the last few lectures we have been investigating Derrida's deconstructive reconstruction of Husserl's theory of the subject. We know why this campaign of neostructuralist theory has to be taken particularly seriously, for according to the neostructuralists, modern metaphysics, in the name of the transcendental unity of the subject, has so far successfully warded off the idea of a difference that subsists prior to the unity of the subject.

This is also true in the instance of Husserl's phenomenology. Due to its own internal logic, according to Derrida, it had to arrive at a modern variant of classical "transcendental idealism," and indeed, it is Husserl himself who chose this phrase for a definitive characterization of phenomenology.[1] Thus it becomes a part of—and I am using Husserl's own words—the "great shift" of modern thought, the "shift to the *ego cogito*, as the apodictically certain and *last basis for judgment* upon which all radical philosophy must be grounded" (*PL*, 7). If self-consciousness becomes the "last basis for judgment," then that means that all other judgments (for example, even those of the so-called a priori sciences like mathematics) derive their evidence from the prior evidence of the *ego cogito*. Of phenomenology Husserl claims that its

> *idealism is nothing other than a consistently carried through self-disclosure*, that is, *in the form of a systematic egological science*, of any meaning of being which makes sense to me, the ego. (*PL*, 33)

The project of such a final foundation (*fondement final*, *OG* [Fr. ed.], 151) of knowledge in an ultimate principle can, of course, be successful only if this principle is evident in and of itself. That is what the term "evident" means. Yet it is precisely this evidence that is obscured in Husserl's phenomenology due to the fact that, first of all, it conceives "self-consciousness" as reflection (as the mirror image of the One in itself, i.e., as a case of self-knowledge which passes through two different moments);[2] and, second, because it views this self-consciousness as being undermined by the flux of internal time consciousness. To be sure, Husserl emphasizes "that all of existence — with its fluctuations, its Heraclitean flux — is one universal synthetic unity" (*PL*, 18). If this were not the case, then the ego would not be capable of simultaneously *knowing* its unity; i.e., it would not be capable of "being for itself what it actually is" (cf. 18). In fact, however, it becomes clear that Husserl has major difficulties in citing the criterion that would allow one to speak of the ekstases of self-consciousness that are extended over different time phases as unities. It would have to be a pretemporal unity, and yet one that would remain stable over the course of time, a unity that at the same time — and this is the most essential point — can be *known* (if it were to transcend knowledge, it could not simultaneously bring about the synthesis of self-consciousness; i.e., the self would be a unity *not* conscious of itself, and this thought is contradictory and goes against all experience). We remember that Husserl attempted to solve the problem with an aporetical construction: he talks about the unity of the self as if it were an "idea in the Kantian sense." And it is exactly at this point that Derrida's deconstructive critique takes hold.

Something that is merely postulated *is* not. What *is*, is the reference of One to itself — however, this reference lacks any criterion to ensure the identity of the two moments, and thus it remains without any certainty about their sameness. Reflection does not lead with total certainty back to its point of departure: thus the circle of self-identification is ruptured, and the evidence of the *ego cogito*, as the ultimate basis for the judgment of all truths, becomes obscure.

It is mainly in the nonidentity inscribed within internal time that Derrida finds grounds for the impossibility of a knowing self-identification. Husserl himself had conceded that "the living self-present" of the ego is swamped by a host of nonpresent things that are not given, and that these undermine the "adequacy" of its self-givenness. Derrida goes one step further and claims that even the self is not given to itself, because the present in which it could coincide with itself is itself not present to itself.

As we have seen, the Living Present is the phenomenological absolute out of which I cannot go because it is that in which, toward which, and starting from which every going out is effected. The Living Present has the irreducible originality of a Now, the ground of a Here, only if it retains (in order to be distinguishable from it) the past Now *as such*, i.e., as the past present of an absolute origin, instead of purely and simply succeeding it in an objective time. But this retention will not be possible without a protention which is its very form: first, because it retains a

Now which was itself an original project, itself retaining another project, and so on; next, because the retention is always the essential modification of a Now always in suspense, always tending toward a next Now. The Absolute of the Living Present, then, is only the indefinite Maintenance [the Nowness] of this double enveloping. But this Maintenance itself appears *as such*, it is the *Living* Present, and it has the *phenomenological* sense of a *consciousness* only if the unity of this movement is given as *indefinite* and if its sense of indefiniteness is *announced* in the Present (i.e., if the openness of the infinite future is, as such, a possibility *experienced* [*vécue*] as sense and right. . . . The unity of infinity, the condition for that temporalization, must then be *thought*, since it is announced without appearing and without being contained in a Present. This thought unity, which makes the phenomenalization of time as such possible, is therefore always the Idea in the Kantian sense which never phenomenalizes itself. (*OG*, 136–37)

This is a complex and, it seems to me, very clear characterization of an essential problem that Husserl was not able to eliminate in his lectures and notes in *The Phenomenology of Internal Time-Consciousness*.[3]

I would like to examine this problem a bit more closely. While he was studying the phenomenon of time, Husserl made a discovery that was obviously quite disconcerting for him and his project of phenomenology: the supposed Archimedean point of the world-constituting consciousness is actually undermined by an even more fundamental entity. This is what, following William James, is called the "stream of consciousness." The flux of internal time divides the identity of consciousness without there being "something" that might be able to be altered and that might flow, for the flow of time is "absolute subjectivity" itself (*T-C*, 100). What phenomenology earlier called — ignoring the internal flux of time — an "act," or "intentional experience," now, on closer investigation, reveals itself to be by no means instantaneous; rather it has been produced in a flux (*T-C*, 101). The asserted absoluteness of the flux — as subject — thus consists in the fact that every individual temporal occurrence "is reduced to such a flux" (150) after the phenomenological reduction. Everything that is temporal is hence *in* flux, except for this flux itself. In this sense, i.e., as pure *form* of change and duration, flux can justifiably be called "absolute."[4]

But doubts arise as soon as one accepts this conclusion: in order to be not merely absolute, but absolute *subjectivity*, the flux of time must have knowledge of itself. But of what sort could this knowledge be?

The consciousness in which all this is reduced, I cannot myself again perceive, however. For this new perceived entity would again be something temporal which referred back to a constitutive consciousness of just such a kind, and so on, *ad infinitum*. The question arises, therefore, whence can I have knowledge of the constitutive flux? (150)

This problem arises because, as we have frequently seen, Husserl thinks of subjectivity in terms of the model of *reflection*: an intentional experience (or even the egoity which carries all experiences) folds back upon itself and becomes its own intentional object. Only if one conceives self-consciousness *in this way* can the dilemma of infinite regress conjured up by Husserl arise. It consists, to be more precise, in the fact that every intentional act has a certain *duration* (thus it is *in* temporality), but that this, however, is not supposed to be the case for the absolute flux of time itself: it is *not* in temporality, and thus it has no duration. Now if there is only consciousness *of* something as intention (and that means *in* temporality), then it follows from this that a flux of time conceived as self-thematization either cannot be absolute or cannot be intended. If it is absolute, then it does not endure, and it thereby overreaches the possibilities of an intentional act; if it can be thematized intentionally, then it is finite (i.e., it is of only a certain limited duration) and thus nonabsolute.

Husserl emphasizes that "there is no doubt that such perception [of the flux of time as such, beyond all duration] exists" (152). If this is the case, however, then the contradiction must be inherent to the theoretical instruments that account for the phenomenon. That means that the model of consciousness *of* something (i.e., intentionality) appears not to be applicable to the self-consciousness of the absolute flux.

Husserl, nevertheless, holds fast to his analogy between consciousness of something and self-consciousness. Self-consciousness is a special case of consciousness: it is a consciousness that, instead of being directed at something other, is directed at itself, and it functions in such a way that two moments—let's refer to them in abbreviated fashion as subject and object—can always be distinguished. A consciousness into which a relation (i.e., an internal contrast) were inlaid could, of course, no longer be called absolute. Husserl therefore has to be careful to think of the absolute self-consciousness of the time flux in a manner different from how he conceives an intention directed at itself (i.e., as reflection). If the flux were the object of an intention that thematizes it, then it would only have the "temporal extension," i.e., "the duration" of this intention itself (152): it would be produced by it and would vanish with it, and thus it would be finite and relative.

This difficulty with the conception of consciousness in his phenomenology forces Husserl into a curious position: on the one hand, he cannot postulate a simply monoform (*einstelliges*) self-consciousness (for then intentionality, which as a beam of consciousness is always directed at something that itself transcends consciousness, would be dependent on something that itself is not intentional in itself, and it therefore would not be primal). On the other hand, he also cannot concede in this particular case that consciousness of the absolute time flux is the result of a self-reflection of the flux, for then this flux would always only have the "duration" of the beam of intentionality that happens to thematize it.

Caught between the Scylla of a monoform consciousness of time flux and the Charybdis of a bipolar-reflective consciousness of time flux, Husserl considers in some groping formulations a model of consciousness that in a mysterious manner would take a middle position between these two: he sometimes calls it an "internal," or "non-posited consciousness" (*T-C*, 175), at other times an "*implicit* intending" (178), a prereflective attending of the "pre-empirical being of the lived experiences" (178), or a "non-objectifying act of meaning" (178).

All these expressions have in common (and that is their function) that they seek to bring into view a certain possibility of self-perception that, *on the one hand*, would be distinct from the intentional and positional reference to an object (in this sense it can be called prereflective); *on the other hand*, however, Husserl cannot imagine that there could be a consciousness in which the poles of subject and object simply coincide, for all consciousness is consciousness *of* something that transcends it. A consciousness deprived of this transcendent *something* as its target would automatically cease to be consciousness.

Retention is just such an immediate intending; it is a consciousness that, at every moment, I have of the most temporally recent phase of the internal influx into my consciousness. Indeed, I can clearly distinguish this consciousness from memory or from "reproduction." Memory explicitly and, as it were, objectifyingly thematizes a past act experience. This is not the case for retention: in the consciousness of the present it preserves an immediately prior consciousness without reflectively objectifying it.

With this Husserl believes he has found an explanation for the consciousness of time flux as such. According to this hypothesis, the absolute subjectivity of the flux would constitute itself neither in the instantaneity of a timeless, nonrelational familiarity nor in an explicit intention, but rather, as it were, by means of an infectious contact between retentions, so that at any given time that retention nearest the present would communicate its temporality (*Zeitlichsein*) to the present one, and so on ad infinitum.

> Since each phase is retentionally cognizant of the preceding one, it encloses in itself, in a chain of mediate intentions, the entire series of retentions which have expired. The unities of duration which are reproduced through the vertical lines of the diagram of time and which are the Objects of the retrospective acts are constituted precisely in this way. In these acts the series of constitutive phases together with the constituted unity (e.g., the enduring sound, retentionally preserved unaltered) attains givenness. It is thanks to retention, therefore, that consciousness can be made an Object. (*T-C*, 162)

The underlying idea is clear: in each consciousness of the present the consciousness of the preceding phase is prereflectively preserved, and the same applies for
this phase in relation to the preceding one, etc. Thus the consciousness of the flux
as a whole arises within the framework of an unclosed and continuing movement,
the end of which can only be death.

There is a major problem, however, in this attempt at an explanation, and Husserl was aware of it. It can be explained in the following manner: if consciousness
of the flux occurred during the transition from consciousness of the present to
retentional consciousness, then there could only ever be time consciousness as
consciousness of the immediate past. This is obviously not the case; on the contrary, we also have consciousness of our present and do not have to "wait," figuratively speaking, until "primal consciousness" has become retention. If this were
the case, then we would never be able to judge that any retention is the most immediately *past* one, since we would need the oppositional concept of the present
in order to make such a judgment. Husserl, however, obviously believes that consciousness of this present subsists only when it becomes the object of a thematization, which, although not reflective, is yet bipolar, by means of the "primal consciousness."

If one were actually to draw this conclusion, then one would lose the possibility of being able to found the evidence of the *ego cogito* in the living self-present,
for precisely this present as a consciousness would be threatened. Since such a
conclusion would be devastating for the legitimation of a transcendental phenomenology as "primal science," Husserl has to lay claim to a fact for whose explanation the theoretical means at his disposal are clearly insufficient: an instant
self-consciousness of the now, that is, a consciousness of itself without any recourse to the bipolar model of reflection. Indeed, Husserl finds himself forced to
move in this very direction.

> We can now raise the question: What about the beginning phase of a
> self-constitutive lived experience? Does it also attain givenness only on
> the basis of retention and should we be "unconscious" of it if no reten-
> tion followed thereon? On this it can be said that the beginning phase
> can become an Object only after its running-off in the way indicated,
> through retention and reflection (or reproduction). But were we aware
> of it only through retention, what its designation as "now" bestowed on
> it would be incomprehensible. The beginning phase could at most only
> be negatively distinguished from its modifications as that phase which
> does not make us retentionally conscious of any preceding ones. But
> consciously it is, of course, positively characterized throughout. It is
> certainly an absurdity to speak of a content of which we are "uncon-
> scious," one of which we are conscious only later. Consciousness is
> necessarily *consciousness* in each of its phases. Just as the retentional
> phase was conscious of the preceding one without making it an object,

so also are we conscious of the primal datum – namely, in the specific form of the "now" – without its being objective. It is precisely this consciousness that goes over into a retentional modification, which then is retention of this consciousness itself and the datum we are cognizant of originarily in it, since both are inseparably one. Were this consciousness not present, no retention would be thinkable, since retention of a content of which we are not conscious is impossible. (*T-C*, 162–63)

This passage once again bears witness to Husserl's self-critical faithfulness to phenomena. Here he encounters a phenomenon whose solution overtaxes the theoretical apparatus of his theory of knowledge. Husserl must now accept what he calls "primal consciousness" as a sort of immanent act of revelation in which something that is prior to constituted temporality (and therefore eternal) is mediated to temporal consciousness in every instant, without itself being capable of becoming the theme of a beam of intention directed at it. This would be the opposite of a consciousness *of* something and to this extent it would be monoform (*einstellig*). If it were *not* to exist, then retention would have nothing *that* it might retain, for one can preserve in immediate memory only something that was previously conscious in its present. But it is precisely the monoformity (*Einstelligkeit*) of primal consciousness that is absolutely unthinkable (for Husserl): he demands it, without elucidating the particular structure of the consciousness in which it is manifest. The fact that he essentially conceives prereflective consciousness as a relation that is analogous to reflection makes itself obvious in the comparison he makes.

Just as the retentional phase was conscious of the preceding one without making it an object, so also are we conscious of the primal datum . . . without its being objective. (162)

Here a parallel is drawn between the reference of a retention to the preceding one and the instantaneous self-consciousness of the primal datum. Now it is easy to distinguish two elements in the relation of a retention to its preceding one: the first and the second retention. The matter is quite different, however, in the case of the primal datum; if one wants to preserve the strict instantaneity of consciousness, then one cannot tolerate here that there be two consciousnesses, one thematizing the other. Husserl apparently is reassured by the addendum that consciousness does not in either case objectify its object, and he emphasizes this frequently in the appendixes to his lectures on internal time consciousness.

One may by no means misinterpret this primal consciousness, this primal apprehension, or whatever he wishes to call it, as an apprehending act. Apart from the fact that it would be an obviously false description of the state of affairs, one would also in this way get involved in insoluble difficulties. If one says that every content attains consciousness only through an act of apprehension directed thereon, then the question immediately arises as to the consciousness in which we are aware of this act, which itself is still a content. Thus the infinite regress is unavoidable. However, if every "content" necessarily and in itself is "unconscious" then the question of an additional dator conscious becomes senseless. (163)

Here Husserl conjures up the classical difficulty of every reflective theory of self-consciousness. If consciousness of consciousness would have to be conceived in analogy to the consciousness *of* something, then only that which in the given instance was just thematiz*ed* (let's call it the object pole) would be illuminated. In order to make conscious that which thematiz*es* (let's call it the subject pole), a new reflection, whose subject position would again remain unconscious, would be necessary, and so on ad infinitum. Self-consciousness, however, *does* exist, and therefore the theory of reflection must be incorrect or inappropriate to it. In the ninth appendix to his lectures, Husserl goes as far as to affirm this conclusion, but he never goes as far as to reject the model of the reflectivity of consciousness. Obviously, he presupposes something like a noetic or *virtual* duality of the primal consciousness that would then be the condition for (worldly, or *actual*) reflection. "Even if reflection is not carried out *ad infinitum* and if, in general, no reflection is necessary, still that which makes this reflection possible and, in principle (or so it seems, at least) possible *ad infinitum* must be given" (154). But how should reflection be made possible if *what* makes it possible does not already carry the predisposition for a future division or duplication in itself?

> Every act is consciousness of something, but every act is also that of which we are conscious. Every lived experience is "sensed," is immanently "perceived" (internal consciousness) although naturally it is not posited or meant ("to perceive" here does not mean intentionally to be directed toward and to apprehend). Every act can be reproduced; to every "internal" consciousness of the act as an act of perception belongs a possible reproductive consciousness, for example, a possible recollection. To be sure, this seems to lead to an infinite regress; for is not the internal consciousness, the perception of the act (of judgment, of external perception, of rejoicing, etc.) now again an act, and hence itself internally perceived, and so on? On the other hand, we can say: every "lived experience" is in the significant sense internally perceived. But internal perception is, in the same sense, not a "lived experience." It is not itself again internally perceived. (*T-C*, 175)

Here the question is whether the nonpositing consciousness is analogous to the positing consciousness, i.e., to that consciousness that thematizes its object. And the answer is yes and no. Yes, because Husserl considers it, first, to be the condition of possibility for reflective retropresencing (*Rückvergegenwärtigung*) (and to this extent it must itself carry the trace of an internal duplication); and, second, because he takes it to be an internal "perceiving," but a "perceiving" nonetheless (perceiving, however, is always a perceiving *of* something). No, because Husserl understands very well that the infinite regress could not be stopped if nonpositing self-consciousness were a case of intention. He therefore chooses this formulation: "Behind this act of perception there stands no other such act, as if this flux were itself a unity in a flux" (176).

However, if we were to lend credence to this last observation, then all traces that allow us to think of the relation between primal consciousness and its immediate presencing as a matter of "internal reflection" (178) would have to be consistently eradicated. Nevertheless, Husserl expresses "internal consciousness" — i.e., each nonpositing self-consciousness of an act of meaning *of* something that is laid into a "positing act of meaning" — by means of a formula in which *two* elements stand side by side, i.e., as "$P_i(A)$." In this formula A stands for "any act known in internal consciousness (which has been constituted in it)," whereas P_i means "the internal consciousness" of A (176). According to this, the complex phenomenon of self-consciousness could be described in this way: there is the intentional act (e.g., looking forward to something, seeing something, thinking of something, etc.), and this act represents a unity, surrounded by the flow of retentions and protentions, *within* the flux of time. An internal perceiving that itself, however, is not an act, but rather a nonpositing familiarity of the act with itself, has been inscribed in this intentional act so that it does not have to wait for its retention in order to become conscious. In short, there are two poles in consciousness: the act, and the consciousness of the act. Precisely here lies the permanent difficulty in Husserl's theory of time consciousness: it is forced to articulate the asserted unity of the phenomenon by means of a duality of moments.[5] A consciousness or self-consciousness that is articulated in itself carries in itself the germ of a *différance* that makes the unity phenomenologically demonstrated to be in it into an idea in the Kantian sense — and exactly this, as we saw, is Derrida's objection.

Unfortunately, Derrida has not specifically interpreted the quoted passages from Husserl's *Phenomenology of Internal Time-Consciousness*, although he frequently relies on the problematics of time consciousness as the focus of his deconstruction: "Husserl's reflections on primordial temporality touch on the most profound region of phenomenological reflection, where darkness risks being no longer the provision of appearing or the field which offers itself to phenomenal light, but the forever nocturnal source of the light itself" (*OG*, 137).

This formulation betrays what Derrida finds fascinating about the aporias in which Husserl's philosophy of time goes astray: it is the problem of "final institution" (*Endstiftung*), of a "final grounding" (*Letztbegründung*) of phenomenology. It is not as if Husserl fails to supply answers to these aporias; as a matter of fact, he emphatically refers to the "transcendental ego" as if it were the supreme evidence from which all other recognitions (*Erkenntnisse*) that lay claim to being "knowledge" (*Wissen*) or "science" (*Wissenschaft*) derive their validity. Yet the ego itself, however, is standing on unstable ground: it is thrown into time and it cannot once more confer upon itself the real ground of its factual subsistence. It constitutes itself *under the presupposition* of a ground that escapes it itself. In other words, the light of evidence in which it dwells is not its own work; an insuperable passivity is prior to its own activity. Derrida speaks of a retreat of the principle and adds that it is this retreat of the principle that first permits phenomena to appear ("without this disappearing of the ground necessary for appearing itself"; *OG*, 138). An unilluminable nonevidence is the real ground for the evidences of consciousness, i.e., of transcendental phenomenology. Now the evidence of phenomena, their being clear in and of themselves, is precisely what Husserl calls his "principle of principles." If one maintains that this principle in reality is not a principle, but rather something that itself is a product of principles, the *principié* of a *fondement-en-retrait*, then one refers the *unity* of the meaning of Being to something that is transcendent to consciousness: this unity becomes, as we know, a merely regulative idea in the Kantian sense, "indefinitely deferred [*différée*] in its content but always evident in its regulative value" (*OG*, 138).

> It is not by chance that there is no phenomenology of the Idea. The latter cannot be given in person, nor determined in an evidence, for it is only the possibility of evidence and the openness of "seeing" itself; it is only *determinability* as the horizon for every intuition in general, the invisible milieu of seeing analogous to the diaphaneity of the Aristotelian Diaphanous, an elemental third, but the one source of the seen and the visible. . . . If there is nothing to say about the Idea *itself*, it is because the Idea is that starting from which something in general can be said. Its own particular presence, then, cannot depend on a phenomenological type of evidence. . . . This space is the *interval* between the Idea of infinity in its formal and finite (yet concrete) evidence and the infinity itself of which there is the Idea. It is on the basis of this horizon-certainty that the historicity of sense and the development of Reason are set free. . . . The *Endstiftung* of phenomenology (phenomenology's ultimate critical legitimation: i.e., what its sense, value, and right tell us about it), then, never directly measures up to a phenomenology. (*OG*, 138–39, 140, 141)

In short, the transcendental condition of possibility for evidence is as such not evident, it is not given in itself; the unity of the transcendental ego escapes itself, it does not possess itself. With this, however, the possibility of deriving the unity of the meaning of the world from the unity of the "living self-present" is obscured. For precisely this unity is a mere, if motivated, *demand*; the unity of the living present "is *present* only in being *deferred-delayed* [*différant*] without respite, this impotence and this impossibility are given in a primordial and pure consciousness of Difference. . . . Difference would be transcendental" (153).

We need to take a closer look at the remarkable formulation at the end of this quotation. "Difference would be transcendental": this is obviously a difficult formulation. It resembles, in a certain sense, Wittgenstein's use of the word "transcendental," as, for example, when he writes in the *Tractatus* that ethics is transcendental (cf. *Tr*, 6.421).[6] As we know, the younger Wittgenstein defines the totality of what can be meaningfully said as the set of possible syntheses between "elementary propositions" (propositions in which experiences are described) and logical judgments. What he calls "logical form" mediates between the two. The logical form is the condition of possibility for any meaningful use of language, but one cannot speak meaningfully about this condition itself. Wittgenstein expresses this in a general way in the assertion that logical form establishes the limits of my world (of the totality of valid statements). *"The limits of my language* mean the limits of my world" (*Tr*, 5.6). "Logic fills the world: the limits of the world are also its limits" (*Tr*, 5.61). This nonreflectivity that Wittgenstein believes inscribed in logic prevents one from making statements about the world, i.e., about its logical form; for in order to accomplish this I would have to transgress the limits of language. Yet precisely this is the intention of all transcendental philosophy, which would like to construct the limits of the world from a transmundane position, for example, from the perspective of the subject. Wittgenstein remarks that such a transcendental subject does not belong to the world; it is, rather, a limit of the world (*Tr*, 5.632), and is therefore something unexpressible:

> *Where in* the world is a metaphysical subject to be noted?
> You say that this case is altogether like that of the eye and the field of sight. But you do *not* really see the eye.
> And from nothing *in the field of sight* can it be concluded that it is seen from an eye. (*Tr*, 5.633)

We do not want to get bogged down in the difficulties of reading the *Tractatus*; rather we only take note of this one point of convergence in Wittgenstein's and Derrida's use of the word "transcendental." Both deny—to be sure, with very different consequences—the possibility of escaping language with the purpose of deriving and mastering its regularities from a point beyond language. Wittgenstein disputes that one can *speak* about the limits of language, since one is imprisoned inside these limits; and Derrida disputes that differentiality can be surmounted by appealing to a transcendental subject. That which is the condition of possibility for meaning and consciousness, and which has until now been called "transcendental," is *Différence* itself. This is the sense in which the intentionally paradoxical phrase "Difference would be transcendental" is valid.

The pure and interminable disquietude of thought striving to "reduce" Difference by going beyond factual infinity toward the infinity of its sense and value, i.e., while maintaining Difference—that disquietude would be transcendental. And Thought's pure certainty would be transcendental, since it can look forward to the already announced Telos only by advancing on (or being in advance of [*en avancant sur*] the Origin that indefinitely reserves itself. Such a certainty never had to learn that Thought would always be to come. (*OG*, 153)

This should not be understood as a sort of continuation of transcendental philosophy by other means: it is both the preservation (*Aufhebung*) and the overthrow of transcendental philosophy simultaneously. To be sure, the term "transcendental" means "condition of possibility for the recognition of something." Whereas, however, the classical idealist concept of the transcendental designates a place of evidence, i.e., something that is not only the condition of possibility for knowledge, but rather *itself* also conscious and, therefore, the *subject* of knowledge, the expression "transcendentality of difference" means something itself not conscious that would be the condition of possibility for consciousness *and* for knowledge.

In *Of Grammatology* Derrida designated as "ultratranscendental" this difference that makes the classical transcendental subject (e.g., of the Kantian critique) possible, and he returns to this conception once more in *Limited Inc*. Here he calls the *différance* that is neither present nor absent the condition of possibility for ontotheological (i.e., metaphysical) discourse, at the same time claiming that it escapes this discourse.

The rest of the trace, its remains [*restance*] are neither present nor absent. They escape the jurisdiction of all ontotheological discourse even if they render the latter at times possible. (*LI*, 225)

What distinguishes this *différance* that makes discourse possible from a transcendental principle is its internal rupture, its lack of origin or root, its nonidentity with itself.

No constituted logic nor any rule of a logical order can, therefore, provide a decision or impose its norms upon these prelogical possibilities of logic. Such possibilities are not "logically" primary or secondary with regard to other possibilities, nor logically primary or secondary with regard to logic itself. They are (topologically?) alien to it, but not as its principle, condition of possibility, or "radical" foundation; for the structure of iterability divides and guts such radicality. (235)

We have to bracket off the term "iterability" in the present context, since at the moment we cannot take cognizance of its implications. For the present I will only say this much: the iterability of concepts or signs can no longer be guaranteed if the criterion for their identity is destroyed simultaneously with the identity of a transcendental subject evident in itself. We can, as a precaution, replace "iterability" with *différance*, and then Derrida's caveat states that we can no longer say of *différance* that it is "a transcendental condition of possibility evoking . . . other phenomena . . . into conditioned effects . . . this kind of (classical) logic is fractured in its code by iterability." (244)

Let's pause here for a moment. In a broad sweep we have analyzed — remaining mostly in the vicinity of Derrida's introduction to *Edmund Husserl's Origin of Geometry* — the difficulties that Husserl (as the last significant representative of a transcendental-philosophical type of philosophy) encountered in his attempt to defend the *ego cogito* as the "principle of principles," i.e., as the supreme evidence and principle from which all other evident "act-experiences" could be derived. Derrida managed to demonstrate that there is a fracture that runs through the heart of self-consciousness, a fracture that places its suitability as the principle of a transcendental philosophy in dispute. But that is not all: Derrida, trying to outdo Husserl, attempts to conceive this difference as the "ultra-transcendental" condition of possibility for self-consciousness (i.e., for transcendentality). That means that transcendentality does not simply resign, but rather that it reflects its posteriority over against something other, with whose relationship with the differential play of language we are already familiar, and which in this context is simply called *différence*.

What I have just described has sometimes been depicted as Derrida's intention to deny the possibility of transcendental philosophy. I believe, however, that such a thesis simply comes up short. In contrast to the early (and, in a certain sense, even the later) Wittgenstein, Derrida does not repudiate the phenomenon of self-consciousness that is evident in itself; to do this would indeed mean falling into absurdity. What Derrida has in mind, if I am correct here, is to provide a *different*, a more illuminating explanation of that same phenomenon that is taken into consideration only within the framework of transcendental philosophy at the price of indissoluble aporias. This, at least, is something he says very clearly in his interview with Jean-Louis Houdebine and Guy Scarpetta entitled "Positions." To be sure, he does not explicitly speak about the subject here, but rather about the referent and about meaning; but we know meanwhile to what extent these concepts are tied together in Derrida's thinking: logocentric metaphysics would like to found the effects of meaning attribution and reference presemiologically in a subject that is present to itself, without having to pass through the "parade of signifiers," i.e., *différance*. Therefore, what Derrida says about these other two "idealities" is a fortiori true for the subject as well.

> In effect, we must avoid having the indispensable critique of a certain naive relationship to the signified or the referent, to sense or meaning, remain fixed in a suspension, that is, a pure and simple suppression, of

meaning or reference. I believe that I have taken precautions on this matter in the propositions that I have advanced. But it is true, and the proofs are not lacking, that this is never sufficient. What we need is to determine *otherwise*, according to a differential system, the *effects* of ideality, of signification, of meaning, and of reference. (*P*, 66)

Let me briefly summarize the essence of this statement. Derrida says that one has to avoid the impression that the work of deconstruction is simply a suppression ("suppression pure and simple") of the phenomena that are to be explained. Such a reductionism, as it commonly occurs in the early phase of logical positivism (e.g., in Carnap), has nothing in common with Derrida's deconstruction of metaphysics. It is not the denial of these phenomena that is necessary; what is necessary is a different, a better, and that means a more plausible explanation than the explanation that was possible within the context of transcendental philosophy.

Now we at least know the direction in which Derrida's demand is moving: that self-consciousness that is called transcendental should not be the explanatory ground (*ratio cognoscendi*) of difference; rather, the latter should be the explanatory ground of self-consciousness. Self-Being and meaning are no longer instituters of differential relations; rather they themselves are results of the difference that precedes them, and which, as our reading of Husserl taught us, cannot be interpreted as a relation of reflection (in a relation of reflection it is always a matter of the difference of two elements that come together in a third; *P*, 58–61), which dialectically transforms the temporality of their opposition into identity. Unfortunately, Derrida never demonstrated concretely what this positive continuation of the thus far purely negative deconstructive work would look like. He has produced no work that, profuse in its detail and based on a thoroughgoing knowledge of modern theories of self-consciousness, unmasks self-consciousness as the effect of differential relations. I find that very unfortunate, for among neostructuralist thinkers, Derrida is hardest on the heels of this phenomenon, and he undoubtedly commands sufficient knowledge of the history of philosophy to approach the issue. It might seem to some that I am distorting matters somewhat by overemphasizing in my lectures the problematics of the subject, and one might claim that, in reality, this problem never concerned neostructuralism. I do not think that such a suspicion has any foundation. The entire early work of Derrida, and basically even everything that he has written since, constantly refers – to be sure, negatively – to the problematics of self-consciousness. One could say that Derrida is more interested in a refutation of the principle that makes subjectivity the point of departure for deductive conclusions than he is in the refutation of any other Western, i.e., metaphysical, principle. And in this Hegel and Husserl are – *ex negativo* – Derrida's constant dialogic partners. Let's not forget that, if one considers the work published by Derrida thus far, the quantitatively greatest portion of his texts is devoted to Husserl and Hegel, the thinkers who uphold self-consciousness as a self-evident principle.[7] His position first took shape, or, at least, first convincingly developed, on the basis of his critique of these two philosophers. However, I believe that—in contrast to Lacan, with whom we will deal later—Derrida has yet to make his *alternative* explanation of the phenomenon of subjectivity compelling; indeed, he has not even been able to present it in an outline. However, we can easily imagine the difficulties he would have had with it, and which now hang over his work as omissions, as blanks, as indications of thoughts he neglected to think. I would like to try to outline some of them here.

First of all, Derrida—with a destructive purpose in mind, to be sure—takes over, from among the positions he criticizes, the view that in the instance of self-consciousness we are dealing with something like a *présence-à-soi*, i.e., a relation of reflection. In a previous lecture we saw that he shares this view, among others, with Heidegger. For both of them this conception has a strategic function. If it is a matter of founding the hypothesis that the history of the West consists in the successive unfolding of a primordial interpretation of Being as presence (*ousía, présence*), then, of course, a self-consciousness conceived as presence to itself (*Anwesenheit bei sich*) (e.g., in Fichte, Hegel, and Husserl) was particularly welcome, for one could demonstrate on its example the will to delusion, i.e., the repression of Being. The zenith of this repression of Being, understood as "presence of the present," in Western metaphysics was attained, according to this interpretation, in Fichte's and Hegel's philosophies of a self-consciousness that autonomously posits itself and its object, sublating it into its innerliness; and the crisis that follows upon this (supposedly first comprehended by Nietzsche) would then be the motive of return, of recollection, a crisis whose most recent and most impressive phase begins with, and as, neostructuralism.

This scenario, you will justifiably interject, is too simple to be true, and, indeed, I consider it to be simply false, first of all, because precisely romantic idealist theory *no longer* took self-consciousness to be a principle, but rather conceived it as something principled (*als ein Prinzipiat*), i.e., as the agency (*Instanz*) in which the self declares its independence of what Schelling calls the "unprethinking Being." In contrast to a still widespread cliché, idealism laid the ground for the "turn" in the Western interpretation of Being that Heidegger and his successors then carried out; and idealism accomplished this in part with considerably more profound, better elaborated, and more fitting arguments than those of the later philosophers.

And second, the foregoing scenario is false because it is not correct to say that idealism consistently conceived of self-consciousness as "presence to itself" (*Anwesenheit bei sich*). On the contrary, we have Fichte and the early romantic philosophers to thank for their clear insight into the impossibility of thinking of the familiarity that consciousness has with itself as a relation of *reflection*. To be sure, the elaboration of this insight produced new difficulties, which, however, are of a quality of which we have no inkling in Derrida's work. Hegel was the only one among the idealists who held on to the theory of reflection in describing self-consciousness: he characterizes it as the coming to itself of a relation, i.e., of a One that was previously already self-relation. Thus he "saw to it that all of Hegelianism would remain dogmatic and unproductive with regard to the theory of consciousness."[8] This is still true for nonidealist Hegel critics, for example, for Heidegger and Derrida. We saw earlier that the apparent "founding" of reflection in the ekstatic structure of understanding and care only repeats this structure of reflection.

For Derrida, who simply remained a negative Hegelian because of his fixation on the model of reflection as the absolute *pudendum*, this reproach applies in an only slightly modified form. If he does not want simply to deny self-consciousness and meaning, as the passage cited earlier certifies, but only "explain it *differently*," namely, as a secondary effect of a prior difference, then he encounters difficulties that are in part analogous to those that were uncovered by Hegel's critics (above all by Schelling), and which are in part even more problematic. Schelling addressed to Hegel the question of how it could be possible for the absolute spirit to recognize itself *as* itself at the end of its path leading to self-knowledge, if it had not already had some knowledge of itself: nothing would be able to recognize itself *as* itself if it did not have a criterion for its identification in the form of a preceding (and self-familiar) knowledge. Hegel's theory of the mind is thus erected on the basis of a theoretical circle, a *petitio principii*.

But the circularity of his argumentation nevertheless lays claim to something — in the form of a presupposition or an assumption — that in itself is not so absurd: the unity of our view of the world. Derrida, it seems to me, lets go of this presupposition and is then confronted with the problem of having to derive self-consciousness from pure difference. Now it may very well be that one has to describe the "structurality of structure" as a centerless play of differences. Still, the mere reference between two marks could never in all eternity produce their sameness, and it certainly could never lead to a *consciousness* of this sameness. Nothing about a "mark," which stands over against another "mark," betrays that they are *the same*. Now Derrida, indeed, does not seem to assume this, since he excludes not only identifiability, but also in particular *cognizant* identification within the structural field. In this case, however, there would be nothing in the self *that* might change and become familiar *as* something changed. But a *pure* change cannot be conceived of; lacking a criterion, it would be indistinguishable from pure nonchange. If *everything* is in flux, then the flux itself can also no longer be recognized; i.e., any statement to the effect that it is so would necessarily nullify itself. This is not true in Hegel, who, presupposing a unity, rescues the "self-consummating skepticism" from total dissolution by interpreting this dissolution as *sublation*, i.e., as the disputing itself of pure difference in the face of the unity of negation inscribed in it, whose autonomy supports the whole structure (*Gebäude*).

Thus Derrida's attack on the dialectical unity of self-consciousness seems to me to miss its target. Even in a radical theory of "indistinguishability" one would still have to be able to demonstrate what significance can be attributed to the expression "identity" in language games. A theory that disputes the applicability of this term no longer interprets the world in which we live and communicate with language. Even temporary (and permanently new and differently articulated) "unities" are unities, and even if they were appearance or illusion, we could demand of philosophy that it make the genesis of this illusion intelligible. To merely point out that behind this illusion of self-identity, and, what is more, of *cognizant* self-identity, there stands pure difference, cannot explain the phenomenon, and it unconsciously strengthens the force of the attacked positions from Fichte, through Hegel, to Husserl — and this even after one admits that they have suffered under the blows of Derrida's critique.

Lecture 17

We followed Derrida's deconstructive reading of Husserl up to the point at which he draws something like a conclusion. This conclusion he formulates very pointedly: "Difference would be transcendental" (*OG*, 153). Derrida later substituted his neologism "différance" for this *Différence* written with a capital letter. *Différance* refers not to a subsisting difference but, to put it poignantly, to that generative gap that can never be sublated (in a Hegelian manner) into a unity in which all determinations (*Bestimmtheiten*) spring up and then dissolve once again. Determination—and this is a leitmotif of neostructuralism—is the effect of differential relations between *marques* of a structure. However, since the differentiality of structure provides no center, the play of differential determination(s) is open, and this means that every signification of a term or of an expression that is marked off by a certain context can interminably be altered by a new differentiation in new contexts. Formulated in this way, *différance* seems to be the ground both of the unity (determination) and of the nonidentity (displacement) of the signification of terms.

This formulation is nearly identical to the one with which Hegel, and Schelling in his intermediary period, designate the principle of their philosophy: the Absolute, they maintained, is not simply the coincidence of something manifold in the One, and also not the unityless manifold itself in its opposition to unity, but rather the "unity of unity and opposition." This formulation, which on first sight seems to be unnecessarily complicated (involuted, in the literal sense of this word), states that in the instance of absolute spirit we are not dealing with a unity that imprints its unity onto the manifold of given experience *from outside* (as is the case with transcendental self-consciousness in the *Critique of Pure Reason*); rather it states that the Absolute is both unity *and* the manifold. According to Schelling, each moment in the self-constitution of the spirit, the positing (unified) as well as the posited (different) "is the *whole* Absolute" (*SW*, I/6, 164); the "doubling of the essence [of the Absolute] represents, in this instance, not a diminution, but an augmentation of unity" (*SW*, I/7, 425). Each moment of self-relation knows itself by means of the act itself through which it is present to itself as "a part of the whole," and even as "the whole indivisible [Absolute] . . . itself" (*SW*, I/6, 165). Not only is this sameness the case, it is, in addition, *conscious* in the Absolute: both what affirms as well as what is affirmed in the absolute spirit *know* themselves as the same; they stand in the *light* of an identity that yet overarches their opposition. In 1804 Schelling expressed this in the following way: not only is that which affirms the same as that which is affirmed, but "the essence of all things [is] the affirming and the affirmed of itself" (*SW*, I/6, 148; italicized in the original). This "of itself" means that what is posited in the difference between the two moments of self-relation is actually not their opposition, but rather the absolute unity of these moments.

> By means of this self-affirmation nothing affirming and nothing affirmed *as such*, nothing subjective and nothing objective, is posited; rather *only God* is posited as the *same* who affirms and is affirmed; the affirming and the affirmed themselves, however, are not posited. (*SW*, I/6, 164)

This is a classical formulation typical of idealism in its heyday: unity is posited *into* the opposition, but it is not posited *as* opposition. All forms of relation can thus be traced back to forms of *self*-relation; and self-relation is nonrelative to that extent that its moments are the affirming and the affirmed *of themselves*, i.e., of the Absolute.

Derrida senses himself to be very close to this concept of a unity of moments that yet is different in itself. In his 1968 lecture to the Société française de philosophie ("La Différance"), he himself emphasized this problematical proximity to Hegel.

> Writing "*différant*" or "*différance*" (with an *a*) would have had the advantage of making it possible to translate Hegel at that particular point—which is also an absolutely decisive point in his discourse—without further notes or specifications. And the translation would be, as it always must be, a transformation of one language by another. I contend, of course, that the word *différance* can also serve other purposes: first, because it marks not only the activity of "originary" difference, but also the temporizing detour of deferral; and above all because *différance* thus written, although maintaining relations of profound affinity with Hegelian discourse (such as it must be read), is also, up to

a certain point, unable to break with that discourse (which has no kind of meaning or chance); but it can operate a kind of infinitesimal and radical displacement of it, whose space I attempt to delineate elsewhere but of which it would be difficult to speak briefly here. (*Margins*, 14)

Thus there are, according to Derrida, profound relationships between *différance* (with an *a*) and Hegelian difference. Both types of difference are, in a certain (if not in the same) sense, authors of differential relations.

Hegel says as much at the end of the *Introduction*, when, following the same procedure as in all his systematic expositions, he presents the sketch of internal division, of self-differentiation as self-determination and self-production of the concept. It is the moment at which the *Einleitung* (introduction) becomes *Einteilung* (division). (*Glas*, 13)

We saw earlier that it would be very unjust to assert that German idealism—allegedly the culmination of the Western repression of Being—overlooked the fact that determination is grounded in contraposition, and thus in negation. Fichte, we recall, spoke of the "law of reflection of all our knowledge." This law states that nothing can be recognized as that which it *is*, without our also thinking that which it is *not*. Even the idea of the principle, of the Absolute, is not excepted from this necessity of having to distinguish itself through contrast with the non-Absolute; in other words, it must transform itself into a relation in order not only to be absolute, but to be *as* the Absolute. Hegel's entire dialectic rests on the unfolding of this basic insight and can be understood as an attempt to reconcile the idea of grounding unity with the idea of difference (without which there would be no determination).

In order to bring out more clearly than Derrida himself does what he calls the "profound affinity" between Hegel's dialectic and the notion of *différance*, I want to summarize Hegel's basic idea in coarsely simplified fashion. Hegel believed that he could derive unity and difference from a single conceptual structure. Unity, or the Universal, is that which only has reference to itself. In contradistinction to this, the particular is that which has its Being in something else or which refers to something else. We note that both definitions, that of the universal as well as that of the particular, employ the category of reference. In the first case it is a matter of the reference of One only to itself; in the second case the referential relation mediates between elements that are different from each other. But the reference as such, Hegel says, is the same in both cases. In the first example the reference is the "immediate," for what does not refer to something other than itself, but rather— like "Being" in the *Logic*—"refers only to itself," can justifiably be called immediate. In the second case we are dealing with something mediated, with mediation: one element refers to another, and the reference between the two establishes a bond or a commensurability between the different elements.

If, in addition to this, both references are to be developed out of the unity of *one* single thought, then one would have to show that the reference to something other is *in truth* a self-reference. And that is precisely the strategy Hegel's *Logic* employs, following a most meticulously structured argument. His intent is to expose the monoform (*einstellige*) relation that is at work in the instance of immediacy as identical to the two-part reference that constitutes the differential relation. That means that he sought to prove the unity of immediacy and mediation, or the unity of unity and difference.

Recent Hegel criticism has characterized this as "Hegel's basic operation."[1] It consists in drawing conclusions from the idea that negation can be considered to be a self-sufficient principle of philosophy. In this case we would be dealing with a negation that would be entirely independent, i.e., a negation that would not first and foremost be the negation *of* something, as in propositional logic, nor would it be a question of a negation executed by a subject that is prior to this negation. Henrich calls this an "autonomous negation."[2] This independence both from an object pregiven to it, as well as from a subject that executes it, is derived from the capacity of such a negation to apply itself to itself, i.e., to become self-referential (a negation of negation). In this self-referential duplication, negation is not related to something other than itself (something that would be independent of it), but rather to itself and *only* to itself. On the other hand, in the case of self-application, negation is still not without an object, i.e., without something other than itself (even if this other is negation itself). One can draw a third conclusion from the thought that negation has become autonomous: self-referential negation has a result that is different from itself, namely, the affirmation or the position that is the result of a negation of negation. We thus can distinguish three elements in the structural totality of autonomous negation: first, nonreferential (or monoform) negation; second, self-referential (or doubled, two-part) negation; and third, pure affirmation or position as a *result* of the self-application of negation. We can add to this the observation that the first and third elements are compatible to the extent that no relation takes place in these instances: in the first example it has not yet taken place, and in the third it no longer takes place; both these types of negation, therefore, can be called "simple" or "immediate." The difference is that the first is the instance of a completely *undetermined* and presuppositionless immediacy, whereas the third is a *determined* (i.e., in itself differentiated) and resultant immediacy. Thus for Hegel the difference between the absence of a presupposition and the supposition of a result becomes "the source of an immanent logical progress" with whose unfolding the *Science of Logic* is concerned.

The notion of an autonomy (in the sense of self-sufficiency) of negation allows for a circumstance—and we must not forget this—in which negation has no object that is different from itself. For the same reason it must be conceived as *self-*referential, since all negation is negation *of* something.

In the classical double negation, the first negation negates a statement [thus something different from the negation], and the second negation negates the first. In this case the duplication of negation by no means implies self-reference in the strict sense, but rather only an application of second-degree negation to first-degree negation. For Hegel's autonomous negation, however, it is the case that it has to be duplicated precisely because it is in this way that it can be made self-referential. This, however, leads to the conclusion that the two negations cannot be distinguished from one another by the fact that they belong to two different degrees. We rather have to conclude that they are not at all different from each other. Negation that negates negation negates *itself*. By the same token, however, we need to add that negation can negate itself only when it can establish a relation with itself of such a sort that we can distinguish it from itself, to the extent that we can distinguish between it as something that is negated and it as something that negates. In autonomous negation, negation is self-negating and is negated by itself. Otherwise one would not be able to identify at all what it means to say that negation is *duplicated*. The consciousness of the fundamental meaning, but also of the logical problematics of all forms of self-reference, is characteristic of post-Kantian idealism. In Hegel's development of autonomous negation this problematics first begins to appear.[3]

In fact, Hegel's *Logic* approaches its goal in three steps: from Being, to essence, to concept. If all three stages are to be understood as forms of autonomous negation, then one should be able to reformulate each one of them in terms of negation: *Being* would then be negation in the state of immediacy, a relation "only to itself," as Hegel says, i.e., not to anything other. *Essence* would be negation in the state of mediation, as a negation that is differentiated in itself and in which what negates encounters what is negated as if it were its Other. In this instance, negation is both immediacy and mediacy at the same time. But it is also more than this: as the relation of something negative to itself, it produces as a result the canceling out of itself of negation and the opening of a space that one could cautiously designate as the absence of negation or, in Hegel's words, as *pure* immediacy or as concept. If we analyze the expression "absence of negation," we realize that the term "negation" is used a third time here; what is actually said is that "the autonomous, the double negation does 'not' exist. Thus negation occurs here three times. In its third occurrence it functions [in the] meaning . . . [of the] Not of difference between irreconcilable states."[4] One might be tempted to believe that with this, negation is simply canceled. In truth, however, the phrase "the autonomous negation does not exist" is itself relational: it relates simple negation to self-negation, and only by virtue of this negative *reference* does negation sublate itself *as* negation. Thus "the thought of the relation to the Other [must be] taken up into the thought of pure self-relation."[5] *Otherness* appears here as a consequence of the *"Not"* that distinguishes the two referential elements from each other.

The conclusion that this position has to be a *result* based on the thought of autonomous negation can also be drawn from the observation that negation is in fact called "autonomous" only because it is not preceded by anything foreign and autonomous. In the classical case of propositional logic the negation of the negation of a statement is its position. In Hegel, however, there is no statement that precedes and is independent of negation, and which would be reinstated in its positivity if negation were to cancel itself out. Accordingly, on the basis of Hegel's premises, positivity, *if* it occurs, can be accounted for only as *result* (not as presupposition) of the double negation, and it is a result that cannot be supplanted by the thought of the self-negating negation (it is its *result*, not its object). If this is the case, then self-referential negation must always be conceived as relation to its opposite (to a state of nonnegativity). In other words, autonomous negation is the reference to an Other—not to an independent or prior Other, but rather to a resultant Other.[6]

To be able to guarantee that this reference, which was just formulated as an *opposition*, is simultaneously a *self*-relation, one has to demonstrate the sameness of the related moments. That which faces negation as its opposite has to be in its essence the same as negation itself. The opposite of autonomous negation, therefore, must also be able to be conceived as autonomous negation; otherwise negation would indeed be heteronomous, i.e., it would have its Being in something Other. Only when the Other proves itself to be identical with autonomous negation (i.e., proves itself to be autonomous negation) has its autonomy been corroborated.

> The full description of its self-relation, therefore, has to be as follows: at the inception there is negation. Then it negates itself. With this, however, it falls away and thus, in its self-reference, which is negative, it is related to its opposite. This relation to an Other can, in a strict sense, be restricted to a self-reference only if the Other is once more negation itself. That means, however, that the opposite of autonomous double negation must itself be a double negation. Double negation can be conceived as self-relation only if it is thought twice. In Hegel's language this would sound something like this: the Absolute is only with itself in its Otherness.[7]

Let me repeat this concisely formulated summary in my own words. Before arriving at the third step, whose understanding presents us with the greatest difficulties, we already saw that the internal structure of autonomous negation includes two modes of Being of negation: negation as mere self-reference (immediacy); and negation as the explicit reference of something that negates to something negated (mediation). However, both these modes of Being do not form an opposition with each other, since they can be thought of as two aspects of one and the same "negative self-relation." In other words, mediacy in duplicated negation (negation that is referred to negation) can be conceived as articulation of that relation that negation has with itself in the state of monoformity (*Einstelligkeit*). Now, however, at the third level at which the logic of autonomous negation unfolds, we are dealing with the relation of a state of negation to a state of absence, i.e., with the relation of negation to an *Other* that is really different from it (to something that itself is *not* negation). This Other is not—as in Schelling or Hölderlin—to be accounted for as a heteronomous *presupposition* of negation, but rather as its *result*. Nevertheless, the question arises as to how negation might be able to *grasp* its opposite *as* a new and different expression of itself. For this to occur, Hegel answers (in his chapter entitled "Determining Reflection"),[8] it is necessary that one not only identify, as has been the case up to this point, negation with itself; rather the entire relation of negation to its Other has to be identified with itself in a further duplication of its structure. In other words, a state in which negation falls away by virtue of self-application (let's call it, following Hegel, "intro-Reflection" [*Reflexion-in-sich*]) is supposed to be identical with another state in which negation is related to the Other of itself (and is therefore not "intro-Reflection," but "reflection upon the Other of itself"). This could occur only if the first state were the faithful mirror image of the second, and, moreover, if it were to reveal itself *as* the last state's mirror image (otherwise the essence would indeed see *itself* undistorted—face to face, as it were—but not *as* itself). Reflection would have to "duplicate" itself in all its previously derived aspects.

> It is, first, that which is presupposed, or that intro-Reflection which is the immediate; and, secondly, it is Reflection which, as negative, refers itself to itself; it refers itself to itself as to that other which is its not-being. (*Logic*, II, 29)

The first synthesis would then be its reflected double in the form of the In-itself (*An-sich*) (immediacy), whereas the second synthesis would mirror and negate the same relation in the form of the For-itself (*Für-sich*) (mediation). This reduplication seems to incorporate an authentic dialectical relation insofar as each related moment contains the entire relation (Hegel calls it "infinite self-relation"; *Logic*, II, 34) to exactly the same extent as, on the other hand, they only are what they are as related moments of this "entire" or "infinite relation" that transcends them. In other words, what is posited as something immediate, independent of reflection, would prove to be itself reflection. With this it undermines by its own action its independence of the Other of the opposing reflection and turns of its own accord into the other related moment; and for this second moment one could demonstrate the operation of the same mechanism. By means of such an exchange of roles, the thought of an autonomous, twice-duplicated negation is indeed confirmed as *self*-determination: in its second aspect autonomous negation posits, negates, and determines itself as the presupposition it is in its first aspect. This seems to make Hegel's project complete: everything happens as if the Being-for-itself of the entire relation were posited. Negative reflection is thoroughly autonomous: in its duplication it consciously has only to do with itself; its determination is transparent to it. The "taking back" into its self-relation of its reference to the Other confirms its "reflection-determinateness" as "the relation to its other-being in itself" (*Logic*, II, 34). Put differently, the Absolute is only with itself in its Otherness, and sameness of the Absolute exists only as the immanent sublation of its Otherness.

At this point we want to pause and formulate two questions. The first is, Can Derrida's idea of *différance* really differentiate itself from Hegel's idea of autonomous negation? The second question is, Do both basic operations, "autonomous negation" on the one hand, and "autonomous play of differences" on the other, really make what we understand under "self-consciousness" and "meaning" comprehensible?

The first of the two questions is a complex one, and it is further complicated by the fact that, first of all, Hegel himself nowhere elaborated on this basic operation as such (Dieter Henrich's text is a summary of the procedure as applied in the section on reflection in Hegel's *Logic*), and, second, that Derrida nowhere deals in a systematic way with Hegel's *Logic* (what he says about Hegel in his most voluminous study primarily traces Hegel's material theses and refers, above all, to the Berlin *Philosophy of Right*). These two difficulties, however, do not undermine the legitimacy of our question itself; we would basically be capable of answering it even without Derrida's help.

We must first of all recall that Derrida—unfortunately, without giving further evidence in support of this—concedes that there is a deep affinity between Hegel's dialectic and his own *différance* (those "relations of profound affinity with Hegelian discourse"; *Margins*, 14). The thought of *différance* cannot simply break with Hegel, "but it can operate a kind of infinitesimal and radical displacement of it, whose space I attempt to delineate elsewhere but of which it would be difficult to speak briefly here" (14). It is too bad that Derrida does not name that place he refers to where he responds to our first question; it is more likely that there is no place at which he systematically responded to this. The dialogue with Hegel remains an *ou topos*, a utopia of neostructuralism.

Let us, therefore, give an answer on our own. What is remarkable at first is that both *différance* and autonomous negation are purely formal. I understand "formal" in the same sense as the editors of Saussure's *Cours*, where one can read that language is not a substance but a pure form. And indeed, if Hegel's negation were supported by something substantial, then it would no longer be autonomous; it would then rather be founded on a substratum that, as such, could not be negative. A One that exists only in relation to an Other could only be thought as heter-onomous, not as autonomous.

This also applies by analogy to Derrida's *différance*. In his lecture to the Société Française de philosophie, Derrida explicitly refers in the discussion of *différance* not only to Hegel but also to Saussure: "In a language, in the *system* of language, there are only differences" (*Margins*, 11). That means that *différ-ance*, thus written, does not "*play*" (*joue*) within a relational system of already *given* facts (or positivities); rather, as it were, it determines or produces the posi-tions of these facts in the first place.

> What is written as *différance*, then, will be the playing movement that "produces"—by means of something that is not simply an activity—these differences, these effects of difference. (*Margins*, 11)

If the meaning-producing movement of *différance* (of differentiation, *différencia-tion*; *Margins*, 13) determines the places of possible positivities, it is not also a positivity itself: it should be considered neither as a subject nor as a substance nor as something present nor even as a something at all. In this sense it can be called "autonomous" like Hegel's negation. This, to be sure, has an implication Derrida does not express *in this way*, one that we, however, need to supply here: *différance* makes relations possible, and it cannot exist without an open field of relations between givens; yet it itself does not participate in the play of these rela-tions (otherwise it would be *something*, and not the condition of possibility), and in this sense it has to be taken to be absolutely singular and relationless, like Hegel's negation. In other words, *différance*, although it is the condition of possi-bility for the play of differentiations, is itself, however, still distinguished from this play: it does not exist *without* this play, but it *is* not the play itself; and it does not exist *due to* this play (in the first case it would be a relation, in the second, an effect; both would stand in contradiction to its transcategorical autonomy).

> It is because of *différance* that the movement of signification is possible only if each so-called "present" element, each element appearing on the scene of presence, is related to something other than itself, thereby keeping within itself the mark of the past element, and already letting itself be vitiated by the mark of its relation to the future element, this trace being related no less to what is called the future than to what is called the past, and constituting what is called the present by means of this very relation to what it is not: what it absolutely is not, not even a past or a future as a modified present. An interval must separate the present from what it is not in order for the present to be itself, but this interval that constitutes it as present must, by the same token, divide the present in and of itself, thereby also dividing, along with the pres-ent, everything that is thought on the basis of the present, that is, in our

metaphysical language, every being, and singularly substance or the subject. (*Margins*, 13)

In Hegel's or Henrich's terminology, this could be formulated something like this: singular and absolutely relationless negation realizes itself as a relation, and in this relation it has to do with the Other as though only with itself. Since, however, this relation must be conceived as autonomous, the Other of negation can only be itself again in a different aspect, and therefore it is negatively related to its singularity and relationlessness. In other words, since we are dealing with a *negative* relation of negation to itself, its simplicity and relationlessness are disputed as such: its originary self-presence is denied it. Precisely this is also the case with Derrida's *différance*: it realizes itself in the form of differences—or it produces them—("Differences, thus, are 'produced'—deferred—by *différance*"; *Margins*, 14). But having become a self-referential phenomenon, it simultaneously disputes the illusion of its own alleged unrelatedness. From this point on, it will never find the way back to itself as something that is identical with itself: it is "deferred" without the possibility of finding its way back to pure immediacy. But it is precisely this possibility that Hegel admits of in the instance of his autonomous negation by duplicating the process of negative duplication once more and as such in a third step: the self-negation of the second step produces a result, namely, the absence of negation. And this state reduplicates itself in its Other, in such a way that this Other now can be grasped as the Other of itself, i.e., as its mirror image and *pure* positivity.

Derrida supported his reference to Hegel by means of a passage from Hegel's *Jena Logic* as translated by Alexandre Koyré. Here Hegel speaks of a "different relation" (*differente Beziehung*) in the thought of the present. The present, Hegel writes,

> "is of an absolutely negative simplicity, which absolutely excludes from itself all multiplicity, and, by virtue of this, is absolutely determined; it is not whole or a *quantum* which would be extended in itself (and) which, in itself, also would have an undetermined moment, a diversity which, as indifferent (*gleichgültig*) or exterior in itself, would be related to an other (*auf ein anderes bezöge*), but in this is a relation absolutely different from the simple (*sondern es ist absolut differente Beziehung*)."
> (*Margins*, 13-14)

Derrida proposes to translate *differente Beziehung*, not as Koyré does, as "different Relation," but rather as "differentiating Relation," thus lending it an active sense (*Margins*, 14); and this translation accords with the question, with which we now are familiar, as to whether there is really a difference between this differentiating relation in Hegel and Derrida's *différance*.

Unfortunately, the essay "La Différance" does not enlighten us any further in this regard. All the negative predicates Derrida applies to the term *la différance* – that it is not a subject, not a substance, nothing present, no cause, no agent, and no essence, but also no linguistic system, etc. – all of this is just as true, in the final analysis, for Hegel's autonomous negation as well. And Hegel's *differente Beziehung* even shares with *différance* the fact that all categories of the intelligible world can be derived from it. To be sure, Derrida does not intend to work up a transformation of Hegel's *Logic*; he does, however, state that the phenomena of "meaning" and "consciousness" are determinations or effects of a system: not one of originary presence, however, but one of *différance* (*Margins*, 16). Hegel could thus correspondingly say that *concepts* like Being, indifference, essence, reflection, existence, identity, ground, concept, idea, etc., are effects or determinations of different stages in the self-unfolding of the play of autonomous negation: they are, in other words, simply "concepts," and not transconceptual entities.

In spite of the almost aporetical confession of a deep affinity between *différance* and absolute negation, Derrida continued to maintain that Hegel himself was a representative of metaphysics, i.e., that he remained caught up in the traditional philosophical grammar that in the end definitively gathers together the unlimited play of differences in the thought of an absolute self-present. Yet Derrida knew quite well that Hegel's variant of metaphysics does not take a principal presence or positivity as its point of departure, but rather that it leads up to it. In *Glas*, for example, he writes:

> The being-near-itself of the mind is actively produced through a limit-less negativity. The mind becomes for-itself, near-itself, only by actively denying everything that limits its freedom from the outside. Its essence is active, dynamic negative. (31–32)

In this passage I presume that Derrida recognizes that negation in Hegel's work has the nature of a principle or of autonomy. He also elaborates quite clearly the difference between a mere being-related and a negative being-related.

> A return to itself, of the mind, consciousness is the simple and immediate contrary of itself. It is that of which it is conscious, that is, its opposite. At once active and passive, identifying itself with its own opposite, it separates itself from itself as its object. . . .
> Theoretical consciousness thus has the form of a contradiction, the form of a relation that is related to something that is not related, does not relate (itself) (*Widerspruch einer Beziehung auf ein absolut nicht Bezogenes*), which absolves itself of the relation. (135, 137)

With the condition that autonomous negation in its full unfolding must be conceived as a reflective relation – but as a negative one – a virtual duality of moments is always preserved. Hegel's intention is to demonstrate that these moments will *prove* to be One and the Same, but they are not One and the Same by nature and from the very beginning (their terminal identity is supposed to be a *result*). Yet when "identity differs, as identity" (*Glas*, 189), i.e., when identity itself has to be conceived as a negative reflective relation—that is, as a contradiction in itself—then the following difficulty arises: either the second moment of the self-relation falls away, in which case identity no longer has a specular tain for reflection and can gain no consciousness of itself; or the Other of identity participates in the play, in which case we are dealing with a difference that, even if both moments really had the same content, would not yet necessarily also produce a *consciousness* of this identity. (These are the circular implications of the model of reflection with which we are already familiar, and which will resurface when we set about answering our second question.)

Derrida seems, at least, to be aware of the difficulties that arise when one tries to overcome the state of negative relation with the goal of working toward either a grounding or a final unity, something Hegel, in fact, attempts to accomplish. Those who have read the left column in *Glas*, which is devoted to Hegel, know that Derrida retranslates the difficulty Hegel had with the idea of absolute reconciliation into the terminology of the philosophy of religion. This puts Derrida's reading of Hegel into close proximity with that of Schelling. Hegel had assumed that although in religion the absolute identity of religion with its opposite was "conceived" (*vorgestellt*), it was not yet "comprehended" (*begriffen*). Derrida thus concludes that if absolute identity—due to the fact that it cannot eradicate the trace of nonidentity or of difference—in fact *can*not be adequately comprehended (*begriffen*), then that religion that holds on to difference receives *ex post facto* a kind of legitimation as a speculatively insuperable position.

> The reconciliation between being and the same, between the being itself of being and the being the same of being is produced, to be sure, in revealed religion, but comes forth there as an object for consciousness that *has* this representation, that has it *before* it. The reconciliation is produced and yet it *does not yet take* place, it is *not present*, but only represented or present as remaining before, preceded, to come, present as not-yet-there and not as a presence of the present. . . .
>
> Consciousness represents unity to itself but it is not there. It is because of this, for that matter, that it has the structure of a consciousness [which for Derrida means simultaneously: of a re-flection], and the phenomenology of mind, the science of the experience of consciousness, finds its necessary limit in this representation.
>
> Absolute religion thus still retains negativity; it remains in a state of conflict, scission, worry. . . .
>
> And if one considers that philosophy—*absolute Knowledge*—is the myth of absolute reappropriation, of presence to oneself absolutely absolved and recentered, then the absolute of revealed religion would have a *critical* effect on *absolute Knowledge*. One would have to keep

to the (opposite) shore, that of religion . . ., in order to resist the lure of *absolute Knowledge*. A combinatory hypothesis. (*Glas*, 246–48)

Let me attempt here to summarize the answer to our first question, namely, can Derrida's thought of *différance* actually be distinguished from Hegel's (or Henrich's) idea of autonomous negation? Both Derrida and Hegel conceive of a pure negation that, in a second step, becomes self-referential, but which from that point onward has to be thought of as *relation* (as divided identity). Hegel tries to think of it as a reflective relation, as self-recognition in the Other. Derrida holds fast to the idea that the trace of nonidentity or of differentiality can also not be eradicated in the formula of reflection (which he accepts as such).[9] In the terminology of Hegel's "Doctrine of Essence," one can say that Derrida comes to a halt at that which Hegel calls "difference" and does not proceed onward to that self-sublation that takes place in "contradiction." In the absolute contradiction, according to Hegel's famous words, difference (in the aspect of opposition) is eliminated, it "falls to the ground" (*zu Grunde gehen*); i.e., it gives way to the category of the "ground."[10] Unfortunately, Derrida has not interpreted this chapter in "The Doctrine of Essence." He has, however, repeatedly alluded to it, as for example in *Glas*, where he paraphrases Hegel's statement with the following words:

This opposition, like opposition in general, will have been at once the manifestation of difference (and consequently of this remainder of time where the void of signification steps aside) *and* the process of its effacement or of its reappropriation. As soon as difference is determined, it is determined in opposition, it is manifested, to be sure, but its manifestation is at the same time (it is the time of the same as effacement of the remainder of time in the itself [*Selbst*]) a reduction of difference, of the remainder, of the step aside. It is the thesis. (*Glas*, 263)

A further allusion can be found in *La Dissémination*, banished to a footnote.

The movement by which Hegel determines difference as contradiction ("Der Unterschied überhaupt ist schon der Widerspruch *an sich*," *The Science of Logic* II, chap. 2) is designed precisely to make possible the ultimate (onto-theo-teleo-logical) sublation [la relève] of difference. *Différance*—which is thus by no means dialectical contradiction in this Hegelian sense—marks the critical limit of the idealizing powers of relief [la relève] wherever they are able, directly or indirectly, to operate. Différance *inscribes* contradiction, or rather, since it remains irreducibly differentiating and disseminating, contradiction*s*. In marking the "productive" (in the sense of general economy and in accordance with the loss of presence) and differentiating movement, the *economic* "concept" of differance does not reduce all contradictions to the homogeneity of a single model. It is the opposite that is likely to happen when Hegel makes difference into a moment within general contradiction. The latter is always ontotheological in its foundation. As is the reduction of the complex general economy of differance to difference. (Belated residual note for a postface.) (*Diss*, 6–7)

This footnote is an interesting piece of evidence, even if it presents itself as purely thetic and makes no effort to prove a point. It is too bad that so many important observations in Derrida's work have the character of such *notes résiduelles et attardées*, which, although he systematically applies them in appropriate contexts, are basically not supported on the basis of arguments. In any case, we can take as one difference between Hegel and Derrida (among many others, of course) the fact that the latter does not believe that the moments that dispute each other in "contradiction" "bring each other to the ground" (*richten sich zugrunde*) in order to become transparent for the pure unity of the ground; rather, Derrida holds on to the thought of an infinite chain of negations which are not sublated in any finite term because their signification is "being other than . . ." and not the contradictory opposition.

A second question remains that, in philological terms, is even more difficult to answer than the first. But if we want to find out whether "autonomous negation" or "autonomous difference" can really make intelligible what we understand as "self-consciousness," then we must put this question not simply to Hegel or Derrida but also to ourselves: *we* want to know about this, and we therefore do not necessarily need to support our observations on the basis of texts.

This is the place to elaborate on a doubt that has accompanied our lectures for quite some time now. I first want to direct it to Hegel, although it applies in modified form just as well to Derrida and, as we will see, to Lacan also. Let me first phrase my doubt in the form of a question: does the successful proof of the identity between the elements of the relation already guarantee that we are dealing with a *cognizant* self-relation? In other words, does self-identification imply *consciousness* of the identity of the identified related elements?

This question is directed at the underlying model used to explain self-consciousness, namely, at the model of reflection. To be sure, Derrida rejects this model, the *présence-à-soi*. Nevertheless, he knows of no other one, and this means that he too remains negatively connected to the model of reflection as the only possibility of thinking of self-consciousness.

Translated literally, the word reflection means "remirroring" (*Widerspiegelung*). If autonomous negation duplicates itself in a final step and faces itself in the totality of its structure, then one can justifiably say that it mirrors itself in itself. Hegel expresses this with the term "intro-Reflection" (an expression Sartre translates as *le jeu reflet-reflétant*). But something that mirrors itself in itself by no means has to have consciousness of the sameness of the two related elements. A tree that mirrors itself in a calm forest lake certainly constitutes a case of reflection without any *knowledge* of the sameness of what is mirrored and what is mirroring; even in the case of the famous myth of Narcissus one can doubt whether Narcissus *knows* that it is *he* whose image smiles lovingly up at him from the water. For nothing about the image betrays that it is the same as the original. Such a consciousness of identity falls outside of the play between reflected and reflecting: if it occurs, it would be the result of a consciousness that is not one with the reflection. For reflection articulates an insuperable duality, whereas identification unifies. In order to be able to identify the two moments of reflection themselves *during* the play of their division, one would have to have a criterion that transcends the limits of the model of reflection. If we apply this to the twice-duplicated negation in Hegel – to what in the "Doctrine of Essence" he calls "positing reflection" – we can say that, although for him the identity of negation and its Other (the absence of negation) is derived, this is not true for reflection itself. But only a reflection that simultaneously implies *consciousness* of the identity of its related elements would be a case of a *cognizant* self-reflection.

It was Schelling who first systematically raised this objection to Hegel's attempt at sublating allegedly heteronomous "Being" into the autonomous play of "reflection." As I have shown elsewhere in considerable detail, Schelling claimed that Hegel's attempt at founding self-consciousness as the result of a reflection does not have at its disposal any criterion for the *knowledge* (*Gewusstsein*) of the identity of the related elements; rather it simply presupposes this identity. Being, conceived as relation *only* to itself, but nevertheless as relation, is identified with another form of relation (that of reflection), whereby this second relation reveals itself to be the mere unfolding of the self-relation that was implicitly presupposed in Being. According to Schelling, however, this argumentative step is not only circular; it does not even prove what Hegel wants to prove, namely, that the identity of Being and essence, of identity and difference, can be *known*.

Let me try to give a highly compact abstract of Schelling's second criticism. The reduction of identical Being to reflection (conceived as duplication of self-relating negation) is, according to Schelling, not only circular; on top of this it believes – incorrectly – that the characteristic feature of the self constitutes itself in the play of two reflexes. In fact, as Schelling already taught in 1804 (that is, several years before the appearance of Hegel's *Phenomenology of Mind*), the synthesis of self-knowledge cannot be grasped as the real ground for our knowledge of the I: neither of the related elements, nor even the concept of relation-as-a-whole, exhibits the trait of being the same as their Other, or the same as that which is grasped by them. This doubt persists regardless of whether one concedes that consciousness of the self only exists in the unity of the same thought in which the relation also carries on its play. As we know, that was Hegel's view, and Schelling does not dispute it. What he claims is simply that two negations related to one another (or the self-relation *of* negation) are the necessary, but not the sufficient condition for founding the existential experience of the *cogito sum*. Although two reflexes that negate each other may very well be able to *de*ny each other's autonomous and independent Being, they are capable of instituting neither the consciousness of the sameness of the related elements nor the consciousness of its indubitable Being. However, since this consciousness of an absolute positivity and identity does exist, Schelling concludes that it must derive from an experience that is prior to the mirror play of negations and that grounds it *in its Being* (see *SW*, I/4, 358; I/6, 185). Even the subsistence of negation *as* negation is already something that cannot be conceived as the effect of negation: existence is not an implication of its concept. If one claims that negation is the ground of a resultant Being (for it does indeed possess, in the possibility of its duplication, the capacity of its self-sublation for the benefit of something positive), then one simultaneously has to keep in mind that it is not already transformed into the generating force of Being simply by virtue of this capacity; it is rather only transformed into the ideal ground of Being. This actually does not say any more than this: there is no *concept* of Being outside the one that appears on the horizon of a self-sublation of reflection. This in turn only means that the doubly reflective negation can retreat for the benefit of Being and thereby allow Being *to appear* (thus it is the ground for the *appearance* of Being); but this also means that neither its own Being, nor the Being of that which it negates, is affirmed. This is both immediately and analytically intelligible: negation can destroy (even itself), but it cannot create. *If* it affirms a Being in its play (for example, its own Being), then by this very affirmation it is granted that we are dealing with something more and other than with an immanent characteristic of negation itself. One could call this, following Sartre, the "ontological proof" of reflection (*EN*, 27ff.). There are several conclusions that can be drawn from it. First of all, one can conclude that Being is prior to consciousness and that this insight is sealed *in the very* failure of the immanent attempt of autonomous self-foundation. Second, one can conclude (and this, of course, is closely related to the first conclusion), that while essence (or reflection) is the knowledge ground of Being (and also of *its* own Being), it is yet not its real ground. *As soon as* it (essence) is, it *is* "unprethinkingly being." That means that, in order simply to fulfill the formal-ontological condition of Being — *essence*, it has previously to *be*. Sartre characterized this state of affairs with the neologism *être été*. With this he means that conceptual being — essence — is supported (carried) in its Being by transreflective Being, since in itself it is actually nonautonomous. Without standing on the firm ground of a Being that is *not* reflection, it would necessarily dissolve into nothingness. That is the meaning of Schelling's notion of a "negative philosophy"; it is characterized by a self-forgetting speculation that absolves itself from its own existing by reducing the "absolutely transcendent Being" to a determination of essence (*Wesensbestimmung*).

All of this is quite difficult to understand and formulate. Nevertheless, we cannot spare ourselves the effort of becoming conscious of the interwovenness of Schelling's two objections. The fact that he introduces the notion of a "transcendent Being" is for Schelling an implicit consequence of the failure of the model of reflection. This perhaps becomes apparent in the following parallel: just as reflection must be grounded in a prereflective and nonrelational familiarity with itself, the synthesis of semblance and resemblance (*Schein und Widerschein*) must be grounded in a presynthetic identity that has to be conceived as nonrelational "Being." However, both prereflective self-consciousness and the Being to which reflection appeals *transgress* the limits of what Lacan calls the *captation narcissique du soi* and open up the theory of self-consciousness for an Other that is no longer, as in Hegel, the Other of itself.

Lecture 18

Our lectures on neostructuralism now stand at the threshold of the question that I consider to be the most decisive one, namely, how neostructuralism explains the phenomenon of subjectivity or how it deconstructs traditional models of subjectivity. One cannot criticize a theory without proving either the nonexistence of the phenomenon to which this theory refers, or the incorrectness of its argumentation with regard to this phenomenon. As to the first of these, the nonexistence of subjectivity designates an exaggeratedly radical position, one William James takes in his provocative essay "Does 'Consciousness' Exist?,"[1] but one that is not taken by Derrida. We saw on the contrary that Derrida does not dispute the phenomenon of self-consciousness, but rather that he wants to explain it in another way than in the language and with the means of modern metaphysics; he describes it as an "effect" of differential relations between the elements of an unlimited play of "marks."

That is nothing new to us. To understand better what Derrida wants to say with this programmatic formula, we picked up an initiative to which Derrida himself encourages us: we tried to discover by means of comparison whether what Derrida calls *différance* is really so different from the (active) "differentiating relation" Hegel proposes in an early version of his *Logic*.

We saw that there is indeed something like a "deep affinity" between these two positions. We made the observation earlier that when Derrida talks about differentiality he uses the term "negation" in the sense of "being other than . . ." That means that each term is what it is by virtue of a differing reference to all other terms. Since this reference leads on into infinity (there is no a priori limit of the differentiating reference to others), there is no definitive identity of a term with itself, and thus there is also no definitive identity of the self with itself.

For Hegel's idea of autonomous negation this last consequence does not hold. To negate, for him, means not only "to distinguish" but also "to sublate." If one applies it to itself, negation has the possibility of canceling itself and thus producing the Other of negation, namely, something positive. In a final intensification of his "basic operation with negation," Hegel tries to show about this Other of negation that it can simultaneously be understood as the Other of negation itself, and thus as identical with it. Derrida does not go along with this speculative conclusion. He stands fast, to put it in Hegelian terms, at the logic of difference and does not advance further to the consequences of what Hegel calls the logic of contradiction, in which the related elements bring each other "to the ground" (*zugrunderichten*) in order to give way to the unity of their "grounding identity."

But we not only compared Hegel's and Derrida's positions; rather we put to both the question of whether they can theoretically explain to us the everyday experience of our Being familiar with ourselves. We saw that Hegel believes that the *knowledge* of this identity was already guaranteed with the proof of the identity of self-referential negation with its Other. This is, however, not the case, or, at least, only at the price of a *petitio principii*. Reflection can recognize as identical to itself only that whose identity it already previously has known. This prior familiarity with itself cannot, however, be the work of autonomous reflection itself, for all reflection is relative; i.e., it is the relation of *two* to each other, and these two are thus to this extent not simply *one*. In other words, the relation of two with each other never explains their identity in the form of something indubitably evident, unless this identity was known previously and is only recognized in the play of reflected-reflecting.

When we talk about self-consciousness, it is not enough to say that in it an identity of two elements related to each other takes place. One also has to be able to demonstrate that and how these two can *know* each other as one and the same; and that is precisely what Hegel's philosophy of reflection cannot do.

One could conclude from this that Derrida has good reasons for not subscribing to this theory. But this is not necessarily the case. For although Derrida rejects the consequences of Hegel's "reconciliation," he still does not dispute that self-consciousness must fundamentally be conceived according to the model of reflection. The difference between him and Hegel in this instance is merely that Hegel believes that reflection leads to the knowledge of a self that is identical with itself, whereas Derrida believes that reflection leads to the knowledge of a self that is not identical with itself. Hence both consider the relation we have in mind when we use the reflexive pronoun "itself" to be a fundamental and insurmountable state of affairs for our notion of the "I" or of "self-consciousness."

But precisely this can be disputed. With regard to Hegel I have already sketched the reasons. Against Derrida I would object that if one sought to make his idea consistent, one would necessarily fall into the absurdity of denying the subsistence of something like familiarity with ourselves. But that would not only be contradictory to what he himself gives as his intention (namely, wanting only to explain self-consciousness *differently* than is done by metaphysics); it would ultimately come down to a denial of the fact that we can associate a meaning with the terms "the self," "consciousness," and "the I" in our everyday language. The functioning of language itself contradicts this.

But let's look a little closer at Derrida's conclusion. Formulated in its most extreme, it states that "self-consciousness" is an effect of differential relations between marks of an unlimited "structure." This statement presupposes that what metaphysics calls consciousness occurs only when something else is also taking place, namely, a relation between a (limited) arbitrarily large set of data (*Gegebenheiten*) differing from one another. Without at least two things or marks and (in the language of the late Saussure) *aposèmes* differing from each other, consciousness (and self-consciousness) does not factually occur.

If one really wants to explain consciousness on the basis of the autonomous play of differences as such, one has to avoid predetermining for this relation something like an originary familiarity of consciousness with itself, which is outside of this play.[2] And Derrida, in fact, avoids exactly this. Second, one would have to avoid attributing the characteristic "conscious" to any states of affairs (or *marques*, or, in Lacan's terminology, *signifiants*) *before* they have been brought into relation to each other (since consciousness is supposed to be a feature, or, to be more correct, an effect of their being related).

As far as this last point is concerned, there is no way of knowing which specific characteristic in the field of a relational structure is supposed to make it possible for me to distinguish conscious relations from unconscious relations (which would lead to the conclusion that there are no unconscious relations: a conclusion that would radically contradict Derrida's notion of a "structural unconscious"). If one can imagine, however, that there are relations between the elements of structure, but that there is not necessarily also consciousness of relations, then the relation of Being other than . . . is "not an appropriate candidate for the description or definition of consciousness."[3] This objection reproduces, *mutatis mutandis*, the objection Schelling directed at Hegel, namely, that nothing in the play of the mutually related elements mediates the information that it is a matter of the *same* elements. In other words, two or more elements related to each other reveal a great deal, but they do not reveal that they are identical to each other and, furthermore, that they are aware of this.

If this negative conclusion is compelling, then the indubitable fact of our familiarity with ourselves has to be explained differently. And this by no means is accomplished, as the overzealous defenders of neostructuralism always assume to be the case for their opponents, by reintroducing a predifferential or presemiological self-consciousness. On the contrary, we already saw that, for example, an idealist philosopher like Schleiermacher, for whom self-consciousness was no principle, but certainly a cardinal theme, a touchstone, so to speak, for the truth of philosophizing, by no means denies that self-consciousness, as he puts it, is "somehow, but regardless of how, determined." This determination can, indeed wants to be understood as a significant imprint, as a *marque non-présente et différentielle*. The decisive difference between Schleiermacher's and Derrida's explanation of consciousness is that the latter is finally forced to sacrifice the phenomenon—certainly, against his own will—whereas the former is able to mediate the thought of our familiarity with ourselves with the other (thought) of the dependency of the self on linguistic structure.

This last possibility in fact exists, if one recalls what I have indicated in earlier contexts, namely, that there are (at least) *two* forms of dependence, and thus, correspondingly, two forms of grounding: dependences of certain states of affairs on thoughts, and dependences of certain states of affairs on other states of affairs. The former is called in the language of metaphysics ideal ground or knowledge ground; the latter is called real ground or Being ground (*rationes cognoscendi versus rationes essendi*).

Now the dependence of consciousness on the differential relations between marks is in no way a real dependence, or, expressed differently, a dependence of consciousness with regard to its reality. Even if the structuralists or the neo-structuralists wanted to appeal in this instance to Saussure, they would not find support for this view even in the official version of the *Cours*. Saussure, rather, rigorously differentiated the oppositive relations, which separate signs from each other and give them their profile, from the relations that connect the material sound and consciousness (meaning) *in* the sign synthesis. According to Saussure there are relations of the type *simile-simile* (e.g., between different phonemes, words, signs, or grammatical categories), and relations of the type *simile-dissimile* (these are the relations between words and ideas) (*CGL*, 115–16). Now Saussure did not propose that what we can call the *semiological synthesis* (i.e., the synthesis of *image acoustique* and *idée*) comes into being exclusively by means of the differential relations between sounds. Differential articulation is no less, but also no more, than a necessary prerequisite for semiological synthesis, but not already its positive Being ground. Saussure's second lecture is even clearer on this point than the version that was edited by Bally and Sechehaye. There he says (and I am blending several passages into one quote):

> The vocal sound . . . is the instrument of thought . . . without existing for itself, independently of thought. . . . The vocal sound is not a word except to the exact, constant extent that a meaning is attached to it. . . .
> On the contrary it is signification which delimits [into units] the words in the spoken mass. . . . The unit does not pre-exist. Significa-

tion is what creates it. The units are not there to receive a signification. (Clearly then, it is meaning that creates the unit.)

The sound, by itself, does not produce significance; we are faced with incorporeal entities. . . .

In itself, [the Greek expression] λεγόμεϑα signifies nothing. . . .

Thought is what delimits units; sound itself does not delimit them in advance: there is always a relation with thought, . . . it is always a matter of the cutting out that thought does in the spoken mass which is amorphous. . . .

Difference is what makes things meaningful, and signification is what creates differences, too. (*CFS*, 15 [1957], 7–8, 41–42, 28, 82, 68, 76)

What all these passages have in common is that they deny a direct causality between differentiality and meaning: meaning is not simply the "effect" of differential relations between *sons*. It is rather the other way round: only by means of an *interpretation*, whose initiator is thought (consciousness, the individual), does an oppositive structure of significants become discourse (*parole*), i.e., something meaningful and conscious. In this sense Saussure can also say that it is interpretation which posits the distinction of units (*CFS*, 15 [1957], 89; cf. 92). For him this follows from the difference between the relations of the type *simile-simile* and those of the type *simile-dissimile*; and while the latter type presupposes the former, it cannot, however, simply be deduced from it.

If we go back to the traditional distinction between real ground and ideal ground, then we could say that the differential relation between the *marques* of structure is not the real ground of the subsistence of consciousness, but rather only the ideal ground of its *determination* (or, to be more precise, of the consciousness of the *determination* of states of affairs). Picking up another traditional distinction, one can also express this by saying that relationality/differentiality is indeed a necessary but by no means a sufficient condition for the existence of consciousness (self-consciousness included).

I would like to make this a little more concrete. It is in fact true (and even a commonplace of late idealist and romantic philosophy) that consciousness (including self-consciousness) is not the author of itself, but rather that it experiences itself as inescapably thrown into the determination of being a self. To that extent it is not master of itself. Indeed, it presupposes, aside from its mere Being, in addition a series of opposites without which it would not be able to determine and grasp itself as that *which* it is. And what could this series of opposites be other than that which the structuralists call structure (of a language, of a discourse, of a tradition, etc.)? But this dependence on structure is not real; rather it is ideal. The dependence of any conceivable determination on a prior *Being* is real. But consciousness as the *knowing* subject is, in the final analysis, dependent on structure. It simply cannot concretize itself *without* referring to an overriding system of relations between marks; but these relations do not simply *produce* consciousness, they serve exclusively its ideal self-determination. This process can by no means be characterized as pure suffering on the side of the subject. One cannot suffer under meanings in the same sense as one suffers under strokes of fortune or material determinations. Significations are beings of a sort that occur only when the marks of the relational structure have previously been interpreted. Interpretation is not a natural occurrence, but rather an act of culture. Cultures determine subjects in terms of motivation: they provide subjects with a system of already interpreted signs, but they never determine fully the sense in which the subject uses them (i.e., interprets or reinterprets them). In other words, the subject is passive and dependent only to the extent that it cannot choose that already interpreted system of marks in which it has to take up its cultural and social identification. But it is free to the extent that it lends meaning to, and brings into expression, the pregiven signs, which, indeed, are nothing other than an ensemble of appeals for our interpretation.

We can therefore agree with Derrida when he disputes that the self is a timeless self-presence. We can also follow him when he says that the differential structure divides the self from itself, without allowing him any return to a predifferential unity. And we can even accept, against Hegel, that under these circumstances no structure is conceivable that exhausts, subdues, and collects its "effects of meaning" in an ultimately valid and terminal concept.

We will take exception only to the simple confusion of the phenomenon of the self with the differentiality of the system. But this conclusion is entirely unneccessary, even if it is a matter of grounding the phenomenon of the nonclosability of structure. For this it is completely sufficient to show that consciousness as such is a being that in its Being is concerned about its Being, as Heidegger says. On the basis of pregiven "symbolic orders" that it did not choose, it transgresses these orders *by virtue of its essential nonidentity with itself.* This nonidentity with itself forces the subject to *interpret* its Being: since it *is* not simply that which is given to it through tradition (through structure), it has to produce its *meaning* by means of a projection into the future. If it were to coincide with structure, it would be identical with it and thus also identical with itself, something Derrida refuses to accept. The only possibility of escaping identification with the pregiven system of signs results from the fact that this system of signs unfolds its meaning only under the condition of an interpretation: viewed as a pure product of nature, every symbolic order remains mute and unarticulated. In other words, signs are hypotheses; they unfold their meaning only for such a being that transgresses their materiality in a projection from which sounds, tones, and graphic traces can be identified as signifiers. It is not sufficient, as we saw, that these signifiers are negatively related to each other: that is also the case for the things in nature, and this is not enough to allow them to gain a human meaning. We simply cannot attribute meaning to any state of affairs *solely* on the basis of its being differentially related to other states of affairs. First of all, the category "meaning" could only mean meaning-for-a-*consciousness* (Lacan, for example, concedes this when he says: "since nothing is represented only for"; *E*, 316); no "signifier" could "signify" solely on the basis of itself, as an object of nature in relation to other objects of nature.[4] Second, the idea of an autonomously conceived differentiality simply does not explain the subsistence of consciousness *for* which signifiers can have a meaning. This certainly does not yet positively describe what self-consciousness is; however, it seems to me to be demonstrated that self-consciousness can justifiably be attributed a manner of reality, and that it can successfully defend its reality against the neostructuralist attempt to let it dissolve (or rather, disappear) in the gap of *différance*.

Let's take a closer look at the thesis that consciousness is not identical with itself. As a being that in its Being relates interpretively to its Being, it is ekstatically always beyond itself. But the "itself" beyond which it is, is first and foremost its structural condition: the pregiven framework of an already interpreted "world" (in Heidegger's language) or of a "symbolic order" (to speak with Lacan). It is separated from this presupposition insofar as it continuously determines anew the meaning of its past by projecting itself onto its future; it accomplishes this in such a way that it never coincides with a specific state of its interpretation. This ekstatic nonidentical Being of the self is even the presupposition for the structurality of structure; for in order not only to constitute an ensemble of *natural* differences, structure requires a transgressing interpretation from which the Being of the sign substances, which in itself is meaningless, is "cleared" and "disclosed" in terms of its (*cultural*, or, if you will, symbolic) value. Now it is completely impossible to determine this meaning, about which the future of the projection will decide, on the basis of its past: the past only then attains its symbolic (i.e., its signifying) quality when it is transgressed. To this extent there is no determinism of structure. The subjective projections by means of which the individuals endowed with the possibility for meaning transgress their having become Being cannot be deduced from the concept of the structure pregiven to them; this is the case because it is *they* (the individuals) who first invent a concept for the whole whose elements they simultaneously are. In other words, the significance of the whole exists nowhere else than in the consciousnesses of the individuals who internalize the pregiven universal in each instance in a particular and singular manner, and reexternalize it again to the general by means of their deeds. This has two implications: first, the concept of the universal (or of structure) is separated from itself by the intervention of an individual, i.e., it loses its semantic and normative identity (in other words, a singular interpretation separates its universality from itself; by the same token, it simultaneously separates the individual from itself, at least to the extent that it in its Being is an element of structure); second, the concept of the universal exists not only in one but in uncontrollably many interpretations (in as many as there are individuals within a community); each one of these interpretations can only subsume another one in the form of a hermeneutic "divination," and each divination carries an index of uncontrollability: none attains the status of an objective, self-identical knowledge.

But, you will probably object, didn't we just abandon the concept of self-consciousness after all? What about the *unity of subjectivity* that has to identify its past by means of a circular movement from its future and that therefore cannot really identify it? Derrida actually reproached the Heidegger of *Being and Time* with half-heartedness for wanting to rescue a sort of circular (i.e., dialectical) *unity* for the ekstatic self ("Ousia and Grammé: Note on a Note from *Being and Time*").

> Can this movement—which one must not hasten to denounce as useless restatement, and which has something essential to do with the movement of thought—be distinguished both from the Hegelian circle of metaphysics or ontotheology, and from that circle into which, Heidegger tells us so often, we must learn to enter *in a certain way*? (*Margins*, 60)[5]

Heidegger, in fact, arrived at his thesis about the circular unity of subjectivity (he calls it *Dasein*) only because he held on to—under modified circumstances, of course—the model of reflection for self-consciousness: according to him, the self does not possess any prior familiarity with itself; it is first of all without any content, and it must be shown *what* it is by that in the direction of which it is projecting itself. Heidegger calls this, as we know, the "relucency" that the self experiences from the ekstatically projected thing. We also recall that Sartre has already objected to this theory (which Derrida will even outdo by denying the possibility of reidentification of the ekstatic self with itself) with the argument that one cannot derive the function of consciousness and self-consciousness from the structure of the ekstatic projection or understanding, except at the price of its self-presupposition:

> We cannot first suppress the dimension "consciousness," not even if it is in order to reestablish it subsequently. Understanding has meaning only if it is consciousness of understanding. (*BN*, 85)

We have gathered additional evidence that supports this objection from the observation that the form of a negative referentiality of marks to each other cannot fundamentally illuminate the function of consciousness because ekstasis or differentiality provides only necessary but no positive conditions for self-Being.

And yet one can indeed assume a prereflective familiarity of consciousness with itself without becoming entangled in comparable circles (like Hegel and Heidegger), and without denying the nonidentity of reflection with itself. In order to accomplish this, one only has to understand that everything *of which* consciousness consists does not itself fall under the immanence of consciousness. It is simply a false explanatory model that conceives self-consciousness as a case of reflection, i.e., as the explicit relation of a consciousness to itself as its own object. If one abandons this self-contradictory and circular idea, then one can see that what we called the nonidentity of the self is only grounded in its ekstatic structure of projection, and by no means in an absence of familiarity with itself. Ekstatically related to the object of its projections, the subject never coincides absolutely with its Being (i.e., with its having become Being); but it certainly has a consciousness of itself *as* a projection that does not coincide with itself. How else would the philosopher be able to express this sentence meaningfully? Identity and nonidentity, furthermore, are relational concepts. If they are to be employed in a nontrivial manner, then something that is not self-understood has to be able to be brought to experience by means of an act of identification or of nonidentification. In this sense it would be totally incorrect to say (and Wittgenstein was completely correct in this) that in the case of self-consciousness we are dealing with the action of an identification. The self that is familiar with itself does not accomplish any self-identification; it *is* familar to itself even before it projects itself onto contents in the light of which it *interprets* its own (as it were, objective) Being. In other words, identification and discrimination presuppose consciousness, yet they are not able and do not want to produce it. "The familiarity of consciousness with itself," Dieter Henrich writes, "can never be understood as the result of an activity."[6] Consciousness can be understood neither as "effect" of differential relations between marks nor as effect of the work of identification: consciousness always already exists when such actions are initiated. In short, self-consciousness is not a phenomenon to which the categories of identity and difference could meaningfully be applied. These categories only first take hold in the field of the ekstatic self-relating of self-consciousness to *something*, be it the object of its own projection directed into the future, or a state of affairs of the world, or even itself as the result of a reflective self-thematization that always already presupposes difference and temporal distance.

We have put numerous critical questions to Derrida regarding his attempt at a deconstruction of the concepts of subjectivity and self-consciousness. We have concerned ourselves primarily with Derrida's work because it puts subjectivity into question on a philosophical level, and in this sense it stands almost entirely alone within the framework of neostructuralism. That, of course, does not mean that other authors have not also made significant contributions to the theme of the subject and self-consciousness. I am thinking above all of Jacques Lacan, in whose work "subjectivity"—in the distinction between a veritable and a narcissistic subjectivity—plays a particularly important role. As a psychoanalyst and psychiatrist Lacan would presumably be somewhat displeased if we were to make him into a philosopher and examine his writings exclusively from the point of view of the epistemological and speculative issues they address. On the other hand, it cannot be denied that neither Derrida's nor Deleuze's nor even Foucault's views about the subject would have been possible without the fundamental impulses derived from Lacan's *Écrits*, impulses they picked up on and altered, each in his own way, to be sure, and often enough in spirited contradiction to the master. The predecessorship of Lacan can be explained to a large extent simply by the fact that an entire generation separates his biography and intellectual growth from those of his younger colleagues and critics. Lacan was born in 1901 (i.e., exactly a year after Gadamer and four years before Sartre). He had already formulated some of his essential ideas in the thirties, i.e., long before the advent of a human-scientific structuralism in France. His most essential and, in terms of their effective-historical reception, most influential texts, however, were written in the fifties and the first half of the sixties. Their appearance thus still predates the year 1968, which we, in a coarsely schematic fashion, marked as the beginning of the actual neostructuralist movement. Taking Lacan into consideration, we might now feel ourselves forced to move this date of inception ahead somewhat, for I believe I will be able to show in what follows that neostructuralism's essential objections to the unity of meaning, system, and subjectivity are outlined (and, often enough, even thoroughly developed) in his texts. Yet it is not difficult to understand why these texts only realize their true effect in the era of neostructuralism: for what Lacan thought always stood in conflict with the classical formation of a taxonomical structuralism.

There is no single essay or set of lectures by Lacan that would sum up the essence of his teaching. Of course, that is just as true for the other authors we are dealing with here. But the basic ideas of Derrida, Deleuze, Foucault, or Lyotard can be distilled much more easily than is the case with Lacan out of an examination of just a few of their works. We can summarize his writings—let's be more cautious and say: his utterances—in a preliminary way by characterizing them as a play of cross-references and allusions whose pertinence can be verified either philologically or through logical argumentation in only a very few cases. Anyone who seeks to get some idea of the implicit unity of Lacan's thought assumes an adventurous interpretive responsibility that, to be sure, can also be called exciting. Lacan's work has just as often served as a thought quarry from which babblers and delirious ravers mine their unconnected fantasies, as it has served as the basis for the primarily interdependent interpretations that comprise the few serious attempts to understand Lacan's fundamental ideas. To understand Lacan means to reformulate him: it means to continue on with what he himself did with those texts on which his work is supported. This maxim is all the more true since Lacan's *écriture* often, if not most of the time, does not so much actually want to clarify the effects of the (Freudian) unconscious, as it wants to represent these effects linguistically and stylistically. Thus his interpreter often steps into traps or snares whose manifest meaning conceals a deeper nonmeaning. (I don't want to deny that the opposite of this also occurs.) On the other hand, it is precisely the elusiveness of Lacan's *Écrits* that presents a special challenge to the interpreter whose conviction about the universality and inescapability of "understanding" will not allow circumvention of any texts. And Lacan, after all, did not conceive his texts as absolute linguistic works of art, but, as he himself asserted again and again, first and foremost as constructive interpretations of the effects and the mechanism of the unconscious. In this sense, the *Écrits* do indeed practice a form of practical hermeneutics with which we must now make ourselves familiar in a general way. In other words, if we fail initially to characterize in principle both the mode of Lacan's *écriture* and the object of his theory, we will have great difficulty in assessing his utterances on that matter that interests us the most, namely, on subjectivity and self-consciousness.

First of all, we should not overlook the fact that it is rather questionable to speak of Lacan's hermeneutics. This is true not only because his work, in spite of all the incursions it never tires of making into neighboring disciplines like philosophy and literary theory, grew completely out of his interest in psychoanalysis; it is also true because his work addresses a series of rather discomforting questions to the notions of "understanding" and "knowing." First of all, there is the question (which we will find again in the neostructuralists) as to whether hermeneutics is not a procedure that aims at moving beyond the expressions (of a text or a discourse) to arrive at their meaning. Hermeneutics, Lacan objects, deals with the business of semantics: it wants to know *what* the text says and *of what* it is speaking. In a certain sense, it wants to get *behind the text* or press on into a sphere beyond the text, where it presumes it can find—not in Gadamer, to be sure, but perhaps in Ricoeur—something like a kernel of truth and unequivocality. This, however, is not at all what Lacan seeks to accomplish. What he himself calls "truth" would rather consist in dissolving an alleged kernel of unequivocality and clarity, returning it to the obscurity from whence it stepped forward as a product of hermeneutical misunderstanding.

What is it, we might then ask, that one can search for in a text if not for its meaning? Perhaps Lacan would answer that one can investigate the *textuality* of the text itself, the manner of its interwovenness, insofar as it and only it is the prerequisite for the *effets de sens*. Certainly, there is something like a *meaning* of the text (Lacan is far from denying this), but for him meaning is an "effect"; i.e., it is nothing originary and it does not stand for any principle.

Now one does not have to imagine the relationship of the text to that which it produces (i.e., to "meaning") as an interaction of two levels of structure, in the sense of something like a deep structure that is prior to or founds the actually spoken surface utterances. Lacan does not believe that there are two languages, the unconscious and the conscious. He rather believes that there is only one, but that this one—our everyday language—carries the traces of the unconscious precisely in its normality. And it is here that the analyst can track them down.

That actually sounds, one might say, like a recasting of the classical hermeneutical procedure into a psychoanalytic form. And, in fact, we can find the expression "interpretation" in Lacan; and it occurs with its affimative and, so to speak, conventional meaning when he says:

> Interpretation is not open to all meanings. It is not just any interpreta-
> tion. It is a significant interpretation, one that must not be missed. This
> does not mean that it is not this signification that is essential to the ad-
> vent of the subject. What is essential is that he should see, beyond this
> signification, to what signifier—to what irreducible, traumatic non-
> meaning—he is, as a subject, subjected.[7]

This passage is a good example for the ambiguity in the use of the word "interpretation" that is characteristic of Lacan. On the one hand, he does not refrain from
portraying himself as an interpreter (and he even adds that there is a minimal
delimitation of nonsense in a text: "the effect of interpretation is to isolate in the
subject a kernel, a *kern*, to use Freud's own term, of *non-sense*").[8] On the other
hand, he insists that the assertion of a semantic kernel in discourse does not stand
in the service of the theory of an autonomous subject that projects its meaning:
the subject and its meaning are "effects" of what he calls the *signifiant*.

Nonetheless, one can still designate Lacan's work as a "hermeneutics." The
reference to Freud, who already understood his *Interpretation of Dreams* in much
this sense, confirms this, and the famous hermeneutical study on Freud by Paul
Ricoeur has the appropriate title *De l'interprétation: Essai sur Freud.*[9] Freud himself stated very clearly what, in his view, is the nature of analytical interpreting.
The task of interpretation is to uncover the latent dream idea within the manifest
dream content. To uncover means to raise to consciousness. The content of a
drive or a wish that is successfully made conscious no longer can be effective as
an unconscious obsession; the subject can now get hold of it.

Psychoanalytic work has often been characterized in German-speaking countries with such a formula or a similar one. In particular the psychoanalytic hermeneutics of the second Frankfurt School tended to interpret this as though it
were a matter of bringing a "systematically distorted" discourse back under control, i.e., of cleansing it of its irrational dross and returning it to the mastery of
a rational, and thus responsible, subject.

There is a famous phrase from the thirty-first lecture of Freud's *New Introductory Lectures on Psycho-Analysis*: "Where id was, there ego shall be."[10] Ricoeur,
Lorenzer, and Habermas, for example, believe that they can base themselves on
this statement when they propose the following interpretation: where once unconsciously oppressive obligations were in power, whose intolerability drove
certain ideational complexes (*Vorstellungskomplexe*) out of the economy of the
personality, the self-conscious I is now to be in charge again. This is basically
in line with the idealist tradition. Already Hegel's *Phenomenology of Mind* described historical process as a battle in which self-consciousness wins out in the
end by understanding everything that came before as its own, still untransparent

content. History is the history of self-consciousness as it comes to itself out of the unconscious. It follows from this that the unconscious is not essentially unconscious, but rather that in its essence, i.e., in its truth, it is identical with consciousness. The unconscious is thus an unpenetrated appearance that attaches itself to consciousness in the condition of its immediacy, and which discloses itself *as* mere appearance over the course of that process of self-enlightenment that idealist philosophy since Schelling has been engaged in describing.

Lacan interprets the quoted statement from Freud's lecture in a totally different manner than that in which until recently it has been interpreted in the German tradition. This interpretation simultaneously demonstrates the direction in which he displaces the signification of the terms "interpretation" and "hermeneutics." Lacan begins by emphasizing – using Freud's statement that has frequently been echoed by modern poets – that "the I is not master in its own house." You are certainly familiar with Kafka's story "A Country Doctor." In a freezing night, a doctor is suddenly called to an uncurably ill patient, but he has no horses. They unexpectedly break out of a pigsty, whereupon we read: "You never know what you're going to find in your own house."[11]

But what does it mean that one never knows this? Lacan gives us the following aid for our reading: in one of his few programmatic texts, in his lecture to the Société Française de philosophie in 1957 on "La psychanalyse et son enseignement," he writes:

> In the unconscious that is less deep than it is inaccessible to conscious study in depth, *id speaks*: a subject in the subject, transcendent to the subject, poses to the philosopher since the *science of dreams* its question. (*E* [Fr. ed.], 437)

This is a difficult and apparently contradictory statement, which at one stroke returns us to the context of our central question regarding the theory of the *subject* in neostructuralism. The statement claims that there are two subjects: one of them is the traditional one itself, which we refer to as the subject (the only one we are acquainted with); the other one is the *id*, i.e., the unconscious (in Freud's sense) that speaks from within the subject, but in such a way that its speech cannot be understood by the conscious subject. After all, Lacan says: "transcendent to the subject."

"Where id was, there ego shall be." Now we can ask the question: which ego is the id supposed to become, since there apparently are two I's or two subjects? In French, unlike in Freud's mother tongue, there are two words that designate the first-person singular pronoun: *je* and *moi*. *Je* is used to characterize the subject as the condition of possibility, be it for an action, a recognition, or a statement; *moi* is used (among other things) if the subject is part of a reflexive relation: "c'est moi qui vient de parler . . .," "or moi, je trouve," etc. The philosophical interpretability of this opposition that French grammar provides is already documented in an early essay by Jean-Paul Sartre from the thirties, "La Transcendance de l'Ego." What is at question here can, of course, be explicated just as well without reflecting on French grammar. Lacan also calls the *Je* (which he usually capitalizes) the "true subject"; the *moi* he calls the "reflective," or even the "narcissistic," "imaginary," or "specular subject."

What is meant by this? If one uses the first-person singular pronoun, then one designates the person who at this given moment is referring to him/herself. To refer to oneself means, in specialized vocabulary, to reflect. "To reflect," moreover (and we must recall issues we have already discussed), is originally a metaphorical expression. It means, simply put, to mirror oneself. Precisely this is what Narcissus does in the ancient myth: he looks into the water and falls in love, being unfamiliar with the nature of the mirror effect (or not thinking about it at the moment), with his own image. Now we understand why Lacan, when he says *moi*, adds that this *moi* is the index word for the designation of the reflective, the specular (from the Latin word *speculum*, meaning "mirror"), the imaginary (reproducing its own image), in short, for the narcissistic ego: for the ego that looks at itself in its own mirror image or that identifies itself by means of its own mirror image. The "other" that this *moi* thinks it perceives as an autonomous being is in truth "imaginary"; i.e., it is only the other of itself. Therefore Lacan spells this type of an "other"/*autre* with a small *a*, and he refers to it as an *objet petit a*.

Nevertheless, there is still the other ego, the *Je*. Lacan also calls it, as I mentioned earlier, "the true subject" or "the subject of the unconscious." He also speaks of the *sujet de l'Autre*, and this time *Autre* is written with a capital *A*. The graphic index indicates that this type of "Other" is really independent of the self-reflection of the subject, and it implies that in this case we are not dealing with the other of itself.

With these explanatory observations I hope to be able to prepare the way for an understanding of Lacan's interpretation of Freud's statement, "Where id was, there ego shall be." He paraphrases Freud's sentence in French by opening up the parentheses, as it were, after each phrase and inserting his comments. We can easily follow this, since text and commentary are given in two different languages:

> *Wo* (Where) *Es* (the subject—devoid of any *das* or other objectivating article) *war* (was—it is a locus of being that is referred to here, and that in this locus) *soll* (must—that is, a duty in the moral sense, as is confirmed by the single sentence that follows and brings the chapter to a close) [Namely: *"Es ist Kulturarbeit etwa die Trockenlegung der Zuydersee"* (It is a civilizing task rather like the drying out of the Zuydersee).] *Ich* (I, there must I—just as one declared, "this am I," before saying "it is I"), *werden* (become—that is to say, not occur (*survenir*), or

even happen (*advenir*), but emerge (*venir au jour*) from this very locus
in so far as it is a locus of being). (*E*, 128)

Let's not be disturbed by the slightly Heideggerian manner of expression. The interpretation retains its validity even without this. For its point is that consciousness or self-consciousness (in the sense of reflection) is not simply supposed to
grow out of the id, as in Hegel, Ricoeur, or Lorenzer; rather, quite to the contrary, out of the id there will grow a subject Other than the reflective subject,
namely "the true subject of the unconscious" (*E*, 128).

Lacan, thus, is of the opinion that the cultural task of psychoanalytic hermeneutics will not consist in making the unconscious conscious, i.e., in reducing
the irreflective *Je* to the reflective *moi*; rather, on the contrary, it will consist in
leading a disturbance, motivated by the defensive reaction of the id, back to the
founding realm of that "absolute subject" to which Lacan attributes the almost
mystical-medial mode of Being of *s'être*. In order to give you a characteristic impression of Lacan's rather free use of language, let me quote the passage in which
he justifies and explains his translation.

> Thus I would agree, against the principles of the economy of significa-
> tion that must dominate a translation, to force a little in French the
> forms of the signifier in order to bring them into line with the weight of
> a still rebellious signification, which the German carries better here,
> and therefore to employ the homophony of the German *es* with the ini-
> tial of the word "*sujet*" (subject). By the same token, I might feel more
> indulgence, for a time at least, to the first translation that was given of
> the word *es*, namely, "*le soi*" (the self). The "*ça*" (id), which not with-
> out very good reason, was eventually preferred, does not seem to me to
> be much more adequate, since it corresponds rather to the German *das*,
> as in the question, "*Was ist das?*," and the answer "*das ist*" ("*c'est*").
> Thus the elided "*c*" that will appear if we hold to the accepted equiva-
> lence, suggests to me the production of a verb, "*s'être*," in which would
> be expressed the mode of absolute subjectivity, in the sense that Freud
> properly discovered it in its radical eccentricity: "There where it was"
> ("*Là où c'était*"), I would like it to be understood, "it is my duty that I
> should come to being." (*E*, 128–29)

Making use of the numerous homophones that so frequently confuse a non-
French speaker, Lacan succeeds at the trick of making us believe that the actual
place of the subject (*Sujet*) is precisely where we would least expect it: in the id,
in the unconscious. *The* subject (*sujet*), by contrast, to which we reduce the unconscious or into which we want to transform the unconscious, precisely this subject Lacan considers to be the place of deception and the place where symptoms
are formed. Its alleged brightness and clarity deceive us about the fact that it is

derived, that it is secondary, that it is an effect of the subject to which Lacan attributes the mode of Being of *s'être* and to which he gives the name *la subjectivité absolue*.

In our next lecture we will study more closely the relationship between these two subjectivities.

Lecture 19

Moving toward a reconstruction of Lacan's theory of the subject we came across the peculiar interpretation of Freud's statement, "Where id was, there ego shall be." Lacan did not, for example, render it as "There where the id was, the *moi* must arise," but rather as "There where id was (or: there where it was/itself was), it is my duty that I should come to being" (*E*, 129). In other words, Lacan used a possibility that French grammar provides for the first-person singular pronoun in order to distinguish *je* and *moi*, not only with regard to their contextual function, but also with regard to their essence. The essence of the *moi* is reflexivity, i.e., the fact that it is its own object, or—and this is only another formulation of the same thing—that it is its own image. One can also express this in the following way: the self-relation that occurs in the specific form of a relation within the *moiité* has the character of the imaginary.

> Literally, the *moi* is an object—an object that fulfills a certain function that we are here calling the function of the imaginary.[1]

But what would be the essence of the *je*, of that subject that Lacan characterizes as the "subject of the unconscious"? Well, Lacan attributes to it the mode of Being of eccentricity, or, as he also likes to say, of "ex-sistence." The *je* is, first of all, not something, but rather itself: it is itself (*il s'est*), as Lacan—exploiting the homophony of the first letter of *s*ubject, Freud's *Es*, and the French reflexive pronoun (*se*), or the pronoun *ça* (read before the subsequent vowel, thus: *s'*, *ç'*)—writes in an almost mystical formulation: the mode of Being of the *je* is the *s'être* or *c'être* (*E*, 128–29). But such a wholly irreflective subject—a subject without

295

a double, without something identical with it—fundamentally has no essence, if essence means "to be something," "to be qualified through characteristics." That means that whatever we can say about this *je* that is curiously enclosed in itself will miss its actual center, its Being. That is precisely why Lacan calls it "ex-sistent" or "ec-centric" and adds that because of its eccentricity it invites misapprehension. This misapprehension consists in the identification of the "true subject" with the *moi*, the subject reflected in itself that incorrectly identifies its reflective opposite with itself. In this misapprehension of the true subject (*je*), Lacan says, consists the actual, indeed, the only function of the *moi*.

> At this point the ambiguity of a failure to recognize that is essential to knowing myself (*un méconnaître essentiel au me connaître*) is introduced. For, in this "rear view" (*rétrovisée*), all that the subject can be certain of is the anticipated image coming to meet him that he catches of himself in his mirror. (*E*, 306)
> The only homogeneous function of consciousness is in the imaginary capture of the *moi* through its specular reflection and in the function of the failure to recognize that remains attached to it. (*E* [Fr. ed.], 832)

In order to be able to characterize the form of apprehending that rules in the self-relation of the *moi* as a form of *mis*apprehending, that which is excluded from the circle of reflective "capture" in the form of, and by virtue of, reflection cannot simply be external: there must be something *that* is misapprehended in reflection and by reflection, and that is precisely the *je*, the true subject without an internal double. In other words, *inside* the *moi* there is something that, misapprehended by the *moi*, is its true kernel; or the imaginary self-identification that occurs in reflection is exposed as an ekstasis of the founding I that has stepped out of its center onto the periphery and thus—ec-centrically—opens up the space of a relation to itself that the *moi* spontaneously uses to *identify* its mirror image with itself.

> It is this subject unknown to the *moi*, misapprehended by the *moi*, *der Kern unseres Wesens*, writes Freud in the chapter of the *Traumdeutung* . . .—when Freud deals with the primary process, he wants to speak of something that has an ontological meaning and that he calls *the kernel of our being*.
> The kernel of our being does not coincide with the *moi*. This is the sense of analytic experience, and it is around this that our experience has been organized. . . .
> Undoubtedly the true *je* is not *moi*. But this is not enough, for it is always possible to set about believing that the *moi* is only an error of the *je*, a partial point of view, whose perspective could be broadened by means of a mere coming to consciousness, enough for the reality that it is a matter of attaining to in the analytic experience to be discovered. What is important is the reciprocal, which must always be present

in our minds—the *moi* is not the *je*, is not an error, in the sense that classical doctrine makes it a partial truth. It is something else—a particular object within the subject's experience. Literally, the *moi* is an object—an object that fulfills a certain function that here we call the imaginary function. . . . All that Freud has written aimed to reestablish the exact perspective of the subject in relation to the *moi*.

I claim that this is essential and that it serves as the center around which everything should be ordered. (*Séminaire*, II, 59, 60)

The quintessence of these passages, it seems to me, is the indication that the function of misapprehension imprinted in the *moi* cannot be interpreted as an error, but rather that the *moi* arrives *necessarily* and for structural reasons at the point at which it misapprehends the kernel of its essence—the true *je*—as the other of itself, as *son semblable*, i.e., as itself. By thus inventing a fictitious *essence* for the *Being* enclosed within it, it throws light on this *je* at exactly that moment at which it pronounces something incorrect about it. The eccentricity of the true subject is in league with necessity, so that nothing can be said about its truth from outside of the center and with the means of the "capture of self that is reflection." If one calls "thinking" a cognitive activity that in some manner thrives—as in Descartes—on the evidence of reflection, then one can characterize the eccentric position of the *moi* to the *je* in the way Lacan himself does in a famous passage.

I think where I am not, therefore I am where I do not think. (*E*, 166)

This does not mean that the evidence that Descartes ascertains does not exist. It means that it only and exclusively exists for the self-experience of the *moi*, of the subject that deceives itself about its *Being*. For the Being that is affirmed in the *cogito sum* is not the Being in itself, but rather only the Being for myself, i.e., only that Being that stands across from me in the circle of reflection as *my* Being, as the being of myself.

Lacan expressly underscores this.

What one ought to say is: I am not wherever I am the plaything of my thought; I think of what I am where I do not think to think. (166)

This passage thus distinguishes between a Being for myself (or, put differently, a Being of the sort that it is what is reflected in a relation of reflection) from a Being of the sort that does not occur in reflection (thus an irreflective or transreflective Being). That is not contradictory to Descartes's argument. Schelling already pointed this out when he showed that Descartes's error was not that he considered the Being evidenced in self-reflection to be immediately certain, but rather that he took this reflected Being to be the entire Being. "That which is first *for me*" does not have to be the first in itself (*SW*, I/10, 4).

Now, obviously the phrase "*I am*" is at the very most a point of departure for me—and *only* for me; the context that is created by a connection to this sentence or to the immediate consciousness of one's own Being can, therefore, always only be a subjectively logical one. . . .
Philosophy thus does not advance at this point any further than to a
subjective certainty. (*SW*, I/10, 5)

Schelling developed this objection in a very clever way (see *SW*, II/1, 301). He
always arrived at the conclusion that with Descartes's *cogito sum*, "philosophy
was banished to the realm of the subjective and to the fact of merely subjective
consciousness" (*SW*, I/10, 8).

The *sum* that is conceptualized in the *cogito* thus only means: *sum qua
cogitans*, I am as thinking, i.e., in this specific mode of Being that is
called thinking and which is only *another* mode of Being than, for example, that of the body, whose mode of Being consists in the fact that
it *fills* space. . . . The *sum* that is enclosed in the *cogito* does not,
therefore, have the meaning of an unconditioned "I am," but rather only
the meaning of an "I am *in a particular way*," namely, as thinking, as
being in the mode that is called thinking. Therefore, the *Ergo sum* cannot imply: "I am in an unconditioned way," but only: "I am in a particular way." (*SW*, I/10, 10–11)

At this point Schelling distinguishes Being itself from its mode of Being.[2] If thinking *is*, he concludes, then it is itself a *mode* of Being, a mode of *how* Being appears, but as appearance of Being and not as Being in itself. But Being does not
appear on its own, but rather by stepping into the circle of reflection: with this,
subsistent Being becomes apparent Being; Being becomes an appearing, or simply appearance: a lucency or appearance (*Schein*) which in reflection is faced with
its relucency or reflection (*Widerschein*). That which was Being becomes the
reflet of that relation whose structural totality Sartre described as *reflet-reflétant*.
The *reflet* or appearance has, of course, in itself no independent Being: it requires
thematization by the *reflétant*; i.e., it is nothing absolute, but rather something
relative, something literally in need of something else, something, as Schelling
says, not conditioned and indubitable, but rather only a being in a particular way
(*SW*, I/10, 11). A being that is only in a certain way is in part a nonbeing, a *néant*
or a μὴ ὄv: a relatively *not*-being in comparison with Being-itself (*SW*, I/10,
283–85). Only this not-being, Schelling concludes, has been affirmed by Descartes as indubitable content of thought. Nothing is stated or determined about
Being as the ground of every mode of Being in this form of argument.

Schelling, by the way, formulates a second objection to Descartes's *cogito
ergo sum*. Let me at least sketch it briefly, since it also shows some parallels to
Lacan's thoughts. Schelling believes, namely, that not only the *esse subsistens*
(the unconditioned and indubitable Being) has not been proved by Descartes;

even the first part of the phrase, the "I think," remains dubitable. The I is nothing originary or immediate, but rather the object of a reflection that thinking directs at itself (*SW*, I/10, 11). To be able to find this object and, above all, to be able to identify it with thinking, this thinking must have existed prior to all reflection and even have been familiar with itself.

> Yes, true thinking must even be objectively independent of that subject reflecting on it, or it will think all the truer the less of the subject [the reflected I] is mixed in with it. Since it is thus two different things, that which thinks and that which reflects on this thinking and posits it as identical with itself, or, put differently, since there is an objective thinking that is independent of me, it could be deceived about that alleged unity precisely because it attributes the *originary* thinking to *itself*; and then the "I think" would mean no more than those other expressions I also use: I digest, I produce fluids, I walk, I ride; for it is not really the thinking being that walks or rides. Something thinks inside me, in me something is thought: that is the fact of the matter, no matter that I state with the same justification: "I dream" and "A dream came to me" [*es träumte mir*]. The certainty that Descartes attributes to the *cogito ergo sum* can thus not bear up under thinking itself. (*SW*, I/10, 11–12)

Lacan, to get back to him, combines both arguments by connecting, or simply identifying, the Being that reflection has not reached (somewhat unprecisely) with the true, i.e., the nonreflected subject. He concludes that the statement *cogito ergo sum* says no more than *ubi cogito, ibi sum* (*E*, 165).

> Of course, this limits me to being there in my being only in so far as I think that I am in my thought. (*E*, 165)

That means that Descartes's statement addresses Being only as the immanent object of thinking (of reflection), as the mere Being for myself of Being. It does not address the true subject whose Being plays outside reflection and which is reduced to appearance, to an image—in short, to something imaginary—when it fulfills the function of that which is reflected. The true subject is, therefore, the Being ground of reflection; not only does the opposite of this not apply, but the *moi* necessarily deludes itself about its position over against the *je*, the latter thought as pure *s'être*.

The famous phrase "I (*je*) am not where I think, therefore, I (*je*) am, where I think not, or where I am not aware that I think" thus must be read against the background of these observations. The *je* is completely unconscious. That may be the case, you will say, but then how can we talk about it at all? We cannot talk about it, Lacan answers, at least if "to talk" means to work with articulate meanings. But we can do something else; we can ask from whence the meanings actually originate with which our consciousness operates and, indeed, in whose light it first becomes comprehensible to itself.

We have arrived at the point at which Lacan's theory of consciousness and sub-jectivity describes *its* kind of *linguistic turn*. We can anticipate vaguely by saying that subjectivity has something to do with sign production, with meaning (*Bedeu-tung*) in the active sense of the word. Sign production, furthermore, has some-thing to do with articulation, with organization, with differentiation of the signify-ing material (see *E*, 149ff., esp. 152–54). That's old hat, you will say. Certainly, but we nevertheless still have to see how Lacan approaches it. Lacan says that both the decentrality of the subject as well as its wish to sublate its ekstatic "ex-sistence" in a conscious unity (that of the *moi*) originate in the organization of the chain of signification—an organization that always simultaneously has to be con-ceived as the dismembering, as the amputation of members in the order of spatial and temporal juxtaposition.

> I am explaining to you that it is insofar as he is engaged in a play of symbols, in a symbolic world, that man is a decentered subject. . . .
> Fascination [inscribed in the specular capture of the *moi*] is abso-lutely essential to the phenomenon of constitution of the *moi*. It is inso-far it is fascinated that the uncoordinated, incoherent diversity of the primal fragmentation acquires its unity. . . .
> The fragmented body finds its unity in the image of the other, which is its own anticipated image. (*Séminaire*, II, 63, 67, 72)

In other words, the true subject has to do with articulation; and the function of the imaginary subject consists in permeating in the space of fiction the primal separation that consciousness experiences in articulation. The wound inflicted by the symbolization of the *je* is imaginarily healed in a vision, indeed, in the image of the *moi* that is identical with what it faces. In this sense, the *moi* exhausts itself in the function of compensation for an originary deficiency, i.e., in the misappre-hension of its true mode of Being. It is this misapprehension that allows self-consciousness to be able to become something imaginary. It becomes something imaginary because despite all this it is the true subject that speaks in the circle of reflection ("in the unconscious, excluded from the system of the *moi*, the sub-ject speaks"; *Séminaire*, II, 79). For even reflection is constructed over a signi-ficant distance in which articulation manifests itself. If one wants to bridge a dis-tance to oneself, this presupposes the acknowledgment of this distance as the more originary phenomenon. The imaginary aspect of the wish to identify oneself with oneself assumes that a real primal division of the subject is the condition of its possibility.

We have to keep in mind that Lacan is neither an epistemologist nor a specula-tive language philosopher; his views, rather, are drawn from his clinical and psy-choanalytic experience. It is into this context of experience that, for a moment, we have to reintegrate his question about the origin of meaning and thus of subjec-tivity.

Lacan begins his observations with the already familiar reflection on the passive form in which in Saussure's terminology *le signifié* is given to us. *Le signifié*: this is a passive form, in contrast to the other side of the sign which is presented to us in the active form as *le signifiant*. Obviously, the speaker receives the meaning of the signs that he uses as a result of the effect of the signifiants, the active signifiers.

This purely grammatical observation opens up for Lacan a dimension that is nourished by his analytical experience. It combines, namely, with the further observation that there is no continual transition from the Being for itself of a meaning and its linguistic (or, as Lacan prefers to say, symbolic) articulation. When a human being is "thrown" into the world, as Heidegger calls it in a realistic and unfriendly way, it is at first still without language: the Latin term *infans* means both child as well as a being without language. The human child, as we know, is born too early, since otherwise it would not be able to pass through the narrow pelvic cavity of the mother. Therefore, it is unique among the mammals where its dependence on its mother is concerned. A child born too early has thousands of needs that its own organism cannot satisfy alone through interaction with external nature. At the beginning the baby does not articulate these needs, rather it expresses them in an unarticulated manner: it cries and starts moving in a still poorly coordinated manner; these indications, however, are absolutely understandable to the mother (or, nowadays, to the parents)—at least within certain limits. You may be familiar with Wilhelm Busch's story about the crying baby that nothing seemed to calm, and in whose diapers the parents has wrapped a pair of scissors by mistake. This shows how advantageous it can be to be able to articulate one's need more clearly than by mere crying. And therefore the baby, the *sujet infans*, should be able to explain its need (*besoin*) to its mother in the form of a demand, i.e., in articulated form. To this end, and for this reason, it is motivated to learn the language of the adults: the so-called symbolic order, the order of articulated and interpreted signs.

But what happens next? The baby or the smaller child that is just learning to speak has to express its need by means of signifiers in order to be comprehensible to the mother. The signifier, however, has already traveled from mouth to mouth (just like the coin travels from hand to hand) before it is able to serve the child for the signification of its wishes. The signifier expresses, in other words, the meaning with which the others (for example, the previous generation of speakers) endowed it, and not that which the child wanted to say. The act the subject wanted to make use of as a transparent means for bringing out its demand no longer radiates back from its expression the familiar traits of its prelinguistic self-consciousness—its narcissistic familiarity with the primal intention of the wish; rather it presents the strange face of an order of the Other. The mere fact of having to speak distorts the prelinguistic—and to this extent imaginary—intention in the medium of linguistic expression and consequently "one receives one's own message from the other, in inverted form" (*Séminaire*, II, 68). This inverting movement thus lets the human being who speaks become that through which "id" (*ça*) speaks, turning its action into passion. The supposedly prior self-possession of meaning has to turn over its authority – i.e., its *auctoritas*, its authorship – to the activity of the signifier, which precisely thereby

> has an active function in determining certain effects in which the signifiable appears as submitting to its mark, by becoming through that passion the signified.
>
> This passion of the signifier now becomes a new dimension of the human condition in that it is not only man who speaks, but that in man and through man *it* speaks (*ça parle*), that his nature is woven by effects in which is to be found the structure of language, of which he becomes the material, and that therefore there resounds in him, beyond what could be conceived of by a psychology of ideas, the relation of speech. (*E*, 284)

Grammar, through the passive form "the signified," points to the circumstance that the symbolically mediated meaning has to be conceived fundamentally as effect, that is, as posterior effect, and that its stability always only consists in the limits within which the "incessant sliding" (*E*, 154) of meaning happens to have come to a halt, that it thus can be retracted by a new "anchoring" (*E*, 154) of meaning on the chain. Since according to Lacan the meaning of a signifying chain is moreover not determined by means of the lexicon, but rather by the memory, inscribed in it, of all unpredictable contexts through which every expression has already passed in the history of its usages, no expression is ever identical with the signification attributed to it by the rule of *langue* (see *E* [Fr. ed.], 503–5). An unconsciousness of a *structural nature* disturbs the unequivocality of meaning in which a subject can abide. (We will return to this in another context.)

At this point we only need to ask how the baby reacts to this. It wanted *something*, and it was given a symbol. A symbol represents a thing, but it is not one itself. The symbol is the ersatz thing par excellence. Whoever symbolically identifies him/herself with him/herself does not identify him/herself in all the fullness of his/her Being. Derrida demonstrated this very nicely when he asserted in his second larger study of Husserl, *Speech and Phenomena*:

> Let us note first that this concept of primordial supplementation not only implies nonplenitude of presence (or, in Husserl's language, the nonfulfillment of an intuition); it designates this function of substitutive supplementation [*suppléance*] in general, the "in the place of" (*für etwas*) structure which belongs to every sign in general. . . . What we would ultimately like to draw attention to is that the for-itself of self-presence (*für-sich*) – traditionally determined in its dative dimension as phenomenological self-giving, whether reflexive or prereflexive – arises

in the role of supplement as primordial substitution, in the form "in the place of" (*für etwas*), that is, as we have seen, in the very operation of significance in general. The *for-itself* would be an *in-the-place-of-itself*: put *for itself*, instead of itself. (*SP*, 88–89)

If we return to the evolutionary-historical context of the symbolization of the human being that is learning to speak, we can concretize this general observation about the nature of the symbolic deferral in the following way: the symbolized *sujet infans* does not attain the object of its need in the manner it intended to as such, but rather over the detour of a representative, a placeholder (*Stellvertreter*). The placeholder not only places – strictly speaking – the desired object at a distance, but also the self of the child that from now on is no longer simply itself, but rather is for itself; i.e., it refers symbolically to itself.

What Lacan calls *le désir* reacts to this fundamental deprivation of world and the self. *Le désir*, Hegel's *Begehren*, Freud's *Wunsch,* is the answer of the human being to his introduction into the order of mere symbols and representatives of full realities; it is the reaction to his constant dissatisfaction and his infinite yearning. The sense of a nonhaving, of a lack, is thus woven into desire, and this lack appears to be an essential characteristic of the symbolic or intersubjective order of speech.

We already know one reason for this: the vital need (*besoin*) is directed toward real people and real things; the word – the element of the symbolic order – mediates a need only verbally, only symbolically (as *demande*): it means, but it *is* not the thing itself. (One wants bread and gets stones instead.)

To this extent, according to Lacan, when one speaks one is always somewhat in the situation of Tantalus who reaches out for foods that recede from his grasp and who stands in water without being able to quench his thirst. The symbolic order was conceived as a means for the satisfaction of desire. Instead of this, it separated the subject of the desire from itself. It now exists on two levels: first, as the narcissistic *moi* of the small child that desperately (futilely) identifies with its mother and uses her breast (insofar as she still offers it these days) as if it were its own organ; and second, as the speaking being that has delivered itself over to the order of the Others. This, according to Lacan, is the reason for the decentering or division of the subject that we have already discussed.

Without digressing too much, I would like to characterize more precisely the ground on the basis of which the symbolic order is experienced as profoundly defective. Without losing sight of the psychoanalytic experience of the mother-child relation, Lacan presents his evidence primarily in the field of linguistics. We know, of course, that Lacan, like all neostructuralists, appeals to Saussure's idea of meaning-producing differentiality. It is the system of differences that, by delineating one sound from another, endows each one with its meaning that is different from all the rest.

We can see right away how well suited this theorem is for providing semiological support for Lacan's psychoanalytic experience. Saussure believes that initially there is no stable meaning that then avails itself of expressions; rather, he believes that, on the contrary, the set of available meanings is produced by the set of differences that subsist among the really existing expressions of the symbolic order. Lacan works this into the thesis that the still prelinguistic subject must entrust its unarticulated desires and its wishes, in order to be comprehensible to others, to the differential (but uniformly different, and thus, on the intersubjective level, valid) system of language (*langue*) that is binding for all speakers of a community. After this, however, these wishes are divided by the differences of language; they no longer have a unity. The most painful part is that the original narcissism of the ego is offended: it learns that not its ego ideal but rather the order of *inter-subjectivity* is its truth, and that its "true subject" is not what it thinks about itself, but what language says about it.[3]

Lacan thus interprets the gap that separates word from word and meaning from meaning as subject, namely, as the unconscious subject. The subject retreats in order to give way to meaning. To this extent we can say three things about this subject: first, that it is always absent and unconscious; second, that it is the ground for the functioning of language and for the reserve of meaning about which we communicate symbolically; third, it is clear that this condition is somewhat unsatisfying and that our ego will always be tempted to include the order of the Other in the imaginary mirror play of its small I (*moi*), i.e., to regress to that narcissism about which Lacan once said, only apparently paradoxically, that it is "the supreme narcissism of the Lost Cause" (*E*, 324).

We have now established a basis upon which we can indicate more exactly how the subjectivity of that which Lacan calls the "true subject" or the "subject of the unconscious" (*sujet de l'inconscient*) relates to what he calls the *ordre symbolique*. We can characterize the relation of both subjects as follows: the "true subject" is a nothing—that is its mode of Being—that is, as it were, borne and preserved in Being by the symbolic order. From this moment on, Lacan continues, this nothing has subsistence because it is now employed in its function as a component of the symbolic order; in this function it survives the act of self-cancellation that makes it into a blank space between the signifiers and thus into something that, compared to the positivities that it brought into Being, is relatively nonbeing.

> The subject only constitutes himself by removing himself from it [the signifying beat] and essentially decompleting it in order to at once count himself in it and fulfill in it only a function of lack. . . .
> The effect of speech is the cause introduced into the subject.
> Through this effect, he is not the cause of himself; he carries within him the worm of the cause that cleaves him. For his cause is the signifier without which there would be no subject in the real. But this sub-

ject is what the signifier represents, and it could not signify anything unless it be for another signifier: to which then the subject who is listening is reduced.

The subject therefore is not spoken to. Id speaks of him, and it is there that he apprehends himself, and this all the more necessarily since before, simply by virtue of the fact that it is addressing him, disappearing as subject under the signifier that he becomes, he was absolutely nothing. But this nothing is supported by its advent, now produced by the appeal made in the Other to the second signifier. (*E* [Fr. ed.], 606-7, 835)

These two quotations, which, it seems to me, are mutually illuminating despite the fact that they are taken from two different contexts, are not as enigmatic as we might think on first reading. In the first passage it is stated that the subject, as it were, renounces its natural positivity and fullness by subtracting itself from the totality of everything positive. But this self-retraction does not simply result in the death of the subject: the subject survives in *such* a way that the positivities that are contrasted with one another due to its disappearance can now be read as signifiers, i.e., as elements of a symbolic order. Even in nature there are intervals and mirrorings; however, they do not make nature decipherable or intelligible in the sense of a script or a text, i.e., in the sense of a texture in whose web the subject has disappeared *as* subject, only to resurface *ex negativo* as the *meaning* of the signifiers and as meaning *by reason of* the signifiers.

We can infer from this how we have to determine the mode of Being of the subject. Compared to the signifiers that step into existence in its stead, the subject undoubtedly has the status of a non-Being. But it is not simply nothing at all, for one can say about it that it is the itself not signifying ground for the significance of the signifiers that have taken its place. The subject is not something that does not exist at all; rather it is Nothing in the sense of something that abandons itself for the benefit of something other. And the other for whose benefit the subject sacrifices itself is the symbolic order. Saussure's famous statement, "in language there are only differences" can thus now be understood to mean that it is the subject that, so to speak, disappears in the gaps between what Saussure calls the "full and positive terms." But it is only because of these gaps that the expressions have any meaning at all, even if it is not that meaning the narcissistic *moi* hoped to embody in these expressions.

The inference of the second passage cited should now also be clear: at that moment when the prelinguistic subject is dissolved in the gaps between the expressions, the symbolic order is established *as* symbolic order (i.e., in its distinctness both from the order of the real and from that of the imaginary). And the subject is now, as Lacan puts it (I am paraphrasing his formulation), that which is "represented" in the play of references between any two signifiers. The subject is no longer its mirror image, no longer identical with itself, and, thus, no longer what it merely thinks it is (but is not); rather, it is that which comes into *Dasein* in the play of reference between any two expressions of the symbolic order as their meaning.

Now we can approach the open question regarding how the true subject is connected to the blinded, the imaginary, or the narcissistic subject. We have to begin by considering the following: *if* the narcissistic subject had a serious possibility of enclosing itself in itself, and thus to remain standing all its life in front of its mirror image, then there would be no compelling motivation for expelling it from this sanctum of consciousness and confronting it with the unsettling experience of the unconscious and the symbolic. But it is the triumph of Lacan's theory that it is able to show that precisely this isolation of the *moi* in itself is not successful, that the imagination *cannot* exclude the unconscious from its calculations.

In this regard, Lacan, as a psychoanalyst and not as a philosopher, makes the following observation: why would we so much like to flee from the Other in the first place? What is behind our wishes for regression, for self-authorship, self-sufficiency, and adequate self-representation? Why do we dream that we are the initiators of the meaning of our world? And why do we even have desire? Are they innate? That would be hard to understand since all desire points to a non-Being, to a condition of dissatisfaction and of lack that our longing seeks to supplement. Since this is the case, would it be less plausible if someone were to tell us that we voluntarily *chose* to be driven by an insatiable longing? No, our wish for narcissistic circumscription was brought about by the unconscious itself (as its utopian, i.e., imaginary, complement), for the unconscious, the Other—this is the symbolic order marked by lack. It was *this order* that canceled out our wish subject; it killed it in the gaps of the differentiations of expressions out of which the language (*langue*) of the Other or the Others arose. This order pricked the wish ego with the thorn of longing that causes prelinguisitic need to exist as desire from that moment onward: to exist as the socially mediated and intersubjectively broken desire that Lacan also ambiguously calls "the desire of the Other."

In *Séminaire* II, under the chapter heading "Beyond the Imaginary: Introduction of the Great Other," Lacan gives a particularly impressive depiction of the effects of being inserted into the symbolic order in which the subject in fact confronts the other subject as an *Other* subject whose individuality can be reduced neither to the specular image of the other (lowercase) that I project of it nor to the grammatical rules that enforce uniformity on all participants in a symbolic order behind their backs, as it were. The truth, the Otherness, and the autonomy of the Other that I confront in speech (*langage*) beyond my narcissism, make themselves recognizable by the fact that I can simultaneously understand the Other and never *entirely* understand it.

I am always aiming for the real subjects, and I must settle for shadows. The subject is separated from the Others, the real ones, by the wall of speech [*langage*].

If the word [*la parole*] is founded in the existence of the Other, the real one, speech is fit to refer us to the other objectivity, to the other with whom we may do what we will, including think that he is an object, that is, that he does not know what he is saying. When we use speech, our relation with the other is always at play in this ambiguity. In other words, speech is as fit to found us in the Other as to prevent us radically from understanding the Other. And this is precisely what is at issue in the analytic experience. (*Séminaire*, II, 286)

We will encounter once again this criterion that states that I recognize the autonomy of the Other by the fact that I never entirely understand it (and this distinguishes understanding from speculative knowledge in Hegel's sense) when we turn to the problem of understanding as such.

At the moment we only have to understand that, and how, Lacan even tracks down the desire of the Other behind the wish for *complete* self-identification. Remaining within the framework of the foregoing passage, it is the experience of the wall that is erected between me and the Other that stirs in me the wish to escape from the dismemberment of the differential order of language (*langue*), or, in other words, to transform the unovercome manifoldness of language into unity.

In this formulation Lacan was also able to interpret the experience of dependence of the narcissistic wish on the desire of the Other in terms of the failure of the dialectical model of reflection for self-consciousness. This model assumes that something that is manifold in itself searches and finds its unity in a mirror image that is held up to it; in this way the disseminally manifold identifies itself as One. It is clear that this formulation is nourished by the psychoanalytic experience, which consists in supplementing the nonwhole of one's own self-perception so that it becomes that unity that I perceive either my own mirror image or the object of my love to be: the dismembered body thus gains the illusion, as Lacan says, of being something integral.

But the shadow of a third element that was repressed by reflection extends into this dual relation (the *moi* as many and the *moi* as one). This third element is the *primally repressed* in Freud's sense: the unappeasable lack that is the basis of the wish for reflective self-identification, a lack that is responsible in the first place for producing the vision of the coincidence of the manifold with itself as One, and which survives as *desire* for narcissistic identification with the *o*ther (with a lowercase *o*). To *desire* the other of oneself (the mother, for example, in the analytical experience) means to know already that the mirror image of reflection, in which one means the other as itself, does not really allow the coincidence with it to be successful: therefore, the subject mirroring itself interprets its desire as an essential "lack" (*Fehl*) of the loved object (in Lacan's theory as the phallus: that which the mother lacks (*fehlt*) and which she, too, desires). This "lack," however, is at the same time the condition of possibility of the desire for identity; for only beyond a lack, a nothing, a gap, a blank space, can I mean something *as* something (for example, as myself). Nevertheless, something that is meant by me is, insofar as it has a determined meaning, first of all separated from me, i.e., articulated; it thus exposes itself as an effect of the symbolic order that the mirror play of the allegedly self-sufficient "dual relation of ego to ego" (*E*, 138, 172ff.) refers to a third element that explodes its self-sufficiency. Even in order to become only illusion, Lacan believes, the imaginary self-entanglement of the *moi* in its *o*ther would have to appeal to the truth of the repressed, i.e., of the great *O*ther, to vouch or testify for it.

> In other words this other is the Other that even my lie invokes as a guarantor of the truth in which it subsists. (*E*, 172; cf. 245ff. and *Séminaire*, II, 74–77, 284ff.)

Now we see how our earlier question can be answered. The question was, If the true I is actually unconscious, how can we know about it? The answer is that we do not know about it, if "to know" means to bring something before our mind's eye, to *re*present something. But we do know about it insofar as in speech we constantly experience a lack that prevents us from endowing a nondifferentiated entity with meaning. Only the dismembered has meaning, and the totality, about which Hegel said that it alone was the true, exposes itself as an illusion that cannot possibly be filled with meaning: it exposes itself as the imaginariness of a *présence-à-soi*. But if the idea of a complete adequation of the *moi* with itself proves to be an illusion ("which is not only imaginary but illusory"; *Séminaire*, II, 286), we have reason to assume that the subject in principle cannot sound out its own ground, i.e., that it experiences itself as grounded on an Other that escapes its own interiority. Lacan formulates this as the analytical hypothesis that the *moi* is by no means the ground of itself, and also not the ground of the meaning in which it holds on to itself, and which helps it to get a principally incomplete understanding of itself.

> The effect of speech is the cause introduced into the subject. Through this effect, he is not the cause of himself; he carries within him the worm of the cause that cleaves him. (*E* [Fr. ed.], 835)

At this point we want to break off our reconstruction of Lacan's theory of the subject and address to it some critical questions. Even if Lacan indisputably deserves the honor of being called the pioneer of a certain (as he likes to call it, subversive) thinking about the mode of Being of subjectivity, he nevertheless is also touched by a series of certain objections that apply to his successors and that we in part, and in modified form, already raised against Heidegger.

We saw that Lacan, as opposed to some of his allegedly more radical successors, is not prepared to sacrifice the concept of the "subject" in his theory. On the contrary, we would not be exaggerating if we said that the problem of the truth of the subject constitutes the nucleus of his deliberations. Taking up observations made earlier, we can even add that Lacan—with entirely different motivations, yet with a comparable result—agrees with Schleiermacher and Sartre that the "true subject" cannot be thought according to the model of reflection. That ego that makes its own acquaintance by means of its mirror image (and fails in this) is rather an epiphenomenon of the true subject. The fact *that* the I (*moi*) fails in its attempt to found itself in the "dual relation of ego to ego" is, for Lacan, not reason enough for henceforth giving up the notion of subjectivity; rather, he draws a conclusion that, within the context of neostructuralism, is quite original, namely, that the reflective ego (*moi*) cannot be the true subject, but that precisely because of its failure it calls for the truth of the Subject (with a capital *S*). Thus, for Lacan reflection is not, as for some representatives of analytical philosophy, a "philosophical pseudoproblem"; rather it is a state of affairs whose subsistence cannot be denied, but which—according to him—does not subsist by virtue of itself, but rather is founded in an Other for which it craves *in* its Being. That means both that this Being is merely relative—it has the mode of Being of a *néant d'être*—and that it appeals to something of absolute Being that it itself is not, i.e., to the great Other.

The structure of this theory of self-consciousness is, although philosophy is not the field of application of Lacan's theory, basically homologous with that which we are familiar with from Schelling and Schleiermacher. There, too, a lack inscribed in the relation of reflection—in the form of a postulate that is necessary for thought—bears testimony to something transcendent on which this relation's merely relative Being is founded. What Sartre calls the "ontological proof of consciousness" remains wholly within the framework of this explanatory model. With this we have said enough about what Lacan has in common with a tradition we are already familiar with and on which hermeneutics also is based.

In contradistinction to this tradition, however, it is very difficult to understand in the case of Lacan what criterion will make it possible in his point of view for the specular I (*moi*) to identify with itself at all. To be sure, Lacan tells us that the specular I (*moi*) is imaginary. But even imaginations have a Being, and this (even if relative) Being has to be clarified in a theory that discusses them. This is particularly true for Lacan's notion of the imaginary I (*moi*), since it justifies the recourse to the "true subject" on the basis of the mere relativity of the mode of Being of the *moi*.

At this juncture the doubts we brought forward when we were faced with Derrida's aporetic deconstruction of the subject also apply to Lacan's theory. His critique of the reflective model of self-consciousness suddenly transports us to the realm of the *grand Autre* to which Lacan attributes the mystical mode of Being of *s'être*, without either explaining or, what is more, justifying the use of the reflexive pronoun in this formulation. Either the true subject is absolutely ir-reflexive, in which case it is impossible to see how one can speak of it as though it were a subject at all, or else with the formulation *s'être* it is in fact ascribed a problematic familiarity with itself about which Lacan does not say a word. This is probably of minor consequence for the interests of the psychoanalytic cure. On the other hand, one also cannot, as soon as one encounters conceptual difficulties, always protect the work of a theoretical writer of Lacan's stature from criticism by referring to the pragmatic needs of concrete psychoanalysis, i.e., by immuniz-ing his work against other ideas. Lacan's writings and seminars are constantly in such close contact with the philosophical tradition; they evolved to such a great extent out of his dialogue with philosophy (and not only with Freud) that we have good reason for not simply breaking off our reflections about the difficulties in Lacan's deliberations at the point where the author and, even more so, his succes-sors want to stop them short.

As far as I can see, Lacan, who—for example, in the *Four Fundamental Con-cepts of Psychoanalysis*—frequently refers to Sartre, did not really grasp the func-tion of the notion of a prereflective or nonthetic *cogito*. In the second *Séminaire*, for example, he quite clearly cites this distinction without, however, acknowledg-ing its legitimacy. Let me quote the entire passage.

> What gives consciousness its apparently primordial character? The phi-losopher seems to start from an indisputable fact when he starts from the transparency of consciousness to itself. If there is consciousness of something, it is not possible, we are told, that this consciousness does not grasp itself as such. Nothing can be experienced without the subject being able to grasp itself inside this experience in a sort of immediate reflection.
>
> In this regard, undoubtedly, philosophers have advanced a few steps since the decisive step taken by Descartes. The question has been posed, which remains open, whether the *je* is immediately grasped in the field of consciousness. But it has already been possible to say of Descartes that he had differentiated thetic consciousness from nonthetic consciousness.
>
> I will go no further into the metaphysical investigation of conscious-ness. I shall propose to you not a working hypothesis—I claim that we are not dealing with a hypothesis—but a way of having done with it, of cutting the Gordian knot. For there are problems that need to be solved that should be dropped without having solved them.
>
> Once again it is a matter of a mirror. (*Séminaire*, II, 61)

One can cut the Gordian knot, according to Lacan, with the claim that self-consciousness, be it thetic or nonthetic, is formed in the mirror play of the narcis-sistic relation: the subject is always shown an objectlike image by means of which, or through which, it henceforth identifies itself.

I beg you to consider . . . that consciousness is produced whenever there is given . . . a surface that is such that it can produce what is called *an image*. This is a materialist definition. (65)

This thesis, particularly in its concrete realization (see *Séminaire*, II, 62–63), is not very far removed from Adorno's thesis of the "preponderance of the object" over the subject, which he likewise called "materialistic."[4] Applied to the theory of self-consciousness, this would be a crass expression for the model of reflection, according to which the ego would identify itself by means of its own object without, however, having a criterion at its disposal that enables it to identify the peculiarity of this object with *itself*. But we have already seen not only that this theory culminates in aporias, but that in the instance of self-consciousness it is not a matter of an act of identification: neither of the self with an image nor of the self with itself.

Interestingly enough, in *Séminaire* II one of Lacan's listeners raises an objection that is wholly in line with this doubt, which Lacan, however, evades. Lefèbvre-Pontalis intervenes in Lacan's lecture with the following comments:

One word, since I think I recognized myself in the anonymous interlocutor who had pointed out to you that you were perhaps dodging consciousness in the beginning only to meet up with it all the more surely at the end. I never said that the *cogito* was an untouchable truth, and that the subject could be defined by this experience of total transparency to oneself. I never said that consciousness exhausted all of subjectivity, which, incidentally, would be difficult what with phenomenology and psychoanalysis, but simply that the *cogito* represented a sort of model of subjectivity, that is, made very palpable this idea that there must be someone for whom the word "as" [or "like": *comme*] has a meaning. And this you seem to omit. For when you had taken [the example of] your apologue of the disappearance of men, you were forgetting only one thing, namely, that men had to come back to grasp the relation between the reflection and the thing reflected. Otherwise, if one considers the object in itself and the film recorded by the camera, it is nothing other than an object. It is not a witness, it is nothing. In the same way, in the example you take of the numbers said at random, in order for the subject to realize that the numbers he said at random are not as random as all that, there must be a phenomenon that you can call what you wish, but which indeed seems to me to be this consciousness. It is not simply the reflection of what the other says to it. I do not really see why it is so important to demolish consciousness if it is to be brought back in the end. (76)

Lefèbvre-Pontalis is referring to the following context: Lacan had followed his first assertion—that even if one assumes a nonthetic consciousness, we are still dealing with a mirror play—with a second one in which he claimed that no consciousness independent of this mirror play is necessary in order to take in the reflex in the mirror.

This, in any case, is what I propose that you admit, so that I may tell you a little apologue that will guide your reflection.

Suppose that all men have disappeared from the earth. I say *men*, given the high value you give to consciousness. This is enough to ask oneself the question—*What is left in the mirror?* But let us go so far as to suppose that all living beings have disappeared. All that is left then is waterfalls and springs—lightning and thunder, too. Do the image in the mirror and the image in the lake still exist?

It is altogether clear that they still exist. And this, for a very simple reason—at the high degree of civilization we have reached, which far surpasses our illusions about consciousness, we have fabricated devices that, without any audacity whatsoever, we can imagine to be complicated enough to develop the films themselves, put them away in little boxes, and place them in the refrigerator. Even though every living being has disappeared, the camera can nonetheless record the image of the mountain in the lake, or that of the Café Flore in the process of crumbling in complete solitude. . . .

So! That is what I propose that you consider as essentially a phenomenon of consciousness, which will have been perceived by no ego [*moi*], which will have been reflected in no experience of the ego's—every sort of ego and consciousness of the I being absent at this time.

You will say to me, *Just a minute, butterfly! The ego is somewhere, it is in the camera.* No, there is not the shadow of an ego in the camera. But, on the other hand, I will gladly admit that the *I* has something to do—not in the camera—with this.

I am explaining to you that it is insofar as he is engaged in a play of symbols, in a symbolic world, that man is a decentered subject. Well then, it is with this same play, this same world, that the machine is constructed. The most complicated machines are made only with words. (62–63)

Here he takes issue with the idea that, in order to perceive the object in the mirror as the reflection or the representative of an object, it is not necessary to have a consciousness *for* which the representation takes place. Instead he maintains that a complicated machine, for example, a Polaroid camera, which could permanently store its copies itself, completely replaces those activities that are usually attibuted to consciousness. The recording camera is egoless (*sans moi*), although it is not without an I (*je*). But even the I (*je*) of this strange camera functions as a centerless entity; although it is not the recording of visual mirror images, it is nevertheless said about it (and elaborated more fully in what follows) that it is formed in a homologous way in the differential screen of expressions that refer to one another (*jeu des symboles*), whose totality is the "symbolic world": "The machine is the structure detached, as it were, from the activity of the subject. The symbolic world is the world of the machine" (*Séminaire*, II, 63).

Lacan not only repeats here—to be sure, in an amusing formulation—the familiar view according to which consciousness arises as an effect of the differential relations between elements of an order (at this point he goes so far as to say: of objects); he even comes quite close to a crude theory of reflective mirroring, according to which the camera can substitute for the function of conscious seeing or of the eye in all essential respects.

> An image means that the energy effects moving out from a given point in the real—imagine them on the order of light, since that is what figures most manifestly as an image in our minds—come to be reflected at some point on a surface, come to strike the same corresponding points in space. The surface of a lake can also be replaced by the *area striata* of the occipital lobe, for the *area striata* with its fibrillary layers is exactly like a mirror. (65)

We will encounter once again in Deleuze and Guattari the dream of a subjectless machine. We can take this as a piece of information about neostructuralism, without denying that Lefèbvre-Pontalis touched the sore spot of this vision: there is nothing intrinsic to the play of visual reflections that would indicate that the mirror images that are sent back and forth are for themselves what they actually are. Even a photographic record does not change anything where this is concerned. The essential difference between an eye and a camera is the trivial one that the eye is an organ and is self-conscious, whereas the camera does not record what it records *for itself*. Consciousness and self-consciousness cannot be reduced to that *without* which they certainly would never come into being, *through* which alone, however, they also cannot be explained. The famous neurophysiologist John C. Eccles recently emphasized this distinction very clearly when he designated consciousness as "a *form of Being which is grounded in itself*," that actively "intervenes by means of interpretation and control" in the processes of the neurological apparatus, to which, however, it cannot be reduced.[5] Eccles undoubtedly would also underscore Lefèbvre-Pontalis's remark that the "relationship between the reflection and the thing reflected" requires a witness *for* which it exists, or, more precisely, for which it exists *as* reflection. And that applies as well, as Lefèbvre-Pontalis further emphasizes, for the differential play of elements in a symbolic order: it is perhaps a necessary, but not a sufficient condition for the constitution of consciousness ("it is not simply the reflection of what the other says to it") that it be inserted in this order and be addressed with expressions taken from its stock. All attempts to derive consciousness from whatever relation between elements, no matter how it is constituted, are philosophically out of the question insofar as they always already presuppose consciousness. This is also correctly emphasized by Lefèbvre-Pontalis when he says that one cannot possibly first want to destroy consciousness, only in order to reintroduce it later. The demolition of consciousness can result in many things, but it cannot generate consciousness, just as nothing comes out of nothing. If, however, in a circular manner one already presupposes consciousness, it becomes meaningless to talk about a derivation of this phenomenon. Any conclusion to the effect that there can be consciousness only when there is then finally already consciousness is purely tautological.

It is disappointing that Lacan's observations on the mode of Being of consciousness supply us with such insufficient information. For even if we do not overlook that Lacan is primarily interested in reinterpreting consciousness as a function of the misapprehension of the unconscious, still the *misapprehending* consciousness must in any case nevertheless be a *consciousness*. But according to what Lacan tells us in the *Séminaire* about the *moi* in Freud's theory, we have to fear that he does not even provide us with any evidence for this; for in order to be *misapprehension*, consciousness would first of all have to be *consciousness*. However, the machine about which Lacan speaks misapprehends neither itself nor the world, since it is not capable of apprehending anything at all.

Lecture 20

Up to this point I have concerned myself very little with the chronology of the texts and ideas presented to us by neostructuralism that deal with the problem of subjectivity, and I intend to continue to let myself be guided by facts that are pertinent to the subject matters at hand. If I were to approach the matter differently, i.e., historically, the thoughts about Lacan that I presented to you in the last lecture would have had to take a place at the very beginning of our series of lectures; for the seminar on the ego (*moi*) in Freud's theory was given in the winter semester of 1954–55, i.e., at a time in which what I have called classical structuralism was still a dominant force in all of Paris, a force, to be sure, that was yet overshadowed by existentialism.

My goal has been to demonstrate that the enterprise of "deconstruction," according to its own intent and to the extent that it understands itself correctly, does not overlap with that of destruction. "Destruction" means demolition, reduction, bringing to the ground (*zu Grunde richten*); "deconstruction," on the other hand, means tearing down to the foundation the walls on which a tradition of thought is erected (and sometimes even taking apart the foundations themselves), so that a new and more convincing thought—or even the same thought in a more convincing form—can be reerected on the same or on different foundations. This reconstructive intent is expressed by the inserted "con," which distinguishes de*con*struction from simple *de*struction. We recall that Derrida explains his newly coined term in approximately this way.

And Lacan, too, as we just saw, by no means intends to show that the problem of subjectivity is only a "philosophical pseudoproblem," as the analytical philosophers put it, following the theoreticians of the Vienna Circle; his aim is, rather, to make a particular and influential philosophical tradition aware (or maybe only remind it) that the "true subject" (*le sujet véritable*) cannot be found where the philosophy of consciousness, the theory of knowledge, and egopsychology commonly look for it, namely, in the mirror play of reflection. He claims, rather, that it can be found "where id speaks" ("là où *ça parle*"): "a subject in the subject, transcendent to the subject, poses to the philosopher since the *science of dreams* its question" (*E* [Fr. ed.], 437). This question, which is explicitly directed at philosophers, has the therapeutic effect of deconstructing the idea of a self-sufficient ego (*moi*) that mirrors itself in itself; i.e., it takes it apart and reconstructs it in a new and different way on new foundations, namely, on the basis of a theory of the absolute dependence of reflection on something prior to it that is not in itself reflective. If we recall what we said earlier about Schleiermacher's founding of hermeneutics in an absolute awareness of dependence, we will be able to agree with the assertion that Lacan's theory of the subject takes up in its own way one of the most profound impulses of the critique of idealism supplied from within idealism itself.

Lacan, to be sure, does this is a form whose concrete realization does not seem satisfactory to us. Let us recall once again our main objection: while critically questioning the subject of reflection by demanding another subject that is not conceived according to the model of reflection, Lacan basically, however, does not have at his disposal any alternative to the reflective model of self-consciousness. Therefore, it is true of his *sujet véritable* either that it is unfamiliar with itself—a completely unarticulated darkness—or that it contains in itself a kind of reflection. In the first case, one would not be able to speak of a subject; in the latter case, one could not speak of an alternative to the *moi*. Lacan, in fact, seizes on the metaphor of the subjectless machine in which reflections are recorded that, however, are no longer somebody's reflections: relations between states of affairs without a subject *whose* relations they are. Thus Lacan's critique of the model of subjectivity as reflection culminates in a model of reflexivity without a subject. That would be either the proverbial night in which all cats are gray, or a recording machine whose records would never be audible to anybody. Thus the deconstructive aim is transformed against its own will into a destructive one, into a denial of the subsistence of the phenomenon it set out to explain.

This criticism, however, applies in a much stronger form to some of Lacan's—should I say "critics," or "successors?"—than it does to Lacan himself. Since this is the case, it seems to me appropriate to have emphasized a consequence that in Lacan is always only a tendency (and, to be sure, an unintended tendency). I am thinking here of Gilles Deleuze and Félix Guattari, the authors of the two-volume work *Capitalisme et schizophrénie* which appeared in 1972 and in 1980, the first volume entitled *L'Anti-Oedipe*, and the second *Mille Plateaux*.[1] In both volumes, whose consciously dadaist and carnivalesque style more or less achieves the provocation it aims to evoke, the notion of the subject-less machine stands in the foreground. Let me try to characterize this notion in the course of a brief examination of the basic ideas presented primarily in *Anti-Oedipus* – although the two authors would certainly be more than a little surprised to see that anyone would like to attend to thoughts that are so unstable, fluid, or imprecise that the mere attempt to get a fix on them seems absurd, or at the very least, comical.

For precisely this reason (the familiar difficulty of nailing a pudding to the wall, or, let's say, in anticipation of our text, of studying a "desiring-machine" [or a "rhizome"] with regard to *one* aspect), we cannot approach the problematics of the subject in *Anti-Oedipus* directly, but only by way of a detour through a characterization of the entire book. We can never really come close to the problem in this way; still, a kind of symptomatological reading can bring us forward. What is of the greatest interest to us about *Anti-Oedipus* is that it is a symptom and, indeed, a particularly glaring one, which, due to the resonance it found especially in the younger generation, has shown us that one cannot simply shrug one's shoulders or laugh and return to the normal academic agenda. To the extent that *Anti-Oedipus* is no less than representative for a thoroughly alarming and rapidly spreading "discontent" in the contemporary condition of our souls and our culture, it must be taken seriously and analyzed as the symptom of a crisis. This does not mean that we have to overestimate the phenomenon. For the present, the effect of the "new thinking" of these two authors can primarily be sensed in the agitation of those it most directly challenged (e.g., orthodox Freudians or Lacanians), or in the whisperings of fan clubs or sectlike groups on the margins of the academic scene; and very little seems to indicate that anyone in France or in Germany who is professionally (or out of interest) engaged in philosophy and/or psychoanalysis would not shake his or her head when he or she hears Foucault's fanfare for Deleuze.

> A fulguration has been produced that will bear the name of Deleuze: a new thought is possible; thought is newly possible. It is not to come, promised by the most distant of new beginnings. It is here, in the texts of Deleuze, leaping, dancing before us, among us . . . one day, perhaps, the age will be Deleuzian.

We are still awaiting this dawn of a new thinking, although, as we said earlier, there are some excited fans who claim already to have seen the new light – partly with concern, partly with hope. But can one deny that the spirit of the times has taken the wind out of the sails of academic philosophy, that one after the other phenomenology, existentialism, Critical Theory, and eventually even structuralism and analytical philosophy are being relegated to the status of "classics" and that their last representatives are longing for a bolt out of the blue that will make thinking possible again?

It is for this reason that criticism and ridicule of Deleuze (and let's not completely forget Guattari) are *one and the same* thing; and even if such criticism and ridicule should have the effect of diverting our attention from the legitimation crises of academic philosophy, we must still first of all seriously accept the — as ever — miscarried challenge of *Anti-Oedipus* and even take it seriously *as* a challenge — to the extent that it is not asking too much to do this.

The text begins with a torrent of sentences that on their own would already have sufficed to attract attention. (I fear that, at the same time, it has the result of diverting our attention *away* from the reading. But I will let you judge for yourself.)

> It is at work everywhere, functioning smoothly at times, at other times in fits and starts. It breathes, it heats, it eats. It shits and fucks. What a mistake to have ever said *the* id. Everywhere *it* is machines — real ones, not figurative ones: machines driving other machines, machines being driven by other machines, with all the necessary couplings and connections. An organ-machine is plugged into an energy-source-machine: the one produces a flow that the other interrupts. The breast is a machine that produces milk, and the mouth a machine coupled to it. The mouth of the anorexic wavers between several functions: its possessor is uncertain as to whether it is an eating-machine, an anal machine, a talking-machine, or a breathing-machine (asthma attacks). Hence we are all handymen: each with his little machines. For every organ-machine, an energy-machine: all the time, flows and interruptions. Judge Schreber has sunbeams in his ass. *A solar anus.* And rest assured that it works: Judge Schreber feels something, produces something, and is capable of explaining the process theoretically. Something is produced: the effects of a machine, not mere metaphors. (*AO*, 1–2)

This is how it begins, and it continues (or better: flows) on in this style for hundreds of pages. What breaks loose here is the vision of a total functioning that occasionally discharges itself in primal screams of conditionless affirmation and adaptation. Affirmation of what, adaptation to what? We will see that this question is irrelevant, for the flow has no aim or meaning whatsoever. Just as in the fourth sentence of the book the nominalization of the *id* is rejected ("What a mistake to have ever said *the* id"), so the teleological directedness and intentionality of the authorless activity — that is how the flowing production is presented to us — is also denied (*AO*, 5). Movement occurs without being the movement of something (i.e., the movement of a substrate or a subject), and, in a strangely sterile reflexivity, it is only directed at itself;[2] that is what constitutes its machinelike aspect (and it is compared to Freud's "primary process").

> The rule of continually producing production, of grafting producing onto the product, is a characteristic of desiring-machines or of primary

production: the production of production . . . which, as we shall see, is what even the very young child does. (7)

This subjectless and aimless production, which, however, is filled to overflowing with and by itself, is most similar, perhaps, to Nietzsche's "life," conceived as the unity of the will to life preservation and the will to life intensification. Deleuze treated this subject in this book on Nietzsche, adding that the nucleus of the "will to power" is the power of "affirmation"—of unreserved affirmation of being-there (*Daseienden*). This love of the Zarathustra-Dionysian "unlimited saying of Yea and Amen" permeates the entire *Anti-Oedipus*, and even the Social Darwinist elitist interpretation of "eternal return" as the Yea to "breeding, to selection" is not missing: a consequence that was at least unwelcome to those who wanted to redeem Nietzsche from the charge of being a predecessor of National Socialism and even an ally of Social Darwinism.[3] I know that this is a broad and very ticklish field, and predecessorship is a particularly questionable concept, because in a certain sense all those who are born earlier are "predecessors" and "precursors" of those who are born later; but there are no grounds for accusing them of complicity simply on this basis alone. At any rate, let's hold on to the structural trait connecting vitalism and Social Darwinism, which consists in the fact of affirming not a rationally founded aim that is attributed to a subject capable of making decisions, but rather the naked, subjectless, and aimless hypostasis "life." Whoever affirms "life" has to affirm it in all its manifestations. If the racial doctrine and the doctrine that affirms the right of those who are better adapted (better adapted to *what?*) has to be considered to be one possibility among others for describing "life," then how are we to reject them?

The unusual and unfamiliar aspect of the neovitalism of the *Anti-Oedipus*, as opposed to the old well-known vitalism, is that it is accompanied by a new affection for the thought of the machine (for which the pseudoromantic vitalism at the close of the nineteenth century had no sympathies whatsoever). For this neovitalism, everything becomes a machine: sky-machines, star-machines, the rainbow-machine, and the mountain-machine—something moans and sighs and rattles and "lives" in the body of the universe in which the delimited body of the (subjectless) vital producer expands. In this cosmic idyll, do we simply have to put up with the "continual whirr of machines" (2), just as we put up with the noise of autos outside our windows? It's inevitable. "One, two / nothing is bad, / everything will work out, / everything is possible . . ." (lyrics of a punk song by Nina Hagen). Even what Max Scheler called "cosmovital empathy"[4] becomes, for the two authors of *Anti-Oedipus*, "a chlorophyll- or photosynthesis-machine, or at least [the desire to] slip his body into such machines as one part among the others" (2).

But if the odd choice of words seems to announce a fashionable rapture, one still cannot say that a topic is addressed that has hitherto been neglected or was previously unheard of. Nietzsche's *Homo natura*, as well as Schelling's and

Feuerbach's "essential unity of the human being and nature," are always in the background (see *AO*, 2ff.). Some formulations even remind one of the magical analogies of romantic nature philosophy—if they were only a little less insipid. In both instances the human being becomes a source for analogies from which the kinship of all cosmological ideas arises; even stars and animals are given over to the human being to protect ("the being who is in intimate contact with the profound life of all forms or all types of beings, who is responsible for even the stars and animal life, and who ceaselessly plugs an organ-machine into an energy-machine, a tree into his body, a breast into his mouth, the sun into his asshole: the eternal custodian of the machines of the universe"; 4). Heidegger's old-fashioned image of the human being as the "shepherd of Being" is futuristically recast under the auspices of the industrial age,[5] turned into the image of the eternal custodian of the machines of the universe (*AO*, 4); indeed the human being is ever their "mechanic" (338, *passim*).

If the human being were the "organizer" of meaning, then we would come into even greater proximity to Lorenz Oken's idea of the unity of the human being and nature, and particularly to his idea of the universal unity of production of nature. Characteristic of Oken's system as well is the universal analogy, the transmutability of realms of Being, the mysticism of the number (in his case it is the number five; in the case of Deleuze and Guattari it is the number three), and the idea that the individual creature exists only as a "partial organism" (particular organ) in the "flowing universe of primal life." Hegel already reproached Oken—and his reproach would also apply in more pointed form to the authors of *Anti-Oedipus*—asserting that in this case a "mostly empty formalism [is at work], an immature brew of half-understood concepts, flat and mostly even silly ideas, and a lack of knowledge of Philosophy itself as well as of the sciences in general";[6] or even calling Oken's work "most crude empiricism with the formalism of materials and poles, embellished with unreasonable analogies and drunken aperçus."[7] All of these criticisms would be even more valid for the authors of *Anti-Oedipus*.

What possible motivation could there be for such a totalization of mechanistic thinking? One motivation is certainly that the machine simply "functions" (a favorite term of those who "say Yea and Amen" to that which is), and certainly another reason is that it is less problematic to experience "pleasure" (to bring into play another favorite concept of these authors) in the machine's dismemberment, its partialization, and its reassembly, than one could expect in the case of the dismemberment of organs and their reattachment. However, they did not consider the horror of being transported to Frankenstein's laboratory: the reader does not attend a slaughterfest, but rather a delirious, or, as Hegel pointedly said, drunken piecing together. Machine parts float about all over (in a figurative language that tends rather toward catachresis than toward metaphor), and they function only under the condition that they are screwed onto other parts or unscrewed from them: conjunctions and incisions abound. The mouth of the machine, for example, is attached to the breast-machine (a "source-machine," as we have already seen, is hooked up to an "organ-machine"). Put in a pseudomathematical way, this means that "desiring-machines are binary machines, obeying a binary law or set of rules governing associations: one machine is always coupled with another" (5). But it is a matter of a binarism ad infinitum: through all this turning of screws and wheels a vitality floods, flows, presses, rages, and raves; a sort of cosmic electricity whose task it is to resist the entropy of the universe, the "antiproduction" and the "body without organs": this vitality is the wish, the Freudian libido, Schopenhauer's and Nietzsche's will to power and will to life, Lacan's desire. The will to life makes things flow, flows itself, and separates the united.

> Amniotic fluid spilling out of the sac and kidney stones; flowing hair; a flow of spittle, a flow of sperm, shit, or urine that are produced by partial objects and constantly cut off by other partial objects, which in turn produce other flows, interrupted by other partial objects. (5–6)

One is hesitant to believe it at first; nonetheless, something remarkable is making itself known. For Deleuze and Guattari it is clear that the machine parts – as partial objects (in the terminology of Melanie Klein) – do not demand any assignment to particular personal bearers. The entities of production are dissoluble and can be arbitrarily recombined; they escape the identity of the compulsion for reference: for example, the compulsion for reference to the breast of the mother Amalie Freud, the spouse of Jacob Freud, in short; they resist the compulsion for reference to the "source-machine" of any armored subject whatsoever that might coincide with itself and which would be unequivocally distinguished from all other subjects.

The act that relates the flows of desire to persons is thus redirected: the result of a jam in the mechanism of the machines that produce the "body without organs" as the space for the inscription of their distinctions (8, 75ff.). The unconscious as such is itself parentless and impersonal (49). It refers to partial objects with which it forms units of production and – if desired – then dissolves again.

> Partial objects are not representations of parental figures or of the basic patterns of family relations; they are parts of desiring-machines, having to do with a process and with relations of production that are both irreducible and prior to anything that may be made to conform to the Oedipal figure. (46)

Desiring-production is thus a "molecular force"; it does not prevent particles that have combined together from forming a more attractive synthesis with different particles at another time. For there is only the process of production, on the one hand, and the relations of production, on the other. That, at least, is the primal condition: the world of desire before the Oedipal figure inscribed itself in desire and transformed it into something primally repressed and unconscious. (We want to take note of the fact that desire thus is *natura sua* not unconscious.)

But how does that transformation of the "desire to desire" (*Wunsch zu wün-schen*) into a craving (*Begehren*) for persons actually occur? How does the productive flow come under the law of the *triangulation familiale* (75f.) (which one at the same time has to imagine as a strangulation, if only because of the rhyme)? By the fact that desire, Deleuze and Guattari answer, is displaced from the level of pure mechanical functioning to the level of signifying (Lacan's *intrusion du signifiant*). Instead of producing realities and remaining with its craving itself within the really existing "identity of the human being with nature," it now produces only images, shadows, and representations (51ff.): it realizes itself indirectly, symbolically; it dies as desire and is reincarnated as (a chain of) signification. (Apparently every representation presupposes a prior presence in which desire, prior to all representation and personalization, is familiar with itself: in his *Logique du sens* Deleuze had already paid tribute to this theorem as Sartre's "decisive" discovery [*LS*, 120, 124], without, to be sure, subscribing to his characterization of it as an impersonal *consciousness*.)[8]

Significations are undoubtedly no natural result of "savage desire," i.e., of the primordial unity of production between the human being and nature. They are formed, as (not for the first time) was shown by Ferdinand de Saussure, in the play of differential relations among material substrates of expression (signifiers), each of them acquiring its identity and thus its determined significance by virtue of the fact that it is unequivocally distinguished from all other expressive substrates. Saussure conceded that he was thinking of the theory of exchange value in political economy when he developed this thought[9] (in fact, the comparison of the semiotic sign to money was already a commonplace in Humboldt's time), and Deleuze and Guattari remember this when they relate the "codification" of desire — the condition for its Oedipalization — with the rise of capitalist commodity production.

The idea in itself is not particularly original. Others have presented it with better arguments and in more depth (of course, the authors reject all talk of "depth"). But lack of originality and a drunken argumentative fluctuation between promises that are never cashed in and superfluous retractions still do not completely wipe out a thought that wants to express itself. The advantage of every brand of eclecticism is that something useful, and even sometimes remarkable, is always caught in its net and, according to the law of coincidence, can even enter into interesting relations. To be sure, one has to deconstruct the ideas, i.e., take them out of their disorder and put them into a new order, which means reformulating them into a communicating discourse.

As far as the idea of representation is concerned — to begin with this issue — Schopenhauer's (and Nietzsche's) predecessorship is evident. For Schopenhauer the "in-itself" (*An-sich*), the desire that holds the world together from within, exists in two manifestations: as will and as representation (*repraesentatio*). One knows this even if one is only familiar with the title of his major work. Only the will is real, of course; representation makes the will ideal and unreal. It transforms the wild drive for life, which makes stones into crystals, which drives the sap into buds and vines, and which pumps the streams of urges through the bodies of animals, into a panopticon of representations whose gruesomeness is made bearable only by the aesthetic distancing that art provides. Except for the pessimistic tone, the same is the case for Deleuze and Guattari: "The objective being of desire is the Real in and of itself" (26–27). And (I am putting the quotation together out of two passages that supplement each other):

> The order of desire is the order of *production*; all production is at once desiring-production and social production. . . . For a *structural unity* is imposed on the desiring-machines that joins them together in a molar aggregate. (296, 306)

This subjugation of the wild flow of production to the structuring order of portrayal, of representation, simultaneously produces the fiction of the unconscious; for the desiring force of production, which is repressed and transformed by the order of representation, lives on as something repressed: it simultaneously both continues to be effective and is excluded from consciousness as something it lacks.

> In reality, social production becomes alienated in allegedly autonomous beliefs at the same time that desiring-production becomes enticed into allegedly unconscious representations. . . . But production is not thereby suppressed, it continues to rumble, to throb beneath the representative agency (*instance représentative*) that suffocates it, and that it in return can make resonate to the breaking point. . . . Now the same is true of both desiring-production and social production: every time that production, rather than being apprehended in its originality, in its reality, becomes *reduced* (*rabattue*) in this manner to representational space, it can no longer have value except by its own absence, and it appears as a lack within this space. . . . once desiring-production has spread out in the space of a representation that allows it to go on living only as an absence and a lack unto itself. (296, 306)

In other words, as opposed to Lacan and Derrida, there is a primal positive for Deleuze and Guattari, namely, desire, which only subsequently gets caught up in the net of the symbolic order and dissociates itself there. For those who assume the standpoint of the order of representation, desiring-production exists only as something that is lacking in the order itself. To be more precise, desiring-production exists for them only as the sacrifice desire has to make in order to become symbol or representation (of craving). The unconscious is thus nothing originary, but rather the effect of a banishment of desire from consciousness. The fact that it appears in this order as a lack does not, however, mean that it is a lack in itself; rather it is the order that breaks down and hollows out the fullness of its positivity. The becoming-sign of desire is the fall from paradise, desire's denial of itself. The will becomes a mere copy and image (*Ab- und Nachbild*); it becomes representation, shadow, illusion: the re-presentation of a primal present.[10]

But that is still quite mildly put, and to the ears of the authors it must sound like a scornful euphemism. Like Nietzsche, they overstress the metaphor of inscription and incision to the point that we find ourselves transported to Kafka's penal colony or similar places of torture: the symbolization of desire—Nietzsche's "mnemotechnique," translated into French as *codage*, *enregistrement*, or *symbolisation*—occurs as a cut in and dissection of the flesh of the will to life. The differentiality of language cuts up and tears up the "full body" of a wildness that dreams again of Wordsworth's "Never-never land." *Style*, *stylo*, *stylet*: three designations for one and the same instrument of torture. Behind this stands (beginning with Nietzsche) "grammar." Its system is

> the movement of culture that is realized in bodies and inscribed on them, belaboring them. That is what cruelty means. . . . It makes men or their organs into parts and wheels of the social machine. The sign is a position of desire; but the first signs are the territorial signs that plant their flags in bodies. (*AO*, 145)

The transformation into a machine, of course, is acceptable (as long as it functions and "nothing is bad"). It is merely the wrong machine that here poses as the agency of flows of desire: a totally alienated machine, i.e., culture. (Yet it is very difficult to imagine how one should conceive "alienation" in a system of mere mechanical functioning—I, at least, cannot conceive of it.)

At any rate, many people from the older generation are familiar with this sort of critique of culture from books that have been successfully suppressed in Germany: Spengler and the representatives of the "conservative revolution" flirted with descriptions of the history of mankind as a process of decay, first the decay of archaic savageness, then of myth, and finally of culture. The zero grade is the totalitarian civilization that the myth of blood, violence, and honor—it is Rosenberg's *Der Mythus des zwanzigsten Jahrhunderts*[11]—is supposed to revert in a revolutionary manner to the Archaic. The most important thing is that the process of culturalization—already in Spengler—is appreciated only when compared to the process of civilization: on the scale that measures decay, it stands pretty close to the bottom, and certain followers of Nietzsche—Gentile, for example—did not, for their part, pass up the opportunity to point out the violent act of "mnemotechnical inscription inherent in it." Let's not forget (in spite of Theweleit) that fascism also knows (and loves) its streams and flows, for example, that "brown flood" (the SA) which, according to Röhm's words of 1933, will "overflow the gray rock [of the military]." In 1947 Sartre, in "What Is Literature?", called opting for the immediate the source of all violence: "Our first duty as a writer is . . . to re-establish language in its dignity. After all, we think with words. We would have to be quite vain to believe that we are concealing ineffable beauties which the word is unworthy of expressing. And then, I distrust the incommunicable; it is the source of all violence."[12]

I will go as far as to assert that the phantasm of the savage flow of craving and of its discursive subdual is the foundation of the minimal consensus of the counterenlightenment, which, as we know, was by no means procapitalist and friendly to the bourgeoisie (Thomas Mann, in his *Doctor Faustus*, called nazism "the completely unbourgeois adventure").[13] This applies to Nietzsche himself, as well as to Spengler, Moeller van den Bruck, Edgar Jung, Heidegger, Alfred Rosenberg, Charles Maurras, or the so-called *Nouvelle Philosophie*, which finds violence in any claim to explanation and symbolic representation of phenomena in terms of the unity of *one* perspective, and which cannot be clearly distinguished from the New Right (*Nouvelle Droite*).

This also applies to Deleuze and Guattari. In a (sometimes stimulating) speculative jaunt through the history of the (decay of the) human species, they distinguish three stages in which the knife of writing cuts into the flesh of desire in order to culminate in the castration of Oedipus. At the beginning (as in Rousseau), there are the savage societies; they constitute themselves by means of codes of kinship relations that make the individual immediately into the representative of the social. To be sure, by means of mere codification they repress with structural necessity the representative of the savage wish. The "savage territorial machine" (which gets its name from its "territorialization" of the boundless, "deterritorialized" streams of archaic desiring-production, dividing it into estates and tracts, parcels and distinctive property) gives way over the course of history to the despotic state in which "the repressive representation"—the "despotic signifier"—establishes its terrorist regime. Precisely how it accomplishes this remains, as usual, obscure. At any rate, the founders of states—a "herd of blonde beasts of prey, a race of conquerors and masters" (Nietzsche, *Works*, XIII, 103; see also 84ff.)[14]—overrun the savage societies in order to pounce "with terrible claws on a population; in numbers possibly tremendously superior, but as yet formless, as yet nomad" (*Works*, XIII, 103) ("which, organized for war and with the ability to organize, unhesitatingly lays its terrible claws upon a populace perhaps tremendously superior in numbers but still formless"; *AO*, 192). The chain of horrors evolves in the following order: the Greek corporate state, Christianity, feudalism, democratic and bourgeois humanism, the industrial society, capitalism, and socialism: "The earth becomes a madhouse" (192).

In order for it to come to this, the play of representations has to consent to its last and devastating *shifting*: accomplished solely through the agency of the *représenté déplacé*, an agency that intensifies the other forms of re-presenting

326 □ LECTURE 20

repression of the savage craving into extremes (its two predecessors are "the repressed representative" and "the repressing representation"; 166).

This is a fairly complicated story, but we have to follow its development, since only at the end do we encounter Oedipus, the guardian and patron of the allegedly universal structure of ego-like centered subjectivity that identifies itself socially by subordinating itself to the morality of the symbolic father, the superego. Oedipus is, therefore, not, as one might have thought, the resulting final product of "grammar" and the compulsions for identification and differentiation inscribed into it (which place persons, subjects, and owners in the stead of the apersonal parts of desiring-machines).

> For Oedipus to be occupied, it is not enough that it be a limit or a displaced represented in the system of representation; it must *migrate* to the heart of this system and itself come to occupy the position of the representative of desire. (177)

This condition is supposed to be fulfilled in capitalism.

With this we have finally arrived at the point where the analogy between the semiological value theory of language and the exchange-value economy of capitalism can be made productive. And this is indeed what happens (240ff.). According to Deleuze and Guattari, capitalism, deceptively enough, is not a system of codification at all. Essential to it is the permanent "decoding" of codes, the "deterritorialization" of territories. Its streams of money, feces, and commodities know no fixed or definitive "limits." They share this with Saussure's (and even more so with Hjelmslev's) "language system," whose "values" (i.e., differentially determined and hollowed-out units) similarly float around their sign hulls (i.e., they "float" as do currencies) over the course of an infinite number of speech applications in order to continually differentiate and identify themselves anew on new and enlarged "speech lattices." With Georges Bataille we could speak of the "unlimiting of economy" that was accomplished in structuralism. Its effect is that codification is replaced by an "axiomatic."[15] This is a strange terminological proposal, for under an "axiomatic" one usually understands a value system or system of principles (which is not subjected to the free market of the exchange of signs) such as is appropriate, for example, to mythical or religious epochs, something that was destroyed, according to Max Weber, by capitalistic rationalism. Be that as it may, the authors designate (if I have counted correctly) five criteria for the distinction of axioms from the code of States. First, they believe that code relations presuppose inequalities (Althusserian "dominancies") between the elements (for example, between the nobility and the serfs). Second, the free market, on the other hand, introduces a purely logical (or economic) differentiality between the exchange values, and it thereby introduces the law of equivalence into the realm of communication. In this manner the signs of power cease completely to be what they were from the standpoint of the code: they become "directly economic coefficients" without duplicating themselves and (by means of representation) referring to noneconomic factors ("they become coefficients that are directly economic instead of being doubles to the economic signs of desire and expressing for their part noneconomic factors determined as dominant"; 249). Third, it is essential to the potency of capital that its axiomatic is never saturated, that it further extend any limit by introducing new axioms: what it decodes or deterritorializes with one hand, for example, religious and ethical obligations, it axiomatizes and reterritorializes with the other (257). Fourth, the capitalist axiomatic can no longer be portrayed as a gruesome instrument of inscription: everything takes place under the appearance of complete nonviolence. Everything seems to be the same as everything else; there are no preferences. Already Marx's *Capital* had emphasized this universalizing potential of unfettered commodity production that dissolves prejudices, breaks through national boundaries, and expands productive forces and necessities ad infinitum. It is based on the fact that capital from now on only marks quantities and no longer pays any attention to qualities: the value of a person loses its aura, the person becomes a "private person" whose identity is not inscribed by God or humanist dignity as an inalienable and intrinsic characteristic but rather is produced by means of the free play of unfettered relations of salability (*Äusserlichkeitsbeziehungen*); the person is what it possesses, and it is "different from all others." This is both the ultimate and the only thing it has in common with other individuals. And fifth, capitalism has the tendency to replace the social machine with technical machines. It is no longer the kinship code or the feudal "filiation" that determines the "value" of a human being (as an element in the system), but rather the machine in the nonfigurative sense. One could say that capitalism — as opposed to those societies described by Lévi-Strauss — makes intersubjective relations into wholly economic relations. For Deleuze and Guattari, this is the reason for the "privatization of the family" (263). In the capitalist stage of the fall from savagery, the family no longer serves economic reproduction; rather it migrates to a place outside it. The processes of socialization that are freed from kinship and filiation now run only by means of the alienated form of economic reproduction; the human being becomes the product of its product that confronts him/her as an independent thing and teaches him/her about its value: "function derived from the flow of capital" (264).

We are by and large familiar with this — in a more convincing and intelligent argumentation — from Karl Marx. But let's not be unjust: the old patriarch, after all, did not bother to enlighten us about the genesis of the Oedipal complex. To speak of enlightenment about it in the case of Deleuze and Guattari would, to be sure, be somewhat of an exaggeration. But now and again — one can only express it with one of the innumerable catachreses with which this book teems — a spark flies out of the "fecal flows" and even out of the "sunbeams in the ass." Oedipus, namely, is the final stage of a process of total abstraction in which all (concrete) relations between human beings are reduced to the final complex of the daddy-

328 □ LECTURE 20

mommy-me: "the despotic sign inherited by daddy, the residual territoriality assumed by mommy, and the divided, split, castrated ego" (265). The function of this language game, which is singularly impoverished as opposed to the richness of filiation, consists in furnishing the abstract private person with his or her last symbolic territory. Capital is in need of this in order not to undermine itself as a functioning mechanism, i.e., in order to impose a certain diet, whose nonobservance would be deadly for the mechanism, on its potentially infinite hunger for decoding.

> It is only in the capitalist formation that the Oedipal limit finds itself not only occupied, but inhabited and lived, in the sense in which the social images produced by the decoded flows actually fall back on restricted familial images invested by desire. It is at this point in the Imaginary that Oedipus is constituted, at the same time as it *completes its migration* in the in-depth elements of representation: *the displaced represented has become, as such, the representation of desire.* (286–87)

Oedipus is thus not an invention of Freud and of ego psychology; with the couch it merely gave Oedipus a new home. And it is true that Freud did not want to see how the familial *images*, as soon as one takes a close look at them, substantially dissolve, thereby allowing us to see through to those social images from which they receive their meaning. If Luther discovered the essence of religion in inwardness, Fichte the essence of the mind in absolute subjectivity, Smith and Ricardo the law of value in the abstract subjective essence of productive activity, then one can view Freud's historical achievement as the discovery of the abstract nature of the libido. But in this case he redirected the savage flow of desire—as if he wanted to excuse himself to the "system" for his discovery—as "the dirty little secret" into the pool of the family, the last bastion of the self-assertion of the subject in its privacy: "In place of the great decoded flows, little streams recoded in mommy's bed. Interiority in place of a new relationship with the outside" (270).

Although impossible to listen to, this is nevertheless intelligible. We can certainly safely concede that the rediscovery, or, put more cautiously, the reapplication of Melanie Klein's theory of partial objects, and the doubts about the transhistorical validity of Freud's psychology of the family and of personality resulting from it, can have a liberating effect. They might even be able to provoke the critical questioning of certain philosophical theories that accept as incontestable that one must approach this matter beginning with the subject. Perhaps "the subject" is in fact a historical, that is, an acquired scheme for our self-interpretation, one that is not grounded in any a priori evidence? One can, indeed, one *must* reflect on these questions, and it is within the framework of such reflections, to which we have granted major significance in our lectures, that we have made an effort to hear what Deleuze and Guattari have to say about it.

It is all the more unfortunate that the authors supplant what they call the "terrorist daddy-mommy language" with the artificially infantilized pee-pee-kaa-kaa language (I say "artificially infantilized" in the knowledge that children speak differently). It is not easy to forget the interruption at the Sartre colloquium at Cerisy in 1979, at which it was admonished: "Why don't we stop all these horse-shit games!" One could easily show, if it were worth proving, how even the im-ages of this language open themselves up to worlds of repression and to the spite-fully overcompensated denial of pleasure. It is not enough to strip away the academic veneer (first of all, because *Anti-Oedipus* is read primarily at universi-ties); until the barriers of terminological, indeed, of jargonlike opposition are re-moved, many things will continue to stand in the way of the liberation of desiring-production, the well-meant Yea in affirmation of the positivity and irreplaceabil-ity of "life." For the sake of several thought-provoking ideas in *Anti-Oedipus*, it is too bad that their "discursive" medium makes them inaccessible to the reader; for the reader cannot help but get the impression that the light that shines on the "ass of Judge Schreber" too seldom illuminates the heads of the authors (at best it heats them up).

But there are more serious objections that can be made. One of them is related to Deleuze and Guattari's theory of schizophrenia. I will take care to avoid incur-sions into a matter about which I am not sufficiently informed (although perhaps not even the authors themselves are). Nevertheless, what Deleuze and Guattari have to say about schizophrenia is closely connected to their reconstruction of the genesis of that persistent overestimation of the ego by which even philosophy— especially philosophy—has been hard hit. Inasmuch as *Anti-Oedipus* makes state-ments about the theory of the subject, we, as philosophers, are directly addressed, and we can, indeed must, put them to a critical test.

According to the view of the two authors, schizophrenia is a disorder that psy-choanalysts and entire schools of ego psychology would like to reduce to neuro-sis; neurosis, however, is an illness that arises out of the incompatibility of savage desires with the law that demands that an "ego" be formed, i.e., that desires be made compatible with the imperatives of the symbolic order (of the superego). Consequently, the cure of psychoanalysis consists in Oedipalizing the "schizo," i.e., in making him into a functional bearer of capitalist order. (Were there no "schizos" in precapitalist times?)

The craving of the schizophrenic, however, is supposed to consist precisely in breaking through the always only relative limit with which capitalism girds the schizophrenic's amoeba-like body, thereby carrying forward the innermost mod-ern spirit that demands the overstepping of limits, curiosity about the world, the undoing of taboos, and emancipation. The "schizo," who dares to go much further than audacious trespassers such as Doctor Faustus or the Flying Dutchman, wants to destroy even this final limit "which causes the flows to travel in a free state on a desocialized body without organs" (246). (The "body without organs" and the "socius" are ciphers for the "antiproduction" that anorganically opposes the originary desiring-production: the material in which punishment and coding are accomplished, closely related to Sartre's *pratico-inerte*.)

> Hence one can say that schizophrenia is the *exterior* limit of capitalism itself or the conclusion of its deepest tendency, but that capitalism only functions on condition that it inhibit this tendency, or that it push back or displace this limit, by substituting for it its own *immanent* relative limits, which it continually reproduces on a widened scale. (246)

The "schizo" (as the authors call him in comradely fashion) is thus produced by capitalism; yet although he is only an extension of its innermost tendency (and thus is completely unsuited to criticize capitalism by means of his craving itself!), in the long run he produces a "socius" for capitalism whose effect, as opposed to the tyrant in the family and at home, Oedipus,[16] threatens to destroy the axiomatic of capitalism. He therefore has to be locked up (confined!) in an insane asylum.

We are already familiar with the basic features of this view from Foucault's archaeology of insanity, on which Deleuze and Guattari also rely. Each generation, it seems, has to construct its contrastive myths out of the material of its experience of real suffering in the existing society. Frequently this occurs in the form of a simple inversion of the dominant axiomatic. In the eighteenth century, for example, the critique of the legitimation of "world curiosity," and particularly of imperial colonialism, becomes stronger in the circles of the ascending bourgeois intelligentsia. The complementary myths of the punished world conquerer (*The Flying Dutchman*) and of the "noble savage" arise at the same time.[17] In the twentieth century, perhaps even since romanticism, these myths seem to have been replaced by the myth of the good madman, of the "schizo" (think of E. T. A. Hoffmann's tale about the insane musician Kreisler or Tieck's novella *Die Reisenden*).[18] If we remain at the level of myth, of the collective imagination of a class or a group at a certain time, it would be very difficult to contradict Deleuze and Guattari's diagnosis. As soon as they recruit their examples from literature (and they do this remarkably often, indeed, they almost never take them from the sphere of the clinic), they can always plausibly prove that the lunatic who is banned from society is imagined as the "better person" in the hidden and poetic dreams of the same society. The "schizo" is the collective suffering subject: the savior with the crown of thorns, but also the revolutionary par excellence; in short, he is the representative bearer of all the forbidden desires and archaically thronging cravings that in their very nature have to be inimical to order, rebellious, and subversive. Each of us can detect this inclination in him/herself. It may very well be true that, in the sense of the colloquial expression, "capitalism drives us all crazy."

Nevertheless, we are still permitted to ask the question as to whether one necessarily has to write about psychosis in the style of psychosis (and not *en poésie* as Beckett, Kafka, Proust, Lawrence, Artaud, or Blanchot did): that is, in a style that over large stretches, one cannot read without sharing with Schopenhauer the pleasure he experienced when he read Hegel.[19]

Even more profound is a doubt of another sort. It concerns the critique of the analogy between Oedipality and subjectivity. In *Anti-Oedipus* this analogy is established by the idea of introducing the savage flows of desire into the order of representation. The "inscribed" subject is not the subject of desire but rather the repressed, displaced, alienated subject that is trained to say I and to obey the code. This formulation is structurally similar to Lacan's delimitation of the narcissistic subject from the true subject. The difference is that Deleuze and Guattari want to understand desire as something nonnegative, or even as pure positivity: the negativity attributed to it is, according to them, itself already the effect of Oedipalization and the related fear of castration; and it is these, moreover, that also make Lacan's *sujet véritable*—conceived as *manque à être* and pure *lacune*—appear unsuited as a means for escaping the I fixation of psychoanalysis.

We cannot treat the posed problem any further here. Instead, we will try to formulate it as clearly as possible and set it as our task for the next lecture: what role does the order of representation (abbreviatedly termed "grammar," following Nietzsche) play in the Oedipalization of the "subject," or, in other words, in the instance of the becoming-subject of desire?

Lecture 21

If there is any thought that helps to unite *Anti-Oedipus* into a text, it is, it seems to me, this one: the savage desire of the *production primaire* – an expression coined in analogy to Freud's "primary process" – is deprived of its natural immediacy and positivity by being inserted into the order of representation, until it can only imagine its uncomplicated fullness as something it lacks, as a *manque à être*. It is, of course, one characteristic feature of representation among others that it replaces a Being with an image, a present with a presencing (or, to be more precise, with a retropresencing). The originary positivity of the thing is thus partly negated by the symbol. The representative of desire, the linguistic sign, for example, is *no* longer desire itself in its Being in itself; rather it is a place-holder (*Stellvertreter*) that "supplies" the absence of that to which it refers. However, in order to be able to accomplish this placeholding, it must subjugate itself to an order: for example, the linguistic sign must subjugate itself to the order of language (of grammar). Now grammar, as we know, achieves the determinateness of its elements only by contrasting them with each other. The identity of the signs, therefore, is grounded, as the condition of its possibility, on the destruction of the unity of the signified: to designate something always already means to incorporate it into a differentiated, a dismembered world. To designate a world by means of a collection of differentiated signs also means to take the loss of the unity of the signified as a part of the bargain. The unity of the signified is replaced by the unity of the signifying structure itself, behind which, itself absent, the shadow of the unity of a sign-instituting subject appears, presuming the order is closed.

The entire affect of the authors of *Anti-Oedipus* is tied up with this notion of structural closure. It is suspected of cutting up, dismembering, violating the natural savageness of the (not yet represented) flows of desire, much as the torture of memory production was dramatically portrayed in Nietzsche's *Genealogy of Morals*.

Is all this supposed to mean that the flows of desire were uniform and unitary *before* their "inscription" into the order of grammar? Not at all; they are manifold and cannot be reduced to any principle of unity (on the contrary, it is grammar that relates them to a—missing—unity whose last savior and guarantor will be Oedipus).

It is in the structure that the fusion of desire with the impossible is performed, with lack defined as castration. From the structure there arises the most austere song in honor of castration—yes, yes, we enter the order of desire through the gates of castration—once desiring-production has spread out in the space of a representation that allows it to go on living only as an absence and a lack unto itself. For a *structural unity* is imposed on the desiring-machines that joins them together in a molar aggregate; the partial objects are referred to a totality that can appear only as that which the partial objects lack, and as that which is lacking unto itself while being lacking in them (the Great Signifier "symbolizable by the inherency of a -1 in the ensemble of signifiers"). Just how far will one go in the development of a lack of lack traversing the structure? Such is the structural operation: it distributes lack in the molar aggregate. The limit of desiring-production—the border line separating the molar aggregates and their molecular elements, the objective representations and the machines of desire—is now completely displaced. The limit now passes only within the molar aggregate itself, inasmuch as the latter is furrowed by the line of castration. The formal operations of the structure are those of extrapolation, application, and biunivocalization, which reduce the social aggregate of departure to a familial aggregate of destination, with the familial relation becoming "metaphorical for all the others" and hindering the molecular productive elements from following their own line of escape. (*AO*, 306-7)

I have purposely quoted a longer, self-contained passage that is meaningful in itself so that you can establish on the basis of the text your own criteria by which to judge the interpretation I am going to give, and about which I myself am fully aware that it stands on very slippery ground. I do believe, however, that one can extrapolate the following view of the subject at hand from the text: "in themselves" the flows of desire do not obey any unity at all. Structure, too—as an order of differentiation (to be sure, of recombination as well, but only on the basis of prior separation)—does not in itself vouch for the subjugation of the represented desires under a principle of unity. However, in order to train the elements—the partial objects, also called molecules (I am not sure why)—to obey the voice of a personal authority (of a *sur-moi*, a great subject, an *ensemble molaire*), one has to invent a principle of unity. This is done by interpreting the variety and manifoldness of the partial ojects in terms of a loss: they are many because, or inasmuch as, they lack unity. However, their movements—their flows—have the *meaning* that they are looking for the missing unity. If one drums this self-understanding into them, then they will consider themselves "castrated": cut through, deprived of their integrity, lacking—and all the more desirous of (craving)—the unity of a point of orientation. This is offered to them in the form of the illusion of the "good identification" of Oedipus, and they gladly seize on it (308).

Apart from the fact that it is hard to see how one can possibly *seduce* the flows of desire into believing in the illusion of Oedipal unity if the possibility of being seduced, i.e., the desire to develop longings of this sort, was not already integral to them, it is also hardly imaginable that a "molecular" multiplicity of desires could possibly exist "in itself"—i.e., *prior* to the entrance into the differentiation of representation. Unity and multiplicity are corresponding ideas; they both originate to the same extent from conceptual work. (The Kantian tradition is probably exerting a distorting influence at this point, since Kant considered "pure manifoldness of sensation" to be preintellectual, and thus untouched by the unitary principle of self-consciousness, whereas multiplicity, rather, is a categorical concept.) Be that as it may, the multiplicity and lack of unity of the desiring-production would, if it existed, by no means permit us to talk about it as a "primary process" or a "savage primordial state," i.e., as something prerepresentative that is prior to the order of grammar, much as Schopenhauer's will is prior to the representation that a subject (misconstruing its In-itself) has of it. The talk about savage desire and its unbroken positivity free of negation is a mere phantasm from a precritical age, and is not deserving of the least attention, except perhaps as a phenomenon and symptom of a thoroughly alarming readiness for flight from civilization and regression in those times when the world, overwrought with codes of all sorts (technical, industrial, pedagogical, bureaucratic, and last but not least, military), justifies the desire to take refuge in relatively precivilized ages.

Yet from the mere fact that already the multiplicity of the flows of desire, for whose emancipation from the order of representation Deleuze and Guattari (if I understand them even a little) are arguing, can be articulated only within the structure of a symbolic (representative) order—otherwise they would have no meaning and would be nobody's desire, since they would be unconscious (and this is precisely what the authors deny)—from all this it does not follow reciprocally that this order serves to train the partial objects for a "molar unity." In coming lectures we will concern ourselves with the idea (that can already be found in Saussure) that the law of differentiality by no means operates in the service of the idea of structural closure. From the fact that I can determine something only when

I bring it into contrast with other things, it by no means follows that I can close the chain of expressions that I distance from one expression, or that I can survey this chain in its entirety. On the contrary, many things speak for the fact that these chains are open and run on into infinity, that new expressions are constantly inscribed while others fall away, and that the form of the *ensemble molaire* is incessantly and uncontrollably changing. In fact, we considered this thought to be one of the basic theoretical insights of all of neostructuralism.

This insight actually is also relevant, however, in an absurdly exaggerated form, for Deleuze and Guattari themselves and their idea of the "boundless and unreserved decoding," i.e., the depreciation of thought in code models. Yet what prevents them from completely developing the consequence of this idea is, in their case as in the case of Foucault, their attachment to a Manichaean dogma of two worlds, something that sends the entire work reeling: on the one side the "order of desire," on the other the "order of representation"; the latter represses the former and trains it, at the end of a long chain of historical transformations, to be obedient to the name of Oedipus—the desired I-identity.

This unsteadiness becomes particularly apparent in the indistinct way in which the differential or indifferential character of either primary production or schizophrenic transgression is described. We recall that the desiring-machines link the partial objects by means of "connective syntheses," which are also called "disjunctive." Now everybody knows that "disjunctive" means mutually exclusive. But that cannot be what Deleuze and Guattari mean, for then the expression "disjunctive synthesis" would be a contradiction in terms. Presumably they mean "disjunctive" in the sense of "disjunctive judgment." A disjunctive judgment, as we all know, has the form: "A is either B or C"; or: "A or B." Thus, here disjunction differentiates, but not necessarily in an exclusionary sense. In the form "A or B" the "or" can be understood as inclusionary, in which case it would indeed accomplish the synthesis of A and B.

This indecision between inclusion and exclusion is allegedly the typical form of conclusion manifest in schizophrenic discourse (*AO*, 75ff.), whereas Oedipalized discourse proceeds in an exclusionary manner.

> The action characteristic of Oedipal recording is the introduction of an exclusive, restrictive, and negative use of the disjunctive synthesis. . . . It becomes nevertheless apparent that schizophrenia teaches us a singular extra-Oedipal lesson, and reveals to us an unknown force of the disjunctive synthesis, an immanent use that would no longer be exclusive or restrictive, but fully affirmative, nonrestrictive, inclusive. A disjunction that remains disjunctive, and that still affirms the disjoined terms, that affirms them throughout their entire distance, *without restricting one by the other or excluding the other from the one*, is perhaps the greatest paradox. "Either . . . or . . . or," instead of "either/or." . . . This is free disjunction; the differential positions persist

in their entirety, they even take on a free quality, but they are all in-
habited by a faceless and transpositional subject. . . . It is because
the exclusive relation introduced by Oedipus comes into play not only
between the various disjunctions conceived as differentiations, *but between the whole of the differentiations that it imposes and an undifferentiated (un indifférencié) that it presupposes.* Oedipus informs us: if you
don't follow the lines of differentiation daddy-mommy-me, and the exclusive alternatives that delineate them, you will fall into the black night
of the undifferentiated. . . . Oedipus says to us: either you will internalize the differential functions that rule over the exclusive disjunctions,
and thereby "resolve" Oedipus, or you will fall into the neurotic night
of imaginary identifications. Either you will follow the lines of the
triangle—lines that structure and differentiate the three terms—or you
will always bring one term into play as if it were one too many in relation to the other two, and you will reproduce in every sense the dual
relations of identification in the undifferentiated. (76, 77, 78, 79)

The resolution of Oedipus thus consists not in the resolution of differentiation but
rather in the nonexclusive use of the disjunctive conclusion, which simultaneously submits what is excluded to identification.

The difference is not between two uses of Oedipus, but between the
anoedipal use of the inclusive, nonrestrictive disjunctions, and the Oedipal use of exclusive disjunctions, whether this last use borrows from the
paths of the Imaginary *or* the values of the Symbolic. (83)

Here are the examples that Deleuze and Guattari provide for what they call the
inclusive use of disjunction:

The schizophrenic is dead *or* alive, not both at once, but each of the
two as the terminal point of a distance over which he glides. He is child
or parent, not both, but the one at the end of the other, like the two
ends of a stick in a nondecomposable space. This is the meaning of the
disjunctions where Beckett records his characters and the events that be-
fall them: *everything divides, but into itself.* . . . "It is midnight. The
rain is beating on the windows. It was not midnight. It was not raining." . . . "I am an Egyptian. I am a red Indian. I am a Negro. I am a
Chinaman. I am a Japanese. I am a foreigner, a stranger. I am a sea
bird. I am a land bird. I am the tree of Tolstoy. I am the roots of Tolstoy." (76, 77)

These examples show very clearly that nonexclusion functions at the level of
judgment, statement, and conclusion, and that it has nothing to do with the discrimination of elementary signs. Of course, I can connect in nonexclusive form
terms that differ on the level of predicative acts, in the judgment "The rose is white
or red," for example. But that does not mean—and it is trivial to point this out—

that the terms "rose," "white," and "red" are not semantically differentiated. Many of the so-called disjunctions which Deleuze and Guattari discuss are logically noncontradictory in the first place, as is the case with the judgments "The rose smells or is white"; or: "I am feeling weak and/or I am feeling strong." "White" and "smell" do not mean the same thing, but they are nevertheless compatible (noncontradictory); and the same person who now feels weak can feel strong at another time (and the authors explicitly emphasize that the disjunctive "or" does not assert simultaneity in the sense of a contrary or contradictory judgment: "It would be a total misunderstanding of this order of thought if we concluded that the schizophrenic substituted vague syntheses of identification of contradictory elements for disjunctions, like the last of the Hegelian philosophers"; 76).

In short, the mode of junction that in these examples is called "inclusive disjunction" does not prove anything in support of the thesis that the flows of desire of "primary production" escape what Lacan calls the "parade of the signifier"; i.e., they do not escape articulation and significance brought on by insertion into a grammar. Let us make certain that the authors actually hold this thesis by citing a few passages that make it quite clear.

> The unconscious poses no problem of meaning, solely problems of use. The question posed by desire is not "What does it mean?" but rather *"How does it work?"* How do these machines, these desiring-machines, work? . . . It represents nothing, but it produces. It means nothing, but it works. Desire makes its entry with the general collapse of the question "What does it mean?" No one has been able to pose the problem of language except to the extent that linguistics and logicians have first eliminated meaning; and the greatest force of language was only discovered once a *work* was viewed as a machine, producing certain effects, amenable to a certain use. (109)[1]

"Primary production" is thus asemantic, senseless, naturelike functioning that is not disturbed in the least by the question about its legitimacy and purposefulness. Because of their adventurous confusion of the logical function of the exclusive disjunctive judgment with the function of semiological differentiation, the authors arrive at the astonishing thesis that Oedipus is the product of a "coding of the savage flow," of an "inscription of the grammar of the desiring-production," whereas the schizophrenic undermines the distinctions of grammar. In reality the "schizo" also *speaks*; "to speak," however, among other things, means to make use of differentiated marks, regardless of how one later combines them into syntagmas and judgments. Be that as it may, Deleuze and Guattari seem to consider the language of the flows of desire to be "primary," and thus to be extragrammatical (otherwise it would be incomprehensible how they can talk about a necessity of "language" (*langue*) or "grammar," rather than of a necessity of logic), and they seem to distinguish "grammar" from this medium of expression.[2]

The structural impossibility of permanently subjugating a term of a linguistic system to the unity of a closed order ("grammar") has here, as it were, sacrificed any claim to more than partial validity: it does not apply to the flows of desire, nor is it relevant—at least not without restrictions—to the "axiomatic of capitalism," which constantly transgresses all limits; it does, however, indeed apply to all codes, including the encoding of the Oedipus complex into the desires of the contemporaries of the capitalist world revolution.

The misunderstanding of grammar as an instrument of punishment and torture, as a prison from which one cannot escape, perhaps goes back to Nietzsche, the main source on which the authors rely. The expression "prison house of language" presupposes the abdication of a subject that, when speaking, makes use of the pregiven signs in order to express, as Lacan says, everything else but that which language (*langue*) prescribes (see *E*, 155–56)—the resignation of a subject, but by no means its empowerment. The protest against the coercion the "code" exercises over the "codified" subjects logically presupposes the death (not only of God, but also) of the subject that in its linguistic activity in some way *relates* to this language, i.e., transgresses and changes it. *If there were* no subject, who would suffer under the coercion of language? And even if there were a subject that would blindly execute those activities conditioned by the code, a subject abandoned in its passivity, then how could one suggest liberation from the code in its name? A machine that *in its essence* is passive (which is moved by external forces, by urge flows) could not even perceive the theft of its freedom by "grammar" as a loss. If, therefore, Deleuze and Guattari—apart from the logical contradiction in the very thought itself—"schizonomadically" (*AO*, 105) demand the abolition of the laws, the "beyond all law" (82), "the destruction of all codes" (250), "a breakthrough in grammar and syntax" (134), "a violence against syntax, a concerted destruction of the signifier" (133) for the benefit of "non-sense erected as a flow, polyvocity that returns to haunt all relations" (133), then they are appealing, it seems to me, to a conception of the human being that has to be able to account for its freedom (or potential for liberation).[3] Nowhere do they provide an account of this, and I also cannot find one in the much more discursive earlier writings of Deleuze. In *Anti-Oedipus* there is not even the slightest trace of a move in this direction—except for two declarations of sympathy with Sartre (256, 377).

"Never," Deleuze and Guattari write, "We'll never go too far with the deterritorialization, the decoding of flows" (382). How is one supposed to conceive the realization of this implied imperative? Certainly not in capitalism, which, although it causes all the flows of desire to flow, nevertheless still sets (movable) limits. Is it to be realized in schizophrenia, which even tears down the "absolute limit," and thereby comes close to the "truth that only breaks open in delirium" (see 4: "for the real truth—the glaring, sober truth that resides in delirium")?

I am not certain whether the authors would absolutely reject this thought. Every "grammaticalization" appears to them to be a "repression of the desiring-machines" (364); accordingly, the unfettering of the flows of desire, the liberation of craving, appears as a revolutionary act ("desire as a revolutionary agency"; 379), as the tearing down of the "last limit" that seeks to confine anarchist craving in an order.

> Completing the process and not arresting it, not making it turn about in the void, not assigning it a goal. (382)

The passage which the authors cite from Pierre Klossowski's *Nietzsche et le cercle vicieux* points in a similar direction.

> The day humans are able to behave as *intentionless phenomena* — for every intention at the level of the human being always obeys the laws of its conservation, its continued existence — on that day a new creature will declare the integrity of existence. . . . Science demonstrates by its very method that the *means* that it constantly elaborates do no more than reproduce, on the outside, an interplay of forces by themselves *without aim or end* whose combinations obtain such and such a result. (368)

Intentionality and directedness at a goal are characteristic features of rationality, be it in the form of logic, in the form of grammar, as control of actions in the name of reason, or as an order of whatever sort. In fact, "we believe in desire as in the irrational of every form of rationality" (379). The "irrational process" of the primary desiring-production operates without repression only if it is not referred to an aim or a purpose ("it must not be viewed as a goal or an end in itself"; 5).

Deleuze and Guattari draw two conclusions from this. The first is that every discursive control of arguments and every reference of actions to an aim (for example, revolution) implies an opting for repression, and against liberation (if somebody now and then adds 2 + 2 = 4, or has the "aim" of fighting against the alienation of the life world, one has to exorcise this purpose by means of "schizoanalysis"). Second, they conclude that any form of limitation has to be considered a form of antiproduction, which is inimical to life.

Let me start with a couple of observations regarding the second conclusion, which is perhaps even weaker than the first one. Try to imagine, just for the fun of it, a completely orderless chaos or a river that does not flow anywhere (and thus has no aim). The sheer impossibility of complying with this request demonstrates immediately that one indeed can imagine that a state of the world does not exhibit the kind of order we wish it had, or that a river takes a different course than we think it has; but we cannot imagine that the arrangement of the parts, in the first instance, and the direction in which the river flows, in the second, cannot be exactly described (as order and as finality). A sea that would stream out in all directions and in all dimensions would no longer flow (since flow presupposes a direction) and would in the end dissolve into standstill and the emptiness of the unlimited universe. The same is true for an aimless desire that fills the entire universe (are there desires that do not desire something?): such a desire would no longer even exist *as* desire; nor would it have an object. Even desire has to differentiate itself in order to experience itself as desire (and not as a nightmare); furthermore, it must constitute a differentiated (thus ordered) world of things that can be desired outside of itself, and it can evolve within an existing "order of production" only as its determined negation.

This might seem sophistic. Nevertheless, no biologist, anthropologist, or philosopher of nature would deny that organic production reaches its (always) preliminary end in the completion of the product; that is, it has to interrupt itself periodically and can articulate itself only in processes that do not destroy the law of "organic equilibrium." (The parts of Deleuze and Guattari's desiring-machine know these "incisions" [*coupures*] [36ff.], which are hastily contrasted with the incisions of structure, with the *articuli* of articulation.) Total dispersion would be entropy. Without a minimum of order, the organism that relies on its environment and on other human beings (or partial objects) could not survive; without minimal predictability of recurring (and thus regulated) experiences, none of us would have the courage to begin the day. No, all organic production is accomplished within orders; however, this does not mean that it does not constantly alter, challenge, and rework the status quo of these orders. In order to be able to transgress the existing order in the direction of another order, one can eliminate neither the idea of directedness at a goal nor that of order as such. Even the "nonsense" with which the authors flirt is relative to a state of sense (of order) and, beyond this relation, would lose its characteristic as the opposite or determined negation of sense.

My objection to the first conclusion, which asserts that one has to help the savage desires attain their rightful place by decoding and definalizing them, is of greater consequence. Even assuming that the authors have in mind something like the liberation of desire—or even an anticapitalist revolution—one has to suppose that they completely misunderstand themselves. Either their book has precisely this *meaning*, the liberation of desire, in which case the rejection of final aims is unintelligible, or it rejects this and all other purposes and pleads for the running amok of Dionysus (who, to be sure, also has his own order, as does everything else that occurs in this world, even if this is not the order that the bourgeois desires).[4]

But one has to pose the question in a more fundamental form, for, as we saw in response to our examination of Foucault, the desire to eliminate order as such can only be a desire that does not know what it desires, i.e., that does not understand itself and that undermines its own basis for existence. If not in the name of some (alternative) order, then in whose name do the authors fight against the order of inscriptions, against the "coding of the savage flow"? One cannot subvert existing circumstances without—in opposition to this reality—referring to a value in whose name that which is can be subjected to criticism. Instead, Deleuze and Guattari identify social (i.e., *actual*) production with desiring-production (see 24ff., a critique of the interpretation of craving as lack). This identification deprives desire of any counterfactual character, something that can be guaranteed only by its displacement onto the level of representation (i.e., of lack, of not having), and which would make the (continually cited) literary text into a quasiethical authority over against the dominant power. The fantasies exiled to the sphere of the unreal now are suing for the happiness of which real society divested itself. A morality, to be sure, would not be very far removed from an (Oedipal) superego and would appeal to concepts like "reason," "purpose," and "meaning." But since the production-machine knows nothing about this (it is enough that it functions), the anarchism of the authors has to remain a matter of caprice and accident, in the worst sense of the word. It is similar to that "simplest surrealist act" of which Breton dreamed ("of going down into the street . . . and firing into the crowd at random as long as you can")[5] and of which Sartre says that this dream found its realization in everyday fascism. The total (and imaginary) destruction of which surrealism dreams, however, does no one any harm ("The total abolition it dreams of does not harm anybody precisely because it is total").[6] The attack here is directed not at this or that order but at the principle of order as such. This makes the guardians of a particular order relax (for example, of the order in which we live and under whose repression we suffer); from this quarter, so they say to themselves, we are not threatened by any real danger.

I consider this universal attack on order as such (whether it manifests itself in the State, in the penal system, in scientific disciplines/disciplinings, in grammar, discourse, family, or even in the conceptual or ethical self-mastery of a subject—in short, everywhere that blind action controls itself by means of the question of its possible legitimation and generalizability) to be a specific exaggeration of Foucault's approach (to which Deleuze not only stands in close proximity, but on which his works are constructed). No one denies that it was Foucault who first directed our attention to the phenomena of "madness and society." But his works—and above all those of his students: Deleuze, the *Nouveaux Philosophes*, and among them, unfortunately, the *Nouvelle Droite* as well—operate with a strongly polysemic concept of reason, that even in its negation is inadequate. Similar to the "dialectic of enlightenment," reason is, on the one hand, a revolutionary and emancipatory medium; one appeals to the reason of the reader when one attacks the conditions of our prisons and asylums. On the other hand, "reason is torture," as Foucault recently said; it is *reason* that locks up nonreason in an asylum, that banishes it from the bourgeois order. That is because reason implies order; but every order is intolerant toward nonorder, this profoundly relative concept, which becomes the opponent of order only according to the axioms of the participants in a worldview (in a "symbolic order") articulated in a certain manner, and which constitutes itself by means of innumerable exclusions. In the thin air of such abstraction, the Foucaultian concept becomes an-archic in an untenable sense: it indeed can no longer be comprehended why one "should distinguish between Stalin and Hitler, Marx and Nietzsche, Bakunin and Gentile" (as the New Philosophers in Paris teach). Every form of control over beings—or, as some say, over "productivity," over the "vital machine"—that is directed by reason is accused of violence; the resigned leftist challengers of yesterday now take theoretical tranquilizers and spiritual analgesics (instead of working through their sorrow and returning to praxis). Because of their factual indifference (i.e., because of their unwillingness to take a position against the existing order and for an alternative order, one that would still be an order of intersubjective coexistence), they become the advance guard of a fatal integration of the individual into the dominant power. A kind of political and intellectual flipping-out, a spiritual Calibanism, a certain uncommon style that barely disguises its poverty of thought behind a flurry of images, and the limitless self-pity of many of our left intellectuals of yesterday; these are the characteristic features of this type of *imitatio* of Foucault. We only have to remind ourselves of the already fascistically colored neovitalisms that, as a result of the rediscovery of Gobineau, Nietzsche, and Chamberlain, are creeping back, this time not so much in Germany, the homeland of blind respect for blind productivity, as in France. And they are all the more dangerous due to their anarchist touch that displeases the average bourgeois. But to displease the bourgeois is, as I have said, in itself not enough: after all, even nazism was a "completely unbourgeois adventure."

It is necessary, it seems to me, to banish a disposition toward action that is not undangerous simply due to the degree of its currency, a disposition I would like to characterize in the following way: out of eagerness to defend the claims of the "schizo" against the terror of norms, one ends up conducting polemics against the concept of norm as such, and thereby becomes a militant supporter of the suicide of those norms with which everyday capitalism presents us. Deleuze and Guattari basically recognize this themselves when they characterize fascism as a "paranoid" reaction to the constant displacement of the limit and to the permanent destruction of the "possibility of believing" (249–51, 257–58). The capitalist state, according to their argument, nourishes fascistoid longings on its very ground; that is, it nourishes the archaic desire for reterritorialization, for reattainment of a firm code (which is impossible under the condition of total economy).

> These neoterritorialities are often artificial, residual, archaic; but they
> are archaisms having a perfectly current function, our modern way of
> "imbricating," of sectioning off, of reintroducing code fragments, resus-
> citating old codes, inventing pseudo codes or jargons. Neoarchaisms, as

Edgar Morin puts it. . . . The fascist State has been without doubt capitalism's most fantastic attempt at economic and political reterritorialization. But the socialist State also has its own minorities, its own territorialities, which re-form themselves against the State, or which the State instigates and organizes. (257–58)

On the other hand: "Completing the process, and not arresting it . . . we'll never go too far with the deterritorialization, the decoding of flows" (382). And since no one proceeds any further than the "schizo," who reaches the "absolute limit," the absurd imperative surfaces, one that demands that one uncover truth in delirium (3).

Once again (for faced with this symptomatic tendency to "dangerous thinking," it seems to me appropriate to "make a memory"[7] for the students of Deleuze and Guattari and to speak to their consciences): one will never defeat the terror of given codes by challenging the concept of the code as such (that would mean both closing one's eyes to all actually existing codes, and remaining silent about the *dominant* structural power in the name of an only *virtual* one). One must rather uncover and explain the repressive effect of this or that concretely analyzed norm, with foresight toward whichever conception of the human being, and of its non-violent coexistence with other human beings, on the basis of which one criticizes this norm. In other words, which contrafactual norm surfaces from the socially repressed fantasies of people like Beckett, Artaud, or Aragon? Whoever poses the question in this way does not "code" morality ("Oedipus"!); rather, he sides with the desiring-production of subjects, and against the apparatuses that obstruct their development. Such a morality of contrafactual political engagement I find at work both in the works of Foucault, as well as in those of Deleuze and Guattari. The unfortunate thing about it is that these authors factually advocate their morality, but can in no way legitimate it on the basis of the premises of their semiotic anarchism. If they thus *have* a morality themselves, it remains principally unfounded, arbitrary, decisionistic, and ideologically exploitable by the Left as well as by the Right. That is a result of their faulty radicalism-universalism: in the end it touches everything and everybody, but nothing and nobody *in particular*, and is just as acceptable to those who dominate as is the universal condemnation of being and its powers by the radical and impotent "No" that Schopenhauer's pessimism launches against the world.

It is true that traditional ethics appeals to a theory of subjectivity, and there are noteworthy reasons (Derrida has presented some of them) for suspending the concepts of the "subject" and of "self-understanding," at least until their function in the text of philosophy, of psychoanalysis, and of the social sciences is illuminated. But that cannot mean that we should liquidate the subject (the actually existing industrial societies and the institutions of the "administered world" are far more adept at this; why compete with them on the level of theory?); rather it can only mean that one has to explain subjectivity better and in a more adequate way than has been done by philosophy up to now. For even if the classical hermeneutic concept of "self-understanding" exhibits conceptual problems, I can still hardly imagine that we can expect a solution of the problem from an alternative theoretical concept that is founded on the principle of the *non*understanding of itself.

"Whoever strives for something infinite," Friedrich Schlegel says in the forty-seventh Lyceum fragment, "does not know what he wants. But this statement cannot be inverted."[8]

Lecture 22

Anti-Oedipus was announced as the first of two volumes devoted to the subject of "capitalism and schizophrenia"; the second volume, which appeared in 1980, is entitled *A Thousand Plateaus.*[1] It is only in a fairly removed sense the continuation of the first volume, primarily because it expounds in even more extreme formulations the polemic against the presumption that a book must have a purpose, a theme, or must engage itself for an issue (for example, the intention of communicating something to somebody — the reader).

This volume is a collection of essays that display a marked disparity of style and are of greatly uneven quality. Some of them fit well into the witty rubric of "most diffuse thoughts," under which the notes of the insane conductor Kreisler are categorized "with truly vicious irony" by his cousin.[2] Other essays, on the other hand, appear to owe their existence to the application of the rules of that party game in which the participants, one after the other, but without communicating about their ideas, have to draw a part of the body: the first person draws the head, the second the upper torso, the third the lower torso down to the knees, the last the calves and feet. The sheet of paper is folded back each time so that the next person has nothing else to go on, except for seeing where to continue drawing the lines. Each level of such a drawing of the body would — in Deleuze and Guattari's terminology — be called a "plateau" (*MP*, 33), and the entire male or female body would be composed of *mille plateaux*, if one folds the paper enough times.

Each morning we got up, and each of us asked himself which plateaus he was going to take, writing five lines here, ten lines elsewhere. We had hallucinatory experiences, we saw lines, like columns of little ants, leave one plateau and go to another. We made converging circles. Each plateau can be read in any place, and brought into relation with any other. A method is needed that indeed makes the multiple; no typographical artfulness, no lexical cleverness, mixture, or creation of words, no syntactic audacity can replace it. The latter, in fact, are most often merely mimetic procedures intended to disseminate or dislocate a unity maintained in another dimension for a book image. Techno-narcissism. Typographical, lexical, or syntactic creations are necessary only if they cease belonging to the form of expression of a hidden unity, and become themselves one of the dimensions of the multiplicity under consideration; we know of very few successes in this genre. We have not been able to do this on our own behalf. We have only used words that, in turn, functioned for us like plateaus. (33)

Many of the essays are indeed composed according to this principle. Yet others, as for example "Postulates of Linguistics" (95–139) and "On Some Orders of Signs" (140–84), turn out, if one judges them *sine ira et studio*, to be better thought through, more stimulating, and theoretically more extensive than that which was presented in *Anti-Oedipus*. I for my part cannot simply agree with the authors when they claim that in the composition of *Mille Plateaux* a nonsignificant recording (*pas de signifiance*, 33, *passim*), indeed, a completely asignificant writing (*écriture tout à fait asignifiante*, 16ff.), was supposed to have been practiced. Nothing is senseless in this book, since it contains mostly well-formed sentences; yet many things in it are nevertheless non-sense (to apply a distinction frequently used in analytical philosophy). Let's rely then, as far as this is concerned, on our own judgment rather than on that of the authors.

Before we close the chapter on "subjectivity" and begin with the third question that we want to address to neostructuralism, I would like to direct your attention to a thematics that was already present in *Anti-Oedipus* and—if the metaphor of the center is still appropriate—which is the central concern of *A Thousand Plateaus*. I am thinking of the idea of a completely unityless multiplicity, whose conceptual opposite is the "subject." Let me begin with the remark that I consider the interest—indeed, not seldom, the pathos—devoted to this topic to be symptomatic and worth some attention; this is true even when the manner in which the authors treat or mistreat the problem appears to us little worthy of imitation, or not even amusing.

Nowhere in neostructuralism, not even in Derrida, does the longing for the unlimiting of the ego, and the dismissal of all requirements that a statement be founded in a principle, find such strong expression as in Deleuze and Guattari. Before we pronounce any judgment on it, this longing itself must first of all be understood and, what is more elementary yet, must be acknowledged as a widespread feeling in our times. To be sure, *A Thousand Plateaus* is a largely wasted chance to bring home to us the importance of the issue, if we *have* not already recognized it; but we also do not want to pay the authors the negative tribute of having diverted us from the significance of the subject matter by the *dégoût* their (by and large) unsubstantial prattle provokes, a subject matter that, however distorted, leaves its mark even in these essays. There are sounder writings that make the opposite mistake of ignoring the entire dimension of contemporary "knowledge interests" articulated in *A Thousand Plateaus* and, as we will see, in a more convincing fashion already in *Différence et répétition*.

The idea of the unityless multiplicity is fundamentally always articulated in metaphors. In *Anti-Oedipus* it was the metaphor of the machine (although this is actually a catachresis rather than a metaphor); in *A Thousand Plateaus* it is the metaphor of the rhizome, taken from botany. "Rhizome" — from the Greek ἡ ῥίζα, the root, the bud, or τὸ ῥίζωμα, rootedness, the stem — refers to a particular metamorphosis of the axis of a plant.

Usually the bud of a plant is an erect, leaf-bearing axis with a terminal growth point: the places at which the leaves are connected to it are the nodes; the sections of the stem between the nodes are called the internodes. The branching off can, in the simplest cases, occur either laterally or dichotomously; in the first case, where the lateral branches remain subordinate to the main stem, botanists speak of monopodia; on the other hand, where the main stem divides into two side shoots, which, for their part, continue to branch off dichotomously (by a further forking of each branch), one speaks of a dichasium (or, when there are more than two shoots, of a pleichasium). These types of shoots, in which all the branches can be traced back to the unity of one stem (and *one* root), are appropriate metaphors, according to Deleuze and Guattari, for a characterization of systematic thinking or thinking that evolves from the unity of one principle, as it is typical of thought in its metaphysical manifestation.

> . . . the law of the One that becomes two, then two that become
> four. . . . Binary logic is the spiritual reality of the tree root. Even a
> discipline as "advanced" as linguistics retains as its basic image this tree
> root, which connects it to classical reflection [and its law of the One
> that doubles back upon itself in becoming two, but in the form of a du-
> ality of which each element boils down to the unity and the unicity of
> the same sole dialectical root] (thus Chomsky and the syntactic tree, be-
> ginning at a point S and developing by means of dichotomy). Which
> comes down to saying that this thought has never understood multiplic-
> ity: it needs to assume a strong main unity in order to get to two fol-
> lowing a spiritual method. (11)

We should add that for Deleuze and Guattari the "subject" of philosophy serves precisely the function of supplying a mental (*geistige*) unity that binds the proliferating multiplicity to the simplicity of one source (one foundation, one root, one origin, one law). This is prototypically the case in the instance of Kant's idea that the manifold of sensual perception must be subordinated to the unity of the categories, and to the unity of self-consciousness, in order to be recognized.

But nature knows metamorphoses of the growth of shoots that are not readily compatible with the metaphor of the dichotomously branching tree of knowledge (or of syntax). Deleuze and Guattari remind us of the *système-radicelle, ou racine fasciculée* (12).

> This time, the main root has aborted, or is rotting toward its tip; then an immediate and commonplace multiplicity of secondary roots come and graft themselves onto it, and begin developing vigorously. This time, the natural reality appears in the abortion of the main root, but its unity nonetheless subsists as past or to come, as possible. (12)

The image is not a bad one. True, we are no longer talking of the growth of shoots, but rather of the growth of roots, and we therefore have to add that, roughly speaking, there are two different kinds of root systems: the stem-based roots of the monocotyledons, and the branching of the main root in the case of the dicotyledons. In the second case—the case of an allorhizomatic root system (think of the carrot, *Daucus carota*)— there is a well-developed main root from which side roots branch off left and right, and these side roots, for their part, can also have further branches. In the first case—the so-called homorhizomatic root system (for example, corn, *Zea mays*)—the branched roots take off at the lower end of the stem itself, so that instead of *one* main root, an entire *bundle* of roots extends into the earth, and each of those roots again sends off side branches.

Books that are composed according to this principle, so say Deleuze and Guattari, only apparently renounce metaphysical unitary thinking, for the swarm of independent and multiple roots comes together in the unity of one single stem.

> The aborters of unity are indeed here makers of angels [*faiseurs d'ange*, abortionists], *doctores angelici*, since they affirm a unity that is properly angelic and superior. The words of Joyce, rightly said to be "of multiple roots," indeed break up the linear unity of the word, or even of language, only by positing a cyclical unity of the sentence, the text, or knowledge. The aphorisms of Nietzsche break up the linear unity of knowledge only by referring to the cyclical unity of the eternal return, present like a not-known of thought. Which comes down to saying that the installment system does not really break with dualism, with the complementarity of a subject and an object, of a natural reality and a spiritual reality: unity is unceasingly thwarted and squelched in the object, whereas a new type of unity wins out in the subject. The world

has lost its pivot, the subject can no longer even make up a dichotomy, but rather accedes to a higher unity of ambivalence or overdetermination, in a dimension that is always supplementary to that of its object. The world has become chaos, but the book remains the image of the world, chaosmos-rootlet rather than cosmos-root. What strange mystification of the book—all the more total by virtue of being fragmented. (12–13)

Finally, there is the rhizome, a further metamorphosis of the stem and the main root. Rhizomes are underground, for the most part horizontally growing clumped shoots whose roots are formed at the stem. In each period of growth they form a shoot that breaks through the surface of the earth and which dies later on, while an underground section of vegetation continues growing in a horizontal direction. In the case of Solomon's seal (*Polygonatum multiflorum*), the main shoot breaks through the surface, while the axis continues to grow under the ground, resulting in a sympodial organization of the rhizome.

It is clear what the rhizome accomplishes as an illustrative vehicle. It serves as the scheme for all Deleuze and Guattari expect from the movement of the flows of desire and of thoughts, but also from the unregulated unfolding of the multiple.

In truth, it does not suffice to say Long live the multiple, though this cry is hard to utter. No bit of typographic, lexical, or even syntactic cleverness will suffice to make it heard. The multiple *must be made*, not by always adding a higher dimension, but on the contrary in the simplest way possible, by dint of sobriety, at the level of the dimensions at one's disposal, always $n - 1$ (only in this way is the one part of the multiple, by always being subtracted). Substract the unique from the multiplicity to be constituted; write at $n - 1$. Such a system could be called rhizome. (13)

The image is supposed to express a decentral growth freed both from the charge of the central root, as well as from that of the root bundle that comes together at one stem. Those shoots (plants) that break through the surface of the earth are not true individuals ("subjects"), but rather partial objects of the total organism: i.e., secondary regressions of the plant world in the direction of the cell colonies of tallophytes, whose parts are absolutely equal to each other (since they are not differentiated), and which react like physiological units, although they are not elements of a central organism: they are aggregates rather than units. This lack of an individuating unity—and "individuation" originally means (for example, in the language of early romanticism) unification, suspension of differentiation/division (*in*differentiation, *in*dividuation)—is supposed to be indicated by the formula $n - 1$ (see also 31): unity is always subtracted anew from the proliferation of multiplicity, so that the chain can never be concluded and completed in a final term, as is the case in the systems of metaphysics (Hegel's, for example).

As inconspicuous and undeveloped as the playfully introduced formula $n - 1$ may be, it nevertheless points involuntarily to the limitations in the exploitability of the image of the decentral or "plagiotropic" (running at a slant to the plant) growth (not only the underground rhizomes, like the lily of the valley, or the bulbous plants, like the potato, but also the plants that form shoots above ground, like the strawberry, belong to the metaphorical complex of what in *A Thousand Plateaus* is called "rhizome"). None of these metamorphoses illustrates the limits of the classical concept of organization, but they show to what extent it can be expanded: in the final analysis even the ecosphere constitues a total organism that overarches all the individual organisms contained in it, without this resulting in the abrogation of the principle of finality. Nobody would doubt the organic character of the brain with the ridiculous remark that the expanding and decentral mesh of axons that connect the neurons has a certain similarity with the plagiotropic connection of the colonies of lily of the valley (24). The fact that channels exist or can be formed between all neurons points to the closure and circularity of the brain functions, which always work for the benefit of the unity of consciousness. To draw conclusions from the material form of cells, axons, synapses, etc., about the form of consciousness of thought would be almost as intelligent as to believe that the perception of a polyhedron would itself be polyhedral or would require an angular head. Nevertheless, Deleuze and Guattari point in this direction.

> Many people have trees in their heads, but the brain itself is more of a weed than a tree. (24)

From which they draw an inference about the rhizomatic nature of the functions of consciousness and memory.

All that is comical at best. The formula $n - 1$, however, teaches us in a more impressive way that in order to determine multiplicity as such, I have to refer negatively to a unity. As soon as I say, for example, that manifoldness is decentral or without unity, I have already negatively referred to a unity without which I would not be able to think multiplicity as that which it is. No one can escape the "law of reflection of all our knowledge: namely, that nothing is *known as what it is*, without our also thinking of what it is *not*."[3] Even the thought of multiplicity either has a meaning (in which case it cannot be all-encompassing, but rather must allow for an oppositional concept), or, on the other hand, it loses this distinction and thereby ceases to designate "multiplicity." (There is something completely analogous to this in Hegel's *Logic* in the case of the purely negative concept of "Being," conceived as "pure indeterminateness" or "relation only to itself"; that is, as what follows in the *Logic* demonstrates, this concept is already determined as negative with foresight to its opposite.)

Deleuze and Guattari's advocacy of the idea of a decentralized multiplicity misses its target at this point. If one can make evident for the thought of an all-encompassing unity (for example, Fichte's "I" or Spinoza's "Absolute") that it can be conceived only under the condition that it include precisely what it would like to exclude (a difference, arising simultaneously to it, which is *not* I and *not* absolute), then its opposite is just as true: a multiplicity that is totally disconnected from the contrastive thought of unity—to whatever extent negatively—could not be a "principle," but rather would be comparable to that zero phoneme about which linguists speak in order to designate a phoneme distinguished from all other phonemes of a language "by the absence of any distinctive features and of any constant sound characteristic."[4]

In other words, one does not escape metaphysics and its unicentrism simply by inverting its premises and turning the privileging of the identity principle into the privileging of multiplicity. Such an abstract opposition is always already metaphysical and does not escape the dialectic of that irrevocable reciprocity that allows neither of the two moments to pose as the totality. Even multiplicity, conceived as an abstract contrastive concept to that of unity, would, if the thought were tenable, have the character of a principle and would be an idea (*Einbildung*) that would not understand itself.

This is a fundamental objection, and for this reason it has bearing on all six "principles" that Deleuze and Guattari mention as the "approximate features" of the rhizome (13). (Here I am skipping over the fact that the frequent mention of "arrangement"—for example, of the "collective arrangement of the act of enunciation" [13]—as well as that of the "principles [of rhizome]" [13]—appeals precisely to *those* concepts that only a short time earlier had been rejected as the constituents of unity and order.)[5]

Deleuze and Guattari seek to characterize the "arrangement" of the rhizome-like connection between individuals with the following "principles":

1st and 2nd principles of connection and heterogeneity (13);
3rd principle of multiplicity (14);
4th principle of asignifying rupture;
5th and 6th principles of cartography and tracing mania. (19)

We are already familiar with most of these "principles" from *Anti-Oedipus* and, by the way, also from Foucault's *Archaeology of Knowledge*. Let's nevertheless see how Deleuze and Guattari try to put into practice the thought of a multiplicity that has no unity.

The principle of connection states that "any point of a rhizome can be connected to any other, and must be. This is very different from the tree or the root, which determines a point, an order" (13). This polemic is primarily directed against systematic linguistics from structuralism to Chomsky, which in all its manifestations is dominated in one way or another by the obsession to derive linguistic events or effects of meaning from a more or less inviolable order (code, grammar). If this were the case, a continuum would exist between the rules of *langue* and the acts of *parole*; the individual speech events would never be any-thing other than the particular cases in which the universal is reproduced without loss of meaning. In order to refute the thought of such a continuity between the individual event and the universal code, the authors introduce the second princi-ple, that of heterogeneity. Applied to the concept of language (*langage*), it asserts:

> A semiotic link is like a tuber agglomerating a great variety of acts— linguistic, but also perceptive, mimic, gestual, and cognitive: there is no language in itself, nor any universality of language, but a concourse of dialects, provincial dialects, slangs, special languages. There is no ideal speaker or listener, any more than there is a homogeneous linguis-tic community. . . . A language is never closed in on itself except in a function of impotence. (14)

In this critique of the scientism of the code model we recognize once again the legitimate kernel thought of what we are calling neostructuralism. We will de-velop it further in the third and final part of our lectures, and at this point we only want to take note that it connects *A Thousand Plateaus*, and already even *Anti-Oedipus*, with the basic theoretical motif of contemporary French philosophy. I believe that this motif is already present in *Anti-Oedipus* in the distinction be-tween the "molar" and the "molecular" aggregates (see, e.g., *ÅO*, 380; *MP*, 260, *passim*). The molar aggregates correspond, if I understand this correctly, by and large to the (social, linguistic, etc.) "structures," the molecular aggregates to the individuals (conceived as irreducible singularities). *Molaire* and *moléculaire* designate "the two poles of social libidinal investment" (*AO*, 366). They can be more closely defined,

> *the one* by the enslavement of production and the desiring-machines to the gregarious aggregates that they constitute on a large scale under a given form of power or selective sovereignty; *the other* by the inverse subordination and the overthrow of power. *The one* by these molar structured aggregates that crush singularities, select them, and regular-ize those that they retain in codes or axiomatics; *the other* by the molecular multiplicities of singularities that on the contrary treat the large aggregates as so many useful materials for their own elaborations. *The one* by the lines of integration and territorialization that arrest the flows, . . . *the other* by lines of escape that follow the decoded and deterritorialized flows, . . . *the one* is defined by subjugated groups, *the other* by subject-groups. (*AO*, 366–67)

It is clear which of the two tendencies (which are also distinguished as the "paranoic" and the "schizophrenic") is most esteemed by the "nomadology" of the authors. What is interesting to us in this context, and in anticipation of future ob-servations, is the particular attention *Capitalism and Schizophrenia* pays to the asystatic and asystematic aspect of singularity and individuality (see *AO*, 76–77, 357–58, 132–34, *passim*). If this sympathy were not expressed in conjunction with an untenable (and self-destructive) polemic against the idea of unity and subjectivity, I, for my own part, would not hesitate to voice my sympathy with it. (I will explain later in which sense and with what restrictions.)

At any rate, the "principle of multiplicity" would present itself in a new light if its formulation were motivated by an interest in saving individual phenomena, in saving both the individuals as well as the individual speech acts they produce. But it is precisely this feature that the authors no longer stress; instead they oppose in the already mentioned self-contradictory and fruitless way the principle of multiplicity to that of unity and, in addition, to that of the subject. The principle of multiplicity, they claim, is not supposed to maintain any relation whatsoever with that of the One as subject or as object (*MP*, 14).

> No unity that serves as a pivot in the object or is divided in the subject. No unity, even one that is aborted in the object, and "comes back" in the subject. A multiplicity has neither subject nor object. (14)

And above all no subject (with whose definition by neostructuralism we are mainly concerned); for – as the authors tell us:

> The notion of unity never appears except when the signifier takes power in a multiplicity, or when a corresponding process of subjectification develops. (15)

Here we once again come across the thesis of *Anti-Oedipus*, according to which the development of the idea of a "homogeneous subject" has something to do with the insertion into the order of representation (of the signifier, of the symbol). Unfortunately, the argument is even more fragmentary here than it is in the form in which we are already familiar with it; it almost seems as if they mean – and the metaphor of the "seizure of power" suggests this – that the thought of a homogeneous subject is formed as the relucence (*Widerschein*) of the unity of a symbolic order, so to speak as the reflection of the "total meaning" of this order. If *that* were the function of a subject, then it would indeed be incompatible with the requirements of precisely those individuals who oppose the prescripts of the symbolic order – including its "total meaning." But even without this regard for the individuals, for the singularities, subjectivity does not have to be thought of as the quasitranscendental unity of a symbolic order, since everyone agrees that this order is differential and decentral. (We need only recall Derrida's text on structure, sign, and play in *WD* [278ff.] and our discussion of it.)

It would be helpful if at this point we recalled one thing further, namely, romantic hermeneutics. Here the singular or the individual is precisely not taken as a principle of identity; whatever else "individuality" might mean, it is at any rate conceived as the direct opponent of the idea of unity and closure of structure. We will come back to this when it is time to analyze the mechanism of change in meaning within the framework of our third question addressed to neostructuralism. At this point it is enough to mention that for Schleiermacher, for example, it is always and fundamentally the individual whose intervention prevents structure (or the signs stored by it) from coinciding with itself. To coincide with itself would mean to be present. Now a structure or a structured sign can never coincide with itself: first of all, because the thought of the differentness of signs presupposes the idea of time; and second, because each use of a sign assumes the iterability of the sign (i.e., its simultaneity). The structuredness of the sign system presupposes time, for it is time, as Hegel already demonstrated quite nicely, that by letting a sound sink into the past (and thus fade out) first allows the following sound to articulate itself in its differentness from the previous one. This applies correspondingly for each sign and for each concatenation of signs: they have to leave the present in order to be able to demarcate themselves in terms of those that are present at any given moment. It is precisely by means of this submerging in time, Hegel continues, that the signs yield their *meaning* (their *intelligence*, as he says): the disappearance of the body of the word, by making room for a second one (which then also fades out) simultaneously allows the internal element – the significance of the sign – to appear.

> The word as something that *sounds* disappears in time; time thereby proves itself in relation to the word to be *abstract*, i.e., merely *destroying* negativity. The *true, concrete* negativity of the linguistic sign, however, is *intelligence*, because it is by means of it that the sign is altered from something *external* to something *internal* and is preserved in this transmogrified form.[6]

This preservation, for its part, is not conceived as mechanical. Precisely because the sign (or the sound) has faded out, it is not (any longer) present to us. The "*reproducing* memory"[7] has to be substituted for the loss of its presence. It "recognizes the object in the name," but it does not accomplish this directly (for both the name and the object designated by it have transpired), but only by means of a hermeneutical hypothesis, which apprehends repeated occurrences of sounds that acoustically are thoroughly distinguishable *as* occasions for the association of the same meaning *by virtue of interpretation*. This identity is thus not one of timeless coincidence, but rather literally an artifact: something that has been uncontrollably restored over the abyss of temporal depresencing.

The second aspect mentioned earlier is closely related to this. In order to be an element of a structure, the sign has to be repeatable. In order to be articulated a second time, the structure first has to step outside of itself in order to be put back together beyond itself. The structure, in other words, is internalized by a speaking individual, only to be subsequently nonidentically reexternalized. It is thus the intervention of an individual that divides the timeless identity of structure from itself. This division occurs in actuality, for the rules that relate to a structure can only extend to the structure itself, but not, however, to the unforeseeable use the individual makes of it. It is precisely for this reason that the individual, as Schleiermacher puts it, cannot be derived from structure, or cannot be "a priori constructed" from it (*HuK*, 172). It is its achievement that it brings the hypothetical identity of signs—which always has to be conceived according to an index of being past—into a state of suspension *by means of* the act of actualizing its meaning (which always presupposes a depresencing of the sign-carrier). Structure cannot guarantee the continuity between the (hypothetical) meaning inscribed in it and always already past in the act of language use, and the new meaning acquired in the individual use: this lack of a criterion for semantic identification, a lack produced by the individual, refers the process of meaning attribution to the infinite (because incalculably open) procedure of hermeneutics (in the romantic sense of the word). One can never definitively make a judgment about the unity of a sign, a sentence, a text, or a symbolically interacting culture, for this unity is constantly produced anew in use and in understanding. To attribute to it a semantic-structural identity exposes itself as a scientist fiction or as a dream of the standstill of the irrevocably depresencing temporization (*Zeitigung*) into which everything touched by the individual is submerged.

It would accordingly be idiotic to reject the subject with the claim that it is an agency that brings the proliferating multiplicity of sign applications to a standstill: "The notion of unity appears only when the signifier comes to power within a multiplicity or when there is a corresponding process of subjectification" (*MP*, 15). I call this fear idiotic because it is simultaneously false on two counts. First, a signifier, on close examination, could for structural reasons never bring the sliding of meaning on its underside to a standstill (whereby the hasty conclusion about a "subject" in the background that acts in the service of the violent instituting of identity becomes untenable). Second, however, the nonfinality of understanding (or, in other words, the insurmountability of multiplicity) does not mean that there is no unity whatsoever of word signs or of speech acts, etc. If that were the case, then not even *A Thousand Plateaus* would have been able to have been written and presented to a reading public. It is absolutely enough, if one does not want to fall into absurdity, to stress that each semiological synthesis has the status of Being of a hermeneutical hypothesis. Lacan saw this very clearly when he spoke of the anchoring of the flow of meaning on the sign chain at certain "anchoring points." This means that the sign chain obviously culminates in the unity of an interpretation, but that this unitary interpretation does not overcome the structural ambiguity of the sign that always exists in nonsimultaneity to itself, without ever concluding itself in an atemporal self-presence. Meaning is always articulated at two different points in time by partners participating in a process of communication, and it is always at least two different subjects that communicate with one another (even in true self-dialogue).[8] From this follows the dualness of the meaning attribution of the sign that could be broken only if one were to entirely eliminate communication — i.e., subjects in general — from the world. The attack on the unity of understanding as such thereby misses the legitimate target of the code model of understanding and flies off into the absurd. For if multiplicity were without unity, then we would not only be able to understand neither provisionally nor incompletely, we would be able to understand nothing; indeed, we would not be able to understand at all. Not even the most delirious statements of *Anti-Oedipus* attain this ideal.

Therefore a detailed criticism of the principle the authors call the "asignifying rupture" (*MP*, 16ff.) is unneccessary. If "asignifying" is supposed to mean incalculable by the code, then we would be the first to agree. But just because it is incalculable by the code (the individual modification that the individual language use induces in the semantic-pragmatic stock of linguistic types) does not mean that it is therefore asignificant, i.e., unintelligible. As acts of hypothetical meaning attribution, modifications are, on the contrary, always motivated (even the "flipping out" of the "schizo" is motivated, and everything that Deleuze and Guattari write about this represents attempts to understand the meaning of this "flipping out," even if they obviously do not reflectively know what they are doing:[9] that simply happens sometimes, and it does not change anything about the truth of the major term). This truth still holds even in view of the fifth and sixth so-called principles, which justifiably claim that "a rhizome cannot be accounted for by any structural or generative model" and that it "is irrelevent to any idea of genetic axis or deep structure" (19ff.).

It seems to me that the argumentation of the authors adheres to the following rule: the model of subsumption, or code model of acting and speaking (which says that each case of acting and speaking is an applied instance that reproduces the rules of a deep structure, of a relational system, of a juridical dispositive, etc., identically *in* application), and the unifying operation of the subject are assigned to each other. Since coded acting and speaking are a case of representation, the idea of the identifiability of the subject thought with that of representation simultaneously surfaces ("Oedipus" — as the symbol for the conditioning of savage desire to say I — is at the same time the end product of its inscription into "grammar"). They thus arrive at the equation of the individual with the subjective and with the significant (against which the passage cited earlier, which increased the value of the singular over against the general, had protested; but the authors lay no claim whatsoever to consistency and scholarliness; *MP*, 33). Let me give a characteristic example of this equation or, in more cautious terms, approximation.

There are only machinic arrangements of desire, and collective arrangements of utterance. No significance, and no subjectification: write at *n*

(every individuated utterance is still imprisoned in the dominant significations, and all signifying desire refers to dominated subjects). (33)

One could probably subscribe to this passage under certain conditions —
conditions that, to be sure, it itself does not fulfill. This is the condition that the
word "significance" refers to the "meaning" (*Bedeutung*) communicated by the
coded sign (which is inscribed in a structure). Yet precisely this universal meaning (I call it universal because it shows exactly the same face to all participants
in the same linguistic circle) is deuniversalized in the act of its individual application. To the degree that the individual application is not "necessitated" by the
universal linguistic law — by the totality of its meanings — it can be called insignificant (it is in this sense that Saussure and Sartre speak of the individual and transformational use of language as the *élément non-signifiant*). In this phrase, however, *non-signifiant* does not mean "senseless" (*sinnlos*), but only: bearing a not
yet universalized, an as yet only individually existing, so to speak virtual meaning
(*Bedeutung*). Such an individual meaning, which has not yet been reexternalized
into the repertoire of universality, is called "sense" (*Sinn*) by Schleiermacher and
Sartre. Sense (*Sinn*) is individual, meaning (*Bedeutung*) universal. But when
sense is nonsignificant, it nevertheless has something to say and can be understood (by means of a hypothesis for understanding on the part of my discussion
partner, and the success of the hypothesis allows sense [*Sinn*] to make the transition to the mode of Being of a meaning [*Bedeutung*]).

But this is not how Deleuze and Guattari make their argument. For them "each
individualized expression" remains the recipient of a command and the prisoner
of the "subject that dominates it," or of the "meanings (*Bedeutungen*) that dominate it." According to the premises of their own work — as unscholarly as it is,
even according to their own intention — this conclusion is in fact irrefutable.
Yet, if we take a closer look, it is destructive for the entire theory. For if
individuation — and individuation, as Saussure already emphasized, is the only
source for transformation of meaning (*Bedeutung*) (see *EC*, I, 28: "changes arise
from an individual") — can*not* break the power of meanings (*Bedeutungen*), then
the power of meanings is absolutely inescapable. In other words, the description
of any code whatsoever as an instrument of coercion or (as Foucault expresses
it) of torture fundamentally presupposes that a code (and not the human beings
that attend to it) *is capable* of coercing. In order to assume this, one has first of
all to conceive — and be it only in order to contradict this view afterwards — the
code just as structurally or generative-grammatically as the linguists and systems
theoreticians do who are ridiculed by Deleuze and Guattari. According to this,
then, the linguist and systems theoretician would simply be correct. Even those
who call for the "decoding" of a code or the "exploding" of the order of discourse
have to face the consequence that such a code, such an order, first of all has to
be viewed as actual. As a matter of fact, if one hopes to show the individual "the

exit from the flytrap," as Wittgenstein put it, then one also has to challenge the *idea* of the code—as Derrida does—and not only its existence.

If, however, it were the case that there are codes—no matter how odious they may seem—and that one cannot escape their power, then the unfettered delirium of *Capitalism and Schizophrenia* would still be blind execution of the order of a discourse that simply does not see through to its own rules of generation, to the requirements of repetition and the obsessive desire that shape it. In short, only those who explode the theoretical framework of the authors' text, and do this with foresight toward a theory of the individual subject that internalizes structures in a nonidentical way and reexternalizes them in an altered form, can liberate their right-minded kernel thought and take it over into a newly defined epistemic framework. That would mean bringing into play a *hermeneutics of individuality* of a sort in which the individual moment is not an opponent, but rather a moment of the structure; that is, a moment of such a type that it prevents the structure from closing itself and thus prevents it from exercising a one-sided determination.[10] Only hermeneutics offers the prospect not only of promising us this liberation but of actually providing it.

Lecture 23

Even if what Deleuze and Guattari try to palm off on us about the genesis of subjectivity in the two volumes of *Capitalism and Schizophrenia* seems to us to be unconvincing, indeed, questionable, we still should not overlook that Gilles Deleuze presented an incomparably more sophisticated and discriminating argumentation at the end of the sixties. I am mainly thinking of *Différence et répétition* of 1968.[1] Although even in this work no room was made for the idea of the subject (as in *Capitalism and Schizophrenia* it is conceived as the agency of the work of unification, as an agent in the service of "representation," and as the adversary of the emancipation of difference); however, one can find in this book notable insights into the mode of Being of individuality (which is strictly opposed to subjectivity). These insights seem to me so noteworthy that I believe our lecture series cannot avoid a discussion of them, especially since they supply us with a particularly good point of departure for our examination of the problematics in the third question we want to address to neostructuralism.

If I am correct, the theoretical approach of *Mille Plateaux* remains far behind that of *Différence et répétition*, inasmuch as the first presents in abstract fashion an "anarcho-structuralist" and impotent polemic against the domination of the model of encoding and representation, whereas in the latter the idea of the code as such is undermined. It makes a big difference whether I first acknowledge the idea of the code (*as* idea) and then reject it (*as* reality), or whether I expose the untenability of the idea that there is a system of structural determination or causality.

This is exactly what Deleuze does in *Différence et répétition*. His attack is here

359

directed at the idea of a self-enclosed system (and that is what justifies an examination of Deleuze's work within the framework of a lecture series on neostructuralism). Such a system, if it existed, would be universal to the extent that its elements would be particular cases that would correspond to the rules of the system. The decisive thing is that an element that is conceived as an applied instance of the general system, insofar as it is a particular of the system, can never contradict the general law of the system or deviate from it. It is from this agreement of particular and general that the universality of the system results, for, trivially enough, whatever is not contradicted in the realm of application is true generally.

This congruity of the general and the particular is verified in the possibility that the particular can be infinitely repeated without loss of meaning. Since from the outset it is defined as the special case in which a universal rule makes itself adequately manifest, it is deprived of all those features by means of which it could maintain its independence over against the universal. That is the difference between the particular and the individual. A concept, for example, is particular and general at the same time. It is particular insofar as it is distinguished from other concepts, but it is simultaneously general because it ignores the individual makeup of the things and states of affairs to which it refers. For it is precisely not the individuality of the objects of which it takes account, but rather the feature they all have in common, the central concern, which gathers an infinite number of individually different elements in the unity of *one* single viewpoint. A concept has this characteristic in common with a word-sign. Both necessarily refer to the common aspect of what can be thought and what can be experienced; both obliterate any regard for the individual. In this sense it would be trivial to say that thought and speech can never be a private matter, for what is expressed in a semiologically articulated thought is always its nonprivate aspect, i.e., that aspect that is communal and general. For the same reason, there is no danger that the repetition of a concept-sign could modify its signification; its generality and communicability rest precisely in the fact that it abstracts from the individual aspects of experience. This abstraction, for its part, which makes a "general speech type" (as Humboldt called it) out of the individual and constantly changing reference to a single state of affairs in the world, guarantees the closure of the conceptual-semantic repertoire on the basis of which I symbolically mediate my living-with-others-in-the-same-world.

The iterability of linguistic "schemes" or conceptual "types" does not, therefore, represent a danger for the univocality of the (conceptual or linguistic) "system" that serves as the basis for their production; rather it guarantees it. Let's cite here John A. Searle, a philosopher of language who supports this view.

Any linguistic element written or spoken, indeed any rule-governed element in any system of representation at all must be repeatable, otherwise the rules would have no scope of application. To say this is just to say that the logician's type-token distinction must apply generally to all the rule-governed elements of language in order that the rules can be applied to new occurrences of the phenomena specified by the rules. Without this feature of iterability there could not be the possibility of producing an infinite number of sentences with a finite list of elements; and this, as philosophers since Frege have recognized, is one of the crucial features of any language.[2]

Under a "token" the logicians mentioned earlier understand the individually applied case of a universal linguistic or conceptual type, or a logical rule. The point of distinction between "type" and "token" is, however, as Searle's formulation very nicely brings out, that it can basically be suffused: from the perspective of experiential reality (of the "phenomenal" world), the unity of the rule of the type has nothing to fear, for its new occurrences are always and necessarily reduced to the already established and unaltered form of the type. The type thus functions as an instrument for the parrying of conceptual or semantic innovation. Searle also formulated this in particularly clear fashion.

Any conventional act involves the notion of the repetition of *the same*. (*R*, 207; emphasis added)

In other words, to the extent that a type is a "conventional act" (i.e., something tied in with a linguistic convention, with an intersubjectively valid code), its repetition can only be the repetition of something that is formally and materially the same. Only what is generally valid, what is common to all, is repeatable (let's be more cautious and add: repeatable with an identical meaning).

Now one has to recognize that the condition that has just been developed with regard to the describability of a language as a grammar is in general a presupposition of the scientific method. A scientist (whether biologist, anthropologist, psychologist, or sociologist) would never maintain about a result he or she has arrived at over the course of his or her work that it has the status of "knowledge" if it were not capable of also laying claim to generalizability. Science knows no individual states of affairs, or rather—since the scientist as a person, of course, knows them very well—the individual states of affairs are sorted out for the benefit of a standardized knowledge about whose validity there is general agreement. (Of course, the universality of canonical knowledge cannot exclude the possibility that it be challenged and that it be in need of revision, as the history of the natural sciences teaches us in just as drastic a fashion as that of the human sciences: but that does not mean—Peirce demonstrated this—that the category of the individual would attain the right to existence in the logic of research.)

The exclusion of the individual is not at all suspicious. It is part and parcel of the concept of calculation or law that dominates the hypothetico-deductive procedure of the exact sciences. In contrast to perceptions, which, according to the classical view, immediately relate to individual things, recognitions are mediate. To be sure, they also refer to things, yet only "by means of a feature which several [and in the case of *pure* concepts, all] things may have in common."[3] Representations (*Vorstellungen*) that are determined by the consciousness of their unity, and therewith elevated to the status of knowledge, are precisely thereby combined according to a *rule*. What is known once will, therefore, behave in exactly the same way under comparable conditions as it did the first time, and each feature that deviates from identity for this reason becomes irrelevant for knowledge.

Repeatability with identical form and meaning—i.e., iteration without loss of semantic identity—is essential to the object of knowledge. If, for example, the linguist examines the grammar of a linguistic community, he or she makes an inventory of the universal rules that govern the set of statements as categorical units of order (i.e., "types") and that make manageable schemes out of its elementary components; these can be reproduced and communicated in different speech situations without serious loss of meaning (each communication presupposes a duplication of meaning into that of the sender and that of the receiver: this duplication does not stand in contradiction to the identity of the message, but rather makes it into what Saussure calls a "social fact").

The individual, in contrast, is, simply according to the etymology of the word, the unpartable (*das Unteilbare*), and thus the unimpartable (*das Unmitteilbare*). It is not indivisible in the sense of the classical model of the atom, where it is a matter of the indivisibility of an infinitesimally small substance that entertains relations "only" with itself (*species infima*); rather the individual is "indivisible" in the sense that it exists without a double and therefore without reference, and thus it literally has no equals. Individuality would be the mode of Being of a being without internal otherness and which refuses to obey the law of iterability (*héteros, alter, ander, autre* are based on the same Indo-European root as *iterum*). The ideas of sameness and repeatability are by no means mutually exclusive in European grammar: they refer to each other. Even the speculative thought of reflecting oneself in the Other adheres to an old Western linguistic convention. "Everything that follows," Derrida says, "may be read as the exploitation of the logic which links repetition to alterity" (*Margins*, 315).

The individual has to be strictly distinguished from the particular, which is always subsumed under the general as a case is subsumed under a rule. Although there were constantly attempts to differentiate both concepts (for example, by Gilbert of Poitier and by Richard of Saint Victor), classical philosophy since antiquity has always insisted that the particularity of the individual can be continuously derived from the general. To be sure, that means that the acknowledged "incommensurability" of the individuals with regard to each other has its limitations; individuals are—according to the doctrines, for example, of Saint Thomas Aquinas and of Leibnitz, who agree on this point—centered on God and can communicate

with one another by means of God – i.e., by means of common participation in
the *esse commune*.

Thus it is not logical incommensurability that has the last word but rather the
symbolic representation of unity in the individuals: taken together they represent
the universe.[4] Leibnitz's infinitesimal calculation finally eliminates the gulf between the universal concept and the *species infima* with rigorous scientific means
by demonstrating that the individual can be derived from the general through a
process of infinite gradation: both are of the same nature, and no dialectic takes
place between them. This is the thesis that the universal and the singular are of
the same species (with the characteristic implication that the individual is a "species," even if only of the smallest sort). God – the highest genus – has a priori the
concept of all individuals at his disposal.

Can one say that this premise, which is just as binding for Fichte's and Hegel's
systems as it is, *mutatis mutandis*, for the natural sciences, constitutes the concept
of science as such and in general? That, at least, is Schleiermacher's view. In a
little-known tradition – which in relation to the official metaphysical tradition one
might call heretical – he does not consider the individual as a place of fullness,
an unerodible kernel of self-identity, and above all a being that could be derived
from a rational ideal by means of processes of deduction. On the contrary, the
individual feeling (i.e., the familiarity of an existing individual with itself) is the
"complement" of a constitutive "lack" inside of each self-consciousness, even the
highest one.[5] It "supplies" and "supplements" the "missing unity" of that movement in which the individual self-consciousness attempts to represent the *universal* condition of truth in itself.[6] The lacuna that separates it from the fullness of
(the Hegelian) concept, and denies it the identity of an originary and complete
self-presencing, causes the individual self to be "open for the totality of the other-
than-us (*Ausser-uns*)."[7] In other words, the absence of a natural signification that
would define it in its essence once and for all forces the individual to turn to interpretation; it has to project its meaning anew in every moment and will never
dissolve the alternating perspectives, in which its own Being and the Being of the
world present themselves to it, "into an identical thinking and eliminate all
differences."[8]

In this way the individual becomes the transcendental condition for meaning
and understanding: it establishes the significations through the exchange of which
communication and intersubjectivity become possible. Yet among these significations there is none that would guarantee a "complete" understanding, i.e., one that
would shake off the "individual component"[9] and which thereby would finally represent (there can be no representation without prior presence). Anything that
once comes into contact with individuality eludes the claim of universality and
verifiability, at least to the extent that "truth" is conceived as "readequation, or
reappropriation as desire to plug the hole."[10] The truth (of symbolic orders) is,
so to speak, hollow. In its heart a hole, as it were, is hollowed out, and this hole

consumes its identity and finality. It is precisely for this reason that the "true" (in the sense of "final") significance of the universal is uncertain: it remains relative to all those interpretations that can be made about it and that are fundamentally infinite. The cause of this is individuality, which interprets every codified concept — in a scientific or linguistic system — in a manner that is particular to it itself; the concept is displaced and, perhaps, nonidentically reexternalized. The universal concepts or significations,[11] Sartre similarly says,

> are only quasi-significations and the set of them taken as a whole constitutes only a quasi-knowledge, *first* because they are elected as the means of *meaning* and *are rooted in meaning* (in other words, they are constituted on the basis of style, are expressed by style and, as such, are blurred from the beginning), and *then* because, in and of themselves, they appear to be, as it were, detached from the universal by a singularity.[12]

As soon as the individual surfaces in the symbolic order, the recursivity of the linguistic types (stressed by Searle) is endangered: no one guarantees that two uses of one and the same sign leave its former signification intact. The iterability of signs does not guarantee their permanence and identity, but rather provides them with an index of uncontrollable transformation. For scientific thinking this is quite a problem: the individual — as opposed to the particular, which always remains masterable by the universal, as an instance is by its rule — is eliminated, as it were, from the universe of "knowable," "significant" propositions, and thus from the universe of propositions that are identical with themselves (within a differential order). Therefore, no knowledge but the conscious position of not-knowing is adequate to it, and it appeals — semiologically — to the "nonsignifying element."[13] For this reason, Sartre calls the hermeneutics that attempts to decipher the individual moment in each sign use on this side of the rules for its codification, as it were, a "hermeneutics of silence" (*une herméneutique du silence*).[14]

Ever since there have been rules for the formation of scientific discourse, i.e., since Parmenides at the latest, the individual — insofar as it is not being in the emphatic sense — has consequently been under thought prohibition. Only with reason (*noeîn*) can one grasp what is universal, present, self-referential, determined in its Being, and unequivocally distinguished from all other beings: in other words, that which can be signified. Whatever lacks one of these criteria *is* not, i.e., it cannot — in the etymological sense of the Greek verb *noeîn* — be perceived (the German words *Vernunft* [reason] and *vernehmen* [to perceive] are related, just as the Greek words *noûs* and *noeîn* are); whatever cannot be perceived or embraced by reason also cannot be inscribed in a symbolic order (that of thought, speech, theoretical behavior in the broadest sense). According to such a theoretical premise, any preference for the nongeneralizable, i.e., for nonbeing relations (*mè ónta*), must simply appear to be insane: it must appear to be a disposition closely related to *idiocy*.

It is worthwhile to ask about the origin of this concept, which Sartre takes up in the title of his *Idiot de la famille*, and which recurs like a leitmotif throughout his *Flaubert*. It signals an appeal to the early Western concept of the human being as the immediately "social creature." In contradiction to the schematic and undifferentiating reconstruction of European intellectual history of which neostructuralism is guilty, one has to insist that the feature of the "singular" (*Eigenen*) and "particular" (*Eigentümlichen*) (*toû idíou* in Greek) was never an outstanding trait of what the Greeks called *lógos* and the Scholastics *ratio*. "Logocentrism" by no means implies a cult of the "singular" (*Eigenen*). Both this concept, and the related one of the private (*tò ídion*), on the contrary, carry the mark of a deprivation (*stérāsis, privatio*): only to a certain extent are they beings, *mè ónta*, creatures that lack truth and the full presence of idea. Over against the public-universal (*tô koinô*)—the realm of that which is bound by "laws" (*nómoi*)—the individual and its particularity (*Eigentümlichkeit*) were always deprecatingly assessed (all words in Greek that are combined with the root *idio* have a deprecatory meaning). The laws (*hoi nómoi*), to be sure, as things established by convention, are revocable (which makes them comparable to hypothetically induced statements of laws in the sciences), but this is by no means true for the thought of regularity or of justice as such.

Plato and Aristotle, of course, do not completely veil the hiatus that separates the universality and exclusivity of the law from the particularity of the situations in which it is applied.[15] These situations are themselves *mè ónta* in their for-itself. Yet both Plato and Aristotle know a sure measure for the identification of the true citizen: he/she immediately recognizes his/her private matter as a public issue, i.e., as a fact that is subject to regularities. This is what distinguishes the true citizen from the private person, from the *idiótäs*.

One could jokingly say—but not without concrete evidence—that the individual in our culture is born to play the role of the idiot. This will not change in the least as long as science upholds the instituted identity in meaning between *Being* and *universality* and allows only those deviations from universality that, like the particular, can be derived from it in deductive steps without altering its essence. Sartre not only alludes to this in the title of his *Idiot de la famille*; he explicitly reminds us at several points of the Parmenidean and Platonic tradition of the proscription of the individual, a tradition that continues to exist both in the bourgeois and in the socialist systems of society, as well as in the theoretical attitude that supports them and that produces those "objective neuroses," which, as symptoms of illness, silently manifest the origin of this proscription.

But what if the individual is not the being-itself (*autò tò ón*)? What then? It must be a *feature* of being, and, in fact, one on the basis of which being comes to its determinedness. All determination is grounded in a negation (*omnis deter-*

minatio est negatio). Can one presume that it is the exclusion of the individual, of the nonsignifying element from the "signifying set," by means of which the *order* of the universal is established and simultaneously the nullity (Sartre says *négatité*) of the ideal ground for this order is explained? In this case the individual would be the ground that is not itself (*der nicht selbst seiende Grund*) (or the ideal ground) for the distinction of being as a universal context of references and assignments in a life world; and it would be through this that the human beings of a given society mediate their communal self-understanding as socialized subjects (*individus communs*, as Sartre says). The individual would thus be *ratio cognoscendi* of this order. For the moment, let's recognize that there are at least three features that connect the individual, defined in the way stated earlier, with Derrida's *différance*: both are conditions of possibility for the subsistence of social or symbolic orders; both establish these orders by subtracting themselves from what they themselves have established; and both are pure nullities (*Verneintheiten*) without a kernel of self-identity and positivity.

Now repetition is defined by Deleuze in a manner very similar to this, and that seemed to me to justify the detour by way of Schleiermacher and Sartre.

Différence et répétition also develops its theoretical approach in direct contradiction to science's opting for the universal and, more specifically, in contradiction to the type-token distinction of the grammatical code model.

Here are the first sentences of the introduction to *Différence et répétition*:

Repetition is not generality. Repetition must be distinguished from generality in several ways. Any formula implying confusion between the two is disturbing, as when we say that two things resemble each other like two peas in a pod; or when we identify "the only science is the science of the general" and "the only science is the science of what is repeated." Between repetition and resemblance—even when the latter is extreme—there is a difference in kind.

Generality presents two great orders: the qualitative order of resemblances and the quantitative order of equivalences. Cycles and equalities are the symbols of these orders. But in any case, generality expresses a point of view according to which one term can be exchanged for another, and one term substituted for another. The exchange or substitution of particulars defines our conduct corresponding to the generality. That is why empiricists are not wrong to present the general idea as a particular idea in itself, on the condition that there be added to this a feeling that it could be replaced by any other particular idea that resembles it in regard to a word. Conversely, it is clear that repetition is a necessary and founded conduct only in relation to what cannot be replaced. Repetition as conduct and as a point of view concerns an unexchangeable, unsubstitutable singularity. Reflections, echoes, doubles, and souls are not in the province of resemblance or equivalence; and just as there is no substitution possible between true twins, there is no possibility of exchanging one's soul. If exchange is the criterion of generality, theft and the bestowal of gifts are the criteria of repetition. There is thus an economic difference between the two. (*DR*, 7)

Let's try to get our bearings in Deleuze's thoughts. What first strikes us is that repetition and universality are conceived as opposites. That can be understood in only *one* way: repetition differs from universality in that it does *not* repeat the same. If science, for the sake of the uniformity of its rules and the identity of meaning of its signs, defines repetition according to the law of equivalent exchange, then there is, in the sense of this definition, no science that deals with that which cannot be exchanged equivalently: a singular soul, for example, as Deleuze rather romantically notes. (Think of the fairy tale about the heart that is exchanged for money in Hauff's *Wirtshaus im Spessart*.)[16] We must recall what we were able to ascertain at the beginning of our lecture series about the structuralist law of transformation. It functions precisely in the sense of an equivalence of one and the same *valeur linguistique* that is filled in each instance by entirely different semantic-phonetic elements. The common feature of an exchange value (for example, the value of a coin: money is, after all, "the universal equivalent," as Marx says) and a word-sign—a linguistic type—is, as Saussure understood very well, their indifference with regard to the individual phonic or physical reality of what they are exchanged for. Just as for five francs I can buy a ticket from Geneva to Nyon, or a paperback book, or even several candy bars, the word-sign can designate an arbitrary number of objects or states of affairs of the same value.

Here as in political economy we are confronted with the notion of *value*; both sciences are concerned with *a system for equating things of different orders*—labor and wages in one and a signified and a signifier in the other. (*CGL*, 79)

To reduce an object or a chain of sounds to its value means to abstract radically from their sensual characteristics. Individuality also belongs to these sensual characteristics (which, as we saw earlier, presents itself not to the concept but to perception, according to the classical view). Only this act of abstraction founds the sign (or the commodity, or the "universal commodity," money) as something that can be repeatedly employed and exchanged without its losing in signification or value (the word stands for that which it signifies if one disregards the individual character of the signified). If this abstraction were not accomplished, then in linguistics (to remain in this sphere) one would have to reckon with the fact that neither the phonic chains nor the significations of a word would remain identical from one linguistic utterance to the next: the (scientifically masterable) system of language would collapse. This consequence, which would be devastating for lin-

guistics, was brought out very nicely by Tullio de Mauro in his introduction to
the vulgate version of Saussure's *Cours.*

> The point of departure of Saussure's reflections is the acute awareness
> of the absolute, unique individuality of each expressive act, which he
> calls *parole.* He asks his students to notice an individual who is speak-
> ing and who exclaims: "War, I tell you, war!" We spontaneously verify
> that the speaker has repeated the word "war" two times. That is true,
> but it is only true in a certain sense. If we are interested in the concrete
> and effective "psychological" content (to use Saussure's term) that "war"
> communicates each time, or rather the concrete phonic act by which
> "war" is realized in each instance, we are confronted by something
> different each time. One person, on saying "war," will have in mind a
> great deal of fanfare, glorious parades, flags blowing in the wind; an-
> other, a killed brother or a destroyed home; von Clausewitz will think
> at length about politics utilizing other means, and the soldier Schweik
> will think about words that out of decency we cannot record here. But
> Saussure means that if the same word is repeated twice, even by the
> same person and in the same discourse, two different things will be
> communicated: "War, I tell you, war!" And the concrete pronunciation
> will be no less different each time, even when—there is no room for
> doubt—the word is pronounced by the same person. . . . The same
> word, repeated in the discourse of the same person, has a different exe-
> cution from one moment to the next: if no detail is really taken in ab-
> straction, the precise meaning, in its concrete reality, will appear from
> one manifestation to the next as if it were formed of different associa-
> tions and emotive resonances; and the real *phonie*, if one considers it as
> an effective whole, has inflections and nuances that are different each
> time. Only Croce has insisted forcefully enough on the individual,
> unique character of the particular expressive act. But what is for Croce
> an end point is for Saussure a point of departure.[17]

We know how Saussure proceeded (and we will return to this later). But at this
point we can already make the observation that the original nonidentity of the *concepts mentaux*, which call forth the linguistic expressions in different speakers,
and the phonic elements during different executions can only hypothetically be
escaped: by operations of that process of abstraction that takes different occurrences of sound images as the occasion for an interpretation that relates these
sound images to a common meaning, and thus considers them as values and no
longer as acoustic bodies. In the final section of this lecture series we will investigate how this happens, according to Saussure's theory, and particularly to what
extent even for him the moment of individuality is preserved in this hypothetical
interpretation that constitutes the identity of the signs.

For Deleuze, at least, this thought is a fundamental one and stands not at the
end of his book but rather at the very beginning. "Repetition is not generality"

was his first sentence. Universality was characterized as the end product of processes of abstraction that identify individually incomparable things by means of their value, i.e., quantitatively by means of equivalence. There is, as Deleuze emphasizes, another procedure: "the qualitative order of resemblances." Here one does not totally abstract from the substantial makeup of things, but rather from that which qualitatively distinguishes them. What remains then as their smallest common feature (of quality) is that which they all have in common – their similarity.

That is trivial. But what is not at all trivial is Deleuze's assertion that repetition belongs neither to the one nor to the other order of universals, whereas for Searle the repeatability of linguistic types was precisely the certifying authority, the touchstone of their semantic identity, i.e., of their transtemporal universality. To be able to hold on to this view, one has to acknowledge the procedure of abstraction (which Saussure also employs) as essentially justified, and that is precisely what Deleuze does not do, if I understand him correctly. For him there is no guarantee that a reiterated word or a repeated gesture, etc., manifests one and the same universal.

> To repeat is to behave, but in relation to something unique and singular that has no likeness or equivalent. (*DR*, 7)

It is not as though there were no universality of repetition. However, the universal aspect of repetition, as Deleuze says, is the universal of a structure, and not of a content. It is generally true – one could formulate it in this paradoxical manner – that because of the intervention of singularizing repetition nothing that is universal holds.

> We are thus opposing generality, as the generality of the particular, and repetition as the universality of the singular. (8)

I do not know whether the terminological distinction between "the generality of the particular" and "the universality of the singular" is an especially appropriate one. On the other hand, we see that Schleiermacher's and Sartre's distinction between the particular and the singular resurfaces here. The particular is what, as one case among other cases (of the same value), is subsumed under a general rule or a universal concept; the individual, on the other hand, is what has no equals and to this extent does not fall under the rule or the concept.

The formulation "that has no likeness or equivalent" is Deleuze's. It stands in a similarly contradictory relation to philosophy's concept of individuality as does the concept of individuality proposed by Schleiermacher and Sartre. Far from being something like a kernel of personal identity in the flux of time (and thus something persistent or permanent), the individual for Schleiermacher, Sartre, and Deleuze is the absolutely nonrepeatable: it is that whose intervention deprives all universal orders of their identity and closure. Individuality is at the same time the opponent of a mechanical conception of communication (A communicates B to C; both partners conceive of the same thing under B). On the contrary, the individual is, in the original sense of the word, the un*part*able and un*imp*artable (*unTEILbar und unMITteilbar*), or "unsharable," which covers both meanings. Not in the sense of the classical model of the atom as the indivisibility of an infinitesimally small substance that entertains relations "only" with itself; rather as that which exists without an internal double and therefore without reference, and which, as a result, literally (as Deleuze says) has no equals and *consequently escapes the criterion of iterability with identical meaning* (and thus also the criterion of the "ideal objectivity" of the propositional statement, of the "intention of a proposition," which can be identically reproduced in an infinite number of formulations). To formulate an individual utterance and to reproduce it in the act of reading (i.e., to recreate it) under these conditions, does *not* mean (and I consider this the decisive factor) *to articulate the same linguistic chain once again* (*and with an identical meaning*), but rather *to undertake another articulation of the same linguistic chain.* For "one can never produce the same thing once again," as August Boeckh says.[18] Robert Musil expresses the same opinion when he calls "the individual something absolutely unique," something "nonfixable . . . , indeed anarchical," which "does not allow for repetition." If one talks about it, then this occurs "in the knowledge that no word can be spoken twice without altering its meaning."[19]

Wilhelm von Humboldt has pointed out what is responsible for this: in each situation of linguistic communication—even in the special cases of self-communication and communicating by means of texts—two modes of conceptualization (*Vorstellungsweisen*) clash with each other, of which only the conventional parts will overlap, whereas "the more individual parts jut beyond."[20] There can be no absolute coinciding "in an unsharable point," for each communication that is mediated by signs or texts provides a historically unstable merging of the universal with an individual *view* of the universal; this view of the universal, however, cannot be universal itself. The effort to communicate would attain objectivity only under the condition that one would be able to control its meaning from an Archimedean point beyond language; but we are once and for all entangled in linguistic occurrences whose untransparency arises from the fact that the rules discourse dictates to us always subsist "at the mercy of the future."[21]

> The synchronic law is general but not imperative. Doubtless it is imposed on individuals by the weight of collective usage . . . , but here I do not have in mind an obligation on the part of speakers. I mean that *in language* no force guarantees the maintenance of a regularity when established on some point. . . . And the arrangement that the law defines is precarious. (*CGL*, 92)

Precisely because the law of language reflects only an actual state of collective speech and is not imperative, each speech act is not only reproductive but creative in a systematically uncontrollable way. *Individual style* always shakes the sign synthesis that connects writing (or spoken word) with meaning; it always displaces the limits of normality that were valid up to that point (but which were not compulsory). Even if one understands this or that in an utterance, innumerable possibilities for meaning remain unexhausted, and, Schleiermacher says, "as long as even only one such possibility is not absolutely dismissed, we cannot speak of a necessary insight" into the semantic structure of the statement or the text (*HuK*, 317).

This productivity of every repetition that is added by the "individual element" (Saussure, *EC*, I, 286) of language (*langue*) in its universality is by no means mysterious. Indeed, it is analytically true that whatever works toward the modification of a general rule cannot be brought into view from the perspective of this rule. If, however, an individuality interpretively intervenes on the basis of a use of a linguistic term (or a speech act executed according to rules), dividing the value of this term or utterance and reexternalizing it nonidentically to the system, then it is clear that the individual could not have been derived from the universal. Already Humboldt and Schleiermacher emphasized that the individual and innovative moment of language use comes to the fore in poetic discourse as such (see, for example, *HuK*, 405), whereas it appears repressed in scientific discourse (see *HuK*, 139). Deleuze differentiates in a similar manner.

> It is rightly said that there are two languages: the language of the sciences, dominated by the symbol of equality, and in which each term can be replaced by others; and lyric language, of which each irreplaceable term can only be repeated. Repetition can always be "represented" as an extreme resemblance or a perfect equivalence. But moving by degrees from one thing to another does not change the fact that there is a difference in kind between the two things. (*DR*, 8)

At this point another concept we already know from *Capitalism and Schizophrenia* is brought into play: it is the concept of "representation." Its mechanism would consist in identifying nonidentical singularities or individualities in terms of their value by relating them to a feature they have in common. If one calls the word-sign a "representation" (as Deleuze does), then one can understand what he means: the individuality of the word uses that appear in the structure of repetition can be reduced to a universal by means of abstracting to the sign value.

> Representation . . . mediates lived experience by ascribing it to the form of an identical or similar object. (*DR*, 29)

That, in very concise form, is what Deleuze has to say about the mechanism of representation, and the thought appears in a much more convincing form than in

Capitalism and Schizophrenia. To represent something means to reduce it either to a similarity or to an equivalence. This reduction implies an idealization of the signified that disregards the constantly changing contents of signs, at the price, to be sure, that the singularity of meaning no longer shows up in what is represented. This not showing up, however, should not be understood to imply that representation would have the last word; indeed, it is rather the case that it is always challenged anew by the nonidentity of repetition.

> It is because repetition differs in kind from representation that the repeated cannot be represented, but must always be signified, masked by what signifies it, itself masking what it signifies. . . .
>
> If repetition is possible, it stems from miracle rather than the law. It is against the law: against the similar form and the equivalent content of the law. If repetition can be found, even in nature, it is in the name of a power that is affirmed against the law and which works under the laws, a power that is perhaps above the laws. If repetition exists, it expresses at once a singularity against the general, a universality against the particular, a remarkable against the ordinary, an instantaneity against variation, an eternity against permanence. In every respect, repetition is transgression. It puts the law into question, it denounces its nominal or general character, in favor of a deeper and more artistic reality. (29, 9)

It is indeed striking how close to Sartre and Schleiermacher Deleuze is here. And this sense of proximity is even heightened when one reads that Deleuze—in spite of his equating the synthetic creation of subjectivity with representation—distinguishes a "true subject of repetition" (*DR*, 29) from precisely this equalizing subjectivity. This true subject is distinct from that of the Kantian "synthesis of apperception" in that it is not a principle by virtue of which the diversity of the individual and the different remains subjugated by means of idealizing abstraction to a unity that is external to it. The true subject of repetition is rather the element that in each repetition escapes the hold of the synthesis and displaces its unities.

> We can rightfully speak of repetition when we are faced with identical elements having absolutely the same concept. But from these discrete elements, from these repeated objects, we must distinguish a secret subject that is repeated through them, the true subject of the repetition. We must think repetition in the pronominal, find the Self of repetition, and the singularity in what is repeated. For there is no repetition without a repeater, nothing repeated without a repeating soul. For that matter, rather than the repeated and the repeater, the object and the subject, we should distinguish two forms of repetition. In any event, repetition is difference without a concept. But in one case, difference is posited as external to the concept, a difference between objects represented under the same concept, falling into the indifference of space and time. In the

other case, difference is internal to the Idea; it is deployed as the pure creative movement of a dynamic space and time that correspond to the Idea. The first repetition is the repetition of the Same, which is explained by the identity of the concept or of the representation; the second is the one that includes difference, and is itself included in the alterity of the Idea, in the heterogeneity of an "appresentation." One is negative, due to the lack of a concept, and the other affirmative, due to the excess of the idea. One is hypothetical, the other categorical. One is static, the other dynamic. One is repetition in the effect, the other in the cause. One, in extension, the other, intensive. One ordinary, the other, remarkable and singular. One is horizontal, the other vertical. One is developed, explained; the other is enveloped, and must be interpreted (etc.). (36)

This passage is noteworthy within the context of our discussion for several reasons. First, because it does not absolutely identify—as opposed to *Anti-Oedipus*—the order of representation with that of subjectivization or Oedipalization; rather, and this is the second point, it emphasizes a "true (individual) subject" that does not work in the service of the identity and permanence of representation, a subject that also receives the romantic designation of "soul." Third, Deleuze establishes a certain dialectic between the uniformity of the universal and the transgressivity of the individual; this dialectic operates in such a manner that the universal *self* breaks down to that extent to which the individual is internal to it. This last consequence is not drawn in the most decisive way, for the adjunction of two types of repetition, one that displaces the unity of the concept and one that does not displace it, has to give the impression (which prevails in *Capitalism and Schizophrenia*) that it is *fundamentally* possible to conceive of a concept that would prove to be resistant to repetition.

Deleuze, as I already mentioned, is not completely unequivocal on this point. On the one hand, he assures us:

The two repetitions are not independent. One is the singular subject, the heart and the interiority of the other, the depth of the other. The other is only the external envelope, the abstract effect. . . . Everywhere the Other [is hidden] in the repetition of the Same. (37)

On the other hand, the metaphor of the "external envelope," used to describe the effect of abstraction that transforms the singular subject into a concept (into a representation), still allows room for the interpretation that this concept could exist as "the other" of the unrepeatable singular subject, i.e., that it could exist in a certain autonomy.

Nevertheless, in *Différence et répétition* there are points at which the thought of a subject identical with itself (as concept) begins to be challenged as such. I want to present these points only briefly, since, with regard to the notion they develop about the subject in classical philosophy, they are completely consistent with the ideas of Lacan and Derrida.

Where he comments, for example, on Descartes's and Kant's *cogito*, Deleuze conceives of the subject in terms of a relation of reflection: "the subject can now represent to itself its own spontaneity only as that of an Other" (82). We saw that already Fichte did *not* (any longer) conceive of the subject in this manner, but Deleuze takes as little notice of more recent theories of self-consciousness as do the neostructuralists as a whole. And Deleuze can easily prove of the subject, conceived in this way, that it can only lay claim in the form of a postulate to the criterion by virtue of which it identifies the two moments in the dyad of reflection as two sides of *the same* thing.

> The unicity and identity of the divine substance are in truth the sole guarantor of the one and identical Self, and God is preserved as long as the Self is kept. (81)

With Kant's attack on rational theology, even the unity of this God (who guarantees the unity of the self) is in danger of collapsing, so that the dividedness of the I that relies on Him as the guarantor of its identity becomes a scarcely solvable problem.

> For when Kant contests rational theology, he introduces *at the same time* a sort of imbalance, a fissure or crack, an alienation of right, insurmountable by right, in the pure Self of the *I think*: the subject can now represent to itself its own spontaneity only as that of an Other, and by this means invoke in the last instance a mysterious coherence that excludes its own coherence, that of the world and that of God. Cogito for a self that has been dissolved: the Self of the *I think* carries within its essence a receptivity of intuition in relation to which, already, I is an other. (82)

In other words, since it is no longer capable of identifying itself either by virtue of its own power, or on the certainty of divine guarantee, the I completely loses its identity (and experiences itself as unpreconceivably altered). (Here I am disregarding the fact—we discussed it at an earlier point—that this view fails to come to terms even on the descriptive level with the phenomenon of our factual familiarity with ourselves: the factual subsistence of our experience of unity speaks for the postulation of a transcendental unity; at this point the undialectical universalization of difference over unity, which we observed in *Capitalism and Schizophrenia*, appears in this work for the first time.)

Be that as it may, Deleuze believes that even in the case of Kant himself difference successfully prevailed over the identifying operation of representation or of reflection. He cites a further event that deepened the division of the I in Kant's philosophy over against the one in Descartes: the discovery of temporality (*DR*,

116ff.), which distributes the two moments of the dyad of reflection over two different positions in time, and which thus makes them exist in a condition of non-simultaneity to themselves. (According to what Deleuze tells us about this, however, it cannot be valid for the transcendental I, but only for the I of "internal meaning." But let's ignore this weakness in Deleuze's argument.)

> Then begins a long inexhaustible story: I is an other, or the paradox of intimate meaning. . . .
> Through and through the I is, as it were, traversed by a crack: it is cracked by the pure and empty form of time. . . .
> . . . the death of God does not allow the identity of the I to subsist, but institutes and interiorizes in it an essential dissimilarity, a "de-mark" rather than the mark or the seal of God. (116, 117)

Before we can even formulate an objection or an addendum, Deleuze himself already makes the observation that it is German romanticism, in particular Hölderlin, "that discovers the void of pure time, and, in this void, at once the continued abduction of the divine, the prolonged crack in the I, and the passion constitutive of the Self" (118). (What Deleuze does not say is that Hölderlin developed a very complicated theory that seeks to illuminate the experiential subsistence of I-ness in the state of its manifest dividedness in reflection; i.e., he by no means wants to sacrifice one for the other.)

Nevertheless, one cannot simply say that Deleuze overlooked the problem that occurs when one grants autonomy to differentiality at the expense of unity. In the next lecture I will demonstrate how he experiments with the thought (borrowed from Heidegger),

> that difference is in itself articulation and link, that it relates the different to the different, without any mediation by the identical or the similar, the analogue or the opposite. There has to be a differentiation of difference, an in-itself as a differentiater, a *Sich-unterscheidende[s]*, by which the different finds itself assembled at the same time, instead of being represented on the condition that there be a prior resemblance, identity, analogy, or opposition. (154)

Lecture 24

In *Différence et répétition* we came across the following conceptual construction: in and of itself repetition does not submit to the law of universality. Repeated events (*événements*/tokens) are not necessarily instances that reproduce the universal rule; rather, they are singularities that, in the act of application, simultaneously transgress and incalculably alter the concept under which they come forward. To a thinking intent on systematization, this characteristic of repetition must appear a particular nuisance, and representation is the means by which the system attempts to integrate deviation. A representation idealizes or abstracts the individuality of singular events up to the point at which (qualitatively or quantitatively) common aspects come to the fore that can be attributed to an essentially unlimited number of singular data as predicates. The agent of this abstraction or idealization is the ego: as the synthesis of the multiplicities of occurrences, it identifies what is by nature nonidentical (i.e., it subjugates it to the external unity of a concept; see especially *DR*, 176ff., 189).

Our question was, Is this synthesis by the ego successful, or is Deleuze able to show that the transcendental synthesis of apperception is actually only an apparent identification or subsumption of the irreducible individuality of the experiential?

We learned on this basis that Deleuze, like one segment of the metaphysical tradition, orients himself around the model of self-consciousness as reflection: the ego is familiar with its essence by means of its representation, by means of its specular double (in contrast to the individual, which exists without an internal or specular double, *sans semblable*, i.e., irreflectively). Conceived as the relation of two elements with each other, the ego is confronted with the peculiar difficulty of being in need of a criterion (transgressing the inwardness of its self-relation) that permits the identification of the two distinctive moments. Deleuze tells us that for Descartes this criterion still consisted in the "divine guarantee." With his attack on rational theology (and metaphysics in general), however, Kant destroys this criterion (for, if it existed, it would be transcendent to human reason, "overexcessive" [*überschwänglich*]); from this it follows that the unity of reason becomes a mere requirement (a postulate). But we are by no means conscious of our familiarity with ourselves as a mere hypothesis: even if the self is not adequately given to itself, it remains an apodictic certainty. From this one could conclude that the model of reflection is inappropriate to the experiential subsistence of self-consciousness. But precisely this conclusion is not drawn by Deleuze. He considers self-consciousness a special case of the interreferentiality of two elements (and thus as a relation of reflection) about which, to be sure, he wants to prove that no (either hypothetical or factual) identity suppresses the differential moment inherent to every repetition: every reflection would thus be a nonidentical mirroring.

Deleuze finds the beginnings for an insight into this situation in Kant himself and in the romantic philosophers. In Kant to the extent that, in his chapter on schematism in his *Critique of Pure Reason*, he conceives the synthesis of self-consciousness as temporal, and thus as a depresenced relation to itself (as nonpresence with itself: *non-présence à soi*). In Hölderlin he finds it insofar as Hölderlin—at the same time as Novalis—emphasized that our consciousness of familiarity with ourselves cannot be obtained from the differences of the relation of reflection as such: either one takes difference to be real (in which case the chance to view it as the manifestation of a grounding unity vanishes), or one represses the reality of difference and thereby loses the possibility of maintaining a *cognitive (erkennende)* reference to unity.[1] Yet we *do have* consciousness of ourselves; we therefore have to postulate a prereflective unity, which is simultaneously conscious, as the basis of the relation of reflection. What this might look like has not yet been satisfactorily illuminated in theory.

Deleuze reflects upon whether our self-consciousness cannot be explained on the basis of the occurrence of differentiation itself—without transcendental recourse to a founding unity. Difference not only separates but also—similar to the "articulation" of the phonic masses—establishes connections and proximities (*DR*, 154), but these are of a sort that do not obey the law of subsumption of what is repeated under the universal or the identical.

> As for these instances [resemblance, identity, analogy, opposition],
> once they cease to be conditions, they are no longer anything but effects
> of the first difference and its differentiation, global or surface effects
> that characterize the denatured world of representation, and which ex-

press the way in which the in-itself of difference hides itself in giving rise to what covers it over. (*DR*, 154)

I shall skip over what Deleuze says about a possible system of "differentially stratified intensities" in order to put my finger on the more fundamental problem, which Deleuze himself articulates in the following way:

> Under what . . . conditions does difference develop this in-itself as a "differentiater," and assemble the different beyond all possible representation? . . . The major difficulty remains: is it indeed difference that relates the different to the different in these intensive systems? Does the difference of difference relate difference to itself with no other intermediary? When we speak of putting things in touch with each other, heterogeneous series, coupling, and resonance, do we not do so on the condition that there be a minimum of resemblance between the series, and identity in the agent that brings about the communication? (154, 156)

In other words, is it possible for different series (for example, sign chains), to which we can attribute the character that they are repetitions of each other, to be brought into relation to each other at all without having recourse to "the identity of a third"—as the criterion for the reference of that which philosophy calls its "ground of relation"?

Deleuze responds with a metaphor that he then loads with a considerable burden of proof.

> The lightning strikes between different intensities, but it is preceded by an invisible, intangible, *somber precursor*, which determines its reverse path in advance, in negative outline as it were. In the same way, every system contains its somber precursor that ensures communication between the border series. . . .
>
> But in any case it is a matter of knowing how the precursor exercises this role. It is not doubtful that *there is* an identity of the precursor, and a resemblance between the series that it puts in touch with each other. But this "there is" remains completely undetermined. . . . Identity and resemblance would then be nothing more than inevitable illusions, that is, *concepts of reflection* that [retrospectively] would account for our inveterate habit of thinking of difference on the basis of the categories of representation, but doing so because the invisible precursor would hide both itself and its functioning, and at the same time would hide the in-itself as the true nature of difference. (156–57).

This—aporetically named—somber precursor displays, as we see, great similarities both to Derrida's *différance*, as well as to Lacan's "true subject," conceived as that which "subtracts itself" from the phenomena of meaning it itself brings to light: "there is no other place than the one in which it is 'missing,' no other identity than the one in which it is missing" (157). The "invisible precursor" has in common with Kant's transcendental subject that it steps into the background for the benefit of those phenomena it brought to light. But the characteristic of possessing identity only in the form of a lack (*manqué*), and thereby eluding the law of reflection and its semiotic fixation as *representamen* (Peirce) – this characteristic it has in common with individuality. Individuality too lets meaning appear as something represent*able*, but it itself is not represented in the representamen and is not representable: for that which is the basis of meaning does not appear as part of the *effect* of meaning. And indeed, there is no integrating third element, no ground of conjunction,[2] which would mediate (intersubjective) *signification* with individual *meaning*; and this is true because meaning cannot be uniformly repeated. Uniformity of significations, therefore, has to be explained as a sort of transcendental appearance, as the precipitate of a differential activity that itself (in its In-itself) does not operate on the level of significations, and which necessarily slips away from its own effects (*[qui] se dérobe nécessairement sous ses propres effets*),

> because it [the somber precursor] is perpetually *displaced* within itself and is perpetually *disguised* in the series. Thus we cannot consider the identity of a third element and the resemblance of the parts to be a condition for the being and the thought of difference, but only a condition for its representation, which expresses a denaturing of this being and this thought, like an optical effect that blurs the true status of the conditions as it is in itself. (157)

All of this is quite transparent. But it does not solve the problem that, within the framework of a satisfactory theory of self-consciousness, interests us most, namely, how something like familiarity of consciousness with itself can be generated beyond nonidentity and "disparity" in repetition. And individuality is distinct from the singularity of objects precisely in that it is not blind, like the blind precursor; rather, it is familiar with itself in a way that can nevertheless be distinguished from the certainty of reflection and the recursivity of representation; for it is a matter of the familiarity of something that is nonrepeatable, and thus of something that is not instantaneous (present).

For this reason we can agree with everything Deleuze negatively says about the mode of Being of that which cannot be repeated (for example, that all meaning rests on the fact that an element that itself is nonsignificant forms its ground [*DR*, 161]). We can even agree with the idea that the individual is different in itself (and not only different from other things: the incalculability of the contexts into which it can enter constantly displaces the margins of its previous unity with itself). On the other hand, the individual is fundamentally distinguished from the somber presurcor in that it, unlike the metaphor Deleuze uses, is not a natural event (*une foudre*) but rather grounded in a *hypothetical judgment*. A judgment, a hypothesis: only an individual could pass a judgment or advance a hypothesis. Even if the coupling of repeated sign chains remains nonidentical here, there is always a *motive* for this being conjoined in such and such a way and in no other; and this motive is the hypothesis that an individual capable of interpretation advances about the unity of the conjoined elements.

To be sure, Deleuze is correct (and Peirce had had this insight a hundred years prior to him) in asserting that there is no transcendental criterion available (such as divine guarantee, for example) that assures the identity of repeated moments. On the other hand, there *is* consciousness of connections and there *is* consciousness (of) consciousness. Thus one could conclude, loosely adapting the basic idea of Peirce's semiotics, that every inference that interprets the repetition of a sign or of an event as the repetition of the *same* is an ampliative inference. An "ampliative inference" designates a nondeductive procedure of inferring. It is nondeductive because precisely that principle is lacking *on the basis of which* the unity of the phenomena connected by the judgment could be derived. It is nevertheless a founded inference to the extent that this principle survives in the form of a reasonable demand: it is that *in expectation of which* every judgment of identity (and, indeed, any judgment at all) already anticipates its founding. This founding, to be sure, occurs only provisionally, since it has no criterion for its truth; but it is provisional in the sense of a well-grounded hypothesis that, although it makes no claim to uncover the thing-in-itself, still could not be replaced by a better-founded judgment.

> By saying that we draw the inference *provisionally*, I mean that we do not hold that we have reached any assigned degree of approximation as yet, but only hold that if our experience be indefinitely extended, and if every fact of whatever nature, as fast as it presents itself, be duly applied, according to the inductive method, in correcting the inferred ratio, then our approximation will become indefinitely close in the long run.[3]

In this sense the inductive-abductive form of inference operates without a prior criterion for identity, yet it is still not adequately described as a bolt of lightning that follows the course in the sky that the "somber precursor" prescribes for an electrical discharge. There is no abductive inference that mediates between the precursor and the lightning itself, but only a blind natural causality. In contrast to this, everything that has meaning is motivated; i.e., it is the result of an interpretive hypothesis. To interpret, for its part, presupposes self-consciousness. And self-consciousness, finally, is, as Dieter Henrich has shown, not an action that could be described as the *identification* of something with something else:[4] this, on the contrary, is rather how the model of reflection, which is not appropriate for describing the phenomenon of self-consciousness, wants to have it. In truth, the familiarity of consciousness with itself has to precede, as part of its prior reserve of knowledge, any reflection of an activity onto itself. "Familiarity with consciousness can by no means be understood as the result of an activity. It always already is present when consciousness occurs."[5]

If this is the case, however, then we can confidently hold on to the notion of self-consciousness, without contradicting what Deleuze says about the nonidentity of repetition, on the one hand, and also without contradicting, on the other hand, the criteria-less conjunction of the different strata of meaning in the wake of the somber precursor. Familiarity with itself is obviously not a state of affairs that is subordinate to the criterion of identity. Hence there are reasons to stick to the opinion that the condition of possibility for the representability of the world, on the one hand, and for the incessant displaceability of this representation, on the other (*DR*, 16), cannot be a preconscious "difference from itself" (or "internal difference," "difference in itself" [*DR*, 157–58]), but that it much rather is a matter of a thoroughly prereflective (and thus a fortiori predifferential) *consciousness*. "Predifferential" does not mean "identical." Both identity and difference, rather, would be "effects" of this prerelational familiarity with itself without which neither meaning attribution nor meaning displacement would be conceivable. Projected into the flow of time (and thus into differentiality), this familiarity with itself would conjoin its utterances and sign chains by means of operations of hypothetical inference in such a way that, on the one hand, every repetition would carry the index of an alteration, and, on the other hand, the set of all alterations would be taken up into the continuity of a *motivated* (i.e., nonblind) succession of interpretations and hypotheses.[6]

But even if the hypothetical nature of inference (only postulated by us, by no means illuminated) comes closer to doing justice to the hermeneutical character of the formation and identification of signs than the obscure metaphor of a somber precursor does, we can still totally agree with Deleuze on the descriptive level: there is no criterion for the identity of a concept, and also none for the continuity of our self-consciousness; every repetition hence implies the alteration of what is repeated as an uncontrollable possibility that is hence a priori irrefutable because it is a *structural possibility*.

We will also not forget that Deleuze—and as far as I can tell, he is the only one among the neostructuralists to have done this—recognized the significance of the individual for the process of meaning attribution and meaning transformation, and that he confirmed this on the basis of lucid phenomenological analyses. To be sure, it is more the idea of "intensity" that serves him (as well as Jean-François Lyotard) as the key concept for the designation of a prerepresentative entity (or rather nonentity) that does not obey the law of identity (see, above all, *DR*, 314ff.; cf. 343 on the mode of Being of intensity as a μὴ ὄν). Nonetheless, intensity— whose primary characteristics are the "difference in itself" (*DR*, 325), non-representativity, and asignificance[7]—does not seem to me to be an essential feature of the Being of individuality (although I would prefer to discuss this point at some other time; for the present, let's simply put it in parentheses without making a decision about it). Be that as it may, Deleuze says: "All individuality is intensive" (317), and "difference is intensive" (342). By means of the common characteristic of intensity, an inner bond is thus established between differentiality and individuality, as we were already able to surmise based on the ideas of Schleiermacher and Sartre.

What Deleuze has to say about this is indeed quite original. For individuality is usually considered a nucleus of self-identity that cannot be further divided. That "the authentic dividual . . . [is] also the authentic individual," is a romantic thought that stands in contradiction to the conceptual history of this term.[8] And Deleuze's thoughts similarly stand in contradiction to the history of this concept.

> The individual is neither a quality nor an extension. Individuation is neither a qualification nor a partition, neither a specification nor an organization. The individual is no more a *species infima* than a composite of parts. Qualitative or extensive interpretations of individuation remain incapable of pinpointing a reason why a quality might cease being general, or why a synthesis of extent might begin here and end there. Qualification and specification already presuppose individuals to be qualified; and extensive parts relate to the individual, rather than the other way around. But precisely, it is insufficient to mark a difference in kind between individuation and differentiation in general. This difference in kind remains unintelligible as long as we do not accept its necessary consequence: that individuation precedes differentiation by right, and that all differentiation presupposes an intense field of prior individuation. It is through the action of the field of individuation that a given set of differential relations, a given set of remarkable points (the preindividual field) are actualized. . . . Individuation does not presuppose any differentiation, but rather provokes it. (318)

The individual is clearly distinguished from the atom that cannot be further divided from the final species, which, as particularities, can still be subordinated to a concept of genus or element (or, in the extreme case, which can be methodically reconciled with the universal by infinitesimal calculation). Moreover, the individual is brought into a delimiting relation with differentiality, of the sort that the former precedes the latter. This reminds us of Sartre, who maintained that the "nonsignifying element," or the individual, installs the significations that are different among themselves in their status of Being in the first place, so that one can say that the significations are projected by the individual and, simultaneously, that "they appear to be, as it were, detached from the universal by a singularity" (*Situations*, VIII, 450) by means of the intervention of an individual. But we could also think of Saussure, who considers differentiality to be a, to be sure, necessary, but not a sufficient condition for the formation of meaning, since the articulation of the phonic mass leads to the constitution of signs only if one has their possible meaning in view. That means that the projection of meaning precedes the shaping of signifiers in a specific sense (or, to formulate it more cautiously, that it proceeds in tandem with it).

> The vocal sound . . . is the instrument of thought . . . without existing for itself, independently of thought. . . . The vocal sound is not a word except to the exact, constant extent that a meaning is attached to it. . . .
>
> On the contrary it is signification that delimits [into units] the words in the spoken mass. . . . The unit does not preexist. Signification is what creates it. The units are not there to receive a signification [after the fact]. (Clearly then, it is meaning that creates the unit). . . .
>
> Thought is what delimits units; sound itself does not delimit them in advance: there is always a relation with thought. . . . it is always a matter of the cutting out that thought does in the spoken mass that is amorphous. . . .
>
> Difference is what makes things meaningful, and signification is what creates differences, too. (*CFS*, 15 [1957], 7–8, 41–42, 68, 76)

All these passages, taken from the second *Cours* of 1908–9, have in common that they establish a dependence of the formation of difference, which according to the popular-structuralist view precedes the formation of meaning (which would boil down to an inverted theory of representation), on the conscious acts of speaking individuals. It is precisely in this sense that Deleuze claims "that individuation precedes differentiation by right, and that all differentiation presupposes an intense field of prior individuation" (*DR*, 318).

This priorness, however, should not be conceived as independence, as if the individual could retain its presemiological identity in its purity over against the play of differences. On the contrary:

> The individual is in no way the indivisible; it is constantly dividing and changing in nature. (*DR*, 331)

The individual, by bringing forth signification—by means of interpreting it—is simultaneously the agent that alters it; this, too, should be understood in the spirit of Saussure, who, to be sure, asserted that "forms and grammar exist only socially," but who also added: "but changes arise from the individual" (*CFS*, 15 [1957], 9). At a later point Saussure specified this and said that no "grammatical form" whatsoever exists independent of the way in which the individual appropriates it, i.e., interprets it: "A grammatical fact . . . is the pure product of interpretation" (100). And in a formulation even clearer, that is more explicitly hermeneutical:

> Language can be considered as something that, from moment to moment, is *interpreted* by the generation that receives it; it is an instrument that people try to *understand*. The present collectivity does not interpret it at all as the preceding generations have done because, since conditions have changed, the means for understanding language are not the same. *Therefore there must be the first act of interpretation, which is active* (earlier, one is placed before a mass to be understood, which is passive). This interpretation will be manifested by the distinctions between units (this is what all the activity of language results in). (89)

This means, first of all, that *langue* does not exercise any determination of the sort realized in individual speech ("nothing guarantees its stability; this order is at the mercy of the future. No sanction is given"; 72). Second, it means that *every* identification of a sign constitutes a hypothetical judgment, namely, an interpretation that, from the system of *langue*, cannot be deduced, an interpretation that takes (understands) the word-hull from generation to generation, indeed, from speech act to speech act, as an always different sign. Third, it means that each identification of a sign, to the extent that it is innovative and interpretive, determines anew the *differentiality* of the sign-units.

Everything Deleuze says about the mode of Being of individuality would be reconcilable with Schleiermacher's and Sartre's view, at least to the degree that Deleuze would attribute a theory of individual self-consciousness to the individual. But this is precisely what he does not do, because he agrees with the representational theory of self-consciousness with which he takes issue insofar as he believes that consciousness fundamentally is constituted as an ego (*ichhaft*).

> A consciousness is nothing without a unifying synthesis, but there is no unifying synthesis of consciousness without a form of the I and a point of view of the Ego. What is neither individual nor personal, on the contrary, are the emissions of singularities inasmuch as they are made on an unconscious surface and enjoy an immanent mobile principle of self-unification through *nomadic distribution*, which is radically distinct from fixed and sedentary distributions as conditions of synthesis of consciousness. Singularities are the true transcendental elements. (*LS*, 124–25)

In a word, Deleuze does not know any other conception of consciousness than that of thought (although consciousness covers a larger field than the field of the acts of thought), and he apparently does not know any other concept of thought than the Kantian conception, according to which a thought owes its characteristic uniformity to the synthetic activity of a founding ego. We already know what Deleuze thinks about this synthesizing action that subjugates the individual to the schema of a concept. Nevertheless, what he says about the "radical" alternative of a mobile and nomadic "self-unification" of all singularities remains highly unsatisfying and indistinct.

This is also true for *Différence et répétition*:

> If the problem [of individuation] acquires a particular urgency with psychic systems, it is because it is not at all certain that the *Je* or the *Moi* belongs to the domain of individuation. Rather, they are the figures of differentiation. (*DR*, 330)

Je is the name for the formal principle of unification that Kant grasps as the transcendental synthesis of apperception; *Moi* designates the psychic organism in the narrower sense. Both are functions in the service of the universalization of individual events of consciousness in anticipation of their regularity and representability.

Yet it is very easy to agree with the thesis that the individual's familiarity with itself is not structured as an ego (*ichhaft*), without simultaneously having also to maintain that it is without consciousness. If it is the individual, as the nonsignificant element, which produces meaning, then it could not possibly be unconscious; an unconscious meaning is a nonthought. But self-consciousness is not consciousness of an I (whether *Je* or *Moi*), but rather consciousness (of) consciousness, which for its part is consciousness *of* something that is not conscious (a state of affairs, for example). This is the reason why we can subscribe to Deleuze's assertions that

> the individuating factors, the implied factors of individuation, thus have neither the form of the *Je* nor the substance of the *Moi*. For the *Je* is not separable from a form of identity, nor the *Moi* from a substance constituted by a continuity of resemblances. . . . Every individuating factor, on the other hand, is already a difference, and a difference of difference. It is constructed on a fundamental disparity, and functions on the borders of this disparity as such. . . . The individual is in no way indivisible; it is constantly dividing and changing in nature. It is not a *Moi* in what it expresses; for it expresses Ideas as internal multiplicities, made of differential relations and remarkable points, preindividual singularities. And it is not a *Je* expression either; for here again it forms an actualizing muliplicity, a condensation of remarkable points as it were, an open collection of intensities. (*DR*, 331)

Although we subscribe to these sentences, we still cannot refrain from demanding an explanation about the way in which the "undetermined, floating, flowing, communicating, enveloping-enveloped" (and not organized as an ego [*ichhaft*]) individual has knowledge of itself (332). This demand has even more weight if one characterizes individuation as that which is unprethinking ("What cannot be surpassed is individuation itself"): "unprethinking" in the sense that it is completed "beyond the *moi* and the *Je*," as pre-ego ("pre-*moi*" and pre-*Je*"), as the itself undetermined ground for all conceivable determination (*DR*, 332), and in this sense related to Plato's μὴ ὄν, which also is not simply "nothing at all" (οὐχ ὄω), but which precedes every affirmation (*DR*, 343). To be sure, to the extent that even the singular participates in Being, it becomes urgent that we ask in what way it is familiar with itself, i.e., how it knows about itself.

But we do not want to follow this line of questioning further at this point (for it would necessarily go beyond the domain of our question about the essence of neostructuralism with regard to a *general* theory of self-consciousness and individuality). Instead of this, we want to reflect on the position of our argumentation. Obviously, we have gradually left—most recently, following texts by Deleuze—the domain of the question about neostructuralism's theory of the subject and are stepping into the realm in which we want to ask about the neostructuralist theory of meaning. And the question of "meaning" is the third question we want to address to neostructuralist theory.

In retrospect we can see that the sequence of our questions, outlined for the purpose of organizing our series of lectures, by no means depicts a merely external order. On the contrary, we have learned that the "archaeology of knowledge"—as a nonhistoricist theory of history—anticipates a certain model of self-consciousness: a model in which, and according to which, the subject can no longer be conceived as the author of history (or, to speak in more general terms, as the author of what Heidegger calls the "meaning of Being"). This deautonomization of subjectivity, in its turn, appeals constantly to a theory of meaning (or let's say, to a semantics, or, more generally, to a semiology); for it is the insertion of the subject in always already existing contexts of meaning (contexts of signs, discourses, institutions, etc.) in whose name this deautonomization occurs. To understand the subject as an effect of meaning (and not as its author) already implies a thesis about the inescapability of the world of signs. In this thesis all those questions we decided to direct at neostructuralism converge. Neostructuralism is essentially language philosophy (a characteristic it shares with its unbeloved relatives, i.e., with analytical philosophy and German hermeneutics); and on the basis of a theory of language and linguistically mediated formation of meaning, the neostructuralists inquire about the Being of history and the status of Being of subjectivity. To this extent, the sequence of our questions turns out to be guided by a certain purpose.

In discussing the problem of the essential impossibility of identical self-reflection and of repetition with identical meaning—theses that are supposed to shake the belief in a self-consciousness identical with itself—we are already standing completely on the ground of sign theory. For, as we know by now, it is, according to the neostructuralist view, the systematically demonstrated impossibility that a sign can be reiterated without a change in meaning that also ruptures the subject—understood as an effect of meaning—and which deprives it of its *présence-à-soi*. Lacan spoke of an "intrusion of the signifier" that robs the subject of its identity; and Derrida, as we recall, talked about the fact that my self-consciousness is preceded by speech, and that this destroys its character as a principle and its coincidence with itself. We thus have to turn to the theory of language in which, in the last instance, the fates of history and subjectivity will be decided.

Meanwhile, we are no longer uninformed nor uncritical about the arguments neostructuralism gave us concerning the mode of Being of signs. Let's first recall that there is a characteristic opposition that separates the neostructuralist from the analytical critique of meaning. The latter—I am overstating this for the sake of a first orientation—considers the givenness of consciousness, which in classical transcendental philosophy was held to be fundamental, to be secondary over against the more fundamental givenness of meaning; but meaning, in turn, is defined as a linguistic category that, in addition, connects the mechanism of language to the compliance with intersubjectively inviolable rules and conventions. Neostructuralism, on the other hand, primarily modified substantially the third of these consequences. For the neostructuralist critique of meaning it is also true that classical philosophy of consciousness is reformulated and newly grounded in terms of a theory of signs; on the other hand, doubts arise about the plausibility of the assertion that language (or, in general, every conceivable system of symbols) can be described—here following Wittgenstein—as "blind compliance with rules." This phrase suggests that "to mean something with something else (an expression)" automatically implies that one has to act according to a convention. One can only say something in a language, and language attributes meaning to its signs, words, and sentences (which stay *typally* identical in different applicational situations) by defining these applicational situations themselves as conventional *types* (for example, as *speech acts*); that is, it subjugates them to an order in which a specific applicational situation (a pragmatic context) is allotted to each expression.

It is precisely this order, as we know, that is no longer guaranteed if one does not take "language" to be the final foundation of meaning attribution, but rather submits it to the play of uncontrollable differentiations. "Order" itself then appears from the outset to be either merely hypothetical and preliminary (from the perspective of a hermeneutical interpretation of this state of affairs) or undecidable and uncontrollable (from the perspective of Derrida and Deleuze). But in neither case is language the last foundation of philosophizing; language rests on something that precedes it and which itself is not subordinate to the category of meaning, but which rather produces it and deprives it of its identity at the same time. A nonidentical meaning could, of course, never be conceived as the result of compliance with a rule; for the distance that separates the identity of the sign from itself also undermines the rule that underlies its creation and deprives it of its pertinence.

This, in any case, is the position that Derrida and Deleuze take, each in his own way. And neither, as I will try to show in our next lecture, develops his views without paying attention to the analytical standpoint, but rather in explicit and critical confrontation with the so-called speech-act theory, which for its part drew certain conclusions from the pragmatic turn of language philosophy based on the work of Peirce and Wittgenstein.

We must begin by acquainting ourselves with the main features that constitute the predecessorship of Peirce and Wittgenstein. But first let's reconstruct the point of conjunction. Earlier I pointed out that one of the characteristic traits of Deleuze's (but also of Derrida's) position is that neither of them lets language stand — as a conventional or traditional sign order — as an inescapable reality (thus as a *principle* of philosophizing): *individuality* precedes linguistic difference. (Derrida, for his part, would say that *différance*, the generative movement of articulation, precedes the existing system of semiological oppositions and prevents it from closing itself in any configuration whatever.) To be sure, both Derrida and Deleuze take issue with the interpretation of individuality or of *différance* as a "transcendental-philosophical" principle (see *LI*, 244: "iterability is, however, not a transcendental condition of possibility"; see also *LI*, 225–26, 234–36). Derrida speaks of *différance* as the "arche-trace," which can also be called "ultratranscendental," insofar as it also still grounds the classical signification of the "transcendental."[9]

> The concept of arche-trace must comply with both that necessity and that erasure. It is in fact contradictory and not acceptable within the logic of identity. The trace is not only the disappearance of origin — within the discourse that we sustain and according to the path that we follow it means that the origin did not even disappear, that it was never constituted except reciprocally by a nonorigin, the trace, which thus becomes the origin of the origin. (*GR*, 61)

In this hyperbolic overstatement, the meaning of "condition of possibility" is preserved in such a way that "language" or the symbolic order cannot be the final quasi-transcendental principles of language philosophy: something, namely *différance*, precedes them as the transcendental principle of meaning constitution.

The neostructuralist theory of meaning shares this movement of "exceeding" — at least at first glance — with that branch of analytical philosophy we know as pragmatism, or, more narrowly, as *speech-act theory*. Its most important precursors are, as we know, Charles Sanders Peirce and Ludwig Wittgenstein. The former asserted (and Derrida cites him approvingly, even if slightly abbreviated in argumentative strength; see *GR*, 48ff.) that linguistic signs and expressions, in order to be able to relate positively or negatively as functions of truth to states of affairs of empirical reality, must before this be provided with a commentary that allows them this reference to the world. Peirce called this commentary the "interpretant"; it permits the sign to signify by virtue of a hypothetical inference that, to be sure, can be motivated by earlier sign uses, but cannot be derived from them. For signs "by nature" have no meaning at all; they acquire it only and principally by virtue of interpretive ascription. If this is the case, then the interpretive creation of meaning, which lends a meaning to a given *sign bearer*, has to be reestablished from one instance to the next, i.e., from one application to the next. To use signs and to understand sign uses thus presupposes ad infinitum preceding interpretations. Radically simplifying this, one could say that language is the order it is in each instance only by virtue of an interpretation that introduces it to this mode of Being, which itself, however, does not have the mode of Being of a linguistic phenomenon (whereby in this context "linguistic" means "of the nature of *langue*," not "of the nature of *langage*." The interpretant is, of course, "linguistic"/*langagier* in this sense, but it is not an element of *langue* as system; this system is in itself mute if it has not been previously interpreted). Derrida gives the following commentary on this thought.

> There is thus no phenomenality reducing the sign or the representer so that the thing signified may be allowed to glow finally in the luminosity of its presence. The so-called "thing itself" is always already a *representamen* shielded from the simplicity of intuitive evidence. The *representamen* functions only by giving rise to an *interpretant* that itself becomes a sign and so on to infinity. The self-identity of the signified conceals itself unceasingly and is always on the move. The property of the *representamen* is to be itself and another, to be produced as a structure of reference, to be separated from itself. The property of the *representamen* is not to be *proper* [*propre*], that is to say absolutely *proximate* to itself (*prope, proprius*). The *represented* is always already a *representamen*. (*GR*, 49–50)

Derrida thus interprets the play of each sign on two levels (that of *langue* and that of *interpretation*) as the originary dividedness of every sign from itself (by virtue of an interpretation that intervenes between itself and its application in a situation). The convergence with the basic idea of pragmatism, at any rate, consists in the fact that for both, language (i.e., the system of signs and of expressive conventions) is not a transcendental principle in itself, but becomes such only by means of a prelanguage-systematic condition of possibility that itself can no longer be characterized as transcendental (individuality for Deleuze, *différance* for Derrida, interpretation for Peirce).

Something very similar is the case in Wittgenstein. To understand the meaning of a word or a chain of words (a proposition) does not mean to know what things or states of affairs are depicted (or designated) by the words. A significant portion of linguistic action does not consist in formulating statements about the existing circumstances of a segment of reality. It could also consist, for example, in "giving orders and obeying them, forming and testing a hypothesis, making up a story, play-acting, singing catches, guessing riddles, making a joke, translating from one language into another, asking, thanking, cursing, greeting, praying, etc."[10] These, in short, are forms of linguistic action in which no substantiating reference is made to reality. From this Wittgenstein draws the conclusion that, to the extent that we understand words or expressions that are used in nonsubstantiating "language games," their signification cannot consist in their appropriateness to a (transsemiological) fact, but rather in the manner of their use, insofar as this use, in its regularity, helps express a collective "form of life." The signification of a word or an expression is, therefore, the nature of its use in conventionalized, i.e., socially determined contexts of actions. Speech is a manner of social action, namely, that of communicating; its regularity points to the underlying social praxis. All forms of life are actions that ipso facto are intersubjective in the sense of being codified. This alone is the ground for their transindividual comprehensibility. (This, after all, was the problem of epistemological solipsism, which Wittgenstein sought to escape by reflecting on the essentially intersubjective character of linguistic signs.)

The germinal thought of so-called speech-act theory is grounded in this consideration. The expression "speech act," although already used by Schleiermacher in the sense of a linguistic "fact" (see *HuK*, 89, 77), was coined by John R. Searle in its specific meaning.[11] Where the main issues are concerned, however, it goes back to the posthumously published Oxford lectures of the language philosopher John L. Austin.[12] Austin had asked himself the important question as to whether previous language philosophy and linguistics had not viewed their subject, the grammatically well-formed phrase, very one-sidedly and only under the assumption that a sentence makes a (descriptive) statement, i.e., communicates something that, if it is true, refers to a fact in the world. The obsession with an Aristotelian model of the *lógos apophanticos*, of the propositional statement, which was also critically restricted by Heidegger, is still at work here. For Austin it is clear what the strategic purpose of this obsession was: only propositional statements can be true or false; therefore they are suited for a language theory in which the functional logic of the truth value always has control over speech events. Now there are, according to Austin, aside from the type of the propositional statement, a large number of nonapophantic forms of expression: one can carry out actions through speech (therefore the designation "act utterances" or "speech acts"); indeed, to speak a language means to apply a rule-governed form of practical behavior. Or, expressed in more accessible terms, to speak means to carry out acts in accordance with rules. Such an action, for example, would be the statement, "I promise not to speak too quickly." Here it is not the case that something is being said about something else; rather, the utterance includes a practical obligation, i.e., an action, for which I assume the responsibility by uttering the sentence. I can also give orders, insult someone, commit a faux pas, recite a prayer, be ironic, etc. In all these cases not (only) is something expressed, but a statement (Searle says: a proposition) is pragmatically *interpreted* on the basis of a superposed form of intentionality: a proposition becomes a speech act if one understands the rule that makes the uttered sentence into the vehicle of a social and, what is more, of an intentional act, such as is the case, for example, in the baptismal or consecrational formula of the priest, who not only wants to state something but also wants to perform an act with this statement. The traditional model of grammar, therefore, would have to be enriched by all those types of statements in which presumed propositional statements in fact express intentional acts. Here "to express" does not necessarily mean "to couch in words," but rather "to mean," for we almost always mean more than we in reality express. Indeed, what we mean can never simply be inferred from what we put into language, but only from the insight into the social rule whose mastery allows communication-ally competent speakers to form utterances (i.e., situationally interpreted statements) out of statements. One can never determine solely on the basis of its grammar what a statement means, i.e., which form of intentionality it expresses. If, for example, someone says: "I am counting to three . . .," then I can take this as a true statement, insofar as he or she really counts to three. However, the threatening gesture and the enraged voice that accompany this statement (which as such do not represent linguistic indexes) should have indicated to me that the speaker wanted to express a serious threat. Austin describes this state of affairs in the following way: a *propositional* (and dependent) *statement content* is interpreted in, and as, a speech act (which he also calls *performative* or *illocutionary act*) in such a way that one can tell—by virtue of mastering the underlying conventions of behavior—which intention it expresses (in this case, a threat).

I have promised to show you that, and how, Deleuze and Derrida in part subscribe to this theory, and in part alter it. I will make good on this promise in the next lecture.

Lecture 25

Let's quickly get back to our examination of the point at which the knowledge interests of a pragmatically oriented language analysis converge with those of neostructuralist language philosophy.

In his major work, *Speech Acts*, John R. Searle formulates what he calls the "principle of expressibility." It states that everything we mean can also be said. This phrase, however, precisely does not mean that every word employed in a statement would have to be, or even be able to be, related on a one-to-one basis to an object (or to a state of affairs, or part of a state of affairs), the recognition of which allows the addressee to recover the meaning of what was said. On the contrary, as Wittgenstein had already pointed out,[1] sentences like "Water!" "Away!" "Ow!" "Help!" "Fine!" and "No!" are neither designations of objects, nor are they incomplete. In such instances it is rather a matter of linguistic acts, and complete ones at that, whose meaning I can recapture by supplying them with the unexpressed conventions for utterances, which however are by no means ineffective or only elliptically stated. What remains unsaid in a grammatically well-formed sentence is that which signifies *in what* (practical) *sense* the sentence is to be understood, i.e., which conventionally codified form of intentionality it expresses; whether, for example, it is to be understood as a descriptive statement, a command, or a request.

Let's keep in mind that Searle holds the view that we frequently mean more than we in fact say. Here, then, the meaning of what is said would depend on something that is not said, namely, an *interpretation* of what was said with a view to a practical, intersubjectively known aim.

392

Austin more effectively designated this dependence of the "meaning-inten-tion"[2] of a sentence or a remark on a form of action that interprets it, calling it the "illocutionary force" of the speech act. The speech act—as the manifestation of a linguistic praxis—has not only a semantic content but also a characteristic force or power. This already comes to expression in the realm of the presumably totally value-neutral judgment we make when we characterize arguments as "strong" or "weak," instead of as "true" or "false." Derrida, in his major confronta-tion with Searle, makes the following remark in this regard:

> In the family of Latin languages, a speech act, whether written or spo-ken, is only said to be *pertinent* when it touches: the object to which it seems to refer, but also—why not?—someone, its addressee, upon whom it produces certain effects, let us say of a perlocutionary sort.
> (*LI*, 177)

Derrida characterizes these effects as "evaluants" and as manifestations of a lin-guistically mediated "violence" (*LI*, 177). If the common premise of speech-act theory and neostructuralism is valid, according to which even the constative utter-ance, i.e., the statement (which has a truth-value function), is dependent on a practical form of intentionality that interprets it as such a statement; and if, fur-ther, it is true that this form of intentionality possesses a certain force, then one can conclude that no conceivable form of language use could in the final analysis be explained in terms of propositional logic. Or, drawing an even more radical conclusion: even logic is the manifestation of a force that precedes and institutes it—totally in keeping with Nietzsche, who identifies the will to power as the prin-ciple of all expressions of force. We saw that even Foucault, in the last phase of his thinking, subscribes to this Nietzschean interpretation, according to which discourses are not simply systems of utterances but rather expressions of power. The discursive unity that is characteristic of them is not inherent in them but rather is the force of exclusion inscribed in them, and by virtue of which they rep-resent precisely this and no other unity. Derrida, too, supported this Nietzschean interpretation of Austin's theory of speech acts to a certain extent by emphasizing, "among other topics of interest," especially:

> Austin had to free the analysis of the performative from the author-ity of the *value of truth*, from the opposition true/false, [". . . two fetishes which I admit to an inclination to play Old Harry with, viz., 1) the true/false fetish, 2) the value/fact fetish."] at least in its classical form, occasionally subsituting for it the value of force, of difference of force (*illocutionary or perlocutionary force*). (It is this, in a thought which is nothing less than Nietzschean, which seems to me to beckon toward Nietzsche; who often recognized in himself a certain affinity with a vein of English thought.) (*Margins*, 322)

Deleuze's appropriation of speech-act theory is very similar, but takes its orientation more decisively from Nietzsche's (and Foucault's) theory of power. All information (which, as such, seems to be purely constative and to have a truth-value function) is suspected of being dependent on an execution of power, or of commands that interpret it pragmatically. Thus Searle's "hypothesis that the speech act is the basic unit of communication" is characteristically transformed into another one (which is gleaned from Nietzsche's *Genealogy of Morals*), according to which "the elementary unity of language—the utterance—is the watchword" (*MP*, 95).

> Rather than common sense, a faculty that centralizes information, an abominable faculty must be defined that consists in emitting, receiving, and transmitting watchwords. Speech is not even meant to be believed, but to obey and make others obey. (*MP*, 95–96)

Even Spengler and other theoreticians from the sphere of the prefascistic theory of power are summoned as witnesses to testify for this position (95–96). This prefascist tradition, whose revitalization we are right now experiencing, is in need of a more penetrating and critical examination than we can provide at this point.

I will limit myself to a presentation of the basic idea of Deleuze's variant of speech-act theory. He reformulates Searle's statement—which claims that the propositional content of an utterance can be understood only if I previously understood the intentional meaning of the entire utterance on a metapropositional level—in such a way that it designates all speech as indirect (*MP*, 97). It is indirect in the sense that its specific applicational meaning is attributed to it from outside of its purely grammatical structure. The ultimate applicational meaning, however, is the "I want," or the "I order you to . . ."

> It is in this sense that speech is the transmission of the word functioning as a watchword, and not the communication of a sign as information. (97)

Deleuze expressly refers to Austin. Deleuze characterizes the so-called *performatives*, which Austin formulated in his "famous theses," in the following way:

> It has been possible to call acts that are internal to speech—these immanent relations of statements with acts—*implicit or nondiscursive presuppositions*, as opposed to the suppositions, which can always be made explicit, according to which a statement refers either to other statements or to an external action (Ducrot). The delimitation of the sphere of the performative, and of the larger sphere of the illocutory already had three important consequences: (1) the impossibility of conceiving of language as a code, since the code is the condition that makes an explanation possible; and the impossibility of conceiving of language as the

communication of a piece of information; to order, to interrogate, to promise, to affirm is not to inform someone of a command, a doubt, a commitment, an assertion, but rather to bring about specific immanent acts that are necessarily implicit; (2) the impossibility of defining a semantics, a syntax, or even a phonetics as scientific zones of speech that are taken to be independent of *pragmatics*; . . . on the contrary, pragmatics becomes the presupposition of all other dimensions, and sneaks in everywhere; (3) the impossibility of maintaining the language-speech distinction, since speech can no longer be defined simply as individual and extrinsic use of a prior meaning, or the variable application of a preexisting syntax: on the contrary, the meaning and syntax of language are what cannot be defined independently of the speech acts that it presupposes. (98)

It seems to me that Austin's basic theses are in fact reiterated in a willful, but essentially correct, manner. And even the step, which neither Austin nor Searle nor Grice considers and which leads to a general theory of institutions and politics (understood as the instituted exercise of power), can certainly be taken on the basis of the premise of speech-act theory. To be sure, this presupposes the view, or, more correctly, the hypothesis that all "socially relevant" utterances, in the final analysis, have to be interpreted as commands that are issued by the subject that represents political power (100). This subject, of course, is not an individual but rather an institution; it explains the "necessarily social character of utterance" (101).

The social character of utterance is intrinsically founded only if it can be shown that the utterance itself refers to *collective arrangements*. Thus it is clear that individuation of the statement and subjectification of the utterance occur only to the extent required and determined by impersonal collective arrangement. . . .

So long as linguistics does not move beyond constants— phonological, morphological, or syntactic—it refers the statement back to a signifier and the utterance back to a subject, and thus misses the point of arrangement, refers circumstances to the outside, closes language in on itself, and makes of pragmatics a residue. (101, 104)

Without a doubt—it is almost trivial to note this—institutions operate not as individuals but rather as collective instruments. Nevertheless, in the end they are run by individuals and have to do with individuals. It is surprising to see to what a great extent Deleuze has changed his opinion in the ten years that separate *A Thousand Plateaus* from *Différence et répétition*. In the earlier work it was the operation of differentiation, which could never be sublated (in Hegelian terms) into a unity, which prevented the "code" from attaining closure. Now language in its entirety (*le langage tout entier*, *MP*, 106) is conceived as an instrument of power, as a political fact, and that also means: as a code. No doubt, it is conceived as a code of another order than that of lexics or of syntax: these two domains are rather put into service by a pragmatics that is interpreted as a politics of language (*La pragmatique est une politique de la langue*"; 105); everything in these realms that lays claim to a certain compulsoriness exhibits a dependence on the dictates of the pragmatic-political code.

> A type of statement can only be evaluated in terms of its pragmatic implications, that is, its relation to the implicit presuppositions, to the immanent acts or incorporeal transformations that it expresses, and which are going to introduce new divisions between bodies. The true intuition is not the judgment of grammaticality, but the evaluation of the internal variables of utterance in relation to the set of circumstances. (106)

In other words, the nonclosure of the grammatical code is explained in terms of its dependence on pragmatics; this, however, can by all means be described as a supercode, or as a code of a second degree. If the former is "direct discourse," then the latter is "indirect discourse": "Indirect discourse is far from presupposing a direct discourse, for the latter is extracted from the former, to the extent that the signifying operations and the processes of subjectification are distributed, attributed, or assigned in an arrangement, or that the variables of the arrangement enter into constant relations, however provisional they may be" (106). It is of little consequence to conjure up the provisional aspect of such second-degree codes, and it is of just as little consequence to multiply them (we are familiar with this from Foucault and Barthes).

> It is obvious that a society is traversed by several semiotics and in fact has mixed orders. . . . A molecular arrangement of utterance . . . assembles many orders of heterogeneous signs. Glossolalia. Writing is perhaps the bringing to light of this arrangement of the unconscious, the selection of the whispering voices, the convocation of the tribes and the secret idioms, from which I extract something I call *Moi*. (106, 107)

The multiplication, and even the "heterogenization," of the code merely always makes the deciphering of each of the schematized forms of intentionality into a deductively certain and predictable event; in contradistinction to this, the individual arrangement, which, for example, is shaped by a style (see 123ff.), can never be derived from a prior code (precisely because it rearranges the elements of this code or these codes in a new, unforeseen combination). Only if the watchword itself is understood as something coded can one believe that individual speech actions and the "ego" (*moi*), which functions as their (grammatical) subject, can be derived from them. But then this pragmatic code ceases to be what Deleuze takes it to be, namely, an indirect discourse. To the extent that it can determine discourses subordinated to it, it itself is something whose rules can be brought to light in a series of propositional statements (in a direct discourse). To codify the subject means to shackle exactly that agency that alone could ground change in meaning and the openness of the code. It is clear that a *moi*, understood as the result of the system, is not capable of performing this task. Only as the subject of indirect discourse would it be adequately defined. It might seem as if Deleuze in fact wants to say exactly this when he writes: "JE is a watchword" (107). At the same time, however, he calls the *cogito* or "self-consciousness" the "incorporeal transformation of a watchword or the result of an indirect discourse" (107). As the *result* of a dictate, however, it could no longer be meaning-creative; rather it would be affected by the inertia of the utterances that can be expressed in the direct discourse.

Once again we have the opportunity to observe in Deleuze's formulation the return of what is repressed, something that inevitably gives itself away in the use of the reflexive pronoun: "Without a doubt, arrangements vary, transform *themselves*" (198; emphasis added). This "itself" (*se*), which is scarcely hidden in this self-reflective movement, could only be the "itself" of a subject capable of meaning: there is no transsubjective reflectivity. Only a subject that relates *itself* to *itself* would be capable, in an act of application, of going beyond a grammatically well-formed phrase and moving in the direction of a form of intentionality that is implicitly inscribed in it. Without the pragmatic provisions (*agencements*), language, according to Deleuze, would remain a pure virtuality (198). That is certainly true; but without the intervention of a real individual even this *agencement* would itself remain such a *pure virtuality* that would make no sense at all on the level of concrete language *use*.

The essentially correct idea that an element of *langue* (and the grammatical rule that generates it) does not already imply its application is thus retracted by the opposite thought, according to which even application has its rules, however provisional they might be. A rule of a higher order could, in fact, never determine the sphere of application of the lower one without for its part being in need of a rule that determines it; and this would lead to an infinite regress. It could be interrupted only by a kind of decision that has the structure of a semantic-pragmatic hypothesis, and this means the structure of an interpretation. Interpretations *have a relation to* provisions and to "semantic-pragmatic codes," but they cannot be determined on the basis of them. This systematic indeterminacy can be characterized as their *freedom*. What is missing in the machine-world of taxonomic pragmatism, as well as in the theoretical universe of *A Thousand Plateaus*, is the regard for the moment of freedom without which social complexes of rules in truth cannot be distinguished from natural determinants and biophysical laws. The idea of a total determination by means of sociopragmatic contexts, or the idea of a closed and saturated context in general, remains far behind Lacan's idea that it is rather the subtraction (and thus the absence of an element in the chain of signifiers) that elevates the remaining elements to the rank of an *order* in the first place and permits them to function *symbolically* (as opposed to a natural order, whose mode of Being would be the law, and whose mechanism would be functionalistic determinism). Order is *symbolic* precisely in the sense that it is *not* closed, and thus cannot have a determining effect. Nondetermination is only the negative expression of the positively designable "fact of freedom." It is missing in any theory that draws inferences from the "meaning-constitutive lack" of the symbolic order, i.e., in neostructuralist pragmatics.

In my opinion, Jacques Derrida undertook a more noteworthy advance in the direction of a reception of Anglo-Saxon pragmatism on the basis of neostructuralism's premises. What is more, Derrida's endeavor is among the very few undertakings in which neostructuralism was prepared to test and even risk its position in a debate with another style of thought (in this case, the Anglo-Saxon style of thought). It is unfortunate that this debate has remained an exception (if one disregards for the moment Derrida's debate with Gadamer)[3] and must also be considered a failure. I am thinking of Derrida's confrontation with John R. Searle in *Glyph*. There is a prehistory that leads up to this confrontation, and I want to call it briefly to mind.

In August 1971 Derrida gave a long paper entitled "Signature événement contexte" at the Congrès international des Sociétés de Philosophie de langue française in Montreal. In the final two sections of this paper he discussed Austin's analysis of performatives, i.e., the theory of speech acts that Austin called "performatives"(Latin: *performare*, to carry something out, a linguistic threat, for example, or a declaration of love, or a promise, etc.). Derrida characterized Austin's analysis as "patient, open, aporetic, in constant transformation, often more fruitful in the recognition of its impasses than in its positions" (*Margins*, 322). For the most part Derrida reflected on possible motives for Austin's banishment of the so-called infelicities from the corpus of *standard or normal performatives*. Normal performatives are those that are carried out according to a convention, i.e., in accordance with what is usual. *Infelicities*, on the other hand, unsuccessful performatives, are those that are ineffective, for example, a threat that could be misunderstood as a statement, because its external appearance was that of an affirmative statement (as in the example cited earlier).

I will limit my discussion first to this aspect. In order to keep the proliferation of infelicities under control, Austin, according to Derrida, has to work with the concept of an exhaustively determinable context. This concept, however, presupposes that the intentional consciousness of the speaker has to be able completely to survey the entire speech act in all its contextual ramifications.

> This conscious presence of the speakers or receivers who participate in the effecting of a performative, their conscious and intentional presence in the totality of the operation, implies teleologically that no *remainder* escapes the present totalization. No remainder, whether in the definition of the requisite conventions, or the internal and linguistic context, or

the grammatical form or semantic determination of the words used; no irreducible polysemia, that is no "dissemination" escaping the horizon of the unity of meaning. (*Margins*, 322)

Yet there *are* those awkward "infelicities," and even Austin himself has to concede that *principally* one cannot exclude the possibility that performatives will fail. Derrida concludes from this that the meaning-effects of speech can never be conventionally mastered with absolute certainty, that there is no preestablished harmony between what Husserl calls the "animating intention" and its "propositional content," and that every new utterance of a type of speech act—a promise, for example—places in question the norm or convention that has been applicable up to that point. Therefore Austin's ostracism of figurative, metaphorical, or fictive speech can only be understood as a theory-strategic move, but it cannot be substantiated.

Derrida consequently asks himself what a theory of linguistic action would look like that could account for the infelicity, for misunderstanding, and for nonunderstanding as principal possibilities of the act of communication with one another.

Searle replied to this question in 1977 in the first volume of *Glyph*, proceeding selectively and limiting his answer to "those [points] that seem to me to [be] the most important and especially [to] those where I disagree with his conclusions" (*R*, 198). As an analytically trained thinker, he concedes that he does not always find Derrida's argumentation very clear. Above all, he thinks the picture Derrida draws of Austin bears no resemblance at all to the original. Now and again he considers a more favorable reading of Derrida, but he cannot shake the impression that "Derrida has a distressing penchant for saying things that are obviously false" (*R*, 203). Derrida, for his part, replied to this position in great detail. His answer is also printed in *Glyph* in an English translation.

I do not want to waste any time describing all the jokes Derrida plays on Searle. Some are very funny, others a little dull. At any rate, Searle broke off the debate, and that is unfortunate. Perhaps Derrida could have prevented this by selecting speech acts that expressed a more benevolent intent.

Derrida calls the debate "improbable," and this is in fact the case, since, as I mentioned, there is scarcely any contact at all between the French and Anglo-Saxon theoreticians of language. But what is just as improbable is the surprising fact that Derrida takes note of a minimal accord between his position and Searle's. This minimal accord consists in the view of both philosophers about the nature of a system of types that establish communication, whereby I am retaining Searle's notion of a "type" in order to characterize with it a sign or a speech act. To be understood, as we know, signs or types have to obey a convention that both speaker and addressee master. Otherwise the meaning or the intention that the one attributes to his or her utterances would not be received by the other. The latter has to be capable of recognizing the perceived sounds as signs with a certain signification or a certain meaning. Searle and Derrida concur that the numerous individual linguistic "events" (or "tokens") are all reducible to a finite number of "types" that I can always use in new combinations when I address you, and with which you are familiar as competent speakers of the language I am using. If you understand me, then you master the grammar of the language I am speaking; and if you recognize the speech acts that I carry out—for example, if you recognize that I am presenting a lecture, that I sometimes make a promise, or that I request your attention when we come to a difficult matter—then you master the conventions of public presentation, of promise, and of request. All these are linguistic types.

Perhaps you will say that this is trivial and self-evident. I think so too, but Searle emphasizes that he does not consider this point to be self-evident and that he is glad to be at one with Derrida at least in this. As a matter of fact, it is the only point at which their opinions converge.

To begin with I want to retrace the path that Searle takes by investigating the conclusions he draws from the aforementioned established principle. First he gives this principle an entirely different semblance: he says that one can also describe the conventionality of linguistic acts as their "iterability." Iterability means repeatability. When a convention has dominion, according to Searle, then it has the effect that I can repeat the type of linguistic action in question, let's say a given promise, in an unlimited number of individual cases without its meaning being changed. In much the same way, adhering to the rules of chess, which always remain the same, you can make an infinite number of different moves or play an infinite number of games. For Searle the criterion of sameness plays the major role here. He says that "any conventional act involves the notion of the repetition *of the same*" (*R*, 207, emphasis added).

Apparently that is a wholly reasonable and innocent statement. It nevertheless forms the point of contention in the confrontation with Derrida. How is that possible? Let me first attempt to uncover some presuppositions that are implied in Searle's definition. I can find four implications. Searle thinks that the iterability of conventional signs or types is, first, a basic requirement of successful communication. That is the minimal consensus with Derrida. Second, he believes that this iterability—by virtue of the "recursivity" of linguistic rules—embraces an "infinite number of possible communications [and of different contents]" (208). Third, he is of the opinion that iterability is necessarily the repetition of *the same*. For if signification changes in the act of communication, then the rules that prescribe language use also change; and if the rules change, then one cannot fix them in a closed system of speech acts, which, however, is exactly what Searle is trying to do. He unambiguously speaks of a "Taxonomy of Illocutionary Acts."[4] Already at this point we note that Searle seeks to expand the traditional model of grammar, which is interested only in propositional statements, by adding to it all other types of speech acts; but he by no means intends to undermine the concept of conventionality itself. Promises, to be sure, are not truth functions, but their success follows a rule that is just as inviolable as that of logic: there is a finite and manageable number of types, of conventions, and of rules that control the contexts. If we recall what we observed a few lectures ago about the model of the code and of decodation, then it will not be difficult to recognize in Searle's third implication the old model of encoding and decoding of types from a code. Formerly they were statements, now they are performances. Language use in situations of practical action thus remains basically masterable for anyone to whom one taught the respective convention by means of education and culture. And since in the case of linguistic *action* intentions are encoded and decoded ("What does the other person want to express by what he says? Does he want to threaten me? Or does he simply want to show me something? Does he want to teach me something? Or is he only talking to himself as he usually does? In short, what is his purpose, his intention?"), since, in other words, even intentions are codified, then I, as a theoretician of speech acts, have to assume that the intention of the speaker does not change in the act of communication. Therefore, and this is the fourth implication of Searle's thesis, the category of intention could never turn up as the troublemaker, as the disruptive element in the system of significations.

With this I have almost betrayed the point of what Derrida calls the metaphysical implications of speech-act theory. One might think that the signification of the signs I utter is secured by grammar and by the lexicon, but that the intention with which I animate them in any given instance (e.g., as threat or promise) is individually assigned to them and can be acquired neither by mastery of a language nor by a good education. But this is precisely what for Searle is not the case: the intention with which a phrase is determined *as* threat or *as* promise is just as universal and just as conventional as the signification of the signs I use. An intention that is supposed to be understood by others can never be mine alone, according to Searle; it has to be capable of being repeated without loss of meaning. All of this follows strictly from his premise. But there is a problem here. Searle maintains that "normally" (i.e., in the "standard case") a speaker or an author means what he says: "understanding the utterance consists in recognizing the illocutionary intentions of the author and these intentions may be more or less perfectly realized by the words uttered, whether written or spoken" (*R*, 202).

Now I ask you: how is it that you know exactly what you mean with an utterance? And above all: how do you know what someone else means with the words he or she utters? Whoever can say what he or she means can just as well *not* say what they mean; logically that is just as feasible. And he or she can "realize" what he or she means "more or less perfectly" in the words uttered. In this "more or less perfectly" lies the entire problem of speech-act theory, and probably of analytical hermeneutics as well. For if meaning and saying can divaricate by even the slightest bit, then the rigid code model of linguistic action seems to have its faults. That is the point on which Derrida puts his finger, and now I would like to present *his* counter to this.

Derrida, like Searle, takes his point of departure from the minimal consensus about the linguistic system and about the iterability of linguistic types. But he draws very different conclusions from this than Searle. I will again proceed by developing these conclusions step by step, and only after having done this will I try them out in the confrontation with Searle. The matter is a relatively complicated one, and I thus will have to turn to that speech act mentioned earlier and ask you for your attention.

First of all, Derrida brings the following feature of communication to light: to be able to function as an intersubjective medium of communication, the code (or convention, if you will) requires a certain distancing of the speaker from his/her utterances. Derrida speaks of *absence*, but if you dislike the term, then replace it with that of utterance. In German, *etwas äussern*, "to utter something," means to put something outside of oneself, to disconnect something from oneself as the speaking subject, to distance oneself from what is uttered. But to what extent do I distance myself from my utterances? Well, I, with my private and singular intentions, have to withdraw behind what I utter, otherwise my message could not be understood by others; i.e., otherwise it would go against the demands of the code. Both demands — that of distancing and that of iterability — are conditions of a structural nature; i.e., one cannot dispose of them by pointing out counterexamples in which the speaker is present "at" his/her utterances or in which an utterance by chance occurs only once.

I first want to present the conclusions Derrida draws from the condition of iterability. Every repetition, he says, differentiates and defers. It differentiates because one can distinguish the first and the second use of a repeated type. And it defers by distributing the two usages over two different points in time. One cannot simultaneously say something and repeat something. That, I think, is evident. Now Derrida asks: who actually proves to me that the signification of a speech act is the same in the second application as it is in the first? Who actually says that it has remained the same after passing through the gap of iteration?

You will say that one can tell by the fact that during the conversation no disturbance occurs. And then I take this continuity as a sign that reciprocal understanding is taking place. When we speak in such a way, we are assuming that there can be understanding only where something identical is understood. But Derrida doubts that such a rigorous attitude is necessary in order to explain linguistic communication.

He first strictly investigates the consequences that follow from his observations and does not concern himself much about objections of a practical nature. He thinks that one cannot deny that time elapses between two uses of a linguistic type, and that this time interval separates the two uses from each other. Separation is thus an ineluctable feature of repeated use. The other requirement is sameness, for otherwise the second use would no longer be repetition but rather perhaps the use of another type. In order to distinguish these contradictory features from those of permanence—a type whose granitic identity could not be eroded by the flow of the history of language would be permanent—Derrida comes up with a ticklish formulation. He speaks of the "nonpresent *remaining* of a differential mark" (*Margins*, 318). At this point, those of us who know our Saussure have to prick up our ears. For what could this nonpresent remaining of a differential mark be other than that which Saussure designates as *aposème* in his *Notes item*? The "remaining mark" and/or the *aposème* designate that minimal remaining of the sign hull without which continuity of communication and of tradition would be inconceivable, but by means of which the respective significations are not simply frozen in their sign hulls like quartz molecules in their crystal lattice at a certain temperature. One could pointedly say that the repetition of a speech act (like any other mark) is not the same use a second time (even if perhaps in a different environment—that is of no consequence for a sufficiently abstract theory), but rather that it is another use of the same remaining mark.

This, then, would be the first conclusion Derrida draws: on the basis of the structural possibility of repetition, the use of every linguistic type bears an index of uncontrollable change. And when we communicate with each other, we always take into account the sliding of meaning underneath the expressions; after all, we learn something from communication with one another or with a book. Our world becomes richer, our supply of meaning grows. How would this be possible if we were those speaking machines the robot theory of analytical philosophy conceives us to be?

Derrida, however, goes a step further and draws an inference that we might find a little adventurous, namely, that iterability not only prevents the gapless *présence-à-soi* of a sign over the course of its multiple applications but that it even undercuts the possibility of recognizing a sign that was *not* repeated as identical with itself (*LI*, 192–98). How can that be? Because, Derrida replies, semiological orders can attribute signification to their elements only by unequivocally distinguishing each one from all others. The key word here is *différance*, as we see. Now the only question is how Derrida brings his basic theorem into our context. This is his argument: whatever can establish its own identity only by taking the detour over all other identities, can, with a certain justification, be said to be separate from itself. Hegel, in his *Science of Logic*, drew this conclusion, and Derrida does so by saying that the sign is debarred from the *immediate* perception of its identity, for between it and itself stands the set of all other signs upon which its "value" is dependent. Now some of us will say that that is surreptitious, for after all the differentiations have been executed, then every sign in a system of course has one and only one signification, and this signification is identical. But Derrida has an answer to this as well. He replies that this is very nice, but that the language system on the basis of which we make this statement, first, has to be cut to the quick by means of a sort of paralyzing incision before we can accomplish this final differentiation in it. In fact, however, language is constantly altered by speech; while speaking we always differentiate the significations of expressions anew; everything is in constant flux, and the identity of a signification is something purely hypothetical. "Meanings are changed *for everyone*," Sartre says, "by each speaker and each day; the meanings of the very words in my mouth are changed by others."[5]

So much for the moment with regard to Derrida's conclusions from the structural feature of iterability. Closely related to this is what he takes to be the second objection to the notion of conventionality: the always possible absence of individual and pertinent (*aktuellen*) intention of the mark (*LI*, 194–95). Derrida does not mean, as Searle insinuates, that intention therefore does not play a role in the execution of a linguistic act. He merely means that my or your current intention, which is completely determined by the discursive situation, temporarily sets (i.e., "fills out") the meaning of the utterance in question. Individual intention never permeates the sign in such a way that it would fuse with it into the unity of an unalterable type. After all, we agreed, as did Derrida and Searle as well, that linguistic signs are only *generally* understood because their signification is not applicable only for me—here and now and in these circumstances. While speaking I distance myself from my individuality. This is the only way in which the totality of signs can even be founded as a sign *system*, i.e., as a *transindividual convention*, in the first place. This, to be sure, leads to the conclusion that the pertinent (*aktuellen*) "animation" of the signs by an *individual* intention is not a fact that could be derived from the concept of convention. The system of linguistic types also has to elevate the forms of intentionality to the rank of types, and precisely by doing this it strictly disregards the singular animations of the types at different times and in different contexts. However, it is exactly these individual intentions, which elude the concept of the code, that undermine the granitic durability of the code by "iterating" and differentiating the linguistic types, i.e., by displacing them in a systematically uncontrollable way. "Once again, iterability makes possible idealization—and thus, a certain identity in repetition that is independent of the multiplicity of factual events—while at the same time limiting the idealization it makes possible: *broaching* and *breaching* it all at once" (*LI*, 200). Derrida seeks to take this into account when he holds up to Austin and Searle, who work with the concept of a "complete context," that the intention of a speech act is never entirely present to itself, that it in part eludes itself. This loss of fullness, which befalls intention by means of the uncontrollable activity of the formation and displacement of differences, is both the condition of codification, and the condition for the *ability of signs to break with their codification* and open up to human language the infinite field of history. Language theory can only step into this field at that moment when it cuts through the shackle of the code and provides the concept of iterability of types with the index of their possible changes in meaning.

And this is precisely what Searle does not do. For him it is clear "that any conventional [or, as Derrida calls it, 'coded'] act involves the notion of the repetition *of the same*" (*R*, 207; emphasis added). The strategic necessity of this assumption is immediately evident. Searle tells us that he understands his theory of speech acts as the linguistic analogue to the idealizing method of most natural sciences (*Speech Acts*, pp. 57-61). In order to attain his goal, he has to assume that intentions are, so to speak, nailed to their expressions and that the imprecision of the available concepts is reducible: one can "idealize" them and free them from "chance" and "impurity." In this way unproblematic and "ideal speech situations" or "pragmatic universals" are generated, under whose protective dominion it is possible to seriously communicate. Well, that is an analytical conclusion drawn on the basis of the methodological premises, but it is by no means a conclusion based on the nature of spoken language. Serious (i.e., "nonfigurative" and nonfictive) speech is accordingly a theoretical construct. Speech-act theory abstracts from the experiential reality of everyday communication until it comes to the point at which it has grouped a finite number of entities and laws that free it from having to give any further consideration to concrete deviations from actual language use, i.e., from considering any irregularity whatsoever. In order to understand a speech act, Searle claims that "it is necessary to know that anyone who said it and meant it would be performing that speech act determined by the rules of the languages that give the sentence its meaning in the first place" (*R*, 202). In other words, idealization methodologically excludes the "parasitic" use—the transforming repetition—of the type and operates with a rigid model of convention that assigns one and only one totally determined applicational meaning to every expressive material according to the performative rules that are to be applied in any given instance. This model *can* function only if the invariability of the signs, i.e., of the codified entities of meaning-expression, remains unshaken, if intention "fills out" expression without any remainder. Since Searle thinks that this is the case and that the model of convention is thus sufficient to explain the effects of "normal" communication, one has to presume that he considers abnormal any use of language that alters meaning; yet without it phenomena such as the evolution of language and progress in knowledge are impossible.

His reaction to unsuccessful speech acts, therefore, is simply to explain them as violations of the norm and thus, complementarily, to explain them on the basis of the explicit rule. What the infelicity cannot achieve is achieved by the theory of infelicity. It heals the malady by deriving it *ex negativo* from the norm. In analogy to the strategy of the rule of three, it supplements to the rule whatever regularity everyday reality lacks: misunderstanding and the "incomplete speech act" are only the shadows thrown by the battlements of the complete act and of total understanding onto the incomplete framing of its structural foundation. This tendency reaches its zenith in H. P. Grice's "Logic and Conversation."[6]

When Derrida disputes that one can ever strictly determine the line that runs between the figurative and the nonfigurative use of language, or, for that matter, as Searle demands, that one can establish a logical relation of dependence between the two, he attacks the fetishism of rule formation and law formation in the human sciences in general. Of course, there is nothing to object to in investigating traditional contexts, societal orders, forms of discourse, speech patterns, or even literary texts with an eye for the structures that make the set of "events" recognizable as cases of universal regularities. The orders mentioned earlier have in common that individuals can acquire a certain competence in regard to them. The concept of competency, which — following Chomsky — was at times substituted for Saussure's *langue*, Hjelmslev's *schematism*, or Humboldt's *system*, designates, much like they do, a capability, a potential, an only virtual being, a *mè ón* in Plato's sense. Yet a merely virtual possibility could never appear as the antecedent in a real causal chain. Competency could have results only under the condition that a self-conscious being, capable of taking action, would realize one or the other possibility. To realize a systematically presented possibility does not mean (as Saussure emphasizes) to be subject to the compulsion of adherence. For such an instance idealist philosophy made the distinction between "necessitation" and "motivation": the former designates causal processes set in motion by a *real* cause; the latter designates those causal processes set in motion by an ideal cause (a ground). An effect is necessitated when, on the basis of certain presuppositions and constellations, it could not possibly *not* occur. An effect is motivated, on the other hand, when, although not coming about without presuppositions, it allows its presuppositions to become effective causes only under the condition that it previously *interpreted* them as such. Now the sort of adherence to a rule that we encounter in the performance of a speech act can proceed only according to the second scheme, for pragmatic universals and the concept of language as system designate pure potentialities that still have to be individualized in order to exist really. But who is supposed to accomplish this individualization? Language itself? There are certain tendencies in analytical philosophy that are inclined to conceive the matter in exactly this way. According to this, language not only would be the master of its own application, but it would propagate totally "on its own," i.e., without the intervention of subjects that are capable of action and that have mastery of meaning. "The rule," according to Wittgenstein, whom I would like to cite here as the representative of numerous Anglo-Saxon philosophies, "once stamped with a particular meaning, traces the lines along which it is to be followed through the whole of space."[7] One can easily understand the motive for this autonomization of language if one recognizes that any other view would be incompatible with the predilection of this theory for the scientific: only when language controls its own statements is it guaranteed that the linguistic event will not challenge the type according to which it is formed. One has to make certain that this does not happen; otherwise the measure of concrete effects of meaning would elude convention, and the anarchy of meaning, as Derrida conceives it, could no longer be contained.

Indeed, with this the weakest link in speech-act theory's chain of argumentation is put under stress. Nobody—not even Searle himself—can overlook that idioms such as the "power of convention" have no place in the realm of serious speech. They borrow from the rhetoric of metonymy by interpreting human deeds as objective forces.

To be sure, there is method in this rhetoric. It bestows upon the pragmatic system what it previously had to take away from meaning-producing individuality: namely, the capacity for reflectivity, for spontaneity, and for continuity. From now on all these capacities are attributed to the language process itself. Yet it is precisely by means of this displacement that this theory confirms—against its own will, of course—that it cannot get along without the power of subjectivity, indeed, that it constantly lays claim to it. The same problem that we already ascertained in the case of Deleuze's pragmatism returns: the concept of a "language that speaks itself" subjectifies language; in this assertion language itself is the grammatical and the personal subject of action. Now according to the classical view, subjectivity is in fact an anarchical capacity: it does what it wants to do. That is why one first has to shackle it by means of conventions; only then does it serve theory like a horse in its bridle.

I am insisting so vigorously on this distortion of subjectivity because it seems to me that it has to do with Derrida's and Searle's minimal consensus about the nature of sign systems. Both, for different reasons, refrain from laying claim to the agency of a subjectivity or individuality that attributes and changes meaning. This seems to me to be connected with the fact that for both, the problem of an *application* of linguistic types does not arise.

In closing this lecture, I would like only to give a prospectus of what is yet to come. Both Derrida and Searle place themselves in the tradition of American pragmatism, above all in that of Charles S. Peirce. I do not want to bring a new name and a new branch of theory into the debate, and thus I will only explain what pragmatism has to do with this. It is the doctrine according to which human beings arrive at knowledge only through actions and practical experience; for example, we arrive at the thesis of the existence of an independent external world through the experience of the unyieldingness of objects. In terms of semiotics this means that human beings arrive at the significations of the signs that they use *by always* specifically (i.e., never once and for all) interpreting them in the given situation. The meaning of a sentence is its use in any given situation. And this also accounts for the evolution of language, for I do not have to use the expression in different situations in exactly the same way.

I have presented this in extremely simplified fashion. But it already becomes clear why I think that Searle, whose speech-act theory itself actualizes certain insights of pragmatism, falls short of Peirce by establishing firm rules for the situations in which signs can be applied, rules that are precisely intended to make these linguistic actions timeless and independent of specific situations. In Derrida's case it is quite different, as we have seen. He takes for granted that the effects of meaning of living language use cannot be derived from contextual rules like an inference can be derived from a premise. Nevertheless, he does not want to subscribe to the assertion that it is individuals, who are firmly rooted in history and who relate *freely* (which does not mean with complete cognizance) to their situations, who are responsible for application and the evolution of language. Must we then assume that the *marques* iterate and alter themselves completely on their own?

It looks this way. Derrida, of course, has one argument against the recourse to the speaking individual subject. He maintains, in a manner similar to that of Wittgenstein or Searle himself, that subjectivity either has a signification or it does not. If it has one, it is an effect of language; if it does not have one, how is one supposed to be able to speak of subjectivity?

If we reflect further on this point we either get to the heart of the problem, or we get into an awful predicament. For the moment I can only hint at what I imagine the solution to be. In my opinion, it does not follow from the statement that without *différance* there would be no significations, and also no change of significations, that significations are generated only *by means of* linguistic differentiality. Linguistic differentiality — the linguistic code, convention — forms the *condition* without which there could be neither speaking nor understanding. But the agency that sees to it *that* meaning can in each instance be produced and understood is subjectivity as individuality. I can only vaguely sketch how this can be conceived in semiotic terms. In every sign that is communicated between speakers there is a universal and an individual element. *Without* the universal element, there would be no understanding; without the individual element, there would be understanding *only* of what is universal and rule-governed. Yet it is a fact that can be repressed, but hardly denied, that universals and rules are challenged over the course of the history of speech; they are distorted, separated from themselves, and thus changed. How might this be possible if the sign were only the instrument that executes the prescriptions of the universal code? How might this be possible if it were not at the same time something other, namely, the individual manner *in which* this code is applied in each instance in a speech act? Now we can see how Searle's aporia can be dissolved. When he writes that every speaker really says what he or she means — at least "more or less perfectly" — only when he or she is serious and is not talking nonsense, i.e., really says what he/she means, then he is confronted with the problem of having to explain any failures in communication in terms of infractions of the rules. If one no longer considers these infractions to be infractions, but rather takes them as what they are: the effective contribution of individual creations of meaning ("individual additives," as Boeckh says), then one can easily comprehend why already Schleiermacher and Humboldt insisted that one never understands what someone else says; that one is always only understood, and always understands, only "more or less perfectly." In each act of communication signs are exchanged. What is identical about them is only their character as marks, as *aposèmes*. Signification, however, has a certain leeway with regard to how it is disposed; it is always inscribed anew—to be sure, within reasonable limits—by individuals into the "mark" and has, as Humboldt says, "no permanent place even in writing."[8] With this we are returned to where we began: to the problem of interpretation and the undecidability of the meaning of a text.

Lecture 26

Philosophical theories tend generally to be less fruitful in those instances where they exhaust themselves in the internal workings of their own execution (and in the formation of a school), than in those cases where they enter into competition with other theories and schools, particularly those that evolve out of different points of departure. Only when they bring the voice of an Other into contact with their own can theories avoid the narcissism of what Husserl, in his *Logical Investigations*, called "the solitary mental life" of an internal self-conversation, and on which Derrida remarked

> that there is no indication in this inner life because there is no communication; that there is no communication because there is no *alter ego*. And when the second person does emerge in inner language, it is a fiction; and, after all, fiction is only fiction. "You have gone wrong, you can't go on like that"—this is only a false communication, a feigned communication. (*SP*, 70)

Feuerbach had reproached Hegel's philosophy of reflection with precisely this: under the pretext of meeting with the Other in its Otherness, it actually only held a speculative monologue with the Other-of-*itself*; Hegel's reflection "*dissimilates*": "It only pretends, but does not mean it seriously; *it plays*."[1]

In this sense we will welcome Derrida's debate with Searle as one of the few fruitful moments in which something like genuine communication took place between Anglo-American pragmatism and neostructuralist language philosophy. To be sure, that does not mean that Derrida generally formulated his critique of the code model of understanding and his critique of the conventionalism of language theory by means of arguments that in themselves were new to his work. On the contrary, it can be shown that the main points of his critique had already been set down in his early examination of the concept of the sign in Husserl's *Logical Investigations*. I would like to support this assertion by means of a short and selective reading of *Speech and Phenomena*, without, however, getting caught up in the internal arguments of his confrontation with Husserl.

There are primarily two complexes of problems that connect *Limited Inc* with the thematics of *Speech and Phenomena*. First of all, it is a question of surveying the field on which the problem of iterability converges with the problem of scientific idealization; and second, it is a question of what results the conclusion, which asserts that the "effects of meaning" cannot be systematically controlled, has for a semantics or pragmatics that wants to hold on to the concept of a subject.

Let's begin by disentangling the strands of the first complex of problems. In *Speech and Phenomena* it appears in the following context, which is different from that of *Limited Inc*: how can the universality of meaning be guaranteed (in Husserl's phenomenology, but for the most part we will disregard this link to Husserl) if meaning is simultaneously a character of "expressions" that for their part are subject to a material basis for expression (Husserl speaks of the "indicative" character)? One cannot totally disregard the materiality of the "indicative carrier of expression," for without it no exchange of information could be organized among real existing subjects in space and time. On the other hand—and meanwhile we know this problematics rather well—the sign carrier, in its materiality, cannot on its own guarantee the identity of the meaning it transports; in fact, it is actualized differently from one articulation to another. If universality is, on the one hand, dependent on communication (*SP*, 37f.), and yet threatened, on the other hand, by the nonidentity in the act of repetition of the expressions, then nothing remains for a theory that strives for objectivity and masterability of meaning other than rigorous abstraction from the reality of the indication (27ff.). The indication has to be "reduced," in Husserl's terminology, to its pure essential subsistence (*Wesens-Bestand*), to that which presents itself to the "solitary mental life" in "authentic intuition" or "living self-presence" as its meaning. I say "as its meaning" because meaning is precisely that which remains when I abstract both from the reality of the empirical subject, which accomplishes the intuition, as well as from the reality of the possible objects to which this subject might relate. Meaning is something unreal, something purely ideal; and if it is attached to "expression," then one has to understand what "expression" means in this context and to what extent the "phenomenological reduction" embraces it. Saussure's *signifiant* is always already disclosed in the light of the meaning (*signifié*) that is assigned to it; thus it itself is nothing that is actually real. Rather it is an "acoustic" or a "graphic *image*" (*image acoustique/graphique*)—as opposed to the *aposème*, the material hull of the word. In much the same manner, what Husserl calls "expression" — as opposed to "indication" — is not a worldly being, but something internal and mental: an ideality (Husserl distinguished between the "empirical body" [*Körper*], which is always sensual, and the "flesh" [*Leib*], which is always spiritual).

> The ideal form of a written signifier, for example, is not in the world, and the distinction between the grapheme and the empirical body of the corresponding graphic sign separates an inside from an outside, phenomenological consciousness from the world. (*SP*, 76)

We can understand in this way why disregarding the existence of the world is not a loss but rather a gain for phenomenology: only the unreality, the worldlessness of meaning could guarantee that ideality in whose sphere every repetition of an expression reproduces with certainty the same meaning. Universality and objectivity: These are idealities themselves. We call universally valid a state of affairs that maintains itself without a change in meaning in infinitely many occurrences (which may well be very different from each other). The same is true for objectivity: what is objective is not the existence of this unrepeatable and fleeting appearance in the midst of the world, but rather what is regular in it and can be preserved in universally valid statements. In a radical turn of the natural attitude toward the world, the true Being of things (Plato's *óntos ón*) is therewith revealed as that which is gained by passing through the abstraction from their worldly Being. Formulated paradoxically, the ideality of pure essential intuition — but also of that which is fixed in scientific laws — is "more being" (*seiender*) than the Being of the real world. Husserl accused classical metaphysics of "blindness" for not (always) having understood this.

> . . . always a blindness to the authentic mode of *ideality*, to that which *is*, to what may be indefinitely *repeated* in the *identity* of its *presence*, because of the very fact that it *does not exist*, is *not real* or is *irreal* — not in the sense of being a fiction, but in another sense which may have several names, whose possibility will permit us to speak of nonreality and essential necessity, the noema, the intelligible object, and in general the nonworldly. This nonworldliness is not another worldliness, this ideality is not an existent that has fallen from the sky; its origin will always be the possible repetition of a productive act. In order that the possibility of this repetition may be open, *ideally* to infinity, one ideal form must assure this unity of the *indefinite* and the *ideal*: this is the present, or rather the presence of the *living present*. The ultimate form of ideality, the ideality of ideality, that in which in the last instance one may anticipate or recall all repetition, is the *living present*, the self-presence of transcendental life. (6)

But, as noted earlier, we want to disregard for our part Husserl's phenomenology, as far as possible, in order to concentrate on the parallel with Searle's assertion that speech-act theory is supposed to secure, by means of the recourse to the type-token distinction, that "every repetition (of a *conventionalized* intention, of a *form* of intentionality) is the repetition *of the same.*" This sameness (as in Husserl) is reached by absolute abstraction from the singular utterance-events (*tokens*), and by means of their reduction to the *type* they have in common, i.e., by means of a gesture of radical idealization. The following applies just as well for speech act theory as it does for phenomenology.

> This ideality is the very form in which the presence of an object in general may be indefinitely repeated as the *same.* . . . Ideality is the preservation of mastery of presence in repetition. (10)

Husserl, of course, tries to found the criterion for the identifiability of repeated expressions in the identity and self-sameness of a transcendental ego-pole (in this he is in accord with the most profound impulse of Kant's critique of knowledge), whereas Searle is satisfied with guaranteeing the return of the same on the basis of conventionality. Derrida nevertheless has reason for insinuating that both of them use, whether directly or indirectly, metaphysical forms of thought (if "metaphysics" means to interpret "Being" as living self-presence and as ideal un-alterability of essence). Both philosophers hope to be able to isolate and identify meaning as the invariable *form* of expressions or manners of utterance. (The tactic directly opposed to this would consist in making meaning dependent on the play of a never uniform repetition of "indications," "word-bodies," "aposemes.")

Both Husserl and Searle further agree insofar as they mistrust the fact of communication. This assertion may sound unjust, at least where Searle is concerned, since communication is a focal point of his language theory. Nonetheless, what Husserl calls the solitary life of the spirit that only speaks with itself essentially overlaps with communication, as Searle describes it, in that in both cases it has been decided beforehand what the *meaning* of the communication is: in phenomenology by the view that the indicative nature of the word-signs — their spatiotemporal concretion as well as the individual-empirical endowment of meaning — remains inessential and external to the significance of what is communicated; in speech-act theory by the precaution that sees to it that every possible sharing of information is accomplished only by employing forms of intentionality whose meaning was known beforehand and which only has to be deciphered by the addressee of the message (i.e., reduced to the intelligible content of meaning, retransformed into idealities). The only new thing in a dialogue, according to this, would be the *informational* content of a statement; the laws, according to which meaning and expression are conjoined, follow an *input-output model*, which Searle very openly introduces as such in the third chapter of *Speech Acts*. "Meaningful speech" is just as strictly determined by conventional frame "conditions" as it is by "appropriate understanding" (see *Speech Acts*, pp. 57-61). In other words, this theory does not tolerate any protestation on the part of concretely accomplished communication that not only exchanges information but can also reciprocally put into question the standpoints and worldviews of speakers, and thus challenge the rules, the "conventions," of "meaningful speech" as such. To concede this power to communication, however, would mean to limit the importance of idealization, i.e., to strip away the "scientific" aspect of the theory of speech acts.

Husserl, for his part, got caught up in an analogous aporia when he had to introduce the existence of the other ego (in his *Cartesian Meditations*). The Other aside from me — for example, my interlocutor — has another self-presence that principally eludes my own; but if the certitude I infallibly have of the meaning of what was said consists in the fact that I can make it present to myself in intuition, without having to make use of another word-body, then the "significative intention" the Other carries out is principally not present to me. What is given to me are merely the "indications" the Other transmits to me (*SP*, 37–38).

> When I listen to another, his lived experience is not present to me "in person," in the original. . . . I may have a primordial intuition, that is, an immediate perception of what is exposed of the other in the world: the visibility of his body, his gestures, what may be understood of the sounds he utters. But the subjective side of his experience, his consciousness, in particular the acts by which he gives sense to his signs, are not immediately and primordially present to me as they are for him and mine are for me. Here there is an irreducible and definitive limit. The lived experience of another is made known to me only insofar as it is mediately indicated by signs involving a physical side. (38–39)

There is thus a fundamental and irreducible alienness in understanding what the Other has said to me, something that I can never transpose into my "living self-present": what the Other wants to tell me I can find out only by conjecture and divination; its meaning is never "given" to me "apodictically." To be sure, I can have memorized all the maxims of discourse established by Grice, and all the rules of speech acts set down by Searle, but in the given instance I still do not know whether the Other also accepts them to the same extent as I, and whether he or she relates them to the same meaning as I. If meaning, however, is indeed — as Searle wants to have it — something transindividual (to attain this, theory *idealizes* it), then it follows that I *alone* cannot make a decision about it: meaning is essentially the meaning of the Other; the Other meaning, or the meaning the Other produces with the signs I uttered, and it is precisely this meaning that escapes my authentic essential "intuition." From this it follows that I also do not "authentically" know my own meaning. And it follows, moreover, that the assumption that the prelinguistic (ideal) unity of meaning guarantees the sameness of the repeated sign proves to be badly founded. For meaning cannot be idealized; it essentially is in need of support from the "indication," the *aposème*, the word-body, the real *externalization* (*Veräusserung*) of the signs (whose necessity Derrida symbolizes by the metaphor of *writing*; 75ff.)

But from all this it by no means follows that there is no ideality of meaning at all. For Derrida it is rather a question of drawing entirely different conclusions from the ideality of meaning than those he calls metaphysical. Already in our previous lecture we saw that he agrees with Searle that all speaking presupposes the structure of iterability. To repeat something undoubtedly means: to be able to represence it. The possibility of producing a sign or an utterance repeatedly *as* this unity idealizes it, i.e., bestows upon it the unity of its signifying.[2] However, Derrida adds, it is not the unity of meaning that makes represencing possible, but, inversely, the unity of meaning—its ideality—is grounded in the structure of represenceability: "The presence-of-the-present is derived from repetition and not the reverse. While this is against Husserl's express intention, it does take into account what is implied by his description of the movement of temporalization and of the relation with the other, as will perhaps become clear later on" (52).

We have already discussed Husserl's theory of time and Derrida's inferences from it within the context of our question about the neostructuralist theory of the subject; I would like to put them aside at this point for reasons of economy. Their function within the current context is immediately evident: if the transcendental ego is the last refuge of evidence, of self-presence, and of the living intuition of meaning, then the unity of meaning has to suffer damage as soon as the unity of this ego is put into question. And this is precisely what happens as soon as one brings into play the internal temporality of subjectivity that ruptures the self-presence of the ego and depresences it from the ground up. This depresencing, we must however note, does not simply end the unity of meaning (as it does that of the ego): it only challenges it and transforms its status of Being from that of an apodictic certitude to that of a motivated *hypothesis*. Both the unity of the self and that of meaning now only exist hypothetically; it does not master, as "principle of principles," the flow of time, or, on the linguistic level, the succession of signs—rather it is constituted by the flow of time, or by the structure of repetition.

> But this ideality, which is but another name for the permanence of the same and the possibility of its repetition, *does not exist* in the world, and it does not come from another world; it depends entirely on the possibility of acts of repetition. It is constituted by this possibility. Its "being" is proportionate to the power of repetition; absolute ideality is the correlate of a possibility of indefinite repetition. (52)

The consequence of this inversion of the relationship between the structure of repetition and the ideality of meaning is, as we see, that the unity of objectivity becomes a hypothesis: a regulative or, as Husserl prefers to say, an "idea in the Kantian sense." The possibility that this idea could ever be intuitively realized in my living self-present is excluded by the *infinity* (i.e., incalculability) of repetition, which is not a priori limited by any principle and which therefore has to be the repetition of something always Other (this follows from the fact that it does not reproduce and represence the sameness of meaning and that it presupposes the loss of "primordial presence" in its Being—even if one conceives what it accomplishes as *re*presencing). Derrida demonstrates very nicely what tensions develop between Husserl's reductionism and the insights of his "phenomenology of internal time-consciousness" (*SP*, 61ff.). We are already familiar with the decisive conclusion that Derrida draws: he maintains that presence is no authority to which one can appeal in order to sublate the dividing power of temporality; it is rather one dimension of time among others that is interwoven in the play of temporization that extends from the past into the future. Whoever says "present" also implies "temporal." And whoever says "temporal" implies "nonidentical": "does not everything that is announced already in this reduction to 'solitary mental life' (the transcendental reduction in all its stages, and notably the reduction to the monadic sphere of 'ownness'—*Eigenheit*—etc.) appear to be stricken in its very possibility by what we are calling time?" (68). This applies for the time dimension of the present in particulary drastic fashion: in the strict sense, it does not have a proper Being. What we call present is rather the differential between the past and the future. Since—as Schelling and subsequently Sartre have shown[3]— the meaning of "Being" is the having-been, and the meaning of "non-Being" is the not-yet or the becoming-Being, one can also characterize this relationship in the following way: the present is the incision, which *itself is not being* (*nicht selbst seiende*), through which Being (the past) mediates its anticipation of non-Being (the future) in order to determine itself from the perspective of this not-yet, i.e., to let its *meaning* be indicated. The old doctrine that states that all determination is grounded in negation thus discloses its temporal meaning. The statement "What-is-not determines what-is" (*BN*, 87) can be rewritten as the claim that the past lets its *meaning* (its determination) be indicated by the future in the manner of a projection (a hypothetical judgment, an interpretation, etc.). The present no longer plays a role in this formulation: it is reduced to a significant gap between two aggregates of Being, to a "merely relative point of indifference," as Schelling expresses it (*SW*, I/6, 276). "Because for the soul it never *is*," it reveals itself to be the realization of that hinge (*brisure*) between Being and Being possible, as the turning point or "crossover" point between "Being and becoming" (*SW*, I/6, 229; I/7, 239). Derrida, by the way, liked to illustrate his idea of *différance* with the metaphor of *brisure*, defined as "crack" and "joint, created by a hinge, in the work of a locksmith" (see *Diss*, 302–3; *GR*, 65ff.). We can draw the following conclusion from this: if the present, looked at carefully, resembles the differentiating *brisure*, then it is the exact opposite of that "living self-present" of which Husserl thinks, and in whose name he hopes to neutralize the depresencing effects of the internal flow of time. It is rather the present itself—as *time* dimension—

whose effect prevents the experiences of consciousness from attaining their real identification. Every time phase contains retentional and protentional retrospections and anticipations *in itself* (i.e., it exists ekstatically, decentrally, and non-presently); in the same way, every repetition of a sign also is a *re*-production of a meaning that was already expressed in anticipation of that meaning that is to be acquired only in the future (reacquired, and reacquired differently). This meaning is thus *de*presenced and *de*actualized in its structure itself.

> How can it be explained that the possibility of reflection and re-presentation belongs by essence to every experience, without this nonself-identity of the presence called primordial? How could it be explained that this possibility belongs, like a pure and ideal freedom, to the essence of consciousness? . . . In all these directions, the presence of the present is thought of as arising from the bending-back of a return, from the movement of repetition, and not the reverse. (*SP*, 67–68)

Now we at least have the hint of an answer to our first question about the connection of scientific idealization to the problem of iteration. Whereas Husserl believes that he is able to guarantee that the repetition of signs is the repetition of *the same* (signs) only through recourse to the "principle of principles," the "living self-present" experienced in the absolute ego, Derrida demonstrates that the possibility for scientific idealization, inversely, is grounded in the possibility of iteration of signs. Yet iteration by no means works in the service of an identity of consciousness, but rather excludes it: since Husserl also does not escape this consequence, the "principle of principles" becomes an "idea in the Kantian sense" for him (*SP*, 9, 100).

The second question we want to pose during the present lecture is closely linked to the first one. Let me repeat it once more in different words: what follows from the decentering of the "principle of principles"—from the depowerment of the idea of an authentic self-present—for a hermeneutics that wants to hold on to the concept of a meaning-conferring subject?

Let's once again take that minimal accord, which connects Derrida's philosophy of language with both Searle's and Husserl's, as a point of departure. This point of consensus is that the iterability, and thus the idealizability of its elements, is a necessary prerequisite for every symbolic order. The two parties only disagree about the consequences of this. For phenomenology, as well as for analytical philosophy, the repeatability and idealizability of types are the recursive condition for the identity of significations; for Derrida, the chain of repetitions, which has become infinite, is deprived of a criterion for identity, and the identification of signification is transformed into a hypothetical judgment about whose truth one cannot finally "decide" (for reasons of principle, not for reasons of methodological insufficiency). Interpretation becomes infinite.

But for Derrida this infinitude of interpretation is nothing that could be explained—hermeneutically—by means of the intervention of a meaning-interpreting and meaning-projecting individual. On the contrary, he is at one with Searle and Husserl in his *rejection of a hermeneutics of individuality.*

Even this consensus can be made comprehensible (for it is far from being dependent on the question of whether significations are "objectively" determinable). If iterability of signs or utterances is a structural possibility of all rule-governed speech and obeys the logic of a recursive model in which an arbitrary number of "tokens" does not threaten the ideality of their "type," then one necessarily has to disregard the individuality of the speaker's consciousness. Only under the condition of their relative independence on the individual, actual, and historically singular meaning-intentions of the speakers can the "tokens" that express them become iterable elements of a transindividual convention—i.e., "types." The individual retreats to make room for the universality of the system.

This reduction of individuality is a necessary condition of every scientific idealization. Frege distinguished "ideas" (*Vorstellungen*) from "thoughts" (*Gedanken*) in this sense; ideas need an owner, "no two men have the same "idea";[4] in contrast to this, a thought expresses what is the case, at least if this thought is true. What is true, however, is principally what not only is valid for a subject but valid for all subjects (according to Frege, a thought—if it is true—is "timelessly true, true independently of whether anyone takes it to be true. It needs no owner").[5] Thus here also truth, in the sense of transindividual validity, is tied up with the disenabling of the first-person singular pronoun, to the extent that this pronoun designates a singular person: "No reason remains for granting an exceptional position to that object which I call 'I'."[6]

Husserl picked up this theme from Frege in his own *Logical Investigations.* There he distinguishes "between *essentially subjective and occasional* expressions, on the one hand, and *objective* expressions, on the other."[7] The first correspond to Frege's ideas, the latter to his thoughts. Thus Husserl can argue:

> Every expression, in fact, that includes a *personal pronoun* lacks an objective sense. The word 'I' names a different person from case to case, and does so by way of an ever altering meaning. . . . If we read the word without knowing who wrote it, it is perhaps not meaningless, but is at least estranged from its normal sense.[8]

Derrida cites this remark, as well as the one that asserts that the index word "I" cannot be immediately significant, but can only have "an indicative function" that cries "as it were, to the hearer 'Your *vis-à-vis* intends himself'."[9] It is "the universal *semantic function* of the word 'I' to designate whoever is speaking, but the notion through which we express this function is not the notion immediately constitutive of its meaning."[10]

One thus has to disregard the continually changing individual meaning of the index word "I" when accomplishing the phenomenological reduction of the objectivity of signification (of a sentence that is introduced by "I" as its grammatical subject). "I," as a name for a constantly changing reality, has no place in the framework of a phenomenology taken as a rigorous science of essence—and it likewise has no place in a scientifically conceived theory of language. Both of these sciences are concerned with ideal objects.

> An ideal object is an object whose showing may be repeated indefinitely, whose presence to *Zeigen* is indefinitely reiterable precisely because, freed from all mundane spatiality, it is a pure noema that I can express without having, at least apparently, to pass through the world. . . . The ideal object is the most objective of objects; independent of the here-and-now acts and events of the empirical subjectivity which intends it, it can be repeated infinitely while remaining the same. (*SP*, 75)

Individuality thus can be phenomenologically reduced: it never offers itself to an originary-presencing intuition; it is essentially nonideal and nonobjective. (One could fittingly designate it as essenceless, something that in a more profound sense it in fact is; this it has in common with Being in the sense of existence, which is likewise systematically excluded from Husserl's phenomenology.) Science and the linguistic *system*, which is indebted to science's axiomatics, have no place for individuality in the framework of their universalizing operations. Individuality is the disrupter par excellence of "thinking" (as it was defined by Frege).[11]

That is also true for Derrida's position. Even if one does not link iterability with the law of identity, it remains true, Derrida concludes, that all rule-governed and repeatable speech includes two moves of distancing: it removes the reference and the respective speaking subject. And it does this not in contradiction to the tendency for idealization, which we know as the implication of the structure of repetition, but rather as its consequence.

> My nonperception, my nonintuition, my *hic et nunc* absence are expressed by that very thing that I say, by *that* which I say and *because* I say it. This structure will never form an "intimately blended unity" with intuition. The absence of intuition—and therefore of the subject of the intuition—is not only *tolerated* by speech; it is *required* by the general structure of signification, when considered *in itself*. It is radically requisite: the total absence of the subject and object of a statement—the death of the writer and/or the disappearance of the objects he was able to describe—does not prevent a text from "meaning" something. On the contrary, this possibility gives birth to meaning as such, gives it out to be heard and read. (93)

Let's disregard in this context the removal of the presence of objects, which Derrida cites as the constitutive feature of all speech (one can talk *about* objects in their absence: the possibility of this abstraction in fact shapes the representational function of the word-sign). This is correspondingly true — and this is the only aspect that interests us at the moment — of the individuality of the speaking subject: whoever speaks has to use words that show the same face to all speakers: their transindividual understandability is founded on this. Even the expressions with which I designate myself must, *as* expressions, be severable from the idiosyncratic consciousness that is proper only to me and that is not communicable. What Derrida calls idealization (or repetition, signification, and the death of the subject) means nothing other than that the sign, in order to open itself up to communicability with Others, has to free itself from the attachment to the "signifying intention" of only One (singular) subject. Searle speaks in the same sense of *"forms* of intentionality": they refer not to my or your but rather to *the* promising, *the* threatening, *the* blessing, *the* commanding, etc. "I" is only a variable, an index word, which in each instance designates the person who at that moment is performing a speech act; however, it designates this person not as a singular being but rather as one about whom statements that are capable of being true, or which at least conform to convention, can be made.

Derrida agrees on this point with Searle as well as with Husserl. He even goes further than the latter in that he challenges Husserl's view that "in solitary speech the meaning of 'I' is essentially realized in the immediate idea of one's own personality."[12]

> Is this certain? Even supposing that such an immediate representation is possible and actually given, does not the appearance of the word *I* in solitary speech (a supplement whose *raison d'être* is not clear if immediate representation is possible) already function as an ideality? Doesn't it give itself out as capable of remaining *the same* for an I-here-now in general, keeping its sense even if my empirical presence is eliminated or radically modified? When I say *I*, even in solitary speech, can I give my statement meaning without implying, there as always, the possible absence of the object of speech — in this case, myself? (95)

In a word, "I" means (*veut dire*) — not *although* the singular empirical "I" is (probably) not given in a presencing "living intuition," but *because* "I" is an ideality, a nonpresence, a *representamen* par excellence. Depresencing is the condition of possibility of its functioning as sign, i.e., as signifier.

> Whether or not I have a present intuition of myself, "I" expresses something; whether or not I am alive, *I am* "means something." Here also the fulfilling intuition is not an "essential component" of expression. Whether or not the *I* functions in solitary speech, with or without the self-presence of the speaking subject, it is *sinnvoll.* . . . The possibility of this nonintuition constitutes the *Bedeutung* as such, the *normal Bedeutung* as such. When the word *I* appears, the identity of its *Bedeutung*, inasmuch as it is distinct from its "object," puts us in what Hus-

serl describes as an abnormal situation—just as if *I* were written by someone unknown. This alone enables us to account for the fact that we understand the word *I* not only when its "author" is unknown but when he is quite fictitious. And when he is dead. The ideality of the *Bedeutung* here has by virtue of its structure the value of a testament. (95, 96)

Derrida believes that he can deduce this directly from Husserl's premises themselves ("it is Husserl's premises themselves that give rise to this astonishment. Husserl continues, 'But since each person, in speaking of himself, says "I," the word has the character of a universally operative indication of this fact' "; 95).

Meanwhile we know that Derrida subjects Husserl's (and correspondingly Searle's) premises to a radical reinterpretation before he draws *his* conclusions. For Husserl—and that applies correspondingly to every view of language that holds to the type-concept of the sign—ideality of meaning is a place of unerodible presence and self-identity (it is only the empirical individual whose signification constantly changes). Searle's concept of conventionality has the same function that Husserl's "principle of principles" serves (somewhat more speculatively, more obviously "metaphysical"), namely, to guarantee that a speech-act type brought into circulation remains *the same* even in repeated use. This view, as we saw earlier, makes out of communication a game whose stakes are determined in advance (except for the function of the accumulation of information on the part of the addressee). The allegedly partner-related act of communication reveals itself to be a speculative monologue (the speakers and the listeners are exchangeable functions, not individuals).

For Derrida, on the other hand, iterability is *not* subject to the axiom of the (metaphysically conceived) self-present. Idealization, which gives rise to significations, must rather be conceived in the final analysis as depresencing: as *différance*. It would bring little if one were to think of it as subjectivity, for precisely also subjectivity—conceived as self-contact—is articulated by means of a difference whose suppression would simultaneously dissolve the *signification* of subjectivity. In this sense difference proves to be irreducible. Even Husserl does not completely elude this consequence: the living present is ultimately transformed into an idea in the Kantian sense, i.e., into something that for its part can never be realized in "living self-present" or given to an experience of consciousness, into something nonintuitable and thus—as a consequence of the metaphorical connotation—into something nonevident. (What is understandable to intuition on its own accord is something "evident.") The demonstrations that show phenomenology to be a strict science are drawn from something in itself nondemonstrable, from something ideal (in the emphatic sense of something unreal). If one renounces the self-contradictory demand of bringing this "idea" into the "living self-present," then a view opens up that allows us to see that the ideality of all meaning and all signifying is grounded in the distancing of a founding subject and in the depresencing of a principle: in a *différance*, conceived as absolute, which is even the ground of *the* ground on the basis of which metaphysics (and the science which is indebted to it) think.

> The [*différance*] is not only the disappearance of origin—within the discourse that we sustain and according to the path that we follow it means that the origin did not even disappear, that it was never constituted except reciprocally by a nonorigin, the [*différance*], which thus becomes the origin of the origin. . . .
> *The trace is in fact the absolute origin of sense in general. Which amounts to saying once again that there is no absolute origin of sense in general. The trace is the differance* which opens appearance [*l'apparaître*] and signification. Articulating the living upon the nonliving in general, origin of all repetition, origin of ideality, the trace is not more ideal than real, not more intelligible than sensible, not more a transparent signification than an opaque energy and *no concept of metaphysics can describe it*. (GR, 61, 65)[13]

To be sure, the radicality of this consequence is impressive (even if it can no longer surprise us), and I would like to add that it was nowhere developed as lucidly and as patiently as in *Speech and Phenomena*—the book on which I would bestow the prize if someone were to ask me to be the judge in a contest for the best philosophical book produced by neostructuralism.

Meanwhile I have already expressed the opinion that I consider this radicality to be excessive. It makes it not only difficult but rather even impossible that one recognize what absolutely legitimate motive drove Husserl to seek refuge in that "idea in the Kantian sense." This motive consisted in the fact that there *is* something like the experience of the unity of self-consciousness—in spite of the uneradicable and unsublateable difference in the notion of the self-present and of "self-affection." It is not true that whoever refers "time" to the concept of unity conceives it metaphysically, that in a countermove against metaphysics one would have to conceive it based on the insight that even within self-contact a difference resides (*SP*, 69). Even if one takes all of Derrida's arguments as a basis, time *cannot* be conceived without taking account of its unifying function, which runs counter to its differential activity. Time, Sartre says in this sense, is differentiation of a particular kind: "a division which reunites" (*BN*, 131). Whoever would not take this unifying activity into account would have to consider time to be a result of moments existing in themselves and completely external to one another, none of which would give me the idea of relating them to each other. Certainly, the opposite thought, which holds that an extratemporal "I think" is impressing its unity onto what is temporally unconnected, without time itself being eternalized or, inversely, thinking being temporalized, is just as untenable. But the untenability of this strictly opposite position (which could with some justification be called "metaphysical") does not make the position taken by Derrida tenable. If *différance* were in fact *absolute*, then this extreme consequence would simultaneously bring with it the consequence that the idea of relation would be annulled (and it is on the basis of this that the differentiality of the sign system is built). If Derrida is correct in emphasizing that the interwovenness of the consciousness of the present (in Husserl) with the retentional-protentional experiences of consciousness fractures the identity of the "living present," then it also remains true that this interwovenness forms a net—a text, a texture—in which the nonidentical present is rescued from its dissolution into mere nonbeing: unity, which as strict self-present and identity proved untenable, now resurfaces as a concept of relation. Schelling demonstrated very convincingly that the time dimension has to be understood on the one hand as a "division" of moments "freed from" unity, but on the other hand as a division that "nevertheless always remains one in this tension—they can *never* be absolutely separated, so that never even for a moment could one be for itself. On the contrary, they are constantly posited as one *in* their separation, and it is precisely this that places them into the necessity of the process; for if they could be totally separated, then there would be no process" (*SW*, II/2, 206).

Applied to Derrida: a minimal continuity is indispensable so that different sign use can continue to be describable as the repeated succession of the same *aposèmes*. The expression "non-present *remaining* of a differential mark" (*Margins*, 318)—i.e., the acknowledgment of a minimal remainder, not of meaning, but of the *marque*—seeks to take this into account. Derrida does this even more clearly in *Limited Inc*.

> The remainder . . . is bound up with the minimal possibility of the re-
> mark . . . and with the structure of iterability. This iterability . . .
> supposes a minimal remainder (as well as a minimum of idealization) in
> order that the identity of the *selfsame* be repeatable and identifiable *in,*
> *through*, and even *in view of* its alteration. For the structure of
> iteration—and this is another of its decisive traits—implies *both* identity
> *and* difference. (189–90)

This coexistence of identity and difference in the process of temporization is called its *continuity*. Continuity implies change (otherwise we would have a static present: a *nunc stans*, a permanence), but it implies change within the framework of a unity. To be sure, this unity is constantly differentiated anew and in every moment challenged and broken down *as* the unity it, in each instance, is. But, we have to add, this occurs in order that new, and just as provisional unities can be constructed. There is absolutely no return to a prior unity that—in Hegel's terms—could be identified as the absolute in the state of its Being-in-itself from the perspective of its goal; no, unity is never originary (in the sense that it can only be looked upon ad infinitum as the modification of a prior unity), and it is never substantial (remaining: barely identified, it is challenged in anticipation of a new conception of unity). On the other hand, there is also no complete destruction of unity such that the singular phases would no longer entertain a relationship with each other. As Derrida correctly remarks, this would mean that one could no longer determine its iterative character – the recurrence of elements that simultaneously carry the index of change, but of a change that occurs within the framework of continuity.

This absurdity, however, seems to me to be a consequence not so much of Derrida's intention as of his conclusion. It no longer allows us to make out – since *différance* is posited as absolute – what distinguishes the reproduction of signs – inasmuch as it is no longer in the service of a self-present that functions as a regulative principle – from the unfettered chaos of unconnected "effects of meaning" (apart from the fact that such a chaos, particularly as the place where meaning is produced, is simply a nonthought). One can most convincingly bring Derrida into difficulties with the *tu quoque* argument that Plato's dialogues and many of Aristotle's writings utilize. By means of this argument one demonstrates "that anyone who disputes certain conditions of reasoning, must already have acknowledged these conditions in order to be able to challenge them, and thus argues in a pragmatically inconsistent way."[14] In order to be able to conceive iterability as the condition of possibility for subjectivity and meaning[15] – for ideality at all – Derrida has to avail himself of the continuity (and thus the framing unity) of the process. He justifiably does so, in my opinion; but then the thrust of his argument is parried, or it can at best be sustained only at the price of self-contradiction. For to the extent that Derrida reminds Husserl's "living present" that the prefix *re-* in the expression "*re*production" (*SP*, 63ff., 66ff.) (as well as in "*re*petition" and "*re*presentation") presupposes the loss of a seamless self-identity of "primordial experience," he for his part has to be reminded by Husserl – and the cited passage from *Limited Inc* acknowledges this as such – that the loss of the self-presence of primordial experience can be marked only within the framework of a *continual process of iteration*, whose formulation in the prefix *re* in the term "*re*marque" indicates a "minimal identity" as something that cannot be theoretically relinquished.

This results, it seems to me, in a series of consequences that all have in common that they can no longer be addressed within the theoretical framework of neostructuralism. They call for a hermeneutics of meaning and of the individual.

Lecture 27

Two lectures ago we discussed Derrida's criticism of Searle's concept of the sign, and in the last lecture we examined his position regarding Husserl's concept of the sign. Although I have made an effort to highlight the conceptual continuity between his arguments against Searle and those against Husserl, this still always occurs in each case in specific contexts that, each according to its own perspective, made the universality of Derrida's approach clear. Because I consider Derrida's arguments to be both complicated as well as significant, I now want to try to reconstruct the essential steps of his critical attack, independent of the reference to Searle and Husserl.

Derrida forces those theoreticians concerned with the systematic constraining of utterances (i.e., of pragmatically interpreted propositions) in a taxonomy of rules to consider that the iterability of utterances, like that of signs generally, is a structural possibility of rule-governed speech. However, in a countermove to the idea of a transtemporal order of speech, Derrida questions the legitimacy of the conclusion that in a functioning grammatical taxonomy every repetition of a sign or of an utterance is necessarily the repetition of the *same*.

According to him, there is no preestablished copresence of author and reader, or of speaker and listener; indeed, strictly speaking, neither the author nor the speaker is ever copresent with what he or she writes or says. For the uttered signs can become elements of an individual message, i.e., types, *faits socials*, only under the condition that the speaker's/writer's intention drops off, as it were, from the signification of the uttered signs: the individual retreats in its singularity in order to make room for the universality of the system. This suspension of individual meaning, however, has the countereffect of making the signs free to take up another (other than) individual interpretation.

From this we can infer that as soon as codified types are exchanged, it must principally be possible—but this does not mean always and in all cases[1]—to replace their first or originary articulation/interpretation with a second one, and thus to depart from convention (which is merely *virtual* anyway, and is constantly annulled by *real* speech). Derrida calls this the "*re*marque": the constant possibility for the speaker, the author, the reader, or the interpreter to mark anew the meaning of a word or sentence.

This possibility, in its turn, follows from the temporality of speech that undermines the notion of the copresence of sender and receiver, just as it undermines that of the synchrony of *concept* and *image acoustique/graphique*. Every form of "being-present-with" (*Gegenwärtig-sein-bei*) has the structure of a differentiation: something is *with* something else, and something is *after* something else. The meaning of a sign or an utterance is separated from itself by every new usage, it is displaced: who can prove that *after* passing through the gap of iteration meaning is joined in the same synthesis with its expressive substratum as at the beginning?

> This etymology, of course, has no value qua proof and were it to be false, the very shift in meaning would confirm the law here indicated: the time and place of the *other time* already at work, altering from the start the start itself, the *first time*, the *at once*. (*LI*, 200)

Saussure expressed a similarly radical idea in the posthumously published *Notes*:

> What has escaped philosophers and logicians here is that, from the moment a system of symbols is *independent* of the objects designated, it was itself subject to undergoing, *by virtue of time*, displacements that are *incalculable for the logician*. (*EC*, II, 23)

But there is a further and more unsettling consequence that Derrida's "rigorous and renewed analysis of the value of presence, a presence to self or to others, of difference and of *différance*" (*LI*, 186) recommends language philosophers to draw. It is not only the repeated sign, he says, that cannot guarantee its identity, but rather even the sign that was only used once. How come? you will ask. Because, Derrida answers, semiological orders—e.g., texts, discourses, orientations in the life world, traditional contexts, etc.—can endow their elements with signification only by distinguishing each singular element from all others. But one can justifiably maintain about something that can only secure its identity over the detour through all other identities that it is separated from itself. For its self is a function of the incalculably open number of all the other sign uses I settle on over the course of an interpretive process and delimit from it by means of distinction.

I would like to portray this thought that seeks to reconcile the notion of the systematic composition of texts with the idea of their historicity and uninterpretability. Since it is quite complicated (and foreign, at least in a German-speaking context), I have decided to approach it in a new way, and I hope I will be excused for repeating things that were already said in other contexts. If meaning and significance are produced in the interrelation of different expressive substances, then the identity of a term could be guaranteed only if the system is in a state of closure and unalterability. The model that underlies both the structural theory of language and texts, as well as Searle's "taxonomy of speech acts" (at least implicitly), is, as we know, the crystal lattice in which all molecules are immovably fixed in their positions, if the temperature is sufficiently low, separated from all the others, but also connected with them. In contrast to the elemental world, the historical-cultural world cannot simply be cooled down to the absolute freezing point (even if all the efforts of the politicians in East or West have the purpose of trying to bring it to this). Language and literature thrive only in a certain warmth that permits flux: the exchange and reconstellation of signs. Texts are always transformations of other and former texts, just as signs are always new articulations of other and former signs (cf. *P*, 26–27; *EC*, I, 160). Why? Because it is simultaneously settled—by means of the thought of differentiation—that no sign is immediately and atemporally present to itself, since it has to take the detour over an incalculable and changing configuration of other signs before it can identify itself. If one in addition comes to understand that this detour runs through infinity, then one has renounced the scientistic idea that there is something like an originary, atemporal presence, one that can be reconstituted by means of textual analysis or discourse analysis, or a familiarity of at least *one* meaning with and by itself (as, for example, is suggested by Greimas's concept of *sens total* or *sens central*); and there certainly is no such self-presence or self-familiarity of the sort that I assuredly would find my way back to—as the *signifié transcendantal*—no matter what paths I happen to take across signs. The paradigm of reflection (of the speculative return to the point of departure, something that one also recognizes in the notion of a "reconstruction of the original meaning of the word or the originally signified intention," which was preserved even through to speech-act theory) does not stand up to the experience of an unlimited economy of semantic oppositions.

Lacan's famous essay "The Agency of the Letter in the Unconscious" had already provided us with some information about the nature of this experience. Lacan spoke of an "incessant sliding of the signified under the signifier" (*E*, 154). The expression "signifier" is undoubtedly incorrectly chosen, for, as Derrida has shown us, the signifier is always only the nonautonomous correspondent of the integral reality of the sign that encompasses it. A signifier is itself an ideality, essentially defined by and constituted in view of the signified (*SP*, 76). It therefore would be self-contradictory to believe that the signified could slide under the signifier, for, as Saussure repeatedly emphasized, the sign can only change as a whole (thus as signifier-signified). It is for this reason that he later called the, as it were, remaining and nonideal part "under" the sign *aposème*: the word hull that allows material-empirical embodiment for the (through and through ideal) sign, without itself entering into the regions of designation (of semiosis). Lacan's thesis can thus be understood quite well if one interprets the term signifier as *aposème* throughout his work. For of course the word hull of a sign can endure, while the sign itself (Lacan says: its meaning) semantically slides.

According to Lacan, this sliding arises from the principal (or, let's say, structural) impossibility of nailing, so to speak, what he calls the signified to what he calls the signifier. To be sure, one can enumerate the rules of grammar and those of the lexicon, but no rule of conjunction or semantic-lexicological definition is capable of accounting in advance for all configurations in which the sign can in fact be used. Now Saussure's principal insight, to which Lacan appeals (*E* [Fr. ed.], 497), is that the signification of a sign is differentially determined: in the contrast to its neighboring signs (which Saussure calls *parasèmes*). According to Lacan, this insight categorically excludes the thought of the closure and fixedness of the lexical-grammatical repertoire (the *batterie signifiante*). It can never be calculated in advance which group of *parasèmes* will in fact determine the semantics of a sign or a sign chain in a historically singular contextual constellation. The meaning of a signifier (as Lacan understands the term) is always defined as an open function (of future, and as such of *at present* incalculable) contexts. Lacan characterizes this fact that every signifier is referred to an open field of semantic determination on the basis of contexts ("only the correlations between signifier and signifier provide the standard for all reasearch into signification") as the anticipation of meaning: "the signifier, by its very nature, always anticipates meaning by unfolding its dimension before it" (*E*, 153). The range of this anticipation cannot be grammatically-lexically limited in advance.

According to Lacan, a second circumstance supervenes that ensures that the identification of meaning according to lexicon and grammar is impossible. That is the fact that the meaning of a statement is always the meaning the other intends with it. Speech is, unless it is viewed as the speculative monologue – as *parole vide* – of the solitary soul with itself, essentially dialogic and interindividual. But that means that the linguistic code, to the extent that it guarantees this interindividual and transindividual dimension of meaning, is totally withdrawn from and unreachable by the individuality of *my* registerings of meaning. The meaning of expressions is thus not determinable by means of my own linguistic competence, and that applies correspondingly and inversely for the Other. Lacan concludes from this:

> What this structure of the signifying chain discloses is the possibility I have, precisely in so far as I have this language in common with other

subjects, that is to say, in so far as it exists as a language, to use it in order to signify *something quite other* than what it says. (155)

This feature of all speech to displace incalculably the meaning of terms in usage (*emploi*, Lacan says [*E*, 153]) comes into view in poetically wrought language as such. Meaning is undecidable, not only on the basis of language's intersubjectivity, which, as it were, takes away from me the monopoly of meaning attribution and democratizes it; and it is not only undecidable by virtue of the fact that every endowment of significance is open to the future (which relativizes the masterability of a sign in anticipation of a still unknown sign constellation); there is, finally, something like a social and contextual memory of signs that incalculably complicates their monosemy. Lacan speaks of former contexts that have been, as it were, vertically attached to the sign and dragged along by it *as* former contexts, and these contexts help determine the horizontal and differential reference to its neighboring sign. The sign preserves the trace of all its former uses; no lexicon could ever give sufficient information about these. These layers of meaning (which originate from the contexts and discursive connections that the signs in question passed through at some earlier time), dragged along by the signs, as it were, beneath their surface, are systematically exploited by poetic language.

> One has only to listen to poetry, which Saussure was no doubt in the habit of doing, for a polyphony to be heard, for it to become clear that all discourse is aligned along the several staves of a score.
> There is in effect no signifying chain that does not have, as if attached to the punctuation of each of its units, a whole articulation of relevant contexts suspended "vertically," as it were, from that point. (154)

Lacan imaginatively illustrates how this can happen on the example of the signifier tree (*arbre*). It is freed from its nominal isolation as lexeme and put in all kinds of relations — which playfully exploit not only its symbolic but also its phonic and graphic substance — that later can no longer be separated from an allegedly "authentic signification" of the lexeme. What "tree" actually signifies cannot be made out: significance is plural inasmuch as it is semantically charged with secondary significations (*parasèmes*).

> Let us take our word "tree" again, this time not as an isolated noun, but at the point of one of these punctuations, and see how it crosses the bar of the Saussurian algorithm. (The anagram of "*arbre*" and "*barre*" should be noted.)
> For even broken down into the double spectre of its vowels and consonants, it can still call up with the robur and the plane tree the signification it takes on, in the context of our flora, of strength and majesty. Drawing on all the symbolic contexts suggested in the Hebrew of the Bible, it erects on a barren hill the shadow of the cross. Then reduces

to the capital Y, the sign of dichotomy which, except for the illustration used by heraldry, would owe nothing to the tree however genealogical we may think it. Circulatory tree, tree of life of the cerebellum, tree of Saturn, tree of Diana, crystals formed in a tree struck by lightning, is it your figure that traces our destiny for us in the tortoise-shell cracked by the fire, or your lightning that causes that slow shift in the axis of being to surge up from an unnamable night into the of Ενπάντα language. (154–55)

Derrida's theorem of the *disseminal* character of the sign is undoubtedly profoundly influenced by Lacan's observations on semantics. There is, nevertheless, a gap, which cannot be overlooked, between their respective views that Derrida likes to emphasize, and which, in his partly admiring and partly polemical analysis of the *Séminaire sur "la lettre volée,"* led him to count Lacan among the hermeneutical thinkers (in proximity to Ricoeur).[2] Here Derrida claims that Lacan has revised the classical view of hermeneutics, according to which an "authentic meaning" hides underneath the textual surface in order to let itself finally be rediscovered by that circular movement that hermeneutics takes as the process of interpretation. Instead of this, the lack, which Lacan defines as subjectivity, takes up residence at exactly the place that classically was occupied by the "transcendental signified" or by the "principle of principles." However, this lack, Derrida ironically remarks, is lacking precisely at its proper place ("The signifier is *missing from its place*"),[3] and analytical hermeneutics finds it at the end of a circle that itself could be called hermeneutical, namely, at the place of "authenticity" and "truth."[4]

The letter was sent from a place and arrived at a place. It is not a subject but a void the lack out of which the subject is constituted. The contour of this void is determinable and magnetizes the entire trajectory of the detour which leads from void to void and from the void to itself and which has, therefore, a circular form. This is a regulated circulation which organizes a return from the detour to the void, and a transcendental reappropriation and readequation which accomplish an authentic contract. . . . Circulation, the payment [*acquittement*] of a debt, steps in to repair the dehiscence which, by opening the debt and the contract, expelled for a time (the time of the signifier) the signified from its proper origin. Circulation allows it to return. This readequation (the truth), therefore, implies a theory of the proper place which itself implies a theory of the letter as an indivisible locality. The signifier should never venture an unreturning loss, destruction or shredding of itself.
    . . . In spite of the appearance of denegation, his is a hermeneutical decipherment.[5]

For Lacan the authentic has been transformed from a self-referential positive fact to a reference of lack to itself (*le propre étant devenu le rapport du manque à lui-*

même);[6] interpretation thus consists – in an entirely traditional fashion – in following the trail of this reference.[7] In the end, the effort involved in this detour is rewarded by the certitude of the represencing of the origin in the sense of Hegelian *sublation*.[8] According to this scheme, "the disseminal structure, i.e., the no-possible-return of the letter, the other scene of its remnance [*restance*]" is misconstrued.[9]

As stimulating as it would be to test Derrida's alternative proposal on Poe's text itself, we have to concentrate on the fundamental aspect of Derrida's objection. One can immediately see what he is getting at without going deeply into details. Lacan's hermeneutics, according to Derrida, does not radically break with the thought of the semantic identifiability of the signifier; it orients interpretation around the criterion of truth and authenticity, and these are epitomized in the idea of the "true subject." Analogous to Hegel's idea of the autonomy of negation, which goes hand in hand with a philosophy of the absolute, Lacan's conception of a detoured self-identification of lack finds its way back to a (vacant but, nevertheless, a) place of truth.

There is something to this. I have shown elsewhere that it is in fact not inappropriate to speak of a hermeneutics in the case of Lacan,[10] and that Lacan himself does not scorn the label of interpreter or hermeneuticist. In *The Four Fundamental Concepts of Psychoanalysis* he very clearly drew the line that separates his psychoanalytical hermeneutics from the thought of disseminal reading. There he says:

> It is false to say, as had been said, that interpretation is open to all meanings under the pretext that it is a question only of the connection of a signifier to a signifier, and consequently of an uncontrollable connection. Interpretation is not open to any meaning. This would be to concede to those who rise up against the character of uncertainty in analytic interpretation that, in effect, all interpretations are possible, which is patently absurd. The fact that I have said that the effect of interpretation is to isolate in the subject a kernel, a *kern*, to use Freud's own term, of *non-sense*, does not mean that interpretation is in itself nonsense.
>
> Interpretation is a signification that is not just any signification. It comes here in the place of the *s* and reverses the relation by which the signifier has the effect, in language, of the signified. It has the effect of bringing out an irreducible signifier. One must interpret at the level of the *s*, which is not open to all meanings, which cannot be just anything, which is a signification, though no doubt only an approximate one.[11]

Let's disregard the theory of metaphor that Lacan addresses in these sentences and concentrate on two statements: first, that interpretation is not arbitrary, but that it can miss its signified; second, that it has the structure of an approximation, i.e., of a conjecture that cannot definitively identify its object. In this way one can simultaneously assert two things about it: interpretation is not simply a criterion-less helter-skelter of meaning attributions; nevertheless, it is neither objective nor definitive. Both statements can be reconciled if one understands identification, which is absolutely necessary for the attribution of meaning, as nonfinal. In this way both statements are granted: first, that interpretation, as Schleiermacher says, is "an infinite task because it is something infinitely past and infinitely future that we want to see in the words" (*HuK*, 94). This, by the way, is absolutely in keeping with Lacan, according to whom speech drags along the past of its former contexts and anticipates a still unspecified future of signification. Second, it is further conceded that the infinitude of interpretation does not put an end to the signifying of signs, but rather merely characterizes meaning as something preliminary and impermanent.

If one were to take Derrida's antihermeneutics seriously in all its radicality, one would have to conclude that the disseminal character of signs – their total nonpresence – not only would make endurable signification impossible for them, but also would prohibit their signification at any point at all. That, to be sure, would be an absurdity that could be maintained only by going contrary to the experience of speaking and understanding. But, as a matter of fact, Derrida's polemics against Husserl's and Searle's and – as it turns out – Lacan's notion of a certain presence of signs has, at its most pointed, precisely this consequence. If it is supposed to follow from the thought of *différance* that interpretation is no longer possible at all, then the category of "meaning" is completely deprived of its basis for existence. Difference would be totalitarian and would break down meaning (instead of multiplying meaning, as in Lacan and Schleiermacher).

In fact, however, difference could never be absolute in the sense that the statement "everything is difference" could be upheld. First, the term *différance* would be meaningless if no other term were joined with it to provide for a distinction (in this context, the term "identity"); second, the mechanism of differentiation could not be understood if the related elements were to be detached from the *reference* that relates them to one another. If the relation of difference has to be understood as one of (determined) negation, and if the operation of negation, following Peirce, can be defined as an operation of distinction (something is negated when it is determined by being different than . . .), then *différance* is not only dividing but also uniting. Put trivially, something can only differ from something else (something determined). Otherness is therefore a relational concept that has something in common with that *whose* other it designates. Fichte formulated this particularly lucidly in his commentaries on the third principle of his first *Science of Knowledge*:

> Every opposite is like its opponent in one respect, = X; and every like
> is opposed to its like in one respect, = X. Such a respect, = X, is
> called the ground, in the first case of *conjunction*, and in the second of

distinction: for to liken or compare opposites is to *conjoin* them; and to set like things in opposition is to *distinguish* them.[12]

In other words, difference is never total but rather always partial. (It occurs within the framework of a continuous field of "divisibility.") If it were conceived as total, then it would detach itself from that *from* which it differs; i.e., it would cease to be a difference.

This insight (as trivial as it is) actually seems to have been taken into consideration in Derrida's idea of the remaining mark (*marque restante*) and the "minimal identity" a sign has to preserve over the process of its incalculable differentiations. But how can this consideration be justified, at least on the basis of his theory, and particularly on the basis of his polemics against Lacan?

Obviously, it cannot be justified through the claim that the *marque* is by nature identical with itself (or continuous). To assume this would mean to fall into the "naturalist fallacy," which Saussure demonstrated to be operable in the "Young Grammarians," and which consists in the belief that natural sounds in themselves are disposed toward the introduction of significations, and that one can conceive of signs as "physical entities." The empirical substrate becomes the carrier of signification in every sign synthesis only as soon as one interprets it as a signifier, i.e., actually relates it to a possible meaning—within the framework of a relational structure. If this relation cannot be understood as that of a "*natural* connection" (and Saussure's linguistic approach draws its theoretical strength primarily from the persuasive refutation of this view), the only other possibility is that one has to conceive it as the result of a hypothetical judgment—of an "abduction" in Peirce's sense. We will investigate its mechanism in a moment. In our present context it is enough to eviscerate the view that with the "minimal identity of a remaining mark" that of a natural sound or of a writing trace could be meant.

If the mark only first distinguishes itself and identifies itself as that which it is by the fact that a meaning is—hypothetically—assigned to it (no identification without signification!), then it is impossible to say, inversely, that meaning is generated out of the mark or out of the relations which it entertains with other marks. Differentiality is certainly a necessary prerequisite for the production of meaning, but it reveals to me the meaning of what was distinguished only under the circular precondition that I ascribe it to the marks in a motivated, yet freely interpretive attribution. A system of marks distinguished "in themselves" would always remain something natural, much like the constellation of molecules in a crystal is something natural. In order to be able to understand relations of marks as segments of a *symbolic* (nonnatural) order, I have to provide them with a meaning—to whatever extent motivated by the framework of the structure itself. And this meaning—as nonnecessitated by the natural side of the sounds, traces, and connections—can only be the result of a free interpretive attribution. (To assume "a little bit of freedom," in order to acknowledge the conditioned character of the pregiven order, would not be much more intelligent than thinking that one is "a little bit pregnant.")

Let's underline the essential point of this still entirely preliminary deliberation: in order to be characterized even only vaguely as a "remaining mark," the mark must have been assigned a meaning. But if assignment of this meaning is the condition under which I can first speak of the unity of the mark at all, then one would necessarily commit a *petitio principii* if one wanted to pass off meaning, for its part, as something determined by the "effect of the mark." In order to be able to exert this meaning-determining effect, the mark—*prior to* all meaning—would have to be composed unitarily. But what could a mark prior to all meaning be, other than a natural object? To assume that natural objects are "distinct in themselves" would mean to fall victim to the "naturalist illusion" whose decisive rejection first opens up the field on which a structuralist and neostructuralist theory of signs is possible.

To be sure, Derrida problematizes the unity of the mark that subsists in itself by adding that it is a nonpresent one (*restance nonprésente de la marque*). If one reads the predicate "nonpresent" in the extreme significance of "bare of every relation to identity," then one not only repeats the indicated absurdity but also strips the term *restance* of precisely that function for whose sake it was introduced, namely, the function of securing for the sign a "minimal identity."

Nonprésente, however, can be interpreted less extremely and more meaningfully than as "without *permanent* identity." That would be an explication reconcilable with Humboldt's statement that the meaning of a sign acquires "no permanent place," and especially not in writing. To have no permanent place, however, does not mean to have no meaning at all. In order to have a meaning, writing (or the *marque*) has to be interpreted again and again. "Again and again" is supposed to express that the unity, into which a given interpretation places the meaning together with its expression, is not permanent but remains relative to the act of employment. Other acts of employment will determine the semantics of the sign *differently*. But this otherness will not be absolute (simply because "absolute otherness" is a nonthought whose signification does not understand itself), but rather relative. An "othering" (*Veranderung*) (to use the term Rosenkranz coined), whose degree of alteration is measured according to the extent of modification it effected on a state of sign synthesis prior to it, can be characterized as determined othering. Here the word "determined," in relation to a new sign synthesis, means that it let itself be motivated by its antecedent. One designates as "motivation" a manner of founding (*Begründung*) that connects to its ground only if it has previously disclosed it *as* ground in light of an interpretation; consequences that are not blindly necessitated, but that relate (freely) to their cause, are motivated. In this sense the semantic transformation of a sign is motivated: since the meaning of the preceding sign itself subsisted only by virtue of a hypothetical judgment (*in itself*, i.e., in its bare naturalness, the mark has no meaning at all, as we saw), this sign's unity of meaning cannot semantically determine a second use of this sign. On the other hand, the first sign use naturally remains the antecedent of the second one, in the sense that since the signification of the first consisted in a hypothesis, this hypothesis can and even *must* be included by a second hypothesis as the motivating force in its own projection. "Must" means here that the second hypothesis is not simply free to determine its antecedent. "Can" means that the first introduction of meaning does not have to be continued in the second on the basis of a kind of natural causality. In this way, a *continuity* would be set up between consecutive interpretations of a sign. This continuity—which is not a continuity in the evolutionary sense, but rather a continuity of hypothetical judgments that motivate each other—could legitimate the notion of a "remaining nonpresent of a differential mark," although on a different theoretical level than the one suggested by Derrida. There would be a remainder insofar as one and the same *aposème* (about whose sameness, to be sure, one has hermeneutically-hypothetically to judge again and again) would be open to an indefinite number of consecutive inscriptions of meaning. This chain would be nonpresent because no inscription would have to continue with identical meaning and form in the (temporally) following one, so that the self-presence of its signifying forms an instant unity that is clouded by no difference.

In the context of the sign chain or chain of interpretation, I speak of *continuity* or *motivation*. The former term I understand in the sense of Peirce's *synechism*, i.e., as the connectedness and cohesiveness of a succession of conclusions in the unity of "one and the same process of the growth of reasonableness."[13] And this connectedness will necessarily have to be continuous, for the phases of the process—the perceptual judgments by virtue of which I am able at all to recognize something *as* something and to place it into relation with something else—are constituted in light of (linguistic) interpretations and in the continuous unity of an (open) stream of consciousness. Only in a world that is already linguistically interpreted can differences be constituted and connections established between elements. This interpretation, which is always already presupposed in every drawing of conclusions and in every meaning (*Meinen*) of something as something, makes my world into a continuum. This is how it is formulated in one of the famous *cotary propositions* with which Peirce, in his lectures in 1903 on pragmatism, sought to "put the edge on" his philosophy (*Coll P*, V, 112). On the basis of the continuity of our stream of consciousness, in which "instants melt into one another without separate individuality," we are justified in abductively-hypothetically inferring the possible "generality" of our judgments (*Coll P*, V, 127). "Continuity is an indispensable element of reality, and . . . continuity is simply what generality becomes in the logic of relatives" (*Coll P*, V, 291).

If the relation that mediates between the linguistically interpreted "perceptual judgments" can be determined as continuity, then the form of causality that mediates between the elements can be more precisely defined as a *motivated inference*.

Motivation is not causation or necessitation. A fact would be necessitated (to use the terminology of the position that Peirce ridicules as *necessitarianism* [*Coll P*, VI, 28–45]), if, on the basis of given empirical causes, it could not possibly not occur. A motive, by contrast, designates a reason (*Grund*) that would be able to determine my actions only in light of an interpretation that would disclose it as the reason for this action.[14] An impetus to an action that unfolds its effectiveness only by virtue of an interpretation (a final idea, for example), which acknowledges and qualifies it as reason, cannot be conceived as the causal basis for an action. Moreover, even physical causes (*Ursachen*) are in the final analysis reasons (*Gründe*), in the sense that the mode of Being of the physical is disclosed as that which it is by means of perceptual judgments (and thus by means of interpretations). Even the laws of mechanics are nothing but motivated inferences on the basis of perceptual judgments whose hypothetical, and thus hermeneutical, character can never be overcome and should never be overcome, because, if it were to vanish, then the understandability of the world in which we observe how mechanical laws operate would vanish with it. The dream of necessitarianism would be to make

the whole action of the mind a part of the physical universe. . . . It enters consciousness under the head of sundries, as a forgotten trifle; its scheme of the universe would be more satisfactory if this little fact could be dropped out of sight. On the other hand, by supposing the rigid exactitude of causation to yield, . . . we gain room to insert mind into our scheme, and to put it into the place where it is needed, into the position which, as the sole self-intelligible thing, it is entitled to occupy, that of the fountain of existence. (*Coll P*, VI, 42–43)

The continuous interpretive process (which refers hypothetically to unity, but is uniform) thus cannot be understood if one simply eliminates the dimensions of consciousness, praxis, and freedom, or if one declares it, with an overhasty reasoning, to be an effect of the differential relations between marks. Hypothetical judgments can be made and motivations executed only within the dimension of a prior consciousness. Inorganic and unconscious nature (according to all that we know about it) knows neither hypotheses nor motivations. Neither, therefore, can be derived from it as secondary effects, unless one presupposes the anticipated result (in a circular fashion).

I conclude from this that the recourse to individuality also should not simply have been given up. For individuality—as Derrida, along with Husserl, concedes—is an agency that offers resistance to the rigorous idealization of the meaning of the sign as something instantaneous and identical (i.e., it accomplishes precisely what is credited to *différance*). Individuality, further, has the advantage over *différance* that it has to be conceived as *self-conscious* (i.e., that it makes motivations and hypothetical judgments possible, this being what interpretations are).

I would like to propose—and I gave detailed reasons for this proposal in *Das individuelle Allgemeine*—that Derrida's *différance* be conceived as *individuality*. It is not "primordially" *différance*, but rather the *élément individuel* that prevents the sign synthesis from coinciding with itself in a transtemporal presence. This noncoincidence, however, does not have the absurd result of causing the interpretation of signs to become a *gratuitous act*, or even of completely thwarting it; rather, it simply has the result of inserting signs into a continuum of nonidentical hypothetical judgments that, however, are motivated by each other. "Nonidentical" means that no sign would be semantically identifiable in an extratemporal sense: it stands, rather, in an openness to incalculable possibilities of interpretation. However, this incalculability of interpretations is not comparable to the anarchy of blind caprice (which, strictly speaking, does not exist: there are rules for running amok, just as there are for gratuitous acts, only they do not have the same rules as those that structure the hundred-yard dash or a musical composition according to a rigid scheme); it is not arbitrary, because each new interpretation of a sign is the reinterpretation of a former sign use. No interpretation can be absolutely new (the concept of absolute innovation is just as self-contradictory as is that of absolute deviation or of absolute difference). The opposite of "absolute" is "relative." Each new interpretation is relative to the interpretation *whose* innovation it brings about; it will thus necessarily take over into itself traces of the previous interpretation. The continuity of this trace, however, has nothing to do with what Husserl calls "living present." For it is obvious that the chain of the incalculable (new) interpretations of already interpreted marks cannot be instantly represented or presenced in authentic intuition. The element of freedom, which we tracked down in the idea of a motivated succession, while intelligible as the action of an individuality capable of meaning, is not—as free transgression—derivable from the signification the respective sign had *up to that point*. Understanding also does not consist in making a semantic deduction out of preestablished premises (a certain state of signification of a language, for example); rather, quite to the contrary, it consists in reproducing in a free and creative "divination" a motivated but grammatically-pragmatically incalculable transformation of meaning as that which it is: *as* novation. The prefix *re-* in the expression "reproduction" does not signify the return to a presumed authenticity of the original meaning or that which was intended by the author (which, if it existed, would only be hypothetically reconstructible, without the assurance of verifiability; and, moreover, this meaning itself is transgressed by the author's meaning projection); *re* means that I have to accomplish once more the creativity of the projected meaning projection as such if I want to understand that, and to what extent, the individual moment cannot rest in the coincidence with the transgressed signification (for logical reasons), but only in the disparity it produced between the old and the new signification. In this sense understanding is *re-* productive: *re*accomplishment not of the former signification, but of the meaning projection that deactualizes, depresences, and irremediably splits up the old signification in the projection of a new one. The fact that understanding—as opposed to that about which the code model of conventionalized semantics/pragmatics dreams—principally lacks final certainty about whether the meaning projection of the other individual has in fact been hit upon, has to be evaluated positively rather than negatively. It expresses that respect of the irreducible otherness of the other human being with requisite radicality, much as it was demonstrated by Derrida in his remarks about Husserl's "analogical appresentation": it is the nonpresence of the meaning of the Other and of the Other meaning, its irreducibility to the presence of a "dator intuition," which the idealization of the code model as well as the idealization of the "eidetic reduction" destroy (*SP,* 39–40, 71). But how shall one destroy this idealization if one has previously denied the existence of the irreducibly Other meaning and of the meaning-of-the-Other—in one word, the individual and nonidentical moment in every accomplishment of meaning—as Derrida has? (Incomprehensibly enough, he even implicitly formulates his argument following Husserl's and Searle's demand for a sameness of signification that excludes the nonidentity of individual meaning, which he, oddly enough, takes as "empirical." If the signification of "I" were to shift from utterance to utterance, he claims, the ideality of this signification would be destroyed: "Doesn't it give itself out as capable of remaining *the same* for an I-here-now in general, keeping its sense even if my empirical presence is eliminated or radically modified? . . . Doesn't speech [*discurs*] and the ideal nature of every *Bedeutung* exclude . . . that a *Bedeutung* is 'ever altering'?" [*SP,* 95]). If one does not conceive the individual moment as effluence or manifestation of an "empirical personality"—which would be absurd, inasmuch as one assumes (as if Peirce had never lived) that something empirical, whether "subjective" or "objective," could be significant in itself—but rather as that which it is: as the nonidentity of signifying in the process of a continuous transformation of sign syntheses, then it sublates, it seems to me, all those accomplishments that Derrida ascribes to *différance* in itself and has the additional advantage of being able to explain a number of phenomena that the reductionism of neostructuralist semantics fails to explain.

By way of conclusion I would like to show how well Derrida, with his view that there is no semantic identity either of the single signs or of complex (conventionally formed) expressions, could have appealed to the authentic Ferdinand de Saussure, whom he, favoring the questionable vulgate version of the *Cours,* never quotes. Saussure himself, on the one hand, contradicts the code model that presupposes, in a completely acommunicative fashion, the identity of significations between speaker and listener; on the other hand, he founds the realizability of the meaning of signs in a hermeneutics whose argumentative force was repressed or went unrecognized, not only by the editors of the first printed version of the *Cours*, but especially by Saussure's allegedly orthodox and structuralist followers. For us the recourse to Saussure has the heuristic purpose of demonstrating once again that structuralism and hermeneutics do not have to be conceived as mutually exclusive alternatives.

Saussure spoke of "a certain floating" between that which the prescripts of the language system demand and that which is left up to the initiative of the speaking individual (*EC*, I, 286). This has to do with the fact that in his view the values of the language system always only unfold their *meaning in actu*; the language system, however, has the modality of mere virtuality. *In actu* means in its succession, in the flow of speech, and thus over time. The unidimensionality of time prevents me from performing two actualizations of *one* and the same sign in one and the same expressive act; and it forces me to articulate my utterances at different times and in different contexts (if there were contextual rules, it would automatically be true of them that even they cannot anticipate and determine the singularity and actuality of the contextual situation in all its details). Time separates the subject of the speaker from itself (and thus mars the idealization of expressions by means of which the speaker designates him/herself); and it separates – at least as a possibility, but this possibility is a principal one – the (former) signification of an expression from each of its future ones. (*Writing* only exemplifies this experience, which we also make in everyday speech in an extreme form.)

In order to account for this experience of the "mutability of signs" language philosophy needs a theory of the linguistic sign of the sort that simultaneously explains its intersubjective understandability (according to a semiotic key that vouches for the "minimal identity" of the signs) *and* the nonidentity or noncontemporaneity of its message.

Now Saussure precisely did not contest his discovery of the systematic constitution – and the ideal character – of language (*langue*) with the idea of an original identity of signs: "Everything [in *langue*] consists in differences" (*CFS*, 15 [1957], 16; see 93: "In *langue*, there is nothing but differences, no positive quantity.") If nothing about the substance of sounds carries meaning in itself, he holds up against the "naturalist illusion" of the "Young Grammarians," then the unity and distinctness of a sign must be produced in a different fashion; namely, on the basis of a cooperation between two principles that mutually supplement and limit each other: the principle of temporal-linear succession and that of a countermoving process of generalization (or idealization) that works counter to the first. (Structuralism and the taxonomical linguistics of analytical philosophy take cognizance of the latter only: the differences of the language system are reduced to a finite number of oppositions in whose lattice time appears to stand still. This view would be metaphysical in the sense that it would not abolish Husserl's "principle of principles.")

Back to Saussure's two principles. On the basis of the first, the unidimensionality of the flow of time, the elements can distinguish themselves from each other: the *chaîne parlée* is founded ad infinitum on a relation of nonidentity, which Saussure understands as the relation of an "other than." Given the term x, from which a second one is distinguished as non-x (and is identified with y, for example), the negation of the set of all $-x$ (thus the double negation of y) yields the continuum of all units of sound that I can legitimately consider as "x."[15]

This principle—it is no other than a better-explicated version of the "principle of differentiality," which we discussed at the beginning of our lecture series—can be designated more clearly by means of formalization. Since this is not my own discovery, but part of an unpublished typescript that Christian Stetter was so kind as to give me, I would like to quote him:

Linguistic sign synthesis is grounded in the principle of nonidentity. If temporally different events in *parole*

$$x_p^1 - x_p^2 - x_p^3 \ldots$$

are acknowledged to be realizations of an *identical* sign, then this is possible only when each of these events is connected with the same series of rudimentary negations, in which the nonidentity of the figure that represents the event to consciousness is established together with all other elements of language. The transition from x_p^1, x_p^2, x_p^3, etc., to x_I, i.e., to an element of *langue*, is thus possible only if

$$x_p^1 \rightarrow a_1 \wedge - b_1 \wedge - c_1 \wedge \ldots,$$

$$x_p^2 \rightarrow a_1 \wedge - b_1 \wedge - c_1 \wedge \ldots,$$

etc., and this in such a manner that none of these series of negations may contain an element the other series do not contain.

We will soon see to what extent the inference from this scheme to a completed and deductively derived identification of signs is problematic. Even the scheme itself makes evident that the bare negativity of differentiation and lapse could never guarantee the consciousness of unity and of iterability with the same meaning of a linguistic type if there were not a principle of "memorization" or "recollection of the successive phonatory units" that works toward an opposite effect (*EC*, II, 39). This, thus, would be a principle that—similar to Kant's "synthesis of recognition"—in memory holds on to the past element and the place of its occurrence within the context of other elements. Saussure speaks of the *recolligibilité* of elements (*EC*, II, 38). *What* is held on to, to be sure, cannot be the element—or the configuration of elements (*Gestalt*)—itself (they are past), but only their placeholder: let's call it x', in conformity with Stetter's scheme. The distinguishing relation does not, as the code model overhastily presupposes, take place between the elements x and −x, but rather between the elements x and x′, between a past-recollected and a currently perceived element that now is interpreted *as* x.

You can see that Saussure's concept of linguistic value—as it was adopted *mutatis mutandis* by the structuralists—originally can by no means be understood as the idea of a timeless-synchronous structure of elements that endurably delimit each other by means of opposition like molecules in a crystal lattice. Just the opposite. Only over time—i.e., as nonpresent—can two values oppose one other (*EC*, II, 38). The concept of value does not exclude that of time, but rather includes it: an element can be delimited and semantically identified only by being followed—in time, outside of its presence—by another one that consciousness recognizes as *non*identical with the former element within the framework of a stream of consciousness that is continuous and which connects its phases on the basis of motivation. And that also applies for the memorized element itself: x′ is not by itself identical with x, by means of its sound configuration or acoustic nature, for example—precisely that would be the "naturalist fallacy"—but rather by virtue of a *creative interpretive operation.*

> This identity always includes an undefinable subjective element. The exact point at which identity exists is always difficult to determine. (*EC*, I, 243)

It is a matter of a hypothetical judgment for which no criteria other than hermeneutical ones are available. In other words, because *event* and *representative of the event* neither exist simultaneously nor are identifiable by means of their sound configuration, an *ampliative inference* is needed (see *Coll P*, VI, 31–32) that first founds the unity of signification (on the level of *langue*) by means of a speaker's consciousness that itself cannot be derived from the rules of *langue*, and which to this extent is transsemiological; and this inference occurs in such a way that it is permanently renounceable and unstable—like all nondeductive inferences.[16] Schleiermacher, who probably was the first to point to this type of ampliative inference in the schematism of the formation and understanding of signs, compared it to a work of art, "but it is not as if its execution would result in a work of art, but rather in such a way that this activity only has the *character* of art because the [grammatical] rules do not also provide their application, i.e., their application cannot be mechanized" (*HuK*, 81). "We call art," he explains, "even in the narrow sense of the word, any composite production in which we are cognizant of general rules whose application, for its part, cannot be reduced to rules."[17] This definition clearly stands in close proximity to Kant's definition of the reflecting (e.g., aesthetic) judgment that is always only looking for the concept that could determine it, but which it for structural reasons cannot find.

The analogy between the hypothetical judgment of meaning attribution (interpretation) and that of aesthetic judgment has often been emphasized since the time of romantic hermeneutics and has been taken as the occasion for extended observations. The semantic uninterpretability of works of art obviously demonstrates in extreme form a characteristic of all speech, including everyday language: its irreducibility to grammar and to the standard of the so-called normal use of words. I would say that poetry expresses this in a radical form, but in fact one can already show on the example of everyday speech that there is no exhaustive understanding, even if one summons up all possible rules and prescripts. For the number and order of oppositions that have to be kept apart from a sign or a textual unit are not a priori determined. Their number can be incalculably expanded by new possibilities of combination and by the hermeneutical imagination of the recipient ("Creative activity will be but a combinatory activity – the creation of new combinations"; *EC*, I, 386). As a consequence of this, the process of semantic identification – i.e., of interpretation – can never be completely executed. The detour by way of the system of differences, by virtue of which I can identify x' with x, leads into infinity. Interpretation therefore is always based on that which Sartre calls a "comprehensive hypothesis": "The truth of this restitution cannot be proven; its plausibility is not measurable" (*IF*, I, 56). Its validity has to be certified always anew in social praxis by means, for example, of the approval of other listeners or of other interpreters.

For this reason, what in Saussure is called *continuous transformation or alteration* of constituted significations is not a deficiency in linguistic theory but rather the prerequisite for the idealization necessary in every theory. If the identity of a sign or a sign chain is grounded in an interpretation – these are Saussure's own words: "Therefore there must be the first act of interpretation, which is active" (*CFS*, 15 [1957], 89; cf. 92, 100); "analogic creation appears as . . . a branch . . . of the general activity of interpretation, of the distinction of units" (*EC*, I, 379) – then interpretations of chains of signs or expressions can be *motivated*, but not, as Schleiermacher says, "mechanized." One hence has to abandon the illusion of a primordially given, self-identical meaning of a text and recognize that utterance (text) and interpretation are not two sides of a divisible labor – of production and reception – but rather that already the signs that are interwoven *in* the utterance (or *in* the text) exist, i.e., acquire the status of signs, only by virtue of an interpretation. It is not the interpretation that in a given instance misses the original meaning of the utterance; rather the utterance itself only has meaning *dià hypóthesin*, only presumably. (Precisely this is what Schleiermacher, and Sartre following him, called the "divinatory act," and sometimes rendered it as "guessing," sometimes as "conjecturing." "On devine en lisant, on crée," wrote Proust.[18]

Not only on the basis of Derrida, but already on that of Saussure, the model of a pragmatic-semantic-syntactic code, from which all elements could be unequivocally derived in methodical and controlled steps, proves untenable.

Todorov was one of the first, at the beginning of the 1970s, to question the systematic masterability of literary texts.[19] Julia Kristeva, the popularizer of Bakhtin's and Voloshinov's concept of *intertextuality*, had shown earlier that the limits of the individual text are blurred in the infinitely open continuum of all other texts. She could have referred to Schleiermacher to support this insight, for he declared interpretation to be an infinite task (*HuK*, 80–81, 94), and added: "No text can be completely understood except in connection with the entire range of ideas out of which it arose, and by means of the knowledge of all life relations both of the authors as well as of those for whom they write."[20] This obviously is an infinite task. Schleiermacher complicated it even further by denying that language (viewed as a system) has the character of finitude (i.e., of self-closure). "Language," he noted laconically, "is something infinite because every element is determinable in a particular way by the others" (*HuK*, 80). This sounds at first like an elliptically formulated allusion to the differential character of the "totality of language" (*HuK*, 78). To be sure, if "differential" were here to be conceived in the sense of the structuralist "opposition"–as a designation for a finite system of terms that are formed by way of an infinite number of oppositions–then one could scarcely comprehend how the infinitude of language is supposed to be explained by precisely this proof ("because"). We have to read more carefully: Schleiermacher does not say that every element is determinable in a determined way, but rather in a "particular" way ("determinable," not simply "determined"). This apparently means that the mode of determination is open and always particular, and thus different in every case. Schleiermacher also gives a less elliptical proof for his thesis of the infinitude of language: "because it is something infinitely past and infinitely future that we want to see in the moment of speech" (*HuK*, 99). This apparently means–and this is the direction indicated by the explanations Schleiermacher devotes to the second canon of *grammatical interpretation* (*HuK*, 116)–that if "the meaning of each word in a given passage (has to be determined) according to its connections with those that surround it," then the "totality of all [meaning-differentiating] exclusions," which "determined" the term in past "uses" and will "determine" it in the future, would have to be known. This reference to time cannot be left out "because language [first] comes into being through speech" (*HuK*, 78), and thus in the unidimensional extension of time in which alone signs can be differentiated from each other. The differentiation of a certain value for a term x (in the flow of speech) is accomplished by the formation of open sequences of oppositions; the *openness* of these sequences makes it structurally impossible to obtain a closed and closable concept of the "system of language."

Derrida coins the expression "text in general" (*P*, 44, 59)–following a line of very similar thoughts, although with reference to Hjelmslev's notion of the "infinite text," which, however, is meant in an entirely different way–in order to draw text-theoretical consequences from the irreducible nonsimultaneity of the signifying substance of a text. He would agree with Saussure and the aforementioned theoreticians, even with Schleiermacher, that the attribution of meaning is a definitively "undecidable" exercise.

"Undecidability" (*indécidabilité*) is actually a key concept in his thought. It not only means that a term, repeated at different times, cannot guarantee the identity of its signifying, but also that it at no time is semantically identifiable.

This last statement however, can be interpreted in different ways, as we have seen. First, it can mean that there is no signification of a term at all, since it lacks even the minimal precondition that would allow it to be characterized semantically (and even if only preliminarily and presumably); this conclusion is absurd, and it is refuted by our communicative experience. It nevertheless seems to me that Derrida has difficulty avoiding this conclusion. Another possible interpretation – that of Schleiermacher and Saussure – says that the attribution of meaning is an infinite exercise because the chain of oppositions, which have to be kept apart from a term (or an utterance) in order to guarantee its identity, is indeterminable for structural and individual reasons. For structural reasons, because no objectively effective law can prescribe how meaning "in the final analysis" can be articulated; for individual reasons, because, depending on the life experience, perspective, worldview, and linguistic competence of different speakers, differentiations of terms can be accomplished whose meaning would only be able to be controlled from a standpoint removed from communication. It is not only the case that there factually is no such standpoint; to demand such a standpoint would be self-contradictory, for words can have a meaning only *in* a communicative situation (and not outside it).

However, it does not follow from this relativizing of the conditions under which we can "make sense" that words or utterances have *no* meaning. What does follow from this is merely that meaning is not objectively (i.e., extracommunicatively) decidable. In other words, meaning has to prove itself over and over again in social praxis (and without a final judicial authority to which it might appeal). "To interpret" means nothing other than this. Something whose objective meaning (if there were such a meaning independent of communication) were known would not have to be interpreted. Only the fact that we can never *entirely* understand each other (i.e., objectify, "know," "recognize" each other) makes it possible that we understand each other. All understanding essentially (and not for reasons that one could reproachfully attribute to the fault or insufficiency of one's interlocutor) implies nonunderstanding. The "complete" understanding of a statement would imply its self-annihilation. This is how Whitehead has taught us to see it: over the course of a process of understanding that would leave nothing in the dark, each individual aspect of what is to be understood, as soon as it was touched on, would have to be part of "what is already clear." "It would thus only be a matter of repeating what is (already) known."[21] Only tautology would guarantee total reprieve from the effort of understanding, which always has an innovative aspect that transgresses our knowledge. Wilhelm von Humboldt and Schleiermacher had already held a comparable view. The former wrote: "Only in the individual does language attain its final distinctness. Nobody conceives in a given word exactly what his neighbor does, and the ever so slight variation skitters through the entire language like concentric ripples over the water. All understanding is simultaneously a noncomprehension, all agreement in ideas and emotions is at the same time a divergence."[22] And Schleiermacher underlines in his speeches for the academy in Berlin, *Ueber den Begriff der Hermeneutik*, that a consequence of the infinitude of interpretation is that "noncomprehension will never entirely be dissolved" (*HuK*, 328).

If understanding is essentially defective (and thus has to deal with undecidables), it still does not follow from this that in the totality of communication no meaning can be determined; nor does it follow from this that interpretations—because they remain without a final criterion—are arbitrary or cannot be assimilated (*nicht nachvollziehbar*). Interpretive hypotheses are always motivated or can be motivated, and if this were not the case they neither could claim validity nor could they prevail in communication (as they do from day to day). If the task of understanding, as Schleiermacher says, is not "mechanizable," then like any other reasonable hypothesis within the field of the so-called exact sciences, it must, on the one hand, be provable, and on the other, it must account for the facts. The interpreter will always make an effort to assimilate (*mitvollziehen*) the innovative act and make evident by which act—according to his divination (*HuK*, 169–70)—the text or the expression in the text (or in the conversation), or even only a certain individual word use in the expression, contrasts itself with a "state of language" by virtue of that "continual activity through which language decomposes the units that are given to it" (*EC*, I, 376). In the case of mere "talk about the weather" (*HuK*, 83), divination can perhaps be dispensed with (although psychoanalysis is of a different opinion: we only need to think about the dispute about Nietzsche's umbrella). But you will agree with me that an analysis, especially of literary texts—if it is not supposed to totally bore us or degenerate into a routine—will have to direct our attention especially to those critical points at which an innovative view of the world demands a creative assimilation on our part: without this, the new aspect—the change—would always be without a name or would disappear under the name of the old. Interpretation takes this new aspect seriously because it is what is proper to the individual; it meiotically accompanies its birth; it is essentially anticonservative. And it knows itself to be in solidarity with one of the profoundest impulses of Critical Theory, which is also a hermeneutics: with the salvation of the nonidentical, of that which deviates from the universal, in short: the salvation of the individual.

> The matters of true philosophical interest at this point in history are
> those in which Hegel, agreeing with tradition, expressed his disinterest.

They are nonconceptuality, individuality, and particularity—things which ever since Plato used to be dismissed as transitory and insignificant, and which Hegel labeled "lazy Existenz." Philosophy's theme would consist of the qualities it downgrades as contingent, as a *quantité négligeable*. A matter of urgency to the concept would be what it fails to cover, what its abstractionist mechanism eliminates, what is not already a case of the concept.[23]

Already *Minima Moralia* was an appeal to regard for "individual existence" (deeply moved by Auschwitz in particular, and by the leveling tendency of commodity-producing society in general), which, to be sure, can no longer be defended "immediately" and naively under the conditions of "damaged life," as it was in the Storm and Stress period, without entering into collusion with these false salvations of individuality. To be silent about individuality would simultaneously have meant common cause with those powers that are responsible for its death.

The dismissive gesture which Hegel, in contradiction to his own insight, constantly accords the individual, derives paradoxically enough from his necessary entanglement in liberalistic thinking. The conception of a totality harmonious through all its antagonisms compels him to assign to individuation, however much he may designate it a driving moment in the process, an inferior status in the construction of the whole. The knowledge that in pre-history the objective tendency asserts itself over the heads of human beings, indeed by virtue of annihilating individual qualities, without the reconciliation of general and particular—constructed in thought—ever yet being accomplished in history, is distorted in Hegel: with serene indifference he opts once again for liquidation of the particular. Nowhere in his work is the primacy of the whole doubted. The more questionable the transition from reflective isolation to glorified totality becomes in history as in Hegelian logic, the more eagerly philosophy, as the justification of what exists, attaches itself to the triumphal car of objective tendencies. The culmination of the social principle of individuation in the triumph of fatality gives philosophy occasion enough to do so. . . . In the period of his decay, the individual's experience of himself and what he encounters contributes once more to knowledge, which he had merely obscured as long as he continued unshaken to construe himself positively as the dominant category. In the face of the totalitarian unison with which the eradication of difference is proclaimed as a purpose in itself, even part of the social force of liberation may have temporarily withdrawn to the individual sphere. If critical theory lingers there, it is not only with a bad conscience.[24]

The same is true for hermeneutics, which seeks to save in the name of the individual whatever is nonconforming, whatever is nonidentical, and whatever, because it is different, is choked and maimed by the executants of power. This purpose inscribes hermeneutics with an ethics that obliges it to rescue the nonuniversal: hermeneutics works not for the leveling reduction of meaning but rather for its differentiation and multiplication; it does not seek to eradicate the singular and subjective (modern industrial society can do this much better), rather it strives for its retention in the memory of humanity. (Above all we need an *archaeology of individuality*.)[25]

No doubt there are hermeneutical schools that want to understand interpretation inversely as the overcoming of this nonidentity—as an approximation of the "ideal objectivity of meaning." These schools might even comprise the majority of those that have arisen in the short history of hermeneutics. But they do not bear the original impulse, the "germinal thought" of romantic hermeneutics. Interpretation does not entail, either for Schleiermacher, for Saussure, or for Sartre (to mention only these three, a minority whose work holds great significance for the future), an identifying of the original meaning of a word or the meaning intended by the author. If this were identifiable, then what sense would there be in declaring hermeneutics to be an "infinite task" and the divinatory formation of hypotheses to be insuperable? The concord in the descriptive realm (in the attestation to the phenomenon of semantic nonidentity) between Derrida, on the one hand, and Schleiermacher and his authentic successors on the other, does not, to be sure, extend into the premises of those theories on the basis of which this description is developed in each case. But philosophy is not only, or at least not essentially, concerned with the correctness of derivations. Rather, the struggle is one that has to do with the foundation of the premises themselves. In this respect Derrida remains an opponent even of that variety of hermeneutics that appeals to Schleiermacher, and in whose tradition recent linguistic research even places the work of Saussure. How must this conflict be theoretically decided? In favor of *différance*? Or in favor of "interpretation"?

Everything that I have said so far indicates in which direction I tend. A more detailed justification of my position would have to be the subject matter of a lecture series other than one whose task it is to inquire into the character of neostructuralism. In *Das individuelle Allgemeine* I hope to have presented reasons why I advise both hermeneutics as well as (neo)structuralism to reconsider the original approach of Friedrich Schleiermacher. I say "original" because the reception of Schleiermacher's hermeneutics reduced it to its psychological aspects, although he, as we know today, derived his germinal idea—namely, the thesis of the "infinity of language" and of the incalculability of the effects of meaning—more from the discovery of a structural deficiency inherent to "grammatical interpretation." Perhaps one should not even say that effective history has systematically misunderstood Schleiermacher. For after all, what would be the measuring stick for the reconstruction of a text in its "originality" now that we have expressed all these questions about the scientistic obsession of modern philosophy of language? Let's say instead that the cultural and historical a priori of the second half of the nineteenth century and the first half of the twentieth century did not allow for the discovery of certain traits in Schleiermacher's hermeneutics that we can bring into focus today. And we owe our ability to do this not so much to hermeneutical thinking itself, as to a theoretical impulse from abroad. Left on its own, I fear that hermeneutics would not have come to the point in the seventies of discovering its basic problem as that of "semantic undecidability." In the light of Derrida's pointed questions—which were meant to shake hermeneutics down to its foundations—it learned to see the insufficiencies of hermeneutical reflection better than its own tradition would otherwise have made possible. As a result of this self-questioning, precursors and contemporaries, who previously would not have been immediately counted as hermeneutical thinkers, came to light: I am thinking, for example, of Wilhelm von Humboldt, Charles Sanders Peirce, the critically edited Ferdinand de Saussure, and Jean-Paul Sartre. And we want to concede one more thing in conclusion: even if the overstating of his radicalism shakes the plausibility of Derrida's arguments and makes it difficult, indeed impossible, for us to follow him to his final conclusion, he still defined the field, and to a certain degree also the level, on which hermeneutics must take up the dialogue with him.

I hope to have presented strong arguments in *Das individuelle Allgemeine* to support the assertion that, in the final analysis, hermeneutics can stand up to the objections of neostructuralism. Hermeneutics can explain the descriptive realms of those states of affairs ascertained by neostructuralism just as well on the basis of its own premises as the latter can, and it avoids a series of aporias that neostructuralism cannot resolve with its own means. If that is reason enough, according to the traditional view, to favor one theory over another, then preference for the hermeneutical orientation would be justified. But that does not mean staying with hermeneutics *telle quelle* and not learning anything new. Hermeneutics should not, and could not, remain as it was when we first perceived neostructuralism's misgivings. Yet the persuasiveness of every theory grows according to its capacity to integrate the arguments of its opponents where they are irrefutable, indeed to appropriate them and to be able to justify them, on the basis of a revised self-understanding, better than the opponents themselves could. *One* meaning of dialectics implies precisely this: the resistance that comes from without has to be made into a resistance within, and it is in the resolution of this conflict that the theory upholds its claim to truth. That is not *parole vide* but, on the contrary, the acknowledgment of the voice of the Other to the extent that I make it into my own (not *reduce* it to my own, but make room for it *inside myself* as that which it is). The methodological pluralism that accepts neostructuralism, analytical philosophy, and hermeneutics as equally plausible articulations of contemporary thought practices the "eunuchlike neutrality" that Droysen ridiculed. In the final analysis, in subscribing to such an attitude one merely takes up a position of resignation and intellectual abdication. The work of conceptualization demands more from those who claim to engage in it than that they execute *their own* thoughts well; it also demands that one confront the thoughts of others in transindividual and, what is more, transcultural and transnational communication. This seems to me to be one thought that we can take over from classical metaphysics, namely, that philosophy in postmetaphysical times satisfies claims to universality, which earlier epochs believed they could ground by appealing to a transtemporal Reason, by means of a will to universal nonrestrictive communication. If West German hermeneutics (particularly that of the younger Frankfurt School) has for the most part failed to make good on the ethics of this imperative, to be sure not in the case of Anglo-Saxon philosophy, but certainly in that of contemporary French philosophy, then this does not mean that neostructuralism should, conversely, neglect hermeneutics.

With this introductory lecture series I hope to have demonstrated readiness on the side of hermeneutics to begin the dialogue with neostructuralism. One can only hope that this will more and more become one that is carried on reciprocally, and that the number of participants in the discussion will grow on all sides. Let me, in conclusion, address to you the request that you take up my appeal to whatever extent possible, always keeping in mind Sartre's caveat that opting for the noncommunicable means opting for the end of communication; and this is the source of all violence.[26]

Notes

Notes

Foreword

1. Frank is a philosopher and German literary scholar whose main areas of interest are German idealism, particularly Schelling, the hermeneutic tradition of the nineteenth century, particularly Schleiermacher (see Schleiermacher, *Hermeneutik und Kritik. Mit einem Anhang sprach-philosophischer Texte Schleiermachers*, herausgegeben und eingeleitet von M. Frank [Frankfurt: Suhrkamp, 1977], and Frank, *Das individuelle Allgemeine: Textstrukturierung und -interpretation nach Schleiermacher* [Frankfurt: Suhrkamp, 1977]), German romanticism (*Das Problem 'Zeit' in der deutschen Romantik* [Munich: Winkler, 1972]), and contemporary French theory (*Das Sagbare und das Unsagbare: Studien zur neuesten französischen Hermeneutik und Texttheorie* [Frankfurt: Suhrkamp, 1980], in addition to *What Is Neostructuralism?*). He has written on topics as diverse as the theory of text and interpretation (*Das individuelle Allgemeine*, and Frank, "Textauslegung," in D. Harth and B. Gebhardt, *Erkenntnis der Literatur* [Stuttgart: Metzler, 1982]), mythology (*Der kommende Gott: Vorlesungen über die neue Mythologie* [Frankfurt: Suhrkamp, 1982]), and individuality (*Die Unhintergehbarkeit von Individualität* [Frankfurt: Suhrkamp, 1986]).

2. The term "antirationalism" is meant to sum up the problematic unity of the French movement. "Antirationalism" describes its common, though by no means united, front against one form of rationalism or other. Whether the theories are also "irrational," a derogatory term denouncing the *absence* of rationality from a "body" of thought, is an open question that should not be prejudged by the label of a movement. Rationalists typically think they are exploring a field that possesses or admits of conceptual order and present their theories discursively, perhaps systematically, whereas antirationalists treat those orders as nonexistent or try to invalidate them.

3. "Basic reality" is here used with a minimum of metaphysical implications. It should not be understood as implying that "reality" exists independently from the discourse in which it is presented, nor that its being basic is the ground or the foundation of other kinds of reality. "Reality" is meant as a topical, not as a metaphysical, term. It designates types of topics or fields authors deal with or present.

453

454 □ NOTES TO PAGES xix-xxvii

4. Tugendhat is one of the rare philosophers to have published extensively on the philosophical tradition (*Ti Kata Tinos: Eine Untersuchung zu Struktur und Ursprung aristotelischer Grundbegriffe* [Freiburg: Alber, 1958]), contemporary Continental philosophy (*Der Wahrheitsbegriff bei Husserl und Heidegger* [Berlin: de Gruyter, 1970], and analytic philosophy (*Traditional and Analytic Philosophy: Lectures on the Philosophy of Language* [Cambridge: Cambridge University Press, 1982] and *Self-Consciousness and Self-Determination* [Cambridge, Mass.: MIT Press, 1986]). Tugendhat's conception of rationality is developed in and evolves through *Traditional and Analytic Philosophy* (theoretical reason), and *Self-Consciousness and Self-Determination* (subjectivity), to *Probleme der Ethik* (Stuttgart: Reclam, 1984) (ethics).

5. Derrida's initial remarks are found in "Signature, Event, Context," reprinted in Derrida, *Margins of Philosophy* (Chicago: University of Chicago Press, 1982). Searle attacks in "Reiterating the Differences: A Reply to Derrida," *Glyph 1* (Baltimore: Johns Hopkins University Press, 1977), pp. 198-208. Derrida replies in "Limited Inc abc . . .;" *Glyph 1*. Compare also Frank, "Zur Entropie der Sprache," in Frank, *Das Sagbare und das Unsagbare*, and Lecture 25 in this book. Many comparisons of analytic philosophy and antirationalism, for instance, by Richard Rorty ("Philosophy as a Kind of Writing: An Essay on Derrida," in Rorty, *Consequences of Pragmatism* (Minneapolis: University of Minnesota Press, 1982), or Henry Staten (*Wittgenstein and Derrida* [Lincoln: University of Nebraska Press, 1984]), are either presentational or stress similarities. The philosophical interest lies in critical confrontation, exhibited, for example, by the French analytic philosopher Jacques Bouveresse. He offers provocative discussions of antirationalism in *Le Philosophe chez les autophages* (Paris: Minuit, 1984) and *Rationalité et cynisme* (Paris: Minuit, 1984).

6. J.-F. Lyotard has triggered the controversy through remarks in *The Postmodern Condition: A Report on Knowledge* (Minneapolis: University of Minnesota Press, 1984). Habermas attacks antirationalism broadly in *The Philosophical Discourse of Modernity* (Cambridge, Mass.: MIT Press, 1987). Rorty, "Habermas and Lyotard on Post-Modernism," in *Praxis International* 4 (1984), pp. 32-44 summarizes the initial controversy. Another topic of the debate has been Foucault's theory of power. See in particular Axel Honneth, *Kritik der Macht* (Frankfurt: Suhrkamp, 1985), and Habermas, *Philosophical Discourse*, chapters 9 and 10. To my knowledge this is the most extended debate between a contemporary rationalism—the Frankfurt School—and contemporary antirationalism.

7. T. W. Adorno and M. Horkheimer, *Dialectic of Enlightenment* (New York: Continuum, 1982). The full title of the German edition from 1944 is *Dialektik der Aufklärung: Philosophische Fragmente* (Amsterdam: Querido, 1944).

8. J. Habermas, *Theorie des kommunikativen Handelns*, 2 vols. (Frankfurt: Suhrkamp, 1981, 1985). One of the two volumes has appeared in translation: *The Theory of Communicative Action*, vol. 1 (Boston: Beacon Press, 1984).

9. Niklas Luhmann is a sociologist and a social philosopher. In Luhmann, *Soziale Systeme: Grundriss einer allgemeinen Theorie* (Frankfurt: Suhrkamp, 1984), he gives a general account of his theory. The translations united in Luhmann, *The Differentiation of Society* (New York: Columbia University Press, 1982), offer a good introduction to his ideas. Several more specialized works are available in translation, among them *Love as Passion: The Codification of Intimacy* (Cambridge, Mass.: Harvard University Press, 1986).

10. Of course, Heidegger's attitude toward hermeneutics has changed in his later writings.

11. My summary is based upon Gadamer, *Truth and Method* (New York: Continuum, 1975). J. C. Weinsheimer, *Gadamer's Hermeneutics: A Reading of Truth and Method* (New Haven, Conn.: Yale University Press, 1985), gives a very helpful presentation of Gadamer's hermeneutics.

12. This is the point where Gadamer clearly sketches a concept of reason. For an exposition of his policy of interpretation, see also his contribution to the debate between French and German philosophers documented in Ph. Forget (ed.), *Text und Interpretation* (Munich: Fink, 1984). I will refer to the debate later. See also notes 25, 29, and 30.

13. It is difficult to choose a sample from Ricoeur's abundant writings. I have found *Freud and Philosophy: An Essay on Interpretation* (New Haven, Conn.: Yale University Press, 1970) and *The Rule of Metaphor* (Toronto: University of Toronto Press, 1977) to be the most valuable expositions of his hermeneutics. The reader may also want to consult Ricoeur, *Interpretation Theory: Discourse and the Surplus of Meaning* (Fort Worth: Texas Christian University Press, 1976), and Ricoeur, *Essais d'hermeneutique* (Paris: Seuil, 1986).

14. See note 1. The two books most relevant for the present context are Frank, *Das individuelle Allgemeine* and Frank, *Die Unhintergehbarkeit von Individualität* .

15. *Das individuelle Allgemeine*; see the chapter "The Unity of Meaning and the Schematism of Language," pp. 185ff.

16. J.-P. Sartre, *L'Idiot de la famille*, 5 vols. (Paris: Gallimard, 1971). Two volumes have appeared in English translation: *The Family Idiot: Gustave Flaubert*, 2 vols. (Chicago: University of Chicago Press, 1981, 1987). Frank has used Sartre's theory in *Das individuelle Allgemeine* in the chapter on the conflict between structuralism and interpretation, pp. 247ff. He also gives a general presentation of *The Family Idiot* in "Archäologie des Individuums: Zur Hermeneutik von Sartres *Flaubert*," printed in *Das Sagbare und das Unsagbare*. See also Lecture 23 in this book.

17. Particularly emphasized in "Archäologie des Individuums. Zur Hermeneutik von Sartres *Flaubert*."

18. For some differences between Deleuze and Derrida see Lectures 23–25; Lyotard and Foucault: Lecture 9; Foucault and Derrida: Lecture 9.

19. *Die Unhintergehbarkeit von Individualität*. See also Frank's previous thought on this topic in *Das individuelle Allgemeine*, pp. 87–121, and the summary in Lecture 23 of this book. Frank's ideas on individuality are indebted to Sartre and to Henrich.

20. Dieter Henrich is perhaps best known as an interpreter of Kant (Henrich, *Identität und Objektivität: Eine Untersuchung über Kants transzendentale Deduktion* [Heidelberg: Winter, 1978]) and Hegel (Henrich, *Hegel im Kontext* [Frankfurt: Suhrkamp, 1971]). For his ideas on subjectivity see *Fichtes ursprüngliche Einsicht* (Frankfurt: Klostermann, 1967), *Selbstverhältnisse* (Stuttgart: Reclam, 1981), *Fluchtlinien: Philosophische Essays* (Frankfurt: Suhrkamp, 1982).

21. See Henrich, *Fichtes ursprüngliche Einsicht*.

22. Frank, *Die Unhintergehbarkeit von Individualität*, pp. 15, 16. See also Lecture 23 in this book. Further elucidation is implicitly given in the passages on Lacan in Lectures 18 and 19.

23. *Die Unhintergehbarkeit von Individualität*, p. 120. See also *Das individuelle Allgemeine*.

24. My critical remarks are directed against hermeneutics only in its present state and as a theory of rationality. They are not meant to discredit the theory of interpretation or the philosophical anthropology (symbolic man) it puts forward.

25. On the Continental scene, J. Greisch, *Hermeneutique et grammatologie* (Paris: Editions du Centre national de la recherche scientifique, 1977), and Frank, *Das individuelle Allgemeine*, are early examples. I mentioned in note 12 that a debate between French and German philosophers about hermeneutics is documented in Forget, *Text und Interpretation*. The volume contains contributions by Gadamer and Derrida. J.-L. Nancy, *Le Partage des voix* (Paris: Galilée, 1982), summarizes deconstructionist views on hermeneutics.

26. Frank has written extensively on the problem throughout his publications. In what follows I draw on his ideas, also as they are expressed in *Das individuelle Allgemeine* and the Appendix to *Was ist Neostrukturalismus?* not contained in the present translation.

27. Derrida, for instance, in his "Purveyor of Truth," reprinted in Derrida, *The Postcard: From Socrates to Freud and Beyond* (Chicago: University of Chicago Press, 1987), pp. 413-96 has relied on the second strategy to discredit Lacan's interpretation of Poe's *The Purloined Letter*.

28. See Lectures 5, 26, and 27 in this book and the untranslated appendix to *Was ist Neostrukturalismus?*

29. Gadamer, "Text und Interpretation," in Forget, *Text und Interpretation*, p. 24.

30. Derrida, "Guter Wille zur Macht I und II," in Forget, *Text und Interpretation*, p. 56.

31. It seems to me that this situation has often prevailed, for instance, in Derrida's debate with Husserl and Saussure, but also in Habermas's discussion of antirationalism. The pattern of the problem is this: A gives an argument to refute B. The conclusion of A's argument attacks B's position. But A's argument against B is based on premises P, not shared by B. Neither of the participants argues for his or against the opponent's premises. Often they are not even mentioned.

32. Antirationalism since Nietzsche has rejected this distinction. It still seems useful to me.

Lecture 1

1. Ferdinand de Saussure, *Cahiers Ferdinand de Saussure*, 15 (1957), p. 72; henceforth cited as *CFS*.

2. TN: The phrase "spiritual situation of the age" refers to Karl Jaspers *Die geistige Situation der Zeit* (Berlin: De Gruyter, 1931); Jürgen Habermas alludes to this title in the collection of essays he edited, *Stichworte zur geistigen Situation der Zeit*, 2 vols. (Frankfurt: Suhrkamp, 1979), selected essays of which have appeared under the title *Observations on the Spiritual Situation of the Age*, trans. Andrew Buckwalter (Cambridge, Mass.: MIT Press, 1984).

3. Pierre Leroux, "Du Cours de Philosophie de Schelling: Aperçu de la situation de la Philosophie en Allemagne," *La Revue indépendante*, 3 (1842), p. 348.

4. Hegel, *The Philosophy of Right*, trans. T. M. Knox (Oxford: Clarendon Press, 1942), pp. 12–13.

5. Hegel, *Science of Logic*, trans. W. H. Johnston and L. G. Struthers, 2 vols. (New York: Macmillan, 1929), II, p. 15; henceforth cited as *Logic*.

6. Schelling, *System of Transcendental Idealism*, trans. Peter Heath (Charlottesville: University of Virginia Press, 1978), p. 232.

7. Nietzsche, *The Joyful Wisdom, The Complete Works of Friedrich Nietzsche*, ed. Oscar Levy, trans. Thomas Common (New York: Macmillan, 1910), X, pp. 167–68. Further references to this edition will be cited as Nietzsche, *Works*, with volume and page number.

8. Nietzsche, *Werke in drei Bänden*, ed. Karl Schlechta (Munich: Hanser, 1966), III, p. 424. Further references to this edition will be cited as Nietzsche, *Werke*, with volume and page number.

9. Georg Wilhelm Friedrich Hegel, *Theorie-Werkausgabe*, ed. Karl. M. Michel and Eva Moldenhauer (Frankfurt: Suhrkamp, 1968ff.), II, p. 432.

10. Cited by Hegel, *Theorie-Werkausgabe*, II, p. 432.

11. Jean-François Lyotard, *The Postmodern Condition: A Report on Knowledge*, trans. Geoff Bennington and Brian Massumi (Minneapolis: University of Minnesota Press, 1984); henceforth cited as *PC*.

Lecture 2

1. Hermann Rauschning, *Die Revolution des Nihilismus* (Zurich: Europa Verlag, 1938); a second edition was brought out by Golo Mann in 1964; TN: Rauschning's book appeared in English under the title *The Revolution of Nihilism* (New York: Alliance, 1939).

2. Ferdinand de Saussure, *Cours de linguistique générale*, Edition critique, ed. Rudolf Engler, 2. vols., (Wiesbaden: Harrassowitz, 1967–74); henceforth cited as *EC* with reference to volume and page number.

3. Ferdinand de Saussure, *Cours de linguistique générale*, published by Charles Bally and Albert Sechehaye, with the collaboration of Albert Riedlinger: Edition critique prepared by Tullio de Mauro, 2nd ed. (Paris: Payot, 1980), pp. 24, 43, 106ff., 115, 157, 182, *passim*. English translations in text are taken from *Course in General Linguistics*, trans. Wade Baskin (New York: McGraw-Hill, 1966),

e.g., pp. 9, 73; henceforth cited as *CGL*. [The translation uses the term "system," not the phrase "a language system."]

4. Cf. Claude Lévi-Strauss, *Anthropologie structurale* (Paris: Plon, 1958), p. 254; published in English as *Structural Anthropology*, trans. Claire Jacobson and Brook Grundfest Schoepf (New York: Doubleday, 1967); henceforth cited as *SA*.

5. Hegel, *Phenomenology of Mind*, trans. J. B. Baillie, 2 vols. (London: Swan Sonnenschein, 1910), pp. 124ff.; see esp. p. 143: "The supersensible world is in this way a quiescent 'kingdom of laws,' no doubt beyond the world of perception—for this exhibits the law only through incessant change—but likewise present in it, and its direct immovable copy or image."

6. Richard Brütting has demonstrated this through the example of the displacement in meaning of the term *texte*, *"Texte" und "écriture" in der französischen Literaturwissenschaft nach dem Strukturalismus* (Bonn: Bouvier, 1976).

7. Derrida, *Positions* (Paris: Minuit, 1972), p. 82. Quotations in the text are taken from *Positions*, trans. Alan Bass (Chicago: University of Chicago Press, 1981); henceforth cited as *P*.

8. I will henceforth quote from the vulgate version of this compilation of lectures using the abbreviation *Cours*, as well as from Tullio de Mauro's "Edition critique," 2nd ed. (Paris: Payot, 1980). Except for de Mauro's introduction and his superb comments, this edition is a reprint of Bally, Sechehaye, and Riedlinger's edition of 1915. [TN: English translations in text are taken from *Course in General Linguistics* (*CGL*).]

9. Derrida, "Limited Inc abc . . . ," supplement to *Glyph 2* (Baltimore: Johns Hopkins University Press, 1977), pp. 162–254; henceforth cited as *LI*.

10. Derrida, *Marges de la philosophie* (Paris: Minuit, 1972), p. 378. Published in English as *Margins of Philosophy*, trans. Alan Bass (Chicago: University of Chicago Press, 1982); henceforth cited as *Margins*. See also *LI*, p. 24.

11. In general the authors of so-called structuralism have concerned themselves astonishingly little with the situation of the manuscripts of the *Cours*. Lévi-Strauss becomes aware of it in 1960 and replaces Saussure's name with the phrase "the editors of the *Course in General Linguistics*" ("the recent documents of which show how the editors of the *Cours* were able to force and schematize the thought of their master"); *Anthropologie structurale deux* (Paris: Plon, 1973), p. 26. On the present situation of the manuscript of the *Cours* see René Amacker, *Linguistique saussurienne* (Geneva: Droz, 1975), and also Ludwig Jäger, "F. de Saussures historisch-hermeneutische Idee der Sprache: Ein Plädoyer für die Rekonstruktion des Saussureschen Denkens in seiner authentischen Gestalt," *Linguistik und Didaktik*, 27 (1976), pp. 210–44.

12. L. Hjelmslev, *Essais linguistiques* (Copenhagen: Nordisk Sprog og Kulturforlag, 1959), p. 21.

13. Jean Piaget, *Structuralism*, trans. Chaniak Mischler (New York: Harper & Row, 1970), p. 14.

Lecture 3

1. "Linguistics occupies a special place among the social sciences, to whose ranks it unquestionably belongs" (*SA*, 29).

2. See Troubetzkoy, "La Phonologie actuelle," *Psychologie du langage* (Paris, 1933), p. 243, to which Lévi-Strauss refers in the following quotation.

3. *Immanuel Kant's Critique of Pure Reason*, trans. Norman Kemp Smith (New York: Humanities Press, 1950), A 140, B 179–80, p. 182.

4. Lévi-Strauss, *The Savage Mind* (London: Weidenfeld and Nicholson, 1966), p. 130.

5. Heidegger, *Being and Time*, trans. John Macquarie and Edward Robinson (New York: Harper & Row, 1962), p. 121; henceforth cited as *BT*.

6. Lévi-Strauss, *Mythologiques* (Paris: Plon, 1964), 4 vols.

7. Benveniste, *Problèmes de linguistique générale* (Paris: Gallimard, 1966), pp. 122ff.

8. Barthes, "Introduction à l'analyse structurale des récits," *Communications*, 8 (1966), pp. 1–27.

9. Ibid., p. 3; emphasis added.

10. See also Derrida, "Semiology and Grammatology," *P*, p. 15.

11. The term "autochthony" denotes a Being-outside-itself of the human being, a Being-an-outgrowth of the earth principle (or of Mother Earth). The limping gait reminds the human being of this "vestige of earth, painful to bear"; that is, it reminds the human being that he/she belongs to living creatures, i.e., is himself/herself admitted into the economy of nature. He/she is an "unhappy animal."

Lecture 4

1. Claude Lévi-Strauss, *The Raw and the Cooked*, vol. 1 of *Introduction to a Science of Mythology*, trans. John and Doreen Weightman (New York: Harper & Row, 1970), p. 5; henceforth cited as *SM 1*.

2. Friedrich Wilhelm Joseph Schelling, *Sämtliche Schriften*, ed. K. F. A. Schelling (Stuttgart and Augsburg: Cotta, 1856–61), part II, vol. 2, pp. 625ff; henceforth cited as *SW* (e.g., *SW* II/2, pp. 625ff.).

3. Ricoeur, "Symbole et temporalité," *Archivio di filosofia*, I–II (1963), p. 24; see also pp. 9–10.

4. Derrida, *Writing and Difference*, trans. Alan Bass (Chicago: University of Chicago Press, 1978), p. 278; henceforth cited as *WD*.

5. *The Naked Man*, vol. 4 of *Introduction to a Science of Mythology*, trans. John and Doreen Weightman (New York: Harper & Row, 1981), p. 625; henceforth cited as *SM 4*.

6. Foucault, *Les Mots et les choses: Une Archéologie des sciences humaines* (Paris: Gallimard, 1966); published in English as *The Order of Things: An Archaeology of the Human Sciences* (New York: Random House [Vintage Books], 1970), p. 387. Henceforth cited as *OT*. Where necessary, the French text is cited (*MC*).

7. Schleiermacher, *Hermeneutik und Kritik*, ed. Manfred Frank (Frankfurt: Suhrkamp, 1977), p. 184; hencefort cited as *HuK*.

8. Geimas, *Sémantique structurale* (Paris: Larousse, 1966), p. 53.

9. Fichte, *Nachgelassene Schriften*, ed. Hans Jacob (Berlin: Junker and Dünnhaupt, 1937), II, p. 368.

10. Ibid.

11. See Fichte, *Sämtliche Werke*, ed. I. H. Fichte (Berlin: Veit, 1845–46), I, p. 522: "You can undoubtedly think thinking: I; and while you are thinking this you innerly find your consciousness to be determined in a certain way; you *only* think something, precisely that which you grasp with that concept of I, and you are conscious of doing this; and you do not think something else which otherwise you could very well think and probably even have thought." This edition is henceforth cited as *FW*, with volume and page numbers.

12. Barthes, *S/Z*, trans. Richard Miller (New York: Hill and Wang, 1974), p. 5. The passage continues as follows: "Let us first posit the image of a triumphant plural, unimpoverished by any constraint of representation (of imitation). In this ideal text, the networks are many and interact, without any one of them being able to surpass the rest; this text is a galaxy of signifiers, not a structure of signifieds."

13. Lévi-Strauss, "Introduction à l'oeuvre de Marcel Mauss," Marcel Mauss, *Sociologie et anthropologie* (Paris: PUF, 1966), pp. ix-lii, here p. l.

14. Lacan, *Écrits: A Selection*, trans. Alan Sheridan (New York: Norton, 1977), pp. 153–54; henceforth cited as *E*. Where necessary, the French text is cited: *Écrits* (Paris: Seuil, 1966), here referred to as *E* (Fr. ed.).

Lecture 5

1. Derrida, *De la grammatologie* (Paris: Seuil, 1967); *Of Grammatology*, trans. Gayatri Spivak (Baltimore: Johns Hopkins University Press, 1976). Henceforth referred to as *GR*.

2. "It is on the basis of the formalist and differential motif present in Saussure's *Cours* that the psychologism, phonologism and exclusion of writing that are no less present in it can be criticized" (*P*, 36).

3. To avoid overburdening myself at this point I refer the reader to Ludwig Jäger's essay "Linearität und Zeichensynthesis: Saussures Entfaltung des semiologischen Form-Substanz-Problems in der Tradition Hegels und Humboldts," *Fugen: Deutsch-Französisches Jahrbuch für Text-Analytik* (Olten: Walter, 1980), pp. 187–205; see also his "Zeichen und Verstehen: Der Saussuresche Begriff des Aposèmes als Grundlagenbegriff einer hermeneutischen Semiologie" (unpublished manuscript).

4. John R. Searle, "Reiterating the Differences: A Reply to Derrida," *Glyph*, 2 (1977), p. 207.

5. "The case of the concept of *structure*, that you also bring up, is certainly more ambiguous. Everything depends upon how one sets it to work" (*P*, 24).

6. Samuel Weber, "Closure and Exclusion," *Diacritics*, 10 (1980), pp. 35–46, see esp. 37–39.

7. Hegel, *Theorie-Werkausgabe*, IX, p. 48.

8. Luhmann, *Legitimation durch Verfahren* (Neuwied: Luchterhand, 1969).

9. I developed this idea in a more argumentative fashion in my paper "Deux siècles de critique de la rationalité: Le Défi de la philosophie actuelle," *Audia philosophica*, 42 (1983).

10. "To the extent that science is differential, its pragmatics provides the antimodel of a stable system. A statement is deemed worth retaining the moment it marks a difference from what is already known, and after an argument and proof in support of it has been found. Science is a model of an 'open system,' in which a statement becomes relevant if it 'generates ideas,' that is, if it generates other statements and other game rules. Science possesses no general metalanguage in which all other languages can be transcribed and evaluated. This is what prevents its identification with the system and, all things considered, with terror. If the division between decision makers and executors exists in the scientific community (and it does), it is a fact of the socioeconomic system and not of the pragmatics of science itself. It is in fact one of the major obstacles to the imaginative development of knowledge" (*PC*, 64).

Lecture 6

1. Gadamer, *Truth and Method* (New York: Crossroad, 1975), p. 269; henceforth cited as *TM*.

2. Gadamer, "On the Problem of Self-Understanding," *Philosophical Hermeneutics*, trans. and ed. David Linge (Berkeley: University of California Press, 1976), p. 55; compare also the decisive formulation from the *Kleine Schriften* (Tübingen: Mohr, 1967), I, p. 127: "Effective-historical consciousness is in an unsuspendable manner more Being than consciousness."

3. See Fichte, *FW*, II, p. 19 and XI, p. 18.

4. Fichte, *FW*, II, p. 62.

5. Schleiermacher, *The Christian Faith*, trans. H. R. Mackintosh and J. S. Stewart (Edinburgh: T. and T. Clark, 1928), p. 8; emphasis added.

6. Schleiermacher, *The Christian Faith*, p. 17. [TN: We have altered the translation slightly.]

7. Schleiermacher, *Dialektik, Sämtliche Werke*, ed. L. Jonas (Berlin: G. Reimer, 1839), section III, part IV/2, pp. 429 (emphasis added) and 430, respectively.

8. We recall that the term "structure" was introduced into philosophy in its specifically modern meaning by Schleiermacher.

9. Foucault, *L'Archéologie du savoir* (Paris: Gallimard, 1969); published in English as *The Archaeology of Knowledge*, trans. A. M. Sheridan Smith (New York: Pantheon, 1971), p. 113. Henceforth cited as *AK*. Where necessary the French text is cited (*AdS*).

10. Althusser and Balibar, *Reading Capital*, trans. Ben Brewster (New York: Pantheon, 1970), p. 25; henceforth cited as *RC*.

11. Foucault uses the drastic formulation "the already 'encoded' eye"; *OT*, xxi.

12. Saussure, "Introduction, *Cours de linguistique générale* [1908-9]," *CFS*, 15 (1957), pp. 1-103, here p. 82.

13. Saussure, *CFS*, 15 (1957), p. 89. My emphasis, M.F.

14. Lacan, *Écrits*; see also p. 304: "the subjection of the subject to the signifier."

15. The French translators characteristically render *reluzent* as *réflectivement*: "de s'interpréter lui-même 'réflectivement' à partir de ce monde"; *L'Etre et le temps*, trans. Rudolf Boehm and Alphonse de Waklhans (Paris: Gallimard, 1964), p. 37.

16. Gerd Lingrün, "Strukturale Linguistik," *Grundzüge der Literatur- und Sprachwissenschaft*, ed. Heinz Ludwig Arnold and Volker Sinemus (Munich: dtv, 1974), II, p. 151.

Lecture 7

1. Foucault, *Die Ordnung der Dinge* (Frankfurt: Suhrkamp, 1971), pp. 15-16; cf. also the "Foreword to the English edition," *OT*, xiv.

2. Sartre, "Jean Paul Sartre répond," *L'Arc*, 30 (1966), p. 87.

3. This is the case despite the fact that one repeatedly comes across formulations that seem to favor such a teleological interpretation, for example, when he talks about *the* reason of the West, which develops in stages ("Western reason is entering the age of judgment"; *OT*, 61).

4. Jean Piaget was correct in comparing the method of describing succeeding *epistemes* genealogically with the theory of paradigm change developed by Thomas S. Kuhn in *The Structure of Scientific Revolutions* (Chicago: University of Chicago Press, 1962); *Structuralism*, trans. Charniak Mischler (New York: Harper & Row, 1970). Piaget also compares Foucault's procedure, although negatively, with the premodern evolutionary-biological model, stating: "His *epistemes* follow upon, but not from, one another, whether formally or dialectically. One *episteme* is not affiliated with another, either genetically or historically. The message of this 'archaeology' of reason is, in short, that reason's self-transformations have no reason and that its structures appear and disappear by fortuitous mutations and as a result of momentary upsurges. The history of reason is, in other words, much like the history of species as biologists conceived of it before cybernetic structuralism came on the scene" (p. 134).

5. "History shows that everything that has been thought will be thought again by a thought that does not yet exist" (*OT*, 372).

6. Piaget uncovered this *petitio principii* in *Structuralism*.

7. In the following I consciously use the term "Enlightenment," although Foucault spans a much larger epoch with the phrase *âge classique*. In reality, however, the guiding concept of *représentation*, as apt as it might be for the illumination of Enlightenment's particular characteristics, seems largely inappropriate as a means for conceptually unifying classical French literature from Pascal to Corneille, not to mention the moralists. Karlheinz Stierle has justifiably objected, in his paper "Die negative Anthropologie der französischen Klassik" (to appear in the documents of the last Romanistentag), that in Foucault's conception the subject is seen as something unfathomable that never completely makes itself available to representation.

Lecture 8

1. Johann Martin Chladen, *Einleitung zur richtigen Auslegung vernünfftiger Reden und Schriften* (Leipzig: Lanckisch, 1742), section 155.

2. Chladen, sections 308ff.

3. Foucault, "Préface," Arnauld and Lancelot, *Grammaire générale et raisonnée* (Paris: Republications Paulet, 1969), pp. iii-iv.

4. *Logigue de Port-Royal*, I, chapter IV, quoted by Foucault, *OT*, pp. 63–64.

5. *Qu'est-ce que le structuralisme?*, ed. François Wahl (Paris: Seuil, 1968), pp. 300ff.

6. Novalis, *Schriften*, ed P. Kluckhohn and R. Samuel (Stuttgart: Kohlhammer, 1960ff.), II, p. 110.

7. Hendrik Birus, "Zwischen den Zeiten: Friedrich Schleiermacher als Klassiker der neuzeitlichen Hermeneutik," *Hermeneutische Positionen*: *Schleiermacher, Dilthey, Heidegger, Gadamer*, ed. Hendrik Birus (Göttingen: Vandenhoeck & Ruprecht, 1982), p. 28.

8. Birus, "Zwischen den Zeiten," p. 28.

9. Cited by Birus, p. 28.

10. See Fichte, *FW*, I, pp. 201 and 538.

11. Another formulation that also interprets double representation as relationship with itself is "duplication of representation in relation to itself" (*OT*, p. 237).

12. This compatibility with the model of self-consciousness that is reflected in itself (for example, in Sartre) can already be gathered from Foucault's terminology. He speaks of the fact that the self-representation of the sign in itself to itself is always "perpendicular" ("la représentation est toujours perpendiculaire à elle-même"). This corresponds to Sartre's "transversality" of self-consciousness that is nonthematically inscribed in each consciousness *of* something. The horizontal consciousness *of* something, because it thematizes this other, is at the same time perpendicularly crossed by an implicit familiarity with this act of thematizing itself: "conscience non-positionelle (de) soi *de* quelque chose d'autre."

13. What became problematical was thus "the relation of representation to that which is posited in it. . . . Representation has lost the power to provide a foundation—with its own being, . . . for the links that can join its various elements together" (*OT*, 238–39).

14. Herder, *Sämtliche Werke*, ed. Bernhard Suphan (Berlin: Weidmann, 1877ff.), XVIII, p. 485.

15. Nietzsche, "On Truth and Falsity in Their Ultramoral Sense," *Works*, II, pp. 171–92.

16. Nietzsche, *Works*, II, p. 180.

17. "The analytic disciplines are found to be epistemologically distinct from those that are bound to make use of synthesis. . . . The ground-plan of that profound event . . . detached the possibility of synthesis from the space of representation" (*OT*, 246).

Lecture 9

1. "What Classical thought reveals is the power of discourse. In other words, language in so far as it represents—language that names, patterns, combines, and connects and disconnects things as it makes them visible in the transparency of words" (*OT*, 310–11).

2. Birus, "Zwischen den Zeiten," p. 28 (see note 7, Lecture 8).

3. Birus, "Zwischen den Zeiten," p. 29.

4. Birus, "Zwischen den Zeiten," p. 49. Cf. Martin Heidegger, "The Age of the World View," *Boundary 2*, 4 (1976), p. 352.

5. I supplied further evidence for this thesis in "Ein Grundelement der historischen Analyse: Die Diskontinuität: Die Epochenwende von 1775 in Foucaults 'Archäologie,'" *Poetik und Hermeneutik XII*: *Epochenschwelle und Epochenbewusstsein*, ed. R. Herzog and R. Koselleck (Munich: Fink/Schöningh, 1984).

6. Karl Marx, *Capital: A Critique of Political Economy*, trans. Samuel Moore and Edward Aveling, ed. Friedrich Engels (Chicago: Charles H. Kerr, 1912), I, p. 186; cf. *Grundrisse: Foundations of the Critique of Political Economy*, trans. Martin Nicolaus (London: Allen Lane, 1973): "the *general possibility* of wealth as subject and as activity" (p. 296).

7. Marx, *Grundrisse*, p. 146.

8. "Life withdraws into the enigma of a force inaccessible in its essence, apprehendable only in the efforts it makes here and there to manifest and maintain itself" (*OT*, 273).

9. "Bopp's analyses were to be of major importance . . . in defining what language may be in

its essence. It is no longer a system of representations which has the power to pattern and recompose other representations; it designates in its roots the most constant of actions, states, and wishes; . . . Language is 'rooted' not in the things perceived, but in the active subject. And perhaps, in that case, it is a product of will and energy, rather than of the memory that duplicates representation. We speak because we act, and not because recognition is a means of cognition. Like action, language expresses a profound will to something. . . . Language is no longer linked to the knowing of things, but to men's freedom" (*OT*, 289, 290, 291).

Lecture 10

1. Cf. the title of a chapter in the second volume of *The World as Will and Representation*, trans. E. F. J. Payne (Indian Hills, Colo.: Falcon's Wing Press, 1958), II, pp. 201ff.: "On the Primacy of the Will in Self-consciousness."

2. Cf. Friedrich Schlegel, *Kritische Ausgabe seiner Schriften*, ed. Ernst Behler (Munich, Paderborn, Vienna: Schöningh, 1958ff.), XVIII, p. 101.

Lecture 11

1. Cf. Peter Sloterdijk, "Michel Foucaults strukturale Theorie der Geschichte," *Philosophisches Jahrbuch*, 79 (1972), pp. 172-75; Gerhard Plumpe and Clemens Kammler, "Wissen ist Macht: Über die theoretische Arbeit Michel Foucaults," *Philosophische Rundschau*, 27 (1980), pp. 185-218, esp. 200ff.; in particular see the excellent essay by Hinrich Fink-Eitel, "Michel Foucaults Analytik der Macht," *Austreibung des Geistes aus den Geisteswissenschaften: Programme des Poststrukturalismus*, ed. Friedrich A. Kittler (Paderborn: Schöningh, 1980), pp. 38-78.

2. See, for example, the preface to his *Phenomenology of Mind*, trans. J. B. Baillie (London: Swan Sonnenschein, 1910), I, p. 47; or the chapter entitled "The Idea" in his *Logic*, II, pp. 395-486.

3. Hegel, *Phenomenology of Mind*, I, p. 21.

4. Cf. the more extensive argumentation in my book *Der unendliche Mangel an Sein: Schellings Hegelkritik und die Anfänge der Marxschen Dialektik* (Frankfurt: Suhrkamp, 1975), pp. 75ff. and 207ff.

5. TN: See H. A. Korff, *Der Geist der Goethezeit: Versuch einer ideellen Entwicklung der klassisch-romantischen Literaturgeschichte*, 4 vols. (Leipzig: Koehler & Amelang, 1964ff.).

6. Cf. Foucault, *L'Ordre du discours* (Paris: Gallimard, 1971), p. 55; henceforth cited as *OD*. Except where indicated, page numbers correspond to *The Archaeology of Knowledge* (*AK*), where *The Order of Discourse* is included as an appendix.

7. Barthes, *S/Z* (Paris: Seuil, 1970); cf. my analysis of the methodological operation of this text, "Textauslegung," *Erkenntnis der Literatur*, ed. Dietrich Harth and Paul Gebhardt (Stuttgart: Metzler, 1983), pp. 123-60, esp. 147ff.

8. Here one finds the well-known statement that "it is permissible to look upon language itself as the expression of the power of the masters"; see *Works*, XIII, p. 20.

Lecture 12

1. The future of the (transgressed) system will be a (new, or alternative, but in any case a) *system*. Sartre has clearly emphasized this: "Since the evolution of the system is the product of its internal reactions and its self-regulations, the observer placed inside the system has no other future than that of the system. And there is not a single element in the system that makes it possible to foresee what will happen after its disappearance. At most it can be said, after a period of disorder, that another system will be constituted, with its structures and its pseudointernal laws that will regulate its life and its death." Jean-Paul Sartre, "Détermination et liberté," *Les Écrits de Sartre: Chronologie, bib-*

liographie commentée, ed. Michel Contat and Michel Rybalka (Paris: Gallimard, 1970), pp. 735–45; here p. 743.

2. Nietzsche, *Works*, XVII, p. 109; cf. also *Werke*, II, pp. 473, 161, 1059, 1089, 1151; III, pp. 1263, 834, 1181.

3. Cf. also Lacan, *E* (Fr. ed.), 505: One can "imprison" no one in language; "in spite of all the *between-the-lines* censures," language still serves at all times "to signify *something quite other* than what it says."

4. Even Althusser's idea of the dominance of one structure (the economic structure) over the others is still too closely related to the idea of a "kernel" or "principle" of structure(s), an idea neostructuralism overcame.

5. This semantic indeterminateness is still present in the Old German verb *wesen* (to be); Schelling and Heidegger point this out.

6. Dieter Henrich, "Kunst und Kunstphilosophie der Gegenwart: Überlegungen mit Rücksicht auf Hegel," *Immanente Aesthetik, ästhetische Reflexion* (Munich: Fink, 1966), p. 18.

7. Henrich, "Kunst und Kunstphilosophie der Gegenwart," pp. 18–19.

8. Sartre coined a famous expression for this experience: "la conscience naît *portée sur* un être qui n'est pas elle," *L'Être et le néant: Essai d'ontologie phénoménologique* (Paris: Gallimard, 1943), p. 28; henceforth cited as *EN*. Cf. also Heidegger, *BI*, p. 330.

9. "Re-presentation" (*Vor-stellung*), "ob-ject" (*Gegen-stand*), and "pre-sence" (*Gegen-wart*) form semantically one and the same metaphorical frame.

10. See for example Fichte, *FW*, I. pp. 526–27.

11. Novalis, *Schriften*, ed. P. Kluckhohn and R. Samuel (Stuttgart: Kohlhammer, 1960ff.), II, p. 112.

12. See Novalis, *Schriften*, II, p. 125. Cf. also the chapter "Nicht-setzendes und setzendes Bewusstsein" in my book *Das Problem "Zeit" in der deutschen Romantik* (Munich: Winkler, 1972), pp. 144ff.

13. Cf. Sinclair, "Philosophische Raisonnements," *Isaak von Sinclair zwischen Fichte, Hölderlin und Hegel*, Hannelore Hegel (Frankfurt: Klostermann, 1971), pp. 243ff., esp. 246, 251ff., 268ff.

14. Schleiermacher, *Dialektik*, ed. Rudolf Odebrecht (Leipzig: F. Meiner, 1942), p. 288; cf. *Dialektik, Sämtliche Werke*, ed. L. Jonas (Berlin: G. Reimer, 1839), p. 429.

15. Frank, *Das Problem "Zeit" in der deutschen Romantik*, pp. 130–232.

16. See also my book *Das individuelle Allgemeine: Textstrukturierung und -interpretation nach Schleiermacher* (Frankfurt: Suhrkamp, 1977), pp. 91–114, esp. p. 95.

17. Schleiermacher, *Dialektik*, ed. Odebrecht, pp. 290 and 291.

18. Schleiermacher, *Dialektik*, ed. Jonas, p. 429.

19. Sartre, *La transcendance de l'Ego: Esquisse d'une description phénoménologique* (Paris: Vrin, 1978).

20. Deleuze, *Logique du sens* (Paris: Minuit, 1969), p. 124; henceforth cited as *LS*.

21. Sartre, *Being and Nothingness: An Essay on Phenomenological Ontology*, trans. Hazel E. Barnes (New York: Philosophical Library, 1956), pp. 100–1, 109–10; henceforth cited as *BN*.

22. Husserl, *L'Origine de la géométrie*, 2nd ed. (Paris: PUF, 1974); translated into English as *Husserl's Origin of Geometry*, trans. John P. Leavey, ed. David B. Allison (Stony Brook, N.Y.: Nicolas Hays, 1978); all references follow this edition and are henceforth cited as *OG*.

23. Sartre, "Conscience de soi et connaisance de soi," *Bulletin de la Societé Française de Philosophie*, 42 (1948), pp. 49–91; here, p. 64.

Lecture 13

1. Schelling, *Philosophie der Offenbarung 1841/2*, ed. Manfred Frank (Frankfurt: Suhrkamp, 1977), pp. 160ff.

2. See also *Works*, XV, p. 40: "It [consciousness] is only a *means of communication*: it was developed by intercourse, and with a view to the interests of intercourse."

3. See *Works*, VI, p. 62: "That the character is unchangeable is not true in a strict sense; this favourite theory means, rather, that during the short lifetime of an individual the new influencing motives cannot penetrate deeply enough to destroy the ingrained marks of many thousands of years."

4. See *Works*, XV, p. 73: "Thus: the indefiniteness and the chaos of sense-impressions are, as it were, *made logical*."

5. "As a matter of fact, logic (like geometry and arithmetic) only holds good of *assumed existences which we have created*. Logic is *the attempt on our part to understand the actual world according to a scheme of Being devised by ourselves; or, more exactly, it is our attempt at making the actual world more calculable and more susceptible to formulation, for our own purposes*" (*Works*, XV, p. 33). Nietzsche, as we know, calls this process "interpretation."

6. Derrida, *La dissémination* (Paris: Seuil, 1972); page numbers correspond to *Dissemination*, trans. Barbara Johnson (Chicago: University of Chicago Press, 1981), henceforth cited as *Diss* (here pp. 340, 341).

7. Heidegger, *Nietzsche*, trans. David Farell Krell (San Francisco: Harper & Row, 1979), I, pp. 200ff.

8. See also my article "Die Aufhebung der Anschauung im Spiel der Metapher," *neue hefte für philosophie*, 18–19 (1980), pp. 58–78.

9. "As may be conjectured, it is not the antithesis of subject and object with which I am here concerned: I leave that distinction to the epistemologists who have remained entangled in the toils of grammar (popular metaphysics). It is still less the antithesis of the 'thing in itself' and phenomenon, for we do not 'know' enough to be entitled even *to make such a distinction*" (*Works*, X, 299–300).

10. See Schleiermacher, *Sämtliche Werke*, (Berlin: Reimer, 1834ff.), III/6, p. 518.

11. See Ernst Tugendhat, *Selbstbewusstsein und Selbstbestimmung* (Frankfurt: Suhrkamp, 1979), pp. 96ff. and 110–11.

12. See Ludwig Wittgenstein, *Philosophical Investigations*, trans. G. E. M. Anscombe (Oxford: Basil Blackwell, 1953), sections 244ff.; henceforth cited as *PI*. See also R. Rhees, ed., "Wittgenstein's Notes for Lectures on 'Private Experience' and 'Sense Data,' " *Philosophical Review*, 77 (1968), pp. 271–320.

13. From this it follows—but Wittgenstein pays no attention to this—that all psychic states and acts have to be *conscious*; if this consciousness cannot be a *knowledge*, then it can only be a matter of a nonpositing *consciousness*.

Lecture 14

1. Ernst Tugendhat, *Vorlesungen zur Einführung in die sprachanalytische Philosophie* (Frankfurt: Suhrkamp, 1976).

2. Tugendhat, *Selbstbewusstsein und Selbstbestimmung* (Frankfurt: Suhrkamp, 1979), p. 7.

3. Tugendhat, *Vorlesungen zur Einführung in die sprachanalytische Philosophie*, p. 63.

4. See his discussion of this in "Phänomenologie und Sprachanalyse," *Hermeneutik und Dialektik: Festschrift für H.-G. Gadamer*, ed. R. Bubner et al. (Tübingen: Mohr, 1970), pp. 3–23.

5. Cf. Tugendhat, "Phänomenologie und Sprachanalyse," p. 23: "Once the understanding of propositions is shown to be primary over against the positing (*Meinen*) of objects, we are faced with the question of where it should be located. That a proposition (*Satz*) is the primary unit of meaning seems to be grounded in the fact that it is the smallest unit of intersubjective understanding. (One can understand a name, but nothing can be communicated with it.) This seems to indicate that, while within the scheme of the subject-object relation this question was approached from the point of the individual subject, the understanding-one-another (*Verstehen*) of propositions should from the outset

be located in an intersubjective understanding (*Verständigung*), and it is for this reason that the 'subject' proves to be secondary over against intersubjectivity."

6. Tugendhat, *Vorlesungen zur Einführung in die sprachanalytische Philosophie*, p. 103.

7. Tugendhat, *Selbstbewusstsein und Selbstbestimmung*, pp. 18–19.

8. Tugendhat, *Selbstbewusstsein und Selbstbestimmung*, p. 19. TN: Unless otherwise indicated, we have translated *Sachverhalt* as "state of affairs" rather than as "proposition." We have opted for this alternative because *Sachverhalt* does not necessarily refer to a linguistic entity, as the word "proposition" seems to indicate, and because we would no longer be able to make the distinction between *Sachverhalt* and *Satz*, the latter word consistently being translated as "proposition." Tugendhat's suggestion that *Sachverhalt* is rendered as "proposition" by Anglo-Saxon philosophers is at least in part fallacious, since in Ogden's translation of Wittgenstein's *Tractatus* the German word is rendered as "atomic fact."

9. Tugendhat, *Selbstbewusstsein und Selbstbestimmung*, p. 21.

10. See Derrida, "Signature événement contexte," *Marges de la philosophie* (Paris: Minuit, 1972), pp. 365–93.

11. Derrida, *La voix et le phénomène: Introduction au problème du signe dans la phénoménologie de Husserl* (Paris: PUF, 1967). Except where cited as *VP*, page numbers correspond to *Speech and Phenomena and Other Essays on Husserl's Theory of Signs*, trans. David B. Allison (Evanston, Ill.: Northwestern University Press, 1973), henceforth cited as *SP*, here p. 8.

12. *L'Origine de la géométrie* (Paris: PUF, 1974). Page numbers correspond to *Edmund Husserl's Origin of Geometry*, trans. John P. Leavey, ed. David B. Allison (Stony Brook, N.Y.: Nicholas Hays, 1978); henceforth cited as *OG*.

13. Husserl, *Ideas: General Introduction to Pure Phenomenology*, trans. W. R. Boyce Gibson (New York: Macmillan, 1931), pp. 318–28; henceforth cited as *Ideas*.

14. It is not inappropriate that Derrida speaks of this alleged preexpressive linguisticality of meaning (*Sinn*) as an *écriture blanche*. Derrida translates the word *Bedeuten* ("meaning something"), which Husserl often uses in an active sense, with *vouloir-dire*.

15. I am disregarding here the problem (which is also discussed by Derrida) of "incomplete expression," where "the upper layer need not extend its expressing function over the entire lower layer" (*Ideas*, 324), as well as the problem of the essential inadequation between individual meaning and its circulating (intersubjectively valid) signification.

Lecture 15

1. "By phenomenological epoché I reduce my natural human Ego and my psychic life – the realm of my *psychological self-experience* – to my transcendental-phenomenological Ego, the realm of *transcendental-phenomenological self-experience*. The Objective world, the world that exists for me, that always has and always will exist for me, the only world that ever can exist for me – this world, with all its Objects, I said, derives its whole sense and its existential status, which it has for me, from me myself, *from me as the transcendental Ego*, the Ego who comes to the fore only with transcendental-phenomenological epoché." Husserl, *Cartesian Meditations: An Introduction to Phenomenology*, trans. Dorion Cairns (The Hague: Nijhoff, 1960), p. 26; henceforth cited as *CM*.

2. "This is the irrepressible philosophical desire to summarize-interiorize-dialecticize-master-*relever* the metaphorical division between the origin and itself, the Oriental difference" (*Margins*, 269).

3. See Klaus Held, *Lebendige Gegenwart: Die Frage nach der Seinsweise des transzendentalen Ich bei Edmund Husserl, entwickelt am Leitfaden der Zeitproblematik* (The Hague: Nijhoff, 1966), pp. 96ff. In my summary of Derrida's critique of Husserl I have intentionally set aside the decisive

point that self- consciousness can never be described as a relation *of* something *to* something, and thus also not as the work of an *identification*.

Lecture 16

1. Husserl, *The Paris Lectures*, trans. Peter Koestenbaum (The Hague: Nijhoff, 1964), p. 33; henceforth cited as *PL*. See also *CM*, pp. 83–88.

2. "Is human transcendental consciousness only the place of reflexive articulation, i.e., the *mediation* of a Logos retaking possession of *itself* through this consciousness?" (*OG*, 146).

3. Husserl, *The Phenomenology of Internal Time-Consciousness*, ed. Martin Heidegger, trans. James S. Churchill (Bloomington: Indiana University Press, 1964); henceforth cited as *T-C*.

4. Something that is absolute is, literally, something that is nonrelative [*ein Unbezügliches*], and its logical opposite, relativity, is a being-related or being-referred to an Other (see Schelling, *SW*, I/6, p. 190). Applied to temporality, relativity takes the form of what Schelling describes in this manner: "A non-being (*Nicht-Wesen*) looks for its reality, which it does not have in and of itself, in the Other; it looks for it in an Other which itself does not have a reality and which, for its part, is also looking to find it in an Other. This infinite interdependence of things . . . is thus itself only testimony to, and expression of, the futility to which they are subjected and the striving back to the unity from which they are torn away and in which only the all (*alles*) is truth" (*SW*, I/6, pp. 195–96; see also I/4, p. 397).

5. When Husserl says that what is given to reflection presents itself as if it were "already there" (*T-C*, 179), then the prereflective asserts a priorness to reflection that cannot be subsumed under positing consciousness. On the other hand, the consciousness of reflection itself is "something of which we are inwardly conscious" (176), and thus it is instantaneous to that prereflective consciousness that it has of itself as reflection. This temporal interval is very difficult to understand if one simultaneously insists on the unity of the modes of Being of consciousness: that which produces consciousness *within* reflection cannot be a different consciousness than the one *of* which reflection is conscious. But this is precisely what Husserl affirms when he distinguishes internal perceiving from the act itself.

6. Ludwig Wittgenstein, *Tractatus Logico-Philosophicus*, 8th ed., trans. and ed. C. K. Ogden (London: Routledge & Kegan Paul, 1960). All references to the *Tractatus* will be cited with the abbreviation *Tr* and the proposition number following this edition.

7. Derrida, *Glas* (Paris: Galilée, 1974).

8. Dieter Henrich, "Selbstbewusstsein: Kritische Einleitung in eine Theorie," *Hermeneutik und Dialektik*, ed. R. Bubner et al. (Tübingen: Mohr, 1970), I, p. 281.

Lecture 17

1. Dieter Henrich, "Hegels Grundoperation: Eine Einleitung in die 'Wissenschaft der Logik'," *Der Idealismus und seine Gegenwart: Festschrift für Werner Marx*, ed. Ute Guzzoni et al. (Hamburg: Meiner, 1976), pp. 208–30.

2. Henrich, "Hegels Grundoperation," p. 215.

3. Henrich, "Hegels Grundoperation," pp. 215–16.

4. Henrich, "Hegels Grundoperation," pp. 217–18.

5. Henrich, "Hegels Grundoperation," p. 218.

6. In this idea resides the motivation for conceiving *Logic* as a process of regulated determination (*Weiterbestimmung*) of terms: it is the difference between the *absence* of a heteronomous *presupposition* and the supposition of a *result* that makes autonomous negation the incitement to a logical progression.

7. Henrich, "Hegels Grundoperation," p. 219.

8. *Logic*, II, pp. 32ff. See also Dieter Henrich, "Hegels Logik der Reflexion," *Hegel im Kontext*

(Frankfurt: Suhrkamp, 1970), pp. 95–156; see also my detailed comments in the book *Der unendliche Mangel an Sein: Schellings Hegelkritik und die Anfänge der Marxschen Dialektik*, (Frankfurt: Suhrkamp, 1975), pp. 32–66, esp. pp. 51ff.

9. Schelling presents a particularly striking formulation for this paradoxical equality of contradiction and identity: "Pure, immediate knowledge . . . [is] a recognition of *contradiction*, or of *absolute identity of the infinite and the finite*, as the Highest" (*SW*, I/8, p. 81).

10. TN: The phrase *zu Grunde gehen* contains an ambiguity in German similar to that inherent in the word *Aufhebung*. *Zu Grunde gehen* means both, literally, "to go to the ground," and simultaneously "to perish" or "to be destroyed." Cf. Hegel's *Logic*, II, p. 70.

Lecture 18

1. William James, "Does 'Consciousness' Exist?" *Essays in Radical Empiricism* (New York: Longmans, Green, 1912), pp. 1–38.

2. I am following here the essay by Dieter Henrich, "Selbstbewusstsein: Kritische Einleitung in eine Theorie," *Hermeneutik und Dialektik*, ed. R. Bubner et. al. (Tübingen: Mohr, 1970), I, pp. 262–63 and 277.

3. Henrich, "Selbstbewusstsein," p. 263.

4. See Saussure himself: "The linguistic entity exists only through the association of the signifier with the signified. . . . Whenever only one element is retained, the entity vanishes; instead of a concrete object we are faced with a mere abstraction. . . . A succession of sounds is linguistic only if it supports an idea. Considered independently, it is material for a physiological study, and nothing more than that" (*CGL*, 102–3).

5. Lacan addressed a similar objection to the behaviorists: *Le Séminaire* (Paris: Seuil, 1978), II, p. 64.

6. Henrich, "Selbstbewusstsein," p. 271.

7. Lacan, *The Four Fundamental Concepts of Psychoanalysis*, ed. Jacques-Alain Miller, trans. Alan Sheridan (New York: Norton, 1978), pp. 250–51.

8. Ibid. p. 250.

9. Paul Ricoeur, *De l'interprétation: Essai sur Freud* (Paris: Seuil, 1965).

10. Freud, *The Standard Edition of the Complete Psychological Works of Sigmund Freud*, ed. and trans. James Strachey (London: Hogarth Press, 1964), XXII, p. 80.

11. Kafka, "A Country Doctor," *The Complete Stories*, ed. Nahum N. Glatzer, trans. Willa Muir and Edwin Muir (New York: Schocken, 1971), p. 220.

Lecture 19

1. Lacan, *Le Séminaire* (Paris: Seuil, 1978), II, p. 60.

2. René Descartes, by the way, himself already did this in relation to the *cogitare/penser*. He asks, for example, in the *Recherches de la Vérité*: "In effect, is doubting anything more than thinking in a certain way?" *Oeuvres et lettres*, ed. André Bridoux (Paris: Gallimard, 1953), p. 897.

3. Derrida also underlined this jumping over of the referential relation that the expression has with a state of affairs, to the relation the expression has with other expressions, and he adds that the relation of an expression to an I or to a mundane state of affairs is grounded in that other reference — in the differentiality of the signifiers. See, for example, *SP* (p. 89): "As a supplement, the signifier does not represent first and simply the absent signified. Rather, it is substituted for another signifier, for another type of signifier that maintains another relation with the deficient present." The distance of the referent from the sign that points to it thus is itself founded in the structure of the ekstatic reference in which — by means of reciprocal delimitation — the expressions get their significance. Whenever a

subject attributes meaning to its acts, this meaning exists in the form of supplementarity, deferral, substitution.

4. Adorno, *Negative Dialectics*, trans. E. B. Ashton (New York: Seabury Press, 1973) pp. 183ff.

5. John C. Eccles, "Hirn und Bewusstsein," *Mannheimer Forum* (1977–78), pp. 15–16; see also his *The Brain and the Unity of the Consciousness Experience* (Cambridge: Cambridge University Press, 1965).

Lecture 20

1. Gilles Deleuze and Félix Guattari, *L'Anti-Oedipe* (Paris: Minuit, 1972), *Mille Plateaux* (Paris: Minuit, 1980); henceforth cited as *AO* and *MP*, respectively. Page numbers for *AO* correspond to *Anti-Oedipus*, trans. Helen R. Lane, Robert Hurley, and Mark Seem (New York: Viking Press, 1977).

2. See also *AO*: "the production of production" (p. 4), "machine of machine" (*passim*).

3. Social Darwinism looked on Nietzsche as an "allied spirit"; we need only think, for example, of the book by Alexander Tille, *Von Darwin bis Nietzsche* (Leipzig: C. G. Naumann, 1885). On the historical context, see Hans-Günter Zmarzlik, "Der Sozialdarwinismus in Deutschland als geschichtliches Problem," *Vierteljahresschrift für Zeitgeschichte*, 11 (1963), pp. 246–73, and Günter Altner, ed., *Der Darwinismus: Die Geschichte einer Theorie* (Darmstadt: Wissenschaftliche Buchgesellschaft, 1981).

4. Max Scheler, *The Nature of Sympathy*, trans. Peter Heath (Hamden, Conn.: Archon Books, 1970).

5. Although it is precisely this age that is once again producing new shepherds.

6. Hegel, "Maximen des Journals der deutschen Literatur," *Theorie-Werkausgabe*, II, p. 571.

7. Hegel, "Maximen des Journals der deutschen Literatur," *Theorie-Werkausgabe*, II, p. 542; cf. also XX, pp. 444f., 452; IX, p. 9; *Phenomenology of Mind*, trans. J. B. Baillie, 2 vols. (London: Swan Sonnenschein, 1910), pp. 108ff.

8. Deleuze, *LS*, p. 124: "This field cannot be determined like that of a consciousness: despite Sartre's attempt, consciousness cannot be viewed as a milieu while rejecting the form of the person and the perspective of individuation. A consciousness is nothing without the unifying synthesis, but there is no unifying synthesis of consciousness without the form of the *I* or the perspective of the self [*Moi*]."

Deleuze has apparently not followed the recent discussion on self-consciousness. He subscribes to the standpoint of Kant and Husserl.

9. *CGL*, pp. 79–80; see de Mauro's comments on pp. 450–51 of his *Edition critique*, 2nd ed. (Paris: Payot, 1980).

10. "Representation is always a social and psychic repression of desiring-production" (p. 184). "The unconscious poses no problem of meaning, solely problems of use" (p. 109).

11. Alfred Rosenberg, *Der Mythus des zwanzigsten Jahrhunderts* (Munich: Hoheneichen, 1936).

12. Sartre, *What Is Literature*? Trans. Bernard Frechtman (New York: Philosophical Library, 1949), pp. 284–85.

13. I presented this view in more detail in my article "Die alte und die neue Mythologie in Thomas Manns *Doktor Faustus*," *Invaliden des Apoll: Motive und Mythen des Dichterleids*, ed. Herbert Anton (Munich: Fink, 1982), pp. 78–94.

14. Let's not forget that Nietzsche characterized this "race" as "the Aryan race," even "physiologically" (*Works*, XIII, p. 26) and "*the Jews*" (p. 30) as the establishers of culture, of law, the penitentiary system: in short, of "resentment." A "cultural-historical" interpretation of these statements does not even come into question, since in the entire *Genealogy of Morals* Nietzsche works with concepts like "blood" ("blood poisoning"), "race," "heredity," and "physiology." (That distinguishes the "genealogical" explanation from the social-historical one which Nietzsche so thoroughly despised!)

15. "It substitutes for the codes an extremely rigorous axiomatic that maintains the energy of the flows in a bound state on the body of capital" (*AO*, 246).

16. Of course, he already has a hard time in late-capitalism. Since the unfettered exchange undermines all values, even that of morality, religion, authority, and the symbolic father, Oedipus fights for his last territory.

17. See my study *Die unendliche Fahrt: Ein Motiv und sein Text* (Frankfurt: Suhrkamp, 1979).

18. E. T. A. Hoffmann, "Kreisleriana," *Fantasie- und Nachtstücke*, ed. Walter Müller-Seidel (Munich: Winkler, 1960); Ludwig Tieck, *Die Reisenden, Gesammelte Novellen* (Berlin: Reimer, 1852), I, 167-270.

19. Schopenhauer, *The World as Will and Representation*, trans. E. F. J. Payne (Indian Hills, Colo.: Falcon's Wing Press, 1958), I, 429: "But the greatest effrontery in serving up sheer nonsense, in scrabbling together senseless and maddening webs of words, such as had previously been heard only in madhouses, finally appeared in Hegel. It became the instrument of the most ponderous and general mystification that has ever existed, with a result that will seem incredible to posterity, and be a lasting monument of German stupidity."

Lecture 21

1. Compare this to the following remark by Husserl, which nicely supplements this context: "But truly senseless speech would be no speech at all: it would be like the rattle of machinery" (*Logical Investigations*, trans. J. N. Findlay [London: Routledge and Kegan Paul, 1970], I, 303).

2. On p. 358 of *AO* one can find the following definition of primary production: "The libido is caught up in molecular desiring-production and knows nothing of persons just as it knows nothing of the ego—even the most undifferentiated ego of narcissism—since its investments are already differentiated, but differentiated according to the prepersonal regime of partial objects, of singularities, of intensities, of gears and parts of machines of desire." Would there accordingly be a presemiotic differentiation? A quasi-natural distinctiveness of individuals?

3. For a fleeting moment the thought occurs to me, like a shooting star, that it is the author himself who, by virtue of the individuality of his writing (*écriture*)—i.e., by virtue of his style—breaks down and alters the universality of grammar: "Yet it has been a long time since Engels demonstrated, already apropos of Balzac, how an author is great because he cannot prevent himself from tracing flows and causing them to circulate, flows that split asunder the catholic and despotic signifier of his work, and that necessarily nourish a revolutionary machine on the horizon. That is what style is, or rather the absence of style—asyntactic, agrammatical: the moment when language is no longer defined by what it says, even less by what makes it a signifying thing, but by what causes it to move, to flow, and to explode—desire. For literature is like schizophrenia: a process and not a goal, a production and not an expression" (*AO*, 133). I will return to the idea of a nonuniversal and nonsignificant individual that undermines the identity of the universal, linked by Deleuze to style, in the context of my reading of *Différence et répétition*; see also *MP*, 123ff.

4. Again and again mention is made in *Anti-Oedipus* of the "[anoedipal] order of production" (p. 100) or of the order of desire (*passim*).

5. Quoted by Sartre, *What is Literature?* Trans. Bernard Frechtman (New York: Philosophical Library, 1949), p. 132.

6. Sartre, *What is Literature?*, pp. 183–84; see also the fantasies of a global inferno and of universal destruction in the work of Nazi authors, cited by Sartre in *Situations*, II, pp. 227–28.

7. Nietzsche, *Works*, XIII, 65.

8. Friedrich Schlegel, *Kritische Ausgabe seiner Schriften*, ed. Ernst Behler (Munich, Paderborn, Vienna: Schöningh, 1958ff.), II, p. 153.

Lecture 22

1. *Thousand Plateaus*, trans. Brian Massumi (Minneapolis: University of Minnesota Press, in press). Page references correspond to *Mille Plateaux* (*MP*).

2. E. T. A. Hoffmann, "Kreisleriana," *Fantasie- und Nachtstücke*, ed. Walter Müller-Seidel (Munich: Winkler, 1960), p. 49.

3. Fichte, *Nachgelassene Schriften*, ed. Hans Jacob (Berlin: Junker and Dünnhaupt, 1957), II, p. 368.

4. R. Jacobsen and J. Lotz, "Notes on the French Phonematic Pattern," *Word*, 5 (1949), p. 155.

5. The same is true for the notion of a *système acentré* (*MP*, 26), which nevertheless would still be a "system."

6. Hegel, *Encyclopädie*, paragraph 462, Zusatz, *Theorie-Werkausgabe*, X, 279–80.

7. Ibid., p. 278.

8. I demonstrated this in greater detail in "Einverständnis und Vielsinnigkeit (oder: Das Aufbrechen der Bedeutungseinheit im 'eigentlichen Gespräch')," *Poetik und Hermeneutik XI: Das Gespräch*, ed. Karlheinz Stierle and Rainer Warning (Munich: Fink, 1984).

9. For example, when they write, "Inexact expressions are needed to designate something exactly" (*MP*, 31): a false conclusion that is structurally similar to the statement that in order to see rectangles we need a rectangular brain.

10. That, of course, does not mean that one would have to deny the coercive character of relations of domination. But it does mean that one attributes this coercion not to structures but rather to individuals. Only individuals can coerce or repress other individuals.

Lecture 23

1. Deleuze, *Différence et répétition* (Paris: PUF, 1968); henceforth cited as *DR*.

2. Searle, "Reiterating the Differences: A Reply to Derrida," *Glyph*, 1 (1977), p. 199; henceforth cited as *R*.

3. *Immanuel Kant's Critique of Pure Reason*, trans. Norman Kemp Smith (New York: Humanities Press, 1950), A 320, B 377, p. 314.

4. See Nikolaus of Cusa, *De docta ignorantia*, Book II, chapter 6.

5. Schleiermacher, *Dialektik*, ed. Rudolf Odebrecht (Leipzig: F. Meiner, 1942), pp. 290 and 295–96.

6. Ibid., pp. 198 and 290.

7. Schleiermacher, *Psychologie*, *Sämtliche Werke*, ed. L. George (Berlin: G. Reimer, 1862), III/4, p. 77.

8. Schleiermacher, *HuK*, p. 411.

9. August Boeckh, *Enzyklopädie und Methodenlehre der philologischen Wissenschaften*, ed. Ernst Bratuschek (Darmstadt: Wissenschaftliche Buchgesellschaft, 1966), p. 83.

10. Derrida, "The Purveyor of Truth," *Yale French Studies*, 52 (1975), p.66.

11. Sartre speaks off *concepts* or *significations* (exactly as do Schleiermacher and Boeckh, incidentally) whenever he wants to designate the communicable product of a process of understanding; on the other hand, he speaks of *meaning* whenever he refers to the process of producing signification as such. He believes that every universal concept is grounded in individual meaning.

12. Sartre, *Situations*, (Paris: Gallimard, 1977), VIII, p. 450.

13. Sartre, *Situations*, VIII, pp. 437, 449–50.

14. Sartre, *L'idiot de la famille*, 3 vols. (Paris: Gallimard, 1971–72), III, 29; henceforth cited as *IF*.

15. Plato, *The Republic*, 293 E ff.; Aristotle, *The Politics*, 1284 a 13–14.

16. See Manfred Frank, *Das kalte Herz* (Frankfurt: Insel, 1981).

17. Tullio de Mauro, "Introduction," in Saussure, *Cours de linguistique générale*, 2nd ed. (Paris: Payot, 1980), pp. v-vi.

18. Boeckh, *Enzyklopädie und Methodenlehre der philologischen Wissenschaften*, p. 126.

19. Robert Musil, *Gesammelte Werke*, ed Adolf Frisé (Reinbek: Rowohlt, 1978), VIII, pp. 1404 and 1151; IV, p. 1212. See also my essay on Musil's treatment of individuality: "Auf der Suche nach einem Grund: Ueber den Umschlag von Erkenntniskritik in Mythologie bei Musil," *Mythos und Moderne*, ed. Karl Heinz Bohrer (Frankfurt: Suhrkamp, 1983), pp. 318-62.

20. Wilhelm von Humboldt, *Gesammelte Schriften*, ed. A. Leitzmann (Darmstadt: Wissenschaftliche Buchgesellschaft, 1968), V, p. 418.

21. Saussure, *CFS*, 15 (1957), p. 72.

Lecture 24

1. I have demonstrated extensively how this is conceived by Hölderlin in my *Der unendliche Mangel an Sein: Schellings Hegelkritik und die Anfänge der Marxschen Dialektik* (Frankfurt: Suhrkamp, 1975), pp. 22-23.

2. I am borrowing this phrase from part I, paragraph 3 of Fichte's *Science of Knowledge*, trans. Peter Heath and John Lucks (1970; reprint, Cambridge: Cambridge University Press, 1982), p. 110: "Every opposite is like its opponent in one respect, = X; and every like is opposed to its like in one respect, = X. Such a respect, = X, is called the ground, in the first case of *conjunction*, and in the second of *distinction*."

3. Charles Sanders Peirce, *Collected Papers*, ed. Charles Hartstone and Paul Weiss (Cambridge, Mass.: Harvard University Press, 1935), VI, p. 32; henceforth cited as *Coll P*.

4. Henrich, "Selbstbewusstsein: Kritische Einleitung in eine Theorie," *Hermeneutik und Dialektik*, ed. R. Bubner et. al. (Tübingen: Mohr, 1970), p. 275: "It is a matter of describing consciousness in such a way that it is neither conscious self-relation nor identification with itself, but conceiving it at the same time in such a way that it is conceded that we are immediately familiar with consciousness."

5. Henrich, ibid., p. 271.

6. Let me add in this context that Derrida began a penetrating investigation into the problematics of self-consciousness in modern philosophy, which he later unfortunately did not continue, in his early essay on "Cogito and the History of Madness" (from 1963, reprinted in *WD*, pp. 31-63). I will leave out the critical reference to Foucault and underline only that Derrida regards the Cartesian *cogito* as a "project of singular and unprecedented excess": "an excess which overflows the totality of that which can be thought, the totality of beings and determined meanings" (*WD*, 57). In other words, the experience of self-consciousness, due to its priorness, goes beyond all other experiences as limited experience *of* something, including the totality of beings and of history, which are only presented in the light of this "hyperbolic extremity" (*WD*, 58). Only the recourse to a divine guarantee connected Descartes's project to that of metaphysics: "As soon as Descartes has reached this extremity, he seeks to reassure himself, to certify the Cogito through God, to identify the act of the Cogito with a reasonable reason. And he does so as soon as he *proffers* and *reflects* the Cogito" (*WD*, 58). According to this, the *cogito*, as the experience of a "familiarity with itself" that is attendant even in madness, would be prereflective; and only in the gesture of wanting to express and reflect would it become "the" *cogito* as the seat of the highest certitude, which, in addition, is founded in God. The decisive aspect of this view is that it distinguishes the *cogito* itself from its (reflective or linguistic) representation (and instrumentalization in the service of a methodical self-certification and world domination), but it does this in such a way that it does not deny consciousness—i.e., subjectivity—to that which precedes representation, as Deleuze seems to do. Derrida also seems to conceive the "hyperbolic act of the Cogito" as individual, since he sharply delimits it from intersubjective communication, "that is, as

soon as he reflects the Cogito for the other, which means for oneself" (*WD*, 59). And finally, he seems to conceive it as *différance* (61–62), so that in the originary *cogito* individuality, self-consciousness, prereflectivity, and differentiality would be united. To be sure, one has to *think* of this unification as a unification, and Derrida is far from doing that.

7. "Asignificance" here does not mean "senselessness" but rather "without significance," following the distinction made earlier.

8. Novalis, *Schriften*, ed. P. Kluckhohn and R. Samuel (Stuttgart: Kohlhammer, 1960ff.), III, p. 451.

9. Derrida, *GR*, pp. 61ff.

10. Wittgenstein, *Philosophical Investigations*, trans. G. E. M. Anscombe (Oxford: Basil Blackwell, 1953), pp. 11–12; henceforth cited as *PI*.

11. John R. Searle, *Speech Acts: An Essay in the Philosophy of Language* (Cambridge: Cambridge University Press, 1969).

12. John L. Austin, *How to Do Things with Words* (Oxford: Clarendon, 1967).

Lecture 25

1. Wittgenstein, *PI*, p. 13.

2. The term was coined by Husserl.

3. For the Derrida-Gadamer debate, see *Text und Interpretation: Deutsch-Französische Debatte*, 2nd ed., ed. Philippe Forget (Munich: Fink, 1983). See also the special issue of the *Revue Internationale de Philosophie*, 151 (1984), ed. Manfred Frank, which documents parts of this debate in French.

4. Searle, "Taxonomy of Illocutionary Acts," *Language, Mind and Society*, ed. Keith Gunderson (Minneapolis: University of Minnesota Press, 1975), pp. 344–69; reprinted in Searle, *Expression and Meaning: Studies in the Theory of Speech Acts* (Cambridge: Cambridge University Press, 1979).

5. Sartre, *Critique of Dialectical Reason. I. Theory of Practical Ensembles*, trans. Alan Sheridan Smith, ed. Jonathan Rée (London: New Left Books, 1976), p. 98.

6. H. P. Grice, "Logic and Conversation," *Speech Acts*, vol. 3, *Syntax and Semantics*, ed. P. Coles and J. L. Morgan (New York: Academic Press, 1975), pp. 41–58. I have argued in detail to what extent this is the case in my reflections devoted to the controversy between Derrida and Searle, "Die Entropie der Sprache," *Das Sagbare und das Unsagbare* (Frankfurt: Suhrkamp, 1980), pp. 141–210, esp. p. 178.

7. Wittgenstein, *PI*, p. 85.

8. Wilhelm von Humboldt, "Grundzüge des allgemeinen Sprachtyps," *Gesammelte Schriften*, ed. A. Leitzmann (Darmstadt: Wissenschaftliche Buchgesellschaft, 1968), V, p. 388; see also Humboldt, *Linguistic Variability and Intellectual Development*, trans. George C. Buck and Frithjof A. Raven (Philadelphia: University of Pennsylvania Press, 1972), pp. 41 and 65.

Lecture 26

1. Ludwig Feuerbach, "Kritik der Hegelschen Philosophie," *Gesammelte Werke*, ed. W. Schuffenhauer (Berlin: Akademie Verlag, 1970), IX, p. 40.

2. For Husserl it is, inversely, the ideality of "meaning" (*Meinung*) (of signification-bestowing intention), which abstracts from the psychophysical act of the intimation of expression or judgment, as well as from the "vanishing noise that can never recur identically" and from the spatiotemporal reference that guarantees the "sameness" or "identity" "in the repetition of the statement." Here the identity in meaning of what is repeated is subordinated to the principle of the *ideal unity of the signified*: ideality commands reality. See *Logical Investigations*, trans. J. N. F. Findlay (London: Routledge and Kegan Paul, 1970), I, pp. 284–89.

3. See Manfred Frank, *Der unendliche Mangel an Sein: Schellings Hegelkritik und die Anfänge der Marxschen Dialektik* (Frankfurt: Suhrkamp, 1975), pp. 236–45; Sartre, *ET*, pp. 150ff.

4. Gottlob Frege, *Logical Investigations*, ed. P. T. Geach, trans. P. T. Geach and R. H. Stoothoff (Oxford: Basil Blackwell, 1977), p. 15.

5. Frege, *Logical Investigations*, p. 17.

6. Frege, *Logical Investigations*, pp. 21–22.

7. Husserl, *Logical Investigations*, I, p. 314.

8. Husserl, *Logical Investigations*, I, p. 315.

9. Husserl, *Logical Investigations*, I, p. 316.

10. Husserl, *Logical Investigations*, pp. 315–16; see also *SP*, pp. 72–73. The distinction between "occasional" and "objective meanings" is first brought up in the *Logical Investigations* on the example of the index word "I," but it is in no way exhausted with the problematics of sentences in which "I" designates an individual subject (which is always qualified by Husserl as being "empirical"). Husserl in general distinguishes—this is a leitmotif of the entire second volume of the German edition of the *Logical Investigations*, from the introduction onward (I, pp. 248ff.)—"between the act of meaning, on the one hand, and meaning itself, on the other, the ideal unity as against the multiplicity of possible acts" (I, p. 312). Meaning made evident in originary essential intuition is transcontextual and transoccasional, it is an "ideal unit of meaning" over against the "shifting acts of meaning" (I, p. 312) as an empirical-grammatical operation in changing situations. Nevertheless, it remains true that Husserl labels all "ambiguous" and "shifting expressions" that deviate from the hypostatized ideal unity of meaning as "*essentially* subjective" (I, p. 321). This means that the function of the index designating an individual can implicitly be found in forms of utterance that do not expressly make use of an "I," given that they are nonobjective, occasional, and shifting according to "subjective idea and thought" (in Frege's sense of "idea"). (See mainly section 28 of Husserl's first investigation, pp. 320–22.) We see that Derrida takes over the methodological imperative of disregarding the occasionality of "signifying" (*des Bedeutens*), in order to guarantee the ideality of "significations," without, to be sure, concluding, as Husserl does, that there is an ideal *identity* of objectively *founded* significations. Expressing it paradoxically, one could say that Derrida assumes an ideal nonidentity (not of individual signifying, but) of signification(s).

11. At least the reduction of individuality is an essential *tendency* of phenomenology. In practice, however, the matter is far more complex. While Husserl considers that index words such as "here, yesterday, this one," etc., are replaceable by "objective expressions," he is of the opinion that the signification of "I" cannot be absolutely sublated into that of an objective or exact (i.e., theoretically defined) expression. The ambiguity of "I" is not the ambiguity of a homonym or an equivocation; it cannot be eliminated by inserting the sum of all proper names, which alternately make use of this expression, into the place of "I." For, according to Husserl, "undoubtedly the idea of self-reference, as well as an implied pointing to the individual idea of the speaker, also belong, *after a certain fashion*," to the semantics of "I" (I, p. 316). "I" can therefore not be reduced to the universal signifying *function* of the index word, it does not coincide semantically with "whatever speaker is designating himself" (I, p. 315). In this it is different from Wittgenstein's and Tugendhat's reductionism. On p. 320 Husserl determines the ineradicability and unomissibility of the implicit and explicit reference to the speaking individual subject as being of a principal nature; the signification of "I" cannot be transformed into an ideal language that would found an ideal-objective signifying of "I" instead of a shifting one (section 28, pp. 320–22).

12. Husserl, *Logical Investigations*, I, p. 316.

13. In the first part of this passage I replaced *la trace* twice with *la différance*, for reasons of adapting it to the context of the passage, and with a justification Derrida himself emphasizes in the second passage cited.

14. See Wolfgang Hogrebe's review article of Herbert Schnädelbach, *Reflexion und Diskurs: Fra-*

gen an eine Logik der Philosophie (Frankfurt: Suhrkamp, 1977), in *Zeitschrift für philosophische Forschung*, 36 (1982), p. 289.

15. Derrida explicitly does this at various points. I will mention only one: "This movement of differance is not something that happens to a transcendental subject; it produces a subject" (*P*, 82).

Lecture 27

1. A structural or principal possibility is not, as Derrida demonstrated very nicely, an eventuality: "have to be able to" does not mean "happens perhaps" (*LI*, 183-86).

2. Derrida, "Le facteur de la vérité," *Poetique*, 21 (1975), pp. 96-147. Published in English as "The Purveyor of Truth," *Yale French Studies*, 52 (1975), pp. 31-113.

3. Derrida, "The Purveyor of Truth," p. 57.

4. Ibid., pp. 92-93.

5. Ibid., pp. 58, 59, 63; see also pp. 65-66, 78-100.

6. Derrida, "La Facteur de la vérité," p. 124 (the English *Yale French Studies* translation skips the section from pp. 122-24).

7. Derrida, "The Purveyor of Truth," pp. 88-89.

8. Ibid., pp. 94-98.

9. Ibid., p. 100.

10. Manfred Frank, "Das 'wahre Subjekt' und sein Doppel: Jacques Lacans Hermeneutik," *Das Sagbare und das Unsagbare* (Frankfurt: Suhrkamp, 1980), pp. 114-40.

11. Lacan, *The Four Fundamental Concepts of Psychoanalysis*, ed. Jacques-Alain Miller, trans. Alan Sheridan (New York: Norton, 1978), pp. 225-26.

12. Fichte, *Science of Knowledge*, trans. Peter Heath and John Lucks (1970; rpt. Cambridge: Cambridge University Press, 1982), p. 110.

13. Peirce, *Coll P*, V, p. 3; see also V, 277-78; VIII, 184, 187-89.

14. Cf. Manfred Frank, *Das individuelle Allgemeine: Textstrukturierung und -interpretation nach Schleiermacher* (Frankfurt: Suhrkamp, 1977), pp. 322ff.

15. See the penetrating remarks by Christian Stetter, "Peirce und Saussure," *Kodikas/Code*, 2 (1979), pp. 124-49, esp. 135-36.

16. The idea of the ultimately determining consciousness of a speaker can actually be found in Saussure himself. It is characterized there as the only measuring stick for the judgments of the linguist (*CFS*, 15 [1957], p. 75).

17. Schleiermacher, *Kurze Darstellung des theologischen Studiums, Sämtliche Werke* (Berlin: Reimer, 1843), I/1, p. 56.

18. Proust, *A la recherche du temps perdu* (Paris: Gallimard, 1954), III, p. 656.

19. Todorov, "Texte," *Dictionnaire encyclopédique des sciences du langage*, ed. Oswald Ducrot and Tzvetan Todorov (Paris: Seuil, 1972), pp. 375-82.

20. Schleiermacher, *Kurze Darstellung des theologischen Studiums, Sämtliche Werke*, I/1, p. 58.

21. A. N. Whitehead, "Verstehen," *Die Hermeneutik und die Wissenschaften*, ed. Hans-Georg Gadamer and G. Boehm (Frankfurt: Suhrkamp, 1978), p. 71; cf. Boehm's preface, p. 27.

22. Humboldt, *Linguistic Variability and Intellectual Development*, trans. George C. Buck and Frithjof A. Raven (Philadelphia: University of Pennsylvania Press, 1972), p. 43.

23. Theodor Adorno, *Negative Dialectics*, trans. E. B. Ashton (New York: Seabury, 1973), p. 8.

24. Adorno, *Minima Moralia: Reflections from Damaged Life*, trans. E. F. N. Jephcott (London: Verso, 1974), pp. 16-18.

25. I gave some indications of the path toward this in *Das Sagbare und das Unsagbare*, pp. 36ff., 85-108, 184-203, esp. 190ff.

26. Sartre, *Situations* (Paris: Gallimard, 1948), II, p. 305.

Index

Index

Theory and History of Literature

Manfred Frank is professor of philosophy at the Universität Tübingen, Germany. He has also taught at the Universities of Geneva and Düsseldorf. In English, Frank's articles have appeared in such journals as *boundary 2*, *Telos*, *Modern Language Notes*, *Glyph*, and *Revue internationale de philosophie*. His books include *Die Grenzen der Verständigung (Lyotard-Habermas)* (1988), *Die Unhintergehbarkeit von Individualität* (1986), *Der Kommende Gott* (1982, 1988), *Das Sagbare und das Unsagbare* (1980), *Die unendliche Fahrt* (1978), *Das individuelle Allgemeine* (1977), four publications on Schelling's philosophy (1975, 1977, 1985), and *Das Problem 'Zeit' in der deutschen Romantik* (1972).

Sabine Wilke, assistant professor of German studies at Stanford University, received her Ph.D. in German from the University of Mainz, Germany. She has taught at the University of California, Davis, and Reed College. Wilke is author of *Zur Dialektik von Exposition und Darstellung* (1988), and contributes to *MLN*, *Telos*, *Husserl Studies*, *The German Quarterly*, *boundary 2*, and other journals.

Richard Gray is associate professor of German at Mills College, California. He earned his Ph.D. in German literature at the University of Virginia in 1981. He has been a visiting assistant professor at Reed College and the University of Virginia. Gray is the author of *Constructive Destruction: Kafka's Aphorisms — Literary Tradition and Literary Transformation* (1987); his work has been published in *The Literary Review*, *Colloquia Germanica*, *German Quarterly*, *Orbis Litterarum*, and other journals.

Martin Schwab is assistant professor of comparative literature and philosophy at the University of California, Irvine. He has studied philosophy at Heidelberg and Oxford, earning a Ph.D. at Bielefeld, West Germany, and he holds a law degree from the University of Heidelberg. Schwab is the author of *Redehandeln* (1981) and has contributed to *Topoi*, *Discourse*, and *Poetik und Hermeneutik*.